MOON

S0-AHM-552

TOKYO
KYOTO & HIROSHIMA

JONATHAN DeHART

TOKYO, KYOTO & HIROSHIMA

Sea of Japan

Nagaoka

Kōriyama

Takaoka

Toyama

Kanazawa

Nagano

kui

Matsumoto

Maebashi

Ūtsunomiya

JAPAN

Kawagoe

NARITA
INTERNATIONAL
AIRPORT

Kōfu

Hachiōji

TOKYO

GIFU

Honshu

Kawasaki

TOKYO
INTERNATIONAL
AIRPORT

NAGOYA

NAGOYA

Yokohama

Mount
Fuji

Kamakura

Shizuoka

Hakone

Tsu

Hamamatsu

PACIFIC OCEAN

0   50 mi

0   50 km

© MOON.COM

Contents

Tokyo, Kyoto & Hiroshima

Fragrant smoke wafts from a food stall under the train tracks beyond Ginza's glitz, where Tokyo office workers unwind over skewers of grilled chicken and beer. In Kyoto, monks rise before the first rays of sunlight spread across a temple's grounds, starting their day reading sutras before an elaborate altar. Meanwhile, in the shadow of Hiroshima's Atomic Bomb Dome, schoolchildren ring a large bronze bell and pray for world peace, their hopes carried aloft with the resonant hum.

Few places offer as wide a range of experiences in such a compact swath of terrain as Japan's cultural and geographic heart, stretching roughly from Tokyo to Hiroshima. Within a few hours by train—and the occasional ferry thrown in—you'll discover high-octane cities, medieval towns, shimmering seascapes, and mouthwatering cuisine, from the greasy to the refined. All throughout, you'll also encounter cutting-edge technology and colorful pop culture balanced by ancient tradition and boundless spiritual depth. In short, within this region, you'll find the very best of Japan.

Beyond the most popular stops—Tokyo, Kyoto, Osaka, Nara, Hiroshima—this region contains Hakone's hot springs, Mount Fuji's snowcapped cone, Uji's

Clockwise from top left: Kyoto; an *izakaya* at night; *yukata; kaiseki ryōri*; visiting the Cupnoodles Museum in Yokohama; Kurama-dera.

tea fields, Himeji's soaring white castle, Okayama's picture-perfect garden, Kura-shiki's romantic canal district, and a constellation of islands strewn across the sparkling Inland Sea, from the funky, forward-looking "art islands" to the holy isle of Miyajima. And this only scratches the surface.

Seasoned globetrotters routinely rate Tokyo and Kyoto among the most sat-isfying cities to visit in the world in polls done by top international travel maga-zines. A trip that combines these two stops with jaunts off the radar will surprise and satisfy even the experienced traveler. And remember: Even Tokyo and Kyoto have their quiet sides.

Wherever you go, a journey to Japan's core is most of all a chance to expe-rience the *omotenashi* (hospitality) of the people, from the faultless service of a restaurant in a Kyoto townhouse to the simple kindness of a family-owned inn. Despite a modern history fraught with challenges, the legendarily welcoming Japanese have continuously reinvented themselves, yet managed to retain their soul. Whether you're craving a culinary quest, a cultural deep-dive, a romantic getaway, a spiritual escape, or an adventure with friends, this accessible slice of Japan has something for everyone. So, go, and savor the essence of this remark-able country, unlike any other.

Clockwise from top left: Shibuya Crossing; Nara; vermillion *torii* of Fushimi Inari-Taisha; swan boats in Ueno-kōen.

10 TOP EXPERIENCES

1 Getting the best vista of **Mount Fuji,** whether viewing it from afar or climbing it up close (page 192).

2 Taking a deep dive into **nightlife in Shinjuku,** Tokyo's most eclectic nightlife zone (page 130).

3 Strolling Kyoto's **Philosopher's Path** (page 229) or the **Arashiyama Bamboo Grove** (page 241) at off-peak hours, finding the city's quiet side.

4 Finding the best fried food in **Dōtombori,** Osaka's lively neon-lit street food center (page 303).

>>>

5 **Cycling the Inland Sea,** traveling over the impressive bridges and shimmering islands of the Shimanami Kaidō, the sea route connecting Western Honshu and Shikoku (page 364).

>>>

6 Reckoning with the ghosts of history at **Hiroshima's Peace Memorial Park** (page 379).

7 Getting acquainted with **Japanese whiskies** at a connoisseur's bar in Tokyo (page 126) or on a distillery tour at **Suntory Yamazaki Distillery** (page 263).

8 Experiencing the Japanese service tradition known as *omotenashi* by **staying the night in a *ryokan*,** where your every need will be anticipated and met (page 266).

9 Visiting Nara's imposing **Tōdai-ji** temple and marveling at the towering bronze Buddha housed within (page 310).

10 Indulging in *kaiseki ryōri,* savoring Japanese cuisine at its most refined (page 255).

Planning Your Time

Where to Go

Tokyo

The high-octane capital should be top priority for any first visit to the country. Tokyo is **quintessential modern Japan,** a pop-cultural and economic juggernaut, and base of the national government. The dynamic city is a feast for the senses, with world-class **food, nightlife,** and **shopping.** It's also the most networked **transport hub** in Japan, with two international airports and extensive rail links to the rest of the country.

Between Tokyo and Kyoto

The dynamic swath of land between Tokyo and Kyoto is packed with attractive destinations, best visited either when traveling between the two cities, or as **side trips** from the capital if you don't have time to make it to Kyoto. South of Tokyo is Japan's second largest city, cosmopolitan **Yokohama,** with a buzzing nightlife scene, and the ancient seaside feudal capital of **Kamakura,** with rich Buddhist heritage. West of there, **Hakone** is a good pick for an *onsen* (hot spring) experience, with Japan's most famous peak, **Mount Fuji,** looming nearby.

Kyoto

Alongside the modern capital of Tokyo, the ancient capital of Kyoto should be top priority for any first journey to Japan. This is the best place to explore **traditional culture,** try a **tea ceremony, shrine- and temple-hop,** eat *kaiseki ryōri* (haute Japanese cuisine), stay in a high-end *ryokan,* and gaze at various styles of

Kyoto

gardens, from landscape to raked gravel. Step away from the top sights to discover a slower, more local side of the city, beyond the tourist throngs.

Kansai

A great complement to Kyoto, the Kansai region is home to **Osaka,** a fun place to eat, drink, and carouse with legendarily friendly locals. Nearby, the small town of **Nara,** home to the famed **Great Buddha of Tōdai-ji,** where you can see traditional Japan, minus Kyoto's crowds. The attractive port city of **Kobe** is known for its high-end beef and jazz, while **Himeji** has Japan's best castle.

Between Kansai and Hiroshima

Moving west from Kansai along the sun-drenched southern (**San'yō**) coast of Honshu, along the gorgeous **Inland Sea** (Seto Naikai), you'll come to the old castle town of **Okayama,** which boasts one of Japan's top gardens, **Kōraku-en.** Nearby, historic **Kurashiki** is split by a romantic canal that was an important artery for the rice trade. Farther west, the salty fishing town of **Onomichi** sits beneath a mountain dotted by **temples.** It is also the starting point for the **Shimanami Kaidō,** or Inland Sea Route, a series of bridges linking Honshu to Shikoku via six islands that can be crossed by bicycle. Elsewhere in the Inland Sea, the "art

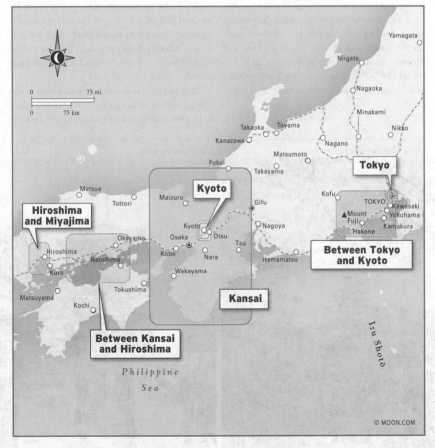

© MOON.COM

islands" of **Naoshima, Teshima,** and **Inujima** give an inspiring glimpse of creative rejuvenation in action.

Hiroshima and Miyajima

Farther west along the urbanized southern coast of Honshu is the vibrant, modern incarnation of **Hiroshima,** as well as the famed "floating" *torii* shrine gate of **Miyajima's Itsukushima-jinja.** East of Hiroshima, the town of **Saijō** has a clutch of *sake* breweries that are a great place to get better acquainted with the drink. West of Hiroshima, the sleepy town of **Iwakuni** is home to **Kintaikyō,** a massive arched wooden bridge that abuts an area that was once a samurai quarter.

Know Before You Go

When to Go

Most of Japan has four distinct seasons, interspersed by a few rainy periods, though the country's diverse geography means the climate varies. **Spring** (roughly late-Mar. through mid-June) and **autumn** (Oct. through early Dec.) are the most pleasant times of year to visit the country on the whole. That said, it's a year-round destination, with each season offering its own draw.

SPRING

Spring begins to creep northward to central Japan **early to mid-March.** Spring tends to be **cool** (8-24°C/46-75°F in Tokyo)—gradually warming through **April** and **May**—with patches of rain. **Cherry blossoms** start to bloom from in late March in Tokyo. Overall, it's a great time to visit.

Most of Japan is wet throughout **June,** when the hit-and-miss *tsuyu* **(rainy season)** takes hold. Overcast skies with patches of rain and the

cherry blossoms at Himeji-jō

Kiyomizu-dera ticket

occasional all-day shower are the norm during this period, though there are plenty of sunny days in between, too.

SUMMER

From **July** through **September,** things can be downright **stifling,** with furnace-like temperatures (23-31°C/73-88°F in Tokyo) and high humidity throughout much of the country. While less amenable than spring, the months of July and August can be a fun time to visit the country due to a plethora of vibrant **festivals** held throughout this sweltering period. Among the best are **Kyoto's Gion Matsuri** (most of July, culminating July 17) and **Osaka's Tenjin Matsuri.** If you're visiting the country during any of these bashes, **book accommodations well in advance** (three months or more, to be safe).

AUTUMN

In **September** and **early October,** it's possible for **typhoons** to whip through the country, with torrential rain and even devastating floods on occasion. These extreme cases aside, it's perfectly safe to travel during this time of year. Just be sure to keep an eye on the weather forecast if you'll be in the country then.

Autumn proper starts from around **early October** and lasts through the first half of **December** for much of the country (10-22°C/50-72°F in Tokyo). This is one of the most pleasant times to visit Japan. As temperatures drop, **blazing foliage** ripples through the country, with November being the highpoint. Rates for accommodations do spike around this time in scenic places, so **book ahead** if you plan to head into nature around this time.

WINTER

Winter sets in from **mid-December** through **mid-March** (2-12°C/36-54°F in Tokyo). The Pacific side of Japan is cold, dry, and crisp, with clear skies and little snow.

HANAMI AND OTHER BUSY TIMES

High season in Japan includes *hanami* (cherry blossom viewing) season (roughly late Mar. through early Apr.), the **Golden Week** holidays (Apr. 29-May 5), **Obon** (roughly Aug. 10-17), and the height of the *kōyō* (autumn foliage) craze in November. To avoid crowds, it's best not to visit the country during these periods, as trains, highways, and hotels will overflow with domestic travelers from around the time the cherry blossoms start to bloom, around late March in Tokyo.

SLOWER MONTHS

Less hectic months include **June,** the **dead of summer** (July, Aug. besides Ōbon, and Sept.), **October,** and **December. January** through **March** is **low season** for most of the country. Deals can be had during any of these off months, especially if you plan several months ahead.

Things generally remain in operation throughout the year, the one exception being the **New Year holidays** (Dec. 29-Jan. 3), when everything but convenience stores, some chain restaurants, and most accommodations (at elevated rates) remain open. While experiencing Japan's New Year traditions is one point in favor of visiting over the New Year holidays, it's probably best to come at another time.

Passports and Visas

To enter Japan, you'll need a **passport** valid for the duration of your trip from the date of your arrival in the country. Although you may not be asked to show it, you're legally obligated to have an onward ticket for either a flight or ferry out of Japan, for a return trip or a future leg of the journey elsewhere. So have something in hand just in case.

If you're coming from the United States, Canada, the UK, most European countries, Australia, or New Zealand, you'll be granted a **90-day single-entry visa** on arrival. South African citizens will need to apply for a **90-day tourist visa** at their closest embassy or consulate. For passport holders from the UK, Ireland,

Choosing Your Side Trips and Day Trips

The cities of Tokyo, Kyoto, and Hiroshima are a classic itinerary for any first-time visitor to Japan, and should be worked into any trip to the country if at all possible. Which of the excursions between and around the cities covered in this book to visit, however, can be a matter of preference. The following chart should help you decide which of the day trips and side trips make the most sense for you to visit:

If you like…	Go to…	Getting There
Cosmopolitan port cities, jazz, craft beer	**Yokohama** has a deep history of engagement with the West and plenty of 19th-century architecture to prove it, plus jazz clubs local brewers (page 156).	Best reached from **Tokyo** by train (30 minutes).
Zen temples, hiking, seaside views	**Kamakura** is home to Kōtoku-in and its Great Buddha, trails through the hills surrounding town, and facing it, the Pacific (page 169).	Best reached from **Tokyo** by train (1 hour).
Hot spring spas, luxury accommodations	**Hakone** is Japan's preeminent *onsen* (hot spring) destination, with high-end lodgings, from *ryokan* to modern hotels, set amid a beautiful environment (page 180).	Best reached from **Tokyo** by train (1.5 hours).
Hiking, breathtaking views	**Mount Fuji** is one of the world's most iconic mountains. It can be hiked overnight or admired from a distance (page 190).	Best reached from **Tokyo** by train (2-2.5 hours) and then bus (depending on far up Mount Fuji you want to go).
Photography, cable cars, scenic boat rides	**Fuji Five Lakes** are an ideal vantage point for viewing Mount Fuji, from lakesides to mountainsides (reached on foot or via cable car) (page 196).	Best reached from **Tokyo** by train (2-2.5 hours).
Architecture, sculpture, lush parks	**Nara** is home to Nara-kōen, a sprawling park where semi-domesticated deer roam freely, and an immense temple that houses the country's largest bronze Buddha statue (page 307).	Best reached from **Kyoto** by train (1 hour) or **Osaka** by train (1 hour).
Street food, neon-lit nightlife	**Osaka** is the best city in Japan for a food crawl, preferably in the rambling lanes that extend from its Dōtombori canal district (page 285).	Best reached from **Kyoto** by train (30 minutes).
Historic neighborhoods, refined food, and jazz	**Kobe** has a posh cluster of old Western architecture, thanks to its community of foreign merchants. Be sure to head to one of its distinguished jazz clubs (page 315).	Best reached from **Kyoto** by train (1 hour) or **Osaka** by train (30 minutes).

If you like...	Go to...	Getting There
Well-preserved castles	**Himeji** boasts Japan's best surviving example of a feudal fortress. Among the country's remaining castles, the city's famed white citadel remains unconquered (page 325).	Best reached from **Kyoto** by train (1 hour), **Osaka** by train (30 minutes-1 hour), or **Kobe** by train (15-40 minutes).
Beautiful gardens	**Okayama** is home to Kōraku-en, a green stroll-garden that calls for leisurely exploration (page 338).	Best reached from **Kyoto** by train (1 hour) or **Hiroshima** by train (40 minutes)
Canal towns, historic architecture	**Kurashiki** has a romantic waterway that runs through an old merchant's quarter. White walls and black tiled roofs form a network of atmospheric lanes (page 342).	Best reached from **Hiroshima** by train (1 hour 10 minutes, with transfers).
Cutting-edge art and design, sunsets, relaxation	**The Art Islands** of the Inland Sea. are heaving with art, innovative museums, and laid-back fishing villages. Don't miss the jaw-dropping sunsets (page 346).	Best reached from **Kyoto** by train and ferry via Uno Port (3 hours 10 minutes) or **Hiroshima** by train and ferry via Uno Port (3 hours).
Temples, walking trails	**Onomichi** is the epitome of a nostalgic port town. Plod up and over the nearby mountains to discover temples, stray cats, and stunning views out to sea (page 356).	Best reached from **Hiroshima** by train (1.5 hours).
Cycling, scenic views	**The Shimanami Kaidō,** a network of bridges linking Honshu to Shikoku, is among the world's most beautiful routes to cycle (page 361).	The Shimanami Kaidō begins at Onomichi (best reached from **Hiroshima** by train, 1.5 hours), accessed by ferry and bicycle.
Idyllic islands, famous shrines	**Miyajima** is an ancient, holy island; on the shore is a shrine gate partly submerged in waves at high tide (page 393).	Best reached from **Hiroshima** by train and ferry (30 minutes).
Historic bridges, scenic rivers, old townscapes	**Iwakuni** has Japan's finest example of an old wooden arched bridge. This marvel of feudal-period engineering leads to a former samurai quarter (page 398).	Best reached from **Hiroshima** by train (50 minutes).

and a number of other European countries, it's possible to extend your visa for another 90 days. This requires a trip to the closest immigration bureau and paying a ¥4,000 fee. For a list of the 68 nations that are not required to apply for a visa before arriving in Japan, visit www.mofa. go.jp/j_info/visit/visa/short/novisa.html.

What to Take

One of the beautiful things about Japan is its well-stocked **convenience stores.** These one-stop shops, selling anything from toiletries and undershirts to bento-box meals and portable phone chargers, umbrellas, cosmetics, and more, are ubiquitous throughout urbanized Japan, making it easy to pick up anything you've forgotten to pack.

Nonetheless, there are a few items you'd be wise to bring. For one: **shoes** that are easy to take on and off (**slip-ons** work best). You'll find yourself likely taking off your shoes much more than you're used to—in someone's home, in a temple, etc. Also pack any **medications** and accompanying **prescriptions** you may need. Be sure to check Japan's strict laws on medication before traveling with medicine. The **U.S. Embassy** provides helpful information on their website about this matter: https:// jp.usembassy.gov/u-s-citizen-services/doctors/ importing-medication.

The electrical outlets in Japan are the same shape as those in the United States, so travelers with devices from the UK or Europe may need a plug adapter. The voltage is 100V; many modern electronics are dual voltage, so a converter may not be necessary, but check your devices to be sure.

It also pays to be aware of Japan's love of **gift-giving.** This is especially important if you plan to meet anyone who may invite you to their home. It need not be expensive. Some kind of a sweet snack or beverage that can be shared, a recording of interesting music, or some kind of decorative item would all do. A little gift goes a long way in Japan.

Planning Ahead

There are a few things that need to be in order before you leave for Japan. First things first, if you plan to get a **Japan Rail Pass** (www.japan-railpass.net), a great value if you plan on making full use of the country's extensive train network, **you must purchase it before traveling to Japan.** You cannot buy a JR Pass once you are in Japan.

If you're planning to travel to some of the more remote parts of Japan and want to rent a car, make sure you've already gotten your **international driver's license** (IDP, aka international driving permit). To learn more about the process of obtaining an IDP, visit https:// internationaldrivingpermit.org, which provides country-by-country information on the process of applying. It doesn't hurt to **book your rental car before your trip** to avoid hassle later.

It also pays to make **reservations** for some meals, attractions, or events, such as a sumo tournament or sporadically held *Noh* theater performance, a few months in advance. Some **popular attractions,** such as Tokyo's Ghibli Museum and Kyoto's "moss temple" Saihō-ji, only allow a set number of visitors per day; you'll need to book your place at these attractions up to a few months in advance as well. If you're determined to snag a seat at a world-class sushi counter, *kaiseki ryōri* restaurant, or any other truly **world-famous restaurants,** some of the wait times are shocking. Aim to book seats months in advance.

Finally, if you happen to be visiting anywhere during a **festival** or one of the **high seasons,** try to book everything—accommodation, rental car, even *shinkansen* (bullet train) tickets—as far in advance as you can (think three, or even six months ahead).

Transportation
GETTING THERE

The vast majority of travelers will arrive in Japan via one of **four main airports:** Tokyo's Narita Airport or Haneda Airport, Osaka's Kansai International Airport, or Nagoya's

Chubu Centrair International Airport. It's also possible to enter the country by sea, with **hydrofoils** and **ferries** shuttling daily between **Busan, South Korea,** and **Fukuoka.** Ferries also make the trip between **Shanghai** and both **Osaka** and **Kobe.**

GETTING AROUND

Once you're on the ground, transportation options are profuse, from trains and planes to buses, ferries, and rental cars.

BY TRAIN

Japan's most efficient mode of transport is its **extensive railway** network. You'll be able to get where you're going aboard a train—whether of the **local, rapid,** or *shinkansen* (bullet train) variety—in the vast majority of cases. Traveling short distances within a city or town is also often best done by train, whether aboveground or subway.

If you plan to rely heavily on the rail network, consider buying a **Japan Rail Pass** (www.japanrailpass.net) before you get to Japan. This pass—which offers unlimited trains on the Japan Rail (JR) network nationwide in increments of one, two, and three weeks—is a steal if you maximize it.

BY BUS

Buses are another option for traveling both long distances and just within town. Although less comfortable than trains, buses are sometimes the only means of reaching some **far-flung destinations.** They are also generally **cheaper** than trains, making them a good option if you're on a serious budget and don't mind the journey taking a bit more time.

BY TAXI

Taxis are abundant. That said, fares are **expensive.** They are best used for only **short distances** within a town or city when there's no cheaper means of getting around, when you're in a rush, or if you have money to burn.

BY CAR

A rental car will be invaluable if you're venturing well **off the beaten path.** Trains still run through some parts of these regions, but their frequency and reach can sometimes be frustratingly limited. Driving is on the **left,** like in the UK. If you plan to drive, you must get an **international driving permit (IDP)** before arriving. Visit https://internationaldrivingpermit.org for country-by-country information on the process of applying.

The Best of Tokyo, Kyoto & Hiroshima

This itinerary is great for a first visit to Japan. Tokyo and Kyoto inevitably form the backbone of any introduction to the country, both its ancient and hyper-modern sides. Also included as a third pole is historically significant Hiroshima.

In between these cities you'll visit Hakone, where you'll experience the pleasures of an *onsen* (hot spring) escape; Nara, where the famed park Nara-kōen houses the temple of Tōdai-ji, the world's largest wooden building, and Japan's largest bronze Buddha statue; Kobe, a cosmopolitan port city with a reputation for world-class beef and jazz; Miyajima, a sacred island famed for its seaside shrine Itsukushishima-Jinja, with an iconic *torii* gate that "floats" at high tide; and Osaka, a brash culinary mecca with some of Japan's friendliest locals.

Besides your flight, it's wise to book any popular hotel a few months or more in advance. In Hakone and Kyoto, in-demand *ryokan* can be booked out upward of half a year in advance, doubly so during peak seasons (spring, late-Mar.-early Apr., and autumn, Nov.-early Dec.). Also, be sure to book your JR Pass ahead of your trip; book any tours or exclusive restaurants (i.e. *kaiseki* in Kyoto, popular restaurants in Tokyo) a month or more ahead to be safe.

DAY 1

After arriving at either **Narita** or **Haneda** airport the night before, sleep off jetlag at your hotel; Tokyo's western districts of **Shinjuku** or **Shibuya,** or the upscale area around **Tokyo Station,** are good bases. The next morning, start at **Meiji Jingū,** Tokyo's most impressive shrine. Proceed down the thoroughfare of **Omotesandō** and its high-end shops to **Aoyama,** where you'll find the **Nezu Museum's** collection of

the entrance to Meiji Jingū

Tokyo National Museum

Omoide Yokochō

premodern Asian art. Make your way to Shibuya, the beating heart of Japanese youth culture and home to the world's busiest intersection, and ascend to **Shibuya Sky** nearby for striking views of the concrete jungle below. Have dinner and drinks at a lively *izakaya* in trendy **Ebisu,** and then go for cocktails or to one of the city's many excellent DJ bars nearby.

DAY 2

Start the day by exploring the slower, old-school neighborhoods on the east side of town. Begin with a trip to the colorful Buddhist temple **Sensō-ji** in **Asakusa,** then head west to **Ueno,** famed for its massive park and the **Tokyo National Museum,** which houses the world's largest collection of Japanese art. Proceed to nearby **Akihabara,** the best spot to get to know *otaku* culture, a catch-all for things geek. End the day in **Shinjuku,** eating dinner in the smoky alleyway of hole-in-the-wall restaurants that is **Omoide Yokochō,** followed by a bar crawl through **Golden Gai's** warren of drinking dens.

DAY 3

In the morning, strike out for the **onsen** (hot spring) resort area of **Hakone,** about 1.5 hours south of Tokyo by train. Arriving by mid- or late-morning, check into a *ryokan.* Spend the afternoon exploring some of Hakone's **art museums,** its larger public bathing complexes, or its abundant **natural beauty.** After enjoying dinner at your accommodation or one of the area's charming restaurants, soothe yourself in an *onsen* pool. This is what Hakone is really about.

DAY 4

After you've fully steeped yourself in hot water, leave Hakone for **Kyoto.** Arriving by around lunchtime, check into your room—**Gion** or **downtown** make convenient bases—grab a bite to eat, and spend the remainder of your daylight hours exploring the hillside temple of **Kiyomizu-dera, Nijō-jō** castle, or **Kinkaku-ji** and **Ryōan-ji.** In the evening, splurge on a once-in-a-lifetime dinner at a *kaiseki ryōri* restaurant, followed by **cocktails** at one of Kyoto's bars, clustered around downtown. Finish the night with

summertime *kaiseki ryōri* meal in Kyoto

a stroll down the dreamy lantern-lit alleyway of **Ponto-chō** and along the **Kamo River,** which is lined with walking paths.

DAY 5

Go deeper on your second day to discover a quieter pocket of town. Head first to western district of **Arashiyama,** most famous for its ethereal **bamboo grove.** Next, make your way across town to the quieter **Higashiyama** neighborhood, where you'll find a number of important temples, from the grand **Nanzen-ji** to **Ginkaku-ji,** the "silver" companion to golden **Kinkaku-ji,** linked by the contemplation-inducing **Philosopher's Path.** Finish your exploration in the southeast of town at **Fushimi Inari-Taisha,** a magical mountainside shrine known for its tunnel of red *torii* shrine gates. Have dinner in the upscale **Gion district.**

DAY 6

Take a side trip to **Nara,** a laid-back complement to Kyoto with deep ties to the spread of Buddhism in Japan. After arriving at either JR Nara Station or Kintetsu-Nara Station by the mid- to late morning, make your way to the lovely garden of **Isui-en.** Proceed next to **Nara-kōen,** the local park that is famously populated by semi-domesticated deer. Go to **Tōdai-ji,** the world's largest wooden structure, and gawp at the immense **bronze Buddha** statue that looms within. Next, proceed east, uphill, to Tōdai-ji's subtemples **Nigatsu-dō** and **Sangatsu-dō,** where you'll have sweeping views over Nara. Have lunch in the park, then press deeper into the forest at **Kasuga Taisha.** Wander throughout the shrine's perimeter and walk along the trail lined with stone lanterns that continues into the surrounding forest. After giving yourself time to soak in the charged ambience, walk west through the heart of Nara-kōen, on into the atmospheric old part of town, **Naramachi.** Stroll through the refined streets and have dinner at one of the area's alluring *izakaya.* You can either spend the night in one of Nara's classic inns or return to Kyoto.

The Art of the Japanese Garden

Evolving over more than a millennium, Japanese gardens have a distinct way of mimicking nature in miniaturized, idealized form. Their elements are diverse—moss, trees, shrubs, stones, lanterns, water—and are often symbolic: raked sand embodies waves, ponds become vast lakes, moss-encrusted boulders evoke mountains in mythic landscapes from Chinese lore or Buddhist scripture.

GARDEN TYPES

Changing with the times, gardens in Japan have ranged from places of spiritual contemplation to aristocratic playgrounds. The earliest examples were the pebble-strewn promenades seen around Shinto shrines. As Chinese culture began to exert its pull in the 6th century, garden design followed the lead of the Middle Kingdom, with large ponds, stone bridges high enough for boats to pass underneath, and gravel areas for parties.

- The latter part of the Heian period (794-1185) saw the emergence of **Pure Land Gardens,** named after the eponymous school of Buddhism. These lofty creations were modeled after the paradise that followers were said to reach after a lifetime of devotion.

- With the ascent of Zen Buddhism and the warrior class during the Kamakura period (1185-1333), up through the Muromachi period (1333-1568), spare, pragmatic *kare-sansui* **(dry landscape) gardens** proliferated. The focus of these gardens is on gravel and sand raked into symmetrical patterns, punctuated by carefully placed large shards of stone. These stark spaces are maintained by contemplative monks.

- The next leap for garden design came in the Azuchi-Momoyama period (1573-1603), with the emergence of the classic **tea garden.** These spaces evolved alongside the development of the tea ceremony and sit beside rustic tea houses flanked by stone lanterns and surrounded by trees and shrubs.

- Tea gardens were largely subsumed into the next trend: *shūyū* **(stroll gardens),** elaborate Edo period (1603-1867) creations that are what you likely see in your mind's eye when you envision a Japanese garden. Paths lead through a fastidiously created landscape, often set beside castles and nobles' estates, with ponds teeming with *koi,* stone bridges, bamboo groves, tea houses, and open-air pavilions.

To dig deeper, good books include *Zen Gardens and Temples of Kyoto* by John Dougill and John Einarsen; *Japanese Gardens: Tranquility, Simplicity, Harmony* by Geeta Mehta, Kimie Tada, and Noboru Murata; and *The Art of the Japanese Garden* by David and Michiko Young.

JAPAN'S BEST GARDENS

The list of great Japanese gardens is long. Here are a few of the best in Tokyo, Kyoto, and beyond.

Kōraku-en

Located in Okayama, Kōraku-en is one the top gardens in all of Japan. This expansive green space, laced with walking paths and streams, all wrapped around a central pond, is a stellar example of a stroll garden. Since its creation in 1700, it has charmed visiting nobility in feudal times to modern-day tourists. There are groves of maple, cherry, plum, and apricot trees, bursts of flowers in spring and summer, and plenty of open-air pavilions to sit and take it all in (page 339).

Tokyo

In Tokyo, fine examples of gardens include centrally located **Hama-rikyū Onshi-teien** (page 57), a striking contrast to the skyscrapers surrounding it; classical **Koishikawa Kōrakuen** (page 75), which plum blossoms in February and irises in June; the serene garden behind the **Nezu Museum** (page 70); and perhaps the capital's most famous example, **Shinjuku Gyōen** (page 74), with a few different gardens within.

Kyoto

In Kyoto, the brilliant imperial grounds of **Katsura Rikyū** (page 242) are a rather formal affair; an application is required to visit. My top pick is the tranquil garden encompassing **Ōkōchi-Sansō** (page 241), just beyond Arashiyama's bamboo grove. You'll also find fine examples of dry landscape gardens on the grounds of **Ginkaku-ji** (page 231), **Daitoku-ji** (page 239), **Tōfuku-ji** (page 222), and **Ryōan-ji** (page 235).

Elsewhere

Beyond Tokyo and Kyoto, other good examples in this book are Nara's **Isui-en** (page 310), with Tōdai-ji temple looming in the background, and Hiroshima's **Shukkei-en** (page 384), where shrunken valleys, mountains, and forest are represented by the careful landscaping.

DAY 7

In the morning, make your way to **Kobe,** aiming to arrive around by 10:30am. Starting from Shin-Kobe Station, traipse downhill through the affluent **Kitano-chō** district, which was home to a burgeoning community of well-heeled expats in the late 19th century. After passing through the heart of **Sannomiya** and then **Chinatown,** pay your respects at **Port of Kobe Earthquake Memorial Park,** where some of the devastation inflicted upon the city's infrastructure is laid bare in a section of the harbor that has been left untouched since that fateful day in January 1995. Return to Sannomiya for lunch, then backtrack to Shin-Kobe Station to hop on a *shinkansen* bound for **Hiroshima** (1 hour 10 minutes-1.5 hours). Arriving in the early to mid-afternoon, check into your hotel and spend the rest of afternoon in **Peace Memorial Park,** taking in all of its museums and memorials, for a sobering lesson on one of the darkest moments in Japan's history. For dinner, try the city's signature spin on *okonomiyaki,* a delicious savory pancake.

DAY 8

In the morning, set out for the island of **Miyajima,** roughly an hour away by train and ferry. First visit its famous shrine, **Itsukushima-jinja,** the base of which is subsumed by waves at high tide. Its iconic "floating" *torii* gate was covered for repairs at the time of writing, but the shrine is nonetheless a beautiful sight. Next, visit the enthralling temple of **Daishō-in,** and then have lunch in town. After you've fueled up, make your way to the **Miyajima Ropeway** and ride to within a 30-minute hike of the top of **Mount Misen.** Take in the numerous temples, monuments, and stunning views of the seascape from this holy peak. Backtrack to Hiroshima, rest and refresh at your accommodation, have dinner downtown—try some **oysters**—and swing by a few of the area's friendly watering holes.

DAY 9

After breakfast, leave Hiroshima by mid-morning aboard a bullet train to **Osaka,** where you'll stay for the night. Make a stop en route at **Himeji,**

okonomiyaki

55 minutes from Hiroshima, home to Japan's best-preserved **castle.** After touring the imposing white fortress, have lunch in Himeji and then continue east to Osaka (about 1 hour). Arriving in Osaka in the early afternoon, leave your bags at your accommodation, then spend the evening soaking up Osaka's brash nighttime vibe in its **Dōtombori** canal-side district on the **Minami** (south) side of town. This is the time to indulge in the city's long list of deep-fried and battered goodies like *okonomiyaki* (distinct from Hiroshima's style), *takoyaki, kushikatsu,* and more. If you've got energy, there is no shortage of **great bars.**

DAY 10
In the morning, make your way back to Tokyo by train and check into your hotel for the night. Revisit any parts of the city that spoke to you, or take care of any remaining **souvenir shopping.** In the evening, relax and prepare for your **return flight** home.

Tokyo, Kyoto & Hiroshima Off the Beaten Path

This itinerary passes through Tokyo, Kyoto, and Hiroshima's most popular neighborhoods, but balances touristy stops with off-the-beaten-path spots. It's good for those who've already visited Japan and don't mind skipping some "must-sees," and can also be mixed with the itinerary above.

Other stops include Yokohama, Tokyo's cosmopolitan, portside southern neighbor; Uji, a town south of Kyoto known for tea production; Kurashiki, a former merchants' town with a romantic canal; Miyajima, the hallowed island that reveals itself more fully to those who stay after tour groups leave; and Iwakuni, a historic town that boasts Japan's most impressive wooden arched bridge and the remnants of a samurai quarter.

Many stops on this route are less likely to be crowded. That said, book accommodations well in advance (half a year or more) if you plan to visit during peak seasons, notably during *hanami* (cherry blossom viewing) in spring (late-Mar.-early Apr.) or during *kōyō* (autumn leaves) in autumn (Nov.-early Dec.). Also be sure to book your JR Pass ahead of your trip. If you have an exclusive meal in mind, it doesn't hurt to book that in advance, too.

DAY 1
Arriving in Narita or Haneda the night prior, base yourself in **Ueno** or **Asakusa** for a more local side of Tokyo. Start your day in Asakusa, the old-school neighborhood beside the Sumida River in the northeast of town that is centered on Tokyo's most popular temple, **Sensō-ji.** After negotiating the bustling temple grounds and surrounding streets, be sure to meander over to the kitchenware mecca of **Kappabashi-dōri.** Head next to the core of the historic neighborhood of **Yanaka,** presided over by an army of cats, and stop at any local temples, shrines, or galleries that may catch your interest. After fueling up at a local coffee shop, walk southeast another 15 minutes through leafy **Ueno-kōen** to Ueno Station. Take the subway to **Tokyo City View** in the entertainment district of Roppongi for striking views of the concrete jungle below. If the current exhibition interests you, also visit the **Mori Art Museum,** just below Tokyo City View. From Roppongi, take the Hibiya line to Ebisu, then transfer one stop on the way to **Daikanyama,** the embodiment of modern Tokyo style. While away the rest of the afternoon perusing the area's tight lanes, lined by fashionable shops. Once you've worked up an appetite, walk westward and

Tasting Your Way Through Japan

Japan is one of the world's truly great food destinations. The list that follows introduces some of the most iconic dishes you'll encounter as you taste your way through Japan's core.

- *Nigiri:* Popularly known simply as sushi (literally "sour tasting"), *nigiri* is a thin slice of raw fish (aka *sashimi*) atop a mound of vinegared rice. It's said to have originated in the late Edo period when street hawker Yohei Hanaya began to sell the simple dish to impatient customers waiting for the older form of sushi, known as *oshi-zushi* ("pressed sushi"). Sushi is ubiquitous across Japan today, but Tokyo has the largest concentration of world-class sushi chefs.

- *Monjayaki:* This Tokyo original is a pancake packed with ingredients like cabbage, meat, seafood, green onions, cheese, and more. Its base is a simple pan-fried batter made from *dashi* (stock), flour, and water. Goes down best with beer.

- **Ramen:** This popular dish consists of wheat noodles, topped with sheets of *nori* (seaweed), chunks of pork, bamboo shoots, green onions, and more, served in broth flavored with miso, pork bones, fish, soy sauce, or some other infusion. Tokyo's Asakusa neighborhood, Kyoto, and Onomichi each have their own spin on the dish.

- **Soba:** Buckwheat noodles served in various ways—in hot soup, cold with dipping sauce, as *yaki-soba* ("grilled soba"), with various fixings. This dish is seen throughout Japan, though some of Kyoto's soba restaurants are noted for elevating the dish to its highest culinary expression.

- **Yakitori:** Chicken and vegetables on skewers, cooked over an open flame or charcoal grill. Pork and even beef are also served at some yakitori (literally "grilled chicken") joints, which range from chic and pricey to cheap eats under the train tracks, like Tokyo's culinary alleys.

- *Tonkatsu:* Breaded, deep-fried pork cutlet, often served with a bowl of rice, miso soup, pickled vegetables, shredded cabbage, and a sweet-savory sauce. This crowd-pleaser originated in Tokyo, where some of the best restaurants serving it are found, but it's popular across Japan.

- **Tempura:** Seafood, vegetables, and more, battered and deep-fried. Originally learned from Portuguese during the 16th century, this dish ranges from cheap to eye-poppingly pricey. Find the best tempura at one of the posh eateries in Tokyo and Kyoto where chefs are masters of the art, but brace yourself for the check.

- *Kaiseki ryōri:* This refined multicourse banquet grew out of the tea ceremony. Ingredients are highly seasonal, preparation methods are masterful, presentation is stunning, and prices match the effort. Given its tea ceremony ties, this culinary tradition is deeply rooted in Kyoto, although high-end *ryokan* across the country are likely to serve it.

- *Shōjin-ryōri:* Simple, healthy vegetarian fare prepared for Buddhist monks. The best place to authentically eat this is at a temple in Kyoto.

- *Wagashi:* Japanese get their sweets fix with very subtle ingredients like *mochi* (rice cake) filled with mildly sweet *azuki* (red bean) paste, or cold arrowroot noodles. The best way to try *wagashi* is by pairing it with a bitter cup of *matcha* (green tea) at a tea house in Kyoto.

- *Okonomiyaki:* This savory pancake packed with vegetables, meat, seafood, cheese, kimchi, and more is an Osaka favorite. Hiroshima also has its own take on this dish, adding noodles to the mix.

- *Takoyaki:* Another Osaka creation, these greasy balls of wheat flour-based batter stuffed with hunks of grilled octopus, green onion, and pickled ginger are cooked inside a special spherical pan. Best eaten in the backstreets of Osaka's Namba district while swilling pints of beer.

- *Kushikatsu:* Another dish with roots in Osaka, *kushikatsu* consists of breaded and deep-fried vegetables and meat (*katsu*) served on skewers (*kushi*). The price ranges from bottom-yen to pricey.

- *Wagyu:* Literally "Japanese beef," *wagyu* is marbled to a degree you've likely not seen elsewhere. When quality and preparation come together right, it literally melts in your mouth. There are a handful of regions in Japan famous for their beef, but Kobe is king.

- **Oysters:** The oysters plucked from the waters off the coasts of Hiroshima and Miyajima are known for their size, juiciness, and tenderness. Restaurants in both prepare fresh oysters any number of ways: grilled, breaded and deep-fried, pickled, steamed.

downhill about 10 minutes to the well-heeled neighborhood of **Ebisu** for dinner. Finish the evening over cocktails or whisky at one of the stylish bars nearby in **Nakameguro.**

DAY 2
Begin the day by transporting yourself to Japan's pop cultural wormhole, **Nakano Broadway,** west of downtown. After surveying the array of shops selling anime, manga, video games, and more, take the train 10 minutes west to **Kichijōji.** Eat lunch in the area, then amble south of Kichijōji Station, through forested **Inokashira-kōen,** and make your way to **Ghibli Museum.** After losing yourself in the imagination of anime director Hayao Miyazaki, stroll northward, back through the park, and grab a **coffee** to drink on the go. Take your time and relax in this suburban escape, centered on a large pond teeming with swan boats. Gradually return to the area around Kichijōji Station and take the train directly to either **Shimokitazawa** or **Kōenji** for dinner and an evening stroll in either of these bohemian

zones. After dinner, simply wandering through the streets in any of these three areas will yield colorful surprises.

DAY 3
Today, head to **Yokohama,** roughly 30 minutes by train south of Tokyo, in the morning. First stop: **Minato Mirai.** To get a sense of the city, ride the elevator to the observation deck atop **Landmark Tower.** Next, visit the nearby **Cupnoodles Museum,** designing your own spin on this prepackaged culinary phenomenon and having a sealed take-home specimen for later consumption. Ramen container in hand, walk south to the seaside park **Yamashita-kōen** and stop at moored World War II-era ship, the **NYK Hikawa Maru.** Next, head to **Chinatown** for lunch. Fueled up, walk south and uphill to the **Yamate** district, which sprawls across a bluff overlooking downtown and the harbor. Stop for a coffee and dessert at **Enokitei Honten** as you explore the area, peppered with handsome 19th-century Western-style homes. For dinner, try **Araiya.** If you've

Ghibli Museum

Arashiyama Bamboo Grove

matcha green tea tasting in Kyoto

got the stamina, do a bar crawl through the adjacent neighborhoods of **Kannai, Bashamichi,** and **Noge.** Return to Tokyo by the last train.

DAY 4

After an early breakfast, travel to Kyoto, arriving by late morning. Start your day early in the northwest of town at **Ryōan-ji,** aiming to arrive right when the gates open to beat the crowds. After gazing for a time at Ryōan-ji's classic rock garden, walk 20 minutes east to **Kinkaku-ji,** the unfortunately crowded, though beautiful "Golden Pavilion." From there, continue another 20 minutes on foot east to mercifully less-crowded **Daitoku-ji.** After exploring its beautiful gardens, have a vegetarian monk's *shōjin-ryōri* lunch at the temple's restaurant. Next, head west to the district of **Arashiyama.** Begin your tour of the area at its undeniably atmospheric (and crowded) **bamboo grove.** After that, don't miss the secluded **Ōkōchi-Sansō** villa, just beyond the grove. To go far beyond where most tourists stop, continue into Arashiyama's backside, where a succession of

quiet temples await, all within 20 minutes' walk of the villa: **Jōjakkō-ji, Nison-in, Giō-ji,** and **Adashino Nenbutsu-ji.** Have dinner downtown to see the city's more modern side.

DAY 5

Begin this full day by exploring **Northern Higashiyama,** which mercifully receives less foot traffic than its southern neighbor, around 9am. Walk via the **Philosopher's Path** from the major temple of **Ginkaku-ji** ("Silver Pavilion") to quiet, mossy **Hōnen-in;** leafy **Eikan-dō;** and **Nanzen-ji,** venturing into the temple's forested backside. Eat a slightly early lunch near Nanzen-ji, then meander over to the nearby hill known as **Yoshidayama,** which sees a fraction of the tourists. Walk up the hill, stopping at the two atmospheric temples of **Konkai-Kōmyō-ji** and **Shinnyo-dō,** followed by **Yoshida-jinja** shrine. From the peak of the hill, continue walking northwest to Demachiyanagi Station, roughly 15 minutes away. From there, ride the Keihan main line to the Keihan Uji line to **Uji,** where you can enjoy

Hanami and *Kōyō* in Tokyo, Kyoto & Hiroshima

In spring, the coming of the *sakura* (cherry blossoms) marks the transition from winter into spring. It is a glorious time to be in the country, underscoring just how much the seasons figure into the nation's psyche. People flock to parks and riversides around the country, sitting under the pink boughs in an annual rite known as *hanami* (flower viewing). In autumn, a more subdued, though equally Japanese pastime known as *kōyō* takes place when the leaves of maples, gingkos, and more blanket the country in an earth-tone palette of red, orange, yellow, tan, and brown.

HOW TO SEE CHERRY BLOSSOMS AND AUTUMN FOLIAGE

Hanami tends to sweep through the region covered in this book around the last week of **March** and the first week of **April**. Peak *kōyō* runs **mid-November-early December**. If you'd love to see the autumn leaves, consider early December, when the rush begins to dwindle.

Being in Japan during either season is magical, but be forewarned: These are **peak travel times**. To ensure you're not left with slim pickings for accommodations, or paying maximum yen, plan any travel during these times *early*. Think 9-12 months in advance. Keep in mind that **weekdays** will be less hectic than weekends. Also, it often gets chilly during both seasons in the evening, so **wear layers**.

THE BEST SPOTS

Tokyo

Some of the best spots to enjoy *hanami* in Tokyo include lovely but thronged **Ueno-kōen, Yoyogi-kōen,** and my personal favorite, **Inokashira-kōen.** More moderately crowded options include **Hama-rikyū Onshi-teien** and **Chidorigafuchi.**

For *kōyō*, visit **Shinjuku Gyōen** and **Koishikawa Kōrakuen.** Tokyo is mercifully quieter during this time than Kyoto, justly famous for its fall season.

Kyoto

Kyoto is inundated with travelers during *hanami* season. You may want to consider avoiding the city at this time if you don't want to deal with crowds; nonetheless, the allure is undeniable. Foremost, **Maruyama-kōen,** the banks of the **Kamo River,** and the **Philosopher's Path** are lovely. **Heian-jingū** and the grounds of **Kyoto Imperial Palace** are a bit less crowded.

Kyoto's best *kōyō* spots range from ubercrowded (**Kinkaku-ji, Kiyomizu-dera, Fushimi Inari-Taisha**) to moderately popular (**Nanzen-ji, Eikan-dō, Hōnen-in, Ginkaku-ji, Tōfuku-ji**) to some lesser-known gems (**Sennyū-ji, Shinnyo-dō**).

Beyond Tokyo and Kyoto

Beyond Tokyo and Kyoto, other great *hanami* spots in the region include the north shore of **Lake Kawaguchi;** in Kansai, the grounds of **Osaka-jō, Nara-kōen,** and the grounds of **Himeji-jō;** Hiroshima's **Peace Memorial Park, Shukkei-en,** and the park surrounding **Hiroshima Castle.**

Prime autumn spots that fall within the scope of this book include **Nara-kōen** (go early in the morning and walk far into the park's backside to get away from the worst of the crowds); Onomichi (**Kōsan-ji** and the **Temple Walk**); Hiroshima's **Mitaki-dera** (expect crowds, but it's stunning); and the entire island of **Miyajima.** Outside Tokyo, **Lake Kawaguchi** is lovely in mid-November, as is **Hakone**—best seen from an *onsen* with a view.

---

a **tea-tasting** session or even a tea-related workshop, and stop by the sweeping temple complex of **Byōdō-in** if you've got time and energy. Return to Kyoto in the early evening for dinner.

DAY 6

Depart Kyoto early in the morning, bound for **Naoshima,** a picturesque island in Japan's gorgeous **Inland Sea** that has developed a reputation for its eclectic modern **art museums,** sculptures dotting the landscape, and laid-back villages. You'll make the journey via *shinkansen*, local train, and ferry, approximately 2 hours altogether. Once you reach the island, drop off your bags at your accommodation, have lunch at one of the charming cafés, and then explore the **Art House Project** (empty houses transformed into works of art in the old village of Honmura), the museum-cum-hotel **Benesse House,** and the **Chichū Art Museum,** built directly into the earth. Don't miss the fiery-orange **sunset** along this southern stretch of coastline.

DAY 7

Early the next morning, return by ferry to the mainland and proceed to nearby **Kurashiki.** Explore its canal district for a few hours and have lunch there. Once you've fueled up, travel west to the nostalgic port town of **Onomichi,** just over an hour away by train. Once in Onomichi, leave your luggage in a locker at the station, then make your way to the port, ride the ferry 40 minutes to the island of **Ikuchi-jima,** and **rent a bicycle** to pedal the massive **Tatara Bridge** to the neighboring island of **Ōmi-shima.** After taking

in the stunning views of the Inland Sea on the **Shimanami Kaidō** cycling route, return by ferry to Onomichi to proceed to Hiroshima.

DAY 8

After the busy previous day, start your day easy in **Hiroshima** with a slow-paced journey through **Peace Memorial Park.** After taking in the numerous reminders and lessons of the horrors of atomic weaponry, decompress by taking the train northwest of downtown to the enigmatic forest temple **Mitaki-dera.** Take your time to explore this enchanting complex, spread over a mountainside and set beside three waterfalls. Descend and return to downtown to sample the city's own spin on the savory pancake dish known as *okonomiyaki.* After dinner, make your way to Miyajima-guchi, about 25 minutes away from Hiroshima Station by train, then take a brief ferry ride to Miyajima, the lush, fabled island just off the coast, for either a one- or two-night stay. Basing yourself on the island for two nights allows you to enjoy the island's quiet and explore it without crowds.

Benesse House

Hiroshima Peace Memorial Park

Miyajima Ropeway to the top of Mount Misen

DAY 9

Start your exploration of the island at its most famous site, the iconic "floating" shrine of **Itsukushima-jinja.** Next, visit the colorful temple of **Daishō-in,** then have lunch in the area. Once you've fueled up, make your way through **Momijidani-kōen,** populated by groups of tame deer, and find the **Miyajima Ropeway.** Ride this to the top of **Mount Misen,** the peak that dominates this hallowed island. As you progress up the mountain, the views of the surrounding sea are increasingly stunning. Once you reach the top ropeway station, hike the remaining 30 minutes to the summit, where the great holy man Kūkai once meditated for 100 days and lit a flame at the **Reikadō,** which is said to have burned continuously for 1,200 years. Go back down the mountain—either by ropeway or on foot, depending on time and energy—and catch your breath at one of the town's cafés if you're so inclined. Once you've caught your breath, return to your accommodation to rest and clean up.

DAY 10

On the last full day, make a half-day trip to **Iwakuni,** a town about 1 hour west of Hiroshima by train or about 25 minutes by train from Miyajimaguchi, famed for its mammoth arched-wooden bridge **Kintaikyō** and old samurai quarter **Kikkō-kōen.** Have lunch there, then return to Hiroshima and there to hop on a *shinkansen* to **Tokyo,** where you'll be in a good position to comfortably catch your return flight home.

Tokyo

Tokyo is more than a city. Japan's sprawling capital bursts at the seams with a population of 37 million to form the largest metro area on the planet. The dizzying metropolis organically congeals around a cluster of hubs the size of cities themselves, giving Tokyo a labyrinthine quality. With the neon nightscapes of Shinjuku and Shibuya evoking *Blade Runner* in the west, the ancient temples and wooden houses of Ueno and Asakusa in the east, and palpable energy coursing throughout, Tokyo packs a strong sensory punch.

The city's dynamism is inextricably linked to its history of continuous reinvention. Long before its ascent on the world stage, Tokyo was a small fishing hamlet known as Edo, located on the banks of the Sumida River. Its clout began to grow when Tokugawa Ieyasu, founder

Highlights

Look for ★ to find recommended sights, activities, dining, and lodging.

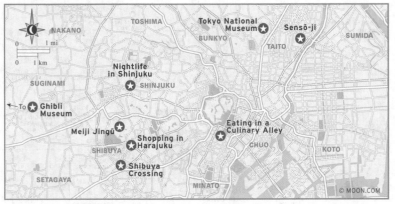

★ **Shibuya Crossing:** Simply crossing the world's busiest pedestrian intersection will leave you gobsmacked by Tokyo's formidable pulse (page 64).

★ **Meiji Jingū:** Surrounded by forest, this majestic Shinto shrine provides an oasis of calm just beyond the fashionable throngs of Harajuku (page 69).

★ **Tokyo National Museum:** If you only have time for one museum in your Tokyo itinerary, make it this one—it holds the world's largest collection of Japanese art (page 77).

★ **Sensō-ji:** Tokyo's most famous temple houses a golden image of the Buddhist Goddess of Mercy (page 79).

★ **Ghibli Museum:** This fantastical museum dedicated to Japan's most beloved anime studio, Studio Ghibli, sits within Inokashira-kōen, one of Tokyo's most appealing parks (page 83).

★ **Shopping in Harajuku:** Ground zero for Japan's colorful youth fashion scene, this neighborhood is full of hip boutiques clustered around the busy thoroughfare of Omotesandō and tucked down a dense tangle of pedestrian-friendly backstreets (page 102).

★ **Eating in a culinary alley:** Take a seat beside locals at a hole-in-the-wall eatery in one of Tokyo's numerous *yokochō* (culinary alleys) for a meal and an experience you won't forget (page 120).

★ **Nightlife in Shinjuku:** Tokyo's most eclectic nightlife zone offers experiences from robot battles to pub crawls through the tumble-down bars of Golden Gai (page 130).

Tokyo

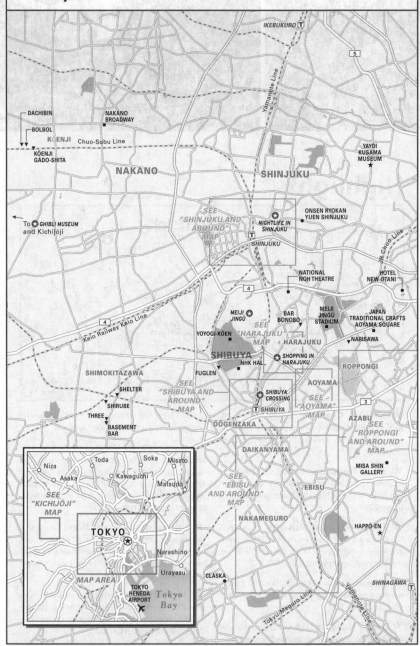

IKEBUKURO T

5

DACHIBIN

BOLBOL
KŌENJI   Chuo-Sobu Line
KŌENJI
GĀDO-SHITA

NAKANO
BROADWAY

YAYOI
KUSAMA
MUSEUM
★

NAKANO

SHINJUKU

SEE
"SHINJUKU AND
AROUND"
MAP

NIGHTLIFE IN
SHINJUKU

ONSEN RYOKAN
YUEN SHINJUKU

To ✪ GHIBLI MUSEUM
and Kichijōji

T
SHINJUKU

NATIONAL
NOH THEATRE

HOTEL
NEW OTANI

4

Keio Railway Keio Line

4

MEIJI
JINGŪ ✪

YOYOGI-KŌEN ■

SEE
"HARAJUKU"
MAP

BAR
BONOBO

MEIJI
JINGŪ
STADIUM

JAPAN
TRADITIONAL CRAFTS
AOYAMA SQUARE

HARAJUKU

NARISAWA

JR Chuo Line

SHIBUYA

NHK HALL

SHOPPING IN
HARAJUKU

ROPPONGI

SHIMOKITAZAWA

SHELTER

SHIRUBE

THREE

BASEMENT
BAR

FUGLEN

SEE
"SHIBUYA AND
AROUND"
MAP

SHIBUYA
CROSSING

AOYAMA

SEE
"AOYAMA"
MAP

3

T SHIBUYA

DŌGENZAKA

AZABU

SEE
"ROPPONGI
AND AROUND"
MAP

DAIKANYAMA

SEE
"EBISU
AND AROUND"
MAP

MISA SHIN
GALLERY

EBISU

Niza   Toda   Soka   Misato

Asaka   Kawaguchi   Matsudo

SEE
"KICHIJŌJI"
MAP

TOKYO ✪

MAP AREA

TOKYO
HENEDA
AIRPORT ✈

Narashino

Urayasu

Tokyo
Bay

NAKAMEGURO

HAPPŌ-EN
★

CLASKA

SHINAGAWA

Tōkyu-Meguro Line

Yamanote Line

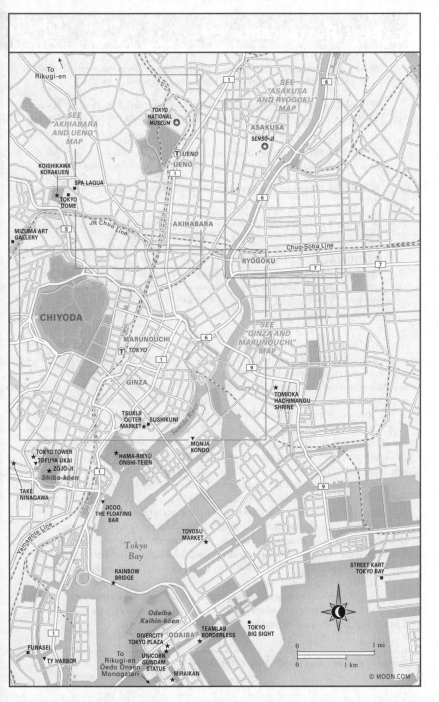

To Rikugi-en

SEE "AKIHABARA AND UENO" MAP

SEE "ASAKUSA AND RYOGOKU" MAP

TOKYO NATIONAL MUSEUM

ASAKUSA

SENSŌ-JI

UENO

UENO

KOISHIKAWA KORAKUEN

SPA LAQUA

TOKYO DOME

MIZUMA ART GALLERY

JR Chuo Line

AKIHABARA

Chuo-Sobu Line

RYOGOKU

CHIYODA

MARUNOUCHI

TOKYO

SEE "GINZA AND MARUNOUCHI" MAP

GINZA

TOMIOKA HACHIMANGU SHRINE

TSUKIJI OUTER MARKET

SUSHIKUNI

Sumida River

MONJA KONDO

TOKYO TOWER

TOFUYA UKAI

ZŌJŌ-JI

Shiba-kōen

HAMA-RIKYŪ ONSHI-TEIEN

TAKE NINAGAWA

JICOO, THE FLOATING BAR

TOYOSU MARKET

Tokyo Bay

RAINBOW BRIDGE

STREET KART TOKYO BAY

Yamanote Line

Odaiba Kaihin-kōen

FUNASEI

TY HARBOR

DIVERCITY TOKYO PLAZA

ODAIBA

TEAMLAB BORDERLESS

TOKYO BIG SIGHT

To Rikugi-en Ōedo Onsen Monogatari

UNICORN GUNDAM STATUE

MIRAIKAN

0   1 mi

0   1 km

© MOON.COM

Best Restaurants

★ **Ginza Kyubey:** For the quintessential sushi experience, reserve a seat at the counter and watch the chefs prepare their delectable creations right before you (page 109).

★ **Tonki:** For the city's best *tonkatsu* (deep-fried breaded pork cutlet), head to this revered restaurant where generations of chefs have been artfully creating the dish since 1939 (page 112).

★ **Shirube:** The open kitchen churns out classics and innovative fare to a boisterous clientele, making dinner here an essential *izakaya* (Japanese pub) experience (page 113).

★ **Sakurai Japanese Tea Experience:** Open your eyes to the wonders of tea (page 117).

★ **Nihon Saisei Sakaba:** It's all about the pig at Nihon Saisei Sakaba, a standing-only *izakaya* that serves essentially every pig part, grilled, on a stick (page 118).

REGIONAL SPECIALTIES

While Tokyo offers everything under the sun, the city is where sushi originated as *nigiri* (sashimi, or raw fish, placed on a bed of rice). Another specialty born in the capital is *monjayaki,* a savory pancake containing hunks of meat, seafood, and vegetables.

of the Tokugawa shogunate, chose to base his government in Edo Castle in 1603. By the mid-18th century, Edo's population swelled to 1 million, making it the world's largest city at the time.

The city was renamed Tokyo (Eastern Capital) in 1868, when the official capital migrated from Kyoto and the Tokugawa shogunate's rule came to an end. It was this pivotal year when political power returned to the emperor via the Meiji Restoration, and Japan opened up to the world beyond after enforcing a policy of self-isolation for more than 250 years. Tokyoites eagerly lapped up the new influences from abroad, from fashion to philosophy, and the contours of the present city began to take shape.

The capital's culinary offerings are truly world-class, from mom-and-pop ramen shops to lavish sushi spreads. It's the best place in Japan to watch traditional kabuki and *Noh*

theater performances, as well as sumo. The city oozes style, with high-end outposts as well as Harajuku's quirky collection of youth-oriented labels. Tokyo is also home to one of the world's most singular pop culture industries, most visible in the gadget paradise of Akihabara's "Electric Town." Moreover, Tokyo simply works. Compared with other major cities, it's positively spic and span. Well-stocked vending machines and convenience stores are reassuringly never more than a few blocks away. And trains full of dapper commuters rarely miss a beat.

But wander away from any busy station and you'll soon discover a dense network of communities with fiercely maintained traditions, where denizens shop at the neighborhood store and rowdy homegrown festivals mark the passing of time, revealing the city at its most hospitable. Embrace the warm welcome, and enjoy getting lost.

Previous: *torii* of Meiji Jingū; Shibuya Crossing; Ghibli Museum.

Best Accommodations

★ **Aman:** Massive yet understated rooms reminiscent of a *ryokan* (traditional inn), each with a *yuzu*-infused stone bathtub and outstanding views of the city at night, offer a high-end respite from the city (page 134).

★ **Hotel New Otani:** A city within the city with a deep sense of history, this hotel has a gorgeous garden, complete with a dramatic waterfall (page 135).

★ **Park Hyatt Tokyo:** This legendary hotel in a prime location amid the skyscrapers of western Shinjuku boasts amazing service, spectacular views of Mount Fuji, and as seen in the film *Lost in Translation,* one of the most dazzling cocktail bars in the world (page 136).

★ **Hanare:** A wonderful *ryokan* in the heart of the charming Yanaka neighborhood includes staff eager to help you explore the city and full of helpful suggestions (page 137).

★ **Gate Hotel Kaminarimon:** In the heart of Asakusa, this hotel is ideally situated for sightseeing in the historic part of town and has a great restaurant, terrace, and bar (page 138).

ORIENTATION

Although Tokyo is commonly thought of as a city, it is in fact one of Japan's 47 prefectures. It's divided into 23 special wards, which function as cities themselves. More than 9 million people live in the 23 special wards, and 13 million reside within the prefecture. The greater metropolitan area is home to a whopping 37.8 million, making it the most populous metro area on the planet.

Wrapping your mind around this massive slice of humanity is daunting, but it's helpful to think of Tokyo not in terms of officially drawn lines but rather as a vast collection of neighborhoods that have grown around a matrix of railway stations. Thankfully, the excellent train and subway system can get you within a short walk of just about anywhere in the city. Key among the railway lines are the roughly ovular **Yamanote line,** which wraps around the city, and the **Chūō line,** which pierces through the center of the city, running east to west. Most travelers stick to major hubs dotting the Yamanote line or inside this loop, with occasional forays west to some of the city's more free-spirited haunts.

While you wouldn't guess it on the street,

Tokyo is a watery realm. All told, upward of 100 rivers and canals flow beneath this concrete jungle, while a handful of broad waterways remain visible, drawing neighborhood boundaries and serving as conduits for pleasure barges and boats bearing goods. The **Sumida River** drifts southward through the heart of Asakusa, passing Ryōgoku, Ginza, and Shimbashi to the west, and Odaiba to the east, and merging with Tokyo Bay. The **Kanda River** spills into the Sumida River just east of Akihabara, after running eastward through the heart of the city from its origin in the central pond of Inokashira-kōen in the western suburb of Kichijōji.

Wherever you are in the city, finding someone fluent in English can be tough. Thankfully, Tokyo residents and police on duty in the city's multitude of *koban* (police boxes) are legendary for going out of their way to help overseas visitors.

Ginza and Marunouchi

Starting near **Tokyo Station,** on the eastern end of the Yamanote line, Tokyo's seat of power is Marunouchi and the sprawling green area around the **Imperial Palace,** set in what's known as the **Chiyoda** district, which has marked the geographic heart of the city since the Edo period. South of Tokyo Station is Ginza, its broad avenues lined with luxury **fashion boutiques, department stores,** and upmarket cafés, restaurants, and bars. It's also home to **Kabuki-za,** where most of the city's kabuki plays are staged.

Tokyo Bay Area

Southeast of the central areas of Ginza and Marunouchi, Tokyo Bay was best known as the home of the Tsukiji Fish Market until it closed in 2018. Across the bay from Tsukiji is **Odaiba,** a human-made island with a number of interesting **museums** and a seaside park, **Odaiba Kaihin-kōen,** that offers some of the best nighttime views of the city.

Roppongi and Around

Inside the southern side of the Yamanote line, a number of cosmopolitan hubs sustain a large share of Tokyo's expat community. Roppongi is at the center of this zone, offering a mix of posh eateries, world-class **art museums,** and one of the city's highest concentrations of **nightlife,** some of it seedy. Nearby, **Azabu** is packed with fine-dining establishments and exclusive shops. These neighborhoods fall under the umbrella of the **Minato** ward, considered one of the capital's priciest areas to call home.

Ebisu and Around

At the southwestern corner of the Yamanote line is upmarket Ebisu, which forms a low-key, sophisticated triangle with neighboring districts **Daikanyama** and **Nakameguro,** chock-full of hip fashion boutiques and excellent options for drinking and dining. Besides bars and restaurants, there are also a handful of worthwhile **museums** in the area, including the **Tokyo Photographic Art Museum,** Tokyo's largest photography exhibition space.

Shibuya and Around

Continuing clockwise on the Yamanote line from Ebisu, Shibuya is one of the best places to experience Tokyo at full tilt. Stepping into the fray at **Shibuya Crossing** is one of the most intensely urban experiences to be had on earth. The bulk of the action is found in the congested streets of **Center Gai** and in the alleys leading away from the station up the hill known as **Dogenzaka.** Just a few stops to the west on the Inokashira line, Counterculture nexus **Shimokitazawa** is directly accessible from Shibuya Station.

Harajuku and Aoyama

Just north of Shibuya, Harajuku is hallowed ground, both as the location of **Meiji Jingū,** perhaps the city's grandest shrine, and for youth trends and streetwear. Neighboring Aoyama is a fashion mecca as well, catering to a much more sophisticated and well-heeled class. Architecture buffs will appreciate the hodgepodge of iconic buildings dotting the wide leafy avenue of **Omotesandō**—the Champs-Elysées of Tokyo—which runs through the heart of both neighborhoods. Besides fashion, both areas are home to a number of **museums,** featuring everything from woodblock prints to Buddhist statuary.

Shinjuku and Around

Though Tokyo's historical and geographic heart may lie in the neighborhoods surrounding the Imperial Palace, in many ways the heartbeat of modern Tokyo is the western hub of Shinjuku, once a sleepy suburb. The sheer energy of **Shinjuku Station,** the world's busiest railway terminal, is tremendous. You'll find a number of the city's nightlife districts here, including **Omoide Yokochō (Memory Lane),** a smoky, raucous pair of lanes tightly packed with small bars and restaurants; **Kabukichō,** the city's largest nightlife zone and home to **Golden Gai,** an iconic collection of tumbledown bars; and the city's lively gay quarter **Shinjuku Ni-chōme.** To the south is **Shinjuku Gyōen,** one of the city's most picturesque parks.

Akihabara and Ueno

Coming on the east side of the Yamanote line's loop, north of Tokyo Station, is the geeked-out zone of Akihabara, devoted almost entirely to supplying the **gadgets** for all manner of quirky hobbies, along with **idol group performances,** cosplay, anime, manga, and more. One stop north is Ueno, a historical and cultural hot spot. The expansive grounds of **Ueno-kōen**—Tokyo's largest park—are home to a number of major museums, from natural history to modern art, with the excellent **Tokyo National Museum** topping the list.

Asakusa and Ryōgoku

North of Ueno, accessible from most of the city only via the Ginza and Toei Asakusa subway lines, Asakusa is Tokyo at its **old-school** best. Like most of the city, much of the area was razed during World War II, but the narrow zigzagging streets, **temples,** aged wooden houses, and shops evoke an earlier time. Across the Sumida River, the neighborhood of Ryōgoku is the nation's foremost center for the ancient sport of **sumo.**

Western Tokyo

There are a few notable areas in Western Tokyo, easily reached from Shinjuku Station along the Chūō line. First is **Nakano,** an *otaku* (geek culture) haven, and farther west, **Kichijōji** is home to luxuriant **Inokashira-kōen** and the whimsical **Ghibli Museum.** Between Nakano and Kichijōji on the Chūō line, **Kōenji** is one of Tokyo's prime countercultural hotspots.

PLANNING YOUR TIME

You can get a good introduction to Tokyo in as little as two or three days; this is enough time to see the highlights of the central part of the city, and to sample the vast culinary, nightlife, and shopping options. With an additional day or two, you can go a bit off the beaten path and explore the more local side of the city. Plan to stay in either **Shibuya** or **Shinjuku** in the west if you want access to the more clamorous, modern side of the city; in the east, **Ueno** and **Asakusa** are good bases

if you'd like an older, slower pace. Meanwhile, **Ginza** and **Marunouchi** have a glut of luxury hotels. The bulk of the city's sights and activities are concentrated in these neighborhoods, with some in trendy residential pockets to the south and west.

In Tokyo **opening times** vary greatly, and many shops, museums, and even restaurants are closed on certain days each week. Some popular sights like **Tokyo Skytree** fill up fast, so it pays to arrive at or just before opening time to beat the rush, or show up from late-afternoon on, after crowds have dispersed.

Weather in the Tokyo area varies significantly by season. **Spring** and **autumn** are the most pleasant times of year, with mild temperatures in the range of 7-19°C (45-66°F) and the arrival of gorgeous cherry blossoms in late March-early April, or beautiful foliage when leaves change color in autumn. **Summer** is humid and can be sweltering (roughly 20-35°C/68-95°F or higher), punctuated by intermittent typhoons in August, September, and sometimes even early October, but it's also a fun time to visit to attend traditional festivals and large music events. **Winter** is cold (average temperatures around 5°C/41°F), but snow is rare; mostly blue skies are the norm. As it's off-season, prices for flights and rooms tend to drop.

Advance Reservations

Other attractions like the **Ghibli Museum,** as well as many popular restaurants, require bookings weeks or even a month or more in advance. Consult the official website of any given attraction beforehand. Pre-planning is key. This is doubly so in light of the impact of **COVID-19.** Some popular attractions have instituted reservation systems to control the flow of foot traffic to help prevent the spread of the virus, a practice that may remain in place beyond the pandemic. To be safe, check the website of any given sight or attraction to confirm whether you need to reserve a spot beforehand.

Itinerary Ideas

TOKYO ON DAY 1

Spend your first day getting to know the hip, modern, young side of Tokyo, focusing on the areas of **Harajuku** and its central thoroughfare Omotesandō, **Aoyama, Shibuya,** and **Ebisu.** You'll discover Tokyo's top shrine, see cutting-edge architecture, and visit a sleek museum before merging with the masses at the world's busiest pedestrian crossing. You'll also eat great meals, sip tea and creative cocktails. All the neighborhoods you'll visit are clustered around the southwestern side of town, which makes them easy to travel between. Most neighborhoods are a 20-minute walk apart, though you can opt to take the train instead (usually just one stop).

1 From Harajuku Station, proceed down the gravel path that leads from the back to Tokyo's grandest shrine, **Meiji Jingū** to explore its grounds and inner sanctum.

2 After backtracking to the towering *torii* gate that marks the entrance to the shrine, begin walking down the famous shopping street Omotesandō, taking in architecture and exploring quirky fashion boutiques tucked in backstreets. Stop for an early lunch at **Maisen,** one of the city's better purveyors of *tonkatsu* (breaded pork cutlet), set in a chicly renovated bathhouse on a Harajuku side street.

3 At the end of Omotesandō, in the posh Aoyama neighborhood, you'll come to the **Nezu Museum.** Explore the collection of East Asian art and religious artifacts in the museum itself, then meander through its beautiful garden.

4 Backtrack down Omotesandō toward **Sakurai Japanese Tea Experience.** Get to know the ancient tradition of Japanese tea in this modern, stylish tearoom.

5 With your appreciation for the humble tea leaf enhanced, walk southwest (about 20 minutes) to Shibuya Station where you'll behold the maelstrom of **Shibuya Crossing.**

6 Spend a bit of time meandering through the belly of the beast in the pedestrian-only Center Gai area, not far from Shibuya Station, to get a visceral sense of Tokyo's pulse. Stop by **Purikura no Mecca** to take some self-portraits in one of the singular photo booths that are all the rage among Japan's youth. (Note that you might not be admitted if you're a guy traveling solo or in a male-only group.)

7 Take a coffee break—and a step back in time—at **Chatei Hatou,** an excellent old-school *kissaten* (tea-drinking place) about a 10-minute walk east of Center Gai, on the opposite side of the Meiji-dōri thoroughfare.

8 As dinnertime approaches, hop on the Yamanote line at Shibuya Station to the stylish neighborhood of Ebisu. Have dinner in rowdy and boisterous **Ebisu Yokochō,** a covered alleyway of no-frills eateries serving grilled meats and vegetables on sticks and in stews, and plenty of booze to wash it all down.

9 If you've got the energy, go for drinks after dinner. **Bar Tram,** a dimly lit bar with a speakeasy vibe known for its absinthe-base cocktails, is a good pick.

TOKYO ON DAY 2

On Day 2, look back on Tokyo's history, starting with a visit to an ancient temple in **Asakusa** and ending in **Shinjuku,** where nostalgic post-war buildings are juxtaposed with towers draped with neon signs. This itinerary gives a taste of Tokyo's dichotomous cultural heritage, from the oldest and best collection of classical Japanese art, the **Tokyo National Museum** in **Ueno,** to the quirky pop-cultural mecca of up-to-the-minute **Akihabara.**

1   Start your day at the famed boisterous temple of **Sensō-ji** in Asakusa, in the older eastern side of town.

2   Hop on the Ginza subway line at Asakusa Station and make your way to Ueno Station and **Tokyo National Museum,** a 10-minute walk northwest of the station and the world's largest collection of Japanese art.

3   Cross Ueno-kōen, Tokyo's largest park, to **Hantei** (about a 15-minute walk west) for a lunch of *kushiage* (battered and deep-fried meat and vegetables on sticks) in a charming Meiji period home.

4   From here, hop on the train at Nezu Station, right outside Hantei. Ride to Nishi-Nippori Station on the Chiyoda subway line, then transfer to the Yamanote line to Akihabara Station. Spend the next few hours getting lost in Akihabara's warren of quirky pop culture. A good starting point is **Mandarake,** a one-stop shop for geeks that sells everything from anime and manga to vintage figurines and cosplay attire.

5   Taking the Hibiya line from Akihabara, make your way to Roppongi. Head to **Tokyo City View and Sky Deck** in the Roppongi Hills complex for stellar views of the city at dusk. If you have time, just underneath Tokyo City View is the Mori Art Museum, one more worthwhile stop for the day.

6   From Roppongi Station, hop on the Ōedo line and make your way to Shinjuku as dinnertime approaches. Eat and drink at one of the many hole-in-the-wall options in **Omoide Yokochō,** one of Tokyo's most atmospheric *yokochō* (culinary alleyways).

7   For a mind-blowing spectacle, walk 7 minutes east to **Robot Restaurant** in the neon-drenched red-light district of Kabukichō after dinner. There's no way to easily sum up this epically kitsch, yet technologically stunning, robot showdown.

8   If you're still going strong, follow this up with a bar crawl through **Golden Gai.** Visitors throng to this former black market to drink their way through a warren of 200 tumbledown bars—each with its own décor, ethos, and regular characters.

TOKYO LIKE A LOCAL

The agenda in this third itinerary is focused on a few local haunts just west of downtown, namely **Kichijōji** and **Shimokitazawa.** Kichijōji is home to **Inokashira-kōen,** a lovely park with a central pond, and the **Ghibli Museum,** linked to the beloved anime film studio helmed by Oscar-winning director Hayao Miyazaki. Head next to hipster-favorite Shimokitazawa, and wend through the scrambled streets lined with hip boutiques, cafes, and record shops.

1   Begin your day in the mid- or even late morning in the appealing suburb of Kichijōji, about 15 minutes west of Shinjuku on the Chūō line. Once you arrive, walk south of the station to the lovely, leafy grounds of **Inokashira-kōen.** If you're so inclined, rent one of the swan boats and ply the waters of Inokashira Pond.

2   Have lunch at the whimsical **Café du Lièvre (Bunny House),** which serves a nice selection of Japanese-style curry dishes and crêpes.

3   After lunch, continue walking south through the less-crowded side of the park to the **Ghibli Museum.** Enjoy taking a tour through this playful, artful ode to Studio Ghibli.

4   When you leave the museum, backtrack to Inokashira-kōen. Get a coffee to-go from **Blue Sky Coffee.**

Itinerary Ideas

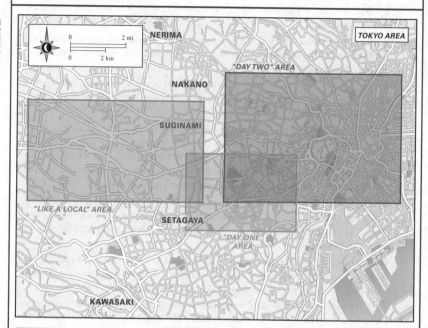

NERIMA

TOKYO AREA

NAKANO

"DAY TWO" AREA

SUGINAMI

"LIKE A LOCAL" AREA

SETAGAYA

"DAY ONE AREA

KAWASAKI

0   2 mi
0   2 km

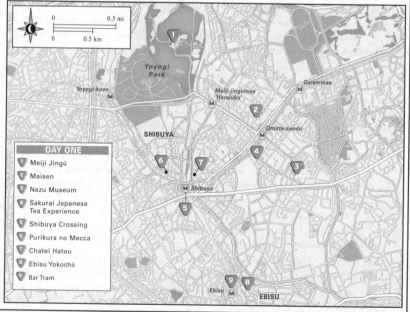

Yoyogi Park

Yoyogi-koen

Meiji-jingumae 'Harajuku'

Gaiemmae

SHIBUYA

Omote-sando

Shibuya

Ebisu

EBISU

0   0.5 mi
0   0.5 km

DAY ONE

1. Meiji Jingū
2. Maisen
3. Nezu Museum
4. Sakurai Japanese Tea Experience
5. Shibuya Crossing
6. Purikura no Mecca
7. Chatei Hatou
8. Ebisu Yokochō
9. Bar Tram

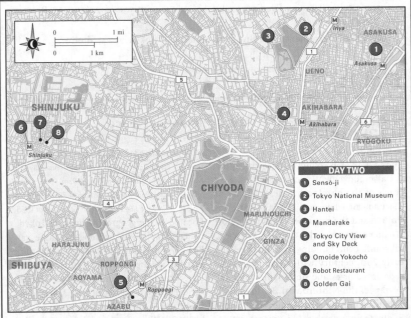

DAY TWO

1. Sensō-ji
2. Tokyo National Museum
3. Hantei
4. Mandarake
5. Tokyo City View and Sky Deck
6. Omoide Yokochō
7. Robot Restaurant
8. Golden Gai

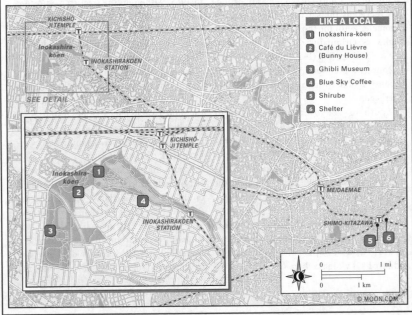

LIKE A LOCAL

1. Inokashira-kōen
2. Café du Lièvre (Bunny House)
3. Ghibli Museum
4. Blue Sky Coffee
5. Shirube
6. Shelter

© MOON.COM

5 Make your way back to Kichijōji Station, stopping to peruse any shops that may catch your eye on the way. Take the Keio-Inokashira line to Shimokitazawa Station (15 minutes, express train) and meander through streets lined by eateries and boutiques with an edgier, countercultural leaning. For dinner, eat at the lively, innovative *izakaya* **Shirube.** Reserve a day ahead to be safe.

6 After dinner, check out the live music scene in Shimokitazawa at **Shelter.**

Sights

GINZA AND MARUNOUCHI
銀座, 丸の内

Today, Ginza is synonymous with glitz. It's also conveniently located within easy reach of the buzzing business district of Marunouchi, where you'll find the **Imperial Palace** and the revamped **Tokyo Station** (1-chōme Marunouchi, Chiyoda-ku; www.tokyoinfo.com) building, which evokes the early 20th century with its appealing facade of red brick and stone. Of historic importance, the **Nihonbashi Bridge** (1-8-1 Nihonbashimuromachi, Chūō-ku), about a 5-minute walk north of Nihonbashi Station, has served as the starting point (marking kilometer zero) for the national network of highways. Originally wooden when built in the early Edo period (1603-1868), today you'll encounter a Meiji period (1868-1912) stone reconstruction, with an expressway running overhead.

South of Tokyo Station, the **Tokyo International Forum** (3-5-1 Marunouchi, Chiyoda-ku; tel. 03/5221-9000; www.t-i-forum.co.jp; 7am-11:30pm daily) is a soaring architectural masterpiece. An ode to natural light envisioned by Uruguayan architect Rafael Viñoly, the ship-like east wing has a spellbinding ceiling of glass and steel. While the building serves primarily as a convention center, it's free to enter for anyone and is worth a quick stop if you're in the area to admire its sky-high ceiling.

Imperial Palace
皇居

1-1 Chiyoda, Chiyoda-ku; tel. 03/3213-1111; https://sankan.kunaicho.go.jp/index.html; 9am-4pm daily Nov.-Feb., 9am-5pm Mar.-mid-Apr., 9am-6pm mid-Apr.-Aug., 9am-5pm Sept., 9am-4:30pm Oct.; free; take Chiyoda line to Ōtemachi Station, exit C13b

Located in the geographic heart of Tokyo, the construction of the Imperial Palace was kicked off by Tokugawa Ieyasu, the first shogun, in 1590. In its heyday, it was the world's largest castle. Today, only the inner circle of the original complex survives. Damaged by fire in 1945, the current palace was rebuilt in 1968. Althought the steel-framed reconstruction is made of concrete, it still looks as you'd expect: sweeping rooflines over white walls, supported by a foundation made from large stones, with a daunting moat crisscrossed by bridges encircling it all. While it commands less attention than the towering original fortress built by Ieyasu must have, the modern-day palace offers respite from the city's hubbub just outside, and the sight of glass-and-steel towers looming nearby offers a striking contrast.

Japan's imperial family resides on the western grounds, which are only open to the public on the emperor's birthday (Feb. 23) and the day after New Year's Day (Jan. 2), when thousands of Japanese try to catch a glimpse of the emperor waving from a palace balcony. The Imperial Household Agency does give two daily **tours** (10am, 1:30pm Tues.-Sat., not held on national holidays; free), each lasting a little more than an hour and delving a bit deeper into the palace grounds. Tours aren't offered during official functions, on public holidays, or during afternoons from late July through August, or December 28-January 4. Spots can be reserved online (http://sankan. kunaicho.go.jp/english/guide/koukyo.html) or by phone as early as a month before you plan to arrive. You can also try your luck and arrive the day of to inquire whether spots are still available; ask at the tour office next to **Kikyo-mon** (Kikyo Gate).

If you decide to forego the tour and explore the grounds on your own, check out the free downloadable **audio guide** (www.kunaicho. go.jp/e-event/app.html). Start in the **Kōkyo-gaien** (www.env.go.jp/garden/kokyogaien), or National Garden, located in the southeastern section of the Imperial Palace grounds. At the western edge of this verdant space, you'll see two iconic bridges. The closer of the two is the **Megane Bridge** ("Eyeglass Bridge"); it was given its nickname because it resembles a pair of spectacles when seen reflected in the moat below. Just behind Megane Bridge stands **Niju Bridge** ("Double Bridge"); its popular name is derived from the fact that it was once a two-level wooden bridge.

EAST GARDEN
皇居東御苑

After either taking a private tour of the palace grounds or capturing a few snapshots in front of these two scenic bridges, proceed to the flawless grounds of the Imperial Palace East Garden. It's a fine example of a Japanese garden, where you can meander along winding paths, over lightly arched bridges, and past stone lanterns, cherry trees, azaleas, and a teahouse. Basking in the pleasant scene, note the stone base of what was once the main tower of Edo Castle, still standing on the lawn. Climb the steps and see the surroundings from atop the last remnants of what was once the world's largest keep.

The garden is best entered via **Ote-mon** (Ote Gate), just west of Ōtemachi Station and roughly a 15-minute walk west of Tokyo Station's Marunouchi North Exit. The **Museum of Imperial Collections** (9am-3:45pm Tues.-Thurs. and Sat.-Sun. Nov.-Feb., 9am-4:45pm Tues.-Thurs. and Sat.-Sun. Mar.-mid-Apr., 9am-5:45pm Tues.-Thurs. and Sat.-Sun. mid-Apr.-Aug., 9am-4:45pm Tues.-Thurs. and Sat.-Sun. Sept., 9am-4:15pm Oct.; free) just beyond Ote-mon, shows off a small selection of the imperial family's more than 9,000 pieces of Japanese art.

Imperial Palace

Ginza and Marunouchi

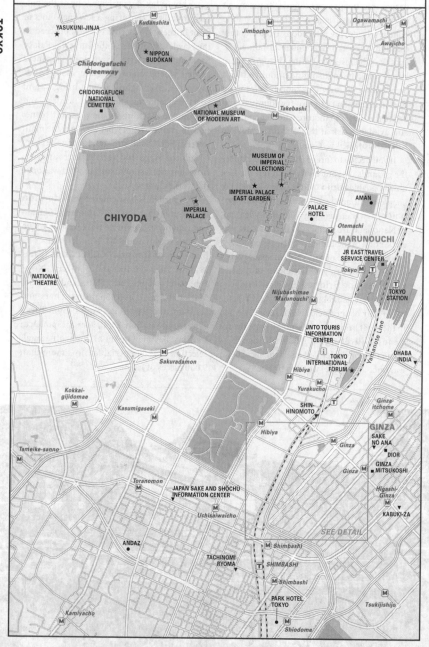

★ YASUKUNI-JINJA

Kudanshita Ⓜ

Jimbocho

Ogawamachi Ⓜ

Awajicho

5

★ NIPPON BUDŌKAN

Chidorigafuchi Greenway

CHIDORIGAFUCHI NATIONAL CEMETERY ■

★ NATIONAL MUSEUM OF MODERN ART

Takebashi Ⓜ

MUSEUM OF IMPERIAL COLLECTIONS

CHIYODA

★ IMPERIAL PALACE EAST GARDEN

★ IMPERIAL PALACE

PALACE HOTEL ●

● AMAN

Otemachi Ⓜ

MARUNOUCHI

JR EAST TRAVEL SERVICE CENTER

Tokyo Ⓜ Ⓣ

■ NATIONAL THEATRE

Nijubashimae *Marunouchi* Ⓜ

Ⓣ TOKYO STATION

Yamanote Line

JNTO TOURIS INFORMATION CENTER ⓘ

Ⓣ TOKYO INTERNATIONAL FORUM ★

DHABA INDIA ▼

Sakuradamon

Hibiya

Yurakucho Ⓜ

Ginza-itchome Ⓜ

Kokkai-gijidomae Ⓜ

Kasumigaseki Ⓜ

SHIN-HINOMOTO

Ⓣ

GINZA

SAKE NO ANA ▼

Tameike-sanno Ⓜ

Hibiya

Ginza Ⓜ

■ DIOR

GINZA MITSUKOSHI ■

Toranomon Ⓜ

Ginza Ⓜ

Higashi-Ginza Ⓜ

JAPAN SAKE AND SHŌCHŪ INFORMATION CENTER

▼ KABUKI-ZA

Uchisaiwaicho

SEE DETAIL

ANDAZ ●

Ⓜ *Shimbashi*

TACHINOMI RYOMA ▼

Ⓣ **SHIMBASHI**

Ⓜ *Shimbashi*

Ⓜ

Kamiyacho Ⓜ

PARK HOTEL TOKYO ●

Tsukijishijo Ⓜ

Shiodome

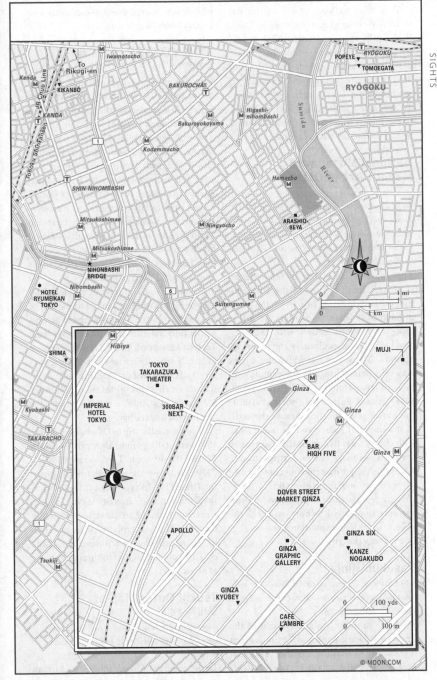

© MOON.COM

Two-hour walking **tours** of the East Garden are offered free of charge by **Tokyo SGG Club,** overseen by the **JNTO Tourist Information Center** (1F Shin Tokyo Bdlg., 3-3-1 Marunouchi, Chiyoda-ku; tel. 03/3201-3331; https://tokyosgg.jp/sp/imperial_palace.html; 1pm Tues.-Thurs. and Sat.-Sun.). To join, arrive at the Tokyo SGG Club's desk at the Tourist Information Center at least 10 minutesbefore the start of a tour.

National Museum of Modern Art (MOMAT)
国立近代美術館

3-1 Kitanomaru-kōen, Chiyoda-ku; tel. 03/5777-8600; www.momat.go.jp/am; 10am-5pm Tues.-Thurs. and Sun., 10am-8pm Fri.-Sat.; adults ¥500, children free, free on 1st Sun. of month; take Tōzai line to Takebashi Station, exit 1b

This massive collection of Japanese art stretches from the turn of the 20th century onward, focusing heavily on the works of modernist Japanese painters, as well as some international artists, with photography, video pieces, sculptures and more also on show. The key theme illustrated by the artworks being shown is the evolution of modern Japan from the Meiji period (1868-1912) onward. Part of the appeal of visiting the museum its location beside the walls of the Imperial Palace and its moat, lined with cherry trees that color the area pink in spring, and foliage blazes during autumn. Alongside the permanent collection, shown across three floors, the ground floor hosts changing special exhibitions, between which the museum shuts its doors, so check the website to see if an exhibition is ongoing before making the trip.

Yasukuni-jinja

3-1-1 Kudankita, Chiyoda-ku; tel. 03/3261-8326; www.yasukuni.or.jp; 6am-6pm daily Mar.-Oct., 6am-5pm Jan.-Feb. and Nov.-Dec.; free

About 15 minutes' walk northwest of the Imperial Palace grounds, or 7 minutes west of Kudanshita Station, sits the Yasukuni-jinja, a shrine that honors Japan's war dead,

historically charged due to associations with Japan's World War II sins.

TOKYO BAY AREA
東京湾

Until recently the area's most famous site was by far the hallowed **Tsukiji Fish Market,** which closed in September 2018. The new market, **Toyoso Market** (6-chōme Toyosu, Koto-ku; tel. 03/3520-8205; www.toyosu-market.or.jp; 5am-3pm Mon.-Sat., often closed Wed. and other irregular times, hours vary for businesses on site; free), which opened in October 2018, remains the world's largest bazaar of fish mongers, but it's unfortunately a somewhat sterile affair compared to its predecessor in Tsukiji. Though it's safe to give the new market a pass, it is still possible to visit Tsukiji's Outer Market of seafood shops and mom-and-pop sushi counters.

Across the bay lies the hyper urbanized development of **Odaiba.** Linked to the rest of Tokyo either by the scenic **Rainbow Bridge** or the fully automated **Yurikamome New Transit Monorail,** Odaiba is a hodgepodge of family-friendly museums, shopping centers, and **Ōedo Onsen Monogatari,** a popular *onsen* (hot spring) theme park. One of Odaiba's biggest draws is its great views of the city from across the bay.

If you make the trip to Odaiba, pass by the 19.7-meter-tall (65-foot) **Unicorn Gundam Statue** (1-1-10 Aomi, Taitō-ku; tel. 03/6380-7800; 10am-9pm daily; free), towering over the **DiverCity Tokyo Plaza** (http://mitsui-shopping-park.com/divercity-tokyo). The life-size statue from the anime series *Mobile Suit Gundam* about giant robots "performs" at select times each day when its head moves and eyes light up, and mist wafts through the area as music plays.

Tsukiji Outer Market
築地場外市場

www.tsukiji.or.jp; take Hibiya line to Tsukiji Station, exits 1, 2, or take Ōedo line to Tsukijishijō Station, exit A1

To the chagrin of many foodies and urban

anthropologists, the colorful, chaotic inner side of the fabled Tsukiji Fish Market, once the site of legendarily intense morning tuna auctions, closed in fall 2018. The market relocated to a massive, sterile new building, Toyosu Market, southeast of Tsukiji. Though it is possible to get a glimpse of the goings on in Toyosu, it's probably okay to skip it; thankfully, Tsukiji's outer market, which once spilled into the streets just northeast of the former inner market, has remained in operation. It's perhaps the one place in the world where sushi for breakfast is recommended.

Starting from mid-morning to early afternoon, stalls sell edibles ranging from freshly bought oysters to sweet yet savory rolled omelets alongside sit-down restaurants and shops hawking pottery and kitchenware of excellent quality. The bulk of these stalls are housed in the newly rebuilt **Tsukiji Uogashi** complex (6-27-1 Tsukiji, Chūō-ku; tel. 03/3544-1906; https://uogashi.tsukiji-dainaka.com; 9am-2pm daily). To glean a bit more insight into the fish business and be guided directly to the best spots for nibbles in Tsukiji, check out the highly rated tour of Tsukiji Outer Market run by **Japan Wonder Travel** (https://japan-wondertravel.com/products/tokyo-fooddrink-tour-tsukiji-fish-market; 3 hours from 8:30am daily; ¥9,500) or the one by **Ninja Food Tours** (www.ninjafoodtours.com/tokyo-foodtours/tsukiji-fish-market; 3 hours from 9am daily; ¥8,800).

Hama-rikyū Onshi-teien
浜離宮恩賜庭園

1-1 Hama Rikyū-teien, Chūō-ku; tel. 03/3541-0200; www.tokyo-park.or.jp; 9am-5pm (last entry 4:30pm) daily; ¥300; take Ōedo, Yurikamome lines to Shiodome Station, exit 10, or take Ginza, Asakusa lines to Shimbashi Station, Shiodome exit

Like all things with deep roots in Tokyo's past, this garden has seen its share of radical transformations, having been flattened during World War II. Today skyscrapers loom just beyond it, but the garden is filled with calm. The garden remains in its original location, south of Ginza, east of Shimbashi, and

right next to the point where the Sumida River mingles with Tokyo Bay. Strolling through the grounds, the space strikes a perfect balance between water and landscape, with numerous native species of vegetation, from hydrangeas to wizened black pines. One pine is said to be 300 years old. Ducks swim in a large central pond that contains two islands, linked by attractive wooden bridges. On one of the islands stands **Nakajima no Ochaya** (9am-4:30pm daily; tea ¥510), an inviting teahouse with one of the best views in the city.

On an island and surrounded by a walled moat, this garden is reachable via the **Minamimon Bridge** or by boat from Asakusa. To reach the garden from Asakusa by boat (35 minutes; ¥1,040, includes garden entrance fee; 1-2 boats per hour), take the Sumida River line operated by **Tokyo Cruise** (www.suijobus.co.jp). Head to **Asakusa Pier** (1-1 Hanakawado, Taito-ku), a stone's throw from Asakusa Station (Ginza, Tobu, Asakusa lines). The **Hama-rikyū Pier** is actually located within the garden itself. For more information, from timetables and routes to pier locations, visit the Tokyo Cruise website.

Miraikan
日本科学未来館

2-3-6 Aomi, Koto-ku; tel. 03/3570-9151; www.miraikan.jst.go.jp; 10am-5pm Wed.-Mon.; adults ¥630, 18 and under ¥210; take Yurikamome line to Telecom Center Station

Miraikan, or the **National Museum of Emerging Science and Innovation,** is a great museum with interactive exhibitions focused on robots and life sciences. There's a globe hanging over the lobby that depicts climate change in action via 851,000 LEDs dotting its 6.5-meter (21-foot) circumference, as well as great displays on outer space and genetics. The museum feels somewhat geared toward kids, but it's fun and interesting for adults, too, and provides good English-language information on its exhibits. As you interact with the androids on display in an exhibit on some of the world's most sophisticated androids, you may find yourself contemplating consciousness and what it really means to be human.

To prevent the spread of coronavirus, admission to the museum was being done through a **reservation system** at the time of writing. Reserve online (www.e-tix.jp/miraikan/en) up to a week ahead of your visit, and no later than 4:30pm on the day you plan to go.

teamLab Borderless
チームラボボーダレス

1-3-8 Aomi, Kōtō-ku; tel. 03/6406-3949; https:// borderless.teamlab.art; 10am-7pm Mon.-Fri., 10am-9pm Sat.-Sun. and holidays, closed 2nd and 4th Tues. every month; adults ¥3,200, children ¥1,000; take Yurikamome line to Aomi Station

Where is digital art and technology heading? Since it opened in 2018, this groundbreaking digital art museum has sought to explore that question in a fun, interactive space—a major hit on Instagram. Everything in the museum is interactive—touching the artworks *is* encouraged for once!—and art is created, with your participation, in real time. The museum is the brainchild of a collective of digital artists and "ultra-technologists" comprised of CG animators, mathematicians, architects, musicians, and engineers. More than 50 works of art are spread over a massive 10,000-square-meter (100,000-square-foot) space, ranging from morphing flowers and waterfalls of light to swimming whales and samurai on the march. If you're active on social media, chances are you've seen images of the **Forest of Resonating Lamps,** in which the mirrored walls, floor, and ceiling, from which hang myriad motion-sensing, color-changing lamps, conjure an otherworldly realm beyond space and time.

This is a particularly wonderful choice if you have kids—though adults will have fun, too. Wear pants (the floors are mirrored in some rooms) and comfortable shoes (some exhibits only admit those wearing flat shoes), and try to dress in a lighter shade (holograms don't interact well with black surfaces). Aim to go in the late afternoon, when it tends to be a bit less crowded. Finally, the number of tickets sold on a given day is limited, so buy yours online (https://ticket.teamlab.art/#) at least a few weeks in advance.

Note that a few of the museum's artworks were temporarily closed at the time of writing to prevent the spread of coronavirus: the Light Sculpture Space, the Floating Nest, and Light Forest Three-dimensional Bouldering.

ROPPONGI AND AROUND
六本木

During the Sino-Japanese War (1894-1895) and the Russo-Japanese War (1905), the Roppongi area was used as a military training ground. Following World War II, Occupation forces moved into newly empty barracks, leading to the development of the sort of nightlife associated with overseas GIs—hence the neighborhood's slightly seedy reputation.

The area, in the heart of the affluent **Minato** ward, has since been developed into an upscale district, with luxury shops, world-class art museums, and towering megacomplexes **Roppongi Hills** (9-7-1 Akasaka, Minato-ku; tel. 03/3475-3100; www.roppongi-hills.com; 11am-9pm daily; free) and **Tokyo Midtown** (9-7-1 Akasaka, Minato-ku; tel. 03/3475-3100; www.tokyo-midtown.com; 11am-9pm daily; free), giving it a cosmopolitan sheen. As the sun falls, however, the area running south from **Roppongi Crossing** fills with shady touts who serve as a reminder that the underbelly still remains. If you can politely but firmly ignore the unsavory characters milling about at night, you'll discover some fantastic dining options and watering holes. Roppongi has also become Tokyo's main hub for contemporary art, with its "Art Triangle" of the **Mori Art Museum,** the **Suntory Museum of Art,** and the **National Art Center, Tokyo.**

Close by, south of Roppongi, the posh neighborhood of **Azabu** boasts great restaurants and swanky cocktail bars, minus the unsavory bits. Looming east of Roppongi and Azabu is **Tokyo Tower** in the **Shiba-kōen** area.

Roppongi and Around

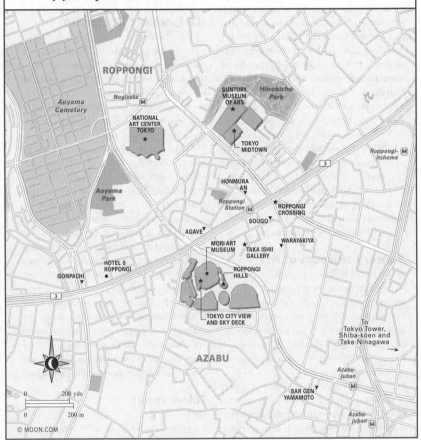

Tokyo City View and Sky Deck
東京シティビュー

52F Roppongi Hills Mori Tower; 6-10-1 Roppongi, Minato-ku; tel. 03/6406-6652; https://tcv. roppongihills.com/jp; 10am-11pm (last entry 10:30pm) Mon.-Fri. and holidays, 10am-1am (last entry midnight) Fri.-Sat. and day before holidays; admission included with ticket to Mori Art Museum; take Hibiya line to Roppongi Station, exit 1C, or Ōedo line to Roppongi Station, exit 3

Tokyo City View offers an almost 360-degree view of the city. For an even more unimpeded view, another ¥500 on top of the admission you've already paid allows you to ride an escalator to the rooftop Sky Deck for a view without windows.

Mori Art Museum
森美術館

53F Roppongi Hills Mori Tower; 6-10-1 Roppongi, Minato-ku; tel. 03/6406-6000; www.mori.art. museum/jp; 10am-10pm (last entry 9:30pm) Wed.-Mon., 10am-5pm (last entry 4:30pm) Tues., adults ¥1,800, students ¥1,200, children ¥600; take Hibiya line to Roppongi Station, exit 1C, or Ōedo line to Roppongi Station, exit 3

If you only visit one contemporary art museum during your time in Tokyo, make it the

Mori Art Museum. One floor above Tokyo City View, this stellar museum consistently hosts sophisticated exhibitions on a range of relevant themes and media from Japan and abroad in a fantastic space designed by American architect Richard Gluckman. Past exhibitions have showcased Japanese visionaries such as Aida Makoto and Takashi Murakami, Chinese hell-raiser Ai Weiwei, and modern Southeast Asian and Middle Eastern art. Note that the museum is closed between exhibitions, so please check the schedule on the website before going. Booking tickets in advance is recommended (and may be compulsory depending on measures in place to combat the coronavirus) and may reduce waiting time to enter. Admission to the museum is included with the ticket for the Tokyo City View, and vice versa.

Suntory Museum of Art
サントリー美術館

3F Tokyo Midtown Galleria, 9-7-4 Akasaka, Minato-ku; tel. 03/3479-8600; www.suntory. com/sma; 10am-6pm Wed.-Thurs. and Sun.-Mon., 10am-8pm Fri.-Sat.; fees vary by exhibition; take Ōedo line or Hibiya line (via underground walkway) to Roppongi Station, exit 8, or Chiyoda line to Nogizaka Station, exit 3

Standing at the western edge of Tokyo Midtown is the Suntory Museum of Art, a "lifestyle art" showcase featuring beautifully crafted everyday objects such as lacquerware, glass, ceramics, and textiles. The museum, designed by architect Kengo Kuma, holds the largest assortment of arts and crafts in Japan. **Tea ceremonies** are held every other Thursday at 1pm, 2pm, and 3pm for up to 50 people total for the day (¥1,000 each; up to two tickets per person). Tickets are sold on the day from the museum's third-floor reception desk. Check the website to confirm which days the ceremonies will be held (www. suntory.com/sma/rental/teaceremonyroom. html). There's also a **café** specializing in morsels from the city of Kanazawa, renowned for its traditional crafts. The **gift shop** carries

exquisitely designed tableware and glassware, some done in the geometric Edo Kiriko style.

National Art Center, Tokyo
国立新美術館

7-22-2 Roppongi, Minato-ku; tel. 03/5777-8600; www.nact.jp; 10am-6pm Wed.-Thurs. and Sun.-Mon., 10am-8pm Fri.-Sat., closed Wed. if Tues. is holiday for exhibitions organized by National Art Center, Tokyo, 10am-6pm Wed.-Mon. for exhibitions organized by artist associations; fees vary by exhibition; take Ōedo line to Roppongi Station, exits 7, 8

With the biggest exhibition space of any art museum in the country, the National Art Center, Tokyo houses 12 galleries in a striking building designed by the late architect Kurokawa Kisho. Standing in front of the massive structure, the curved green windows of its front wall appear to undulate as it allows natural light to flood the soaring atrium. The museum doesn't have a collection of its own. Instead, it hosts meticulously curated shows ranging from the surrealist mindscapes of Salvador Dalí to the polka-dot infused world of Yayoi Kusama, alongside a host of other exhibitions overseen by various art collectives and associations throughout Japan. The museum also boasts two restaurants, a café, and a stellar gift shop, **Souvenir From Tokyo.**

Tokyo Tower
東京タワー

4-2-8 Shiba-kōen, Minato-ku; tel. 03/3433-5111; www.tokyotower.co.jp.html; 10:30am-9:30pm, last entry 9pm Mon.-Fri., 9am-10pm, last entry 9:30pm Sat.-Sun.; adults ¥1,200, 16-18 years old ¥1,000, junior high and elementary school students ¥700; take Ōedo line to Akabanebashi Station, Akabanebashiguchi exit

Finished in 1958, Tokyo Tower was originally intended to commemorate the city's phoenix-like rise after World War II. Its resemblance to the Eiffel Tower is overt, as is the fact that it stands 13 meters taller than its Parisian inspiration. The structure still serves

1: Tokyo Tower 2: fountain at Meiji Jingū
3: Shibuya Crossing 4: Tokyo Metropolitan Teien Art Museum

as a radio and television broadcast tower, but the words "tourist trap" are admittedly hard to avoid when thinking of it today. Its extra attractions—a wax museum, an aquarium, and an exhibit dedicated to the anime program *One Piece*—only reinforce this impression. People still flock to it nonetheless, and the white-and-orange behemoth remains one of the most recognizable points in the city's skyline. The observation decks of the Tokyo Metropolitan Government Building, Tokyo Skytree, or Tokyo City View provide more sweeping views. But if you feel the pull of vintage charm, Tokyo Tower still offers thrilling views of the Minato area skyline at night. If you're coming from Roppongi on foot, the tower is about 20 minutes' walk southeast of Roppongi Crossing (intersection of Gaien-higashi Dōri and Roppongi Dōri). You'll see it looming in the distance as you head southeast down Gaien-higashi Dōri.

EBISU AND AROUND
恵比寿

Ebisu is a sophisticated neighborhood, a welcome relief from the chaos of nearby Shibuya to the northwest on the Saikyo line. A mix of locals and expats congregate here to eat and drink at an impressive array of restaurants and drinking dens.

Ebisu has long been associated with food and, more specifically, drink, as its very origin is linked to the founding of a brewery, Yebisu Beer, in the late 1920s. Both neighborhood and brewery are named for the god of prosperity, embodied in a jolly looking statue next to the train station. **Yebisu Garden Place** (4-20 Ebisu, Shibuya-ku; tel. 03/5423-7111; www.gotokyo.org; daily; free), site of the **Museum of Yebisu Beer** (B1F Sapporo Beer Headquarters, Yebisu Garden Place, 4-20-1 Ebisu, Shibuya-ku; tel. 03/5423-7255; www.sapporobeer.jp; 11am-7pm Tues.-Sun., tasting salon last order 6:30pm, closed Tues. if Mon. is holiday), is a city within a city, with a pleasing blend of greenery, shops, and cultural offerings oriented around a spacious central square.

The nearby neighborhoods of **Daikanyama** and **Nakameguro** have a similar vibe, with high-end fashion boutiques and hipster cafés. The mellow streets are worth wandering for the sake of putting yourself in serendipity's way.

Tokyo Photographic Art Museum
東京都写真美術館

Yebisu Garden Place, 1-13-3 Mita, Meguro-ku; tel. 03/3280-0099; https://topmuseum.jp; 10am-6pm Tues.-Sun., last entry 5:30pm, closed Tues. if Mon. falls on holiday; entry fee varies by exhibition; take Yamanote line to Ebisu station, east exit, or Hibiya line to Ebisu Station, exit 1

Tokyo's premier photography museum, colloquially shortened to **TOP Museum,** is housed in a four-story building toward the back of Yebisu Garden Place. The space boasts a library, studio, research laboratory, film screening hall, and multimedia gallery. Its permanent collection includes works by greats such as Ansel Adams, W. Eugene Smith, and Gustave Le Gray, as well as Japan's own photographic legends, such as Nobuyoshi Araki, Daido Moriyama, Miyako Ishiuchi, Rinko Kawauchi, and Mika Ninagawa, among many others.

A café on the museum's first floor, run by the trendy Maison Ichi bakery in nearby Daikanyama, provides a space to relax with a beverage or light meal after enjoying the visual feast.

Tokyo Metropolitan Teien Art Museum
東京都庭園美術館

5-21-9 Shirokanedai, Minato-ku; tel. 03/3443-0201; www.teien-art-museum.ne.jp; 10am-6pm daily, last entry 5:30pm, closed the 2nd and 4th Wed. each month, closed Thurs. if Wed. falls on holiday; entry fee varies by exhibition, garden only adults ¥200, college students ¥160, high school and junior high school students ¥100; take Yamanote line to Meguro Station, east exit, or Mita, Namboku lines to Shirokanedai Station, exit 1

The Tokyo Metropolitan Teien Art Museum's

Ebisu and Around

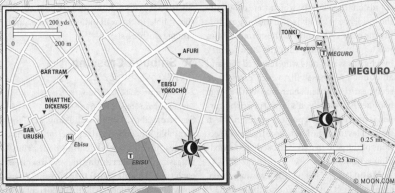

DAIKANYAMA

DEBRIS

OKURA

T-SITE

OJINJO

SEE DETAIL

DAIKAN-YAMA

SOLFA

EBISU

Ⓜ Ebisu Ⓣ EBISU

EBISU

Naka-meguro Ⓜ

CABIN NAKAMEGURO

MUSEUM OF YEBISU BEER ★

YEBISU GARDEN PLACE ★

TOKYO KYŌSAI HOSPITAL

Naka-Meguro park

TOKYO PHOTOGRAPHIC ART MUSEUM ★

Institute for Nature Study

NAKAMEGURO

Meguro River

TOKYO METROPOLITAN TEIEN ART MUSEUM ★

TONKI

Ⓜ Meguro Ⓣ MEGURO

MEGURO

0   200 yds
0   200 m

AFURI

BAR TRAM

EBISU YOKOCHŌ

WHAT THE DICKENS!

BAR URUSHI

Ⓜ Ebisu

Ⓣ EBISU

0   0.25 mi
0   0.25 km

© MOON.COM

main draw is the building itself. Completed in 1933, the mansion is a stunning example of art deco architecture, with both a rose garden and a Japanese landscape garden. It was formerly the residence of Emperor Hirohito's uncle, Prince Asaka Yasuhiko, and Princess Nobuko, Emperor Meiji's eighth daughter. Prince Asaka returned from a stint in 1920s Paris, inspired to build a modern home. He enlisted French architect Henri Rapin and glass designer René Lalique, along with a team of Japanese architects, to produce the dazzling result. In 2014, the structures were restored and a new annex was added by artist Sugimoto Hiroshi. A visit to the museum today means exploring the enchanting mansion, with its crystal chandeliers and lush grounds, just as much as seeing whatever exhibition—likely in the decorative arts genre—is taking place at the time.

Happo-en
八芳園

1-1-1 Shirokanedai, Minato-ku; tel. 03/3443-3111; www.happo-en.com; 10am-10pm daily; free; take Namboku, Mita lines to Shirokanedai Station, exit 2

Happo-en, which means "garden of eight views," is aptly named: It looks beautiful from any angle. Serene paths wind through the beautifully landscaped garden, which has a pond at its heart and is dotted by bonsai trees, some of which are centuries old. A stone lantern said to have been carved by the warrior Taira-no Munekiyo some 800 years ago also stands on the grounds, which were originally the residence of an advisor to the shogun during the early 17th century. The current design was largely realized in the early 20th century by a business magnate who acquired the land and built a Japanese villa, which can still be seen near the garden's entrance. With a large banquet hall on-site, it's no surprise the garden is one of the most popular places in Tokyo for couples to tie the knot. Note that small sections of the garden may be closed off if a wedding is underway.

Muan (tel. 03/3443-3775; www.happo-en.com/banquet/plan_en/detail.php?p=837;

11am-4pm daily), a teahouse, is also tucked away in the garden, offering sets of *matcha* (powdered green tea with a highly caffeinated kick) and Japanese-style sweets, as well as small tea ceremonies if you book ahead. Overlooking Happo-en is also the excellent **Thrush Café** (tel. 03/3443-3105; www.happo-en.com/restaurant/thrushcafe; 10am-10pm Mon.-Fri., 9am-10pm Sat.-Sun., food last order 8pm, drink last order 9:30pm), which offers a more substantial menu for a meal in the serene setting.

SHIBUYA
渋谷

As recently as the late 19th century, Shibuya was open countryside with a reputation for producing excellent tea. Today at **Shibuya Crossing,** pedestrians briskly walk in all directions, bombarded by advertisements and music clips playing on television screens mounted on glass and steel shopping complexes.

Shibuya is in the midst of an ambitious spate of development: A major commercial complex known as **Shibuya Stream** (3-21-3 Shibuya, Shibuya-ku; tel. 0570/050-428; https://shibuyastream.jp; 10am-9pm daily) opened in 2019, and a skyscraper called **Shibuya Sky,** with a massive rooftop terrace with views of Shibuya Crossing and Tokyo as a whole, opened in November 2019.

Four stops west on the local Keio-Inokashira line, or just one stop on the express train, is the counterculture nexus of **Shimokitazawa,** home to artisanal coffee shops, hole-in-the-wall indie rock venues, and vintage clothing shops.

★ Shibuya Crossing
渋谷スクランブル交差点

2-2 Dogenzaka, Shibuya-ku; www.sibch.tv; take JR lines to Shibuya Station, Hachikō exit

Seen from above, Shibuya Crossing, aka "the scramble," resembles a giant free-for-all, with hordes of cell phone-wielding pedestrians amassing and then rushing in every direction each time the walk signal turns green. When you visit, you're propelled into the current and

Views of Shibuya Crossing

To fully grasp the scale of Shibuya Crossing's foot traffic, head to the hallway linking the JR station to the Keio-Inokashira line on the second floor of the **Shibuya Mark City** commercial complex. Windows lining the passageway offer views of the frenzy below. You'll also be able to see the *Myth of Tomorrow,* a vivid mural by Tarō Okamoto, dramatically depicting Japan's traumatic relationship with nuclear weapons in its abstractly dread-inducing depiction of the atomic bombing of Hiroshima.

Another good vantage point is **Shibuya Hikarie** (2-21-1 Shibuya, Shibuya-ku; tel. 03/5468-5892; www.hikarie.jp; 10am-9pm daily; free), a complex of boutiques, eateries, and artistic offerings accessible from Shibuya Station's east exit; from the 11th floor, you'll have a view of the spectacle of the fabled Shibuya Scramble, set within a wider view of Shibuya as a whole.

There's also a plexiglass-enclosed viewing platform in **Mag's Park** (1-23-10 Jinnan, Shibuya-ku; https://magnetbyshibuya109.jp/en/mags-park; 11am-11pm daily, last entry 10:30pm; ¥1,000), a rooftop space that opened in 2018 atop the **Shibuya 109** department store. Its location on one corner of the scramble gives unimpeded views of the intersection.

Looming highest of them all is **Shibuya Sky,** an open-air, 360-degree rooftop viewing platform.

become part of the flow. For maximum impact, try coming on a Friday night or anytime Saturday, when the trend-conscious masses come out to shop, eat, and play.

This is Tokyo at its rawest, the perfect visceral place to soak in the sheer energy of the world's largest metropolis. It's also the gateway to a district at the heart of Japanese youth culture, thriving in the teeming streets of Shibuya's **Center Gai;** it's also where you'll find an entry point to **Dogenzaka,** a district bursting at the seams with options for dining and nightlife of every shade, as well as one of Tokyo's most well-known agglomerations of love hotels.

In the frantic square next to the crossing is perhaps Tokyo's most beloved meeting point: **Hachikō Square,** with a bronze statue of the legendarily loyal dog for which it's named. The canine came to meet his master, a professor, at the station as he returned home from work every day, and continued to make his daily trek to Shibuya Station nearly a decade after his master died in 1925.

Shibuya Sky

2-24-12 Shibuya, Shibuya-ku; tel. 03/4221-0229; www.shibuya-scramble-square.com/sky; 9am-11pm daily, last entry 10pm; online adults ¥1,800, junior high and high school students ¥1,400, elementary school students ¥900, children 3-5 years old ¥500; in-person adults ¥2,000, junior high and high school students ¥1,600, elementary school students ¥1,000, children 3-5 years old ¥600; JR lines to Shibuya Station, east exit

On the rooftop of a new cloud-scraping complex called Shibuya Scramble Square, at 755 feet (230 meters) above ground, this observatory, known as Sky Stage, is the highest point in the neighborhood. Besides offering a bird's-eye view of the frantic crossing below, you'll also get sweeping views of Tokyo's sprawl, extending all the way to Mount Fuji on clear days. There's a smattering of hammocks, sofas, and, come nighttime, a show of 18 colored light beams shooting skyward from the roof. Indoors, just under the viewing deck, you'll find **Sky Gallery** (46F), a window-encased corridor open rain or shine, with a collection of digital displays showing Tokyo from unique angles. There's also a **café** and **bar** where you can quaff cappuccino or craft beer as you take in the jaw-dropping views.

Tickets are for a set time and date. You can either purchase them online in advance, or at the counter on the 14th floor. Buying them online in advance is recommended to avoid queuing and to save a little money. You'll be

Shibuya and Around

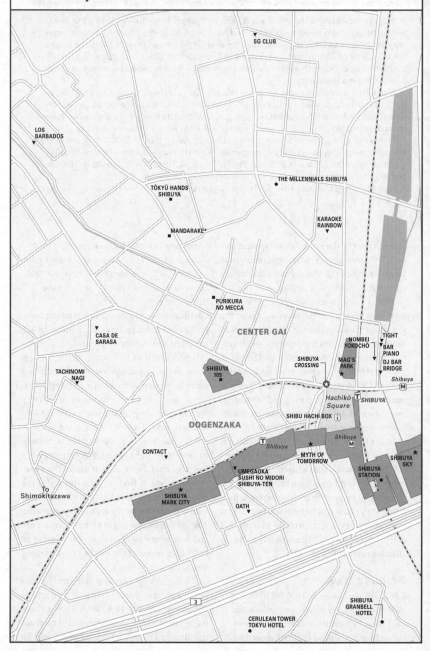

SG CLUB

LOS
BARBADOS

THE MILLENNIALS SHIBUYA

TŌKYŪ HANDS
SHIBUYA

KARAOKE
RAINBOW

MANDARAKE

PURIKURA
NO MECCA

CASA DE
SARASA

CENTER GAI

NOMBEI   TIGHT
YOKOCHŌ
                BAR
SHIBUYA   PIANO
CROSSING   MAG'S DJ BAR
TACHINOMI   PARK BRIDGE
NAGI
SHIBUYA   Shibuya
109   Ⓜ

Hachikō Ⓣ SHIBUYA
Square

SHIBU HACHI BOX ⓘ

DOGENZAKA

CONTACT   Ⓣ Shibuya

                 Shibuya
                   Ⓜ
UMEGAOKA   MYTH OF
SUSHI NO MIDORI TOMORROW
SHIBUYA-TEN
                        SHIBUYA   SHIBUYA
To   STATION   SKY
Shimokitazawa
SHIBUYA   OATH
MARK CITY

3

                                    SHIBUYA
                                    GRANBELL
CERULEAN TOWER   HOTEL
TOKYU HOTEL

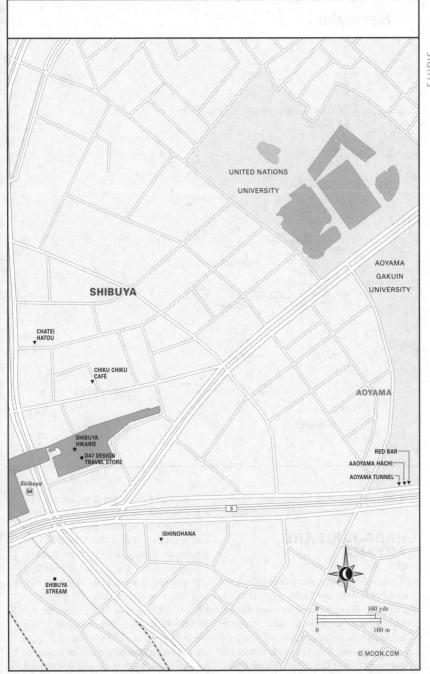

UNITED NATIONS

UNIVERSITY

AOYAMA

GAKUIN

UNIVERSITY

SHIBUYA

CHATEI
HATOU
▼

CHIKU CHIKU
CAFÉ
▼

AOYAMA

SHIBUYA
HIKARIE
★
■ D47 DESIGN
TRAVEL STORE

RED BAR
AAOYAMA HACHI
AOYAMA TUNNEL
▼ ▼ ▼

Shibuya
Ⓜ

3

ISHINOHANA
▼

■
SHIBUYA
STREAM

0   100 yds

0   100 m

© MOON.COM

Harajuku

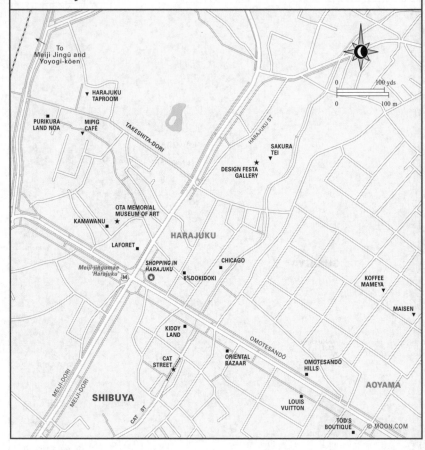

required to store your belongings in a locker free of charge before heading up to the roof.

HARAJUKU AND AOYAMA
原宿, 青山

Harajuku and Aoyama have deep roots in the world of fashion, and in the spiritual world, thanks to the city's most majestic shrine, **Meiji Jingū.** But the area is also notable to architecture buffs. Buildings of note along the area's main drag, **Omotesandō,** include the **Dior** store (5-9-11 Jingūmae, Shibuya-ku; tel.

03/5464-6260; 11am-8pm daily), located a few minutes' walk south of Meiji-dōri, designed by Pritzker Prize-winning duo Sejima Kazuyo and Nishizawa Ryūe; **Louis Vuitton** (5-7-5 Jingūmae, Shibuya-ku; tel. 0120/26-4115; 11am-8pm daily), just up the hill from Dior and resembling a giant pile of trunks connected by a maze of corridors; **Omotesandō Hills** (4-12-10 Jingūmae, Shibuya-ku; tel. 03/3497-0310; 11am-9pm Mon.-Sat., 11am-10pm Sun.), a sleek, high-end mall built around a cavernous central atrium, across the street from Louis Vuitton; and **Tod's** (1-5-8

Aoyama

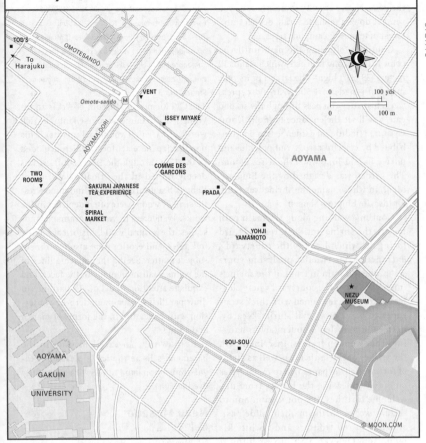

Jingūmae, Shibuya-ku; tel. 03/6419-2055; 11am-8pm daily), just a few buildings up from Louis Vuitton, which architect Itō Toyo designed to play on the theme of Zelkova trees with its intersecting concrete beams. Heading farther along the leafy avenue into the posh district of Aoyama, you'll come to the **Prada** store (5-2-6 Minamiaoyama, Minato-ku; tel. 03/6418-0400; 11am-8pm daily), a six-story, five-sided architectural marvel wrapped in diamond-shape convex windows, giving it a bubble-like appearance.

★ Meiji Jingū
明治神宮

*1-1 Yoyogi Kamizonochō, Shibuya-ku; www.meijijingu.
or.jp; sunrise-sunset daily; free; take Yamanote line
to Harajuku Station, Omotesandō exit, or Chiyoda,
Fukutoshin lines to Meiji-Jingūmae Station, exit 2*

One of Tokyo's most iconic Shinto shrines, originally built in 1920, Meiji Jingū is set in a sprawling swath of green. When you reach the large *torii* gate with the imperial crest in its lintel, offer a light bow for good measure before crossing the threshold, delineating the sacred space from the din outside, and be sure to remain on either side of the gravel pathway, as the middle is reserved for the gods. Notice the city sounds fade as you venture down the shaded trail, deeper into a forest of towering camphor trees.

Continue following the path until you come to the second *torii* gate, which stands 12 meters (39 feet) high—the largest of its type in Japan—made of 1,500-year-old cypress trees. Just after you pass through the second gate, you'll see the entrance to **Meiji Jingū Gyōen,** a traditional garden with a pond inhabited by colorful carp, a riot of white and purple in mid-June when the irises bloom. The garden was designed by the Emperor Meiji, in whose name the shrine was built, for his wife Empress Shoken.

Continue walking along the main path toward the shrine until you reach a third *torii* gate, which leads to the courtyard's entrance. After ritually purifying yourself at the fountain in front of the shrine's inner gate, enter the courtyard where clusters of trees are festooned with thick straw ropes to drive away evil spirits. Nearby, notice the countless wooden tablets hanging from wooden frames, inscribed with the wishes of the faithful, as well as strips of fortune-telling paper tied to metal wires en masse, releasing the buyers from unwelcome fortunes. It's not uncommon to see a *miko,* or shrine maiden, glide past, adorned in red trousers and a white kimono top. Or even a Shinto wedding if your timing is lucky. The **Honden** (central hall) is the courtyard's centerpiece, with its cypress-wood exterior and gently curved copper-clad roof offset by bronze lanterns hanging from its eaves.

To see Meiji Jingū at its most lively, visit during festivals. Foremost among these is the **New Year,** when some three million people mob Meiji Jingū for *hatsumode,* their first Shinto shrine trip of the year, to pray for a successful year ahead. **Musical performances** and dances are staged in the shrine's courtyard April 29-May 3 and November 1-3.

Ota Memorial Museum of Art
浮世絵 太田記念美術館

1-10-10 Jingūmae, Shibuya-ku; tel. 03/3403/0880; www.ukiyoe-ota-muse.jp; 10:30am-5:30pm Tues.-Sun., last entry 5pm, closed Tues. if Mon. falls on holiday; admission varies by exhibition; take Yamanote line to Harajuku Station, Omotesandō exit, or Chiyoda, Fukutoshin lines to Meiji-Jingūmae Station, exit 5

The Ota Memorial Museum of Art is an inviting space to immerse yourself into the rich world of *ukiyo-e* (woodblock prints). This popular Japanese art form, which exploded in the 17th through the 19th centuries, was deeply rooted in the "floating world" of Kabuki, beautiful courtesans, and sumo wrestlers, all of whom were often depicted in the works. Wanderers traversing dramatic landscapes, the natural world, historical scenes, folk tales, and erotica were also prominent subject matter. Seeing the intricate lines of the prints, realism in many of the faces, and exquisite attention to detail, it's hard not to draw parallels to Japan's modern-day obsession with caricature in the forms of manga and anime.

Kamawanu, an excellent shop in the basement, sells aesthetically pleasing *tenugui,* thin cotton hand towels with beautifully dyed designs.

Nezu Museum
根津美術館

6-5-1 Minami-Aoyama, Minato-ku; tel. 03/3400-2536; www.nezu-muse.or.jp; 10am-5pm Tues.-Sun.; adults ¥1,300, students ¥1,000, children free; take Chiyoda, Ginza, Hanzomon lines to Omotesandō Station, exit A5

This sublime museum has excellent exhibitions of East Asian art, a relaxing café with beautiful garden views of wisteria and irises, and a dazzling mix of traditional and modern architecture. Combined, these elements create an understated ambience exuding elegance; you'll sense you've stumbled onto something special.

The Nezu Museum first opened in 1941, standing on the same land where once stood the private residence of late Tobu Railway founder Nezu Kaichiro, whose private collection of Japanese and Asian art served as the foundation for the museum's collection. After the original museum was destroyed during World War II, the current structure, designed by Kengo Kuma, reopened in 2009.

The collection includes more than 7,000 artworks from across Japan and East Asia, including exquisite bronze statutes from China's Shang and Zhou dynasties, Japanese paintings, and Korean ceramics. The **café** overlooking the lush garden in back offers good options for a light lunch or afternoon tea. And the 17,000-square-meter (180,000-square-foot) Japanese **garden** beckons visitors to stroll and discover two traditional teahouses and myriad stone lanterns and Buddha statues.

To prevent the spread of coronavirus, the museum was using a timed-entry system for admission at the time of writing, requiring an **online reservation** to buy tickets for groups of up to four.

SHINJUKU AND AROUND
新宿
Tokyo Metropolitan Government Building
東京都庁

2-8-1 Nishi-Shinjuku, Shinjuku-ku; www.metro.tokyo. jp; 10am-8pm daily, last admission 7:30pm (south observatory), 10am-5:30pm daily, last entry 5pm (north observatory), south observatory closed 1st and 3rd Tues. of month, north observatory closed 2nd and 4th Mon. of month; free; take JR lines to Shinjuku Station, west exit, or Ōedo line to Tochōmae Station, exit A4

The headquarters of the city's army of civil servants is the brainchild of Pritzker Prize-winning architect Tange Kenzo. This colossal structure has dominated western Shinjuku's skyline since it opened in 1991. Kenzo drew inspiration from Notre Dame in Paris, as evidenced in the archetypal twin-tower form, but this is where the similarities to Paris's medieval masterpiece

end. But what the glass-and-granite Tokyo Metropolitan Government Building lacks in old-world charm, it makes up for in stunning views.

Reach either of the two towers' observation decks via an elevator on the ground floor of Building 1, which also houses a tourist office that offers free **tours** of the complex (weekdays only except for national holidays and the first and third Tues. every month; first-come, first-served). At 202 meters (662 feet) high, both observatories offer similar views, but the southern tower tends to be less crowded. The southern tower's main advantage is that it stays open later. At the time of writing, hours were reduced to prevent coronavirus spread. Check the website for updates.

Hanazono-jinja
花園神社

5-17-3 Shinjuku, Shinjuku-ku; tel. 03/3209-5265; www.hanazono-jinja.or.jp; 8am-8pm daily; free; take JR, Odakyu, Keio lines to Shinjuku Station, east exit, or take Marunouchi, Shinjuku lines to Shinjuku-Sanchōme Station, exit B3

In a very unlikely spot for a shrine, abutting Tokyo's largest red-light district. To enter the shrine grounds from Yasukuni-dōri, you walk between two copper lion statues standing guard at the entrance before passing down a cobblestone path flanked by wooden lanterns painted vermillion. Inside, you'll discover a main prayer hall and a handful of sub-shrines dotting the grounds. Dedicated to the fox god Inari, overseer of money and success, the shrine is a magnet for proprietors of businesses, aboveboard and not, and entertainers who work in neighboring Kabukichō. It's said that yakuza, the Japanese mafia, often run food stalls and other businesses at the shrine's lively festivals, including the **Reitaisai Matsuri,** which falls on the closest weekend to May 28 every year. On January 8, those who purchased talismans for success in business during the previous year line up to toss their old charms into a fire.

Shinjuku and Around

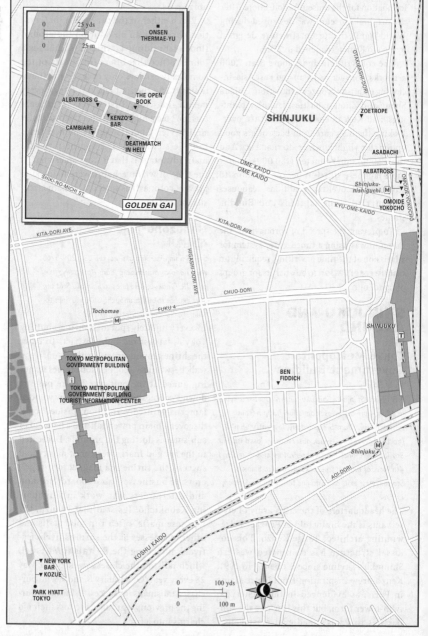

ONSEN
THERMAE-YU

THE OPEN
BOOK

ALBATROSS G

KENZO'S
BAR

CAMBIARE

DEATHMATCH
IN HELL

SHIKI-NO-MICHI ST.

0   25 yds
0   25 m

GOLDEN GAI

SHINJUKU

ZOETROPE

ASADACHI

ALBATROSS

Shinjuku-nishiguchi

OMOIDE
YOKOCHŌ

OMOIDE-YOKOCHŌ

OTAKARASHI-DORI

OME KAIDO
OME KAIDO

KYU-OME-KAIDO

KITA-DORI AVE.

KITA-DORI AVE.

HIGASHI-DORI AVE.

CHUO-DORI

FUKU 4

Tochomae

SHINJUKU

TOKYO METROPOLITAN
GOVERNMENT BUILDING

TOKYO METROPOLITAN
GOVERNMENT BUILDING
TOURIST INFORMATION CENTER

BEN
FIDDICH

Shinjuku

AOI-DORI

KOSHU KAIDO

NEW YORK
BAR

KOZUE

PARK HYATT
TOKYO

0   100 yds
0   100 m

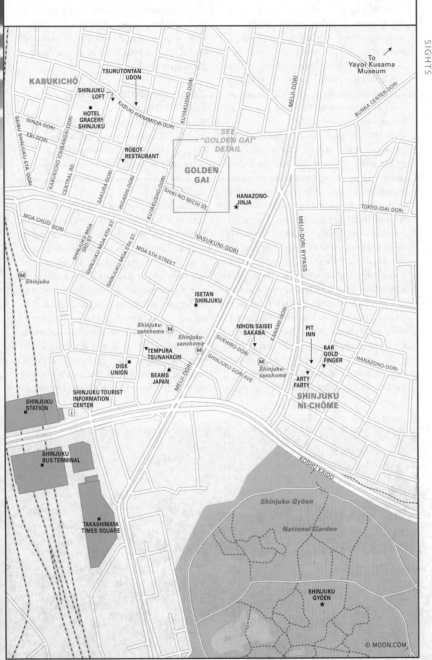

Shinjuku Gyōen
新宿御苑

11 Naito-machi, Shinjuku-ku; tel. 03/3350-0151; www.env.go.jp; 9am-4pm Tues.-Sun. Oct. 1-Mar. 14, 9am-5:30pm Tues.-Sun. Mar. 15-June 30 and Aug. 21-Sept. 30, 9am-6:30pm July 1-Aug. 20, closed Tues. if Mon. is a holiday; adults ¥500, university and high school students ¥250, children 15 and younger free; take Marunouchi line to Shinjuku Gyōen-mae Station, exit 1

This 150-acre green space is Tokyo's biggest garden and one of its best situated, in the heart of Shinjuku. What makes Shinjuku Gyōen unique is its diversity of landscaping styles. A formal French garden occupies the northern part, which is defined by neat lines of carefully planted trees and flowers. The south is a classically Japanese garden complete with stone lanterns, ponds with islands reachable by arched bridges, and a welcoming teahouse. A typically English-style open lawn sprawls across the center. The grounds are also home to a greenhouse growing subtropical plants, including orchids, an imperial villa dating to 1869, and Taiwan-kaku Pavilion, built to celebrate Emperor Hirohito's wedding in 1927.

The garden is at its most beautiful in spring when hundreds of cherry trees blossom, filling the garden with an ocean of pink petals.

The onset of autumn also injects added color to the already beautiful scene, when the leaves of the garden's more than 20,000 trees transform into a mosaic of color. Note that alcohol and sports are prohibited in the garden, but picnics are ideal.

Yayoi Kusama Museum
草間彌生美術館

107 Bentenchō, Shinjuku-ku; tel. 03/5273-1778; https://yayoikusamamuseum.jp; 11am-5:30pm Thurs.-Mon. and national holidays; adults ¥1,100, children 6-18 ¥600; take Ōedo line to Ushigome-Yanagichō Station, east exit, or Tozai line to Waseda Station, exit 1

For full immersion in a surreal polka-dotted landscape housing mirrored infinity rooms, loudly colored geometric and patterned paintings, and multitudinous phallic sculptures, head to the Yayoi Kusama Museum. The five-story white building full of windows and warm light stands out markedly from the drab apartment blocks surrounding it. The museum hosts two exhibitions per year, drawing on the artist's prodigious body of work. Active since the 1950s, and once a figure in New York City's avant-garde in the 1970s, Kusama, known for her trademark bob-cut red wig, has honed a singular style that has

Shinjuku Gyōen in springtime

made her one of Japan's most famous contemporary artists. Her work is inspired by the hallucinatory visions of forms superimposed on the world around her, which she's experienced since childhood.

Two floors are dedicated to Kusama's paintings, one floor houses installations for visitors to lose themselves in, and the top floor has a reading room. Tickets must be purchased in advance online, and the museum admits ticket holders according to six 90-minute time slots daily (11am-12:30pm, noon-1:30pm, 1pm-2:30pm, 2pm-3:30pm, 3pm-4:30pm, 4pm-5:30pm). Tickets are often sold out far in advance. If you plan to visit, book your spot early through the official website.

AKIHABARA AND UENO
秋葉原，上野

Akihabara has long been associated with commerce, from bicycles and radios during World War II to a flourishing black market that specialized in supplying radios to information-starved civilians in the postwar years. Whether you indulge in one of the obsessions catered to by the neighborhood's myriad niche shops or not, a visit will surely leave you feeling like you've experienced a bona fide slice of Japanese subculture. If you crave a break from all the gadgets, the nearby classical garden of **Koishikawa Kōrakuen** to the west is well worth a detour, too.

To the north are **Ueno-kōen** and **Ueno Station.** West of Ueno you'll discover the laid-back **Yanaka,** a charming neighborhood of mom-and-pop restaurants, shops selling locally made crafts, art galleries, old-school cafés, and a number of serene temples and shrines.

Kanda Myōjin
神田明神

2-16-2 Sotokanda, Chiyoda-ku; tel. 03/3254-0753; www.kandamyoujin.or.jp; free; take Chūō, Sōbu, Marunouchi lines to Ochanomizu Station, exit 1, or Yamanote, Hibiya lines to Akihabara Station, Electric Town exit

It's somewhat counterintuitive that one of Tokyo's oldest shrines, Kanda Myōjin, has become so deeply associated with Akihabara, Tokyo's most technology-crazed neighborhood. Founded in AD 730, the current shrine is in fact a concrete re-creation of the original one. It is dedicated to three gods: Ebisu (god of commerce and fishermen), Daikokuten (guardian of farmers, harvests, and wealth), and Masakado (full name: Taira no Masakado, a guardian deity). Visitors to the shrine typically come to pray for luck in marriage and business.

Passing through the shrine's magnificently carved vermillion gate today, you'll soon discover indicators of its proximity to "Electric Town," such as *omamori* (amulets purchased for blessing or protection at temples and shrines) to protect electronic gadgets and a glut of *ema* (wooden prayer plaques) adorned with precise hand-drawn portraits of suppliants' favorite anime and manga characters alongside their prayers. In mid-May during oddly numbered years, the **Kanda Matsuri,** seen as one of Tokyo's top-three festivals, begins at the shrine and then spills out into the area's streets.

Origami Kaikan
おりがみ会館

1-7-14 Yushima, Bunkyō-ku; tel. 03/3811-4025; www.origamikaikan.co.jp; 9:30am-5:30pm Mon.-Sat.; free to enter gallery, fees for classes vary; take Chūō, Sōbu, Marunouchi lines to Ochanomizu Station, exit 1

Established in 1859, Origami Kaikan is regarded as the place where the art of origami paper-folding was born. The building houses an exhibition space, a workshop where you can see origami paper being created, and a shop devoted to origami papers, books, and more. There are also Japanese-language classes on origami priced according to the class's level of difficulty on any given day.

Koishikawa Kōrakuen
小石川後楽園

1-6-6 Koraku, Bunkyō-ku; tel. 03/3811-3015; www.tokyo-park.or.jp; 9am-5pm daily; ¥300; take Chūō,

Akihabara and Ueno

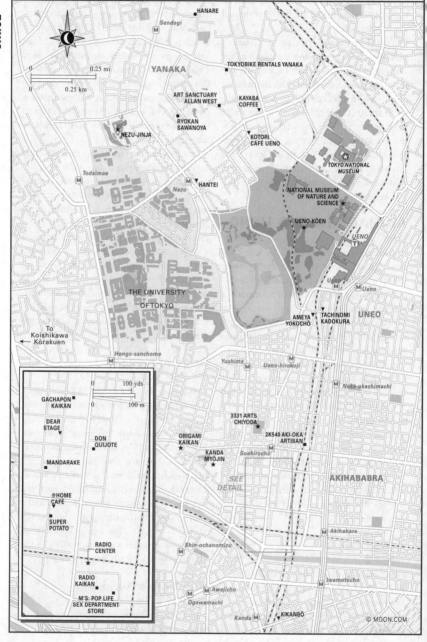

HANARE

Sendagi

YANAKA

TOKYOBIKE RENTALS YANAKA

0   0.25 mi
0   0.25 km

ART SANCTUARY
ALLAN WEST

KAYABA
COFFEE

RYOKAN
SAWANOYA

NEZU-JINJA

KOTORI
CAFÉ UENO

Todaimae

TOKYO NATIONAL
MUSEUM

Nezu   HANTEI

NATIONAL MUSEUM
OF NATURE AND
SCIENCE

UENO-KŌEN

UENO

THE UNIVERSITY
OF TOKYO

Ueno

Ueno

To
Koishikawa
Kōrakuen

AMEYA   TACHINOMI   UNEO
YOKOCHŌ   KADOKURA

Hongo-sanchome

Yushima   Ueno-hirokoji

Naka-okachimachi

GACHAPON
KAIKAN

0   100 yds
0   100 m

DEAR
STAGE

DON
QUIJOTE

3331 ARTS
CHIYODA

2K540 AKI-OKA
ARTISAN

MANDARAKE

ORIGAMI
KAIKAN

KANDA
MYŌJIN

Suehirocho

AKIHABABRA

@HOME
CAFÉ

SUPER
POTATO

SEE
DETAIL

RADIO
CENTER

Akihabara

RADIO
KAIKAN

Shin-ochanomizu

M'S: POP LIFE
SEX DEPARTMENT
STORE

Iwamotocho

Awajicho

Ogawamachi

Kanda   KIKANBŌ

© MOON.COM

Sōbu, Ōedo, Tōzai, Namboku, Yurakuchō lines to
Iidabashi Station, east exit (JR station) and exit C3
(subway)

West of Akihabara on the Chūō line is the station of Iidabashi, the closest stop to one of Tokyo's most beautiful Japanese-style gardens: Koishikawa Kōrakuen. The origin of this Edo-period garden dates back to 1629 when it was four times as large and the property of Yorifusa Tokugawa, head of the influential Mito Tokugawa clan. The original garden was larger than the current incarnation, but its essence remains. Landscapes from Chinese legend and Japan's natural wonders are re-created in miniature throughout the garden, which erupts in colorful plum blossoms in February and irises in June. The changing color of leaves in autumn is also a draw. The grounds are graced by a lotus pond, small waterways, and bridges, including the famous Full-Moon Bridge (Engetsu-kyo).

★ Tokyo National Museum
東京国立博物館

13-9 Ueno-kōen, Taitō-ku; tel. 03/5777-8600;
www.tnm.jp; 9:30am-5pm Tues.-Thurs. and Sun.,
9:30am-9pm Fri.-Sat., closed on Tues. if Mon. is
holiday, last entry 30 minutes before closing; adults
¥1,000, college students ¥500, ages 18 and under
free; take Yamanote line to Ueno Station, Ueno-kōen
exit

At the opulent Tokyo National Museum you'll see the most extensive collection of Japanese art on the planet, including Buddhist sculptures, swords, *Noh* masks, delicate ceramics, colorful kimonos, and sacred scrolls. All told, there are more than 110,000 pieces in the collection, with around 4,000 items on display at any one time.

The backbone of the collection is in the Honkan (Japanese Gallery), a 25-room space that hosts rotating exhibitions of Japanese art and antiquities. The five-floor Toyokan on the right exhibits art from China, Korea, Southeast Asia, Central Asia, India, and Egypt; the oft-closed Hyokeikan, constructed in 1909 to honor the emperor's wedding, is on the left. Behind the Honkan is the Heiseikan, which displays artifacts from prehistoric Japan, occasionally hosts special exhibitions of Japanese art, and houses a gift shop and a few eateries. Behind the Hyoeikan is the newest addition to the museum, the Gallery of Hōryū-ji Treasures. This spectacular collection shows off some objects from a 7th-century temple in built in Nara Prefecture. If you're pressed for time, focus on exploring the Honkan and the Gallery of Hōryū-ji Treasures.

Beyond the galleries, a garden and several teahouses can be found behind the Honkan, but these facilities are only open to the public in spring (mid-Mar.-mid-Apr.), when its cherry trees explode with pink petals, and in autumn (late Oct.-early Dec.), when the leaves become a riot of earth tones. Excellent English signage and audio tours are available for the museum's main collections, but are not always available for special shows.

To prevent the spread of coronavirus, all visitors must book a ticket ahead of their visit. Tickets go on sale for the following week starting every Friday at noon during the week before. See the official website for details.

National Museum of Nature and Science
国立科学博物館

7-20 Ueno-kōen, Taito-ku; tel. 03/5777-8600; www.
kahaku.go.jp; 9am-5pm Tues.-Thurs. and Sun.,
9am-8pm Fri.-Sat.; ¥630; take Yamanote line to Ueno
Station, Ueno-kōen exit

From dinosaur bones to a large chunk of a meteorite that fell into China in the 16th century, the National Museum of Nature and Science is the best place to get a glimpse of the natural forces underlying the Japanese archipelago. Spread across two buildings, the Japan Gallery and the Global Gallery, this museum has collections on outer space, evolution, Japan's flora and fauna, and the crucially important role that rice has played in the development of Japan.

Multilingual touch screen displays are conveniently available throughout the museum, along with optional English audio

Geek Paradise: Akihabara and *Otaku* Culture

The district of Akihabara is ground zero for all things geek, or *otaku*, in Japan. Long before geekdom invaded these streets, however, the area was home to a post-World War II black market where tech-savvy university students known as "radio boys" sold transistor radio parts—often pilfered from the occupation forces—to information-starved citizens.

Throughout the 1960s, Akihabara expanded its reach beyond the humble radio and became the premier destination for popular new items like televisions, refrigerators, and washing machines. Since the mid-1980s, Akihabara has exploded into full geek mode. This is the place to find performances by idol groups—pop music groups composed of teenagers who have been picked, preened, and marketed for mass appeal—cafés where patrons are served coffee by cosplay butlers and maids, and high-rise buildings full of shops selling anime, manga, plastic figurines, video games, and more.

RADIO CENTER

1-14-2 Sotokanda, Chiyoda-ku; tel. 03/3251-0614; www.radiocenter.jp; 10am-7pm daily; free; take Yamanote, Chūō lines to Akihabara Station, Electric Town exit

For a glimpse of Akihabara of old, head to the run-down two-floor Radio Center under the Sōbu line train tracks. Here you'll find tumbledown shops peddling parts for all manner of electronic devices.

@HOME CAFÉ

1-11-4 Sotokanda, Chiyoda-ku; tel. 03/5207-9779; www.cafe-athome.com; 11am-10pm daily; ¥700 cover charge

Aside from wandering the neighborhood's many fascinating shops, to get a taste of the Akihabara of today head to @Home Café, the easiest place to wrap your head around the country's maid café phenomenon.

tours (¥300). This is a good rainy-day option for those traveling with kids.

Due to the coronavirus, visitors must book a timed-entry ticket online in advance. Tickets go on sale for a given date 30 days in advance and can be bought for groups of up to five. See the official website for details.

Nezu-jinja
根津神社

1-28-9, Nezu, Bunkyō-ku; tel. 03/3822-0753; www. nedujinja.or.jp; 6am-5pm daily; free; take Chiyoda line to Nezu Station, exit 1

With its long tunnel of red *torii* gates, koi ponds, some 3,000 azaleas that explode with color in spring, beautiful grounds, and an ornate main building reminiscent of the famed Tōshō-gū shrine in Nikkō outside Tokyo, Nezu-jinja is one of Tokyo's more beautiful shrines. This shrine is also one of the country's oldest; the main structure dates to 1706, having miraculously survived World War II. In fact, it is said to have stood in Sendagi, just north of the shrine's current location, 1,900 years ago, before being relocated to its current spot to celebrate the fifth shogun Tsunayoshi choosing his nephew Ienobu as his successor.

The shrine can get crowded during spring, but the best thing about Nezu-jinja is its relative lack of popularity, compared to big-name religious sites in the city like Meiji Jingū, and Sensō-ji. For these reasons, it's worth going just a bit out of the way to see it, especially if you won't be venturing outside Tokyo.

ASAKUSA AND RYŌGOKU
浅草, 両国

DON QUIJOTE

4-3-3-Sotokanda, Chiyoda-ku

Akihabara's branch of Don Quijote, a maze-like chain store selling everything under the sun at cheap prices, also hosts daily performances (go to http://ticket.akb48-group.com/home/top.php for tickets) by idol group AKB48 in an event space on its top floor.

GACHAPON KAIKAN

3-15-5 Sotokanda, Chiyoda-ku; tel. 03/5209-6020; www.akibagacha.com; 11am-7pm daily

For a glimpse into the wondrous world of *gachapon,* or toys dispensed in capsules from vending machines, head to the Gachapon Kaikan, where avid collectors zealously part ways with ¥100 coins in their quest for figurines and models of everything from animals to mushrooms.

DEAR STAGE

3-15-5 Sotokanda, Chiyoda-ku; tel. 03/5209-6020; www.akibagacha.com; 11am-7pm daily

To see idols in the making, check out live music performance space Dear Stage. Performances take place in the evenings, and sometimes in the afternoons. In the evenings, there are also two upper-floor bars staffed by bubbly young women in maid outfits (¥500 per hour). Check the website calendar to confirm start times and more.

INFORMATION AND TOURS

For an English map to help you navigate the delightfully baffling labyrinth of Akihabara, head to **Travel Cube Akihabara Tourist Information Center** (1-13 Kanda Sakuma-chō, Chiyoda-ku; tel. 03/6262-9432; www.facebook.com/OficinadeInformacionTuristicadeAkihabara; noon-5pm daily). If you're keen to peek behind Tokyo's geek curtain but feel timid, check out the well-rated **Akihabara Anime & Manga Culture Guided Tour** (www.getyourguide.com; 2.5 hours; ¥4,500).

Asakusa first emerged as a neighborhood during the early part of the Edo period. The area's location northeast of the shogun's castle was believed to place it in an unlucky direction, according to principles of Chinese geomancy. Thus, Shogun Tokugawa Ieyasu called for the construction of the great temple of **Sensō-ji** in 1590 to keep evil spirits at bay.

Southeast across the **Sumida River,** the neighborhood of Ryōgoku centers around **sumo.**

★ Sensō-ji
浅草寺

2-3-1 Asakusa, Taitō-ku; tel. 03-3842-0181; www. senso-ji.jp; temple grounds always open, main hall 6am-5pm daily Apr.-Sept., 6:30am-5pm Oct.-Mar.; free; take Ginza, Asakusa lines to Asakusa Station, exit 1

Tokyo's oldest temple, Sensō-ji, or Asakusa Kannon, is a testament to the capital's turbulent past. Originally completed in AD 645, the temple is said to have been inspired by two fishermen brothers who miraculously found a golden statue of Kannon, the Buddhist goddess of compassion, wrapped in nets they had cast into the nearby Sumida River. It is said that the golden object still resides in the temple, but it remains hidden from sight.

The temple was mostly razed during World War II, but it has been fully reconstructed. Its current iteration is made of concrete rather than wood, but the atmosphere remains intact. Enter the grounds via the imposing **Kaminari-mon** (Thunder Gate), recognizable by its giant red lantern and flanked by statues of Fujin and Raijin, the rather wrathful-looking deities of wind and

Asakusa and Ryōgoku

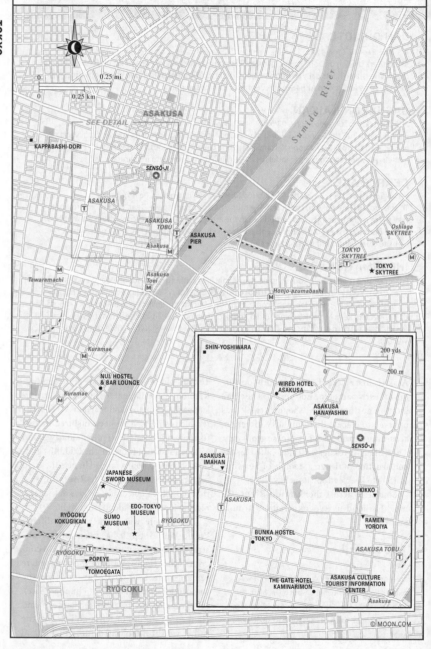

ASAKUSA

SEE DETAIL

KAPPABASHI-DORI

SENSŌ-JI

ASAKUSA

ASAKUSA TOBU

ASAKUSA PIER

Asakusa

Tawaramachi

Asakusa Toei

Kuramae

NUI HOSTEL & BAR LOUNGE

Kuramae

JAPANESE SWORD MUSEUM

EDO-TOKYO MUSEUM

RYŌGOKU KOKUGIKAN

SUMO MUSEUM

RYŌGOKU

RYŌGOKU

POPEYE

TOMOEGATA

RYOGOKU

Sumida River

Oshiage 'SKYTREE'

TOKYO SKYTREE

TOKYO SKYTREE

Honjo-azumabashi

0   0.25 mi
0   0.25 km

SHIN-YOSHIWARA

WIRED HOTEL ASAKUSA

ASAKUSA HANAYASHIKI

SENSŌ-JI

ASAKUSA IMAHAN

ASAKUSA

WAENTEI-KIKKO

RAMEN YOROIYA

BUNKA HOSTEL TOKYO

ASAKUSA TOBU

THE GATE HOTEL KAMINARIMON

ASAKUSA CULTURE TOURIST INFORMATION CENTER

Asakusa

0   200 yds
0   200 m

© MOON.COM

thunder. Crossing the threshold, amble along **Nakamise-dōri,** a row of shops and food stalls hawking charms, traditional crafts, and rice crackers and red bean cakes.

At the far end of Nakamise-dōri, where the shops end, stands a second large gate called **Hozo-mon,** and just beyond it is the temple's main hall, **Kannon Hall.** Worshippers gather around a large cauldron to bathe in the smoke, believed to impart good health. If you're inclined, buy a bundle of incense sticks to light and place in the cauldron yourself. Looming to the left of Kannon Hall is a five-story pagoda. And to the east of Kannon Hall is **Asakusa-jinja,** a shrine built in 1649 to commemorate the two fishermen who snagged the golden statue of Kannon almost 1,400 years ago.

With more than 30 million annual visitors, the temple is jam-packed any day of the week. Avoid visiting on weekends, and instead try to go in the late afternoon or after dusk when crowds are thinner.

Tokyo Skytree
東京スカイツリー

1-1-2 Oshiage, Sumida-ku; tel. 03/5302-3470; www. tokyo-skytree.jp; 9am-9pm daily, last entry 8pm; Tembo Deck ¥2,100 Mon.-Fri., ¥2,300 Sat.-Sun. and holidays, Tembo Galleria ¥1,000 Mon.-Fri., ¥1,100 Sat.-Sun. and holidays, combination tickets ¥3,100 Mon.-Fri., ¥3,400 Sat.-Sun.; take Hanzōmon line to Oshiage Station, Tokyo Skytree exit

The world's tallest freestanding tower, Tokyo Skytree rises 634 meters (2,080 feet) above the east bank of the Sumida River. The only human-made structure taller is the 830-meter (2,723-foot) Burj Khalifa in Dubai (which is considered a skyscraper rather than tower). It opened in 2012 to serve as the capital's new and improved television broadcasting tower. The structure itself, a central pillar enmeshed in a giant steel frame, incorporates principles of traditional Japanese and temple architecture in its delicate balance of both convex and concave curves.

But the tower's real draw is the 310 restaurants and shops situated around its base in a complex called **Tokyo Skytree Town,** and two dizzyingly high observation decks. Reaching these fantastically high perches isn't cheap. A ticket to the **Tembō Deck**—standing 350 meters (1,148 feet) with 360-degree views, a glass-floor paneled section, and a snack bar—sets an adult back ¥2,100 on weekdays (¥2,300 on weekends). Another ¥1,000 on weekdays (¥1,100 on weekends) gives you a combination ticket that sends you via high-speed elevator to the **Tembō Galleria,** which is 100 meters (328 feet) higher and includes a 110-meter-long (360-foot-long) glass floor. Daytime views from either platform are stunning and reach all the way to Mount Fuji when the sky is clear. Arriving just before dusk ensures an awesome view, as the vast blanket of Tokyo's twinkling lights is seemingly endless.

Purchase tickets on the fourth floor, where current wait times are indicated in English. Try showing up in the morning or at night on weekdays to avoid the crowds.

If you're approaching from Asakusa Station and Sensō-ji, Skytree is located about 20 minutes on foot to the east, on the opposite (east) side of the Sumida River.

Japanese Sword Museum
刀剣博物館

1-12-9, Yokoami, Sumida-ku; tel. 03/6284-1000; www. touken.or.jp; 9:30am-5pm Tues.-Sun., closed Tues. if Mon. falls on holiday; adults ¥1,000, students ¥500, 15 and under free; take Sōbu, Ōedo lines to Ryōgoku Station, west exit (JR station) or exit A1 (subway station)

If you enjoy geeking out on history or samurai cinema, the Japanese Sword Museum is well worth visiting. Its collection of blades came into being thanks to the Ministry of Education's creation of a society and museum dedicated to keeping Japan's rich tradition of sword-making alive after *katana* seized by U.S. occupation forces were returned to Japan in 1948. Dozens of steel specimens, displaying exceptionally high levels of craftsmanship and decorative flourishes, as well as a large collection of handles and sheaths, are on display with clear English signage. Armor and other

artifacts from the Heian and Edo periods are also on show.

From the third floor, step out on the landing to look over the neighboring **Former Yasuda Garden,** which dates to the late 17th century and is free to enter.

If you're approaching on foot from Asakusa's more popular sights, it's about 20 minutes' walk south of Sensōji and 30 minutes' walk south of Tokyo Skytree.

Edo-Tokyo Museum
江戸東京博物館

1-4-1 Yokoami, Sumida-ku; tel. 03/3626-9974; www. edo-tokyo-museum.or.jp; 9:30am-5:30pm Tues.-Sun., closed Tues. if Mon. is a holiday; adults ¥600, college students ¥480, high school and junior high school students ¥300, elementary school students and younger free; take Ōedo line to Ryōgoku Station, exits A3, A4, or Sōbu line, west exit

Visit this museum for an engaging overview of Tokyo's history from feudal days to modern metropolis. Behind an exterior resembling a massive spaceship, the museum illustrates the dramatic ups and downs of the city's past, from the 1923 Great Kanto Earthquake to incineration by American B-29 bombers during World War II. All of this, followed by the dramatic transformation that swept the city during post-World War II "economic miracle," and the subsequent popping of the bubble economy, have molded the city into what it is today. These traumas and transformations are powerfully illustrated through a wide range of displays, including miniature models of entire city districts, a reconstruction of a typical post-World War II apartment, and a hodgepodge of items from daily life, such as vehicles and household objects.

English signs are ubiquitous, and English-speaking volunteer guides are available 10am-3pm daily, reservable on the spot at the sixth-floor Permanent Exhibition Volunteer Guide Reception Center or by phone two weeks in advance. It's also possible to take a self-guided tour with an English-language audio guide, available for a ¥1,000 deposit. Choose your course and leave the museum with a deeper appreciation for the historical journey of the multilayered city around you.

Like the Japanese Sword Museum, it's located a bit of a hike south of Asakusa (25-30 minutes, depending on where you're starting from). At the time of writing, the museum had suspended its extended hours on Saturdays due to coronavirus. Check the website for updates regarding opening hours and more.

WESTERN TOKYO
★ Ghibli Museum
三鷹のジブリ美術館

1-1-83 Shimorenjaku, Mitaka-shi; tel. 0570/05-5777; www.ghibli-museum.jp; 10am-6pm Wed.-Mon.; adults ¥1,000, children ¥100-700; take Chūō line running west from Shinjuku's JR Station to reach both Mitaka Station and Kichijōji Station, which sit beside each other, Chūō, Sōbu lines to Mitaka, south exit, or Kichijōji, park exit

If you're only going to visit one sight outside downtown, make it the Ghibli Museum. Arriving at the whimsical facade of the complex on the edge of the heavily wooded Inokashira-kōen, you'll fittingly feel as if you've just wandered into the imagination of legendary anime director Hayao Miyazaki. It's a must-see for Ghibli fans and doesn't disappoint even those with only a passing interest. The museum, located west of downtown, is a seamless ode to Miyazaki's vision, which has produced classic films such as *Spirited Away* and *Princess Mononoke.*

The first floor showcases animation techniques, original Ghibli drawings, and a richly illustrated history of the art form; there's also a theater playing short Ghibli flicks that are only viewable at the museum. Special thematic exhibitions, such as the place of food in Ghibli films, are featured on a rotating basis on the second floor. The rooftop boasts a garden inhabited by Ghibli characters, including a towering robot soldier from *Castle in the Sky,* and there's even a giant cat bus

---

1: Tokyo National Museum 2: Nezu-jinja 3: Sensō-ji
4: Ghibli Museum

Kichijōji

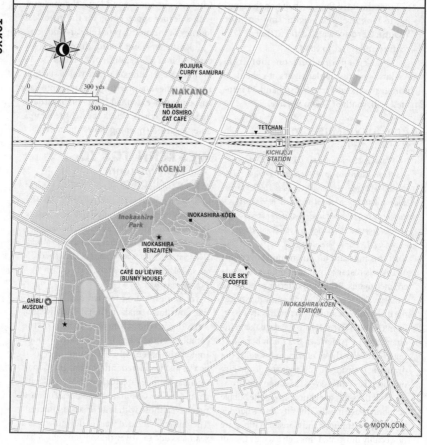

ROJIURA
CURRY SAMURAI

NAKANO

TEMARI
NO OSHIRO
CAT CAFÉ

TETCHAN

KICHIJŌJI
STATION

KŌENJI

Inokashira
Park

INOKASHIRA-KŌEN

★ INOKASHIRA
BENZAITEN

CAFÉ DU LIÈVRE
(BUNNY HOUSE)

BLUE SKY
COFFEE

GHIBLI
MUSEUM

INOKASHIRA-KŌEN
STATION

★

0   300 yds
0   300 m

© MOON.COM

brought to life from Miyazaki's hallmark *My Neighbor Totoro,* and both adults and kids can hop aboard.

The museum is extremely popular and limits the number of its daily visitors. Tickets are only valid for the date and time you book and can be purchased up to three months in advance. For example, tickets for October would

be sold from July 1. Reserve as early as you can within that timeframe.

Ghibli Museum can be reached either via bus from Mitaka Station (¥320 round trip, ¥210 one-way; 10 minutes one-way), or a 20-minute walk from Kichijōji Station through leafy Inokashira Park. The latter option greatly enhances the experience.

Nakano Broadway: An Akihabara Alternative

If you're seeking a less touristy slice of *otaku* than Akihabara, consider heading to Nakano Broadway (5-52-15 Nakano, Nakano-ku; https://nakano-broadway.com; store hours vary, roughly noon-8pm), a huge collection of shops hawking *otaku* goods just north of Nakano Station on the Chūō line, less than 10 minutes from Shinjuku Station. The area has become more popular in recent years, but hasn't yet succumbed to the deluge of duty-free shops catering to the tourists now flooding Akihabara. At Nakano Broadway, all the shops you would want to see are located under one sprawling roof, rather than scattered around a hectic neighborhood.

- Make a beeline for the flagship Mandarake store, spread across several floors; Mandarake Henya (4F) specializes in vintage collectibles.

- You'll also find four establishments owned by artist Takashi Murakami, famous for his collaborations with Louis Vuitton, among other things: Bar Zingaro (2F), which sells great coffee; contemporary art gallery and shop Hidari Zingaro (3F); contemporary ceramics showcase Oz Zingaro (4F); and *otaku*-influenced art space pivix Zingaro (2F).

- Sing karaoke with maids at Anison Karaoke Bar Z (301 No. 2 Sankyō Bldg., 5-57-9 Nakano, Nakano-ku; tel. 03/6454-0790; www.anisonkaraokebar-z.com; 6pm-11:30pm daily), or visit the Daikaiju Salon (1F Lions Mansion Nakano, 1-14-16 Arai, Nakano-ku; tel. 03/5942-7382; http://daikaijyu-salon.com; 3pm-11pm Mon.-Fri., 1pm-11pm Sun.), a bar/café revolving around Japan's pantheon of monsters, located about 5 minutes' walk north of Nakano Broadway. Patrons must order at least one food or drink item per hour.

Entertainment and Events

From kabuki to elegant, traditional *Noh* theater, to edgy forms of dance and theater such as *butō*, Tokyo has a flourishing performance arts scene.

For more information on other Japanese performing arts, go to the Performing Arts Network Japan website (www.performingarts.jp/index.html). Another useful resource is the official site of the Japan Arts Council (www.ntj.jac.go.jp), where it's also possible to get tickets for performances at Japan's national theaters. To get a sense of the city's edgier contemporary performing arts scene, check out Tokyo Stages (https://tokyostages.wordpress.com), compiled by Tokyo-based writer and translator William Andrews.

THEATER
Ginza and Marunouchi
KABUKI-ZA

4-12-15 Ginza, Chūō-ku; tel. 03/3545-6800; www. kabukiweb.net; full performance ¥4,000-20,000, one act ¥800-2,000; take Hibiya, Asakusa lines to Higashi-Ginza Station, exit 3

Kabuki-za is the place to see kabuki in Tokyo. The building itself evokes a drama that is decidedly Japanese: the sweeping curves of its roof, pillars dotting its exterior walls, and an arched entryway reminiscent of a shrine over which paper lanterns hang. Even if you don't have time to watch a kabuki performance, pay a visit to this marvelous Ginza landmark.

A key thing to be aware of before watching kabuki is its slow pace. Showtimes tend to run either from 11am to around 3:30pm or 4:30pm to 9pm. If sitting through a full performance sounds daunting, it's also possible to watch just one act; 90 seats and 60 standing positions at the back of the theater are reserved on the day of each performance for this purpose.

Booking **tickets** is simple thanks to the official English-language website, which offers a clear breakdown of the various plays and showtimes. If you prefer to reserve tickets over the phone, just dial 03/6745-0888. There is usually an English-speaking member of staff available 10am-5pm daily. At the time of writing, tickets could only be booked by phone. Check the theater's official website for any potential updates. For a full performance, it's best to book a few months in advance to snag a good seat. When you reserve your place, be sure to rent a headset if you'd like a running interpretation of the performance in English (¥500 with ¥1,000 refundable deposit for one act, ¥1,000 and personal ID for full performance). And if you plan to see a full performance and think you'll get hungry, bring something to snack on, or perhaps even a bento box meal. On the fifth floor of the complex behind the theater, you'll find a gallery showcasing kabuki-related memorabilia and outfits, and an excellent **café.**

NATIONAL THEATRE

4-1 Hayabusa-chō, Chiyoda-ku; tel. 03/3265-7411; www.ntj.jac.go.jp; ¥1,800-12,800, headsets with English-language interpretation ¥700 with refundable ¥1,000 deposit; take Hanzōmon line to Hanzōmon Station, exit 1

Tokyo's top traditional performance space stages not only kabuki, but also *bunraku*, a form of theater using oversized puppets that originated in Osaka, as well as *gagaku* (imperial court music) concerts. Check the website for performance schedules and to reserve tickets in advance.

KANZE NŌGAKUDŌ

Ginza Six B3F, 6-10-1 Ginza, Chūō-ku; tel. 03/6274-6579; www.kanze.net; take Ginza, Hibiya, Marunouchi lines to Ginza Station, exit A3

Found in the third-level basement floor of Ginza Six, this is the new incarnation of the Kanze association, which performed at a renowned theater in Shibuya from in 1901 until 2017, when they relocated. In its current home, you can catch performances featuring just the final acts of three *Noh* plays. This is a good way to receive an enjoyable, not overwhelming introduction to this highbrow form of dance theater, but unfortunately performances at Kanze Nōgakudō are often sold out months in advance, and there is no English-language website for booking tickets.

Kabuki-za

The performing arts have a rich history in Tokyo, stretching back to the hedonistic *ukiyo* (floating world) that took shape during the Edo period, in which samurai and sumo wrestlers gathered with geishas in teahouses. The word *ukiyo*, loaded with connotations of extravagance, transgression, and ennui, also produced a great deal of art, from poetry and music to painting and woodblock prints known as *ukiyo-e*.

This was the heyday of kabuki, a traditional form of theater with flamboyant costumes, riveting music, and extravagant stage sets. Today, the art form continues to thrive in the capital, the best place in the country to see it, as well as traditional arts like the more rarefied *Noh* dance theater, known for its music and poetry.

KABUKI

A kabuki play is visual spectacle above all else: elaborate, billowing costumes of varying hues; dramatic mask-like makeup; a troupe of traditional musicians who provide an evocative soundtrack; elaborate set design including revolving stages and trap doors through which actors appear and disappear; and of course, the fine-tuned gestures, poses, facial expressions, and vocalizations of the highly trained, male-only actors, who command serious presence and occasionally even zip through the air on wires.

When watching kabuki, the audience is often well-heeled and vocal, shouting out in support of their favorite actors at key moments—a practice that had been curtailed at the time of writing due to coronavirus. If you can, try to get a spot near the *hanamichi* ("flower path"), along which actors make their dramatic entrances and exits, and act out key scenes. The stories depicted often involve star-crossed lovers or samurai of yore. **Kabuki-za** is the best place to see kabuki in Tokyo.

NOH

A *Noh* play is even slower-paced than a kabuki performance. Originating in the 14th century, this stark form of dance theater is a highly standardized art form, largely due to the fact that it was deemed the shogunate's ceremonial art of choice during the Tokugawa Period (1603-1868). This background explains why the origins of *Noh* are commonly viewed as "higher" than kabuki's "low culture" pedigree.

Today, five troupes continue to perform the austere form of theater, portrayed through slow movements, poetic archaic language, flamboyant costumes, and famously minimal masks. Story lines usually involve incidents from history, literature, legend, and even recent events, and sometimes have a supernatural thread. The *shite* (main character) wears an array of masks made from Japanese cypress, artfully carved to portray anything from old women to demons and ghosts. These masks evoke a range of emotions and facial expressions. Complementing the actors is a chorus that gives vocal assistance to the lead actor as the story unfolds, as well as a four-piece ensemble that provides a soundtrack of drums and flute. See a Noh performance at the **National Noh Theatre.**

To see a show, call at least two months in advance to talk with an English speaker; there are a few on staff. Tickets usually start from around ¥4,000, and performances, which last two to three hours, tend to be held on weekend afternoons from 1pm. It's also possible to catch the last act of a play from the unreserved seating section by purchasing a special ticket on the day of a performance (¥3,000).

TOKYO TAKARAZUKA THEATER

1-1-3 Yurakuchō, Chiyoda-ku; tel. 0570/00-5100; https://kageki.hankyu.co.jp; ¥2,500-12,500; take Yamanote line to Yurakuchō Station, or take Chiyoda, Hibiya, Mita lines to Hibiya Station

The Tokyo outpost of the Takarazuka Revue, based in the town of its namesake near Kobe, features all female performers. The performers fit into one of five troupes of around 80 members each: *hana* (flower), *tsuki* (moon), *yuki* (snow), *hoshi* (star), *sora* (cosmos), and a sixth group of superstars known as *senka* who rotate in and out of the other five troupes. Think: grand, flamboyant, musical, dance, extravaganza. Check the website for the performance schedule. Arrive at the theater early to queue, as tickets go fast. Worst case, there are nosebleed seats with slightly obstructed views that tend to be easier to snag.

Harajuku and Aoyama
NATIONAL NOH THEATRE

4-18-1 Sendagaya, Shibuya-ku; tel. 03/3423-1331; www.ntj.jac.go.jp; ¥2,800-5,000; take Sōbu line to Sendagaya Station or the Ōedo line to Kokuritsu-kyogijō Station

At the National Noh Theatre, *Noh* performances are acted out on a beautiful stage crafted from cypress wood. All action takes place on a square wooden stage supported at its four corners by pillars, entered by actors along a bridge that leads into the stage. *Noh* has a mysterious air that may not be everyone's cup of tea, but it's a singular art form that will prove fascinating for those who like to explore rarefied forms of traditional culture. Shows are sporadic, but when they take place, this is a great venue, as it offers English-language translation on a screen provided at each seat. Check the English-language website for details on show times and prices, which vary by performance, and to book tickets in advance.

ART GALLERIES

If you're into art, Tokyo provides ample choices for gallery-hopping. The following galleries stand out for their cutting-edge work by artists both Japanese and international. For extensive gallery listings, exhibition information, and more, **Tokyo Art Beat** (www.tokyoartbeat.com) is an excellent resource. And if you're really keen to dive deep into Tokyo's art world, it's worth looking at the **Grutt Pass** (www.rekibun.or.jp/grutto/english.html), a coupon booklet for more than 70 museums around the city.

Ginza and Marunouchi
GINZA GRAPHIC GALLERY

1F DNP Ginza Bldg., 7-7-2 Ginza, Chūō-ku; tel. 03/3571-5206; www.dnp.co.jp; 11am-7pm Mon.-Sat.; free; take Ginza, Hibiya, Marunouchi lines to Ginza Station, exit A2

Run by a Japanese printing giant, the Ginza Graphic Gallery focuses on the best in design and graphic arts.

Roppongi and Around
TAKA ISHII GALLERY TOKYO

3F Complex 665, 6-5-24 Roppongi, Minato-ku; tel. 03/6434-7010; www.takaishiigallery.com; 11am-7pm Tues.-Sat.; fee varies by exhibition; take Hibiya line to Roppongi Station, exit 3

Taka Ishii Gallery showcases work by big-name Japanese and international photographers. Past exhibits have included Nobuyoshi Araki, Daido Moriyama, and Thomas Demand.

TAKE NINAGAWA

2-12-4 Higashi-Azabu, Minato-ku; tel. 03/5571-5844; www.takeninagawa.com; 11am-7pm Tues.-Sat.; fee varies by exhibition; take Namboku, Ōedo lines to Azabun-Jūban Station, exit 6

This gallery often features pioneering young Japanese artists.

Harajuku and Aoyama
DESIGN FESTA GALLERY

East: 3-20-2, West: 3-20-18, Jingū-mae, Shibuya-ku; tel. 03/3479-1442; www.designfestagallery.com; 11am-8pm daily; free; take Yamanote line to Harajuku Station, Omotesandō exit, or take Chiyoda, Fukutoshin lines to Meiji-Jingūmae Station, exit 5

Design Festa Gallery is the brainchild of three local artists who had a vision for a dilapidated apartment block in Harajuku's backstreets. Spread across three floors, some of the rooms are overseen by the creators themselves, who rent space from the gallery. The gallery space offers a glimpse into Tokyo's art scene at the young, grass-roots level, and is connected to **Design Festa**, the country's largest art and design fair held twice a year. If you're thirsty or hungry after perusing the eclectic offerings, there's also a funky café and an *okonomiyaki* (savory pancake) restaurant on-site.

ESPACE LOUIS VUITTON TOKYO

7F Louis Vuitton Omotesandō, 5-7-5 Jingū-mae, Shibuya-ku; tel. 03/5766-1094; www. espacelouisvuittontokyo.com; noon-8pm during exhibitions; free; take Ginza, Hanzomon, Chiyoda lines to Omotesandō Station, A1, or Chiyoda, Fukutoshin lines to Meiji-Jingūmae Station, exit 4

On the seventh floor of the Omotesandō Louis Vuitton store is an airy, well-lit space that has hosted shows by artists from Japan, as well as from Finland, India, the United States, and Brazil.

Akihabara and Ueno

3331 ARTS CHIYODA

6-11-14 Sotokanda, Chiyoda-ku; tel. 03/6803-2441; www.3331.jp; 10am-9pm daily; fee varies by exhibition; take Ginza line to Suehirocho Station, exit 4, or take Yamanote, Sōbu lines to Akihabara Station, Electric City exit

This experimental art space is housed in a former junior high school. The facility includes private galleries, a large exhibition space, and recording studios, and the schoolyard is now a public park. As with many of Tokyo's galleries, it also has an attractive café and a gift shop stocked with locally created pieces. If you want to feel the pulse of Tokyo's creative world, be sure to pay a visit to this inspired hub.

ART SANCTUARY ALLAN WEST

1-6-17 Yanaka, Taitō-ku; tel. 03/3827-1907; www.allanwest.jp; 1:30pm-4:30pm Mon.-Wed. and Thurs.-Fri., 3pm-4:30pm Sun.; take Chiyoda subway line to Nezu Station, then walk 10 minutes northeast

Set in the heart of the charming Yanaka neighborhood, in a beautifully renovated wooden building with handsome sliding doors, exposed beams, and tatami mats throughout, this is the gallery and studio of artist Allan West. Originally hailing from Washington DC, West moved to Tokyo in 1982 to study under master painter Kayama Matazo at Tokyo University of the Arts. Today, he paints brilliantly in the traditional Nihonga style, from prints and scrolls to screens. He is a strict traditionalist, even making his own paint. You can just look or even buy his work. Prices start from as little as ¥5,000, but shoot to upward of ¥5 million from there. It's a great reason to meander into this charming local side of town.

FESTIVALS AND EVENTS

This list of Tokyo events, from celebrations of contemporary art to centuries-old rites, is by no means comprehensive, but these are some of the city's biggest and best. Though all major events and festivals were cancelled in 2020 due to the coronavirus, hopes are high that they will be reinstated in 2021. Check websites and local restrictions for confirmation.

Spring

ART FAIR TOKYO

Citywide; https://artfairtokyo.com; early Mar.; 1-day pass ¥4,000 for one, ¥6,000 for two

Art Fair Tokyo provides a great chance to dive into Tokyo's art scene, with some 150 galleries participating every March, normally for about a week during the first half of the month. It is a four-day event that requires purchasing a ticket to attend. Participating galleries and museums offer discounted admission for those holding an Art Fair pass.

TOKYO RAINBOW PRIDE

Yoyogi-kōen and around; http://tokyorainbowpride.com; first week of May; free

Thousands suit up in fancy attire for a parade with floats to celebrate LGBTQ pride at Tokyo Rainbow Pride. The parade goes from Yoyogi-kōen toward Shibuya Station. A festival is also held in Yoyogi-kōen.

DESIGN FESTA

Tokyo Big Sight; http://designfesta.com; May, Aug., and Nov.; ¥800 one day, ¥1,000 for one-day tickets bought day of entry, ¥1,500 two days, ¥1,800 for two-day tickets bought day of entry; take Rinkai line to Kokusai-Tenjijo Station or Yurikamome line to Kokusai-Tenjijo-Seimon Station

Taking place three times a year in May, August, and November, Design Festa is a massive event showcasing the work of the city's newest crop of artists and designers. As the name indicates, it's linked to the Design Festa Gallery in Harajuku. It takes place over a weekend at **Tokyo Big Sight** (3-11-1 Ariake, Kōtō-ku; tel. 03/5530-1111; www.bigsight.jp), a massive exhibition space in Odaiba made of four upside-down pyramids on massive pillars resembling something out of *Star Wars*. There's plenty of food and amenities, but the point is the performances, workshops, and artwork on display.

KANDA MATSURI

Kanda Myōjin and around; closest weekend to May 15 in odd numbered years; free

Kanda Matsuri is one of Tokyo's three biggest festivals. Thousands flood the streets all the way from Kanda to Nihonbashi and Marunouchi, with hundreds of floats and *omikoshi* (portable shrines) carried by sweaty participants to the great shrine of **Kanda Myōjin.** It's a spectacle to behold. The festival begins Friday afternoon before the weekend closest to May 15 and goes until around early evening. Saturday's festivities begin from around noon and last till late afternoon. Sunday starts around 6am and goes all the way through evening.

SANJA MATSURI

Asakusa-jinja and around; www.asakusajinja.jp/en/sanjamatsuri; third weekend of May; free

The largest festival in Tokyo, drawing a crowd of almost two million, this three-day bash takes place the third weekend of May each year, beginning from Friday afternoon. It celebrates the three founders of Tokyo's most famous Buddhist temple, **Sensō-ji** in Asakusa, which sits next to the Shinto shrine of **Asakusa-jinja,** where the three founders are enshrined. The most visually stunning aspect is about 100 elaborate *mikoshi* (portable shrines), which symbolically house deities,

being paraded through the nearby streets by men and women decked out in Edo-period attire in the hopes of bringing prosperity to the area. The neighborhood around Sensō-ji is overflowing with *yatai* (foot stalls), games, and plenty of locals beating drums, playing bamboo flutes, and milling around in *yukata* (lightweight kimono). The festivities culminate on Sunday when three massive *mikoshi* owned by Asakusa-jinja make their rounds.

ROPPONGI ART NIGHT

Roppongi; www.roppongiartnight.com; last weekend of May; free

During the last weekend of May each year, Roppongi, where three major contemporary art museums are clustered, hosts a two-day overnight event showcasing art, design, film, music, and live performances. Walk through the district, from Roppongi Hills to Tokyo Midtown to the National Art Center, and explore. Stalls selling food and drinks dot the area, too, giving it a lively, even rowdy atmosphere as the night wears on.

Summer
SUMIDAGAWA FIREWORKS

Asakusa; www.sumidagawa-hanabi.com; 7pm last Sat. of July; free

The Sumidagawa Fireworks is Tokyo's largest fireworks show, on the banks of the Sumida River. Crowds of up to one million around Asakusa, the center of the action, are intense, and the displays awesome. To get a good spot, plan on arriving several hours before of the show. Even then, be prepared to jostle for a decent position.

COMIKET

Tokyo Big Sight; www.comiket.co.jp; early Aug., late Dec.; free

This one's for the *otaku* out there. Comic Market, or Comiket, is Tokyo's largest manga sale, held twice a year in August and December. Each edition takes place over the course of four days at **Tokyo Big Sight** (3-11-1 Ariake, Kōtō-ku; tel. 03/5530-1111; www.bigsight.jp), which also hosts Design Festa.

Hordes of cosplayers and manga fans, to the tune of 200,000, gather for the event, so be prepared for serious crowds.

ASAKUSA SAMBA CARNIVAL

Asakusa; www.asakusa-samba.org; last Sat. of Aug.; free

You'd think you were in Brazil at the Asakusa Samba Carnival, a huge celebration with music, floats, and flamboyantly costumed dancers with the requisite tail feathers. The event serves as a reminder of the deep historic ties between Brazil and Japan: Brazil is home to the biggest Japanese diaspora of any country in the world. In celebration, around 20 teams parade down Asakusa's major thoroughfare of Umamichi-dōri, moving past the Kaminarimon gate of Sensō-ji temple in the direction of Tawaramachi. The lively festival draws some 500,000 spectators.

KŌENJI AWA ODORI

Kōenji; www.koenji-awaodori.com; last weekend of Aug.; free

Kōenji Awa Odori is a pulsating, fun, and rowdy festival, by far Tokyo's best *awa-odori* dance festival. These take place in August during O-bon season, when Buddhist tradition holds that the ancestors return to the world of the living. The festival's roots are actually in Tokushima, Shikoku, where the festival has been going strong for more than 400 years. Each year, more than one million people flock to the suburb of Kōenji to watch troupes of musicians and dancers weave through the neighborhood's streets. This is one of my personal favorites. The street parade begins around 5pm and ends around 8pm or 9pm, although people stick around to eat and drink into the night. All you have to do is ride the Chūō line west of Shinjuku to Kōenji (about 7 minutes); you will be immediately propelled into the action as you exit the station.

Fall

TOKYO JAZZ FESTIVAL

Multiple venues; www.tokyo-jazz.com; Sept.; from ¥3,800 depending on seat class and event, free performances also held

Tokyo Jazz Festival brings together a world-class lineup of jazz stars from Japan and abroad for Japan's biggest jazz event. It's definitely recommended for serious devotees of the art. It takes place over a weekend, usually around the end of August or early September, mostly in Shibuya and Harajuku, with some outdoor performances

musicians in Kōenji Awa Odori

in Yoyogi-kōen and some indoor performances at NHK Hall (2-2-1 Jinnan, Shibuya-ku), among other venues in Shibuya and around (see website). Tickets go on sale starting around late June and sell out relatively fast, so keep an eye on the website if you're keen to attend. Note that there are some free performances in Yoyogi-kōen.

Sports and Recreation

Tokyo's sights, food, nightlife, and shopping will probably be more than enough to keep you busy during your time in the city, but if you feel the need for some recreation, a number of great parks can be found throughout the city. There's also a classic amusement park, Asakusa Hanayashiki, in the heart of the old part of town.

PARKS
Ginza and Marunouchi
CHIDORIGAFUCHI
千鳥ヶ淵

From 2-chōme Kudanminami to 2-chōme Sanbanchō; tel. 03/5211-4243; www.gotokyo.org; free; take Hanzōmon, Shinjuku, Tōzai lines to Kudanshita Station, exit 2

Just beyond the Imperial Palace, Chidorigafuchi runs along the western side of Hanzo Moat. The park is divided into three sections. The Chidorigafuchi Greenway runs south to the Chidorigafuchi National Cemetery, the burial site of 352,297 unidentified casualties of World War II, including civilians who died from air raids and the atomic bombs dropped on Hiroshima and Nagasaki. Farther south of the cemetery, there's also a park area, Chidorigafuchi-kōen.

The Chidorigafuchi Greenway, lined by cherry trees, is one of the Tokyo's most quintessential *hanami* (cherry blossom viewing) spots. In the middle of the park, you'll find a boathouse where you can rent paddleboats between April and November and ply the moat (30 minutes; ¥500). During *hanami* season, when the trees lining the moat explode into a riot of pink, expect considerable wait times for boat rentals and limited space to snap pictures amid the legion of photographers.

Tokyo Bay Area
ODAIBA KAIHIN-KŌEN
お台場海浜公園

1 Daiba, Minato-ku; tel. 03/5500-2455; www.tptc. co.jp; 24 hours daily; take Yurikamome line to Odaiba Kaihin-kōen Station

Across the Rainbow Bridge from the rest of the city, you'll find Odaiba Kaihin-kōen. This seaside park reminds you that Tokyo is in fact a maritime city—something that's easy to forget. Take in some of the best views of Tokyo from across the bay from this 800-meter-long (2,624-foot-long) human-made beach, complete with walking paths, a promenade, and even a Statue of Liberty knockoff. This popular date spot is especially romantic at dusk, as the Rainbow Bridge and city light up and petite cruise boats fill the bay. Windsurfing and kayaking are permitted, and the necessary equipment can be rented at the boathouse next to the beach, but swimming is forbidden.

Shibuya and Around
YOYOGI-KŌEN
代々木公園

2-1 Yoyogi Kamizonocho, Shibuya-ku; www. yoyogipark.info; 24 hours daily; free; take Yamanote line to Harajuku Station, Omotesandō exit; Chiyoda line to Yoyogi-Kōen Station, exit 3

Perhaps Tokyo's most popular public park, there are often large weekend festivals held here during spring and summer, and the place is absolutely jam-packed during *hanami* (cherry-blossom viewing), when the sprawling green space erupts in color as the park's myriad cherry trees blossom. The park is also known as a place for street performers of all kinds, including the famed rockabilly dancers who congregate every Sunday to bust a move to 1950s rock tunes at the park's main entrance near Harajuku Station.

Akihabara and Ueno
UENO-KŌEN
上野公園

5-20 Ueno-kōen, Taitō-ku; tel. 03/3828-5644; www.tokyo-park.or.jp; 5am-11pm daily; free; take Yamanote line to Ueno Station, Ueno-kōen, Shinobazu exits

This sizable public park is dotted with shrines and temples. It contains Shinobazu Pond, stocked with abundant lotus flowers and waterfowl, and Japan's oldest zoo. Ueno-kōen is also blessed with a large proliferation of cherry trees that burst colorfully to life each spring to make the park one of the city's most popular spots for *hanami*. The park's real draw is its abundance of museums, with Tokyo National Museum at the head of the pack. The National Museum of Nature and Science is also worth a visit.

Western Tokyo
INOKASHIRA-KŌEN
井の頭恩賜公園

1-18-31 Gotenyama, Musashino-shi; www.kensetsu. metro.tokyo.jp; 24 hours daily; free; take Sōbu, Chūō, Inokashira lines to Kichijōji Station, Kōen exit

If you want to get a bit outside downtown, Inokashira-kōen is highly recommended. This lovely park is located in the bustling suburb of Kichijōji, which always hovers near the top of any list of Tokyo's most desirable places to call home. The park has a central walking loop that circles a large pond, where you can rent paddle boats shaped like large swans. On weekends, performers attract crowds and locals sell their wares, from jewelry to photographs and paintings. On an island at the western edge of the park's large pond, you'll find Inokashira Benzaiten, a shrine dedicated to Benzaiten, patron of the arts. At the back of the park, you'll find the immensely

popular Ghibli Museum. There are also some excellent cafés and restaurants in and around Inokashira, so take your time and enjoy this special place.

TOURS

The most rewarding discoveries in Tokyo often come through serendipity and wandering on your own, but sometimes a tour can help unlock facets of the city. For basic walking tours, Tokyo Metropolitan Government Tours (www.gotokyo.org/en/tourists/guideservice/guideservice/index.html; average 3 hours; free or only covering costs incurred by guides) and Tokyo Systemized Goodwill Guide (SGG) Club (http://tokyosgg.jp/guide.html; average 1.5-2 hours; free) provide good options.

With more eateries than any city on the planet, it's no surprise that Tokyo is also full of food tours. A few operators include Food Tours Tokyo (http://foodtourstokyo.com; average 3 hours; ¥18,000 for group of up to 4, ¥4,500 pp for group over 4, food costs of about ¥5,000-6,000 not included, costs incurred by guide must be covered), Japan Wonder Travel (https://japanwondertravel.com; average 3 hours; ¥9,000-14,500, includes some food and drinks), Ninja Food Tours (www.ninjafoodtours.com; 2-3.5 hours; ¥7,500-10,800, includes some food and drinks), and Oishii Food Tours (www.oishiitours.com; 3.5 hours; ¥12,000-15,000, includes some food and drinks).

Nightlife Tours

If you're interested in joining a tour down the rabbit hole that is nightlife in Tokyo, here are a few to consider.

BACKSTREET GUIDES
https://thebackstreetguides.com; 6 hours Wed., Fri., Sun.; ¥13,000, includes some food and drinks

Night Out Tokyo Tour by Backstreet Guides starts with a few sights, followed by yakitori and drinks in Shibuya then Shinjuku, and ends with an introduction to the rowdy district of Roppongi with a few photo ops.

TOKYO URBAN ADVENTURES

www.urbanadventures.com; 2.5-3 hours; ¥11,065, includes snacks, two drinks

Kanpai Tokyo: Shinjuku Drinks and Neon Lights by Tokyo Urban Adventures leads customers through a tour of Shinjuku's endless array of bars and restaurants, with a focus on the red-light district of **Kabukichō** and the drinking dens of **Golden Gai.**

OKAWARI BAR CRAWLS

tel. 806/514-4647; https://okawaribarcrawls.com; Tues.-Wed., Fri.-Sun.; 4 hours; $65 (roughly ¥7,000), includes two rounds of drinks

For a great tour through a more local culinary alleyway and drinking zone, Okawari Bar Crawls offers tours for solo travelers or groups of up to 8. This is a great option if you want to mingle with locals outside the major downtown hubs typically covered by nightlife tours.

"SHIBUYA STRAY CAT"

www.airbnb.com/experiences/64941; 5 hours; ¥10,500, includes drinks

My personal recommendation: Go deeper than all these tours with "Shibuya Stray Cat" Tatsuya, a seasoned journalist, bona fide character, and Tokyo old hand who has been drinking and befriending his way through Shibuya's backstreets for decades. A gregarious, boisterous host and guide, Tatsuya's perspective on the colorful neighborhood stretching back to the 1970s is fascinating. His tours veer well off the beaten track.

Cultural Tours
GAIJIN TOURS

www.gaijintours.com; 2-4 hours; ¥4,000-20,000

For culturally focused street-level introductions to Tokyo neighborhoods, Gaijin Tours offers a number of interesting options, from exploring the pop-cultural maze of Akihabara to the old-school neighborhood of Yanaka, west of Ueno.

EYEXPLORE

www.eyexplore.com; 2.5 hours; ¥9,900-28,000, other tours as high as ¥120,000

If you're a keen street photographer, check out Eyexplore. This outfit offers photography walking tours with a variety of themes, including the city at night, architecture, and temples.

Bus Tours
HATO BUS TOURS

www.hatobus.com; tel. 03/3435-6081; 4 hours; adults ¥5,000-12,000, children ¥3,160-8,000 for Tokyo tours

Hato Bus Tours is the best-known provider, offering English-language half-day and full-day tours of Tokyo, as well as points of interest around the capital from Kamakura and Nikkō to Mount Fuji and Hakone.

GRAY LINE

www.jgl.co.jp/inbound; tel. 03/3595-5948; adults ¥4,900-9,800, children 6-11 ¥2,600-6,600

Gray Line offers both half-day and full-day tours of Tokyo's major sights. Tours depart from Dai-Ichi Hotel in Shinbashi, although pickup from some major hotels can be arranged.

SKYBUS

www.skybus.jp; tel. 03/3215-0008; four times daily; adults ¥1,600, children ¥700

Skybus gives tours lasting roughly an hour through various areas of the city in red double-decker buses with open tops. If you just want a quick introduction, this is the way to go.

Bike Tours
TOKYO BICYCLE TOURS

www.tokyobicycletours.com; 3-6.5 hours; ¥5,000-9,000

If you're interested in combining a tour with a bike ride, try Tokyo Bicycle Tours, which offers tours of central Tokyo and the Tokyo Bay Area by reservation only, for a minimum of two riders.

TOKYO GREAT CYCLING TOUR

tel. 03/4590-2995; www.tokyocycling.jp; 1.5-6 hours; adults ¥5,000-13,000, ages 12 and under ¥2,500-6,500

The Tokyo Great Cycling Tour offers a wide range of cycling routes.

BAY CRUISES

Stand at the banks of the Sumida River in Asakusa during the evening and you will most likely see a number of low-slung boats festooned with paper lanterns gliding in both directions on the river. These are traditional houseboats known as *yakatabune*. It's possible to ride one of these crafts up and down the Sumida River, and around the contours of Tokyo Bay, eating and drinking as you go. While the food is hit-or-miss, the views of the city from the water are romantic.

Thoroughly modern compact cruise boats also sail the waters around Tokyo. Choosing a cruise provider can be daunting, given the sheer number of them and the language barrier (some do have English-language reservation services). To get a sense for what your options are, visit the website of the **Tokyo Yakatabune Association** (www.yakatabune-kumiai.jp/en/index.php).

FUNASEI

1-16-8 Kita-Shinagawa, Shinagawa-ku; tel. 03/5770-5131; www.funasei.com; 2.5 hours; adults from ¥10,800, children ¥4,000-8,000

This *yakatabune* (traditional houseboat) cruise provider operates six traditional boats and one private charter yacht, seating 20 to 120, depending on the craft. The boats depart from Shinagawa (located south of Ginza and the Tokyo Tower, on the west side of Tokyo Bay) and sail northward, up the Sumida River to Tokyo Skytree in Asakusa, before returning via Odaiba. The meals served on board are Japanese—tempura, sashimi, and more—and booze is unlimited. Note that the liaison by phone is an English-speaking travel agency. Inquire directly with them about cruise schedules and availability.

BASEBALL

An interesting counterpoint to deeply indigenous sumo, the relatively recent import of baseball reveals many of the nation's cultural quirks. Although Tokyo's baseball fans are less fervent than the rabid supporters of Kansai's Hanshin Tigers, the capital boasts two major teams, the **Yomiuri Giants** and **Yakult Swallows.** Stadium capacity was reduced over the course of the coronavirus pandemic, but it has been possible to catch a game for the most part.

TOKYO DOME

1-3-61 Koraku, Bunkyō-ku; tel. 03/5800-9999; www.tokyo-dome.co.jp, tickets sold at www.giants.jp; tickets ¥1,800-6,500; take Marunouchi, Namboku lines to Korakuen Station, exit 1, or JR Chūō, Sōbu to Suidōbashi Station, west exit, or Mita subway line to Suidōbashi Station, exit A5

Home to Japan's winningest team, the Yomiuri Giants, this center in the geographic heart of the city is a great place for the authentic Japanese baseball experience. More popular than Tokyo's second team, the Yakult Swallows, tickets sell out well in advance. Plan and purchase as far ahead as you can.

MEIJI JINGŪ STADIUM

3-1 Kasumigaoka-machi, Shinjuku-ku; tel. 0180/993-589; www.jingu-stadium.com; tickets ¥1,600-5,900; take Ginza line to Gaienmae Station, exit 3

This historic (built in 1926), 37,000-seater stadium is home to the Yakult Swallows. If the Giants are akin to New York's Yankees, the Swallows are the Mets. Nicely located near Aoyama, Harajuku, Shibuya, and Shinjuku, this is a convenient place to experience Japan's true national pastime.

THEME PARKS

Tokyo has its fair share of theme and amusement parks, with **Tokyo Disneyland** and **Tokyo DisneySea,** located just east of town in Chiba Prefecture, firmly atop the list.

The Lowdown on Sumo

There aren't too many sports more deeply associated with Japan in the popular imagination than sumo. The sport is deeply rooted in ancient Shinto rites meant to entertain the gods in hopes of a good harvest. And in many ways, it remains more ritual than action even today. Ryōgoku, south of Asakusa and east of Marunouchi, across the Sumida River, is the center of sumo in Tokyo.

If you're lucky enough to attend a match, upon entering the arena, look up. The roof suspended above the ring is the roof of a Shinto shrine. The bulk of the activity taking place under this sacred cover consists of the referees intoning chants and the wrestlers cleansing their mouths with water, throwing salt to symbolically purify the ring (where women are, controversially, not allowed to enter), and repeatedly performing the choreographed show of strength known as *shiko*, in which they squat, clap their hands, raise each leg, and stamp each foot. The matches themselves sometimes last only seconds, but in rare cases can stretch to around a minute. The first man who leaves the ring or touches its earthen surface with any part of his body but the soles of his feet loses the match. Hence the effort to pack on the pounds by alternating calorie-rich meals with long naps.

Here are the best ways to catch a glimpse into the fascinating world of sumo during your time in Tokyo.

CATCH A MATCH

The best place to see a sumo match is at Ryōgoku Kokugikan (1-3-28 Yokoami, Sumida-ku; tel. 03/3623-5111; take Sōbu line to Ryōgoku Station, west exit) in Tokyo. Fifteen-day tournaments are held at this stadium three times a year (Jan., May, and Sept.). The day kicks off around 8am, but it gets interesting around 3pm when the top wrestlers begin to enter the ring. The tournaments usually end around 6pm.

Buy your tickets a month in advance (http://sumo.or.jp, http://buysumotickets.com, or http://sumo.pia.jp/en; ¥3,800-47,800, average ¥18,000 around tournament time). There's also a box office near the station's main entrance that sells a few hundred tickets for nosebleed seats (¥2,100) on the day of each match, but you'll need to arrive no later than 5:30am or 6am to have a shot at landing one. You can rent a headset that provides English-language commentary (¥100 with ¥2,000 deposit).

Tournaments are also held in Osaka in March. Advance tickets (book a month beforehand; ¥2,500-12,300) can be purchased online: http://sumo.or.jp, http://buysumotickets.com, and http://sumo.pia.jp.

WATCH A PRACTICE

If you're not in town during tournament season, it's also possible to watch the wrestlers colliding up close on an intimate visit to a stable, or *beya*, where *asa-keiko* (morning practice) can be observed through a window.

ASAKUSA HANAYASHIKI

2-28-1 Asakusa, Taito-ku; tel. 03/3842-8780; www.hanayashiki.net; 10am-6pm daily; ages 7-12 ¥500, ages 13 and up ¥1,000; free ride pass ¥2,000 6 years old and younger, ¥2,200 ages 7-12, ¥2,500 ages 13 and up; individual ride ticket ¥100, coupon book of 11 tickets ¥1,000

This old-school amusement park in Asakusa has been running since 1883. While the park's 20 or so rides won't wow you with thrills, they will certainly inspire a sense of nostalgia. Among them are Japan's oldest rollercoaster, which runs on a steel track, and an old-fashioned haunted house. This is by no means a must-see, but if you feel like doing something offbeat, are traveling with kids, or need a break from temples and shrines, Hanayashiki is a fun option.

TOKYO DISNEY RESORT

1-1 Maihama, Urayasu-shi, Chiba Prefecture; domestic tel. 0570/00-8632, from overseas +81 45/330-5211; www.tokyodisneyresort.jp; opening hours vary by season; adults ¥7,400, junior high and

Arashio Beya (2-47-2 Hama-chō, Nihonbashi, Chūō-ku; tel. 03/3666-7646; www.arashio. net/tour_e.html; 7:30am-10am daily Dec.-Feb., Apr.-Jun., Aug.-Oct.; free; take Tōei Shinjuku line to Hamachō Station, exit A2), west across the Sumida River from Ryōgoku Kokugikan, accommodates guests who are willing to respect some rules: no talking, filming, flash photography, eating, drinking, or chewing gum. Note that aside from being closed during tournament time, the stable's doors are also shut to the public for one week after each grand tournament. Reservations aren't possible, so it's wise to call the day before sometime between 4pm-8pm to confirm practice will be held the next morning. There's a Japanese-language script on the website, written in *romaji* (Roman alphabet) with an English translation, that you can use in the call.

There are also sporadically held stable tours with knowledgeable locals offered through the websites Voyagin (www.govoyagin.com) and Magical Trip (www.magical-trip.com).

EAT *CHANKO NABE*

The calorie-dense hot pot loaded with vegetables, seafood, and meat is scarfed down by wrestlers daily. Try Tomoegata (2-17-6 Ryōgoku, Sumida-ku; tel. 03/3632-5600; www.tomoegata.com; 11:30am-2pm and 5pm-10:30pm Tues.-Fri., 11:30am-2pm and 4:30pm-10:30pm Sat.-Sun., holidays), located in the heart of sumo territory in Ryōgoku. Alternatively, you can get a small bowl of the stuff (¥300) in the basement of the Ryōgoku Kokugikan on a tournament day.

LEARN MORE

The Sumo Museum (1F Ryōgoku Kokugikan, 1-3-28 Yokoami, Sumida-ku; tel. 03/3622-0366; www.sumo.or.jp; 10am-4:30pm Mon.-Fri., sporadically closed Mon. and national holidays; free) houses memorabilia and woodblock prints related to the sport. It also holds special exhibitions six times a year. Note that the museum closes between special exhibitions and is only open to tournament ticketholders during the grand tournaments held at the Ryōgoku Kokugikan three times a year (Jan., May, and Sept.) in Tokyo. Before making the trip, check the museum's schedule online (http://sumo.or.jp/EnSumoMuseum/schedule) to be safe.

At the Tomioka Hachimangu Shrine (1-20-3 Tomioka, Koto-ku; tel. 03/3642-1315; www. tomiokahachimangu.or.jp; 24 hours daily; free; take Ōedo, Tōzai lines to Monzen-nakachō Station, exit 1), southeast of Ryōgoku Kokugikan, sumo bouts were held for about 100 years during the Edo period. Monuments bearing the names of wrestlers who became *yokozuna* (grand champions) and *ozeki* (second-highest rank) dot the grounds. Look to your right as you enter and find the humblingly massive handprints in stone of some sumo superstars. It's also an impressive shrine in its own right.

high school students ages 12-17 ¥6,400, children ages 4-11 ¥4,800; take JR Keiyo line to Maihama Station, south exit

Operating under the banner of Tokyo Disney Resort, Tokyo Disneyland and Tokyo DisneySea are located about 15 minutes on the train east of Tokyo Station (¥220). While the Disneyland side of the park is essentially modeled on the one in California, DisneySea is the only park run by Disney with a nautical theme. The park consists of seven areas modeled after various watery settings, from real places (Mediterranean Harbor) to the fantastic (Mermaid Lagoon). While both parks can be a lot of fun for a family, DisneySea is a bit more appealing to adults.

A few things to bear in mind before a trip to either park. One, it is crowded. To avoid the worst, have a look at this calendar (www15.plala.or.jp/gcap/disney), which gives an idea of how crowded the park is likely to be on a specific day. Two, book your ticket online through the website—a requirement at the time of writing due to the impact of coronavirus. Three, arrive as early in the day as you possibly can. Finally, make use of the Fastpass system: Put your park ticket into a machine for a specific attraction and receive a pass that lets you know when to return to join the Fastpass line. Thoroughly read through the website to check for updates on ticketing procedures and more, as the situation continues to evolve amid the coronavirus pandemic.

To reach Tokyo Disneyland, exit Maihama Station and walk 5 minutes southeast to Resort Gate Way on the Disney Resort line and take the monorail one stop to Tokyo Disneyland Station (2 minutes; ¥260). To reach Tokyo DisneySea, take the same monorail to Tokyo DisneySea Station (9 minutes; ¥260).

ONSEN
Tokyo Bay Area
ŌEDO ONSEN MONOGATARI

2-6-3 Aomi, Kōtō-ku; tel. 03/5500-1126; https:// daiba.ooedoonsen.jp; 11am-9am daily, last entry 7am; adults ¥2,768, children age 4-12 ¥1,078 on weekdays, adults ¥2,988, children age 4-12 ¥1,078 on Sat.-Sun. and holidays, adults ¥2,218 surcharge for 6pm-2am on weekdays and ¥2,438 on Sat.-Sun., adults surcharge for 2am-5am ¥2,200 daily, adults ¥1,580, children age 4-12 ¥1,078 for 5am-7am admission daily; take Yurikamome line to Telecom Center Station, or Rinkai line to Tokyo Teleport Station, then board shuttle

Change your street clothes for a *yukata* (lightweight kimono) and get acquainted with the *onsen* experience at this kitschy, surprisingly family-friendly hot-spring theme park across Tokyo Bay in Odaiba. This massive complex has gender-separated indoor and outdoor baths fed with water from beneath Tokyo Bay, and a mixed outdoor foot bath wherein small fish chomp away dead skin on your feet. There are also food stalls, old-school festival games, and restaurants in a kitschy recreation of Tokyo as it once looked in the old days. No tattoos allowed.

Asakusa and Ryōgoku
ONSEN THERMAE-YU

1-1-2 Kabukichō, Shinjuku-ku; tel. 03/5285-1726; www.thermae-yu.jp; 11am-9am daily, irregular closings; ¥2,405 Mon.-Fri., ¥1,100 surcharge from midnight-9am daily, ¥880 surcharge on Sat.-Sun. and holidays; take Marunouchi, Fukutoshin, Shinjuku lines to Shinjuku-Sanchōme Station, exit E1, or Chūō, Sōbu lines to Shinjuku Station, east exit

Besides the spic-and-span sex-separated indoor and outdoor pools at this impressive new *onsen* complex, there are also saunas, a beauty salon, and various exfoliation scrubdowns, as well as a bar, café, and eatery on site. The water is pumped in daily from Izu Peninsula, southwest of Tokyo. A good choice in the heart of Kabukichō. Uncovered tattoos aren't permitted, but coverings can be purchased for ¥300.

Akihabara and Ueno
SPA LAQUA

5-9F Tokyo Dome City, 1-1-1 Kasuga, Bunkyō-ku; tel. 03/5800-9999; www.laqua.jp; 11am-9am daily, last entry 8am; adults ¥2,900, children 6-17 years old ¥2,090, ¥1,980 surcharge from 1am-6am, ¥350 surcharge Sat.-Sun. and holidays; take Marunouchi line to Kōrakuen Station, exit 2

Real *onsen* water is piped into the stylish indoor and outdoor pools at this hot-spring complex not far from Koishikawa Korakuen, west of Akihabara, from 1,700 meters (5,577 feet) beneath the earth, said to bestow health benefits such as improved circulation. This huge complex is spread across five floors, which also house facilities for treatments ranging from Thai massages to Korean body exfoliation scrubbing sessions. No tattoos allowed.

Shopping

GINZA AND MARUNOUCHI
銀座, 丸の内

Ginza is home to an array of shops dedicated to high-end fashion and luxury goods, both produced in Japan and overseas. Think world-class brands in sophisticated boutiques and swanky, sprawling emporiums offering an entire city's worth of consumer opulence under one roof.

Fashion
DOVER STREET MARKET GINZA

6-9-5 Ginza, Chūō-ku; tel. 03/6228-5080; http://ginza.doverstreetmarket.com; 11am-8pm daily; take Ginza line to Ginza Station, exit A2

If this seven-floor complex feels like a shopping mall as seen through the eyes of a design renegade with avant-garde sensibilities, that's because it is. Legendary designer Rei Kawakubo, whose label Comme des Garçons exploded onto the world's runways in the 1980s, has revived Ginza's fashion cred with Dover Street Market Ginza, a bleeding-edge, high-concept shopping mall brimming with top-end brands from Japan and overseas.

GINZA SIX

6-10 Ginza, Chūō-ku; http://ginza6.tokyo; 10:30am-8:30pm daily; take Ginza, Hibiya, Marunouchi lines to Ginza Station, exit A3

Ginza's largest shrine to commerce is enormous, with 241 brands under one very exclusive roof. You'll also find an exquisitely designed Tsutaya Books on the sixth floor and even a *Noh* theater in the basement. Splash out some serious cash and you can even hire a personal stylist to advise you on your shopping spree. And it's not just clothes. If you're in search of that perfect bottle of booze made in Japan (*nihonshū, shōchū*, whiskey, gin), a fantastic choice in this complex is *Imadeya* (B2F Ginza Six; tel. 03/6264-5537; www.imadeya.co.jp/shops/ginza; 10:30am-8:30pm daily).

OKURA

20-11 Sarugaku-chō, Shibuya-ku; tel. 03/3461-8511; www.hrm.co.jp/okura; 11:30am-8pm Mon.-Fri., 11am-8:30pm Sat.-Sun. and holidays; take Tōkyū Tōyoko line to Daikanyama Station

Situated on a fashionable street behind T-Site, Okura (オクラ) is a great place to get acquainted with Japan's centuries-old indigo dyeing tradition. The threads here are all made using old-school indigo dyeing techniques. A mix of old and modern-style attire are sold, from *tabi* (split-toed socks) to jackets, jeans, T-shirts, and scarves. The tastefully rustic building that houses the shop is a pleasure to explore, too. As there's no English sign, look out for the squat, traditional-style shopfront, which normally has some indigo-dyed specimen on display out front.

Souvenirs
MUJI

3-3-5 Ginza, Chūō-ku; https://shop.muji.com/jp/ginza; 10am-9pm daily; take Ginza, Marunouchi, Hibiya subway lines to Ginza Station, exit B4, then walk 3 minutes northeast, or take JR Yamanote line to Yūrakuchō Station, central exit, then walk 5 minutes southeast

This is the seven-floor global flagship of Muji, a brand that has developed a reputation beyond Japan for its classically minimal, affordable, practical, and smartly designed products, from kitchenware and furniture to stationery, clothing, and snacks. There's also a diner and bakery on-site.

EBISU AND AROUND
恵比寿

There's a hip pocket of town located upon a hill between Ebisu and Shibuya called **Daikanyama.** The streets, lined with trendy boutiques and cafés, beg to be strolled. This is one of many places where stylish locals shop.

Japan's Big Three of Fashion

As you walk down Omotesandō, which is lined with architecturally stunning designer shops, you'll pass the flagships of the designers that make up Japan's big three names in fashion when you reach the Aoyama area on the southeastern end of the avenue.

ISSEY MIYAKE

3-18-11 Minami Aoyama, Minato-ku; tel. 03/3423-1408; www.isseymiyake.com; 11am-8pm daily
Crossing the large four-way intersection with Aoyama-dōri, you'll come to the Issey Miyake shop on the first corner on the left. Exploding on the scene in the late 1980s, he became famous for his experimental approach, involving fresh uses of fabric, geometric forms, and materials ranging from rough and natural to brightly colored plastic.

COMME DES GARÇONS

5-2-1 Minami Aoyama, Minato-ku; tel. 03/3406-3951; www.comme-des-garcons.com; 11am-8pm daily
Cross the street at the crosswalk and enter the flagship of legendary fashion label Comme des Garçons. Launched in the early 1980s by renowned designer Rei Kawakubo, here you'll find her renegade-chic style on full display. Fashion aside, the striking building, with its dramatic lines and spare interior, is worth a visit in its own right.

YOHJI YAMAMOTO

5-3-6 Minami Aoyama, Minato-ku; tel. 03/3409-6006; www.yohjiyamamoto.co.jp; 11am-8pm daily
Finally, continue up the right side of the street to see the flagship of the third name in Japan's high-fashion trinity, Yohji Yamamoto, who is renowned for his tailoring, which incorporates Japanese techniques onto distinctive black flowing garments.

Bookstores
T-SITE

17-5 Sarugaku-chō; tel. 03/3770-2525; https://store.tsite.jp/daikanyama/; 7am-2am daily; take Tōkyū Tōyoko line to Daikanyama Station

This has to be among the world's coolest bookstores. The design of the complex, which appears to be enmeshed in a knit exterior of countless letter Ts, has won awards for architecture firm Klein Dytham. There's a solid selection of books and magazines on travel, art, architecture, food, and culture, including some in English, and Anjin, a chic café and lounge-bar, is on the second floor. A great place to chill for a few hours.

SHIBUYA
渋谷

A number of large, eclectic shops carrying quirky lifestyle goods, as well as a number of youth fashion retailers, can be found in Shibuya. Teenybopper fashion emporium Shibuya 109 (www.shibuya109.jp), housed in an iconic multi-floor tower just west of Shibuya Crossing, is the neighborhood's most recognizable fashion landmark. Affordable designer items can be found, too, if you know where to look.

Souvenirs
TŌKYŪ HANDS SHIBUYA

12-18 Udagawachō, Shibuya-ku; 03/5489-5111; https://shibuya.tokyu-hands.co.jp; 10am-9pm daily; take Yamanote line to Shibuya, Hachikō exit

It's all about household items at Tōkyū Hands Shibuya, from the useful to the downright bizarre. The eight-floor Shibuya branch of this quirky purveyor of miscellaneous goods is Tokyo's largest, with everything from sundry

---

1: rainy shopping day in Shinjuku 2: shopping along Takeshita-dōri in Harajuku 3: women in *yukata* crossing the street in Ginza

Purikura

Purikura, a shortened form of "print club," is a massive industry in Japan, attracting giggling teens en masse to take cutesy photos with friends. They are essentially photo booths, but the photos can be souped up with various digital enhancements. Often located in game centers, *purikura* booths are popular nationwide, although major cities like Tokyo and Osaka command a particularly large number.

HOW IT WORKS

Many of booths have a preset theme; for example, a dessert-themed booth may add little digital slices of cake to your photos. Insert money in the slot and step inside. After you've input the settings of your choice—doe eyes and rosy cheeks, perhaps—strike a silly pose and let the camera do its work. After the images have been taken, you'll have the option to do further editing with a stylus in an editing booth outside. Once you've modified your photos to your liking, simply press the "end" button on the screen to print them out. Voila: a cheap, quirky souvenir.

PURIKURA PLACES

A few good bets to try out a *purikura* booth include **Purikura no Mecca** (3F, 29-1 Udagawachō, Shibuya-ku; open 24/7; take Yamanote line to Shibuya Station, Hachikō exit) and **Purikura Land Noa** (1-17-5 Jingūmae, Shibuya-ku; tel. 03/6206-8090; 8am-11:30pm daily; take Yamanote line to Harajuku Station, Takeshita exit) on Takeshita-dōri. Here you'll find collections of *purikura* booths to snap away to your heart's content.

Note that some *purikura* spots loosely enforce a rule that prohibits men, whether solo or in a group, from entering without at least one woman accompanying them. You'll be less likely to face an issue in an arcade than in a place solely dedicated to the booths.

---

materials for DIY projects to kitchenware shaped like cartoon characters, light fixtures, and more than 400 types of toothbrushes. If you can dream it, Tōkyū Hands likely has it.

D47 DESIGN TRAVEL STORE

8F Shibuya Hikarie, 2-21-1, Shibuya, Shibuya-ku; tel. 03/6427-2301; www.hikarie8.com/ d47designtravelstore; noon-8pm Thurs.-Tues.; take Yamanote line to Shibuya Station, east exit

As the name suggests, the D47 Design Travel Store features the unique flavors, arts, and specialties of the 47 prefectures that comprise the Japanese archipelago. Japan may not be a huge country geographically speaking, but a trip to this store will likely impress you with the true extent of its diversity.

★ HARAJUKU AND AOYAMA
原宿, 青山

These neighborhoods are home to the highest concentration of trendsetting shops in the city. Funky Harajuku caters to the young. But if you head down **Omotesandō** toward Aoyama, you'll be dazzled by some of the most bleeding-edge high fashion anywhere, artfully displayed in stunning boutiques.

Another great place for urban strolling is the jam-packed pedestrian shopping street of **Takeshita-dōri,** Harajuku at its most youthful and saccharine, directly in front of Harajuku Station's Takeshita exit. Some of the hippest boutiques are located along **Cat Street,** near the intersection of Meiji-dōri and Omotesandō, about a 7-minute walk southeast of Harajuku Station's Omotesandō exit, and in the tangle of backstreets to the north of Omotesandō and east of Meiji-dōri.

Fashion
LAFORET

1-11-6 Jingūmae, Shibuya-ku; tel. 03/3475-0411; www. laforet.ne.jp; 11am-8pm daily; take Yamanote line to Harajuku Station, Omotesandō exit

For a quick introduction to youth fashion

trends, come to LaForet in Harajuku. Inside you'll find a smorgasbord of boutiques hawking brightly colored clothes for hip young things, as well as various exhibitions and events. Check out the goth-lolita offerings and local labels Monomania and H>Fractal, all found in the basement, and the legendary, bleeding-edge **GR8** on floor 2.5, incongruously fronted by a traditional garden with stone lanterns and bonsais.

CHICAGO

2F Mansion 31, 6-31-15, Shibuya-ku; tel. 03/6427-5505; www.chicago.co.jp; 11am-8pm daily; take Yamanote line to Harajuku Station, Omotesandō exit

A fixture in Harajuku's always evolving fashion landscape, Chicago has the largest selection of vintage threads of any branch in the chain. The strong suit here is vintage kimonos and lighter cotton versions called *yukata,* which are sold at prices that won't break the bank.

6%DOKIDOKI

2F TX101 Bldg., 4-28-16 Jingūmae, Shibuya-ku; tel. 03/3479-6116; https://6dokidoki.com; noon-8pm daily; take Yamanote line to Harajuku Station, Omotesandō exit

Vivid clothing and accessories, adorned in unicorns, hearts, and ice-cream cones assault your vision at 6%Dokidoki, which translates to "6% Excitement." It's no shock to learn the shop's founder Sebastian Masuda often works with Kyary Pamyu Pamyu, a J-Pop starlet who is *kawaii* (cute) incarnate. Come here for the full Harajuku experience. Seeing is believing.

SOU-SOU

1F A-La Croce Bldg., 5-4-24Minami-Aoyama, Minato-ku; tel. 03/3407-7877; http://sousounetshop. jp; noon-8pm daily; take Ginza, Hanzōmon lines to Omotesandō Station, exit B1

Sou-Sou is a Kyoto brand that injects modern flare into classic Japanese fashions. At its outpost in trendy Aoyama, you'll find a range of excellent souvenir options from cool T-shirts

and split-toe trainers to *yukatas* designed with a modern twist.

HOUSE @MIKIRI HASSIN

5-42-1 Jingūmae, Shibuya-ku; tel. 03/3486-7673; https://shop.mikirihassin.co.jp; noon-9pm Thurs.-Tues.; take Chiyoda, Ginza, or Hanzomon line to Ōmotesandō, exit B2, then walk 6 minutes west

This bleedingly cool purveyor of fashion deep in the backstreets of Harajuku is a great place to see what Japan's fresh crop of designers are up to. Think Harajuku's new vanguard. The neon shop sign reads "ハウス."

Souvenirs
ORIENTAL BAZAAR

5-9-13 Jingūmae, Shibuya-ku; tel. 03/3400-3933; www.orientalbazaar.co.jp/en; noon-6pm Sat.-Sun. and holidays; take Yamanote line to Harajuku Station, Omotesandō exit, or Chiyoda, Fukutoshin lines to Meiji-Jingūmae Station, exit 4

Harajuku's Oriental Bazaar is a one-stop souvenir shop with English-speaking staff and reasonable prices. If you have limited time and want to take home a few items, they have it all: origami earrings, *sake* cup sets, tableware, antiques, *yukata, ukiyo-e* prints.

SPIRAL MARKET AOYAMA

5-6-23 Minamiaoyama, Minato-ku; tel. 03/3498-1171; www.spiral.co.jp; building opens 11am daily, shop closing hours vary; take Ginza, Hanzōmon, Chiyoda lines to Ōmotesandō Station, exit B1

This arts complex, beautifully designed by Pritzker Prize-winning architect Fumihiko Maki, is built around an ascending spiral at the core of its interior. You'll find shops selling homeware, accessories, stationery, ceramics, and various handmade crafts from around Japan, complemented by an art gallery, cafe, restaurants, and more.

JAPAN TRADITIONAL CRAFTS AOYAMA SQUARE

1F Akasaka Oji Bldg., 8-1-22 Akasaka, Minato-ku; tel. 03/5785-1301; http://kougeihin.jp; 11am-7pm daily; take Ginza, Hanzōmon lines to Aoyama Itchōme Station, exit 4 north

Youth Fashion

Harajuku has been a center of fashion and youth culture since at least the 1990s. Its heyday was well documented in photographer Shoichi Aoki's legendary magazine, *FRUiTS,* when creativity flourished in the neighborhood's then-pedestrian-only smaller streets. Although recent years have seen *FRUiTS* cease publication (resulting in declarations of the demise of Harajuku as a global fashion hub) and car traffic flowing through those streets that were once youth hangouts, the neighborhood's fashion landscape is far from dead, but rather, in a state of flux.

A host of new fashion leaders are establishing themselves in the scene, such as Peco and Aiba Runa, whose brand **RRR By Sugar Spot Factory** and social media imprint have made her one of Harajuku's new stars. Similarly, new magazines, such as *Fanatic* and *Melt Magazine,* are popping up. For an easy-to-access look down the rabbit hole that is Japan's fashion subcultural universe, as well as other quirky bits of obscure travel, peruse the blog of writer and TV host **La Carmina** (www.lacarmina.com/blog).

A young man shows off his outfit in the Harajuku district.

HARAJUKU SUBCULTURES

Although not as prevalent as they once were, many lively fashion subcultures continue to be visible in Harajuku's streets:

- **Cosplay:** "Costume play" is about dressing as an anime, manga, or video game character, and is the most widely recognizable of Harajuku's subcultures.

Another excellent one-stop shop east of Harjuku and Aoyama is Japan Traditional Crafts Aoyama Square, a showcase for traditional crafts from all over Japan that receives funding from the government. Crafts on sale incorporate a wide range of materials, from lacquer and textiles to bamboo, metal, ceramics, and glass. Artisans practice their craft in the store, which features their work on a rotating basis. Items sold here are of a uniformly high quality. Check the artist schedule online.

Toys
KIDDY LAND

6-1-9 Jingūmae, Shibuya-ku; tel. 03/3409-3431; www.kiddyland.co.jp/harajuku; 11am-9pm Mon.-Fri., 10:30am-9pm Sat.-Sun., holidays; take Yamanote line to Harajuku Station, Omotesandō exit, or Chiyoda, Fukutoshin lines to Meiji-Jingūmae Station, exit 4

Kiddy Land is a monument to toys. The enormous shop is chockablock with characters from Studio Ghibli and Disney films, Doraemon dolls, Godzilla models, Star Wars figures, and Sanrio mascots. If you're buying gifts for kids, this shop ticks all boxes.

SHINJUKU AND AROUND
新宿

While Shinjuku has a hodgepodge of everything, from vinyl records to punk-rock fashion shops, department stores are the defining feature. A number of mammoth electronics stores also dot the area.

- **Kawaii:** The "cute" aesthetic extends far beyond the realm of fashion; perhaps no other country has placed such emphasis on the culture of cuteness. The most universally recognizable manifestation of this aesthetic is the iconic character Hello Kitty.

- **Lolita:** Another major trend with roots in Harajuku, this genre sees mostly young women donning knee-high stockings and knee-length skirts with petticoats, sometimes adding a corset or headdress, Victorian-style. There are numerous spins on this style, from **Gothic Lolita** to **Punk Lolita** and beyond.

- **Gyaru:** Based on the English word "gal," the key elements include hair dyed blond or brown, heavy makeup, provocative clothing, and a bit of a devil-may-care attitude to go with it.

- **Visual *kei*:** The "visual style" trend has roots in a Japanese rock movement akin to glam rock. Young male followers suit up in loud outfits and sport flashy hairstyles and makeup.

- **Fairy *kei*:** It doesn't get much more saccharine than this: pastel hair bows, decorative stars, babies, angels and polka dots, leg warmers, tights, baggy shirts, oversized glasses, and more. Stop by **Spank!** (4F Nakano Broadway, 5-52-15 Nakano, Nakano-ku; tel. 08/03404-3809; http://spankworld.jp; 12:30pm-7:30pm Thurs.-Tues.), the store that hatched this trend.

- **Dolly *kei*:** This style is inspired by European fairy tales and religious symbols, filtered through a Harajuku lens.

- **Genderless *kei*:** A relatively new development, this style draws on flourishes of *kawaii* to blur the boundaries of gender. Boys have been the predominant force in this movement, which idealizes a slim figure, bright eyes, makeup, expertly coifed hair, painted eyebrows, showy clothing, and plenty of *kawaii* accoutrements from hats to handbags.

- **Decora:** In this style, accessories, legwarmers, and knee-socks are layered over each other to the point of overpowering the rest of an already quirky outfit, funky dental mask, and tutu included.

Souvenirs
BEAMS JAPAN

3-32-6 Shinjuku, Shinjuku-ku; tel. 03/5368-7300; www.beams.co.jp/global/shop/j; 11am-8pm daily; take Yamanote line to Shinjuku Station, east exit

The Beams Japan flagship carries some of Japan's best designs, from fashion to art and housewares. It also houses a gallery that exhibits works by photographers and artists. If you get hungry while browsing the shop's six floors, head to the basement, where you'll find a restaurant serving Japanese takes on Western staples and curry, as well as a café.

Vinyl Records
DISK UNION SHINJUKU

3-31-4 Shinjuku, Shinjuku-ku; tel. differs for each shop; https://diskunion.net; 11am-9pm Mon.-Sat., 11am-8pm Sun.

Tokyo is legendary among record collectors—"crate diggers"—as one of the best cities in the world to find vinyl treasure. Sprawling over eight floors, this legendary record shop in Shinjuku's hectic core covers any genre under the sun. Note that there is a heavy emphasis on the old compact disc here, but there's a decent selection of vinyl, too. To see a map breaking it all down in English, visit https://diskunion.net/pdf/shop/e_shop_areamap.pdf.

AKIHABARA AND UENO
秋葉原, 上野

Akihabara is the preeminent place to experience the wonderful and wacky world of *otaku* culture. Here you'll find all manner of electronic products and parts, multistory complexes filled with anime and manga, video game emporiums, maid and butler cafés, a

Top Souvenirs

If you can dream it, you can likely buy it in Tokyo. What follows should give you a starting point for thinking about what to take home from your trip.

FUNKY FASHION

Try Beams Japan (page 105) in Shinjuku or any boutique in Harajuku's youth fashion mecca LaForet (page 102).

KIMONOS AND *YUKATA*

Head to Chicago (page 103) in Harajuku for vintage options, Jotaro Saito in Ginza Six (page 99) for high-end, and Sou-Sou (page 103) in Aoyama for traditional items with a contemporary twist.

CRAFT AND DESIGN

For traditional crafts like lacquerware, folding fans, and ceramics, check out Oriental Bazaar (page 103) or Japan Traditional Crafts Aoyama Square (page 103). For great contemporary design, try D47 Design Travel Store (page 102) or 2K540 Aki-Oka Artisan (page 107).

HOUSEWARES

Tokyo is home to a number of multi-floor "lifestyle goods" emporiums like Tōkyū Hands Shibuya (page 101) where everything under the sun is on sale. The famed shopping street Kappabashi-dōri (page 107) has a huge selection of knives, kitchenware, and crowd-pleasing fake plastic food samples.

POP CULTURE PICKS

For items like manga and anime merchandise, head to Mandarake (page 106). For retro video games, check out Super Potato (page 107).

shocking number of vending machines, and plenty of cosplayers milling about.

Pop Culture
RADIO KAIKAN

1-15-16 Sotokanda, Chiyoda-ku; www.akihabara-radiokaikan.co.jp; 10am-8pm daily; take Yamanote, Sōbu, Hibiya lines to Akihabara Station, Electric Town exit

A 10-story tower to geekdom with deep historical roots, stretching back to the years immediately following the war when radios were a premium item, Radio Kaikan carries a hodgepodge of figurines, dolls, manga, trading cards, and much more. Even if you don't plan to buy anything, it's worth stopping to peruse the merchandise to get a sense of the

jaw-dropping extent of the depth and breadth of hobbies catered to in Akihabara.

MANDARAKE

3-11-12 Sotokanda, Chiyoda-ku; tel. 03/3252-7007; http://mandarake.co.jp; noon-8pm daily; take Yamanote, Sōbu, Hibiya lines to Akihabara Station, Electric Town exit

Mandarake is an eight-floor shop at Akihabara's epicenter that has it all: manga, anime, cosplay items, rare art, dolls, *doujinshi* (a wildly popular genre of self-published manga that's often highly risqué), video games, consoles, vintage figurines and models, card games, and loads of toys. If you don't find what you need at Radio Kaikan, try Mandarake instead.

SUPER POTATO

3F-5F Kitabayashi Bldg., 1-11-2 Sotokanda, Chiyoda-ku; tel. 03/5289-9933; www.superpotato. com/akihabara; 11am-8pm Mon.-Fri., 10am-8pm Sat.-Sun., holidays; take Yamanote, Sōbu, Hibiya lines to Akihabara Station, Electric Town exit

There may be no better spot for retro video games on earth than the awesomely named Super Potato. This secondhand bazaar of 8- and 16-bit games, from the Super Mario Brothers to Sonic the Hedgehog and Link (The Legend of Zelda), packs a surprisingly powerful nostalgic punch for those who came of age at the dawn of the video game era in the 1980s. Even if you don't buy anything, stopping by this shop is like stepping into a museum dedicated to the heroes and heroines of your lost youth. Be sure to have a few coins handy to play a few rounds of old-school arcade games on the fifth floor.

M'S: POP LIFE SEX DEPARTMENT STORE

1-15-13 Sotokanda, Chiyoda-ku; tel. 03/3252-6166; www.ms-online.co.jp; 10am-11pm daily; take Yamanote, Sōbu, Hibiya lines to Akihabara Station, Electric Town exit

It's an open secret that everyone who has spent any amount of time exploring Akihabara's maze of curiosities has snuck into M's: Pop Life Sex Department Store. If nothing else, I'd be remiss not to mention this one for its, ahem, value as a cultural case study. While the name speaks for itself, the sheer scale of the shop and its happy-go-lucky atmosphere are worth marveling at. Its seven floors are overflowing with sex toys, lingerie, costumes, whips, chains, life-sized dolls, DVDs—basically every imaginable product catering to the flesh. And it all feels normalized, with shoppers perusing merchandise as if they're in a sporting goods store.

Souvenirs
2K540 AKI-OKA ARTISAN

5-9 Ueno, Taito-ku; www.jrtk.jp/2k540; 11am-7pm Thurs.-Tues.; take Yamanote line to Akihabara Station, Akihabara Electric Town exit, Yamanote line to Okachimachi Station, south exit 1, or Ginza line to Suehirocho Station, exit 2

2K540 Aki-Oka Artisan is a unique space under rail tracks that houses a smattering of shops selling both traditional goods and quirkier, more modern items. The eclectic emporium's name derives from its distance from Tokyo Station—2 km and 540 meters (about 1.5 mi)—and its location between Akihabara and Okachimachi. The key thread tying its shops together is the fact that they all sell wares made in Japan, from kaleidoscopes and hats to figurines, sneakers, furniture, and toys. The space also holds occasional hands-on workshops related to traditional crafts.

ASAKUSA AND RYŌGOKU
浅草, 両国

True to its locale in the heart of old-school Tokyo, Asakusa is a great place to find traditional crafts and souvenirs that you would associate with Japan. It's also a good place to indulge in a bit of kitsch.

Kitchenware
KAPPABASHI-DŌRI

take Ginza line to Tawaramachi Station, exit 3

A short walk from Sensō-ji brings you to Kappabashi-dōri, a busy road lined with store after store dedicated to the culinary arts. Starting at the corner of Asakusa-dōri and running along Shinbori–dōri, you'll find shops selling tableware, knives, crockery, signage for restaurants, utensils, and more. Some stores worth a look include knife emporiums **Kama-Asa Shoten** (2-24-1 Matsugaya, Taito-ku; tel. 03/3841-9355; www.kama-asa.co.jp; 10am-5:30pm daily) and **Kamata Hakensha Knife Shop** (2-12-6 Matsugaya, Taito-ku; tel. 03/3841-4205; www.kap-kam.com; 10am-6pm daily), and shops selling hyperreal plastic food models and other kitchen-related souvenirs of all kinds, such as **Ganso Shokuhin Sample-ya** (3-7-6 Nishiasakusa, Taito-ku; tel. 0120-171-839; www.ganso-sample.com;

10am-5:30pm daily). When you spot the huge head of a chef protruding from atop the Niimi building, you'll know you've come to the right place.

Souvenirs
SHIN-YOSHIWARA

102, 3-27-10 Nishiasakusa, Taito-ku; www. shin-yoshiwara.com; noon-6pm daily; take Ginza line Tawaramachi Station, exit 3

This cheeky souvenir shop is a one-off. Inspired by the carnal essence of Yoshiwara, Edo's legendary red-light district that once stood in the same area, designer Yayoi Okano decided to open Shin-Yoshiwara, a shop that sells traditional items with a sassy twist. Here you'll find Japanese hair ornaments shaped like voluptuous nude women, ceramic dishes etched with two female breasts containing the characters of the shop's name inside them, *ukiyo-e* style prints depicting tatted-up *yakuza* at public baths, and more. Okano's sexy merchandise initially received a mixed response from locals, but feelings have slowly warmed and the shop's reputation has grown.

Food

It's not a stretch to say that Tokyo may have the best food on the planet. The level of mastery among chefs, premium ingredients, and sheer number of cooking styles found in Japanese cuisine put the city in a league of its own. Japan's capital boasts more Michelin stars than any other city on earth, to the chagrin of Paris and New York. And where the Big Apple is said to have about 30,000 restaurants, estimates put that number anywhere from 150,000 to 300,000 for Tokyo.

Embarking on a voyage into this vast culinary seventh heaven can be a life-changing experience. Japanese cooking aims to bring out the natural flavors inherent in a given preparation; so rather than dowsing dishes in a heavy layer of sauce, food is more likely to be lightly dipped in *shoyu* (soy sauce) or seasoned with a pinch of sea salt. An aesthetic sense is also a fundamental tenet—hence, the importance of seasonality and presentation. It's routine to see food so beautifully presented in elegant vessels made of lacquer, stone, wood, clay, ceramic, or glass that the meal is nearly elevated to art.

Restaurant options run the gamut, from **sushi** and **sashimi** to Japanese-style hot pot dishes **sukiyaki** and **shabu-shabu**. *Kaiseki* is a multicourse affair that evolved from the tea ceremony, comprising appetizers through a series of dishes that have been grilled, raw, fried, simmered, and steamed, and ending with a light seasonally appropriate dessert. *Okonomiyaki* is a savory pancake cooked on a grill in front of you.

Then there are meals cooked over an open flame, such as **yakiniku** and **robatayaki**. Noodles, from **ramen** and **udon** to summer favorites **somen** and **soba,** are ubiquitous and served in a staggering variety of broths.

Highly evolved **foreign cuisines** are also readily on offer, from French and Italian to Indian, with chefs routinely going overseas to study their cuisine of choice before coming back to open their own shop and putting twists on the menu.

GINZA AND MARUNOUCHI
銀座, 丸の内
Izakaya
SAKE NO ANA

3-5-8 Ginza, Chūō-ku; tel. 03/3567-1133; www. sakenoana.com; 11:30am-10pm Mon.-Sat., 11:30am-9pm Sun. and holidays; lunch sets ¥1,050-2,200, dinner courses ¥5,400-6,480; take Ginza, Marunouchi, Hibiya lines to Ginza Station on, A13 exit

Here, the focus is n on serving food that goes best with *sake*. This restaurant is a fantastic place to go for a crash course on the Japanese rice-based brew, thanks to an in-house *sake* sommelier, Sakamoto-san, who is happy to give you a taste-based tour by pairing different varieties with dishes like a *natto* (fermented soy bean) omelet or deep-fried fugu (puffer fish).

TACHINOMI RYOMA

ALC Bldg. 1F, 2-13-3 Shimbashi; tel. 03/3591-1757; 4:30pm-12:30am Mon.-Sat., closed holidays; ¥4,000; take Yamanote, Ginza, Asakusa lines to Shimbashi Station, Karasumori exit

This welcoming *tachinomi* (standing-drinking) in the heart of the salaryman stronghold of Shimbashi, bordering Ginza's southern edge, has an extensive *shōchū* menu with more than 100 varieties. It's a great place to sample a number of varieties with a booze-friendly menu of choices like *karage* (fried chicken) and sashimi. The bartenders here really know their stuff and are happy to make suggestions.

SHIN-HINOMOTO

2-4-4 Yūrakuchō, Chiyoda-ku; tel. 03/3214-8021; http://shin-hinomoto.com; 5pm-midnight Mon.-Sat.; courses ¥4,500; take Yamanote, Yūrakuchō lines to Yūrakuchō Station, Hibiya exit

Alongside being owned by a Brit, Shin-Hinomoto, aka Andy's Fish, has another twist: It's under the train tracks, so don't be surprised if you feel a rumble each time the cars on the Yamanote line roll overhead. This is a great place to go for the full *izakaya* experience, complete with cramped quarters, lively customers exclaiming "*kanpai*" ("cheers") with each round of drinks, and cheap but tasty grub. The menu is heavily weighted toward seafood and is helpfully available in English. As you enter the restaurant, there's a cubby hole lined with vending machines selling booze to the right side of the entrance. The sidewalk here is a favorite place for salarymen to congregate for a canned alcoholic beverage of choice after leaving the office. Reserve a day or two ahead to be safe—by telephone only—especially if you're visiting on the weekend.

Sushi
★ GINZA KYUBEY

8-7-6 Ginza, Chūō-ku; tel. 03/3571-6523; www. kyubey.jp/en; 11:30am-2pm and 5pm-10pm Tues.-Sat.; lunch ¥5,500-23,000, dinner ¥10,000-30,000; take Ginza line to Shimbashi Station, exit 3

Ginza Kyubey is the ideal spot for the full sushi experience. Take a seat at the counter and watch as master chefs work their magic in front of you. Although this place is not cheap, the prices feel commensurate with the ambience and fare. One of the great things about Kyubey is that the atmosphere isn't stuffy, which can sometimes be the case at high-end sushi shops, where a small number of customers sit at one counter as the master does his work, and people converse in hushed tones. By contrast, Kyubey seats more 17 and has a relatively lively atmosphere, striking the right balance of high quality and friendly ambience. Reservations, made via your hotel concierge, are recommended. If this restaurant is fully booked, try the branch at Hotel New Otani.

Café
CAFÉ L'AMBRE

8-10-15 Ginza, Chūō-ku; tel. 03/3571-1551; www. cafedelambre.com; noon-8pm (last order 7:30pm) Mon.-Fri., noon-7pm (last order 6:30pm) Sat.-Sun. and holidays; ¥1,000; take Yamanote line to Shimbashi Station, exit 1

This legendary coffeehouse in the heart of Ginza has been caffeinating the masses since 1948, though its interior looks more recent. Although some old-school Tokyo coffeehouses can be a bit full of themselves, this is a relaxed place for a caffeine hit and conversation. The English-language menu offers more than 30 varieties, including some exotic concoctions. How about coffee with Cognac?

International
DHABA INDIA

Sagami Bldg. 1F, 2-7-9 Yaesu, Chūō-ku; tel. 03/3272-7160; http://dhabaindiatokyo.com; 11:15am-2:30pm and 5pm-9pm Mon.-Fri., 11:30am-3pm and 5pm-9pm Sat.-Sun. and holidays;

Food Underground: Discover Japan's *Depachika*

A typical Japanese department store (*depato*) is 5-10 floors high, with women's fashion on the first couple of floors, fashion and sports gear for men on the floors above that, and lifestyle items, stationery, and furniture on the next few floors. A restaurant floor is at the top, usually offering an impressive range of cuisines, including Italian, Korean, Chinese, and Japanese. Some department stores turn their rooftops into beer gardens in warmer months. But the floor that proves to be the biggest revelation for many is the basement level, where you'll typically find an extensive gourmet food hall known as a *depachika*. Excellent seasonal produce, sushi, tempura, bento box lunches, tofu, fresh ginger, yakitori, *tonkatsu*, croquettes, premade salads, sandwiches, cheese, Western and Japanese desserts… the list goes on.

For the full *depato* experience, with an emphasis on the best subterranean food halls, check out the following department stores:

GINZA MITSUKOSHI

4-6-16 Ginza, Chūō-ku; tel. 03/3562-1111; www.mitsukoshi.co.jp; 10am-8pm Mon.-Sat., 10am-7:30pm Sun. and last day of holiday periods; take Ginza, Hibiya, Marunouchi lines to Ginza Station, exits A7, A8, A11

Ginza Mitsukoshi has a vast array of decadent culinary options in its sprawling basement food hall. Head to the rooftop garden to eat them.

ISETAN SHINJUKU

3-14-1 Shinjuku, Shinjuku-ku; tel. 03/3352-1111; https://isetan.mistore.jp/store/index.html; 10am-8pm; take Marunouchi, Shinjuku, Fukutoshin lines to Shinjuku-Sanchōme Station, exits B3, B4, B5; or Chūō, Sōbu lines to Shinjuku Station, east exit; or Ōedo line to Shinjuku Station, exit 1

Isetan Shinjuku is the flagship of this hip chain. It's renowned for its artistic, attention-grabbing window displays, but the showstopper here is its opulent *depachika*. Caviar, giant legs of Iberico ham, Japanese sweets, and a stunning array of booze, from champagne to whisky and *nihonshū*.

TAKASHIMAYA TIMES SQUARE

5-24-2 Sendagaya, Shibuya-ku; tel. 03/5361-1111; www.takashimaya-global.com; 10am-8pm Sun.-Thurs., 10am-8:30pm Fri.-Sat.; take Chūō, Sōbu lines to Shinjuku Station, South Exit

Takashimaya Times Square () has a swanky sensibility, with a glut of luxury brands. Head down to the basement to see how this is applied to food. Take note of the haute bento box meals prepared by the chefs at *kaiseki ryōri* purveyor Kikunoi. There's a rooftop garden here, too.

---

lunch ¥1,200, dinner ¥2,200; take Ginza line to Kyobashi Station, exit 5

Dhaba India is a splendid South Indian restaurant that has it all: chefs recruited straight from Tamil Nadu and Kerala, a soothing ambience thanks to dark blue walls and a turquoise floor, and knock-out food. The menu's range is impressive, too, from lemon prawn curry served with delectably thin puri to a mean masala dosa. And perhaps most importantly, the chefs don't tone the spice down to suit local tastes. If northern Indian fare is more to your liking, check out nearby sister shop **Khyber** (Ginza 1-chōme Bldg. 1F, 1-14-6 Ginza, Chūō-ku; from ¥1,000).

Steakhouse
SHIMA

3-5-12 Nihonbashi, Chūō-ku; tel. 03/3271-7889; www.jimu-uke.co.jp/shima_site; noon-1pm (last order) and 6pm-9pm (last order), closed Sun. and two irregular days each month; lunch ¥8,000, dinner ¥23,000; take Ginza line to Kyobashi Station, exit 6

If you want to go big on one steak meal in Tokyo, Shima is an excellent choice. The immaculately marbled beef, sourced from a Kyoto farm, is phenomenal. Thanks to the warm presence of Chef Oshima Manabu, a Kyoto native, the atmosphere at this discrete basement eatery is friendly, too. Patrons seated at the counter can be heard chatting away with the chefs. It's not cheap, but some Tokyo eateries charge three to four times as much for a similar meal. Reservations required for dinner. Call ahead a few days or more in advance to be safe.

TOKYO BAY AREA
東京湾
Monjayaki
MONJA KONDO

3-12-10 Tsukishima, Chūō-ku; tel. 03/3533-4555; www.monja.gr.jp/kondohonten.html; 5pm-11pm Mon.-Fri., 11:30am-11pm Sat.-Sun.; lunch ¥1,500, dinner ¥2,500; take Ōedo line to Tsukishima Station, exit 8

Doing brisk business since 1950, Monja Kondo is said to be Tokyo's first restaurant to serve *monjayaki*, the Tokyo-born cousin of *okonomiyaki*, a savory pancake-like dish with stronger ties to Osaka and Hiroshima. The menu boasts a whopping 90 toppings to choose from, and friendly staff are on standby to help you cook your meal at your table's teppanyaki grill.

Sushi
SUSHIKUNI

4-14-15 Tsukiji, Chūō-ku; tel. 03/3545-8234; https://ameblo.jp/sushikuni; 10am-3pm and 5pm-9pm Thurs.-Tues.; lunch ¥2,000-3,000, dinner ¥5,000-6,000; take Ōedo line to Tsukijishijō Station, exit A1

A stand-out in Tsukiji Outer Market, Sushikuni is known for its *kaisen-don*, or raw fish served over rice. The specialties here are *ikura* (salmon roe) and *uni* (sea urchin roe). Queues do form, but they move relatively fast.

International
TY HARBOR

2-1-3 Higashi-Shinagawa, Shinagawa-ku; tel. 03/5479-4555; www.tysons.jp/tyharbor/en; 11:30am-2pm and 5:30pm-10pm Mon.-Fri., 11:30am-3pm and 5:30pm-10pm Sat.-Sun. and holidays; lunch ¥1,300-3,200, dinner ¥1,300-5,800; take Tokyo Monorail or Rinkai line to Tennozu Isle Station, central exit

For a maritime city, Tokyo admittedly has few options for wining and dining with a view of the bay. TY Harbor remedies that. It includes a chic bar serving dark and light California-style beers, and a restaurant serving Western cuisine, from steaks and salads to burgers made with fine cuts of *wagyu* beef.

ROPPONGI AND AROUND
六本木
Izakaya
GONPACHI

1-13-11 Nishi-Azabu, Minato-ku; tel. 03/5771-0170; www.gonpachi.jp; 11:30am-3:30am (food last order 2:45am, drink last order 3am); lunch ¥1,000-3,500, dinner ¥4,500-8,900; take Ōedo, Hibiya lines to Roppongi Station, exit 2

This towering *izakaya* is said to be the restaurant that inspired a particularly gory scene in the film *Kill Bill*. Gonpachi has garnered a reputation as a lively spot with a wide-ranging menu of countryside standards like yakitori and grilled fish. Adding to the atmosphere are a soundtrack of the three-stringed *shamisen* and servers in traditional coats. There is a more upscale sushi restaurant with an open terrace on the third floor as well.

WARAYAKIYA

Roppongi Gordy Bldg. 1F, 6-8-8 Roppongi, Minato-ku; tel. 03/6778-5495; www.dd-holdings.jp/shops/warayakiya/roppongi#; 5pm-5am Mon.-Sat., last order 4am, 5pm-11pm Sun.-Mon. and holidays, last order 10pm; ¥3,980; take Ōedo, Hibiya lines to Roppongi Station, exit 3

Warayakiya is a great *izakaya* focused on a grilling method that uses straw instead of charcoal. This style originates from Kōchi Prefecture on the Pacific side of Shikoku. With the leaping fire reaching temperatures up to 900°C (1,652°F), it's worth getting a counter seat so you can watch the chefs expertly sear fish, meat, and vegetables to perfection. The seared bonito is a hit, and the place is lively and often packed, so booking ahead is recommended.

Kaiseki
TOFUYA UKAI

4-4-13 Shiba Kōen, Minato-ku; tel. 03/3436-1028; www.ukai.co.jp/english/shiba; 11:45am-3pm and 5pm-7:30pm (last order) Mon.-Fri., 11am-7:30pm (last order) Sat.-Sun. and holidays; closed two Mon. every month; lunch ¥5,940-7,960, dinner ¥10,800-16,200; take Ōedo line to Akabanebashi Station, Akabanebashiguchi exit

Tofuya Ukai, just a stone's throw from Tokyo Tower, is the best place to taste the wonders of tofu. Impressively, this *kaiseki* restaurant even makes its own tofu at a shop in the foothills of the Okutama mountain range west of Tokyo. Set amid readily visible gardens with ponds teeming with colorful carp, the restaurant is set within a relocated *sake* brewery that was originally built in Yamagata Prefecture more than 200 years ago. Staff in kimonos serve up to 500 guests in the wooden complex's 55 tatami-mat private rooms. Book ahead for a seat and to settle on your dining course, which must be determined beforehand.

Soba
HONMURA AN

7-14-18 Roppongi, Minato-ku; tel. 03/5772-6657; www.honmuraantokyo.com; noon-2pm and 5:30pm-9pm Mon.-Fri., noon-2pm and 5pm-9pm Sat.-Sun. and holidays; lunch ¥1,600, dinner ¥7,400; take Ōedo, Hibiya lines to Roppongi Station, exit 4b

Honmura An elevates the humble buckwheat noodle to an art form. Owner Koichi Kobari returned to Tokyo from New York in 2007 to take over his late father's soba shop, leaving a legion of disappointed fans in his wake. The shop defies the image of soba as being something eaten on the fly or from a bento box, and encourages diners to savor the noodles, which are served both hot and cold. The menu fluctuates by season and is fully bilingual. Prices are shockingly cheap for the quality of the food. A ¥350 seating charge applies at dinner. Reserve over the phone up to a month in advance, then be sure to reconfirm your reservation the day before you are scheduled to dine.

Vegetarian
SOUGO

Roppongi Green Bldg. 3F, 6-1-8 Roppongi, Minato-ku; tel. 03/5414-1133; www.sougo.tokyo; 11:30am-3pm lunch, 2pm-5pm café time, 6pm-11:30pm dinner (last order 10pm); lunch ¥1,500-5,000, café time ¥600-1,200, dinner ¥8,000-10,000; take Ōedo or Hibiya line to Roppongi Station, exit 3

A stellar vegetarian option in a city with limited choices for those who don't eat meat, Sougo has garnered a reputation for its accessible *shōjin-ryōri*, or vegetarian food eaten by Buddhist monks. It's offered at a price and level of accessibility sadly lacking at most restaurants serving the spiritually inspired cuisine. Bucking tradition, there is an open kitchen fronted by a bar. The menu is seasonal and experimental, and incorporates some nonvegan items such as dashi stock and even cheese. Vegan meals can be ordered a day beforehand.

EBISU AND AROUND
恵比寿

Izakaya
★ TONKI

1-1-2 Shimomeguro, Meguro-ku; tel. 03/3491-9928; 4pm-10:45pm Wed.-Mon., closed third Mon. every month; ¥2,100; take Yamanote line to Meguro Station, west exit

Serving *tonkatsu* since 1939, Tonki is an institution, a short walk from Meguro Station. The entrance may look commonplace, but slide open the wooden door, lift the curtain, and you'll enter a surprisingly expansive first floor, with an open kitchen full of diligent chefs at work and surrounded by a counter on three sides. Queues are commonplace, especially for a seat on the first floor, where customers can watch the masterful chefs perform. For quicker seating, choose the second floor. Set meals, including rice, trimmings, and miso soup, are ¥1,900 for both fatty and lean cuts of pork.

OJINJO

2-2-10 Ebusi, Shibuya-ku; tel. 03/5784-1775; www. facebook.com/OJINJO; 5pm-12:30am Mon.-Fri.,

4pm-12:30am Sat.-Sun. and holidays; ¥4,000; take Yamanote line to Ebisu Station, west exit

This lively *izakaya* hidden down a side street in Ebisu is renowned for the quality and variety of its *chūhai*, or *shōchū* mixed with soda and freshly squeezed lemon juice. With a menu containing six spins on the classic *izakaya* beverage (with crushed ice, mint, etc.), it's a great place to get acquainted with this commonly quaffed cocktail, which is often flavored with other types of fruit juice, such as grapefruit, plum, and more. The *shōchū*-friendly food menu is likewise diverse, from Okinawa stir-fries and grilled fish to oysters. Reserve a few days in advance to snag a spot.

Ramen
AFURI

1117 Bldg. 1F, 1-1-7 Ebisu; Shibuya-ku; tel. 03/5795-0750; http://afuri.com; 11am-5am daily; ¥1,000; take Yamanote line to Ebisu Station, west exit

Just outside the backdoor of the always boisterous Ebisu Yokochō, you'll find the flagship of hit ramen shop Afuri. Soup stock here is infused with a mix of chicken, seaweed, and seafood, in varying degrees of fattiness. The most popular variety is *shio* (salt-based) ramen. I recommend selecting the citrus yuzu-infused *shio* broth with thick hunks of *chashu* (pork belly). The thin noodles and surprisingly light broth leave you feeling satisfied without the food coma triggered by some varieties of ramen.

Street Food
EBISU YOKOCHŌ

1-7-4 Ebisu, Shibuya-ku; www.ebisu-yokocho.com; 5pm-late daily; ¥3,000; take JR Yamanote line to Ebisu Station, east exit

Tokyo may lack the cred of a city like Bangkok, but you can find pockets of good, gritty street food. In Ebisu Yokochō, a bustling arcade with a retro feel, small *izakaya* line a narrow concrete foot path, selling everything from grilled fish and yakitori to *yakisoba*, even raw horse and whale. Somewhat out of sync with the DIY décor—rickety stools, tables made of beer crates—there are even a few wine bars. It

gets rowdy on Friday nights when people meet to wash away the cares of the workweek over frosty pints of beer. While you must order drinks from the store where you're seated, it's possible to order food from other establishments from within the *yokochō*. At the time of writing, some stores were closing earlier than usual due to coronavirus.

SHIBUYA AND AROUND
渋谷

Izakaya
TACHINOMI NAGI

2-20-7 Dogenzaka, Shibuya-ku; tel. 03/6416-5257; http://tachinomi-nagi.com; 5pm-midnight Mon.-Sat., closed on public holidays; ¥3,000; take Yamanote line to Shibuya Station, Hachikō exit

Tucked down a quiet street on Dogenzaka's "love hotel hill," this standing bar—*izakaya*, really—is a great place to sample *nihonshū* (commonly known as *sake* in the west), paired with casual nibbles. It's fronted by a row of bamboo and bottles of the brew it specializes in. In particular, the shop is known for its collection of *nihonshū* brewed in Fukushima Prefecture. The staff are experts at pairing your booze of choice with food, from sashimi to vegetable medleys to rice dishes. *Nihonshū*-tasting flights start from a surprisingly reasonable ¥500. Recommended.

★ SHIRUBE

Pinecrest Kitazawa 1F, 2-18-2 Kitazawa, Setagaya-ku; tel. 03/3413-3785; 5:30pm-midnight (food last order 11pm, drink last order 11:30pm) daily; ¥4,000; take Keio-Inokashira, Odakyu lines to Shimokitazawa Station, south exit

Shirube is the place to come for the quintessential *izakaya* experience. Pull aside the white curtains in front of the door that reads "Izaka-ya-ism," slip off your shoes inside, and take a seat. At the center of the buzzing restaurant is its large open kitchen, where you can see the energetic team of chefs at work. The friendly staff will be happy to help you navigate the diverse menu, also available in English, which features classics such as sashimi, *nikujaga* (stewed beef with potatoes

and onions), and more. These staples are complemented by a number of innovative fusion dishes like cheese tofu and avocado-tuna dip with toast. The simplest (and most recommended) option is the ¥4,000 *nomihōdai* (all-you-can-drink) plan, which comes with a set meal and lasts 90 minutes. The place gets packed; reservations recommended.

Sushi
UMEGAOKA SUSHI NO MIDORI SHIBUYA-TEN

4F Mark City East, 1-12-3 Dogenzaka, Shibuya-ku; tel. 03/5458-0002; www.sushinomidori.co.jp/shop.php?name=shibuya; 11am-10pm daily, last order 9:45pm Mon.-Sat. and 9:30pm Sun.; courses ¥850-2,800, à la carte from ¥50; take JR lines, Tōyoko line, or Ginza, Fukutoshin, Hanzōmon subway lines to Shibuya Station

For cost performance and convenience, this sushi joint is hard to beat. Your choices will range from sea urchin to a whole boiled conger eel. Sushi platters come with green tea and miso soup. Unfortunately, with excellent value comes queues. If you'd like to avoid the longest wait times, aim to come for a late lunch (around 2:30pm), a late dinner (try 9pm), or during off hours (between the lunch and dinner rush). Also note that the restaurant has eight branches, so have a look at the website and consider another branch to avoid the heaviest crowds.

Cafés
FUGLEN

1-16-11 Tomigaya, Shibuya-ku; tel. 03/3481-0884; www.fuglen.com; 8am-10pm Mon.-Tues., 8am-1am Wed.-Thurs., 8am-2am Fri., 9am-2am Sat., 9am-midnight Sun.; café from ¥250, bar from ¥1,250; take Chiyoda line to Yoyogi-kōen Station, exit 2

A sister cafe to Oslo's fashionable coffee spot of the same name, Fuglen is the central nexus in Tomigaya, an enclave for in-the-know locals on the backside of Shibuya. Although it's

firmly on the hipster map, this bar and café has the substance to complement its style. Seating includes a counter, a few tables, and a sofa. They serve excellent coffee and a range of tasty baked goods. From 7pm, they sell well-made cocktails that make for good aperitifs.

CHATEI HATOU

1-15-19 Shibuya, Shibuya-ku; tel. 03/3400-9088; 11am-11pm daily; ¥1,000; take Yamanote line to Shibuya Station, east exit

With an entrance reminiscent of a lodge in the Alps, Chatei Hatou is a venerable café extolled by serious coffee drinkers the world over, including Blue Bottle Coffee CEO James Freeman. Upon entering, the master selects the cup you'll use from among an eclectic array standing on a shelf behind the counter. A cup from the impressive menu may cost upward of ¥1,500, but if you want a real *kissaten* experience, it's worth it.

International
LOS BARBADOS

104, 41-26 Udagawachō, Shibuya-ku; tel. 03/3496-7157; www7b.biglobe.ne.jp/~los-barbados; noon-3pm and 6-11pm Mon.-Sat.; plates ¥700-1,100; take Yamanote line to Shibuya Station, Hachikō exit

This eight-seat restaurant and bar is an off-the-radar gem in the backstreets of Shibuya, serving surprisingly good African and Middle Eastern fare, including some solid vegetarian options. The cozy space is run by a friendly Japanese couple, Daisuke and Mayumi Uekawa, who developed a passion for the region after spending extended time in central Africa. It's also a bar with a good selection of beer, wine, and rum.

CASA DE SARASA

Shimada Bldg. 2F, 2-25-5 Dogenzaka, Shibuya-ku; tel. 03/5428-6155; www.facebook.com/CasaDeSarasa; 3pm-10pm daily; ¥2,000-3,500; take Yamanote line to Shibuya Station, Hachikō exit

Good Mexican food is hard to come by in Japan. Thanks to this restaurant, Tokyoites in need of an authentic taco fix now have relief. The impressive variety of

---

1: Omoide Yokochō 2: yakitori 3: a bowl of *chirashi* 4: Sakurai Japanese Tea Experience

Tokyo's Animal Cafés

Tokyo is ground zero for the animal café phenomenon that has swept the globe. What started with the humble cat café—essentially, a café where felines are simply allowed to play, purr, eat, sleep, and strut around as they please—has grown to include a mushrooming menagerie of staggering variety. Today, you can find cafés inhabited by owls, rabbits, dogs, foxes, hedgehogs, snakes, penguins—the list goes on.

A core concern when visiting any animal café is the welfare of its critters. Some things to consider: Are the animals caged? Do they have space to roam? Do they seem at ease? Do they get breaks from customers' attention? Are they well-fed, scrubbed, and groomed? Before visiting, do your research on a given animal café, and on whether a given species may not be well-suited to the experience of being in such an environment. Owl cafés, in particular, have been the subject of animal rights activists' ire for confining the birds and exposing them to excessive contact with people—neither healthy things for birds of prey. Ditto for dogs, which seem overly cooped up in many of the cafés that keep them.

With these ethical concerns in mind, here are some of Tokyo's best animal cafés.

TEMARI NO OSHIRO CAT CAFÉ

Kichijōji Petit Mura, 2-33-2 Kichijōji-Honchō, Musashino-shi; tel. 0422/27-5962; https://temarinooshiro. com; 10am-9pm daily; ¥1,200, ¥1,600 Sat., Sun., and holidays, ¥700 from 7pm, all prices before tax; take Chūo, Sōbu, Inokashira lines to Kichijoji Station

Beyond a whimsical facade that gives you the impression you're entering a fairy-tale realm, around 20 felines lounge on platforms, sleep in nooks, and frolic with customers. As a bonus, the cat-shaped sweets are surprisingly good. Children under 10 are not admitted.

KOTORI CAFÉ UENO

1-8-6 Ueno Sakuragi, Taito-ku; tel. 03/6427-5115; http://kotoricafe.jp; 11am-6pm daily; no cover charge, one-drink minimum; take Chiyoda line to Nezu Station

At this colorful, chirpy café in Ueno, you'll meet a range of avians, from a cockatoo and parrots to canaries and lovebirds. Most of the time the birds are left to flap and sing in peace, but five-minute petting sessions are available for ¥500. During peak time, you may be limited to a one-hour stay.

MIPIG CAFÉ

1F Barubizon, 1-15-4 Jingūmae, Shibuya-ku; tel. 03/6384-5899; https://mipig.cafe; 10am-8pm daily; ¥1,000 per hour, one-drink minimum; take Yamanote line to Harajuku Station, Omotesandō exit, or Chiyoda, Fukutoshin lines to Meiji-Jingūmae Station, exit 2

At this welcoming café in the heart of teenybopper Harajuku, you can play with a breed of cute, micro pigs as you quaff coffee. It's wildly popular, so it's wise to book ahead through the website (in English).

CHIKU CHIKU CAFÉ

2F Daikyousibuya Bldg., 1-13-5 Shibuya, Shibuya-ku; tel. 03/6450-6673; https://hedgehoghome.cafe; 1pm-6pm daily; ¥1,300 per 30 minutes, ¥2,400 per 60 minutes; take JR lines to Shibuya Station, Hachikō exit

This cheerful café ups the cuteness ante once more with hedgehogs. Here you can pet, feed, and photograph the furry little mammals, which have ample room to explore miniature settings made to look like traditional Japanese-style tatami rooms, classrooms, lavatories, and more. Reservations are recommended and can be made in English online.

taco fillings ranges from stewed pork with freshly squeezed orange and herb to stir-fried shrimp in garlic oil. There are plenty of sides—cheese-filled battered jalapenos, totopos with guacamole, nachos—and the drink menu is extensive, with a range of Mexican beers and a long list of tequilas. It's a little bit on the pricy side, but the quality and frankly, rarity, of the offerings makes up for it. Recommended.

HARAJUKU AND AOYAMA
原宿, 青山

Okonomiyaki
SAKURA TEI

3-10-1 Jingūmae, Shibuya-ku; tel. 03/3479-0039; www.sakuratei.co.jp/en; 11am-9pm Mon.-Thurs., 11am-10pm Fri.-Sun. and holidays; lunch ¥1,050-1,500; take Yamanote line to Harajuku Station, Takeshita exit

Connected to Design Festa Gallery is a bright, lively restaurant called Sakura Tei. While some *okonomiyaki* joints cook the dish for you, here you do it yourself on a teppanyaki plate at your table. Don't fret; there's a photo guide at each table instructing you how to properly get the job done. The English-language menu includes both *okonomiyaki* and *monjayaki* (batter topped with meat, vegetables, and seafood, then cooked to a loose texture resembling a scrambled egg), from classics like pork, kimchi, and seafood medleys, to the experimental, like a carbonara version.

Tonkatsu
MAISEN

4-8-5 Jingūmae, Shibuya-ku; tel. 0120/428-485; https://mai-sen.com; 11am-9pm (last order 8pm) daily; ¥1,580-5,000; take Ginza, Hanzomon, Chiyoda lines to Omotesandō Station, exit A2

Set in what used to be a bathhouse, with soaring ceilings and a small garden in back, Maisen is a popular and excellent *tonkatsu* restaurant located amid the back lanes of Harajuku. You can choose from a range of pork dishes, from *hire katsu* (pork filet) to *rosu katsu* (pork loin). Set meals come with a small dish of pickled radish, rice, and soup.

Cafés
KOFFEE MAMEYA

4-15-3 Jingūmae, Shibuya-ku; tel. 03/5413-9422; www.koffee-mameya.com; 10am-6pm daily; from ¥450; take Ginza, Hanzomon lines to Omotesandō Station, exit A2

Koffee Mameya is the new incarnation of once legendary Omotesandō Koffee, which closed in 2015. Fortunately, the same impeccable standards of quality have been maintained. There's no seating at this popular bean specialist, but it's a great place to grab a coffee or espresso to-go while exploring Harajuku's backstreets. If you want to purchase beans to brew at home, 15-20 types are available, sourced from five roasteries.

★ SAKURAI JAPANESE TEA EXPERIENCE

Spiral Bldg. 5F, 5-6-23 Minami-Aoyama, Minato-ku; tel. 03/6451-1539; www.sakurai-tea.jp; 11am-10pm Mon.-Fri., 11am-8pm Sat.-Sun.; tea ¥1,400, tasting course ¥4,800; take Ginza, Hanzomon lines to Omotesandō Staion, exit B1

Owner Shinya Sakurai takes his tea seriously. After spending 12 years becoming a master in the realm of tea, he finally felt ready to open his exceptional Aoyama café, Sakurai Japanese Tea Experience. This attractive café, which doubles as a chic, innovative tea-ceremony space, is stocked with jars containing tea leaves sourced from around Japan, which Sakurai personally travels to procure. There's an area to sit and quaff your brew of choice, with samples of single varieties priced at ¥380 each. For the full experience, including the opportunity to sit back and watch the master at work, try a tasting course of five different tea varieties; it costs ¥4,800 but is worth it. As you wait for your brew to reach peak drinkability, Sakurai will share details surrounding the delicate coaxing that each type of leaf requires for optimal preparation. The range of options is eye-opening, with some tea served with surprising accents, like lime, or infused with spirits. Some tea leaves can be eaten after being prepared. Paired with a traditional Japanese sweet, the combination is exquisite.

International
NARISAWA

2-6-15 Minami Aoyama, Minato-ku; tel. 03/5785-0799; www.narisawa-yoshihiro.com/en/openning.html; noon-3 pm (last order 1pm) and 6pm-10pm (last order 7pm), Tues.-Sat. with other sporadic closings; lunch ¥27,000, dinner ¥32,400; take Ginza, Hanzomon, Ōedo lines to Aoyama-itchōme Station, exit 5

At Narisawa, creativity and attunement to nature are the hallmarks of the culinary creations of pioneering chef Yoshihiro Narisawa. Working away in his immaculate Aoyama kitchen, Narisawa brings a singular sensibility to a host of European cooking techniques—primarily French. He forages his own herbs and adds seasonal touches to every meal. His visually striking creations range from *wagyu* beef to edible soil, and a range of innovative desserts. The restaurant has an extensive selection of wines and cheeses, too. Reservations for a given month are accepted from the beginning of the month prior through the restaurant's website. In other words, if you want to reserve a table in September, you can reserve from August 1. Be prepared to act promptly when the reservation period officially opens.

SHINJUKU AND AROUND
新宿
Izakaya
★ NIHON SAISEI SAKABA

Marunaka Bldg. 1F, 3-7-3 Shinjuku, Shinjuku-ku; tel. 03/3354-4829; http://ishii-world.jp/nihonsaisei/shinjuku3; 3pm-11pm (last order 10:30pm) Mon.-Sat.; ¥3,000; take Marunouchi, Fukutoshin, Toei Shinjuku lines to Shinjuku San-chōme Station, exit C3

It's all about the pig at Nihon Saisei Sakaba, a standing-only *izakaya* that serves essentially every pig part, grilled, on a stick. This Shinjuku institution has a friendly, gritty

ambience, with smoke wafting into the street where customers stand around makeshift tables made of empty beer crates and drink from frosty mugs. Have a look at the English menu: colon, spleen, womb, even birth canal. Don't worry; there are standard grilled bits, too. For a fun night out with the chance to mingle with fellow customers, this spot is hard to beat.

Kaiseki
KOZUE

Park Hyatt Tokyo 40F, 3-7-1-2 Nishinjuku, Shinjuku-ku; tel. 03/5323-3460; http://restaurants. tokyo.park.hyatt.co.jp/en/koz.html; 11:30am-2:30pm and 5:30pm-10pm; lunch ¥2,300-10,000, dinner ¥13,000-22,000; take Ōedo line to Tochomae Station, exit A4

Kozue serves haute Japanese cuisine with fabulous views on the 40th floor of the Park Hyatt Tokyo. The high-end *kaiseki* restaurant serves seasonal fare—for instance, fugu in winter, freshly foraged mushrooms in autumn—in artisan-made earthenware, porcelain, and lacquer dishes. Views of the city at night are outstanding year-round, and on clear afternoons you'll be able to see Mount Fuji. It's a spectacular dining experience. Book either online or over the phone a few days in advance to be on the safe side. Book a week or more ahead and make a special request for a window seat.

Street Food
OMOIDE YOKOCHŌ

1-2-11 Nishi-Shinjuku, Shinjuku-ku; http://shinjuku-omoide.com; take Yamanote line to Shinjuku Station, west exit

This atmospheric alley, lit by red lanterns and filled with smoke, is packed with small, gritty bars and restaurants serving down-and-dirty fare consisting of animal parts and vegetables cooked over an open flame, washed down with prodigious amounts of booze. It once lacked public restrooms—hence its colloquial name "Piss Alley." Thankfully, restrooms with dubious levels of privacy are now crammed into one part of the alley, but everything else remains more or less un-changed. The colorful lanes run alongside the train tracks on the west side of Shinjuku Station, though the area is best reached via a tunnel that cuts under the train tracks near the East Exit. Talk of redevelopment is fre-quent, but for now the structures still stand in all their dilapidated glory.

As for picking a restaurant, **Asadachi** (1-2-14 Nishi-Shinjuku, Shinjuku-ku; noon-11pm Tues.-Sun.) is a lively spot. Beware of the more mysterious entries on the rather unconventional menu; those include exotic fare such as raw pig testicles and grilled sal-amander. But don't worry—plenty of other options exist, including grilled fatty salmon belly, mushrooms and grated daikon (rad-ish), and boiled tripe. Asadachi, recognizable for its turtle shells hanging over the coun-ter (yes, they serve them too) is only one of dozens of options in the alleyway. The best way to dine in Omoide Yokochō is to stroll the lane and take a seat at any counter that draws you.

And for drinks, try **Albatross** (1-2-11 Nishi-Shinjuku, Shinjuku-ku; 5pm-2am Sun.-Thurs., 5pm-5am Fri.-Sat.), a classic watering hole decked out in chandeliers and red velvet that occupies three cramped floors. The top floor is a partially covered rooftop balcony with *Blade Runner*-like views of Shinjuku at night. Note that a ¥300 per person table charge applies.

Tempura
TEMPURA TSUNAHACHI
3-31-8 Shinjuku, Shinjuku-ku; tel. 03/3352-1012; www.tunahachi.co.jp/en; 11am-10:30pm (last order 10pm) daily; lunch ¥1,512, dinner ¥2,484-5,400; take Yamanote line to Shinjuku Station, south exit
Tempura Tsunahachi is the perfect place to eat excellent tempura that doesn't break the bank. Housed in an old wooden building, the shop has been serving customers from kabuki actors to pro baseball stars since 1923. If you go for lunch, sets start from ¥1,500, which is downright cheap for the level of quality com-pared to similar spots. Don't be shocked if

there's a queue out front when it opens for lunch. This a great, cost-effective option if you're willing to wait.

Udon
TSURUTONTAN UDON
Amimoto Bldg. B1F, 2-26-3 Kabukichō, Shinjuku-ku; tel. 03/5287-2626; www.tsurutontan.co.jp/shop/ shinjuku-udon; 11am-8pm daily; ¥880-1,980; take Yamanote line to Shinjuku Station, east exit
Tsurutontan Udon boasts an expansive menu packed with photos of the numerous creative spins the shop puts on this wheat flour-based noodle dish. It's a good choice for a meal be-fore or after a night out. There are both hot and cold dishes, prepared using both Japanese and overtly Western flavors like carbonara.

AKIHABARA AND UENO
秋葉原, 上野
Izakaya
TACHINOMI KADOKURA
Forum Aji Bldg. 1F, 6-13-1 Ueno, Taito-ku; tel. 03/3832-5335; http://taishoen.co.jp/kadokura; 11am-11pm daily, last order 10:30pm; à la carte ¥150-600; take Yamanote line to Ueno JR station, Iriya exit, or Hibiya or Ginza line to Ueno subway station, exit 5a
Stand alongside locals at Tachinomi Kadokura, a no-frills bar that serves cheap, delicious pub fare: sashimi, a fried and breaded ham cutlet, an omelet with vegeta-bles grilled on a hotplate at your table. It all goes down well with beer. An English menu is available.

Kushiage
HANTEI
2-12-15 Nezu, Bunkyo-ku; tel. 03/3828-1440; http:// hantei.co.jp; 11:30am-2pm and 5pm-9:30pm daily; closed Mon. or Tues. if Mon. is a holiday; lunch ¥3,200-4,300, dinner from ¥5,000-7,000; take Chiyoda line to Nezu Station, exit 2
Pull back the curtain and step inside Hantei, set in an old three-story wooden building that hints at what the rest of this charming neighborhood once looked like. *Kushiage*, or deep-fried vegetables, meat, and fish on

☆ Tokyo's Culinary Alleys

One of the great experiences of any trip to Tokyo is a visit to the city's atmospheric alleyways known as *yokochō*, preferably with a twofold agenda: eating grilled meats and swilling back draft beer alongside locals. Smoky, crowded, friendly, sometimes even rowdy, the alleys offer a wonderful way to get up close and personal with Tokyo's earthier and historic side, as well as to make connections with the locals. As an added bonus, you get amazing food at a bargain price. Don't be afraid of the offal. It can be surprisingly good.

A growing trend of new shops opening in some of the city's trendier *yokochō* has added a buzz around them in recent years. So you've come at a fortunate time. Lucky you, these amazing alleyways are scattered all around the city. Besides Omoide Yokochō (page 118), Kōenji Gādo-shita (page 122), and Ebisu Yokochō (page 113), here are some other culinary alleyways worth visiting:

YŪRAKUCHŌ GĀDO-SHITA

2-3 Yūrakuchō, Chiyoda-ku

Ramshackle restaurant zone *Gādo-shita* means "beneath the girder," which makes perfect sense: Extending north and south of Yūrakuchō Station—toward Tokyo Station to the north and Shimbashi Station to the south—this extensive network of watering holes and *izakaya* is a lively after-work hub for office workers keen to blow off steam on weekday evenings. The densest cluster of restaurants is south of Yūrakuchō Station's central west exit, across the major east-west artery of Harumi-dōri, where you'll begin to smell grilled meat and see tipsy salarymen emerging from under the tracks of the JR Yamanote line on your left.

sticks is the specialty at this old-school restaurant. Lunch courses consist of either 8 or 12 skewers. For dinner, servers bring out six sticks at first, with the option to call for six additional sticks (¥1,500) or three (¥800) at a time. Diners also have the option of adding either white rice, pickles, and red-bean miso soup, or rice topped with kelp and seaweed and pickles (¥600).

Ramen
KIKANBŌ

2-10-9 Kajichō, Chiyoda-ku; tel. 03/6206-0239; http://kikanbo.co.jp; ¥1,000; 11am-9:30pm Mon.-Sat., 11am-4pm Sun.; take Chūō, Sōbu lines to Kanda Station, east exit, or walk 8 minutes south of Akihabara Station, Electric Town exit

"Ogre's iron club" is the literal meaning of this restaurant's name. After experiencing the kick from a bowl of ramen at this well-loved noodle spot, you'll understand why. You'll have to choose your spice level (1 to 5) for *kara* (chili) and *shibi* (*sansho* pepper, akin to the mouth-numbing pepper served in much Sichuan-style Chinese cuisine). The broth is made from

a mix of miso, meat, and fish, and the noodles are topped with hunks of pork and other fixings (bean sprouts, baby corn, optional boiled egg for ¥100). The fiery theme is reinforced by an all-black interior, demon masks hanging from the walls, and *taiko* (traditional drum) soundtrack. Recommended for those with a penchant for spice, but proceed with caution.

Café
KAYABA COFFEE

6-1-29 Yanaka, Taitō-ku; tel. 03/3823-3545; http://taireki.com/en/kayaba.html; 8am-11pm Mon.-Sat., 8am-6pm Sun.; à la carte ¥250-600, lunch sets ¥1,000; take Keihin-Tōhoku, Yamanote, Keisei lines to Nippori Station, north exit, or Chiyoda line to Nezu Station

Housed in a traditional wooden home built in 1916, Kayaba Coffee was founded by Kayaba Inosuke and his wife Kimi in 1938. This charming institution is a stellar example of a *kissaten*, as Tokyo's retro coffee houses are known. About 5 minutes' walk west of Ueno-kōen, this café is a local landmark with its ambience intact, from the yellow sign out front

NOMBEI YOKOCHŌ

1-25-10 Shibuya, Shibuya-ku

"Drunkard's Alley," a 1-minute walk from Shibuya Crossing, is another classic *yokochō*, firmly on the tourist radar but retaining its old-school atmosphere. To reach it from Shibuya Station's Hachiko exit, cross Shibuya Crossing, turn right and walk under the train tracks, where you'll see the alleyway on your left, lined with hanging lanterns. A few good spots are Tight (1-25-10, Shibuya-ku; tel. 03/3499-7668; www.2004-tight.com; 6pm-2am Mon.-Sat.), an appropriately named bar squeezed into a remarkably tiny space, and Bar Piano (tel. 03/5467-0258; opening times vary, generally 8pm-late daily), which was visited by the late globe-trotting chef, writer, and food personality Anthony Bourdain.

AMEYA YOKOCHŌ

4 to 6 Ueno, Taito-ku

This jumble of streets beside and under the elevated train tracks a few minutes' walk south of Ueno Station is known as "Ameyoko" by locals, named for the abundance of candy (*ame*) that was sold here in the postwar years. *Ame* also denotes "America," as black-market American goods were also hawked in the area after the war. The mostly outdoor market has an indoor mall, where you'll find all manner of cheap clothing and sneakers. Outside, some 500 stalls and hole-in-the-wall eateries make this one of Tokyo's most sprawling and bustling marketplaces.

and retro furniture to the dark wood paneling and brick counter. The menu consists of classic *kissaten* fare like egg sandwiches and, of course, great coffee. Note that queues do form sometimes, particularly during weekend lunch hours.

ASAKUSA AND RYŌGOKU
浅草, 両国
Ramen
RAMEN YOROIYA

1-36-7 Asakusa, Taitō-ku; tel. 03/3845-4618; https:// yoroiya.jp; 11am-8:30pm Mon.-Fri., 11am-9pm Sat.-Sun. and holidays; ¥1,000; take Ginza or Asakusa line to Asakusa Station, exit 1

The ramen at this Asakusa institution is delicious, and service is fast, friendly, and (mostly) off the tourist track. Ramen Yoroiya specializes in ramen served in a *shoyu* (soy sauce-based) broth. This style of ramen, usually topped with a double-yolk boiled egg, originated right in the neighborhood. While it's less crowded than many eateries around Sensō-ji, which can be rammed during lunch

hours, a queue sometimes forms during peak hours. It moves relatively quickly, but to avoid this, arrive early or in mid-afternoon after the rush passes. English menu available.

Kaiseki
WAENTEI-KIKKO

2-2-13 Asakusa, Taito-ku; tel. 03/5828-8833; https:// waentei-kikko.com/english; 11:30am-2:30pm and 5:30pm-10:30pm Thurs.-Tues.; lunch ¥2,500-3,500, dinner ¥6,800-13,800; take Ginza or Asakusa line to Asakusa Station, exit 1

Set in an old house near Sensō-ji, Waentei-kikko has tatami-mat floors, sliding doors framed with translucent paper, dark wooden rafters, and most importantly, four daily performances (12:15pm, 1:30pm, 6:30pm, and 8pm) by Fukui Kodai, one of the restaurant's managers and a master at the three-stringed Tsugaru-*shamisen*. The restaurant serves seasonal set meals for both lunch and dinner, the former more casual in a bento box and the latter in the form of a *kaiseki* course. This is a wonderful way to experience traditional Japanese music in an intimate setting. Reservations recommended.

Shabu-Shabu/Sukiyaki
ASAKUSA IMAHAN

3-1-12 Nishi-Asakusa, Taito-ku; tel. 03/3841-1114; www.asakusaimahan.co.jp/english; 11:30am-9:30pm (last order 8:30pm) daily; lunch ¥1,500-10,000, dinner ¥8,000-25,000; take Tsukuba Express to Asakusa Station, exit A2, or Ginza line to Tawaramachi Station, exit 3

Take a seat at the Asakusa branch of this butcher-cum-sukiyaki restaurant. Watch as the server places succulent cuts of perfectly marbled *wagyu* into a soy-based soup in the pot on your table, heated by a flame, with mushrooms, tofu, green onions, and other vegetables. When the dish is cooked just enough, pull out a slice of beef and dip it in the small dish of raw free-range (and perfectly safe) egg. It's pricey but delicious.

WESTERN TOKYO
Izakaya
DACHIBIN

3-2-13 Kōenji-Kita, Suginami-ku; tel. 03/3337-1352; www.dachibin.com; 5pm-5am daily; ¥3,000; take Chūō, Sobu lines to Kōenji Station, north exit

Dachibin serves great Okinawan fare made with ingredients sourced from the southern islands, including a healthy list of *awamori*, their fiery variety of *shōchū*. The atmosphere is rowdy and inviting, the staff friendly, and once a month there's a live jam session featuring the *sanshin*, a three-stringed instrument native to Okinawa. This place has been doing a brisk business for more than three decades.

Soup Curry
ROJIURA CURRY SAMURAI

2-27-2 Kichijōji-Honchō, Musashino-shi; tel. 0422/27-6043; http://samurai-curry.com; 11:30am-3:30pm and 5:30pm-10:30pm daily; ¥1,500; take Chūō, Keio-Inokashira lines to Kichijōji Station, north exit

Here, you'll find excellent ingredients, from Hokkaido-sourced vegetables to thick cuts of fatty pork, with no additives and a surprisingly spicy kick: This soup curry restaurant with roots in Sapporo is the real deal. The list of customizable options is extensive, from cheese topping to extra helpings of vegetables like burdock root and okra. The *sakusaku* (crispy) broccoli is amazingly flavorsome. Beware: even at the lower end of the spice spectrum—there are 10 levels—you'll likely be putting out the fire with regular sips of water.

Street Food
KŌENJI GĀDO-SHITA

3-chōme Kōenji-Minami, Suginami-ku; ¥3,000; take Chūō, Sobu lines to Kōenji Station, north exit

Perhaps the most legitimate street food option of Tokyo's vast array of alleyways known as *yokochō*, Gādo-shita is a hodgepodge of smoky, boisterous bars and restaurants with seating both inside and out, running along the train tracks west of Kōenji Station. It gets rowdy on weekends and is a great place for a night out with locals in one of Tokyo's most bohemian neighborhoods.

Yakitori
TETCHAN

1-1-2 Honchō, Musashino-shi; tel. 0422/20-5950; http://hamoyoko.jp/menu/kichijoji_tecchan; 3pm-midnight Mon.-Fri., noon-midnight Sat.-Sun. and holidays; ¥3,000

One of the numerous eateries spread throughout the maze of **Harmonica Yokochō**, another of Tokyo's culinary alleys in the neighborhood of Kichijōji, is Tetchan, a funky yakitori joint designed by famed architect Kengo Kuma with risqué wall art downstairs. This lively spot has a handful of tables, a long wrap-around bar that looks onto the kitchen, and a few standing tables. The menu includes a tasty range of grilled chicken on skewers, a bit of pork, lamb, and beef, and vegetable side dishes.

International
BOLBOL

3-2-15 Kōenjikita Suginami; tel. 03/3223-3277; http://bolbol.jp/english.html; 11:30am-3pm and

5pm-10pm Thurs.-Tues.; lunch ¥650-1,000, dinner ¥1,000-4,600; take Chūō, Sobu lines to Kōenji Station, north exit

BolBol offers excellent Persian food and is run by a friendly owner from Iran and his Japanese wife. The atmosphere evokes Iran, from the Persian rugs on the floor to the ornate tableware and instruments hanging on the wall. Try the dinner course, which includes buttered rice, lamb, and chicken on skewers, grilled tomatoes, and pickled vegetables. Combine it with draft beer or wine. If you're so inclined, relax with a hookah after dinner. Belly dance shows that encourage participation from willing audience members are held on Friday and Saturday nights. The showtimes for these performances vary, but are usually from 8pm or later.

Cafés
BLUE SKY COFFEE

4-1-1 Inokashira, Mitaka-shi; http://blueskycoffee.jp; 10am-6pm Thurs.-Tues., closed on some rainy days; ¥250; take Chūō, Sōbu, Keio-Inokashira lines to Kichijōji Station, park exit, or Keio-Inokashira line to Inokashira-kōen Station

Housed in charmingly worn wooden building, this café sits right in the heart of Inokashira-kōen. They brew great coffee using top-notch equipment and sell a smattering of sweets, too. A great spot for a coffee to-go in the park.

CAFÉ DU LIÈVRE (BUNNY HOUSE)

1-19-43 Gotenyama, Musashino-shi; tel. 0422/43-0015; 10:30am-7pm (last order 6pm) daily; ¥1,000-2,000; take Chūō, Sōbu, Keio-Inokashira lines to Kichijōji Station, park exit

Set in the forested backside of Inokashira-kōen, this charming café with accents of French décor is a great stop for a bite either on the way to or after visiting the nearby Ghibli Museum. Using high-quality buckwheat flour sourced from Hokkaido, the restaurant and café whips up tasty *galettes* with toppings like eggs, pesto, tomatoes, mushrooms, and other veggies. There are also sweet crêpes and a handful of tasty curry-and-rice dishes.

Bars and Nightlife

Befitting a city its size, Tokyo has seemingly infinite options to drink, dance, and mingle once the sun goes down: swanky cocktail bars, thumping clubs, party boats, whisky dens, rambling red-light zones, and live houses where indie rockers jam.

For the connoisseur, the capital is a perfect place to get acquainted with Japan's unique alcoholic heritage, from *nihonshū* to *shōchū*. It's also home to visionary mixologists who craft cocktails in dreamy hideaways, and masters of malt who helm bars stocked with encyclopedic whisky menus.

Audiophiles will appreciate the city's DJ bars and night clubs, which are renowned for their exacting standards when it comes to sound, as well as their carefully curated artist lineups. In hipster enclaves like Shimokitazawa, venues host live performances by indie bards and rowdy punk rockers. If you prefer something with a bit more swing, the city's love of live jazz runs deep, too.

And in the concrete canyons of Shinjuku, the country's largest red-light zone is found in the neon-splashed streets of Kabukichō. Here, you can watch a robot battle or drink your way through a maze of pint-sized bars where five is a crowd. A brief stroll away, you'll also find Tokyo's friendly gay district, Shinjuku Ni-chōme.

Above all else, exploring Tokyo at night reveals the city with its hair down. Be prepared to make some new friends.

GINZA AND MARUNOUCHI

銀座, 丸の内

Bars

BAR HIGH FIVE

Efflore Ginza 5 Bldg. B1F, 5-4-15 Ginza, Chūō-ku; tel. 03/3571-5815; www.barhighfive.com; 5pm-1am Mon.-Sat. (last entry 11:30pm); table/cover charge ¥1,000; take Ginza, Marunouchi, Hibiya lines to Ginza Station, exit B5

Located in a basement, amid the Ginza area's glitz, is Bar High Five, with mixologist extraordinaire Hidetsugu Ueno at the helm and a long counter facing an impressive wall of bottles. In addition to world-renowned cocktails, the bar offers a serious selection of scotch and whisky. The owner speaks fluent English, too. This probably won't be the best choice if you're looking to socialize—the atmosphere is a bit buttoned-down and there's a clearly written list of rules (posted in English on the bar's website) that must be upheld by customers. But if you're a keen connoisseur of nuanced drinks, this is among the very best bars in all Asia.

300BAR NEXT

Murasaki Bldg. B1F, 1-2-14 Yūrakuchō, Chiyoda-ku; tel. 03/3593-8300; www.300bar-next.com; 5pm-11pm Mon.-Thurs., 5pm-2am Fri., 3pm-2am Sat., 3pm-11pm Sun. and holidays; take Ginza, Hibiya, Marunouchi lines to Ginza Station, exit C2, or Yamanote, Yūrakuchō lines to Yūrakuchō Station, Hibiya exit

For a budget option in Ginza—yes, you read that right—300Bar Next can't be beat, with all drinks and food costing only ¥300 per item. If you happen to be in Ginza and don't feel like splashing out, this is your best option. The bartenders are friendly and know their drinks (and make a mean mojito), and the crowd is lively and welcoming. It's a fun place to warm up for a big night out.

TOKYO BAY AREA

東京湾

Night Cruise

JICOO, THE FLOATING BAR

2-7-104 Kaigan, Minato-ku; tel. 03/5733-2939; www.jicoofloatingbar.com; 6pm-9pm daily; ¥2,600 entry; take Yurikamome line to Hinode Station; Yamamote, Keihin-Tohoku lines or Tokyo Monorail to Hamamatsucho Station, or Asakusa, Ōedo lines to Daimon Station

This futuristic looking boat, complete with bar, DJ deck, and multicolored lights, offers nighttime cruises through Tokyo Bay from Hinode Pier to Odaiba, taking in dazzling views of Rainbow Bridge along the way. Jicoo, The Floating Bar leaves Hinode Pier at 8pm, 9pm, and 10pm on Thursday, Friday, and Saturday nights. The music and vibe on Thursday and Friday nights are mellower, while Saturday nights get a bit rowdier. It's a fun alternative to partying on land and a good way to see Tokyo's lights from the water.

ROPPONGI

六本木

Bars

AGAVE

DM Bldg. B1F, 7-18-11 Roppongi, Minato-ku; tel. 03/3497-0229; http://agave.jp; 6:30pm-2am Mon.-Thurs., 6:30pm-4am Fri.-Sat.; take Hibiya, Ōedo lines to Roppongi Station, exit 2

Frida Kahlo paintings, Zapata posters, and Mexican tunes waft through a room with orange stone walls. There's a humidor full of cigars, and behind the bar, an array of some 550 varieties of tequila and mescal. You'd swear you were in Mexico, but Agave is in fact a basement with the ambience of an upscale cantina. It's located near Roppongi's main drag and is seriously committed to the drink derived from the blue-leafed plant after which it's named. Beware that a single pour from the cheaper end of the menu starts at around ¥1,000, while rarer offerings go for upward of ¥9,000.

Sake 101

In Japanese culture, *sake* is sacred, worthy of gifting to the gods, inseparable from the cycle of the seasons and the rice harvest. What is popularly known as *sake* overseas is actually called *nihonshū* (literally: "Japanese alcohol") in Japan, where *sake* denotes all forms of alcohol, from wine and whisky to beer. That said, even in Japan, *sake* is sometimes used to refer to *nihonshū* (i.e. "*sake* bar" or "*sake* specialist" would tend to imply *nihonshū* rather than any other type of alcoholic drink).

While Japanese love an ice-cold beer as much as anyone, two tipples unique to the nation are *nihonshū* and *shōchū*. Keeping things as simple as possible, *nihonshū* is a fermented, rice-based, 15-18% alcohol drink, often served with fine cuisine. *Shōchū* is the fun-loving distilled cousin, more likely to show up at casual gatherings or rowdy *izakayas*, usually in the 25-30% alcohol range, and made with a laundry list of potential ingredients, from barley to sweet potatoes to fruits.

To go deeper, check out the books *Food Sake Tokyo* by Tokyo-based culinary extraordinaire Yukari Sakamoto, and *The Complete Guide to Japanese Drinks*, an award-winning ode to Japan's drinkable offerings by Stephen Lyman and Chris Bunting. Then, swing by the **Japan Sake and Shōchū Information Center** (1-6-15 Nishishinbashi, Minato-ku; tel. 03/3519-2091; www.japansake.or.jp/sake/english/goto/jssic.html; 10am-6pm Mon.-Fri.) for a crash course with one of the sommeliers on staff.

Once you've grasped the basics, here are some of the best spots to drink *nihonshū* and *shōchū* in Tokyo.

- **Sake no Ana** (page 108): A Ginza restaurant with a fantastic *nihonshū* and a sommelier on staff with a knack for food pairing.

- **Tachinomi Nagi** (page 113): A friendly standing *izakaya* (*tachinomi*) and *nihonshū* specialist in Shibuya.

- **Tachinomi Ryoma** (page 109): True to its name (*tachinomi* means "standing bar"), there are 100 types of *shōchū* here, which you can drink elbow-to-elbow with salarymen.

- **Ojinjo** (page 112): A lively, tightly packed *izakaya* in upscale Ebisu renowned for its lemon *chūhai* (*shōchū* with soda and fresh lemon juice).

BAR GEN YAMAMOTO

1-6-4 Azabu-Juban, Minato-ku; tel. 03/6434-0652; http://genyamamoto.jp; 3pm-11pm Tues.-Sun., closed Aug. 18-28; cover charge ¥1,000; take Namboku, Ōedo lines to Azabu-jūban Station, exit 5B

About 5 minutes' walk southeast of the massive Roppongi Hills complex in the affluent neighborhood of Azabu-Juban, you'll find legendary cocktail wizard Gen Yamamoto at work. Bar Gen Yamamoto is a model of simplicity: eight seats at the bar, no soundtrack, minimalist interior. It's just Yamamoto mixing renowned cocktails using seasonal fruits and vegetables from around Japan: lemons and tomatoes from Shikoku, pears from Hokkaido, grapes from Okayama. Rather than measuring everything like a chemist in a lab, he masterfully eyeballs most ingredients in his concoctions. For the full range of flavors, from sweet to savory, try one of the tasting sets of four, six, or seven drinks (¥4,600, ¥6,800, or ¥7,900). It's not cheap, but the quality and craft are phenomenal.

EBISU AND AROUND
恵比寿
Bars
BAR TRAM

Swing Bldg. 2F, 1-7-13 Ebisu-Nishi, Shibuya-ku; tel. 03/5489-5514; http://small-axe.net/bar-tram; 6:30pm-2am daily; cover charge ¥500; take Yamanote line to Ebisu Station, west exit, or take Hibiya line to Ebisu Station, west exit

Bar Tram and sister bar **Bar Trench** (102 DIS Bldg., 1-5-8 Ebisu-Nishi, Shibuya-ku; tel. 03/3780-5291; http://small-axe.net/

Tokyo's Best Whisky Bars

"For relaxing times, make it," Bill Murray dramatically pauses for effect, "Suntory time." Few could have guessed the heights to which Suntory Whisky, and Japanese whisky in general, would soar back in 2003 when Murray's character Bob Harris uttered this now classic line in the moody Tokyo-set film *Lost in Translation*.

Still, around that time, there were signs that Japan's distillers were destined for greatness. First came the "Best of the Best" nod from *Whisky Magazine* to Japanese whisky maker Nikka for its 10-Year Yoichi in 2001. Then, in 2015, *Whisky Bible* declared Suntory's now legendary Yamazaki Sherry Cask 2013 the world's best whisky. This shook the foundations of the whisky world, previously dominated by the United Kingdom and Ireland. In the ensuing five years, Japanese whisky sales to the U.S. market skyrocketed 1,000%. Awards haven't stopped rolling in since, with makers like Suntory, Nikka, and Chichibu mopping up global prizes. Most recently, Suntory's Hakushu Single Malt 25 Year Old was crowned best single malt in the 2020 World Whisky Awards.

To learn more about Japanese whisky's stratospheric ascent, check out *Japanese Whisky: The Ultimate Guide to the World's Most Desirable Spirit with Tasting Notes from Japan's Leading Whisky Blogger*, by Brian Ashcraft, and *Whisky Rising: The Definitive Guide to the Finest Whiskies and Distillers of Japan*, by Stefan Van Eycken.

Better yet, taste it for yourself in one (or more) of Tokyo's glut of world-class whisky bars.

APOLLO
B1F, 8-2-15 Ginza, Chūō-ku; tel. 03/6280-6282; http://theapollo.jp; 11:30am-10pm, last order 9pm daily, closed 4pm-5pm Mon.-Fri.
This classy spot in Ginza has a deep whisky selection, a Tom Waits soundtrack, and a friendly, erudite bartender.

BAR URUSHI
Uchida Bldg. 2F, 1-12-9 Ebisu-nishi, Shibuya-ku; tel. 03/6416-4518; www.bar-urushi-j.com; 7pm-3am Mon.-Sat.
A casual, sophisticated hideout in Ebisu with an affable bartender and an extensive whisky selection.

CABIN NAKAMEGURO
Riverside Terrace 101, 1-10-23 Naka-Meguro, Meguro-ku; tel. 03/6303-2220; www.cabintokyo.com; 7pm-late Mon.-Thurs., 7pm-2am Fri.-Sat., last order 1am, closed on holidays
A great whisky menu in trendy Ebisu.

ZOETROPE
3F, 7-10-14 Nishi-Shinjuku, Shinjuku-ku; tel. 03/3363-0162; www.facebook.com/ShotBarZoetrope/; 5pm-midnight Mon.-Fri., 5pm-11:30pm Sat.; ¥1,000 cover charge
A film buff's bar in Shinjuku with more than 300 bottles of domestic whisky.

bar-trench; 6pm-1am Mon.-Sat., 6pm-1am Sun. and holidays; cover charge ¥500) specialize in herbal liqueur and absinthe-infused cocktails. Dimly lit atmospheric hideouts with a whiff of 19th-century Paris about them, both bars are a short walk from Ebisu Station, and just around the corner from each other. The bartenders are dressed for the job—white shirt, necktie, vest—of navigating more than 70 varieties of the green fairy at Bar Tram alone. Bar Trench boasts the largest collection of bitters in Japan and has an equally quirky list of cocktail names. Monkey Gland, anyone? Note that both bars' opening hours were shortened at the time of writing to prevent

Clubs
SOLFA

1-20-5 Aobadai, Meguro-ku; tel. 03/6231-9051; www. nakameguro-solfa.com; opening hours vary by event (check calendar on website); fee varies by event; take Tōkyū Tōyoko line to Nakameguro Station, main exit

Located in the hip neighborhood of Nakameguro, one train stop or a 15-minute walk from Ebisu Station, Solfa is a wonderfully intimate nightclub. The dance floor accommodates up to 100 people, and the lounge can squeeze in a bit more. DJs on deck usually play artfully chosen techno and house, with some hip-hop nights, too. If you feel like going to a more discerning club that isn't an overwhelmingly crowded, sweaty affair, this one's for you.

DEBRIS

B1F, 11-12 Daikanyama-chō, Shibuya-ku; tel. 03/6416-4334; https://debrispace.com; 7pm-midnight Mon.-Sat.; take Tōkyū Tōyoko line to Daikanyama Station

Descend the stairs and open the door to this unique space with a speakeasy vibe. Farther inside, the aesthetic is urbanized Asian chic. The eclectic décor was conceived by a team of artists and creators involved in throwing outdoor festivals around Japan, and the space was launched by the crew that organizes Zipang, an annual beachside electronic music festival. Events range from music—the sound system is serious—to occasional film screenings and art shows. Cocktails are creatively made. P.B. Restaurant, serving Chinese food, is attached on the ground floor.

Live Music
WHAT THE DICKENS!

4F, 1-13-3 Ebisu-Nishi, Shibuya-ku; tel. 03/3780-2099; www.whatthedickens.jp; 5pm-midnight Tues.-Sun.; no cover

This foreigner-friendly faux British pub (shepherd's pie and fish-and-chips included) is a favored haunt of Tokyo's expat community and a healthy number of Japanese regulars, too. Local acts jam every evening.

SHIBUYA AND AROUND
渋谷

Bars
ISHINOHANA

B1F, 3-6-2 Shibuya, Shibuya-ku; tel. 03/5485-8405; http://ishinohana.com; 5pm-midnight Mon.-Sat.; cover charge ¥500; take Yamanote line to Shibuya Station, east exit

It's all about seasonality at Ishinohana, evidenced by the owner's obsession with fresh produce at this cocktail den near Shibuya Station. This bar is also thankfully devoid of the pomp on display at some of Ginza's swankier cocktail lounges. There's a menu with myriad takes on the martini and another featuring only infinite variations on the mojito. Exotic fruits and vegetables are injected into classics, alongside a host of cocktails originating from this shop, including the award-winning Claudia, a martini infused with caramel syrup and pineapple juice.

SG CLUB

1-7-8 Jinnan, Shibuya-ku; tel. 03/6427-0204; http://sg-management.jp; 5pm-1am Sun.-Thurs., 5pm-2am Fri.-Sat.; take Yamanote line to Shibuya Station, Hachikō exit

This bar has gained serious cred in recent years, coming in at number nine in the 2020 Asia's 50 Best Bars awards. Helmed by fabled bartender Shingo Gokan, this stylish space is spread over two floors: "Guzzle" (ground floor) and "Sip" (downstairs). Guzzle, the more casual of the two, has a 19th-century saloon vibe with subtle Japanese touches, such as menus printed on paper imprinted with kimono designs from the mid-1800s. Sip is dimly lit by Edo-period street lamps, with a jazz soundtrack and industrial décor. Standouts cocktails include the Wagyu Mafia Fashioned, made with bourbon, A5 *wagyu* beef fat, and organic raw honey, and the LOL (aged Scotch, melon, and aged plum liqueur).

Clubs
CONTACT

2-10-12 Dogenzaka, Shibuya-ku; tel. 03/6427-8107;
www.contacttokyo.com; times and fees vary by
event; take Yamanote line to Shibuya Station,
Hachikō exit

Contact is a great choice for discriminating
clubbers. There's a clear separation between
the dance space and the bar area. A no-drinks
policy is in effect on the dance floor, where
flashes of lasers and strobes penetrate air
cooled by mist machines, all enveloped by a
superb sound system. This venue is the latest
entry by organizer Global Hearts, who made
a mark in Tokyo's electronic music scene with
now-closed Yellow and Air. Keep an eye on
the website; major international DJs routinely
perform.

Karaoke
KARAOKE RAINBOW

Shibuya Modi 8F, 1-21-3 Shibuya, Shibuya-ku; tel.
03/6455-3240; www.karaoke-rainbow.com/pc/shop/
shibuya.html; 11am-5am daily; ¥140 per 30 minutes
(until 7pm), ¥380 per 30 minutes (after 7pm), first
hour free Mon.-Fri. (until 7pm) and Mon.-Thurs.
(after 7pm); take Yamanote line to Shibuya Station,
Hachikō exit

Karaoke Rainbow is a chic karaoke spot in
Shibuya with a large English-language cata-
log of songs. It nicely dodges the garish neon
and worn rooms seen in many chains, instead
taking its style cues from, say, Brooklyn: art
on the walls, plants, streetlamps, and benches
in the corridors. Note that while you do get a
free hour of crooning before 7pm on Mon.-
Fri. and even after 7pm on Mon.-Thurs.,
you'll still need to buy a drink during the
first hour.

DJ Bars
DJ BAR BRIDGE

Parkside Kyodo Bldg. 10F, 1-25-6 Shibuya,
Shibuya-ku; tel. 03/6427-6568; https://
bridge-shibuya.com; 8pm-5am daily; cover charge
¥1,000 (includes one drink); take Yamanote line to
Shibuya Station, Hachikō exit

On the 10th floor of a building next to
Shibuya Station, DJ Bar Bridge boasts views
of the pedestrian scramble below, a friendly
crowd, affordable drinks, and a great roster
of resident DJs. Most important, its sound
system is fantastic. Given its convenient location, this is a great place to begin a night
in the area.

OATH

Tosei Bldg. B1F, 1-6-5 Dogenzaka, Shibuya-ku; tel.
03/3461-1225; www.djbar-oath.com; cover charge
¥1,000 (includes one drink); 8pm-5am Mon.-Sat.;
take Yamanote line to Shibuya Station, Hachikō exit

Descend the stairs and enter this compact
club, a vital node in Tokyo's underground
scene that hosts performances by a long list
of regular local DJs. Opulent chandeliers
hang from the ceiling and ornately kitsch
mirrors are mounted on the walls. After
paying the cover charge, drinks are priced
at a reasonable ¥500. But the real draw is the
great sound system.

AOYAMA TUNNEL

Aoyama Bldg. B1F, 4-5-9 Shibuya, Shibuya-ku; http://
aoyama-tunnel.com; 8pm-5am Tues.-Sat.; cover
charge ¥1,000 (includes one drink); take Ginza,
Chiyoda, Hanzōmon lines to Omotesandō Station,
exit B1, or Yamanote line to Shibuya, Hachikō exit

Aoyama Tunnel is the ideal environment for
an all-nighter. Cheap drinks, a good DJ list,
and stellar sound keep the revelers coming.
It's about a 10-minute trek from Shibuya
station up a busy main road rammed with
traffic, but once you arrive you'll enjoy
yourself. For a change of pace, head upstairs
to the worn (and storied) multi-floor club
of **Aoyama Hachi** (Aoyama Bldg. 1F-4F,
4-5-9 Shibuya, Shibuya-ku; tel. 03/5766-
4887; www.aoyama-hachi.net; hours and
fee vary by event), or next door on the first
floor, the afterhours hot spot **Red Bar** (tel.
03/5888-5847; 8pm-late daily; cover charge
¥1,000, includes one drink), which is bathed
in red light as the name suggests, and scope
out the vibe.

The Spectacle of Kabukichō

Tokyo's largest red-light zone, neon-lit Kabukichō ("Kabuki Town"), occupies 360,000 square meters (89 acres) just north of Yasukuni-dōri.

THE HISTORY

Once known as Tsunohazu, it was a residential zone that was razed during World War II bombing raids. Postwar plans to resurrect the area as a family-friendly entertainment center with a kabuki theater never materialized. Instead, host and hostess bars, strip clubs, soaplands (brothels masquerading as bathhouses), and love hotels proliferated, and the *yakuza* (Japanese mafia) and Chinese investors moved in. By the 1990s, Kabukichō had become a *fuzoku* (pink trade) zone, which it remains to this day.

EXPLORING KABUKICHŌ

Despite its seedy reputation, there are security cameras dotting the area and it's a safe place for a stroll if you keep your wits about you and ignore the persistent touts. "Cleanup" efforts are ongoing, as exemplified in the recent opening of the large Toho cinema and shopping complex right in the heart of the action. Definitely go to the unmissable, uncharacterizable Robot Restaurant, but otherwise, just walking around the neighborhood, taking in its atmosphere, and then moving on to Golden Gai is the best way to experience the area.

ROBOT RESTAURANT

Shinjuku Robot Bldg. B2F, 1-7-1 Kabukichō, Shinjuku-ku; tel. 03/3200-5500; www.shinjuku-robot.com; 4pm-11pm daily; ¥8,000; take Shinjuku, Ōedo Marunouchi lines to Shinjuku-Sanchōme Station, exit B3 or E1, or take JR lines to Shinjuku Station, east exit

Robot Restaurant must be experienced to be fully comprehended. But to give an idea, four 90-minute shows happen nightly in a basement in Kabukichō, featuring women in bikinis riding mechanical flame-spewing dragons and towering robots, engaged in a war with a legion of other robots, all set amid a heavily mirrored landscape, drenched in eye-searing neon and with a nonstop din of music and battle sounds (earplugs definitely recommended).

This singular spectacle cost a whopping ¥10 billion to create, which is perhaps reflected in the hefty price of admission. You can book your tickets online in advance, or at the venue. If you opt for the latter, there are often discount vouchers available at tourist information centers and some accommodations that can shave as much as ¥2,000 off the cost of admission. "Restaurant" is a misnomer; the food here is on par with a convenience store bento. Ditto for the drink menu, which extends to canned alcoholic drinks and bottles of tea. This has very much become a "tourist-only" affair, but if you enjoy a zany spectacle, go and leave with your mind blown.

Live Music
SHELTER

Senda Bldg. B1F, 2-6-10 Kitazawa, Setagaya-ku; tel: 03/3466-7430; www.loft-prj.co.jp/SHELTER/index.html; hours and fee vary by event; take Keio-Inokashira, Odakyu lines to Shimokitazawa Station, south exit

Shelter is a compact venue at the center of Shimokitazawa's vibrant rock scene. Domestic and occasional overseas acts jam here nightly. Go early to be sure you get in.

THREE AND BASEMENT BAR

5-18-1 Daizawa, Setagaya-ku; take Keio-Inokashira, Odakyu lines to Shimokitazawa Station, south exit

Three (tel. 03/5486-8804; www.toos.co.jp/3; hours and fee vary by event) and Basement Bar (tel. 03/5481-6366; http://toos.co.jp/basementbar; 6pm-midnight) sit side-by-side in the same building. Basement Bar provides a space for indie rockers to jam on the cheap, and Three does the same, with a lounge for a little class. Rough around the edges, they are vital outposts in Tokyo's indie scene.

HARAJUKU AND AOYAMA

原宿, 青山

Bars

HARAJUKU TAPROOM

2F, 1-20-13 Jingūmae, Shibuya-ku; tel. 03/6438-0450; https://bairdbeer.com/ja/taprooms/harajuku; 5pm-midnight Mon.-Fri., noon-midnight Sat.-Sun.; take Yamanote line to Harajuku Station, Takeshita exit

A stone's throw from the youth fashion catwalk of Takeshita-dōri isn't the most likely spot for a craft beer bar to thrive, but Harajuku Taproom, by Baird Brewing, manages to do just that. Its restaurant has an *izakaya*-inspired menu and serves 15 of Baird Brewing's fantastic microbrews. On weekends and national holidays, it opens at noon for lunch.

TWO ROOMS

3-11-7 Kita-Aoyama, Minato-ku; tel. 033/498-0222; www.tworooms.jp; 11:30am-2am Mon.-Sat., 11:am-10pm Sun.; take Ginza line to Omotesandō Station, exit B2; or take Fukutoshin line to Kitasandō Station

Two Rooms is a sleekly decorated bar with excellent fish grilled teppanyaki-style, succulent steaks, a motherlode of wine, and a plush outdoor terrace with spectacular views of the city. It's popular as both a sophisticated nightlife spot and a restaurant. On weekends, Two Rooms serves an amazing brunch.

BAR BONOBO

2-23-4 Jingūmae, Shibuya-ku; tel. 03/6804-5542; http://bonobo.jp; hours vary by event (see schedule on website); cover charge ¥1,000 (includes one drink); take Yamanote line to Harajuku Station, Takeshita exit

Bar Bonobo, tucked away on a Harajuku backstreet, is a converted two-story house with a great sound system and friendly vibe. There's a bar on the first floor, a DJ booth upstairs where various music events are held, and a rooftop terrace. A bit off the beaten path, it's worth the detour if you're looking for a laidback place with a slightly underground feel. Start times vary by night, but the action goes late into the night.

Clubs

VENT

Festa Omotesandō Bldg. B1F, 3-18-19 Minami-Aoyama, Minato-ku; tel. 03/6804-6652; http://vent-tokyo.net; 11pm-late on nights with events; fee varies; take Ginza, Chiyoda, Hanzomon lines to Omotesandō Station, exit 4

Great DJ lineups and a dance floor with a spectacular sound system are the main selling points at Vent. This newcomer to Tokyo's electronic music scene is located at the corner of Omotesandō and Aoyama Dōri. Its chic interior is minimal and contains a lounge that provides a great place to socialize and drink without being drowned in decibels. These elements tend to attract an aurally savvy crowd who are in-the-know yet friendly. Both local DJs and big names from overseas are routinely scheduled to spin.

TOP EXPERIENCE

★ SHINJUKU AND AROUND

新宿

Tokyo offers a great variety of nightlife, but Shinjuku stands above the crowd in terms of depth and variety. Served by the world's busiest train station, the area is home to **Kabukichō,** the city's biggest red-light district; **Golden Gai,** a warren of more than 200 small bars; and the city's gay quarter centered in **Shinjuku Ni-chōme.**

Bars

BEN FIDDICH

Yamatoya Bldg. 9F, 1-13-7 Nishi-Shinjuku, Shinjuku-ku; tel. 03/6279-4223; www.facebook.com/BarBenfiddich; 5pm-3am Mon., Tues., Thurs., and Sat., 5pm-2am Wed. and Fri., closed holidays; take JR lines to Shinjuku, west exit

At Ben Fiddich there are roots and spices in jars, perfectly sculpted ice cubes, pestles and mortars, and organic mixing ingredients sourced from bar master Hiroyasu Kayama's family farm in neighboring Saitama Prefecture. What you won't find is a menu;

just sit back with an open mind and let the bar master work his magic.

NEW YORK BAR

Park Hyatt, 3-7-1-2 Nishi-Shinjuku, Shinjuku-ku; tel. 03/5323-3458; http://tokyo.park.hyatt.com; 5pm-11pm Sun.-Thurs., 5pm-midnight Fri.-Sat.; ¥2,500 cover charge after 8pm Mon.-Sat., or after 7pm Sun.; take Ōedo line to Tochōmae Station, exit A4

Made famous by Sofia Coppola's film *Lost in Translation,* this bar is a true gem and offers some of the most dazzling views of the city at night. Perched on the 52nd floor of the Park Hyatt Tokyo, in Shinjuku's skyscraper district, New York Bar is the pinnacle of elegance, with its dark wood and floor-to-ceiling windows from which Mount Fuji can be glimpsed on clear days. Here you'll find top-notch cocktails; an array of booze, including the most varieties of wine from the United States in Japan; and excellent steak and pizza.

BAR GOLD FINGER

2-12-11 Shinjuku, Shinjuku-ku; tel. 03/6383-4649; www.goldfingerparty.com; 6pm-2am Sun.-Thurs., 6pm-5am Fri.-Sat.; take Fukutoshin, Marunouchi, Shinjuku lines to Shinjuku Sanchōme Station, exit C8

This bubbly bar is a mainstay in the Shinjuku Ni-chōme area, with revelers sometimes spilling into the street outside. Note that it's women-only on Saturdays.

ARTY FARTY

Kyutei Bldg. 2F, 2-11-7 Shinjuku, Shinjuku-ku; tel. 03/5362-9720; www.arty-farty.net; 8pm-late

Perhaps the most popular of the lot in in Ni-chōme, this is a great place to end the night. Note that women are required to come with a gay friend for admission on weekends when the dance floor gets jumping.

Live Music
SHINJUKU PIT INN

B1, 2-12-4 Shinjuku, Shinjuku-ku; tel. 03/3354-2024; www.pit-inn.com/index.html; 2:30pm, 7:30pm; hours and fee vary by event; take Marunouchi line to Shinjuku-Sanchōme Station, exit C5

An eminent jazz spot imbued with history and blessed by a consistently stellar lineup of both Japanese and overseas artists. There are daily matinee and evening shows.

SHINJUKU LOFT

Tatehana Bldg. B2F, 1-12-9 Kabukichō, Shinjuku-ku; tel. 03/5272-0382; www.loft-prj.co.jp; hours and fee vary by event; take Yamanote line to Shinjuku Station, east exit

A stalwart of Tokyo's live music scene. One

Shinjuku's Kabukichō nightlife district

Pub Crawl Through Golden Gai

The endless bars and cramped clubs of Golden Gai make for a perfect pub crawl, perhaps after first gorging on grilled meats in Omoide Yokochō or Shinjuku Sanchōme, and having your mind blown by the trippy, cacophonous spectacle that is Robot Restaurant.

Golden Gai has a rich, bohemian lore, frequented by writers like Japanese literary prize winners Saki Ryūzō and Nakagami Kenji and film directors such as Quentin Tarantino. When in Golden Gai, adhere to some basic rules. First, try to avoid going in groups of more than three. Space is at a premium. Second, confirm whether the bar has a cover charge before entering so that you're not shocked by the bill. Third, be respectful and friendly with the whole bar, but avoid getting rowdy. Fourth, move on to the next bar after a few drinks. The key word is bar *hopping*. Finally, don't smoke or drink in the street, or take photos without permission.

To get there, take the Shinjuku, Ōedo, or Marunouchi line to Shinjuku-Sanchōme Station, exit B3 or E1; or take JR lines to Shinjuku Station, east exit. Just a few minutes' walk from Golden Gai is Ni-Chōme, Tokyo's friendly, compact gay district, accessible directly from Shinjuku-Sanchōme Station (Shinjuku, Ōedo, Marunouchi lines, exits C5, C8).

- Begin your pub crawl at Kenzo's Bar (1-1-7 Kabukichō, Shinjuku-ku; tel. 090/9847-5563; https://twitter.com/KENZOS_BAR; 8pm-5am daily), a leopard-spot printed bolt-hole with a 1980s soundtrack overseen by the gregarious Kenzo himself, who's adept at easing first timers into Golden Gai.

- Leaving Kenzo's, turn right and walk to the T-junction, then turn right, and then right again so that you're in the alleyway parallel to the one where Kenzo's is located. Walk roughly halfway down the alley until you see Albatross G (1-1-7 Kabukichō, Shinjuku-ku; tel. 03/3203-3699; www.alba-s.com; 5pm-2am Sun.-Thurs., 5pm-5am Fri.-Sat.) on the right. This cramped bar has red walls, lots of crystal chandeliers, and friendly bartenders who appeared in one of the late Anthony Bourdain's Tokyo episodes for his show *Parts Unknown*.

- When you exit Albatross G, turn right out of the door and walk straight ahead. On your left, toward the end of the alley, you'll come to a large, unmarked wooden door. Slide it open and step inside The Open Book (1-1-6 Kabukichō, Shinjuku-ku; tel. 080/4112-0273; www.facebook.com/theopenbook2016; 7pm-midnight daily). This lemon sour (*shōchū*, soda, and lemon juice) specialist offers the ideal spot to get acquainted with this versatile drink, which patrons sip beside a wall overflowing with books.

- Upon exiting, turn left and walk to the road ahead. Turn right and then right again down the first lane, which is the same one Kenzo's Bar is located on. On the right side of the lane, not far from the road, you'll come to Cambiare (1-1-7 Kabukichō, Hanazono Sanban-gai 2F, Shinjuku-ku; https://twitter.com/CambiareB; 6pm-2am Mon.-Thurs., 6pm-5am Fri.-Sat.). Ascend the stairs and enter this lurid space of reds, blues, yellows, and psychedelic floral patterns, inspired by Dario Argento's cult classic Italian horror flick *Suspiria*. Horror chic aside, the bartenders and patrons are lovely.

- End your journey at Deathmatch in Hell (1-1-8 Kabukichō, Golden-Gai 3rd street, Shinjuku-ku; tel. 090/2524- 5575; www.facebook.com/deathmatchinhell; 8pm-3am Mon.-Sat., closed holidays). Brace yourself. This legendary bar is bursting with horror and sci-fi movie posters, a heavy metal soundtrack, and splatter films playing on TV. The long-haired owner is a bona fide character, and the crowd is fun.

room hosts the main show and a smaller one near the bar hosts more intimate performances.

ASAKUSA AND RYŌGOKU

浅草、両国

Bars

POPEYE

2-18-7 Ryōgoku, Sumida-ku; tel. 03/3633-2120; www.lares.dti.ne.jp/~ppy; 5pm-11:30pm Mon.-Thurs., 3:30pm-11:30pm Fri., 3pm-11:30pm Sat. and holidays; take Sōbu line to Ryōgoku Station, west exit

Popeye has 70 beers on tap, with the bulk brewed by Japanese craft outfits. In fact, the microbrew mecca has more Japanese microbrews on tap than any other bar worldwide. Try to get a place at the counter, where the approachable staff will be happy to guide you in your journey through the islands' best offerings. Be warned that many of the beers aren't cheap, and the British pub fare leaves something to be desired. But if you're a craft brew aficionado and unearthing hidden gems is your aim, this is the best spot in the capital to explore Japan's microbrew scene.

Accommodations

When choosing accommodation in Tokyo, the most important factor is convenience. The most popular areas are the zone surrounding Tokyo Station, centered on **Ginza** and **Marunouchi,** and in the western part of the city, **Shinjuku** and **Shibuya.** The draws of these core areas are proximity to the city's best food, shopping, and nightlife. Further, Tokyo, Shibuya, and Shinjuku stations are on the Yamanote line, which runs in a loop around the city, while Ginza has several subway links (Ginza, Hibiya, Marunouchi lines).

Roppongi is also a solid base in the heart of downtown with good subway links (Oedo, Hibiya lines). That said, it's very much "on" 24 hours a day and can feel somewhat seedy at nighttime, particularly along the main drag of Gaien-Higashi-dōri. As such, it's best suited to night owls and those traveling without kids. The same caveat applies to Shinjuku's **Kabukichō** district—it's a very colorful area, but it doesn't score the highest marks for family friendliness at nighttime.

Another area worth considering is the older side of town in the city's northeast, centered on **Ueno** and **Asakusa.** These two neighborhoods have more affordable options and plenty of local character but are also less central.

If you end up staying outside of these core areas, aim to at the very least find a room near a station on the Yamanote loop line, the east-west Chūō/Sōbu line, or a subway station not too far from the city's core, encompassing the area inside the Yamanote line.

GINZA AND MARUNOUCHI

銀座、丸の内

¥20,000-30,000

HOTEL RYUMEIKAN TOKYO

1-3-22 Yaesu, Chūō-ku; tel. 03/3272-0971; www. ryumeikan-tokyo.jp; ¥24,000 d; take Yamanote line to Tokyo Station, Yaesu North exit

Next to Tokyo Station, Hotel Ryumeikan Tokyo is a branch of the Ryokan Ryumeikan Honten, which has been running since 1899. The rooms are petite but smart, and feature free Wi-Fi access. Helpful staff are ready to assist you in sending your luggage to the airport so you don't have to carry it with you. This is a good option for those wanting an affordable place to sleep, but not much else.

¥30,000-40,000

PARK HOTEL TOKYO

1-7-1 Higashi-Shimbashi, Minato-ku; tel. 03/6252-1111; www.parkhotel-tokyo.com; ¥36,000 d; take Yamanote, Ginza, Asakusa lines to Shimbashi Station,

Shiodome exit for JR station, exit 1d for subway
station, or take Yurikamome, Ōedo lines to Shiodome
Station, exits 7, 8

The Park Hotel Tokyo is a Design Hotel with reasonable rates—not an easy find in Tokyo. The first hotel in the capital launched by Berlin-based Design Hotels, this property in Shiodome boasts a floor with more than 30 rooms, each uniquely painted by Japanese artists. The walls of these special rooms feature contemporary takes on everything from Mount Fuji and the book *Tale of Genji* to samurai and kabuki. The hotel even has pillow consultants on staff and collaborates with pillow maker Lofty to provide guests with versions that offer maximum rest.

Over ¥40,000
IMPERIAL HOTEL TOKYO

1-1-1 Uchisaiwaicho, Chiyoda-ku; tel. 03/3504-1111;
www.imperialhotel.co.jp; ¥47,200 d; take Chiyoda,
Hibiya, Mita lines to Hibiya Station, exits A5, A13,
or Yamanote, Yūrakuchō lines to Yūrakuchō Station,
Hibiya exit

The Imperial Hotel Tokyo has more history coursing through its halls than just about any other hotel in the city. It has been standing on its current site, overlooking the Palace, Hibiya Park, and Ginza, in some form since 1890. Its second incarnation, which opened (and remained standing) the same day that the 1923 Great Kanto Earthquake struck the capital, was designed by Frank Lloyd Wright. Its current main building opened in 1970 and boasts 13 restaurants and three bars, including the superb Imperial Lounge Aqua and the legendary Old Imperial Bar, originally designed by Frank Lloyd Wright and still graced by the same furniture and motifs. The hotel's proximity to Hibiya, Ginza, and Yūrakuchō stations ensures easy access to anywhere in the city.

ANDAZ

1-23-4, Toranomon, Minato-ku; tel. 03/6830-1234;
https://tokyo.andaz.hyatt.com; ¥115,515 d; take Ginza
line to Toranomon Station, exit 4

Atop Tokyo's second tallest building and most recent skyscraper development project, Toranomon Hills, the Andaz is notable for its superb views and rooftop bar that hosts a variety of seasonal events. Chic, contemporary Japanese flourishes, such as lanterns and washi paper dividers grace the lounge. And thanks to the hotel's boutique sensibility, there's no need to visit a check-in desk; instead, friendly staff wielding small electronic tablets are happy to serve you anywhere you may meet. The area may feel too business-like for some, but it's in the midst of a significant sprucing-up to be finished in 2023, giving the district around the hotel a nice buzz.

PALACE HOTEL

1-1-1 Marunouchi, Chiyoda-ku; tel. 03/3211-5211;
https://en.palacehoteltokyo.com; ¥124,600; take
Chiyoda line to Ōtemachi station, exit C13b

The recently revamped historic Palace Hotel is long on views, with its south-facing rooms with balconies—a rare luxury in Tokyo—overlooking the Imperial Palace moat and gardens, with the skyscrapers jutting skyward in the backdrop. The spacious rooms have earth-tone décor that exudes a hushed elegance in harmony with the green space sprawling outside the window. It's also within walking distance of Hibiya Park and the shopping districts of Ginza and Yūrakuchō, and it has phenomenal Japanese and Western food on-site. Cultural events are often held in the lobby to reflect the seasons, such as traditional rice cake-making performances on New Year's Day and cherry blossom events in spring.

★ AMAN

The Ōtemachi Tower, 1-5-6 Ōtemachi,
Chiyoda-ku; tel. 03/5224-3333; www.aman.com;
¥100,000-330,000 d; take Marunouchi line to
Ōtemachi station, exit A5

Luxury resort giant Aman operates an exclusive hotel on the top six floors of Ōtemachi Tower. The lavish 84-room property is a departure for Aman, being its first in an urban setting. While the brand is a haven for celebrities who want to keep a low profile, this hotel is in the heart of the bustling Ōtemachi business district, only a short walk from Tokyo Station. Friendly, attentive staff are ready to guide you to deluxe facilities, including fine dining, a two-floor spa, a lounge, and a café. And the rooms are massive.

ROPPONGI AND AROUND
六本木
¥20,000-30,000
HOTEL S ROPPONGI

1-11-6 Nishi-Azabu, Minato-ku; tel. 03/5771-2469; http://hr-roppongi.jp; ¥27,045 d; take Hibiya line to Roppongi Station, exit 2

Sleek Japanese aesthetics in many of the rooms and a shared ground-floor lounge with computers, periodicals, and art books give Hotel S Roppongi a sophisticated sheen. The well-designed hotel shares space with serviced apartments and restaurants. The Zen suite comes with a round bathtub made of Hinoki cypress. Located a stone's throw from Nishi-Azabu crossing, a diverse range of eateries and nightlife options are close at hand. The only drawback is that it's about a 10-minute walk from the nearest train station, Roppongi.

HARAJUKU AND AOYAMA
Over ¥40,000
★ HOTEL NEW OTANI

4-1 Kioi-cho, Chiyoda-ku; tel. 03/3265-1111; www. newotani.co.jp/en/tokyo; ¥45,980 d; take Ginza, Marunouchi lines to Akasaka-Mitsuke Station, exit 7

One of the biggest hotels in Japan, the Hotel New Otani is like a small city with a long, colorful history. It was used as the backdrop for the corporate villain's HQ in the 1965 James Bond film *You Only Live Twice*. There are more than 30 places to wine and dine, a plethora of gift shops, fashion boutiques, a spa, florist, supermarket, even a dentist and a doctor. The high point is the 400-year-old 10-acre garden brimming with trees, flowers, koi ponds, and a surprisingly large waterfall. One drawback: The swimming pool is open in summer only.

EBISU AND AROUND
恵比寿
¥30,000-40,000
CLASKA

1-3-18 Chūō-cho, Meguro-ku; tel. 03/3719-8121; www. claska.com/en; ¥30,250 d; take Tōkyū Tōyoko line to Gakugei Daigaku station, east exit

Design is the key word at Claska, where Japanese elements infuse each of the 20 rooms. Galleries, art studios, a shop, and event spaces are found on some of the floors, and the rooftop is graced by a terrace. A ground-floor restaurant serves Japanese and European fare, and some of the rooms can be reserved on a weekly basis for longer-term guests. The one downside is that it's a bit far at around 2 km (1.25 mi) from the nearest station, Meguro, so guests may end up using taxis.

SHIBUYA
渋谷
Under ¥10,000
MILLENNIALS SHIBUYA

1-20-13 Jinnan, Shibuya-ku; tel. 03/6824-9410; www.themillennials.jp/shibuya; pods from ¥4,700 with breakfast; take JR lines, Tōyoko line, or Ginza, Fukutoshin, Hanzōmon subway lines to Shibuya Station, Hachiko exit, then walk 7 minutes north

Sleep in a "smart pod"—essentially a well-appointed capsule—kitted out with plug and USB socket and comfortable bedding at this chicly minimal hostel. There's a shared workspace, free Wi-Fi throughout, and coffee, breakfast, and beer are all served for free.

¥20,000-30,000
SHIBUYA GRANBELL HOTEL

15-17 Sakuragaoka-cho, Shibuya-ku; tel. 03/5457-2681; www.granbellhotel.jp; ¥21,700 d; take Yamanote line to Shibuya station, south exit

Located just a stone's throw from Shibuya Station, the Shibuya Granbell Hotel is a good option for those on a midrange budget who want to be near the action. Room design is several cuts above a standard budget hotel, thanks to the involvement of the same company responsible for decking out the fashionable Claska. Think funky pop-art prints adorning curtains, minimalist color schemes, and appliances with a hip edge. Top-floor suites can be booked for longer-term stays. Free Wi-Fi is available in all rooms, which is a good thing given the hotel's popularity among young movers and shakers.

¥30,000-40,000
CERULEAN TOWER TOKYŪ HOTEL

26-1 Sakuragaoka-chō, Shibuya-ku; tel. 03/3476-3000; www.tokyuhotels.co.jp/cerulean-h; doubles from ¥32,000, from ¥35,300 with breakfast; take JR lines, Tōyoko line, or Ginza, Fukutoshin, Hanzōmon subway lines to Shibuya Station, west exit, then walk 3 minutes southwest

Occupying floors 19-37, this high-rise hotel has smart, spacious rooms with great views of the city. Bathrooms are well-appointed, there are several restaurants and a bar on site, and there's a fitness center with a pool. A good pick if you'd like to stay in Shibuya and want something classy.

SHINJUKU AND AROUND
新宿
¥10,000-20,000
ONSEN RYOKAN YUEN SHINJUKU

5-3-18 Shinjuku, Shinjuku-ku; tel. 03/5361-8355; www.uds-hotels.com/yuen/shinjuku; doubles from ¥12,000; take Fukutoshin, Marunouchi or Shinjuku subway lines to Shinjuku San-chōme Station, exit C7, then walk 8 minutes northeast, or take JR lines to Shinjuku Station, east exit, then walk 17 minutes east

Just beyond Shinjuku's hubbub, this modern *ryokan* has chic, zen-like rooms, some with good views of the surrounding cityscape. All rooms have well-appointed private baths, as well as access to a shared, gender-separated *onsen*. The rooms are on the petite side but are a great value, given the hotel's location and price point. There's a restaurant on-site serving Japanese food (breakfast: ¥1,800). A good budget pick.

¥20,000-30,000
HOTEL GRACERY SHINJUKU

1-19-1 Kabukichō, Shinjuku-ku; tel. 03/6833-2489; http://shinjuku.gracery.com; ¥25,000 d; take Yamanote line to Shinjuku Station, east exit

The Gracery Shinjuku is for Godzilla fans. A 12-meter (39-foot) statue of the monster bellows and exhales smoke on the hour noon-8pm on the hotel's eighth-floor terrace. Set in the heart of Shinjuku's Kabukichō entertainment district, the 30-floor tower offers guests at the higher levels impressive views of Tokyo—just like the monster would have. The rooms, of which there are almost 1,000, are small but well designed. For serious fans, there's a room with a statue of the creature inside.

Over ¥40,000
★ PARK HYATT TOKYO

3-7-1-2 Nishi-Shinjuku, Shinjuku-Ku; tel. 03/5322-1234; http://tokyo.park.hyatt.com; ¥144,600 d; take Ōedo line to Tochōmae station, exit A4

Park Hyatt Tokyo is a rock-star hotel that owes much of its fame to Sofia Coppola's 2003 film *Lost in Translation,* staring Bill Murray as jaded action star Bob Harris, fresh in Tokyo to film a whisky commercial. It's hard not to visualize scenes from the movie when passing through the lobby, taking a dip in the pool, or, perhaps most of all, having drinks in the supremely atmospheric New York Bar. Clean lines and minimalist décor imbue the hotel with understated elegance, and Mount Fuji can be glimpsed on clear days.

AKIHABARA AND UENO
秋葉原, 上野
¥10,000-20,000
RYOKAN SAWANOYA

2-3-11 Yanaka, Taitō-ku; tel. 03/3822-2251; www.sawanoya.com; ¥11,880 d; take Chiyoda line to Nezu Station, exit 1

Ryokan Sawanoya is a great Yanaka-area inn. At this family-run *ryokan*, the traditional touches are all in place: tatami floors,

Japanese-style ceramic and cypress-wood baths (both shared and private in some rooms), paper lanterns, futons in place of beds, and traditional dance performances at select times. The affable owners are happy to help, providing a slew of travel information, local recommendations, and bicycle rentals to guests. What's more, there is English-language information throughout the *ryokan,* educating guests on such topics as bathing etiquette.

¥20,000-30,000
★ HANARE

3-10-25 Hagiso, Yanaka, Taitō-ku; tel. 03/5834-7301; http://hanare.hagiso.jp; ¥22,000 d; take Chiyoda line to Sendagi, exit 2

Hanare is a gem in the heart of Yanaka, one of Tokyo's most charming neighborhoods. This *ryokan* is run by wonderful staff who encourage guests to get out and experience the city. They're always armed with suggestions for the best shrines, public baths, bike rentals, mom-and-pop restaurants, and traditional craft shops. All five rooms have tatami floors, and the bathroom is shared. The inn shares a building with a café, a gift shop, and a gallery.

ASAKUSA AND RYŌGOKU
浅草, 両国
Under ¥10,000
BUNKA HOSTEL TOKYO

1-13-5 Asakusa, Taitō-ku; tel. 03/5806-3444, http://bunkahostel.jp; ¥2,555 single bunk bed in mixed dorm; take Tsukuba Express to Asakusa Station, exit 4

Bunka Hostel Tokyo appeals to backpackers who want a bit more comfort. Housed in a renovated office building in the heart of Asakusa, the hostel has options ranging from bunk beds to family rooms. It also offers a shared dining room, free Wi-Fi, and an *izakaya* on the first floor, open to guests and non-guests alike.

NUI. HOSTEL & BAR LOUNGE

2-14-13 Kuramae, Taitō-ku; tel. 03/6240-9854; https://backpackersjapan.co.jp; ¥3,500 single bunk bed in mixed dorm, ¥9,000 twin bunk bed in private room; take Ōedo line to Kuramae Station, exit A7

Nui. Hostel & Bar Lounge is roughly a 15-minute walk from Asakusa, set in the trendy district of Kuramae. This is another hostel with all the right touches, including a first-floor bar-café that draws guests and non-guests together and creates a nice social buzz. Mixed dorms and doubles share

dine with a view at Park Hyatt Tokyo

bathrooms and a kitchen, and Wi-Fi is free. Common areas close at midnight.

¥10,000-20,000
WIRED HOTEL ASAKUSA

2-16-2 Asakusa, Taitō-ku; tel. 03/5830-7931; http:// wiredhotel.com; ¥16,000 d; take Ginza line to Asakusa Station, exit A

With design and branding by a Portland-based creative outfit, Wired Hotel Asakusa ticks all the artisanal boxes. On the first floor you'll find a café-bar open to all and serving soy-based snacks, naturally. Single rooms, doubles, and even a penthouse suite ensure that all types of travelers' needs are met. Décor feels more New York studio than old-school Tokyo, but this boutique hideaway is indeed in the middle of Asakusa, the heart of the city's old downtown district.

¥20,000-30,000
★ THE GATE HOTEL KAMINARIMON

2-16-11, Kaminarimon, Taitō-ku; tel. 03/6263-8233; www.gate-hotel.jp; ¥28,614 d; take Ginza line to Asakusa Station, exit 2

Located just across from Sensō-ji's iconic Kaminarimon Gate, the Gate Hotel Kaminarimon designed by Shigeru Uchida, a renowned designer whose mastery extends from architectural interiors to furniture and urban planning, offers a stylish option in the heart of old Tokyo. The lobby shares the 13th floor with an eatery specializing in French fusion cuisine. One floor up, there's also a terrace and bar. May-October guests can take an elevator to the rooftop for excellent views of Tokyo Skytree and surroundings. For those seeking a good option in the old part of town, this hotel offers great bang for buck.

Information and Services

TOURIST INFORMATION

The easiest way to gather information is from your hotel's front desk, but if you're hitting the pavement and need to stop somewhere for additional help, there are a number of tourist information centers scattered around Tokyo. Thankfully, many are located in areas you'll likely pass through as you explore. For a full list of tourist information centers around town, visit https://tokyotouristinfo.com/en.

In the Marunouchi area, you'll find the Japan National Tourism Organization's **JNTO Tourist Information Center** (3-3-1 Marunouchi, Shin-Tokyo Building, Chiyoda-ku; tel. 03/3201-3331; www.jnto. go.jp; 9am-5pm daily; take Chiyoda line to Nijubashimae, exit 1). Here you can get information not only on Tokyo but also on Japan as a whole. There are also branches at Narita Airport terminals 1 and 2. Also in Marunouchi is the **JR East Travel Service Center** (1-9-1 Marunouchi, Tokyo Station, Chiyoda-ku; www.jreast.co.jp/e/

customer_support/service_center_tokyo. html; 7:30am-8:30pm daily; take JR Yamanote line to Tokyo, Marunouchi North exit), with English information on booking getaways within Japan.

In Shibuya, you'll find **Shibu Hachi Box** (2-1 Dōgenzaka, Shibuya-ku; tel. 03/3462-8311; https://tokyotouristinfo.com/en/detail/ M0123; 10am-8pm daily) next to Shibuya's beloved canine statue of Hachikō.

In Shinjuku, you can pick up information in English on various practicalities at the **Tokyo Metropolitan Government Building Tourist Information Center** (2-8-1 Nishi-Shinjuku, Shinjuku-ku, Tokyo Metropolitan Government Building 1F; tel. 03/5321-3077; 9:30am-6:30pm daily; take Ōedo line to Tochomae, exit A4). The **Shinjuku Tourist Information Center** is outside the South East Exit of JR Shinjuku Station (3-37-2 Shinjuku, Shinjukuku; tel. 03/3344-3160; www.kanko-shinjuku.jp/office/-/index.html; 10am-7pm daily).

For help with navigating the eastern districts of Ueno and Asakusa, the **Asakusa Culture Tourist Information Center** (2-18-9 Kaminarimon, Taitō-ku; tel. 03/3842-5566; 9am-8pm daily; take Ginza line to Asakusa, exit 2) is your best bet.

BANKS AND CURRENCY EXCHANGE

ATMs are ubiquitous throughout Tokyo, from convenience stores to banks. To the chagrin of many travelers, however, they often don't cooperate with foreign-issued cards, even when they bear the logos of Visa, MasterCard, American Express, Plus, or any other major card.

For currency exchange, most banks such as **Mizuho, Mitsubishi UFJ,** and **Sumitomo Mitsui** do the job, but only on weekdays 9am-3pm. If you need to exchange currency, it's best to handle it upon arriving at an international airport. You can also exchange money in Marunouchi at **Exchangers** (Shin-Tokyo Bldg. 1F; 3-3-1 Marunouchi, Chiyoda-ku; tel. 03/6269-9466; www.exchangers.co.jp; 10am-6pm Mon.-Fri.).

POSTAL SERVICES

Japan's postal service is efficient and dependable, and Tokyo has local branches in every district, typically open 9am-5pm Monday-Friday and Saturday 9am-noon. Sending packages via airmail to the United States normally takes about one week, while surface deliveries require a month or two.

For the best service, go to any ward's central post office, which will have English-speaking staff. These larger main branches also tend to have longer hours of operation, such as 9am-9pm on weekdays and 9am-7pm on weekends. Your best bet is **Tokyo Central Post Office** (2-7-2 Marunouchi, Chiyoda-ku; tel. 03/3217-5231; Tokyo Station, Marunouchi South Exit), which operates 24 hours.

Also note that **FedEx** (tel. 0120-003/200 toll free; www.fedex.com) has locations dotted around the city's major business districts.

Rates aren't cheap, but this is a reliable way to send a package overseas.

INTERNET ACCESS

It's a common complaint that Tokyo has a dearth of Wi-Fi in public spaces like cafés compared with other cities, but the situation is improving. Signal strength varies, but Wi-Fi is available on subway station platforms, in some convenience stores, and even on the streets of some neighborhoods. Many shops and attractions provide Wi-Fi for customers as well. Most hotels provide Wi-Fi for guests, sometimes for a fee, or at least have shared computers in the lobby. There are also Internet cafés, which will have computer booths that you can typically rent in 30-minute or one-hour increments.

Free Wi-Fi Japan (www.flets.com) allows you to connect at various hot spots around Tokyo after registering and getting log-in credentials online or at a tourist center. **Travel Japan Wi-Fi** (http://japanfreewifi.com) allows access at some 200,000 spots around Japan for iOS and Android devices after registering online.

But the best way to ensure you remain connected is by renting a pocket Wi-Fi either at the airport on arrival—there are numerous providers with clear English signage—or via **Japan Wireless** (http://japan-wireless.com), which ships devices to travelers who have already checked into their hotels.

PHARMACIES AND MEDICAL SERVICES

For emergency fire and ambulance services, dial 119. Most operators don't speak English, but will transfer you to someone who does. A multilingual service that can connect you to English-speaking doctors of various kinds is the **Tokyo Metropolitan Health and Medical Information Center** (tel. 03/5285-8181; www.himawari.metro.tokyo.jp; 9am-8pm daily). Call the number and request English assistance. They will put you in touch with an operator who can help.

Aside from seeking assistance from one of

these services, English-speaking physicians are limited. For emergency room services with English-speaking care, go to St. Luke's International Hospital (9-1 Akashi-cho, Chūō-ku; tel. 03/3541-5151; http://hospital. luke.ac.jp; take Hibiya line to Tsukiji, exit 3).

DIPLOMATIC SERVICES

The U.S. Embassy and Consulate (1-10-5 Akasaka, Minato-ku; tel. 03/3224-5000; http://jp.usembassy.gov; take Namboku line to Tameike-Sanno, exit 13) is open weekdays 8:30am-5:30pm.

The Embassy of Canada to Japan (7-3-38 Akasaka, Minato-ku; tel. 03/5412-6200; www.canadainternational.gc.ca/japan-japon; take Ginza, Ōedo, Hanzōmon lines to Aoyama-Itchōme Station, exit 4) is open weekdays 9am-5:30pm.

The British Embassy Tokyo (No. 1 Ichiban-chō, Chiyoda-ku; tel. 03/5211-1100; www.gov.uk/world/organisations/british-embassy-tokyo; take Hanzōmon line to Hanzōmon Station, exit 4) is open weekdays 9:30am-4:30pm.

The Australian Embassy Tokyo (2-1-14 Mita, Minato-ku; tel. 03/5232-4111; https://japan.embassy.gov.au; take Ōedo, Nanboku lines to Azabu-jūban Station, exit 2, or take Mita, Asakusa lines to Mita Station, exit A3) is open weekdays 9am-12:30pm and 1:30pm-5pm.

The New Zealand Embassy, Tokyo (20-40 Kamiyama-chō, Shibuya-ku; tel. 03/3467-2271; www.nzembassy.com/japan; take Chiyoda line to Yoyogi-kōen Station, exit 1) is open weekdays 9am-5:30pm.

The South African Embassy in Japan (Hanzōmon First Building 4F, 1-4 Kojimachi, Chiyoda-ku; tel. 03/3265-3366; www.sajapan.org; take Hanzōmon line to Hanzōmon Station, exit 3a) is open weekdays 9am-5:30pm.

USEFUL WEBSITES

Tokyo Cheapo (www.tokyocheapo.com) is a great resource packed with tips on how to make your yen go further in Tokyo.

TimeOut Tokyo (www.timeout.jp/en/tokyo) offers extensive listings of the best events, restaurants, bars, and more. Check the calendar for events that will be taking place when you're going to be in Tokyo. They also publish a free quarterly print edition.

Savvy Tokyo (https://savvytokyo.com) is a lifestyle website geared toward women living in Japan, operated by the same media outfit that runs Gaijinpot. Another solid resource.

Tokyo Art Beat (www.tokyoartbeat.com) is the best website for keeping tabs on happenings in Tokyo's art scene. There are extensive gallery and museum listings.

Go Tokyo (www.gotokyo.org/en) offers information on things to do, shopping, transportation, accommodations and just about anything else you'll need for your time in the capital.

Tokyo Dross (http://tokyodross.blogspot.jp) provides extensive gig listings with an underground bent. This is a source you should check out if you're keen to experience the best musical offerings in the city, from electronic to punk.

Tokyo Jazz Site (http://tokyojazzsite.com) is a fantastic website dedicated to exploring the capital's deep jazz scene, from old-school cafés with extraordinary sound systems to underground haunts well off the tourist path.

Getting There

AIR

Tokyo is served by Narita Airport (tel. 0476-34-8000; www.narita-airport.jp) and Haneda Airport (03/6428-0888; www.tokyo-airport-bldg.co.jp/en). Narita is about 60 km (37 mi) east of the city, and Haneda is south of the city near the Tokyo Bay. Haneda, Japan's busiest airport, is undeniably more convenient than Narita, but more international flights come and go from the latter.

Narita has three terminals, with **Terminals 1** and **2** handling international flights and **Terminal 3** catering to budget airlines. Be careful to confirm the right terminal for your departing flight; going to the wrong terminal can result in lost time, but don't panic. Free shuttle buses run between the three terminals every 15-30 minutes (7am-9:30pm), departing from the ground floor of each one. If anything is unclear, there are information desks with English-speaking staff all across the airport who can point you in the right direction.

Whether arriving via Narita or Haneda, if you plan to get to Tokyo by train, it may be worth sending your baggage to your destination in Tokyo via courier service, as navigating the trains with luggage can be challenging. Simply inquire about the nearest **luggage courier service** at an information desk if you don't see one. Signage is clear and in English. Ask the staff at the kiosk about how to send your baggage back to the airport on your return.

From Narita Airport

The trip into Tokyo from Narita by bus takes 1.5-2 hours, depending on traffic. By train, it takes 36-80 minutes, depending on your destination.

TRAIN

One of the simplest options for reaching Tokyo from the airport is the **Narita Express** (www.jreast.co.jp/e/nex; 7:45am-9:45pm daily; adults ¥3,070-3,250, roughly half for children). The Narita Express (N'EX) runs to a host of stations downtown, including Tokyo (1 hour), Shinjuku, Shibuya, Ikebukuro, and Shinagawa. All seats are reserved and can be purchased at an airport N'EX counter, with trains leaving approximately every 30 minutes. The best deal is the round-trip fare of ¥4,070 for adults, available to foreign travelers (must be used within two weeks).

The **Keisei Skyliner** (www.keisei.co.jp; 7:30am-10pm daily) is actually quicker than N'EX, but the destinations are more limited, with half-hourly trains making the roughly 40-minute trip to either Ueno or Nippori station. One-way tickets for both destinations are ¥2,520 and must be reserved at the Keisei ticket counter in Terminal 1 or 2. After arriving at either Ueno or Nippori, you'll then have the option of transferring to the JR Yamanote line. The Skyliner & Tokyo Subway Ticket that allows travelers to purchase a one-way or return ticket on the Skyliner along with receiving a subway pass for between one and three days. If your destination happens to be in the northeastern part of Tokyo, the Skyliner makes sense, but the N'EX offers easier access to other parts of the city.

For those on a tighter budget, the **Keisei Main line** (6:30am-10:30pm) offers a rapid train every 20 minutes (¥1,030) that takes about 65 minutes to reach Nippori and just over 70 minutes to reach Ueno at the northeastern corner of the JR Yamanote line. This line essentially takes the same path as the Skyliner, but makes extra stops. Another option offered by Keisei is the Narita Sky Access Express, (5:40am-11pm daily; ¥1,290-1,520), which runs every 40 minutes and follows the same route as the Keisei Main line, but veers southwest at Aoto Station and travels to Nihonbashi Station (59 minutes), Shimbashi (62 minutes), and Shinagawa (72 minutes), all of which are connected to the convenient Ginza line.

BUS

Taking the bus from Narita is straightforward, with tickets sold at counters in the arrivals hall. One of the most popular bus services is the **Airport Limousine Bus** (www.limousinebus.co.jp/en; ¥3,200 adults, ¥1,600 children), which runs at scheduled times to a number of major hotels and major train stations in the capital. The average journey takes around 1.5 hours, or a bit more in heavy traffic. Tickets can be purchased in all terminals, and most staff speak English. This service is particularly good for those staying at a hotel that is directly linked or closer to the Airport Limousine's route.

The **Keisei Bus Tokyo Shuttle** (www.keiseibus.co.jp/inbound/tokyoshuttle/en/; ¥1,000) is a good budget option. This service runs every 20 minutes 6am-11pm. Tickets are sold at the Keisei Bus Counter in the arrivals lobby in Terminals 1 and 2. The list of destinations isn't as extensive as it is for the Limousine Bus, but the price is lower and it gets the job done by taking passengers to Tokyo Station, Sukiyabashi crossing in the heart of Ginza, and Shinonomeshako in Koto-ku, east of Odaiba. Keisei buses also run from Tokyo Station to terminals 2 and 3 from 11pm-6am (¥2,000), though less frequently. Inquire at the ticket counter or check the website for more information.

One more option worth considering is **Access Narita** (tel. 0120-600-366; www.accessnarita.jp; 7:25am-10:45pm; ¥1,000 adults, ¥500 children 6-12, free for children 5 and under), which is available at all terminals and allows you to buy a ticket as you board the bus. The bus runs three times an hour and takes passengers to either Tokyo Station or Sukiyabashi crossing in Ginza. When you leave the airport, look for the blue sign for Access Narita and head there.

TAXI

Taking a taxi from Narita is, simply put, not economical. But if money is no object, you can take a cab at a fixed rate of ¥20,000-22,000, with a surcharge of 20 percent 10pm-5am, to most places in downtown Tokyo (60-90 minutes). Taxis from the airport can be paid with credit card. To catch a taxi, head to taxi stand no. 15, just outside Terminal 1, south exit S2. For more information, see www.narita-airport.jp/en/access/taxi.

From Haneda Airport

Although the city is closer to Haneda, many of the flights coming into the airport arrive late at night, which means trains into Tokyo may have already stopped running. The good news is that buses run late into the night from Haneda, and taxis are significantly more affordable than from Narita. By bus, the journey is 30-90 minutes, depending on traffic, and by train, it takes as little as 15 minutes.

TRAIN

Making the trip into Tokyo from Haneda Airport by train is a brief affair, with the **Tokyo Monorail Haneda Airport line** (www.tokyo-monorail.co.jp/english; 5am-midnight daily; ¥500 one-way) running local, rapid, and express service trains between Haneda Airport and JR Hamamatsucho Station on the southeastern side of the JR Yamanote line. Trains run every 5-10 minutes, and the ride to JR Hamamatsucho Station only takes about 15 minutes.

Another option is the **Keikyū Airport Express** (tel. 03/5789-8686; www.haneda-tokyo-access.com/en; 5:30am-midnight; ¥300-500), which stops at Haneda's domestic and international terminals. This train runs several times hourly to Shinagawa Station in about 15 minutes, and then some of the trains continue on along the Toei Asakusa subway line to stations such as Ginza and Asakusa. Shinagawa is a major hub, linked to the Yamaote line, among others.

BUS

The simplest bus option is the **Airport Limousine Bus** (www.limousinebus.co.jp/en; ¥950-1,250 adults depending on destination, half-price for children). Some of the hubs the bus links to include Shinjuku, Shibuya, Roppongi, and Ginza. Travel times are 20-90 minutes, depending on traffic and the distance of the destination. Late-night buses run to Shinjuku Bus Terminal (12:20am, 1am) and Shibuya Station (12:15am, 12:50am, 2:20am). Note that prices double midnight-5am.

TAXI

It's more reasonable to take a taxi from Haneda than from Narita Airport (though it's still not cheap), with taxis running to some of Tokyo's major hubs for ¥5,600 (to **Ginza**) at the lower end of the scale, up to ¥8,500 (to Ikebukuro) at the higher end. Note that a surcharge of 20 percent applies for all rides 10pm-5am. Taxis from the airport can be paid for with credit card. You can get a taxi at the first-floor curbside area, reachable by escalator from the arrival lobby on the second floor (www.haneda-airport.jp/inter/en/access/taxi.html).

TRAIN

Tokyo is by far the most connected city in Japan when it comes to train travel. There are three main train stations in the city that travelers arrive at when traveling by *shinkansen* (bullet train), which is the simplest, most pleasant, and most efficient way of reaching the city by train.

Tokyo Station is the final station for bullet trains traveling to the capital from all over the country, whether from Kyoto (average 2 hours 15 minutes; ¥14,170), Shin-Osaka (average 2.5 hours; ¥14,720), or Hiroshima (4 hours; ¥19,440). While it's possible to make the trip on a wide range of train types operating at the local level—local, express, rapid, limited express, etc.—in most cases, doing so will increase cost and complexity exponentially, with frequent transfers.

Shinagawa Station, on the south side of downtown, is one stop before Tokyo for bullet trains coming from Kyoto, Osaka, Hiroshima, Kyushu, and all other stops to the west. Meanwhile, the hub of Ueno on the northeast side of town, which also serves as a *shinkansen* terminal, receives trains coming from the northeast (Tohoku and Hokkaido) before they finally reach Tokyo.

Generally speaking, Tokyo Station is a safe bet for your terminus of choice, as the station is also linked to the Yamanote line, which runs in a loop around Tokyo's downtown, and the Chūō and Sōbu lines, which run east-west through the city, as well as the Marunouchi subway line. Ueno, serviced by the Yamanote, Hibiya, and Ginza lines, may be worth considering as your terminus if you're heading in the city's north or east,

and Shinagawa, on the Yamanote and Toei Asakusa line, may be a good pick if you're heading to somewhere in the city's south or west.

BUS

If you're arriving in Tokyo domestically by land, thanks to the JR Highway Bus (03/3844-1950; www.jrbuskanto.co.jp) and a few other highway bus companies you can travel between the capital and other major cities around Japan overnight for less than you'd pay for a train ticket. But you get what you pay for, as journeys are significantly prolonged on the road. Further, some buses have toilets, while others don't, although all make stops for restroom breaks.

JR Highway Bus terminals in Tokyo are located near the new south exit of Shinjuku Station (6:20am-midnight) and the Yaesu South Exit of Tokyo Station (6am-12:30am). As there's no easy English-language ticketing website for JR Highway Bus, your best bet is to inquire about tickets directly at the JR ticket window at one of these terminals.

Perhaps the most popular bus route into Tokyo is from Kyoto, from where JR operates night buses that depart daily, usually from midnight. The trip takes around 7.5 hours and costs ¥9,000-9,500. Another popular trip is from Osaka, which takes about 8 hours and costs ¥9,500-10,000.

Among the numerous private bus operators, discount player Willer Express (https://willerexpress.com/en), stands out, offering some trips between Tokyo and Kyoto or Osaka for as little as ¥3,000. On the website of Kosoku Bus (www.kosokubus.com/en), you'll find bus trips for as little as ¥2,800 (Osaka to Tokyo). The website allows you to search for and purchase tickets in English for a variety of routes and providers around the country.

Private operators often start and end journeys at terminals elsewhere in Tokyo, beyond the Shinjuku and Tokyo stations. Just be sure to know how to navigate to or from the departure or arrival point, wherever it is in the city, before setting off. Tokyo is a good jumping-off point for highway bus journeys to elsewhere in the country; to get a sense of the kinds of trips that can be taken from Shinjuku Station's bus terminal, for example, visit http://shinjuku-busterminal.co.jp/en/search.

Car

Renting a car might make sense for some journeys beyond the capital to or from more remote areas that may be less accessible by train. That said, rather than driving all the way to Tokyo from somewhere far-flung, a more likely scenario would be to drop off your rental car at the nearest major train hub, then simply go to Tokyo by rail.

Getting Around

Tokyo has, bar none, one of the best public transport systems of any major global city. Buses, trains, subway lines, and taxis shuttle millions around the city daily. There are also growing numbers of cyclists and plenty of people putting their drivers licenses to use, too. But for the vast majority of travelers, the city's vast network of above-ground trains and subway lines are sufficient for all of their transportation needs.

TRAIN

While Tokyo's train system can feel daunting, don't fret. It's actually not that difficult to navigate once you've grasped a few key things. For starters, the two most important above-ground JR lines (covered by the Japan Rail Pass) for most travelers will be the oval-shaped Yamanote line that runs around the core of the city, and the Chūō line that shoots directly through the Yamanote line, linking Tokyo's eastern and western suburbs. Key stations on the Yamanote line include Tokyo, Shinagawa, Shibuya, Shinjuku, and Ikebukuro, while major stations on the Chūō line, from east to west, include Tokyo, Shinjuku, and the western suburb of Mitaka. Most trains run roughly from around 5am to midnight, with some running a bit later than that.

There are a number of private lines that you may occasionally need to use to reach some more local stations. Some key ones to be aware of include the Keio-Inokashira line, which runs between Shibuya and Kichijōji with Shimokitazawa in between; the Tōkyū Tōyoko line, linking Shibuya to Daikanyama, Nakameguro, and, much farther along, Yokohama; the Odakyu line, which links Shinjuku to Shimokitazawa; and the Yurikamome line, which links Odaiba to the rest of downtown across Tokyo Bay. Again, the Suica or Pasmo can be used freely on these lines. Of course, you can also simply purchase a ticket too.

TICKETS

The easiest way to navigate different train and subway lines is by simply getting a Suica (www.jreast.co.jp/e) or Pasmo (www.pasmo.co.jp/en) card as soon as you begin to use Tokyo's public transport system, but it's also possible to buy paper tickets for these trains as you go. To do this, calculate your price based on the fare chart on the wall above ticket machines at all stations. Generally speaking, single fares within Tokyo for the JR lines range from ¥130 to around ¥390, with fares increasing if you ride beyond the bounds of Tokyo proper. If your route involves transferring to the subway or to other private lines, this will also raise the total fare. There will usually be an English-language station breakdown, but the easiest way to calculate fares is by planning ahead, using the website Hyperdia (www.hyperdia.com), which allows you to calculate rail fares anywhere in the country, including above-ground and subway lines, adjusting for date and either the intended time of departure or arrival.

If you plan on traveling heavily within the city for a day, using a mix of lines, the Tokyo Combination Ticket (www.jreast.co.jp/e/pass/tokyo_free.html; ¥1,590 adults, ¥800 children) allows unlimited travel for one calendar day on all 13 subway lines, all JR East lines (excluding those with reserved seats), the Nippori-Toneri Liner, Tokyo Toei streetcars, and even the Toei Bus system. This ticket can be purchased through the ticket machines at some JR East reserved-seat ticket machines, JR Ticket Offices (Midori no Madoguchi), and the JR EAST Travel Service Centers. This ticket can also be purchased at Tokyo Metro and Toei Subway stations, with some exceptions. Note that the ticket will not work outside Tokyo's core metropolitan area—it wouldn't cover travel to Mitaka, where the Ghibli Museum is.

SUBWAY

A total of 13 color-coded subway lines, operated by Tokyo Metro (www.tokyometro. jp/en) and Toei (www.kotsu.metro.tokyo.jp/eng), both government-run, crisscross the city. The fare for one-way journeys is ¥170-240 (¥90-120 for children) for Tokyo Metro lines, and ¥180-320 (¥90-160 for children) for Toei lines. Changing between lines operated by Tokyo Metro and Toei requires a special transfer ticket, which can be slightly complicated for the uninitiated. The easiest way to handle all the tricky transfers between different rail lines is by purchasing either a Suica (www.jreast.co.jp/e) from a JR ticket machine or a Pasmo (www.pasmo.co.jp/en) from a Tokyo Metro ticket machine. The subway runs roughly 5am-midnight.

While all of Tokyo's subway lines may prove useful to you, there are a handful that connect to the majority of locations you'll be most likely to visit. These include the Ginza line, which stops at Shibuya, Omotesandō, Ginza, Ueno, and Asakusa stations; the Marunouchi line (Shinjuku, Shinjuku-Gyōenmae, Ginza, and Tokyo); the Hibiya line (Nakameguro,

Ebisu, Roppongi, Ginza, Tsukiji, Akihabara, and Ueno); the Chiyoda line (Meiji-jingūmae and Omotesandō); Hanzōmon line (Shibuya, Omotesandō, Ōtemachi, and Oshiage); Fukutoshin line (Shinjuku Sanchōme, Meiji-jingūmae, and Shibuya); Toei-Ōedo line (Roppongi, Tsukijishijō, Ryōgoku, and Ueno-Okachimachi); and Toei-Shinjuku line (Shinjuku and Shinjuku Sanchōme). Note that a few subway lines continue on as a separate aboveground line once they reach the terminal stop.

If you'll be using the Tokyo Metro system heavily, it's worth looking into the Tokyo Metro 24-Hour Ticket (www.tokyometro. jp/en; ¥600 adults, ¥300 children). You can buy this ticket at any Tokyo Metro station and use it for unlimited travel on any Tokyo Metro line. For even greater access, including both the Tokyo Metro and Toei subway lines, there's also the Common One-Day Ticket for Tokyo Metro & Toei Subway Lines (www.tokyometro.jp/en; ¥900 adults, ¥450 children). This ticket allows unlimited travel on all subway lines for one calendar day, either on the day of purchase for a same-day ticket or for any day within six months of the date of purchase for the advance ticket option.

BUS

Bus stops dot every area of the city, with Toei (www.kotsu.metro.tokyo.jp/eng) buses linking every corner. No matter how far you ride, all fare is capped at ¥210 (¥110 for children). Simply hop aboard, drop your money (in coins) into the electronic box next to the driver's seat at the front of the bus and ride until your intended stop. If you've only got bills on hand, a machine that changes ¥1,000 notes is at the front of every bus, but you won't get any money back if you drop more than the required fare in coins into the box. While buses are plentiful and easy to use, the train and subway networks are so convenient that buses tend only to be necessary in special cases outside the city center where train lines may not reach.

BICYCLE

Tokyo's streets are mercifully safe thanks to drivers' conscientiousness. While you should be cognizant of pedestrians, sidewalks around town are generally considered acceptable places to navigate a bicycle, too. Some guesthouses and *ryokan* rent bikes to guests, and there are also a number of bike rental services around town.

Take a look at **Tokyobike Rentals Yanaka** (4-2-39 Yanaka Taitō-ku; tel. 03/5809-0980; https://tokyobikerentals. com; 10am-7pm Wed.-Mon.), a bicycle designer with a hipster bent located in Yanaka. Advance bookings are required via the website, which is bilingual, with a one-day rental priced at ¥3,000 and ¥1,500 for each extra day.

TAXI

Taxis in Tokyo are pricey, starting at ¥410 for the first 1.059 km (0.6 mi), after which the fare jumps ¥80 for each additional 237 meters (777 feet). A surcharge of 20 percent is often applied 10pm-5am. With rates like these, taxis rarely make economic sense unless you're splitting the fare with other passengers and not going too far. That said, they are an option for late-night rides after the train and subway lines stop running. The vast majority accept credit cards. There are a few taxi companies with English-speaking services,

including **MK Taxi** (03/5547-5547; www.to-kyomk.com) and **Nihon Kotsu** (03/5755-2336; www.nihon-kotsu.co.jp). For more information on taking taxis in Tokyo, see the website of the **Tokyo-Taxi Hire Association** (www.taxi-tokyo.or.jp).

CAR

Driving a car in Tokyo rarely makes sense due to the tricky network of one-way streets and significant difficulty and expense of parking. The excellent train and subway systems make driving unnecessary.

If you do plan to get around in a car, parking is only had at a premium, starting at ¥100-500 per 30 minutes, to upward of ¥2,800 for 12 hours, or more for 24 hours. The actual parking lots range from self-service lots to underground car parks, often attached to department stores or other large shops, and the very Japanese phenomenon of the parking tower, in which cars are mechanically lifted and lowered by attendants who effectively stack them in shelves.

You can find parking spaces and gauge the rates at www.parkme.com/tokyo-jp-parking. It's ill-advised to try and park beside the street if there is no parking meter present, as police sometimes patrol for illegally parked cars, and don't park in the lot of a restaurant or business where you're not actually a customer, which can result in a fine.

Between Tokyo and Kyoto

For visitors craving a break from the bustle of

Tokyo or the crowds of Kyoto, Japan's excellent public transport provides easy access to a number of destinations in between, perfectly suited for a day trip or an overnight stay.

Only 30 minutes from Tokyo by train to the south, the cosmopolitan port city of Yokohama offers a fascinating look into Japan's history. Near the scene of Commodore Perry's second arrival in 1854, the city rose as an international port as Japan opened itself to trade. The spirit of international exchange is strongly felt in its expansive Chinatown, too. After dark, the city's burgeoning craft beer and live jazz scenes offer the promise of a great night out.

For a dose of traditional culture and relaxation, head just south

Highlights

Look for ★ to find recommended sights, activities, dining, and lodging.

© MOON.COM

★ **Bar-Hopping in Yokohama:** Yokohama's accessible, low-key nightlife is mostly known for its craft beer and live jazz. Check out the neighborhoods of Kannai, Bashamichi, and Noge (page 166).

★ **Great Buddha at Kōtoku-in:** The temple of Kōtoku-in houses the famed bronze Daibutsu (Great Buddha), which stands 11.4 meters (37 feet) tall (page 173).

★ **Onsen in Hakone:** The Japanese have been enjoying a variety of *onsen* in the Hakone area since the 16th century (page 185).

★ **Views of Mount Fuji:** Japan's most sacred peak looms larger in the national psyche than perhaps any other mountain on earth (page 192).

Best Restaurants

★ **Araiya:** This is the place to sample Yokohama's famed beef hot pot, a fixture of the city's culinary scene since the Meiji period (page 165).

★ **Tsuruya:** This mom-and-pop shop has served broiled eel on rice since 1929 and was once a favorite of Nobel Prize-winning novelist Yasunari Kawabata, who lived nearby (page 178).

★ **Sanrokuen:** Diners occupy cushions on the wooden floor, grilling skewers of meat, seafood, and mountain vegetables over a sunken hearth at this countryside gem near Lake Kawaguchi (page 199).

of Yokohama to the beachside town of Kamakura, Japan's first feudal capital. The earthy town has lovely seaside views and is dotted with temples, including Kōtoku-in, which houses the famed bronze Daibutsu (Great Buddha). The town is surrounded by green hills lined with hiking trails.

For spectacular views of Mount Fuji, take a train about two hours west of Tokyo and three hours from Kyoto to the countryside town of Hakone, nestled in the beautiful Fuji-Hakone-Izu National Park. Here, you can book a room in a *ryokan*, peruse art museums in lush outdoor settings, and soak in an *onsen*. But to get up close and personal with Mount Fuji itself, official climbing season runs from July through August. Or bask in the mountain's presence from the comfort of a hot spring near the Fuji Five Lakes, which form an arc around Mount Fuji's northern base. Among them, Lake Kawaguchi is an accessible, pristine vantage point with a wealth of excellent hotels built for the sole purpose of relaxing within close range of the almost perfectly symmetrical peak.

ORIENTATION

Yokohama and **Kamakura**, both in Kanagawa Prefecture, lie to the south of Tokyo and are within commuting distance from the city. Moving farther south/southwest, **Fuji-Hakone-Izu National Park** (富士箱根伊

豆国立公園; www.fujihakoneizu.com) covers 1,227 square km (474 square mi) and comprises **Hakone, Fuji Five Lakes,** and **Mount Fuji** itself. The park spreads across parts of three prefectures: Yamanashi, Shizuoka, and Kanagawa.

PLANNING YOUR TIME

If your trip is largely confined to Tokyo, you don't need to go too far to get a well-rounded taste of what Japan has to offer. **Yokohama** is only 30 minutes to the south of Tokyo by train, and **Kamakura** is only another 30 minutes south from there. Both cities are easy day trips, and neither requires an overnight stay. Yokohama tends to be somewhat busy any day of the week, while the pace of Kamakura shifts from relatively sleepy on weekdays to boisterous and oftentimes overcrowded on weekends, with beaches filling up from the second half of June through the first half of September. Plan accordingly, avoiding the weekends if possible.

Venturing slightly farther, on a long day trip from Tokyo, it's possible to visit the **Mount Fuji** and **Fuji Five Lakes region.** But to really soak up the experience, an overnight stay is recommended. The return trip is enough to exhaust a seasoned traveler. And at least in the case of the Fuji Five Lakes region, which is geared toward downtime, rushing back to the hubbub of Tokyo defeats the

Previous: Mount Fuji; Great Buddha at Kōtoku-in; private room at Hakone Yuryō Onsen.

Between Tokyo and Kyoto

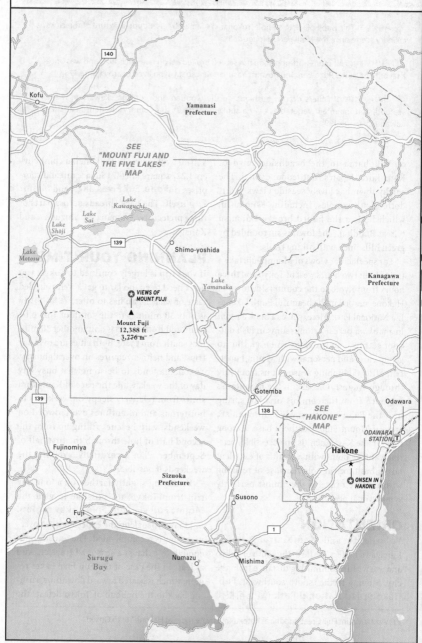

140

Kofu

Yamanasi
Prefecture

SEE
"MOUNT FUJI AND
THE FIVE LAKES"
MAP

Lake
Kawaguchi

Lake
Sai

Lake
Shōji

Lake
Motosu

139

Shimo-yoshida

Kanagawa
Prefecture

Lake
Yamanaka

⭐ VIEWS OF
MOUNT FUJI

▲
Mount Fuji
12,388 ft
3,776 m

Gotemba

139

138

SEE
"HAKONE"
MAP

Odawara

ODAWARA
STATION

Hakone

⭐ ONSEN IN
HAKONE

Fujinomiya

Sizuoka
Prefecture

Susono

1

Fuji

Suruga
Bay

Numazu

Mishima

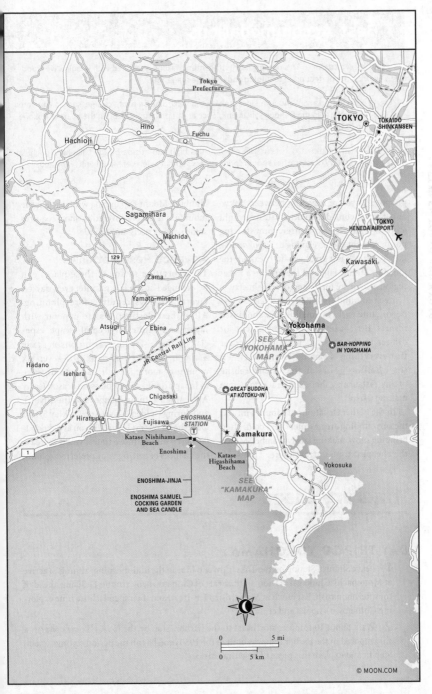

Best Accommodations

★ **Fukuzumiro:** This dreamy late-19th-century Hakone gem filled with imaginative wood-work is the perfect place to unplug and recharge (page 188).

★ **Gōra Kadan:** Wander the incense-scented halls, dine on haute cuisine, soak in a private bath, and bask in the tranquil sylvan ambience at this premium *ryokan* in the heart of Hakone (page 188).

★ **Shuhokaku Kogetsu:** The *onsen* at this high-end escape beside Lake Kawaguchi, a *sakura* (cherry blossom) hot spot in spring, offers stunning views of Mount Fuji (page 200).

purpose. If you're traveling between Tokyo and Kyoto, consider making an overnight stop in Hakone, no matter your starting point. A night spent relaxing at a *ryokan* in a hot spring tub is a great way to break up the journey. Mount Fuji and the Fuji Five Lakes region also make for a good overnight stay.

Keep in mind that many businesses close down quite early in small towns and *onsen* resorts. It's not uncommon to step out for dinner in the early evening and discover that everything is closed. Be sure to check the opening hours on the official website of any restaurant, shop, or attraction before making a trip.

In the higher elevations of Mount Fuji and the surrounding area, winters very cold, often bringing snow, making late November-March the cheapest time to travel here. That said,

climbing Mount Fuji during winter when the mountain is deeply covered in snow requires some serious skills and a guide.

Advance Reservations

Transportation to any of these places can be arranged at the last minute, even day-of. Overnight stays require more planning. All of these destinations are popular with Japanese urbanites in need of escape, especially Hakone. Try to arrange *onsen* stays as far in advance as possible—even six months or more. *Ryokan* reservations spike in Japan around cherry blossom season (early Apr.), when autumn foliage pops (mid-Nov.), and during Golden Week (Apr. 29-May 5) and Obon holidays (mid-Aug.). If you avoid popular *onsen* during those times, you'll increase the chances of getting your preferred room.

Itinerary Ideas

DAY TRIP TO YOKOHAMA

1 Leave Shibuya Station on the Tōkyū Toyoko Line in the mid-morning, aiming to arrive at Motomachi-Chūkagai Station, in the heart of Chinatown, by around 11:30am, ahead of the afternoon rush. Eat lunch at Manchinro Honten, and then spend a little time exploring Chinatown's nooks and crannies.

2 Walk about 10 minutes northeast to the harbor. Stop by the NYK Hikawa Maru, a ship moored in the harbor that was built in the 1930s and has all the period stylings intact. Step in and explore this piece of maritime history.

3 To learn more about Yokohama and its long engagement with the West, walk about 10 minutes northwest, staying near the harbor, to the **Yokohama Archives of History.**

4 Next, in the futuristic Minato Mirai area, visit the quirky **Cupnoodles Museum,** where you can direct the creation of your own one-off cup of noodles yourself for a nominal fee of ¥400.

5 Personalized Cupnoodles in hand, ascend to the observation deck atop nearby **Landmark Tower** for sweeping views over the city and harbor.

6 As dinnertime starts to approach, choose **Araiya,** a great spot to try Yokohama's spin on beef hot pot, located near Minato Mirai.

7 Go on a bar crawl through Yokohama's lively nightlife districts. **Yokohama Bay Brewing Kannai** is a great place to start.

DAY TRIP TO KAMAKURA

On this full day of temple-hopping, plan to get an early start and eat breakfast at your hotel, so you can jump right in.

1 Begin your exploration of Kamakura in the north side of town, starting from **Kita-Kamakura Station.** Aim to arrive by around 9:30-10am.

2 Walk about 6 minutes west of the station to the temple of Jōchi-ji. After exploring the temple's grounds and slowing down to Kamakura time, find the entrance to the **Daibutsu Hiking Course,** located next to the temple grounds. Follow the well-marked course, passing a number of small temples and shrines like the atmospheric Zeniarai Benten, tucked away in the forested hills around the seaside town.

3 You'll know you've reached the end of the hiking course when you reach the temple of **Kōtoku-in,** which houses the famed Daibutsu, or Great Buddha, statue, after which the trail is named.

4 After admiring the 90-ton spectacle, walk 10 minutes south to **Hase-dera,** a temple known for its 11-faced 9-meter-tall (30-foot-tall) wooden visage of Kannon, goddess of mercy.

5 From here, head to nearby **Good Mellows** for a satisfying burger.

6 After eating lunch, walk to Hase Station, on the Enoden train line. Ride this local railway to Kamakura Station, then stroll along the famed shopping street of Komachi-dōri, alert for any interesting shops that may catch your eye. Proceed until the end of the street, where you'll reach the entrance to **Tsurugaoka Hachiman-gū.** This shrine, which sits atop a cliff overlooking the ocean, is dedicated to the god of war, Hachiman, serving as a reminder of Kamakura's deeply martial past.

7 To see a magical bamboo grove, walk about 20 minutes deeper into the eastern part of town to the temple of **Hōkoku-ji.**

8 For dinner, return to the center of town to try Japan's unique spin on curry at the nostalgic greasy spoon **Caraway Curry House.**

Itinerary Ideas

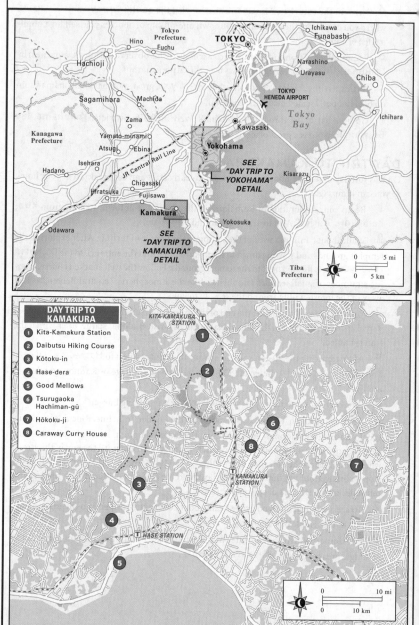

DAY TRIP TO KAMAKURA

1. Kita-Kamakura Station
2. Daibutsu Hiking Course
3. Kōtoku-in
4. Hase-dera
5. Good Mellows
6. Tsurugaoka Hachiman-gū
7. Hōkoku-ji
8. Caraway Curry House

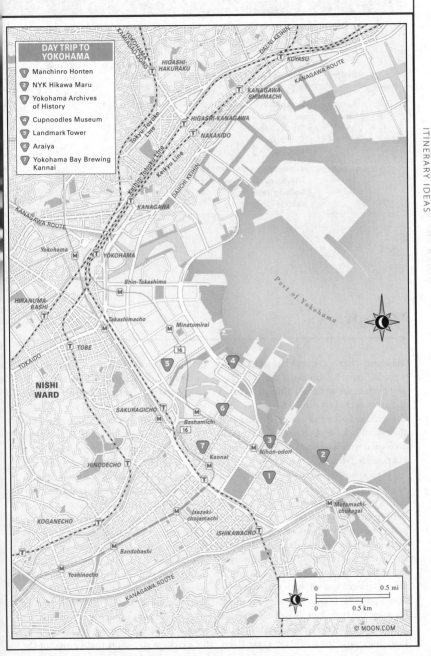

DAY TRIP TO YOKOHAMA

1 Manchinro Honten
2 NYK Hikawa Maru
3 Yokohama Archives of History
4 Cupnoodles Museum
5 Landmark Tower
6 Araiya
7 Yokohama Bay Brewing Kannai

Port of Yokohama

NISHI WARD

HIGASHI-HAKURAKU
KOYASU
KANAGAWA ROUTE
KANAGAWA SHIMMACHI
HIGASHI-KANAGAWA
NAKAKIDO
KANAGAWA
YOKOHAMA
Yokohama
Shin-Takashima
HIRANUMA-BASHI
Takashimacho
Minatomirai
TOBE
TOKAIDO
SAKURAGICHO
Bashamichi
HINODECHO
Kannai
Nihon-odori
Motomachi-chukagai
KOGANECHO
Isazaki-chojamachi
ISHIKAWACHO
Bandobashi
Yoshinocho
KANAGAWA ROUTE

DAINI KEIHIN
YOKOHAMA-KAMASAC-DORO
Tokyu-Toyoko Line
Keihin-Tohoku Line
Keikyu Line
DAIICHI KEIHIN
KANAGAWA ROUTE

0   0.5 mi
0   0.5 km

© MOON.COM

Where to Go from Tokyo and Kyoto

When traveling in this region, Nozomi *shinkansen* are often the quickest way to get from place to place, but note that these trains are not covered by the JR Pass, while Hikari and Kodama trains are.

Destination	Why Go?	Getting There from Tokyo	Getting There from Kyoto	How Long to Stay
Yokohama	cosmopolitan port history, jazz scene, Japan's largest Chinatown, craft beer	Train: 20-40 minutes, ¥280-570	Train: 2-2.5 hours, ¥12,980-13,300	Half-day-one day
Kamakura	Zen temples, hills, forested walking trails, seaside views	Train: 45 minutes-1 hour, ¥730-940	Train: 2-2.5 hours, ¥13,300	One day

Yokohama 横浜

Yokohama, Japan's second-largest city with a population of 3.7 million, is one of the biggest ports in the world. It's ultimately part of the urban sprawl emanating from Tokyo, but has a relaxed pace and a sense of space that the capital lacks, with its panoramic bayside views and wide avenues. Yokohama is lively but rarely feels frantic or overwhelming, making it an appealing escape for an afternoon or evening.

In a word, Yokohama is cosmopolitan. This defining trait is inseparable from the city's past as the entry point for Commodore Perry's black ships, which heralded the end of Japan's 250-year period of self-isolation and the signing of the Kanagawa Treaty in Yokohama in 1854. Declared one of Japan's five international ports in 1858, Yokohama became a booming silk trade hub, as well as a channel for foreign technology and ideas during the powerfully transformative Meiji period. It was the home of Japan's first brewery, bakery, and ice cream shop. Sakuragichō Station, still in service, was the terminus of Japan's first train, which ran to Shinbashi in Tokyo.

Remnants of Yokohama's legacy are visible throughout the city today, from its Port Museum and the moored Nippon Maru ship to graceful 19th-century Victorian homes in affluent hillside neighborhoods, where early foreign residents did their best to make themselves feel at home. The city's melting-pot heritage is also evident in the meandering lanes of dumpling shops, temples, and teahouses of its Chinatown, Japan's largest and a great place to dine. Other dining hot spots include the areas of Kannai, Bashamichi, and Noge: boozy neighborhoods infused with faded Shōwa-period (1925-1989) charm. A number of craft beer pubs in these areas make for a great night of bar-hopping, rounded out by the excellent jazz clubs that opened in the

Destination	Why Go?	Getting There from Tokyo	Getting There from Kyoto	How Long to Stay
Hakone	*onsen* hot spring resorts, swanky *ryokan*, quality museums, scenic views	Train: 90 minutes, ¥2,330	Train: 2 hours, ¥12,100	Overnight
Mount Fuji	views of one of the world's most famous mountains, bucket list hikes, dazzling sunrises and sunsets	Train: 2.5 hours, ¥2,380 Bus: 1.5 hours, ¥2,000	Train and bus: 4 hours, ¥13,400 Bus: 9.5 hours, ¥6,600	One day–overnight
Fuji Five Lakes	great photographs of Mount Fuji, fun and relaxation by Lake Kawaguchi	Train: 2.5 hours, ¥2,500 Bus: 1 hour 40 minutes, ¥2,000	Train and bus: 4 hours, ¥13,400 Bus: 9.5 hours, ¥6,600	One day–overnight

decades following its rebirth from the ashes of World War II.

But Yokohama is far from being stuck in the past. The future-facing bayside development Minato Mirai 21, smack in the middle of downtown, looms large in the city's image today. But wander away from the harbor, and historic alleys remain.

ORIENTATION

Compared to Tokyo, most of Yokohama's highly walkable streets are mercifully uncrowded. The main entry point into the city is Yokohama Station, located at the northern side of town, with the modern bayside development of Minato Mirai and the adjacent human-made island of Shinkō to the southeast.

South of the Minato Mirai area, which includes Shinkō, and running roughly parallel with the bay, is the wide boulevard of Nihon-ōdōri, once the key roadway of Yokohama. Continuing eastward, the bay leads to the waterfront park of Yamashita-Kōen, with neighboring Chinatown (Motomachi-Chūkagai) to the southwest. South of Chinatown is the charming shopping district of Motomachi, where much of Yokohama's foreign population lived in the 19th century; many of the city's pioneering foreign residents are buried in the Yokohama Foreign General Cemetery. Overlooking it all is Yamate, a historic district full of 19th-century buildings atop a bluff just south of Motomachi.

Heading northwest of Yamate, either on foot (20 minutes) or one stop on the train from Ishikawachō Station (10 minutes' walk northwest of Yamate) on the Negishi line, you'll arrive at the southern edge of the neighborhoods of Kannai, Bashamichi, about 5 minutes' walk northeast of Kannai and south of the Ōka River; and Noge, a rambling nightlife zone on the north bank of the river. All these zones are packed with great options for eating and drinking. Other useful public transport hubs in this area are Sakuragichō Station, on the Negishi line and the blue subway line. West of Noge is Hinodechō Station, on the Keikyū line.

Yokohama

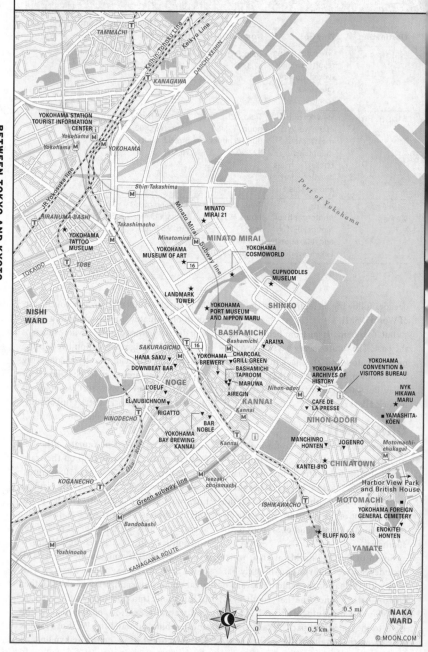

TAMMACHI

Keihin-Tohoku Line
Keikyu Line
DAICHI KEIHIN

KANAGAWA

YOKOHAMA STATION
TOURIST INFORMATION
CENTER
Yokohama
Yokohama
YOKOHAMA

JR Yokosuke Line

Shin-Takashima

Port of Yokohama

MINATO
MIRAI 21

HIRANUMA-BASHI

Takashimacho
Minato Mirai Subway line

YOKOHAMA
TATTOO
MUSEUM

Minatomirai
MINATO MIRAI

YOKOHAMA
COSMOWORLD

TOKAIDO
TOBE

YOKOHAMA
MUSEUM OF ART
16

CUPNOODLES
MUSEUM

NISHI
WARD

LANDMARK
TOWER

YOKOHAMA
PORT MUSEUM
AND NIPPON MARU

SHINKO

BASHAMICHI
Bashamichi

16
SAKURAGICHO

ARAIYA

HANA SAKU
DOWNBEAT BAR

YOKOHAMA
BREWERY

CHARCOAL
GRILL GREEN

YOKOHAMA
ARCHIVES OF
HISTORY

YOKOHAMA
CONVENTION &
VISITORS BUREAU

L'OEUF

BASHAMICHI
TAPROOM
MARUWA

Nihon-odori

NYK
HIKAWA
MARU

NOGE

EL NUBICHNOM

AIREGIN

CAFE DE
LA PRESSE

YAMASHITA-
KOEN

RIGATTO

KANNAI
Kannai

NIHON-ODORI

HINODECHO

BAR
NOBLE

YOKOHAMA
BAY BREWING
KANNAI

Kannai

MANCHINRO
HONTEN

JOGENRO

Motomachi-
chukagai

KOGANECHO

Isezaki-
chojamachi

KANTEI-BYO

CHINATOWN

To
Harbor View Park
and British House

Green subway line

ISHIKAWACHO

MOTOMACHI

Bandobashi

YOKOHAMA FOREIGN
GENERAL CEMETERY

ENOKITEI
HONTEN

Yoshinocho

BLUFF NO. 18

YAMATE

KANAGAWA ROUTE

0   0.5 mi

0   0.5 km

NAKA
WARD

© MOON.COM

SIGHTS
Minato Mirai and Shinkō
みなとみらい, 新港

Minato Mirai 21 (http://minatomirai21.com) is an ambitious urban development next to the bay in downtown Yokohama, including a smattering of shops, restaurants, museums, hotels, one of Japan's highest observation decks, and even a small amusement park. In this "harbor of the future," as its name literally means, you'll find the bulk of the structures that make up Yokohama's skyline.

As you'll notice from the high perch of Landmark Tower, development has spilled across a small inlet to Shinkō, an artificial island containing restaurants, shops, and more.

YOKOHAMA PORT MUSEUM AND NIPPON MARU
横浜みなと博物館、帆船日本丸

2-1-1 Minato Mirai, Naka-ku; tel. 045/221-0280; www.nippon-maru.or.jp; 10am-5pm Tues.-Sun., closed on Tues. when Mon. is a holiday; adults ¥600, children ¥300; take JR Negishi line, Yokohama Subway line to Sakuragichō Station

While Yokohama does have a cultured side, in truth the city is more mercantile than avant-garde. To get a sense of its role as a center of maritime commerce, visit the Yokohama Port Museum. While the museum may feel slightly dry if you're not a history buff, the accompanying tour of the anchored 1930 ship, the Nippon Maru, is worth the price of admission. Originally launched as a training vessel for officers of the merchant marine, the elegant ship was then used for training during World War II, and as a transport ship following the war. Its history comes alive as you amble along the deck and through its halls. At 97 meters (318 feet) long, the ship is quite a sight when its sails are raised.

LANDMARK TOWER
ランドマークタワー

2-2-1 Minato Mirai, Nishi-ku; tel. 045/222-5015; www.yokohama-landmark.jp

The 296-meter-high (971-foot-high) Landmark Tower is worth a visit for its Sky Garden (69F The Landmark Tower Yokohama; tel. 045/222-5030; www.yokohama-landmark.jp/skygarden/web/english; 10am-9pm (last entry 8:30pm) Sun.-Fri., 10am-10pm (last entry 9:30pm) Sat. and summer holidays; adults ¥1,000, elementary and junior high students ¥500, high school students and over 65 ¥800, children over 4 years old ¥200). At 273 meters (895 feet) above the ground, this observation deck is the best place to survey the development, as well as views of Mount Fuji and Tokyo when the sky is clear. The elevator, which climbs at a speed of 750 meters (2,460 feet) per minute, ensures that the ride to the top is fun, too.

YOKOHAMA MUSEUM OF ART
横浜美術館

3-4-1 Minato Mirai, Nishi-ku; tel. 045/221-0300; http://yokohama.art.museum/eng/index.html; 10am-6pm Fri.-Wed.; adults ¥500, university and high school students ¥300, free for children under 12; take Minato Mirai line to Minato Mirai Station, exit 3

A showcase of contemporary art and photography, the Yokohama Museum of Art is another one of Minato Mirai 21's major draws. The space features Western and Japanese artists, with exhibitions ranging from conservative to groundbreaking (check the schedule). As an added bonus, the building was designed by Pritzker Prize winner Tange Kenzo—something worth appreciating as you pass through the rays of natural light beaming into the courtyard entrance from a soaring skylight. At the time of writing, the museum was operating on a timed admission system to combat coronavirus spread, requiring a reservation.

YOKOHAMA COSMOWORLD
横浜コスモワールド

2-8-1 Shinkō, Naka-ku; tel. 045/641-6591; http://cosmoworld.jp; 11am-9pm Mon.-Fri., 11am-10pm Sat.-Sun.; most rides ¥300-800; take Minato Mirai line to Minato Mirai Station, exit 3, or JR Negishi line, Yokohama Subway line to Sakuragichō Station

The most notable point of interest on Shinkō island, a human-made addition to Yokohama's

Yokohama Tattoo Museum and Japan's Relationship with Ink

From ocean waves rolling over an arm to a flamboyant tiger on one's back, Japanese tattoos, or *irezumi* (literally "insert ink"), are among the most sought-after styles among ink aficionados. A traditional Japanese tattoo calls for a major commitment of time and money, potentially involving tens of thousands of dollars and continuous weekly visits for as long as five years. The artist and client hold ongoing discussions about the design, and the master has the right to refuse service.

When this dance is carried to its conclusion, a full-body suit covers the arms, legs, chest, and back—only ending in places where clothing stops. There are complex social reasons for this. While tattoos are a matter of fashion in the West, and foreign enthusiasts may clamor for a place under the needle of a great master, the art is weighed down by taboo in Japan—an irony, given its deep history with the art.

THE TATTOO TABOO

In the ancient past, Okinawan women tattooed their hands with talismans and shamanic symbols using a blend of ink and the island's very own firewater, *awamori*. Japan's indigenous Ainu people have an ancient tradition of using soot from the fireside to mark their faces and arms with designs intended to ward off evil spirits and ensure safe passage into the afterlife. The modern tattoo tradition took root on the islands more recently, during the Edo period (1603-1868), in the red-light zones of Edo and Osaka. During this period, the motifs we think of as "Japanese" today began to emerge. The explosion of woodblock prints (*ukiyo-e*) in the art world grew hand in hand with tattooing.

Although the art form was strictly banned, members of the underclass, from dock workers to firefighters and palanquin bearers, proudly rebelled and got inked in droves. The *yakuza* (mafia) got inked as well, fueled by the belief that tatting up—painful, permanent—took courage, loyalty, and, as a bonus, disregard for the law. Furthermore, the cost accrued from a full-body suit came to be viewed as a signifier of financial success. To learn more, check out *Japanese Tattoos: History, Culture, Design*, by Brian Ashcraft (with Hori Benny).

This historical mix of reasons took hold in the public's imagination, and the art form still has never achieved social acceptability. Even today, tattooing remains a very private affair, done discretely and by appointment only. Most *onsen* and fitness centers still ban those sporting ink.

YOKOHAMA TATTOO MUSEUM

1-11-7 Hiranuma, Nishi-ku; tel. 045/323-1073; www.ne.jp/asahi/tattoo/horiyoshi3; noon-6pm Wed.-Mon.; ¥1,000; take Keikyū line for Kanazawa-Bunko to Tobe station

The Yokohama Tattoo Museum, run by legendary master Horiyoshi III and his wife, is an excellent place to go for a nuanced view of the rich history and impressive level of skill that goes into this art form. The cramped space is positively overflowing with tools of the trade and related memorabilia. Note that the museum is closed on the 1st, 10th, and 20th of every month.

waterfront, is Yokohama Cosmoworld, a small but lively amusement park famed for the **Cosmo Clock 21,** a Ferris wheel that stands 112.5 meters (369 feet) above the crowds and has a massive clock plastered to its side. One rotation on the ride, which was the world's tallest Ferris wheel when it opened, takes 15 minutes and offers stunning views of the city below. It's an ideal attraction if you're traveling with kids.

CUPNOODLES MUSEUM
カップヌードルミュージアム

2-3-4 Shinkō, Naka-ku; tel. 045/345-0918; www. cupnoodles-museum.jp; 10am-6pm Wed.-Mon., closed Wed. if Tues. is holiday; take Minato Mirai line to Minato Mirai Station, exit 3, or JR Negishi line, Yokohama Subway line to Sakuragichō Station

Also in the Shinkō district, the Cupnoodles

1: Cupnoodles Museum **2:** Yokohama Chinatown

Museum is a surprisingly inspirational ode to the humble instant meal, a staple among college students worldwide. Following a sleek visual presentation, including a short animated film on creator Momofuku Ando, the inventor of instant noodles and how he overcame adversity and created a new industry, you can oversee the creation of your own signature noodle variety for a nominal fee (¥400), including the packaging and toppings. With advance reservations, you can even learn to knead your own instant noodles. This is another fun option for those traveling with kids. At the time of writing, the museum was operating on a timed admission system to fight the spread of coronavirus. Check the website for details.

Nihon-ōdōri
日本大通り

Heading south of Minato Mirai and Shinkō brings you to the roughly northeast-southwest avenue of Nihon-ōdōri. This historic thoroughfare was once the heart of Yokohama, reflected in some of the grand architecture seen in the buildings, some of which date to the 19th century. Sitting at the northeast edge of this avenue is the **Yokohama Archives of History.** Running alongside the harbor just east of this historic street is the waterfront park of **Yamashita-Kōen,** with the **NYK Hikawa Maru,** a 1930s-era ship that has all the period fixings intact and can be entered and explored.

YOKOHAMA ARCHIVES OF HISTORY
横浜開港資料館

3 Nihon-ōdōri, Naka-ku, Yokohama; tel. 045/201-2100; www.kaikou.city.yokohama.jp/ en/index.html; 9:30am-5pm Tues.-Sun., closed Tues. if Mon. is holiday; adults ¥200, children ¥100; take Minatomirai line to Nihon-odori Station, exit 3

This one's for the history buffs. If you want to get a sense of what Japan was like when it was first opening up to the wider world after the arrival of Commodore Perry's black ships, the Yokohama Archives of History museum

includes more than 200,000 artifacts from that pivotal historical time, up through the beginning of the Showa period (1926-1989). Maps, newspaper clippings, photographs, prints, models of ships, and more allow you to peer into Yokohama's past.

Adding to the museum's historical significance is the fact that it is situated in the same building where the Treaty of Kanagawa was signed between the shogunate and the U.S. government on March 31, 1854, bringing an end to Japan's 250-year lockdown. One tree in the museum's inner courtyard is supposedly an offspring of the incense tree seen in many sketches of Perry's dramatic arrival at that very spot.

NYK HIKAWA MARU
日本郵船氷川丸

Yamashita-kōen, Naka-ku; tel. 045/641-4362; https:// hikawamaru.nyk.com; 10am-5pm Tues.-Sun., closed on Tues. if Mon. is holiday; adults ¥300, children ¥100; take Minato Mirai line to Motomachi-Chūkagai Station

The city's other grand vessel from the decadent 1930s is docked on the east side of Yamashita-Kōen. Among the distinguished passengers who traveled aboard the ship in its heyday, when it traversed the Pacific, was Charlie Chaplin. For a small fee, you can roam through its cabins and salons, inspect its engine room, saunter along its deck, and enter its bridge to see where it was commanded.

Chinatown
横浜中華街

As with many port cities, Yokohama is home to a bustling Chinatown. Just as the city became one of Japan's first ports to welcome foreign trade, many Chinese were seeking to escape political turmoil found a home here. Among the Chinese who wound up in Yokohama were those who fled Shanghai after the Opium War, finding a new life as go-betweens who helped Western merchants navigate the tricky waters of Japan's unfamiliar business customs.

Yamate Walk

Begin this 1.8-km (1.1-mi), 35-minute walk through this charming, historic hillside neighborhood known as "the Bluff" by trundling 500 meters (1,640 feet) uphill from Motomachi-Chūkagai Station until you reach the scenic **Harbor View Park** (114 Yamate-chō, Naka-ku; tel. 045/671-3648; 24 hours daily; free). This lofty park sits at Yamate's eastern end.

- After admiring the sweeping views of the bustling bay, walk 2 minutes west, heading toward the heart of the neighborhood. Drop into **British House** (115-3 Yamate-chō, Naka-ku; tel. 045/623-7812; www.hama-midorinokyokai.or.jp/yamate-seiyoukan/british-house/#; 9:30am-5pm daily, closed 4th Wed. of month or next day if Wed. falls on holiday; free). This classic house, built in 1937 to serve as the residence of the British consul, is beside a rose garden that blooms April-June, then again in October and November.

- Continue your walk into this formerly well-heeled side of town, once home to a buzzing expat community, by paying your respects at the **Yokohama Foreign General Cemetery** (96 Yamate-chō, Naka-ku; tel. 045/622-1311; www.yfgc-japan.com). Although this graveyard is normally closed, if you happen to be in the area either from February-July or September-December on a Saturday, Sunday, or national holiday, drop by between noon and 4pm and give a donation of ¥200-300 to enter the grounds. Whether you enter the cemetery proper or not, there are sweeping views from there over Yokohama's downtown.

- Leaving the cemetery, walk south along Yamate-hondōri for about 3 minutes until you reach **Enokitei Honten** (89-6 Yamatechō, Naka-ku; tel. 045/623-2288; www.enokitei.co.jp; 11am-7pm (last order 6:30pm) Tues.-Sun.; from ¥600; take Keikyū line to Hinodechō Station, then walk 3 minutes east). If you're feeling like dessert, a caffeine break, or even a light lunch, this nostalgic café set in the former home of an American prosecutor sits in the heart of Yamate.

- Continue west along Yamate-hondōri another 10 minutes, then turn right and proceed to **Bluff No. 18** (16 Yamate-chō, Naka-ku; tel. 045/662-6318; www.hama-midorinokyokai.or.jp/yamate-seiyoukan/bluff18; 9:30am-5pm daily, open until 6pm Jul.-Aug., closed 2nd Wed. of month or next day if Wed. falls on national holiday; free), once the home of a local Catholic priest, moved to its current location in 1992.

Chinatown, or Yokohama Chūkagai, remains vital in part thanks to China's ascent in recent decades. Stores hawk a mix of items, from touristy trinkets to lanterns and tea. Its main draw is its sheer energy and some 200 eateries, which generate a steady flow of foot traffic, especially on weekends.

KANTEI-BYŌ
关帝庙

140 Yamashita-chō, Naka-ku; tel. 045/226-2636; www.yokohama-kanteibyo.com; 9am-7pm daily; free; take Minato Mirai line to Motomachi-Chūkagai Station, or JR Negishi line to Ishikawachō Station

Kantei-byō is a temple dedicated to Guan Yu, a Han war general from China's Three Kingdoms period who is now seen as a guardian of wealth, making the temple a spiritual haven among businesses owners in the area. Facing the temple's opulent gate, you'll notice the dragons on its roof and the hanging red lanterns. Walk up the first set of steps, lined with stone dragons, past two guardian dogs, and up another staircase to the main hall. Inside, under a ceiling festooned with myriad shimmering golden ornaments, Guan Yu is powerfully seated at the center, ready to help the finances of the faithful. If you draw a straight line from Chinatown's main north and south gates, as well as between the main east and west gates, Kantei-byō lies at the intersection of these two lines: Feng Shui is in full effect, maximizing the power of this sacred spot to boost the neighborhood's bottom line.

ENTERTAINMENT AND EVENTS

GREAT JAPAN BEER FESTIVAL YOKOHAMA

www.beertaster.org; usually held on two or three days in mid-Apr. and mid-Sept.; ¥5,000 for unlimited tasting ticket

This massive beer festival, popularly known as BeerFest Yokohama, attracts the most crowds of any locale to host this annual celebration of all things hoppy. The focus is firmly on Japanese craft beers, although some imports do make an appearance. All told, a few hundred tipples are on tap across the city. Check the website for additional details.

YOKOHAMA JAZZ PROMENADE

tel. 045/211-1510; http://jazzpro.jp/english; first full weekend of early Oct., performances 9am-10pm; one-day ticket ¥5,000 adults, ¥1,000 junior high and high school students, free for primary school students and younger

Japan's biggest jazz festival, Yokohama Jazz Promenade transforms the port city into one giant stage. Jazz bands from Japan and abroad jam in the streets, in the city's numerous jazz clubs, and at large venues like Minatomirai Hall, Yokohama Kannai Hall, and Motomachi's main shopping street, among many others. See the website for a schedule and information about getting tickets.

PARKS

YAMASHITA-KŌEN

山下公園

279 Yamashita-chō, Naka-ku; tel. 045/671-3648; www.city.yokohama.lg.jp/kurashi/machizukuri-kankyo/midori-koen/koen/koen/daihyoteki/kouen008.html; 24 hours daily; free

This bustling park features a broad waterside promenade with open views of the bay, where ships glide by. Within the park, you'll spot a smattering of statuary, ranging from a monument to a Filipino general, an effigy of a girl scout, and even a large head-shaped statue immortalizing the import of Western-style methods of trimming hair to Japan. Most

visible of all the park's nearby features is the iconic 1930 ocean liner, the **NYK Hikawa Maru.**

FOOD

Nihon-ōdōri

日本大通り

CAFÉ DE LA PRESSE

Yokohama Media & Communications Center 2f, 11 Nihon-ōdōri, Naka-ku; tel. 045/222-3348; www.alteliebe.co.jp; 10am-8pm Tues.-Sun.; drinks ¥480-900, food ¥800-1,800; take subway Blue line to Nihon-ōdōri, exit 3

A French-style café on historic tree-lined Nihon-ōdōri, Café de la Presse is located on the second floor of the Yokohama Media & Communications Center. It's good for a pit stop if you're in the area, whether it's for a caffeine hit, cocktail, or an aperitif. The menu includes a good selection of Western dishes, from quiches and sandwiches to soups and salads, as well as European desserts.

Chinatown

横浜中華街

JOGENRO

191 Yamashita-chō, Naka-ku; tel. 045/641-8888; www.jogen.co.jp/jgr_yokohama; 11:30am-10:30pm Mon.-Thurs. and Sun., 11:30am-11pm Fri.-Sat. and day before any holiday; lunch sets ¥1,100-3,300, dinner courses ¥4,500-20,000; take Minatomirai line to Motomachi-Chūkagai Station, exit 2

Chinatown's maze of eateries is not solely devoted to Cantonese-style cooking. To shake things up Shanghai-style, try Jogenro. This restaurant sprawls across five floors, each with its own theme. Opulent furniture and décor you'd expect to see in a colonial townhouse in early-20th-century Shanghai evoke the Pearl of the Orient. The menu includes a solid range of soup dumplings, as well as stir-fried and grilled meats, vegetables, noodles, and rice.

MANCHINRO HONTEN

153 Yamashita-chō, Naka-ku; tel. 045/681-4004; https://en.manchinro.com; 11am-10pm daily; lunch sets ¥1,200-3,000, dinner courses ¥6,000-21,000;

take Minatomirai line to Motomachi-Chūkagai Station, exit 2

This classy spot serves good Cantonese cuisine, rustled up by a chef who trained in Hong Kong and ran a restaurant in Shanghai before relocating to Yokohama. The multicourse feasts are made using local ingredients, while remaining loyal to the principles of the Cantonese kitchen. Check out the extensive breakdown of the menu, available in English on the restaurant's website. If the main shop is fully booked, there's a second branch, **Manchinro Tenshinpo** (156 Yamashitachō, Naka-ku; tel. 045/664-4004; 11am-10pm daily; lunch sets ¥1,200-3,200, dinner courses ¥4,200-13,000) just around the corner, only a 1-minute walk away. This second restaurant is slightly more reasonably priced and its menu is more focused on dim sum. Reserve a table online at either restaurant before making the trip for dinner. It's a little pricey, but this is reflected in the quality.

Kannai, Bashamichi, and Noge
関内, 馬車道, 野毛

HANA SAKU

2-60 Hanasakichō, Naka-ku; tel. 045/325-9215; http://kulakula.info/hanasaku/index.html; 5pm-11:30pm daily; ¥180-880 per plate; take subway Blue line to Sakuragichō Station, south exit 1

An *izakaya* in Sakuragichō with a minimalist interior of clean lines, wood, and metal, Hana Saku is all about *sake*. The bartender is happy to introduce patrons to the wonders of *sake*, from sweet to dry, choosing from more than 20 varieties. The food menu is based on Kyoto-style side dishes of pickled and cooked vegetables, grilled meats and stews, and creative takes on tofu.

MARUWA

5-61 Sumiyoshichō, Naka-ku; tel. 045/641-0640; 11:30am-2pm and 5:30pm-8pm Mon.-Fri., 11:30am-2pm Sat.; lunch ¥1,000-2,000, dinner ¥2,000-3,000; take Minatomirai line to Bashamichi Station, exit 5

For perhaps the best *tonkatsu* in the city, head to Maruwa in Bashamichi. The shop's no-frills décor and lack of music allow you to fully direct your attention to the delectable breaded cutlets of pork. At lunchtime, be ready for a queue. Arrive around 11:15am to avoid standing in a long line. Alternatively, come for dinner when it's less crowded (though pricier). All meals include miso soup, pickled vegetables, and refillable rice and shredded cabbage.

CHARCOAL GRILL GREEN

6-79 Benten-dōri, Naka-ku; tel. 045/263-8976; www. greenyokohama.com; 11:30am-2pm and 5pm-11:30pm Mon.-Fri., 11:30am-3pm and 5pm-11:30pm Sat.-Sun.; ¥1,400-4,800; take Minatomirai line to Bashamichi Station, exit 3

Charcoal Grill Green is a bistro in the heart of Bashamichi, focused on charcoal-grilled meat (chicken, lamb, steak, duck) and seafood, as well as a good range of salads, soups, and other starters. The drink menu has a good selection of local craft beers and wines from California. This is a good place for either a few bites with drinks or a full meal.

★ ARAIYA

4-23 Kaigan-dōri, Naka-ku; tel. 045/226-5003; www. araiya.co.jp; 11am-2:30pm and 5pm-10pm daily; lunch ¥2,000-4,000, dinner ¥7,500-12,500; take Minatomirai line to Bashamichi Station, 6 Akarenga Soko exit

Araiya has a menu of rice bowls topped with strips of beef and *sukiyaki,* and extensive *shabu-shabu* courses. But its signature dish, *gyū-nabe,* consists of lean cuts of beef, leeks, shiitake mushrooms, and thin strands of jelly made from *konnyaku* (a plant from the taro family). The dish is cooked in a delicately balanced sauce that is both sweet and savory in a cast-iron pot at the table and dipped in raw egg, and the result is delicious.

RIGATTO

2-39-4 Miyagawachō, Naka-ku; tel. 045/253-6116; www.rigatto.jp; 5pm-midnight (last order 11pm) daily; courses from ¥3,000, à la carte ¥380-2,800; take Keikyū line to Hinodechō Station

This chic eatery—its airy wooden interior dimly lit—in the heart of the nightlife action near the Ōka River, serves superb Italian fare—salami platters, salads, pizzas, pastas, meat and seafood mains, and more—paired with an extensive Italian wine list. The staff are welcoming, there's an English menu available, and food is made from scratch. Reserve a few days ahead to be safe.

★ BARS AND NIGHTLIFE
Kannai, Bashamichi, and Noge
関内, 馬車道, 野毛

If Yokohama's nightlife could be summed up in a few words, they would be "craft beer and jazz." The city's craft beer zone is primarily centered in the neighborhoods of Kannai, Bashamichi, and Noge, all within walking distance of each other. Kannai is in the most southern position of the group, with Bashamichi northeast of there, while Noge is northwest of Kannai, across the Ōka River. The street lined with bars known as **Yoshidamachi** is also wedged into this quarter, between Kannai to the south and Noge to the north. It's possible to walk across the entire area in 10-15 minutes.

YOKOHAMA BAY BREWING KANNAI

2-15 Higashidōri, Naka-ku; tel. 045/341-0450; www. yokohamabaybrewing.jp; 4:30pm-11pm Mon.-Fri., 1pm-11pm Sat.-Sun.; take JR Negishi, Blue line to Kannai Station

Yokohama Bay Brewing is a good spot to begin a bar-hop through Yokohama's craft beer zone. This shop was opened in 2011 by Suzuki Shinya, trained in the Czech Republic and Germany and formerly the head brewer of Yokohama Brewery. Of the seven or so beers on tap, four or five are carefully selected from local outfits around Japan; the others are Suzuki's creations, always anticipated by his diehard fans. Simple bar nibbles are also on the menu.

BASHAMICHI TAPROOM

5-63-1 Sumiyoshichō, Naka-ku; tel. 045/264-4961; https://bairdbeer.com; 5pm-midnight Mon.-Fri.,

noon-midnight Sat.-Sun and holidays; take subway Blue line to Kannai Station, exit 3

Seven minutes' walk northeast of Yokohama Bay Brewing Kannai, you'll find another craft-beer gem, the three-floor Bashamichi Taproom, run by Shizuoka-based Baird Brewing Company. Around 20 beers, from light lagers to punchy ales and dark, honeyed stouts are on tap at the ground-floor bar. There's a spacious second-floor seating area and a rooftop terrace that beckons in warmer months. The kitchen also whips up excellent platters of barbecued tender pork, beef brisket, and ribs, smoked overnight in an oven imported from Texas and flavored with sauces made in house.

YOKOHAMA BREWERY

6-68-1 Sumiyoshichō, Naka-ku; tel. 045/641-9901; www.yokohamabeer.com; 11:30am-3pm and 6pm-11pm Mon.-Fri., 11:30am-11pm Sat., 11:30am-9pm Sun.; take Minato Mirai line to Bashamichi Station, exit 3

Two minutes up the road from Bashamichi Taproom, you'll find the city's oldest craft-beer brewery, Yokohama Brewery. Founded in 1995, the brewpub serves a range of pilsners and sweeter Belgian-style beers. Above the brewery is Umaya, a restaurant serving Western and Asian cuisine.

BAR NOBLE

2-7 Yoshidamachi, Naka-ku; tel. 045/243-1673; http://noble-aqua.com; 6pm-1:30am daily; table charge ¥800 per person; take Blue line to Kannai Station, exit 6, or JR Negishi line to Kannai Station, Isezakichō exit

If you'd like to take a break from craft beer or are just feeling like a cocktail, head to Bar Noble, located right around the corner from Yokohama Bay Brewing Kannai. You'll get a whiff of the sort of sophistication emanating from Ginza's swanky cocktail strongholds here, down to the dapper bartenders. Ambient lighting, a Zelkova countertop, and tunes lightly wafting from unseen speakers deepen the spell. With more than 500 types of booze on the shelf, rest assured, the bartenders know how to mix a drink. Try Great Sunrise, the bar's signature cocktail, which won the World Cocktail Championship in November 2011. This deep-yellow concoction is meant to signify the hope of a new day following the March 11 Tohoku earthquake and tsunami.

AIREGIN

5-60 Sumiyoshichō; tel. 045/641-9191; www.airegin. yokohama; 7pm-10:30pm daily; ¥2,500 cover charge includes one drink; take Blue line to Kannai Station, exit 8

Airegin (Nigeria spelled backward) is a standout in the city's vibrant jazz scene. Originally opened as a jazz *kissa* (jazz café) in Shinjuku, Tokyo, by a jazz-loving couple in 1969, it relocated to Yokohama where became established as a stalwart in the local scene. This archetypal jazz joint is cozy and smoky and draws a dedicated crowd of connoisseurs. Look for the large yellow sign on the sidewalk. It's located a few doors down from Bashamichi Taproom.

EL NUBICHNOM

1-1 Miyagawachō, Naka-ku; tel. 045/231-3626; https://ameblo.jp/el-nubichnom; 5:30pm-10:30pm Mon. and Wed.-Thurs., 5:30pm-11:30pm Fri., 3pm-11:30pm Sat., 3pm-8pm Sun.; take subway Blue line, JR lines to Sakuragichō Station, exit 1

El Nubichnom claims to be the world's smallest craft-beer bar. This standing-only bolthole, overlooking the Ōka River, is run by a friendly, passionate beer judge named Kajisan. Five or six Japanese craft brews are on tap at any given time, and often include some rare ones. This is a fun, cramped spot for a drink or two.

Note that the two-story building that houses El Nubichnom is home to an array of bars. To see the options on the second floor, ascend the staircase on either side of the building to the corridor that runs along the back of the building, where you'll find the entrances to all second-floor bars.

L'OEUF

2-23-4 Miyagawachō, Naka-ku; tel. 045/315-5517; https://oeuf-yokohama.jimdo.com; 6pm-11pm

Wed.-Sat., 5pm-11pm Sun.; take subway Blue line, JR lines to Sakuragichō Station, exit 1, or Keikyū line to Hinodechō Station

Swing open the massive wooden door and step inside the unique space that is L'Oeuf. The bar's dark-wood interior has a European flavor, inspired no doubt by the decade its owner, Ikuo Mitsuhashi, spent in Paris as a pantomime artist. Next to the door is a piano, and at the center of the room is a pole for dance performances. The bar, run by the friendly English and French-speaking Mitsuhashi-san, is in the back, and there's additional seating upstairs.

DOWNBEAT BAR

1-43 Hanasakichō, 2F Miyamoto Bldg., Naka-ku; tel. 045/241-6167; www.yokohama-downbeat.com; 4pm-11:30pm Mon.-Sat.; cover charge for some events; take subway Blue line, JR lines to Sakuragichō Station, exit 2

A good place to end the journey through Yokohama's jazz landscape is at one of the best jazz joints in the city, Downbeat Bar is a classic old-school jazz *kissa* with dim lighting and worn posters plastered on the walls and ceiling. Tunes chosen from a gold mine of some 3,700 records are played through a stellar sound system. It also hosts gigs sometimes.

INFORMATION AND SERVICES

For information on the city in English, your first port of call in Yokohama is the **Yokohama Station Tourist Information Center** (tel. 045/441-7300; 9am-7pm daily). Located about 7 minutes' walk from Nihon-ōdōri Station, near the western edge of Yamashita-Kōen, **Yokohama Convention & Visitors Bureau** (Sangyō-Bōeki Center 1F, 2 Yamashita-chō; tel. 045/221-2111; www. welcome.city.yokohama.jp/eng/convention; 9am-5pm Mon.-Fri.; take subway Blue line to Nihon-ōdōri, exit 3) is well stocked with English-language maps and flyers and is run by friendly English-speaking staff. And for information on Chinatown, head to the **Chinatown 80** (80 Yamashita-chō;

tel. 045/681-6022; 10am-8pm Sun.-Thurs., 10am-9pm Fri.-Sat.; take Minatomirai line to Motomachi-Chūkagai, exit 2).

There are also a few good local resources online. **Yokohama Seasider** (www.yokohamaseasider.com) has event listings, interviews with local movers and shakers, restaurant, café, and bar recommendations, and more. Last but not least, the **Yokohama Official Visitor's Guide** (www.yokohamajapan.com) has recommendations and transportation information.

GETTING THERE

The train ride from Tokyo to Yokohama is easy and surprisingly quick. There are a number of options for getting to Yokohama, but for simplicity's sake I recommend starting your journey from either Shibuya, Shinjuku, Tokyo, or Shinagawa station.

If you leave from Shibuya station, take the **Tōkyū Toyoko Line** straight to **Yokohama Station**. You can catch the express or limited express train from Shibuya Station, depositing you at Yokohama Station in as little as 30 minutes. The fares for these faster rides are the same as the local train (¥280 one-way). The Tōkyū Toyoko Line also continues as the **Minato Mirai Line** to **Motomachi-Chukagai,** the best stop to access Chinatown. If you need to go to a station in downtown Yokohama that is not serviced by express or limited express trains, you can transfer to a local train at Yokohama Station. Also departing from Shibuya Station is the **JR Shonan-Shinjuku Line** (25 minutes; ¥400 one-way), which also leaves from Shinjuku Station (30 minutes; ¥570).

Two other Tokyo hubs with easy access to Yokohama are Tokyo and Shinagawa stations. The **JR Tōkaidō line, JR Yokosuka line,** and **JR Keihin-Tohoku line** run from both stations. From Tokyo station, the train takes 30-40 minutes and costs ¥480, and from Shinagawa, the journey takes 20-30 minutes and costs ¥300.

Coming from Kyoto, take the *shinkansen* to Shin-Yokohama Station (2 hours; ¥13,300), then transfer to the **Blue subway line** or the **JR Yokohama line** to make your way into the city from there.

GETTING AROUND

Many of Yokohama's sights, clustered around Minato Mirai 21 and the areas of Motomachi and Chinatown, are within walking distance of each other.

Train and Subway

The city is served by a subway system with two easily navigable lines, simply called the **Blue and Green lines,** which run north-south (¥210-520). There is also the local aboveground **JR Negishi line** that runs through the city. But chances are, you won't even need to use these lines. The vast majority of sights you'll likely visit in Yokohama are easily accessed from stops on the **Minato Mirai line,** which is simply the continuation of the Tōkyū Toyoko line that runs directly to Yokohama from Shibuya.

Bus

In addition to train and subway lines, there's an **Akai-Kutsu** bus service (www.yokohamajapan.com/information/getting-around-yokohama/akaikutsu.php), which shuttles visitors to popular sights in Minato Mirai 21, Chinatown, and Motomachi. Buses leave from Sakuragichō Station, located on the Blue subway line and JR Negishi line. A trip on one of these buses costs ¥220 for adults and ¥110 for children ages 11 and under, which you can pay when you get on the bus, and station announcements are made in English.

Kamakura

鎌倉

One hour south of Tokyo by train, Kamakura is the closest place to the capital to deeply experience Japanese Buddhism in its various forms. Located next to the ocean, hemmed in by mountains laced with hiking trails, the city is home to more than 80 temples and shrines. If you're going to make only one trip beyond Tokyo, make it Kamakura.

The vast majority of Kamakura's religious complexes were built during the Kamakura period (1185-1333) by monks who absconded from China during the Song Dynasty, when the climate began to turn against Buddhism. At the same time, the religion was spreading in Japan, particularly the Zen school. During this brief period, Japan's first shogun, Minamoto no Yoritomo (1147-1199), chose to base his rather makeshift government here after wresting power from Kyoto, resulting in a temple construction boom.

Modern-day Kamakura has the feeling of a beach town, which it is. Down-to-earth locals, artisan cafés, and restaurants selling health-conscious food vaguely evoke coastal California. Surfers and sunbathers fill the beaches along the coast heading west to Enoshima, a small island off the coast. Especially on holidays and weekends, the lively shopping street of Komachi-dōri and the town's more popular temples and shrines are thronged with tourists.

The town begs to be explored on foot. Next to the grounds of Jōchi-ji you'll find the trailhead to the Daibutsu Hiking Course, a pleasant hike that leads southward through the mountains to the iconic Great Buddha statue at the temple of Kōtoku-in.

ORIENTATION

Kamakura's time in the political spotlight was turbulent and brief, but its spiritual legacy is readily visible today, with clusters of temples and a handful of key shrines located throughout the city. The main concentrations can be accessed on foot or by bus from **Kita-Kamakura Station** in the north; **Kamakura Station** in the city center, where you'll also find the major shopping thoroughfare of **Komachi-dōri;** and **Hase Station** in the southwest, where you'll find the **Great Buddha at Kōtoku-in.** Beyond the religious sights, the trails weaving through the hills surrounding the city and around the nearby Shōnan coast give a chance to experience a quieter side of Japan, without going far from Tokyo.

Six stops west of Hase Station on the Enoden line is **Enoshima Station,** the gateway (by rail) to the nearby island of **Enoshima.** Sitting roughly 8 km (5 mi) west of Kamakura's downtown, this island is linked to the mainland by a bridge, and has east-west stretches of sandy beachfront flanking its north side, namely, **Katase Higashihama** stretching eastward, and **Katase Nishihama,** rolling westward, with Mount Fuji seen hovering in the backdrop on clear days.

The city's three most important Zen temples, in order of importance, are **Kenchō-ji, Engaku-ji,** and **Jōchi-ji.** In truth, this hardly scratches the surface. If you're keen to temple-hop all day, ask the kind staff at the tourist information center next to Kamakura Station for more information on the town's many gems.

SIGHTS
Kita-Kamakura
ENGAKU-JI
円覚寺

409 Yamanouchi; tel. 0467/22-0478; www.engakuji. or.jp/top.html; 8am-4:30pm daily Mar.-Nov., 8am-4pm daily Dec.-Feb.; adults ¥300, junior high and elementary school students ¥100; take JR Yokosuka line to Kita-Kamakura Station

Of Kamakura's five great Zen temples, Engaku-ji is the biggest. Founded in 1282 by Hōjō regent Tokimune, the complex originally

Kamakura

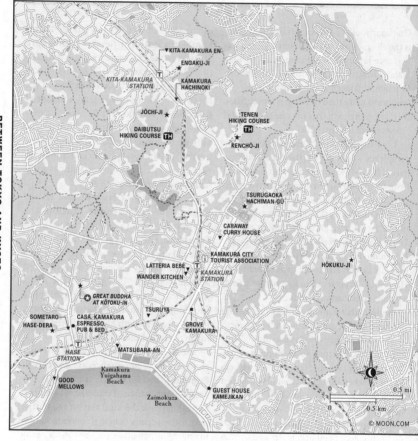

▼ KITA-KAMAKURA EN
ENGAKU-JI ★
KITA-KAMAKURA STATION
KAMAKURA HACHINOKI
JŌCHI-JI ★
TENEN HIKING COURSE
DAIBUTSU HIKING COURSE TH
KENCHŌ-JI ★
TSURUGAOKA HACHIMAN-GŪ
CARAWAY CURRY HOUSE
KAMAKURA CITY TOURIST ASSOCIATION
LATTERIA BEBE
WANDER KITCHEN
KAMAKURA STATION
HŌKOKU-JI ★
GREAT BUDDHA AT KŌTOKU-IN
TSURUYA ▼
SOMETARO
HASE-DERA ★
CASA KAMAKURA ESPRESSO PUB & BED
GROVE KAMAKURA
HASE STATION
MATSUBARA-AN
Kamakura Yuigahama Beach
GOOD MELLOWS ▼
Zaimokuza Beach
GUEST HOUSE KAMEJIKAN

0   0.5 mi
0   0.5 km

© MOON.COM

had more than 40 subtemples on its grounds, of which 17 are still standing. The temple's bell, cast in 1301, is Kamakura's biggest and today is only rung to celebrate the new year.

Attesting to the temple's deep antiquity, the Shozoku-in subtemple showcases some of the best touches of Zen architecture from China's Song Dynasty of any temple in Japan and contains a tooth of the Buddha. (Note that this building is not open to the public for most of the year, but can be glimpsed through a gate at other times.) Yasunari Kawabata, the first Japanese writer to win the Nobel Prize for literature, set much of his novel *Thousand*

Cranes on the temple's grounds, dense with history and ambience. Also, legendary film director Yasujiro Ozu is buried in the temple's cemetery.

Before leaving, be sure to relax and sip a tea at the **teahouse** (8am-4:30pm daily Mar.-Nov., 8am-4pm daily Dec.-Feb.) located on the grounds near the large bell. English menu available. The temple also holds free *zazen* (seated meditation) sessions (6am-7am daily, 1:20pm-2:20pm every Sat., 10am-11am every 2nd and 4th Sun. of month, no sessions Jan. 1-8 and Oct. 1-5). You must show up before a given session starts to join, so be sure to get there with time to spare. Sitting still for an hour is a surprising ordeal for some—be sure you're up to the challenge before setting out.

KENCHŌ-JI
建長寺

8 Yamanouchi; tel. 0467/22-0981; www.kenchoji.com; 8:30am-4:30pm daily; adults ¥500, children ¥200; take JR Yokosuka line to Kita-Kamakura Station

Kenchō-ji is Japan's oldest Zen monastery, founded by the Hōjō regent Tokiyori in 1253 and constructed by Rankei Doryu, a Chinese priest who came to spread the message of Zen in Japan. Only 10 buildings now dot the grounds (there were about 49 subtemples and seven main halls at its peak) but vestiges of its greatness remain, from a bell cast in 1255 and classified a National Treasure to an atmospheric grove of juniper trees as much as 700 years told, said to have sprung from seeds from China and been planted by Rankei himself. Other interesting elements include an effigy of Jizō Bosatsu, guardian of criminals, a grim reminder of the area's use as an execution ground long ago, and a pond shaped like the character for "spirit."

On Friday and Saturday (www.kenchoji.com/zazen; 4:30pm-5:30pm), the temple holds free crash courses on *zazen* (seated meditation), open to all, in Japanese. Even if you don't understand the instructions, it's perfectly acceptable to show up and join in, following visual cues. Show up about 15 minutes before 4:30pm to join. Brace yourself: You'll be sitting in one position for more than 30 minutes.

Central Kamakura
TSURUGAOKA HACHIMAN-GŪ
鶴岡八幡宮

2-1-31 Yukinoshita; tel. 0467/22-0315; www. tsurugaoka-hachimangu.jp; 5am-8:30pm daily Apr.-Sept., 6am-8:30 daily Oct.-Mar.; free

Given Kamakura's samurai legacy, steeped in power struggle and war, it's appropriate that the first shogun, Minamoto Yoritomo, chose to put the god of war, Hachiman, front and center at the city's largest shrine. Tsurugaoka Hachiman-gū sits at the top of a high bluff, with great views of the city and coast. The design and layout of the shrine were so colored by Minamoto's battle-hardened worldview that even the bridges cutting through the pond on its grounds were meant to symbolize the fissure between the eternally feuding Minamoto and Taira clans.

Be sure to have a look at the marvelous collection of Buddhist statuary held at the **Kamakura National Treasure Museum** (2-1-1 Yukinoshita; tel. 0467/22-0753; www.city.kamakura.kanagawa.jp/kokuhoukan; 9am-4:30pm Tues.-Sun.; adults ¥400, children ¥200; take JR Yokosuka line to Kamakura station, east exit) behind the pond on the shrine's grounds. The works on display range from wild-eyed temple guardians brandishing swords to beatific, haloed bodhisattvas and *jizō*, as the oft-bibbed stone statues of the protector of children, travelers, and unborn are known.

HŌKOKU-JI
報国寺

2-7-4 Jomyo-ji; tel. 0467/22-0777; www.houkokuji. or.jp; 9am-4pm daily; ¥300; take bus 23, 24, 36 from Kamakura Station to sixth stop for Jōmyō-ji

Hōkoku-ji, a Rinzai temple built in 1334, is a slight detour, but its atmospheric bamboo grove makes the trip worthwhile. The temple is also home to a raked rock garden, a smattering of Buddhist statuary, and a small **teahouse** in a pavilion. While you're there, stop at the space with a roof in the grove to sit and slow down with a cup of green tea and a sweet (9am-3:30pm daily; ¥600). While sitting, clearing the mind, and doing nothing may not appeal to all, the temple holds basic Zen seated meditation sessions, or *zazen,* on Sunday mornings (7:30am-10:30am; free) for those who'd like to add a little Zen to their lives.

Hase
HASE-DERA
長谷寺

3-11-2 Hase; tel. 0467/22-6300; www.hasedera.jp/ en; 8am-5:30pm (last entry 5pm) daily Mar.-Sept.,

*8am-5pm (last entry 4:30pm) Oct.-Feb.; adults
¥400, children ages 6-11 ¥200; take Enoshima
Dentesu line to Hase Station*

At Hase-dera, a veritable storeroom of evocative Buddhist relics, an 11-faced Kannon (the goddess of mercy) with a colorful backstory is the temple's centerpiece. Legend states the statue was one of two carved from a camphor tree found by a monk named Tokudo Shonin in AD 721, in a village called Hase, near Nara, where the other one still stands. The one in Kamakura is said to have washed ashore on a nearby beach after having been cast into the ocean near Osaka in the faith that it would resurface. Hase-dera was built to commemorate its miraculous discovery.

Along with this multifaced statue of the bodhisattva of compassion, 33 other carvings at the temple depict Kannon's range of avatars. The complex also houses a sutra library, a bell cast in 1264, and an army of stone *jizō* statues clad in red bibs encircling a hall dedicated to the guardian of children and travelers. Walk past the *jizō* and enter the cave beyond, where you'll find a serene candlelit space and exquisite reliefs of Buddha and other sacred figures carved into the walls. Alongside Kōtoku-un, Hase-dera is one of the best temples to visit in Kamakura.

★ GREAT BUDDHA AT KŌTOKU-IN
高徳院

*4-2-28 Hase; tel. 0467/22-0703; www.kotoku-in.jp/
en; 8am-5pm daily; adults ¥200, children ¥150; take
Enoshima Dentesu line to Hase Station*

The 11.3-meter-tall (37-foot-tall), 81-tonne (90-ton) bronze statue of Amida Buddha, the Great Buddha at Kōtoku-in (aka Daibutsu), a temple of the Jōdo (Pure Land) sect, is a symbol of Kamakura itself. Said to be based on the famed gold-encrusted Buddha occupying Tōdai-ji in Nara, the Buddha's calm pose is accentuated by its palms, facing upward in a mudra known as the *jobon-josho,* believed to maximize potential enlightenment.

This tranquility is impressive, given the fact that the Daibutsu, about a 10-minute walk from Hase-dera, has seen its fair share of calamity, from earthquakes to tidal waves and fires. The original sat in a large hall, destroyed by a monumental typhoon that leveled the city in 1494. Today, it remains seated in blissful meditation—its 1-meter-wide (3.3-foot-wide) eyes half-closed—wearing the same expression of serenity it had when it was cast in 1252. Although temporarily closed at the time of writing to prevent coronavirus spread, it has traditionally been possible to pay an extra ¥20 to enter the statue itself and see the impressive bronze-work from the inside; there's even a stairway leading to shoulder-height.

The temple complex itself consists of spacious grounds and a handful of buildings topped with black-tile roofs. More than anything though, these structures serve as the backdrop for the magnificent statue.

Enoshima
江の島

A short detour from Kamakura's sights, along the charming Enoden line, will take you to the tiny island of Enoshima. Exiting Katase Enoshima Station, walk across the bridge from the beach to the small craggy spit of land just off the coast. From Kamakura Station, just hop on the laid-back Enoshima line and chug your way to Enoshima Station (23 minutes; ¥260). From there, walk 15 minutes south, crossing a bridge from the coast of the mainland to the island. The island's main attractions are its park, a pair of caves, and, most of all, its shrine. Along the island's main strip, you'll find plenty of stalls serving seafood, cafés, and, hugging its perimeter, eateries with shimmering views. If the sky is clear, you can see Mount Fuji cutting a beautiful profile in the distance.

Note that swimming is not allowed on the beaches directly attached to Enoshima itself. However, **Katase Higashihama Beach,** just east of Enoshima on the mainland, and **Katase Nishihama Beach,** fanning out to the west, fill with sunbathers and swimmers

---

1: Engaku-ji **2:** Kenchō-ji **3:** tea at Hōkoku-ji

in the scorching summer months, while surfers flock to the beaches farther to the east and west.

ENOSHIMA-JINJA
江の島神社

2-3-8 Enoshima; tel. 0466/22-4020; http:// enoshimajinja.or.jp; 8:30am-5pm daily; free entrance, ¥200 to view Benzaiten statue

Once you've reached the island, wander its atmospheric (and often crowded) main thoroughfare toward the main part of this prominent shrine, which is distributed throughout the island in three parts. This holy place is dedicated to Benzaiten, the Japanese incarnation of Sarasvati and goddess of water, knowledge, the arts, and good fortune—hence why some come to wash their money in the shrine's pond. According to legend, Benzaiten created Enoshima, then vanquished a dragon with five heads that was wreaking havoc on the area. The statue of Benzaiten housed here is considered one of the three most venerated in Japan.

ENOSHIMA IWAYA CAVES
江の島岩屋

2 Enoshima; tel. 0466/24-4141; www.fujisawa-kanko. jp/spot/enoshima/17.html; 9am-5pm daily Mar.-Oct., 9am-4pm daily Nov.-Feb.; adults ¥500, junior high and elementary school students ¥200

Hollowed by erosion over the millennia, these two caves on the craggy southern side of the island are reached via a stone staircase. The first cave is occupied by Buddhist statuary; the second is devoted to the five-headed dragon that once terrified the residents of the area until it was banished by the goddess Benzaiten.

ENOSHIMA SAMUEL COCKING GARDEN AND SEA CANDLE
江の島サムエル・コッキング
苑, 江の島シーキャンドル

2-3-28 Enoshima; tel. 0466/23-2444; https://

enoshima-seacandle.com; 9am-8pm daily; adults ¥700, elementary school students ¥350, includes garden entry

At the top of the island you'll find this botanical garden of camellias, roses, and more. Named after an English merchant who arrived in Yokohama in 1869, soon after Japan reopened to the outside world, and who lived in the area until his death in 1914, this garden was originally the botanical experiment of Cocking, who built a villa on the island in 1882. Ruins of the greenhouse Cocking had built still stand today. For good coastal views, ascend to the viewing deck of the candle-shaped lighthouse, a modern construction known as the Sea Candle. Built with the same materials used to build the original lighthouse that once stood in Cocking's garden, it stands 59 meters (194 feet) tall. Unfortunately, the 360-degree vista from the observation deck is partly hindered by windows, but you can see all the way to Mount Fuji on clear days. Look north and see if you can spot Yokohama's Landmark Tower or even Tokyo SkyTree looming far in the horizon beyond.

SPORTS AND RECREATION
Hiking

Pick up information about hiking options and maps, or ask questions to the English-speaking staff, at the **Kamakura City Tourist Association,** which sits just beside Kamakura Station's east exit.

DAIBUTSU HIKING COURSE
Hiking Distance: *3 km (1.9 mi) one-way*
Time: *1-1.5 hours one-way*
Information and maps: *Kamakura City Tourist Association*
Trailhead: *Jōchi-ji*

This hiking course is a great way to explore the city's riches on foot. The route links the temple of **Jōchi-ji** (1402 Yamanouchi; tel. 0467/22-3943; https://jochiji.com/en/; 9am-4:30pm daily; adults ¥200, children ¥100), located about 8 minutes' walk southwest of Kita-Kamakura Station with the **Daibutsu**

1: Hase-dera **2:** Enoshima-jinja **3:** Great Buddha at Kōtoku-in

(Great Buddha) in the south, passing the atmospheric shrine of **Zeniarai Benten** (2-25-16 Sasuke; tel. 0467/25-1081; 8am-4:30pm daily; free) on the way. You'll also take in **Genjiyama Park** (4-7-1 Ogigayatsu, Kamakura; 24 hours daily; free), the neighboring **Kuzuharagaoka Shrine** (5-9-1 Kajiwara, Kamakura; tel. 0467/45-9002; 24 hours daily; free), and **Sasuke Inari Shrine** (2-22-10 Sasuke; tel. 0467/22-4711; 24 hours daily; free). From the shrine, the hike continues for about 20 more minutes, at which point you find yourself at the foot of the temple of **Kōtoku-in** and its famed Great Buddha.

TENEN HIKING COURSE

Hiking Distance: 6 km/3.7 mi

Time: 2 hours

Information and maps: Kamakura City Tourist Association

Trailhead: Kenchō-ji

If you are interested in hiking around Kamakura but the Daibutsu Hiking Course seems prohibitively crowded, there are other hiking trails in the hills around Kamakura, including the recommended Tenen Hiking Course, which runs through the hills on the northern edge of town. You'll find the trailhead on the grounds of the temple Kenchō-ji, on the north side of town. Here, to the left side of the main hall you'll see the path leads down into a valley. Walk down this path until you reach a large concrete *torii* gate, and ascend the steep stone steps, lined with protruding-nosed statues of the mythological Tengu. The official start of the Tenen Hiking Course lies just beyond the small rest area at the top of the steps.

Beaches

Sunbathers, swimmers, and surfers from around the greater Tokyo area flock to the beaches around Kamakura in the summer months. There is roughly 7 km (4.3 mi) of coastline stretching toward the island of Enoshima.

Official swimming season is considered to be July 1-August 31, when food shacks and various amenities are in operation, and **lifeguards** are on duty 9am-5pm daily. Alcohol, having a barbecue, and smoking are prohibited on the beach; some restaurants near the water serve booze and allow smoking. According to local law, tattoos must be covered on the beach.

ZAIMOKUZA BEACH
材木座海岸

5-chōme Zaimoku area, Kamakura-shi; http://zaimokuza.net/english; beach open 24 hours daily, official swimming season 9am-5pm daily Jul. 1-Aug. 31; free

One of Kamakura's top picks come summertime, together with neighboring beach Yuigahama, this long stretch of sand spans about 1 km (0.6 mi), with Zaimokuza Beach at the eastern side and Yuigahama to the west, split by the **Nameri River.** Zaimokuza Beach, which is Kamakura's longest, is sandy and shallow with mellow waves. There are good amenities on both beaches during summer: beach huts, rental shops (surfboards, wet suits, wakeboards, life jackets, parasols, and more), changing rooms, showers, cafés, bars, and food shacks. To reach Zaimokuza Beach, take the Keikyū bus bound for Izu from Kamakura Station to Zaimokuza bus stop, then walk 2 minutes, or take the Enoden line from Kamakura Station to Yuigahama Station, then walk 15 minutes southeast.

YUIGAHAMA BEACH
由比ヶ浜海岸

2-chōme Hase area, Kamakura-shi; https://yuigahama.sos.gr.jp/en; beach open 24 hours daily, official swimming season 9am-5pm daily Jul. 1-Aug. 31; free

Yuigahama tends to be slightly more crowded than Zaimokuza Beach and has been popular since the Meiji period. Like Zaimokuza Beach, the beach is sandy, and the water is shallow and calm. The easy accessibility of both beaches makes them popular with families in summer, and the amenities are comparable at both. To reach Yuigahama Beach, take the Enoden line to Yuigahama Station, then walk 5 minutes south from there. If you don't mind walking, you can also make your way on foot from Kamakura Station in about 25 minutes. It's also easy to walk between Zaimokuza Beach and Yuigahama.

KATASE HIGASHIHAMA BEACH
腰越海水浴場, 片瀬東浜海水浴場

from 3-chōme Koshigoe area, Kamakura-shi in the east, to 1-chōme Katasekaigan, Fujisawa in the west; http://travelenoshima.jp/place/katase_sea.html; beach open 24 hours daily, official swimming season 9am-5pm daily Jul. 1-Aug. 31; free

Extending roughly 1 km (0.6 mi) east to west, facing the northeastern corner of Enoshima, this beach is well-known across Japan. It's historic and has been drawing visitors since the Meiji period. Later, the glut of U.S. troops who sought escape on the beach during the Korean War inspired its nickname of Miami Beach of the East. For better or worse, there's a grain of truth to this moniker. Its clean sand, calm waves, and profuse amenities ensure that this beach is often thronged at summer's sweltering peak. To reach this beach, take the Enoden line to Enoshima Station, then walk 10 minutes south.

KATASE NISHIHAMA BEACH

from 2-chōme to 3-chōme Katasekaigan area, Fujisawa; beach open 24 hours daily, official swimming season 9am-5pm daily Jul. 1-Aug. 31; free

Even bigger and more crowded than its neighbor to the east, Katase Nishihama Beach occupies about 1 km (0.6 mi) of sand. This continuation of the area's eastern answer to Miami Beach is where Japan played its first beach volleyball match and surfed its first waves. While it isn't exactly Oahu's north shore, decent waves do build here when the wind picks up. Like its neighbor, amenities and options for dining, rental shops, and more are readily available. Take the Enoden line to Enoshima Station, then walk 15 minutes southwest, crossing the bridge over the Sakai River, which separates Katase Nishihama Beach from Katase Higashihama Beach.

FOOD
Kita-Kamakura
KAMAKURA HACHINOKI

350 Yamanouchi; tel. 0467/23-3723; www.hachinoki. co.jp; 11:30am-2:30pm Mon.-Fri., 11am-3pm Sat.-Sun. and holidays, 5pm-7pm Thurs.-Tues., dinner only by reservation a day early; lunch ¥3,600-4,500, dinner ¥6,800-14,250; take JR lines to Kita-Kamakura Station

Kamakura Hachinoki is a Michelin-starred restaurant serving *shōjin-ryōri* (Buddhist vegetarian cuisine traditionally reserved for Zen monks). Set in an old Japanese house, with tatami mats and exquisite old wooden furniture, the meal is a multicourse banquet. Allow a full evening to properly enjoy it. English menu available.

KITA-KAMAKURA EN

501 Yamanouchi; tel. 0467/23-6232; www. kitakamakura-en.com; 11:30am-2pm (last order 1:30pm) lunch, 5pm-8pm (last order 6:30pm) dinner Tues.-Sun., reservation required for dinner; lunch ¥5,000, dinner ¥10,000; take JR lines to Kita-Kamakura Station, west exit

This fantastic family-run *kaiseki* restaurant overlooks a pond and Zen temple grounds. Kita-Kamakura En is a simple space with an earthy color scheme, free of the stuffy atmosphere often associated with *kaiseki*. Set courses change with the seasons, and ingredients are sourced from around the country. On the second floor of the ochre building outside Kita-Kamakura Station's main exit. Reserve a month or more in advance. Alternatively, stop by at teatime if it's fully booked.

Central Kamakura
CARAWAY CURRY HOUSE

2-12-20 Komachi; tel. 0467/25-0927; 11:30am-7:30pm Tues.-Sun.; from ¥660; walk 6 minutes northeast of JR Kamakura Station

With its nostalgic interior, kind staff, and reasonably priced heaving portions, this Japanese curry joint really hits the spot. The contents of the curry—chicken, pork, beef, squid, cheese, or egg—are smoothly shredded into a puree-like consistency, with the curry served on the side of rice and a salad. Get the small rice if you don't want to leave feeling overstuffed. It's a popular spot and sometimes attracts a queue, which tends to move quickly. A recommended place to try one of Japan's classic comfort foods.

WANDER KITCHEN

10-15 Onarimachi; tel. 0467/61-4751; http:// wanderkitchen.net; noon-8pm daily; ¥1,000; take JR, Enoden lines to Kamakura Station

Down a quiet side street near Onari shopping street, Wander Kitchen is a cozy, chic spot for a casual lunch or dinner. Its affordably priced menu casts a wide net, from spicy Southeast Asian and Indian curries to European and Latin American fare. Friendly staff are ready to help you navigate the Japanese menu. Look for the pink flamingo at the entrance to the small side street. Free Wi-Fi.

LATTERIA BEBE

11-17 Onarimachi; tel. 0467/81-3440; http:// latteria-bebe.com; 11am-9pm Tues.-Sun.; ¥850-2,200; take JR, Enoden lines to Kamakura Station

Latteria Bebe is an excellent pizzeria owned by two brothers who apprenticed as chefs in Italy (one making pizza, the other cheese). Set in an old wooden house about 5 minutes' walk from Kamakura Station, the restaurant has a wood-fire oven and offers on-site cheese workshops where guests make their own mozzarella. The menu includes seasonal ingredients and local seafood. Lunch sets are a good value. Book ahead a few days in advance if possible; otherwise, be prepared to wait. Limited English spoken.

★ TSURUYA

3-3-27 Yuigahama; tel. 0467/22-0727; http:// arai-kikaku-site.com/tsuruya; 11:30am-7pm Wed.-Mon.; ¥2,200-4,400; take Enoden line to Wadazuka Station

It's all about eel at Tsuruya. This Michelin-starred restaurant has been serving a simple menu since 1929 consisting of broiled eel atop rice—either in a stylish wooden box or a

bowl—or with rice on the side, delicately flavored with a variety of dipping sauces. The shop has literary associations thanks to the fact it was frequented by novelist Yasunari Kawabata, the first Japanese writer to win the Nobel Prize for literature, who lived in the area toward the end of his life. It's advisable to book a few days in advance.

Hase
SOMETARO

3-12-11 Hase; tel. 0467/22-8694; www. okonomi-sometaro.com; 11:30am-9pm Thurs.-Mon.; ¥1,000; take Enoden line to Hase Station

Just around the corner from Kannon Coffee you'll find Sometaro, a great *okonomiyaki* restaurant. Here you can cook your own fully customizable savory pancake (toppings include cheese, kimchi, egg, and more) or *yakisoba* (stir-fried *soba* noodles) on a hotplate at your table. If you're new to the process, affable staff are happy to help you get the job done.

GOOD MELLOWS

27-39 Sakanoshita; tel. 0467/24-9655; http:// goodmellows.jp; 10:30am-6:30pm Wed.-Mon.; ¥1,200; take Enoden line to Hase Station

About 12 minutes' walk from Hase-dera, Good Mellows is a great beachside option serving reasonably priced burgers, beers, and the kinds of sides you'd expect to see at a bar stateside (buffalo wings, fries, salads). The burgers can be customized with a range of toppings (pineapple, avocado, bacon, and a slew of cheeses). English menu available. The place closes early, so it's better as an option for lunch.

MATSUBARA-AN

4-10-3 Yuigahama; tel. 0467/61-3838; http:// matsubara-an.com; 11am-10pm (last order 9pm) daily; lunch ¥2,000-3,000, dinner ¥3,000-4,000; take Enoden line to Yuigahama Station

Set in an atmospheric old Japanese house, Matsubara-an is a soba restaurant firmly on the foodie map. Guests have a choice between a chic indoor dining area and outdoor seating in a quiet garden. The restaurant makes its own noodles, which it serves both *kake* (hot) and *zaru* (cold), along with sides like tempura and sashimi. Lunch sets come with starters like roast duck and veggies with *bagna cauda* (Italian hot garlic and anchovy) dip. Reserve a few days in advance for dinner; lunch is first-come, first-served.

ACCOMMODATIONS

Kamakura is a comfortable day trip from Tokyo. That said, if you happen to be traveling between Tokyo and Kyoto, or would simply like to slow down, consider staying overnight. One night, preferably not too far from the beach, is recommended.

GUESTHOUSE KAMEJIKAN

3-17-21 Zaimokuza; tel. 0467/25-1166; https:// kamejikan.com; mixed dorm from ¥3,200, double ¥9,000 pp, ¥12,000 double, ¥16,000 for four people; take bus no. 12, 40 or 41 from Kamakura Station to Kuhonji bus stop, or walk 25 minutes southeast from Kamakura Station

The name of this languid, renovated wooden home, nearly a century old, appropriately translates to "Turtle Time." There's a private room for two, a private room for up to four, or a mixed dorm with six beds, which all share two toilets and one shower. The property sits about 250 meters (820 feet) inland from Zaimokuza Beach. There's also a cozy café and bar on site that operates on weekends (noon-5pm Sat.-Sun.).

CASA. KAMAKURA ESPRESSO. PUB & BED

1-15-5 Hase; tel. 0467/55-9077; https://casa-kamakura-espresso-pub-amp-bed-jp.book.direct/ ja-jp; double ¥14,200, twin with bunk beds ¥12,000 for two, includes breakfast; take Enoden line to Hase Station, then walk 3 minutes north

This inn in Hase sits right beside the road that leads to Hase-dera, and is about 7 minutes' walk north of Yuigahama Beach. There are just two rooms: a double with two twin beds, and another private room with a bunk bed. Both have an en suite toilet and shower. There's also a shared lounge and a café on site

where an American-style breakfast is served (included in the price).

INFORMATION AND SERVICES

Exit Kamakura Station's east exit and you'll be right in front of the **Kamakura City Tourist Association** (1-1-1 Komachi; tel. 0467/22-3350; www.trip-kamakura.com; 9am-5pm daily). Here you'll find English-language maps, pamphlets, and booklets on the town's history and culture. The center has friendly English-speaking staff who are happy to answer questions. The website **Kamakura Today** (www.city.kamakura.kanagawa.jp/vis-itkamakura/en) also provides good information in English about the town's sights, food, shopping, and more. Finally, for more information on Enoshima and the beaches lying to its north that fall within the boundaries of the city of Fujisawa, check out the **Discover Fujisawa** website (www.fujisawa-kanko.jp).

GETTING THERE

The **JR Yokosuka line** runs from Tokyo and Shinagawa stations in Tokyo, as well as Yokohama Station to Kamakura Station (25 minutes-1 hour; ¥350-¥940). Another option is the **JR Shōnan-Shinjuku line,** which directly links Shinjuku and Shibuya to Kamakura in roughly an hour (¥940). In order to reach Kamakura station on this train, you'll need to transfer at Ofuna, unless you catch a train bound for Zushi.

From Kyoto Station, take the **Tōkaidō** *shinkansen* (1 hour 55 minutes; ¥13,500) to Shin-Yokohama Station. There, you'll transfer to the **JR Yokohama line** and ride to Yokohama Station (15 minutes; ¥170), where you'll transfer again to the **JR Shōnan-Shinjuku line** or the **JR Yokosuka line,** either of which goes directly to both Kita-Kamakura (20 minutes; ¥310) and Kamakura Station (25 minutes; ¥350).

GETTING AROUND

The beautiful thing about Kamakura is its sheer walkability. That said, if you want to save a bit of time, you can get around the city and its major sights, clustered around Kita-Kamakura, Kamakura, and Hase stations, by taking the train, bus, or even riding a bike.

Train

Aside from the JR lines that connect Kita-Kamakura and Kamakura stations, the **Enoden (Enoshima Electric Railway) line** is a classic old-school tram that goes from Kamakura station to Hase, near the Great Buddha, before moving slowly on through the city's coastal neighborhoods and to the island of Enoshima (23 minutes; ¥260 from Kamakura Station).

Bus

There is also a network of city **buses** leaving from Kamakura Station and connecting to all the main sights. Blue buses are run by **Keikyū** (https://timetablenavi-en.keikyu-bus.co.jp/en/route/dia/landmark); orange by **Enoden** (www.enoden.co.jp/en/bus; from ¥180). These two bus companies tend to share bus stops around town, although they each have a respective terminal stand outside Kamakura Station's east exit. Fares start from ¥180.

For a map of town that includes information on bus terminals closest to popular sights and more, visit www.trip-kamakura.com/img/downloadcontents/map-english.pdf.

The **Kamakura Free Kankyo Tegata** is a special ticket deal that allows you to ride freely on any bus running through the city, as well as most stretches of the Enoden line (www.city.kamakura.kanagawa.jp/visitkamakura/en/access/index.html; adults ¥570, children ¥290). These passes can be purchased at tourist information centers in Kamakura Station, near the east exit of Enoden Kamakura station, Hase Station, and handful of sights around town, including the gift shop at Engaku-ji.

Cycling

While Kamakura is an ideal city to explore on foot, there are options for bicycle rentals for those who would like to cover more terrain. The heart of town is relatively flat, although you may encounter some hills as you pedal inland, toward the low-lying mountains that ring the city. There are no designated cycling routes per se, but traffic tends to be fairly calm and the scale of the town is such that a bicycle can take you everywhere you want to go.

Grove Kamakura (2-1-3 Yuigahama, Kamakura-shi; tel. 0467/23-6667; www.grove-kamakura.com; 10am-7pm Thurs.-Tues.), located about 8 minutes' walk from Kamakura Station, rents front-suspension bikes for ¥2,500 and dual suspension bikes for ¥3,000 per day.

Hakone 箱根

Hakone has been known for its wealth of natural beauty, from verdant mountains to a plethora of *onsen,* since the 16th century. It is said that Hideyoshi Toyotomi (1537-1598), the great samurai warrior and one of Japan's "three unifiers," treated himself to a bit of R&R in Hakone following the Siege of Odawara in 1590. He could think of no better option than relaxing in the soothing waters after conquering nearby Odawara Castle, then the world's largest, and ousting the Hōjō clan to become the new ruler of Japan. Located

in the heart of **Fuji-Hakone-Izu National Park** (www.fujihakoneizu.com), Hakone's natural splendor and diverse artistic offerings—many of them displayed outdoors—are understandably a draw to busy 21st-century Tokyo-ites, too.

The traditional approach to exploring Hakone is to make a loop, completed via a succession of quirky transportation options, from a quaint local train line and a cable car to a ropeway over a dramatically vaporous valley and a galleon-like sightseeing boat on

Hakone

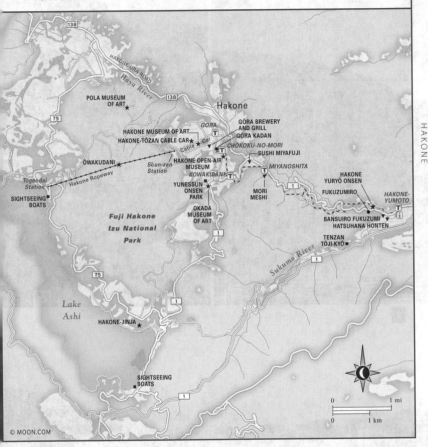

138

HAKONE-URA ROAD

Haya River

POLA MUSEUM
OF ART

138

Hakone

75

GŌRA
GŌRA BREWERY
AND GRILL
HAKONE MUSEUM OF ART
GŌRA KADAN
HAKONE-TŌZAN CABLE CAR
CHŌKOKU-NO-MORI
Cable Car
SUSHI MIYAFUJI

ŌWAKUDANI
Sōun-zan
Station
HAKONE OPEN-AIR
MUSEUM
MIYANOSHITA

Hakone Ropeway
KOWAKIDANI
HAKONE
YURYŌ ONSEN

Tōgendai
Station
YUNESSUN
ONSEN
PARK
MORI
MESHI
FUKUZUMIRO

SIGHTSEEING
BOATS
OKADA
MUSEUM
OF ART
HAKONE-
YUMOTO

Fuji Hakone
Izu National
Park
BANSUIRO FUKUZUMI
HATSUHANA HONTEN

1
TENZAN
TŌJI-KYŌ

Sukumo River

75

1

Lake
Ashi

1

HAKONE-JINJA

SIGHTSEEING
BOATS

1

© MOON.COM

0   1 mi
0   1 km

Lake Ashi (Ashi-no-ko), which occupies a caldera and offers stunning views of Mount Fuji looming in the backdrop. While fun, following this well-worn path can feel a bit formulaic. It can pay to follow your own curiosity in Hakone and blaze your own trail. Or, perhaps the simplest plan of all, vegging out in an *onsen* resort and gorging on haute cuisine wearing only a robe and slippers for a few days.

With so many things to do in one place, it's no wonder that Hakone is a destination of choice for day trips and weekend escapes from the capital. The upside of this is that a trip to the area is certain to be a good mix of relaxation and stimulation. The downside is that the place is inundated on weekends, holidays, and in peak season. To minimize the impact of crowds on your experience, come on a weekday and hit the popular spots early in the day.

ORIENTATION

A good way to navigate this area is the **Hakone-Tozan line,** which starts in the city of **Odawara**, east of Hakone, and winds westward almost to the foot of **Mount Hakone.** The first stop of note is

Hakone-Yumoto, a town on Hakone's eastern edge. The primary draw here is the wealth of *onsen* options, including **Hakone Yuryō Onsen** and **Tenzan Tōji-kyō**. Back on the Hakone-Tōzan line, if you continue west you'll come to **Miyanoshita**, a good area to stop for a bite to eat or stay overnight, and **Kowakidani**, where you'll find the stunning **Okada Museum of Art** and the fun **Yunessun Onsen Park**. Push farther west on the Hakone-Tōzan railway line to its final two stops, **Chōkoku-no-mori**, where you'll find the crowd-pleasing **Hakone Open-Air Museum**, and **Gōra**, home to the **Hakone Museum of Art** and a good area to sleep if you plan to stay at one of the area's many *ryokan*. From there, a cable car links Gōra to **Sōun-zan**, from where hiking trails begin and the **Hakone Ropeway** descends to **Lake Ashi** at Hakone's southwestern edge, hovering above the dramatically volcanic landscape of **Ōwakudani** below.

SIGHTS
Around Kowakidani
OKADA MUSEUM OF ART
岡田美術館

493-1 Kowakudani; tel. 0460/87-3931; www. okada-museum.com/en; 9am-5pm daily; adults and university students ¥2,800, children ¥1,800; from Hakone-Yumoto station, take bus to Koakien bus stop

Since it opened in 2013, the Okada Museum of Art has been wowing visitors with its collection of East Asian art, both ancient and modern, from Chinese pottery to Japanese scrolls. Situated on a mountain blanketed in forest, the museum is the creation of casino magnate Kazuo Okada, a self-professed art lover who began to set aside pieces with the express intention to one day open a museum. He succeeded brilliantly. The result is this cutting-edge structure spread over five floors, behind which you'll find a lush stroll garden and laid-back café. There's also a footbath at the entrance where museumgoers can refresh themselves before gawking at the many beautiful artistic specimens in the private collection for the next few hours.

Around Chōkoku-no-mori
HAKONE OPEN-AIR MUSEUM
箱根 彫刻の森美術館

1121 Ninotaira; tel. 0460/82-1161; www.hakone-oam. or.jp; 9am-5pm daily; adults ¥1,600, university and high school students ¥1,200, middle school and elementary school students ¥800; take electric train to Chōkoku-no-Mori Station

Japan does art in natural settings exceptionally well, and Hakone Open-Air Museum is a superb example. Imagine traipsing through a sculpture garden dotted by works by masters both European and Japanese, from Miró and Rodin to Henry Moore and Morie Ogiwara, set against a backdrop of verdant mountains and valleys. You've just pictured this refreshing museum in your mind's eye.

For Picasso fans, there's a pavilion devoted entirely to his work, with some 300 pieces. Another noteworthy work is the Symphonic Sculpture, a spiral staircase encased by a colorful swirl of glass, leading up to a viewing platform where the lush natural surroundings can be appreciated.

Those traveling with kids will be relieved to find Zig Zag World, a sculpture-inspired playground. And if you want to soak and relax after a day spent walking, there's even an outdoor foot bath.

Around Gōra
HAKONE MUSEUM OF ART
箱根美術館

1300 Gōra; tel. 0460/82-2623; www.moaart.or.jp/ hakone; 9:30am-4:30pm Fri.-Mon. Apr.-Nov., until 4pm Dec.-Mar., open if Thurs. falls on national holiday; adults ¥900, high school students ¥400, junior school students and younger free; take Hakone Tozan cable car to Gōra Station

Exquisite Asian pottery and art, a traditional teahouse, and an enigmatic moss garden that crackles with color in autumn are some of the discoveries that await at the Hakone Museum of Art. Built on the collection of art

---

1: Hakone-jinja **2:** sulphur vents of Ōwakudani **3:** Hakone Open-Air Museum

The Hakone Loop

Getting around the central area of Hakone, including Mount Hakone and lovely Lake Ashi, is part of the fun of making the trip. Seeing the region's sights involves a combination of jumping between local trains, cable cars, ropeways, buses, and boats. A caveat: While this is the "classic" way to see Hakone, in truth it's a bit cookie-cutter (read: touristy). If there are specific things that appeal to you in the area that don't fit neatly into this route, the best way to see Hakone can actually be limiting the number of things you see and do, while maximizing down time, perhaps soaking in an *onsen*.

The easiest way to complete the full route is to get a **Hakone Freepass** (www.odakyu.jp/english/passes/hakone), which can be picked up at any train station on the Odakyū line. This pass can either be purchased for a two-day trip from Shinjuku (adults ¥5,700, children ¥1,500) or Odawara (adults ¥4,600, children ¥1,000), or as a three-day pass from Shinjuku (adults ¥6,100, children ¥1,750). For detailed information on where the pass can be bought, visit www.odakyu.jp/english/support/center/.

TRAIN AND CABLE CAR

The **Hakone-Tōzan railway,** which begins at Odawara, passes through a number of stops where some of the area's best resorts and museums are located, ultimately ending up in the heart of Hakone at **Gōra.** From there, most visitors take a 10-minute ride on the **Hakone-Tōzan cable car,** connected directly to Gōra Station, 1.2 km (0.75 mi) to **Sōun-zan Station** (¥430).

ROPEWAY

At Sōun-zan you have the option of floating over **Ōwakudani** (Great Boiling Valley) aboard the **Hakone Ropeway** (1-15-1 Shiroyama, Odawara; tel. 0460/32-2205; www.hakoneropeway.

aficionado Okada Mokichi (1882-1955), some of the earthenware pieces date as far back as the Jomon period (13,000-300 BC).

POLA MUSEUM OF ART
ポーラ美術館

1285 Kozukayama; tel. 0460-84-2111; www. polamuseum.or.jp; 9am-5pm daily, adults ¥1,800, children ¥700; from Gōra Station, take Hakone Tōzan bus for Shissei Kaen to Pola Bijutsukan bus stop

This eye-catching, largely subterranean complex full of windows and light shows off the art collection amassed by the late owner of the POLA skin care and beauty products group, Suzuki Tsuneshi. Discreetly set within a hillside hidden in a beech forest, where some trees are three centuries old, the museum's collection extends from modern paintings—including Japanese artists like Sugiyama Yasushi and some heavy Western hitters like Picasso, Monet, Renoir, and Cezanne—to surrealists (Dalí), sculptures, Ming Dynasty vases,

and glassware delicately crafted mostly by Japanese and European artists. In a word, it's eclectic. Buses bound for the museum depart Gōra Station 4-5 times hourly.

Around Sōun-zan
ŌWAKUDANI
大涌谷

tel. 0460/84-5201; www.kanagawa-park.or.jp/ owakudani; cable car 9am-5pm daily Mar.-Nov., 9am-4:15pm daily Dec.-Feb.; ¥820 with Hakone Free Pass, ¥1,580 round-trip without Hakone Free Pass; from Gōra Station, ride Hakone-Tōzan to Sōun-zan Station, transfer to cable car and ride one stop to Ōwakudani Station

Ride in a cable car over this geologically tortured landscape. Ōwakudani means "Valley of Hell," named for the desolate, steamy valley emitting the strong scent of sulfur that formed 3,000 years ago when Kamiyama erupted, an event that also created the nearby Lake Ashi. If the sulfur fumes get to you, consider that co.jp/foreign/en; 9am-5pm daily Feb.-Nov., 9am-4:15pm Dec.-Jan.; adults ¥1,600, children ¥800 Sōun-zan to Ōwakudani round-trip, covered by Hakone Freepass). Gondolas on this line depart about once every minute and carry up to about 18 passengers.

Exiting the infernal valley, proceed along the ropeway to **Tōgendai** on the northeastern shore of the alpine **Lake Ashi**. The entire journey, from Sōun-zan to Tōgendai, takes about 30 minutes (adults ¥1,450, children ¥730 Sōun-zan to Tōgendai one-way, covered by Hakone Freepass).

CRUISE

Head for the dock to take a cruise over the gorgeous Lake Ashi, which offers excellent views of Mount Fuji when the sky is clear (colder months, early morning, and late afternoon are the best times to catch a glimpse of the peak).

Cruise boats are operated by **Hakone Sightseeing Boats** (www.hakone-kankosen.co.jp/foreign/en; 9:30am-5:30pm Mar. 20-Nov. 30, 10am-4:40pm daily Dec. 1-Mar. 19; 30 minutes; adults ¥1,000; children ¥500, covered by Hakone Freepass) and run between **Hakone-machi** and **Moto-Hakone** (10 minutes; adults ¥360; children ¥180) on the lake's south side and Tōgendai on the northern side. From Moto-Hakone, a great option is to walk to **Hakone-jinja,** a scenic shrine only 5 minutes from town on foot.

BUS

Complete the loop by traveling on the **Hakone Tōzan Bus** (www.hakone-tozanbus.co.jp/english) from Motohakone-ko bus stop back to Hakone-Yumoto, the buzzing gateway to Hakone at the eastern edge of the resort area. The ride takes about 35 minutes and buses depart from every 20-30 minutes (¥1,150; covered by Hakone Freepass).

the Japanese government's Ministry of the Environment concluded that the stench ranks among Japan's most prevalent 100 odors. The upshot of all this is that the area is known to turn out tasty *onsen tamago*: eggs boiled until turning black in the sulfurous springs.

Southern Lake Ashi
HAKONE-JINJA
箱根神社

80-1 Motohakone; tel. 0460/83-7123; http://hakonejinja.or.jp; 9am-4pm daily; from Hakone-Yumoto Station, take Hakone Tōzan bus (line H) to Hakone-jinja Iriguchi bus stops

Built in 757, Hakone-jinja is a picturesque shrine on the shore of Lake Ashi; it is at its most dramatic when it's shrouded in mist. To reach the shrine, take the 5-minute stroll from the Moto-Hakone boat pier and continue along an ascending path lined by lanterns and marked by an imposing and very photogenic *torii* gate. Definitely stop

by this shrine if you're exploring the Lake Ashi area.

★ ONSEN
Around Hakone-Yumoto
HAKONE YURYŌ ONSEN
箱根湯寮

4 Tōnosawa; tel. 0460/85-8411; www.hakoneyuryo.jp/english; 10am-8pm (last entry 7pm) Mon.-Fri., 10am-10pm (last entry 9pm) Sat.-Sun. and holidays; adults ¥1,500, children ages 6-12 ¥1,000; take shuttle bus from Hakone-Yumoto station, or Hakone-Tōzan line to Tōnosawa Station

For the classic countryside *onsen* experience within easy reach of Tokyo, Hakone Yuryō Onsen ticks all boxes. Surrounded by lushly forested hills, the outdoor baths here are excellent, with serene views of foliage on all sides and baths ranging from large single-sex communal pools to 19 private open-air ones rented by the hour (from ¥4,000). Book a private bath up to a month in advance by phone. Alongside baths, massages are offered in relaxation rooms, and an on-site restaurant serves food cooked over an *iori* (open hearth).

As is the case with most *onsen*, if you're sporting any ink you will need to keep it under wraps at the reception desk. Further, the communal baths will not be an option. Conceal what tattoos you have until reaching your reserved private bath, however, and you'll still be able to enjoy the experience.

TENZAN TŌJI-KYŌ
天山湯治郷

208 Yumoto-chaya; tel. 0460/86-4126; www.tenzan. jp; 9am-10pm daily; adults ¥1,300, children ¥650; take shuttle bus "B" from Hakone-Yumoto Station

If you're a person with tattoos, this sprawling *onsen* complex, which doesn't have a policy against tattoos, is your best bet in Hakone. Tenzan Tōji-kyō has indoor and outdoor baths, uniquely designed and surrounded by lush foliage, set at a range of temperatures, from merely warm to exfoliation-inducing. For maximum relaxation, head to one of the complex's saunas or massage rooms.

Around Kowakidani
YUNESSUN ONSEN PARK
根小涌園ユネッサン

1297 Ninotaira; tel. 0460/82-4126; www.yunessun. com/en; swimwear area 10am-6pm Mon.-Fri., 9am-7pm Sat.-Sun. and holidays, area where swimwear is not permitted 11am-7pm Mon.-Fri., 11am-8pm Sat.-Sun. and holidays; swimwear area for adults ¥2,500, children ¥1,400, area where swimwear is not permitted adults ¥1,500, children ¥1,000, all-area pass adults ¥3,500, children ¥1,800; from Gōra, Hakone-machi, or Hakone-Yumoto, take a bus to Kowakien

If you've ever dreamed of dunking yourself in a massive bathtub full of coffee, tea, or something harder like wine, Yunessun Onsen Park gives you that chance. There are also waterslides, mixed open-air baths with sweeping views of nature, and numerous other options for immersing yourself in hot rejuvenating liquid concoctions at this hot spring theme park—bathing suit required.

For a more traditional *onsen* experience, the adjoining **Mori-no-Yu** (11am-7pm Mon.-Fri., 11am-8pm Sat.-Sun. and holidays; adults ¥1,500, children ¥1,000) offers single-sex, clothing-optional bathing both in and outdoors, including tubs under gazebos amid traditional gardens, and private baths that can be rented for ¥5,000 per hour.

If you'd like to experience the whole gamut, admission to both parts of the park is

---

communal bath at Hakone Yuryō Onsen

¥3,500 adults, ¥1,800 children. And if you're too relaxed to bother leaving after all that soaking, there are four official hotels connected to the park. Tattoos, no matter how small, are not permitted at Yunessun.

FOOD
Around Hakone-Yumoto
HATSUHANA HONTEN

635 Yumoto; tel. 0460/85-8287; www.hatsuhana. co.jp; 10am-7pm Thurs.-Tues.; ¥1,000-1,400; take Hakone Tōzan railway to Hakone-Yumoto Station

Set in an old wooden building overlooking the Hayakawa River, Hatsuhana Honten has been serving its distinctive style of *soba* noodles since 1934. When wheat flour was scarce during World War II, the restaurant's owner tried making the noodles with only buckwheat flour and eggs, then dipping them in mineral-rich sticky yam called *jinenjo*. An unexpected hit, the recipe survives to this day. Try the original *seiro soba*, known for its distinctive chewy texture, made without water and dipped in sticky yam.

Miyanoshita
SUSHI MIYAFUJI

310 Miyanoshita; tel. 0460/82-2139; www. miyanoshita.com/miyafuji; 11:30am-2:30pm and 5:30pm-7:30pm Thurs.-Mon.; ¥1,500-2,000; take Hakone Tōzan railway to Miyanoshita Station

Sushi Miyafuji is an old-school family-run sushi joint that brings in fish from the port of Odawara daily. The most popular items on its menu are rice bowls topped with fish, including the *aji-don* (rice bowl topped with brook trout) and the fisherman's bowl (horse mackerel and squid over rice). Located 5 minutes' walk up a slope from the Fujiya Hotel.

MORI MESHI

404-13 Miyanoshita; tel. 0460/83-8886; https:// morimeshi.jp; 11:30am-3pm and 5pm-9pm daily; courses from ¥3,000, à la carte from ¥400; take Tōzan line to Miyanoshita Station

This bistro with a classic, all-wood interior and *izakaya* vibes sits right outside Miyashita Station. It's a great place for a healthy lunch

or dinner made with quality ingredients and generous helpings of fresh produce. The menu of tapa-like Japanese dishes includes a mix of salads, *oden*, sashimi, tempura, Japanese curry, noodles, and more. The staff are friendly and attentive. English menu available. Restaurants in the area are often full. Reserve ahead a day before or at least earlier the same day to be safe.

Around Gōra
GŌRA BREWERY AND GRILL

1300-72 Gōra; tel. 050/5461-3081; 1pm-9:30pm (last order 8:30pm) daily; lunch ¥3,000, dinner ¥5,000; take Tōzan line to Gōra Station

This stylish brewpub with dark wood paneling, a large tree supporting the vaulted ceiling at the center of the dining space, and a large window behind the bar looking out onto a landscape garden set into a hillside, is a great place for some craft beer and a meal. The grub matches the drink: salads, grilled vegetable platters, sausages, *gyoza* (fried dumplings), burdock root chips, sautéed shiitake mushrooms, and much more. It's popular, so reserve ahead a day or two to be safe.

ACCOMMODATIONS
Around Hakone-Yumoto
BANSUIRO FUKUZUMI

643 Yumoto; tel. 0460/85-5531; www.2923.co.jp; ¥28,000 with two meals; take Hakone Tōzan railway to Hakone-Yumoto Station

With a history stretching back to 1625 and old-school ambience intact, Bansuiro Fukuzumi weaves a spell on guests. Rebuilt now several times, the current iteration of this majestic old inn is a product of the Meiji period, when Japanese and Western architectural styles were often blended in experimental ways. Hence, wood, stone, and metal coexist seamlessly in the same building. It was no surprise that this inn—one of Hakone's oldest—was declared an important cultural property in 2002. The cuisine offered is similarly excellent, and there are private *onsen* baths to boot.

★ **FUKUZUMIRO**

74 Tōnosawa; tel. 0460/85-5301; www.fukuzumi-ro. com; doubles from ¥44,000 with two meals; from Hakone-Yumoto Station, take Hakone Tōzan railway to Tōnozawa Station

Fukuzumiro is another old-school gem, in business since 1890. Next to the Hayakawa River, the atmospheric property sprawls across three floors with 17 rooms, each with its own unique flourishes. Creativity is built into the *ryokan's* exquisite woodwork—look for the "lucky bat" carvings scattered throughout—and the inn is known as a retreat for writers and artists, including novelist Natsume Sōseki, Nobel Laureate Yasunari Kawabata, and actor Tsumasaburo Bando. Food courses featuring a range of seafood and vegetables are delivered to guests' rooms.

Around Gōra
★ **GŌRA KADAN**

1300 Gōra; tel. 0460/82-3331; www.gorakadan.com; ¥100,000 with two meals; take Hakone Tōzan railway from Hakone-Yumoto Station to Gōra Station

Gōra Kadan is a legendary *ryokan* so luxurious, the premium price tag actually feels justified. Top-notch *kaiseki* cuisine is presented like art in a European-style building, where flower-scented incense infuses the halls. Gorgeous tatami rooms filled with antiques and separated by sliding rice-paper walls have private gardens and open-air baths. And, of course, the hospitality is refined to the hilt. No detail is missed, no edges left unsmoothed. Amenities include a pool, spa, and salon. This property is world-class in every sense. If you can manage to book a room—do so as far in advance as possible—this is the Hakone hotel worthy of a serious splurge.

INFORMATION AND SERVICES

There is a **tourist information center** at Hakone-Yumoto Station (706-35 Yumoto Hakone-machi; tel. 0460/85-8911; www.hakone.or.jp; 9am-5:45pm daily) where you can ask questions of helpful English-speaking staff, and pick up English-language maps and

more. Online, **https://hakone-japan.com** provides plenty of information on things to see and do in Hakone.

GETTING THERE

To reach Hakone from Tokyo, take the **Odakyū line** from Shinjuku Station to **Hakone-Yumoto Station.** The speedy Romance Car reaches Hakone-Yumoto in 90 minutes (¥2,330), while the *kyūkō* (express) train will get you there in 2 hours (¥1,220). Note that you may need to change trains at Odawara if you take the cheaper express train.

If you have a JR Pass, you can also take the **JR Tōkaidō *shinkansen*** (Kodama, Hikari trains only) about 30 minutes to **Odawara Station.** You can then transfer to the local **Hakone-Tōzan line**—not covered by the JR Pass—to access the rest of the Hakone area.

The easiest way to reach Hakone from Kyoto is by taking the **JR Tōkaidō Shinkansen** (Hikari trains only) to **Odawara Station** (2 hours 5 minutes; ¥12,300), then hopping on the Hakone-Tōzan line and traveling west into Hakone proper from there. As is the case with any long-distance journey, there are other potential iterations on this basic route (e.g., taking the Nozomi *shinkansen,* which is not covered by the JR Pass, to Nagoya, then transferring to the Hikari *shinkansen,* which is covered by the JR Pass, and riding to Odawara from there). Just be aware that the JR Pass does not cover all *shinkansen* types, which can complicate and inflate fares if you're traveling with a JR Pass.

Travel Passes

If you're traveling from Tokyo to the Hakone region, the **Hakone Freepass** (www.odakyu.jp/english/passes/hakone; adults ¥5,700, children ¥1,500 for two-day pass, adults ¥6,100, children ¥1,750 for three-day pass) includes travel round-trip between Shinjuku and Hakone-Yumoto and use of the area's various modes of transportation (local train, cable car, Hakone Ropeway, boat). It also allows you to see many of the area's attractions at discounted rates. You can buy a

2- to 3-day pass at any Odakyū line train station, or buy the two-day pass online (www.japan-rail-pass.com/pass-regional/east/hakone-free-pass?ap=j0095g).

If you're combining travel from Tokyo to both Kamakura and Hakone, the **Hakone Kamakura Pass** (www.odakyu.jp/english/passes/hakone_kamakura; adults ¥7,000, children ¥2,250) covers your round-trip between Shinjuku, Kamakura, and Hakone, with free access to all Odakyū trains, buses, boats, cable cars, and ropeways around Hakone, as well as the Enoden railway that links Kamakura and Enoshima. The pass also gives you access to many area attractions at discounted rates. Valid for three days, the pass is only available at Shinjuku Station's Odakyū Sightseeing Service Center.

Finally, the **Fuji Hakone Pass** (www.odakyu.jp/english/passes/fujihakone) allows you to travel freely for three days within Fuji-Hakone and receive discounts at more than 90 attractions throughout the area. You have the option to add round-trip train fare from Shinjuku (adults ¥9,780, children ¥3,590) or to begin using the pass from Odawara Station (adults ¥7,180, children ¥2,290). You can buy this pass at the Odakyū Sightseeing Service Center in either Shinjuku Station or Odawara Station.

GETTING AROUND

The local train line servicing the Hakone area is the **Hakone-Tōzan line,** which connects Odawara to Gōra, a 1-hour journey, stopping at Hakone-Yumoto, Tōnosawa, Kokakidani, and near the Hakone Open-Air Museum and Okada Museum of Art, among other stations, along the way.

The cheapest way to get around the Hakone Loop is to purchase the **Hakone Freepass** (www.odakyu.jp/english/passes/hakone; adults ¥5,700, children ¥1,500 for two-day pass, adults ¥6,100, children ¥1,750 for three-day pass).

Cable Car and Ropeway

From the Hakone-Tōzan line's terminus at Gōra Station, where you'll find the Hakone Art Museum, the classic route includes taking the **Hakone-Tōzan Cable Car** (¥430, covered by Hakone Freepass) from within Gōra Station to Sōun-zan. From here, take the **Hakone Ropeway** (1-15-1 Shiroyama, Odawara; tel. 0460/32-2205; www.hakoneropeway.co.jp/foreign/en; 9am-5pm daily Feb.-Nov., 9am-4:15pm Dec.-Jan.; adults ¥1,600, children ¥800 Sōun-zan to Ōwakudani round-trip, covered by Hakone Freepass) to Ōwakudani, where plenty of steaming and bubbling volcanic activity is in full view, and then to Tōgendai on the shore of Lake Ashi (adults ¥1,450, children ¥730 Sōun-zan to Tōgendai one-way, covered by Hakone Freepass).

Boat Cruise

Tōgendai is the jumping-off point for a **boat cruise** to Hakone-machi and Moto-Hakone. Cruises are operated by **Hakone Sightseeing Boats** (www.hakone-kankosen.co.jp/foreign/en; 9:30am-5:30pm daily Mar. 20-Nov. 30, 10am-4:40pm daily Dec. 1-Mar. 19, 30 minutes, adults ¥1,000; children ¥500, covered by Hakone Freepass) and **Izuhakone Sightseeing Boats** (www.izuhakone.co.jp/ashinokoboatcruise/info/en.html; 8:30am-5pm daily year-round, not covered by Hakone Freepass) run between Hakone-machi and Moto-Hakone (10 minutes; adults ¥360, children ¥180).

Bus

From Moto-Hakone, return to Hakone-Yumoto by **bus** (35 minutes; ¥1,150, covered by Hakone Freepass). Catch the bus from the Hakone Tōzan Bus Information Center (6 Moto-Hakone; tel. 0460/83-6171; www.hakone-tozanbus.co.jp/english), located about 15 minutes' walk southeast of Hakone-jinja.

Mount Fuji

富士山

The Japanese have a word to describe the rush of emotion that ensues in the moments just before the first rays of the sun break over the horizon when viewed from a mountain top: *go-raiko*. The phrase, roughly meaning "honorable coming of the light," seeks to capture a feeling that is hard to pin down, an innate sense that witnessing the sunrise from a mountain peak is an extraordinary, even spiritual experience. Seeing the sky fill with the colors of dawn followed by sunrise from atop Mount Fuji, Japan's highest peak at 3,776 meters (12,388 feet), is the ultimate way to grasp the essence of *go-raiko* and to understand why the mountain holds such sway over the national psyche.

Since time immemorial, Mount Fuji has stood as nature's most sacred spot in Japan. The goddess of Mount Fuji, Princess Konohanasakuya—daughter of the mountain god and deity of all volcanoes—is honored at small shrines dotting its slopes. The privilege to climb to the summit was not granted for laypeople until about 150 years ago. Women were not permitted to make the ascent until 1868. Even today, steadfast hikers with mystical leanings approach the mountain only after purifying themselves at Sengen-jinja, a shrine in a dense old-growth forest at the mountain's base. Today, the inner sanctum of Sengen-jinja still stands atop the peak, serving as a reminder of these sacred roots.

Rather than a trickle of holy men, weekend warriors and overseas travelers now crowd the mountain, which is the crowning jewel of **Fuji-Hakone-Izu National Park** (www.fujihakoneizu.com). The summit is flush with the same amenities you'd expected to find in any Japanese town, from 24-hour ramen stalls to a weather station and even a post office. But those who witness sunrise from the summit cannot deny the deeper stirrings felt by seekers who made the same journey centuries ago.

HIKING

For most travelers, glimpsing Mount Fuji from afar is enough. But during the official climbing season (July-Aug.), well-established paths beckon to those keen to get up close and personal with the sacred peak. Once you've reached the top, the amenities available may shock you. You can mail a postcard, buy a charm at a shrine, circumnavigate the volcanic crater (a 2-hour walk), and slurp ramen at a food stall perched near the caldera's rim. Mount Fuji is one of the most climbed mountains in the world. But don't let the legions of grannies and middle-aged salarymen fool you—the ascent can be arduous. As the old adage goes: "A wise man climbs Fuji once; a fool climbs it twice."

Planning Your Hike

Temperature differences between the base and summit are as much as 20°C (36°F) in summer. Although Mount Fuji's last eruption was in 1707, its soil still contains a thick layer of granular volcanic ash, prone to shifting as you walk. Wear sturdy boots suited for hiking, a hat that can be fastened to prevent losing it in the wind, sunscreen, gloves, sunglasses, a headlamp if you're hiking at night, sufficient water (3 liters is wise), vitamin-infused drinks, calorific snacks, and a trash bag. In short, prepare for the unexpected. Thick wool socks and waterproof clothes could save you from a multihour slog while drenched in the rain.

Depending on where you start and which trail you take, the journey from one of the main fifth stations up the top half of Mount Fuji is usually a five- to six-hour affair. Most begin the journey at night—around 8pm if they're starting from the first station, or 11pm if they're starting from the fifth station—and walk until morning. Another popular way to make the ascent is to start in the afternoon, stay in a hut overnight at

Mount Fuji and the Five Lakes

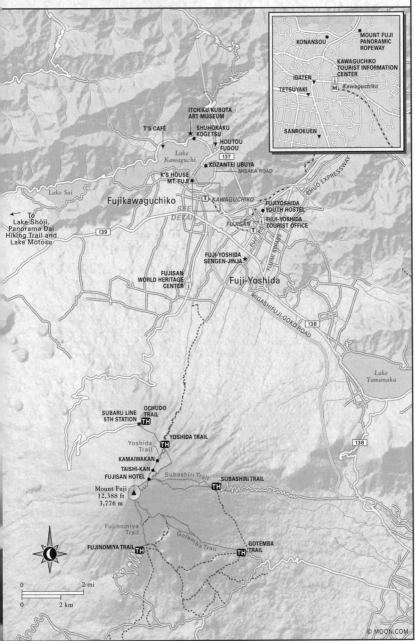

KONANSOU

MOUNT FUJI
PANORAMIC
ROPEWAY

KAWAGUCHIKO
TOURIST INFORMATION
CENTER

IDATEN

TETSUYAKI

SANROKUEN

Kawaguchiko

ITCHIKU KUBOTA
ART MUSEUM

T'S CAFÉ

SHUHOKAKU
KOGETSU

HOUTOU
FUDOU

Lake
Kawaguchi

KOZANTEI UBUYA

MISAKA ROAD

K'S HOUSE
MT. FUJI

CHUO EXPRESSWAY

Lake Sai

Fujikawaguchiko

KAWAGUCHIKO

FUJIYOSHIDA
YOUTH HOSTEL

FUJISAN

FUJI-YOSHIDA
TOURIST OFFICE

To
Lake Shōji,
Panorama Dai
Hiking Trail and
Lake Motosu

139

FUJI-YOSHIDA
SENGEN-JINJA

Fuji-Yoshida

FUJISAN
WORLD HERITAGE
CENTER

HIGASHIFUJI-GOKO ROAD

138

Lake
Yamanaka

138

SUBARU LINE
5TH STATION

OCHUDO
TRAIL

YOSHIDA TRAIL

Yoshida
Trail

KAMAIWAKAN

TAISHI-KAN
FUJISAN HOTEL

Subashiri Trail

SUBASHIRI TRAIL

Mount Fuji
12,388 ft
3,776 m

Fujinomiya
Trail

Gotemba Trail

FUJINOMIYA TRAIL

GOTEMBA
TRAIL

0   2 mi

0   2 km

© MOON.COM

☆ Views of Mount Fuji

Seen from afar, Mount Fuji's symmetry is stunning. Its near-perfect cone, snow-capped most of the year, is one of the most iconic mountains in the world. Whether in the background of a 17th-century woodblock print or looming behind the pastoral foreground view from a bullet train, it's easily one of the most immediately recognizable mountains anywhere. It's on the ¥1,000 note, is seen plastered across *sento* (public bath) walls nationwide, and is a favorite motif in traditional crafts, from exquisitely painted porcelain cups to the scabbards of samurai swords. Its special status as a natural object of such widespread recognition was attested to when it was declared a World Heritage site in 2013—a rare feat for a landform.

A NATIONAL SYMBOL

Since the Heian period (794-1185), Mount Fuji has been the object of poetic admiration, appearing in the 8th-century *Manyoshu*, Japan's first poetry anthology. During the Edo period (1603-1868), as the seat of political power drifted from Kyoto to Edo (now Tokyo), Mount Fuji's status grew. An increasing number of feudal lords and merchants traversed the country, moving east to west, passing by the increasingly idealized peak. During this time, pilgrims formed associations dedicated to making the journey and even built temples using rocks and plants taken from the sacred mount, in the hopes of channeling some of its sacred power. Meanwhile, devout lords had small hills built on their property in Edo from which they viewed the summit, not yet obscured by high-rises as it is across most of Tokyo today.

But the most enduring tributes to Mount Fuji to emerge during the Edo period were in the arts, from the poems of haiku masters such as Matsuo Basho (1644-1694) to, most notably, *ukiyo-e* woodblock prints by masters like Katsushika Hokusai (1760-1849) and Utagawa Hiroshige (1797-1858). In fact, Fuji appears in one of the most recognizable paintings of all time, Hokusai's immortal *Great Wave Off Kanagawa*, in which its snowy summit looms in the background, behind the brave souls navigating turbulent ocean currents in long wooden boats. While *Great Wave* is undoubtedly Hokusai's most famous work, his series *One Hundred Views of Mount Fuji*, which he finished at age 75, is regarded as a masterpiece through which he achieved immortality both for himself and the mountain, which has become a symbol of Japan itself.

BEST VISTAS

Regardless of where you gaze at Fuji from, note that weather around the peak can be fickle. Its summit is often hidden by clouds in spring, summer, and autumn. Crisp winter days provide some of the best views, particularly in the morning. While there are no guarantees the weather will cooperate, here are a few of the best spots to try and catch a glimpse of the timeless peak. That said, if you don't have time to visit the region surrounding the mountain itself, be sure to at least take a peek out the window of the bullet train as you shuttle past the mountain.

- West of Kamakura, the island of **Enoshima** offers some magnificent views of the peak on clear days, contrasting beautifully with the rugged Shōnan coast. Try **Katase Nishihama Beach,** just west of the island on the mainland, or the observation deck of the lighthouse known as the Sea Candle, located atop the island within the **Samuel Cocking Garden** (page 173).

- In Hakone, the southeast corner of **Lake Ashi** offers splendid views of the distant peak, with **Hakone-jinja** in the foreground (page 185).

- Closer to the Mount Fuji itself, the Five Lakes region has some excellent viewing spots. **Lake Kawaguchi** offers some of the best, particularly from its north shore, as does the **Panorama Dai hiking trail** (page 197).

- If you'd like to hike around Mount Fuji without approaching the summit, the **Ochudo trail** is a good hike for a day trip (page 195).

the seventh or eighth stage, and then proceed to the summit in the early morning. Walking at either of these times allows hikers to avoid the sun at its peak and to see the sunrise from the top.

Resources packed with Fuji tips include the online guide **Climbing Mount Fuji** (www17. plala.or.jp/climb_fujiyama) and the official **Mount Fuji Climbing website** (www. fujisan-climb.jp).

Safety

Be mindful of your own condition along the way. Around the time you enter the eighth stage, altitude sickness becomes a real concern. If you begin to feel nauseous or uncharacteristically exhausted, don't ignore the warning signs. Turn back if these symptoms arise.

Making the ascent outside of July and August requires legit skills hiking in icy conditions, and the capacity and gear to handle extremes. Hikers keen to summit Fuji during the off-season should register with local authorities at the **Lake Kawaguchi Tourist Information Center** (3641-1 Funatsu; tel. 0555/72-6700; www.fujisan.ne.jp; 8am-6pm daily) and keep an eye on the weather forecast, respecting the risk involved. Finally, hire a guide.

Guides

Fuji Mountain Guides (tel. 042/445-0798; www.fujimountainguides.com; ¥44,000 pp for 2-day tours), run by bilingual American guides, offer tours year-round. **Discover Japan Tours** (www.discover-japan-tours. com/en; ¥10,000 pp for 2-day tours) offer tours for groups of at least two. If you're ill equipped to summit the peak and would like to rent gear or attire, check out the offerings of **Yamarent** (tel. 050/5865-1615; contact by phone 10am-5pm daily; www.yamarent. com), which rents anything you'll realistically need and then some: boots, rainwear, crampons, even avalanche beacons. Have a look at the website first, and then either call or email (via the website) ahead before you make a trip to one of its branches, where an appointment is required.

Routes

If you'd like to climb Fuji, the popular **Yoshida trail** runs along the mountain's north face in Yamanashi Prefecture, while the **Subashiri** runs up the eastern face (the less popular **Fujinomiya** and **Gotemba** trails line the south face in Shizuoka Prefecture). For a map outlining Fuji's main trails, visit www.fujimountainguides.com/ uploads/1/5/3/1/15315858/fuji_climbing_ map_all4trails.pdf. Each trail is broken into 10 stations, with the fifth being where most climbers start their ascent. Given Fuji's immense popularity, you might find yourself sharing the slopes with loads of hikers, particularly on weekends during the climbing season, with the Ōbon holidays in mid-August being the busiest time. Foot traffic can be so heavy that queues form at bottlenecks in the trail. Although merging with the crowd is part of the journey, it's helpful to climb on a weekday, preferably in July, and to undertake the majority of the ascent overnight.

YOSHIDA TRAIL

Distance: 15 km (9 mi) round-trip
Time: 9-12 hours round-trip
Information and maps: Fuji-Yoshida Tourist Office or Fujisan World Heritage Center; www.japan. travel/en/spot/2328; www.fujimountainguides.com/ uploads/1/5/3/1/15315858/yoshida_trail_map.pdf
Trailhead: Subaru Line Fifth Station

By far the most popular route to the top of Fuji involves starting from the fifth station of the well-trodden Yoshida trail. Known as the **Subaru Line Fifth Station** (aka **Kawaguchi-ko Fifth Station** or **Yoshidaguchi Fifth Station**), this station sits at an elevation of 2,305 meters (7,562 feet) and is by far the most developed of the mountain's fifth stations, including the most mountain huts (20) of all major routes. The ascent takes about 6-7 hours and the descent takes 3-5. The fifth station can be reached by bus—seat reservations unavailable—from either Kawaguchiko Station or Fujisan Station, operated by **Fujikyū Bus** (tel. 0555/72-6877; http://bus-en.fujikyu.co.jp; 50 minutes, buses start from 6:20am, 1-2 depart hourly; ¥1,570 one-way, ¥2,300 round-trip). For a simplified English explanation of how to take this bus, check out the clear primer at http://bus-en.fujikyu.co.jp/get-on-bus/.

While starting at the fifth station will more than likely be all you need to scratch your Fuji itch, for experience seekers with a slightly masochistic bent, it's entirely possible to climb Fuji the same way that spiritual pilgrims of yore once did. In the town of Fuji-Yoshida, near Lake Kawaguchi at the mountain's eastern base, pilgrims gravitate to **Fuji-Yoshida Sengen-jinja** (aka Kitaguchi Hongū Fuji Sengen-jinja; 5558 Kami-Yoshida; tel. 0555/22-0221; www.sengenjinja.jp; 24 hours daily), a shrine dedicated to the mountain's chief deity, Princess Konohanasakuya. The Yoshida trail, which goes from the base to the summit, starts from this shrine. Sticklers for tradition swear by this trail, which entails roughly a 12-hour, 19-km (11.8-mi) ascent from base to summit, followed by a descent that takes 3-5 hours.

SUBASHIRI TRAIL

Hiking distance: *14 km (8.75 mi) round-trip*
Time: *10-12 hours round-trip*
Information and maps: *www.japan.travel/en/fuji-guide/mt-fuji-subashiri-trail; www.alltrails.com/trail/japan/shizuoka/mount-fuji-trail-subashiri-trail*
Trailhead: *Subashiri Fifth Station*

On the south face of the mountain, the Subashiri trail begins from the **Subashiri Fifth Station** (1,950 meters/6,398 feet) and has relatively well-developed infrastructure with 12 huts along the way. This is the second-best option overall, and is particularly appealing if you happen to be coming from Lake Yamanaka rather than Lake Kawaguchi. It winds through forests and is less crowded. In fact, it merges with the more accessible, developed, afnd crowded Yoshida trail from the eighth station onward. The ascent (8 km/5 mi) takes around 7-9 hours, while the descent (6 km/3.75 mi) takes about 3 hours.

To reach Subashiri Fifth Station, take the JR Tokaido line from Tokyo to Kozu (1.25 hours; ¥1,320), then transfer to the JR Gotemba line and ride until Gotemba Station (50 minutes; ¥670). From Gotemba, take the bus to Subashiri Fifth Station (1 hour; ¥1,540 one-way, ¥2,060 round-trip).

hiking the Yoshida trail on Mount Fuji

OCHUDO TRAIL

Hiking distance: *6 km (3.7 mi) round-trip*
Time: *2-3 hours round-trip*
Information and maps: *www. yamanashi-kankou.jp/kokuritsukoen/en/miryoku/ hiking/course2.html; www.fujisan-climb.jp/en/ m3oati0000002q40-att/2016Reiho_Climbing_ Edition.pdf*
Trailhead: *Subaru Fifth Station*

If you'd like to hike around Mount Fuji without approaching the summit, the Ochudo trail, which begins from the Subaru Fifth Station and moves westward at a roughly constant elevation, is a good hike for a day trip.

ACCOMMODATIONS

Reserving a space at one of Mount Fuji's mountain huts can be tricky during climbing season. **Fuji Mountain Guides** (www. fujimountainguides.com/mountain-hut-reservations.html) offers a reservation service for a nominal fee of ¥1,000.

KAMAIWAKAN

Yoshida trail, seventh station; tel. 080/1299-0223; http://kamaiwakan.jpn.org; ¥8,000, depending on day and meal option

Clean and revamped, Kamaiwakan is a good option at 2,790 meters (9,153 feet) with free Wi-Fi and two optional meals. Some English is spoken. Book two months ahead.

TAISHI-KAN

Yoshida trail, eighth station; tel. 0555/22-1947; www. mfi.or.jp/w3/home0/taisikan; ¥9,000, depending on day

Taishi-kan is a tried-and-true mountain hut for Fuji hikers. It sleeps 350 hikers in sleeping bags. Two meals (including vegetarian and halal on request) are included in the price. Checkout time is 5am. Soft drinks and snacks are sold. Some English is spoken. Book two months in advance.

FUJISAN HOTEL

Yoshida trail, eighth station; tel. 0555/22-0237; www. fujisanhotel.com; ¥8,000, depending on day and meal option chosen

Fujisan Hotel is a very popular option, given its location at the 3,400-meter (11,154-foot) junction of the Lake Kawaguchi and Subashiri trails. The lodge will hold onto your bag while you walk the final 60 minutes of the path to the summit. Breakfast and dinner are optional. Book two months in advance.

INFORMATION AND SERVICES

For maps and English-language information on the area, visit **Fuji-Yoshida Tourist Office** beside (Fuji-Yoshida) Fujisan Station (tel. 0555/22-7000; www.fujisan.ne.jp; 9am-5pm daily), the **Lake Kawaguchi Tourist Information Center** (3641-1 Funatsu, Fujikawaguchiko; tel. 0555/72-6700; www. fujisan.ne.jp; 9am-5pm daily), or **Fujisan World Heritage Center** (6663-1 Funatsu, Fujikawaguchiko; tel. 0555/72-0259; www. fujisan-whc.jp/en/index.html; 8:30am-7pm daily late July-Aug. 26, 8:30am-6pm Aug. 27-Sept., 8:30am-5pm rest of year) on the north face of the mountain, south of Lake Kawaguchi.

GETTING THERE

Straddling the border of Yamanashi and Shizuoka prefectures, Mount Fuji is within easy reach of Tokyo by bus or train. The main transit hubs for accessing the Mount Fuji area include the town of **Fuji-Yoshida** and **Lake Kawaguchi,** which are served by buses and trains from Tokyo.

Train

To come via train, starting from Shinjuku, take the **Chūō line** west to **Otsuki.** The limited express (*tokkyū*) train takes 1 hour 10 minutes (¥2,360), while the regular (*futsū*) train takes about 1 hour 30 minutes (¥1,340) and may require a transfer at Takao Station. From Otsuki, transfer to the **Fuji Kyūkō line** to Fuji-Yoshida (Fujisan Station; 50 minutes; ¥1,040). Note that the JR Pass covers the leg of the trip up to Otsuki, but does not cover the Fuji Kyūkō line.

Bus

If you'd rather take a bus—in some ways the simpler option—buses operated by **Keiō Dentetsu** (tel. 03/5376-2222; http://highway-buses.jp; adults ¥2,000, children ¥1,000) and **Fujikyū Express** (http://bus-en.fujikyu.co.jp/highway; adults ¥2,000, children ¥1,000) depart once or twice hourly from the Shinjuku Highway Bus Terminal (Shinjuku Station west exit; https://highway-buses.jp/terminal/shinjuku.php) and run to both the town of Fuji-Yoshida (Fujisan Station) and Kawaguchiko Station. The journey to either stop takes about 1 hour 40 minutes.

If you want to take a bus from downtown Tokyo straight to the fifth station, Keiō Dentetsu runs buses directly to the fifth station of the Subaru Line Fifth Station, partly up the mountain from Shinjuku Highway Bus Terminal (tel. 03/5376-2222; http://highway-buses.jp; adults ¥2,900, children ¥1,450 one-way). You must reserve a seat in advance.

Fujikyū (http://bus-en.fujikyu.co.jp/highway) and **JR Kanto Bus** (www.jrbuskanto.co.jp.e.wn.hp.transer.com) also operate buses between Yaesu South Exit of Tokyo Station and Kawaguchiko Station (2 hours; ¥2,000 one-way). Fujikyū also operates buses that depart near the Mark City shopping complex attached to Shibuya Station and run to both Kawaguchiko Station and Fujisan Station (2-2.5 hours; ¥2,000 one-way). From Kyoto, board the **Tōkaidō *shinkansen* Kodama line** and ride to **Mishima Station** (2 hours 40 minutes; ¥11,110). From the south exit of Mishima Station, catch a **Fujikyūkō bus** (http://bus-en.fujikyu.co.jp/highway) to Kawaguchiko Station. This last leg of the journey takes anywhere from 1.5 hours to more than 2 hours, depending on road conditions, and costs ¥2,300 one-way.

To reserve a seat online with minimum fuss for any of the above routes, visit the website of **Japan Bus Online** (https://japanbusonline.com/en) or **Willer Express** (https://willerexpress.com/en).

GETTING AROUND

Once you've arrived in either the hub of Fuji-Yoshida (Fujisan Station) or Kawaguchiko Station, buses operated by **Fujikyū Bus** (tel. 0555/72-6877; http://bus-en.fujikyu.co.jp) connect to the five lakes and other area attractions.

To get farther up the mountain by bus, you can travel about one hour from either Kawaguchiko Station or Fujisan Station to the **Subaru Fifth Station** (¥1,570 one-way, ¥2,300 round-trip). During the official climbing season, buses run to the fifth station 7am-8pm, and return 8am-9pm. Note that buses run much less frequently throughout the rest of the year—roughly 9am-3pm. For more details, see the **Fujikyū Yamanashi** website (http://bus-en.fujikyu.co.jp/route). All buses running to the fifth station operate mid-April-early December. As these buses are essentially local, there's no reservation system. Plan on showing up and buying a ticket on the same day in person. Find detailed English instructions at http://bus-en.fujikyu.co.jp/get-on-bus.

Fuji Five Lakes 富士五湖

Five lakes surrounding the iconic peak teem with visitors, particularly in summer, reaching fever pitch during climbing season. **Lake Yamanaka** is a favorite for water sports lovers, while **Lake Sai** is a good place to camp and, in summer, to swim. **Lake Shōji,** the smallest of the five, and **Lake Motosu,** famed for its appearance on the ¥1,000 note, are both west of Lake Sai. Farther from Tokyo than the other three lakes, they offer fewer amenities and don't warrant a detour for those with limited time. **Lake Kawaguchi,** on the north face of the mountain, is the most developed and easy to access from Tokyo, and therefore the one covered here.

Along with the neighboring town of

Fuji-Yoshida, the town surrounding Lake Kawaguchi, known as **Fujikawaguchiko,** makes for a good overnight stay before or after climbing Fuji. Of the five lakes at the base of the revered volcano, Kawaguchi is the one worth a stop for those on a short trip, due to its easy access from Tokyo and its well-developed infrastructure. The town is teeming with *onsen* resorts, most offering unobstructed views of Fuji, which looms to the south. The southern shore is admittedly touristy and can become jammed with visitors during summer. But the lake's east side and less-developed northern shore offer spectacular views of the mountain and are home to a few museums worth visiting. Lake Kawaguchi is a great choice if you want to appreciate Fuji at a distance, preferably while lounging around a *ryokan* clad in a *yukata* or soaking in an *onsen* tub.

SIGHTS
Itchiku Kubota Art Museum

2255 Kawaguchi; tel. 0555/76-8811; www. itchiku-museum.com; 9:30am-5:30pm Wed.-Mon. Apr.-Nov., 10am-4:30pm Wed.-Mon. Dec.-Mar., closed Wed. if holiday falls on Tues., open daily Oct.-Nov.; adults ¥1,600, college and high school students ¥900, junior high and elementary students ¥400; from Kawaguchiko Station take Kawaguchiko bus (Kawaguchiko line) to Itchiku Kubota Art Museum bus stop

In Kawaguchi, the Itchiku Kubota Art Museum showcases textiles woven by master artist Kubota Itchiku (1917-2003), who elevated the kimono to stunning heights. The museum itself is housed in a pyramidal building and presents Kubota's stunning vision in the artwork called *Symphony of Light,* containing 80 kimonos, of which 30 are shown at any one time. Each hefty garment in this work is three to four times heavier than a normal kimono and incorporates dyeing techniques dating to the 14th-17th centuries. There's a **café** with a glass beads gallery on site (coffee or tea ¥500), as well as a garden with a **teahouse** on the grounds (10am-2:30pm daily; tea ¥1,000, tea with sweets sets ¥1,300-2,500).

Mount Fuji Panoramic Ropeway

1163-1 Azagawa; tel. 0555/72-0363; www. mtfujiropeway.jp; 9:30am-4:30pm (last descent 4:50pm) daily Mar.-Nov., 9:30am-3:30pm (last descent 3:50pm) daily Dec.-Feb.; adults ¥500, children ¥250 one-way, adults ¥900, children ¥450 round-trip

At the southeastern edge of Lake Kawaguchi, the Mount Fuji Panoramic Ropeway will transport you 1,104 meters (3,622 feet) up to a viewing deck with superb views of Mount Fuji. You won't get views of Japan's most famous peak better than this.

HIKING
PANORAMA DAI HIKING TRAIL

Hiking distance: *5.1 km (3.2 mi) round-trip*
Time: *2-3 hours round-trip*
Information and maps: *https:// nowrongturnsblog.wordpress.com/2017/05/10/ itinerary-for-an-unforgettable-trip-to-mt-fuji*
Trailhead: *Panorama-dai-shita bus stop*

Traveling westward from Lake Kawaguchi by car (30 minutes) or bus (40 minutes), start hiking from the northwestern shore of Lake Shoji along the Panorama Dai hiking trail. After following the moderately difficult path for about 1 hour, you'll reach a breathtaking lookout point (elevation 1,325 m/4,347 ft) directly facing Fuji. Note that the signage is almost entirely in Japanese—just look for the boards indicating the Panorama Dai (パノラマ 台) and stick to the path, which entails walking roughly 45 minutes uphill to a junction, then veering left and forging on for another 15 minutes to the lookout point.

A caveat: The buses running between Kawaguchi-ko Station and Panorama Dai Shita bus stop, next to this trailhead, are very sporadic (Blue line bus, 4-5 daily; ¥1,040 one-way from Kawaguchi-ko Station). For this trip to make sense, I would only recommend making it if you have a rental car. Also note that there are numerous locations called "Panorama Dai" in the region. If you're using Google Maps, instead search for the GPS coordinates 35°29'25.9"N 138°36'09.3"E. Here,

you'll find a small parking lot next to the bus stop. The trailhead is right across the street. Alternatively, search for the Yamadaya Hotel in Google Maps. The trailhead is about 200 m (656 ft), or a 3-minute walk south, from there.

FOOD

T'S CAFÉ

Ridge E 1F, 1477-1 Ōishi; tel. 0555/25-7055; www. fujioishihanaterasu.com; 10am-6pm daily in summer, 10:30am-5pm daily in winter; ¥700-1,200; take Fuji Kyūkō line to Kawaguchiko Station, then take Kawaguchiko "retro bus" (Kawaguchiko line) to Kawaguchiko Natural Living Center bus stop

Tucked away in Fuji Ōishi Hanaterrace—a cluster of shops next to Ōishi Park dedicated to locally produced foods and goods—T's Café offers a reasonably priced menu of drinks, snacks, light meals, and ice cream, all made using locally sourced ingredients. Views of lavender fields and Mount Fuji are an added bonus. This is a good pick if you're on the lake's north shore.

TETSUYAKI

3486-1 Funatsu; tel. 070/4075-1683; https:// tetsuyaki.business.site; 11:30am-2pm and 5pm-9:30pm daily; ¥800-1,000; take Fuji Kyūkō line to Kawaguchiko Station

Two minutes' walk from Kawaguchiko Station, Tetsuyaki offers good greasy-spoon options on a budget-friendly menu. You'll find chicken and rice dishes, steak and fries, *okonomiyaki,* ginger pork, and booze. It's a good option if you're searching for a bite after dark, as many restaurants close early around town.

IDATEN

3486-4 Funatsu; tel. 0555/73-9218; http://ida-ten. jp; 11am-1am (last order midnight) daily; ¥880-1,180; take Fuji Kyūkō line to Kawaguchiko Station

Generous portions of tempura are the focus of the menu at Idaten. Sit in a counter seat for a view of the kitchen, where you can see the chefs at work. Optional sets include rice, miso soup, and *udon.* English menu is available. This is a good choice if you're on the south side of the lake, near Kawaguchiko Station.

HOUTOU FUDOU

707 Kawaguchi; tel. 0555/76-7011; www. houtou-fudou.jp/index.html; 11am-7pm daily; ¥1,050; take Fuji Kyūkō line to Kawaguchiko Station, then take Kawaguchiko "retro bus" (Kawaguchiko line) to Kawaguchiko Music Forest bus stop

Houtou Fudou, on the eastern shore of the lake, is a good restaurant to sample *houtou,* a dish that includes flat noodles akin to *udon* in a bowl of miso-based stew and vegetables. This dish is a specialty of Yamanashi Prefecture and a local favorite. Along with *houtou,* the menu also includes *soba* noodles, minced tuna with rice, *basashi* (raw horse meat), and *inari* sushi (sweetened tofu pouches stuffed with sushi rice). Call ahead if you plan to visit the store after 4pm on a weekday.

★ SANROKUEN

3370-1 Funatsu; tel. 0555/73-1000; 11am-7:30pm Fri.-Wed.; ¥2,100-4,200; take Fuji Kyūkō line to Kawaguchiko Station

A 15-minute walk from Kawaguchiko Station, Sanrokuen is an atmospheric restaurant set in a thatched-roof house, built 150 years ago. Guests sit on the floor around a sunken hearth and slow-grill five-course sets of meat, fish, vegetables, and tofu on spears over an open charcoal pit. While rainbow trout, duck, pork, beef, and a variety of delicious local vegetables feature heavily on the menu, some items are not your everyday fare. Barbecued jellyfish, anyone? This is a good choice for a unique, homey meal with friendly hosts. It's wise to book a week in advance or more to ensure a seat. English is spoken.

1: Lake Kawaguchi from the top of the Mount Fuji Panoramic Ropeway **2:** passengers boarding the ropeway car

ACCOMMODATIONS

FUJIYOSHIDA YOUTH HOSTEL

3-6-51 Shimoyoshida, Fujiyoshidashi; tel.
0555/22-0533; www.jyh.or.jp/e/i.php?jyhno=2803;
¥3,200 dorm; take JR Chūō line to Otsuki Station,
then take Fuji Kyūkō railway to Shimoyoshida Station

Given that its no-frills rooms are private, the name Fujiyoshida Youth Hostel is a bit of a misnomer. Guests share a clean bathroom and sleep on futons on tatami-mat floors in the six rooms of this tiny inn, which is a Japanese-style home run by a family who lives on the first floor. The owners are extremely hospitable and are happy to help with local recommendations. This is a solid budget option in the town of Fuji-Yoshida, away from the more touristy Lake Kawaguchi. Breakfast is available for an additional ¥600.

K'S HOUSE MT. FUJI

6713-108 Funatsu; tel. 0555/83-5556; https://
kshouse.jp; ¥3,300 dorm, ¥8,400 private room
without bathroom, ¥8,800 private room with
bathroom; take Fuji Kyūkō line to Kawaguchiko
Station

Popular among backpackers and hikers who are in town to climb Mount Fuji, K's House Mt. Fuji offers clean, cozy Japanese-style private rooms with tatami-mat floors and dorm-style rooms, including some that are female-only, at reasonable rates. Guests have access to a shared lounge and kitchen, and the hostel is close to a convenience store, supermarket, and a few eateries. It's located only a 3-minute walk from the south side of the lake. This is a solid budget option for those seeking to meet fellow travelers.

KONANSOU

4020-2 Funatsu; tel. 0555/72-2166; www.konansou.
com; ¥42,000 with two meals; take Fuji Kyūkō line to
Kawaguchiko Station

Konansou is a *ryokan* with modern Japanese and Western-style rooms, some with private outdoor bathtubs, at the southeastern corner

of Lake Kawaguchi. There are fantastic views of Mount Fuji and the lake throughout the hotel. Alongside gender-separated indoor and outdoor public *onsen* baths, there is a rooftop garden with an *onsen* footbath and private *onsen* baths that can be reserved in 50-minute increments. Guests can opt for a breakfast buffet and dinner plan comprising *kaiseki* fare, either eaten in the restaurant or delivered to the room.

★ SHUHOKAKU KOGETSU

2312 Kawaguchi; tel. 0555/76-8888; www.kogetu.
com; ¥45,000 with two meals; pickup from
Kawaguchiko Station available for guests

The biggest draw at this plush *onsen ryokan* is the stunning view of Fuji, seen from both the men's and women's open-air pools. Sitting on the northern shore of Lake Kawaguchi, this luxury spot has all the bells and whistles you'd expect—top-notch hospitality, *kaiseki* meals made with the finest seasonal ingredients served directly to the rooms, and large, well-appointed Japanese-style rooms with views of the lake and peak looming beyond. There's also a stunning garden and a private lakeside beach. If you've got the cash, this is a worthy splurge.

KOZANTEI UBUYA

10 Asakawa; tel. 0555/72-1145; www.ubuya.co.jp;
¥58,000 with two meals; take Fuji Kyūkō line to
Kawaguchiko Station; hotel shuttle bus available from
there upon request

Kozantei Ubuya is a high-end *ryokan* on the east side of Lake Kawaguchi with phenomenal lakeside views of Mount Fuji from its indoor and outdoor *onsen* baths. Antifogging windows in the bathrooms of even standard suites offer unhindered vistas of the famed peak. Spacious rooms come in both Japanese and Western styles, and deluxe suites have private outdoor bathtubs. Optional breakfast and dinner are prepared with locally sourced ingredients.

1: room at Shuhokaku Kogetsu **2:** Mount Fuji looms over Fujikawaguchiko

1

2

INFORMATION AND SERVICES

Just outside Kawaguchiko Station, on your right-hand side as you exit the station, the **Kawaguchiko Tourist Information Center** (3641-1 Funatsu; tel. 0555/72-6700; 9am-5pm daily) has English speakers on staff, as well as pamphlets about the area's *onsen* and maps for its hiking trails.

GETTING THERE AND AROUND

As **Kawaguchiko Station** is one of the major gateways to Mount Fuji itself, making a trip from Tokyo to Lake Kawaguchi, which is next to Kawaguchiko Station, means taking essentially the same route you would if you were traveling to Mount Fuji, as described above. This applies to both train and bus routes.

If you're coming from Tokyo by train, take the Chūō line limited express train (1 hour 10 minutes; ¥2,360) or the regular train (1 hour 30 minutes; ¥1,340; may require transfer at Takao Station) west from Shinjuku Station to Otsuki. When you've reached Otsuki, change trains to the Fuji Kyūkō line and ride until Kawaguchiko Station (1 hour; ¥1,170). Note that the JR Pass does not cover rides on the Fuji Kyūkō line.

Traveling from Tokyo by bus, either take one of the buses operated by **Keiō Dentetsu** (tel. 03/5376-2222; http://highway-buses.jp; adults ¥2,000, children ¥1,000) or **Fujikyū Express** (http://bus-en.fujikyu.co.jp/ highway; adults ¥2,000, children ¥1,000), both running once or twice hourly, from the Shinjuku Highway Bus Terminal (Shinjuku Station west exit; https://highway-buses.jp/ terminal/shinjuku.php) to Kawaguchiko Station. The trip takes roughly 1 hour 40 minutes. Alternatively, ride a bus operated by **Fujikyū** (http://bus-en.fujikyu.co.jp/ highway) or **JR Kanto Bus** (www.jrbus-kanto.co.jp.e.wn.hp.transer.com) from Tokyo Station's Yaesu South exit to Kawaguchiko Station (2 hours; ¥2,000 one-way). Fujikyū runs another route that starts from near the Mark City commercial complex linked to Shibuya Station and runs to Kawaguchiko Station (2-2.5 hours, depending on traffic; ¥2,000 one-way).

Likewise, if you are coming to Lake Kawaguchi from Kyoto, or a closer hub, such as Nagoya, you would follow the same route as the one described above to reach Mount Fuji from the west. The simplest way is by taking the Tōkaidō *shinkansen* **Kodama line** to **Mishima Station** (2 hours 40 minutes; ¥11,110). Near Mishima Station's south exit, ride a **Fujikyū bus** (http://bus-en.fujikyu. co.jp/highway) to **Kawaguchiko Station** (1.5-2 hours depending on road conditions; ¥2,300).

You can book a seat online for any of these bus routes—recommended—at **Japan Bus Online** (https://japanbusonline.com/en) or **Willer Express** (https://willerexpress.com/ en).

Kyoto 京都

The ancient Japanese capital hardly needs an introduction. It provides the source material for the vision many hold of Japan: geisha, tea ceremony, and more than 1,400 temples and shrines. With more than 12 centuries of heritage, Kyoto is inarguably one of the world's most culturally rich cities. In many ways, it is traditional Japan boiled down to its essence, where its history, spiritual life, aesthetics, ambience, and culinary genius coalesce. But there's plenty of modernity and industriousness here, too. It's the ideal complement to Tokyo for any first-time trip to the country.

Kyoto was Japan's capital for almost a millennium. Besides the Kamakura period (1185-1333), when the temporary feudal government moved its political base to Kamakura, the emperor ruled from

Highlights

Look for ★ to find recommended sights, activities, dining, and lodging.

© MOON.COM

★ **Fushimi Inari-Taisha:** At Kyoto's must-see Shinto shrine, the main complex is merely the prelude to a long mountain trail lined with 10,000 vivid *torii* gates (page 219).

★ **Kiyomizu-dera:** This temple sits imposingly atop a hill in the Southern Higashiyama district, affording sweeping views (page 225).

★ **Nanzen-ji:** One of Kyoto's grandest temples, it's surrounded by sub-temples, gardens, an aqueduct, and a hilly trail that leads to a sacred grotto (page 228).

★ **Philosopher's Path:** Seek tranquility with a stroll along this flower-lined pedestrian path, which stretches from Nyakuoji-bashi Bridge to the temple of Ginkaku-ji (page 229).

★ **Kinkaku-ji:** The upper two floors of this famed pavilion, once the retirement villa of shogun Yoshimitsu Ashikaga and now a temple of the Rinzai sect of Zen Buddhism, are gold-plated—an homage to the extravagance of Kyoto's aristocratic past (page 236).

★ **Arashiyama Bamboo Grove:** This magical bamboo grove stretches from the north gate of temple Tenryū-ji to Ōkōchi-Sansō villa (page 241).

★ **Gion Matsuri:** One of Japan's biggest festivals commemorates a purification ritual aimed at appeasing the gods of fire, earthquakes, and floods. Every July, this rite transforms Kyoto's streets into passageways for massive floats, pulled by locals donning colorful traditional attire (page 243).

Best Restaurants

★ **Kikunoi Honten:** This family-run restaurant set on an evocative street between Maruyama-kōen and Kōdai-ji serves some of the best and most gorgeous *kaiseki* fare in the city (page 252).

★ **Kagizen Yoshifusa Kōdai-ji:** This cozy branch of an iconic traditional dessert café is a great spot to sample a traditional sweet with a cup of powdered green tea (page 252).

★ **Omen:** This *udon* shop is an ideal place to stop for lunch as you walk along the Philosopher's Path in one of the most tranquil parts of the city (page 253).

★ **Tōsuirō:** Enjoy exploring creative spins on tofu and *yuba* (tofu skin) at this atmospheric riverside restaurant (page 257).

★ **Café Bibliotic Hello!:** This chic café is a hip hideaway, ideal for a coffee break or light meal off the tourist trail, tucked down a quiet street in the center of downtown (page 258).

★ **Izusen Daijinten:** Sample Buddhism's unique culinary contribution to global food culture, *shōjin-ryōri*, at this idyllic restaurant situated in a temple complex (page 258).

★ **Shoraian:** Feast on a surprisingly affordable *kaiseki* spread in this lovely restaurant in the hills of Arashiyama, overlooking the Katsura River (page 259).

REGIONAL SPECIALTIES

Kaiseki ryōri is essentially Japanese fine dining. These elaborate multi-course meals grew out of what were long ago simpler meals served after tea ceremonies. Dishes in a *kaiseki* meal are served in a very specific order, often beginning with an aperitif such as a small cup of *nihonshū* (rice wine) and a small appetizer, followed by soup, sashimi, and individual dishes that are, respectively, boiled, grilled, deep-fried, steamed, and served in a vinegar-based sauce. This is generally followed by rice, pickled vegetables, and miso soup, and finally, a light dessert, which is often fresh fruit or **wagashi** (Japanese sweets), which are themselves another Kyoto specialty.

Kyoto from 794 to 1868. The foundations of Japanese traditional culture and aesthetics, especially the austerity and restraint of Zen Buddhism, were laid by the aristocracy here in the Heian period (794-1185). Over its long history, Kyoto was struck by fires and wars, but was mercifully spared bombing raids during WWII due to its extraordinary historical and cultural value.

At its heart, Kyoto is a city of temples. "Kyoto and Zen go together like love and Paris," wrote scholar and scribe John Dougill in the insightful and beautifully photographed *Zen Gardens and Temples of Kyoto*.

Monks practice *zazen* (seated meditation) in rooms adorned with brushstrokes of flowing calligraphy and paintings of misty landscapes and serpentine dragons. They eat elaborate vegetarian feasts (*shōjin-ryōri*) and gaze at the simple lines and symbolically placed stones of enigmatic rock gardens.

Beyond the city's temples and shrines, Kyoto is a gourmand's dream. Culinary arts are refined to painstaking levels, with the multicourse haute cuisine known as *kaiseki ryōri* at the pinnacle, often served in atmospheric *machiya* (narrow wooden townhouses known as "bedrooms for eels")

Previous: Fushimi Inari-Taisha; Kiyomizu-dera; Philosopher's Path in springtime.

Best Accommodations

★ **Hotel Granvia:** This clean modern hotel, literally in the Kyoto Station building, wins big points for convenience (page 265).

★ **Hotel The Celestine Kyoto Gion:** A phenomenal new modern hotel in a quiet pocket of Gion, this is a fantastic option at the higher end of midrange hotels (page 267).

★ **Yuzuya Ryokan:** This refined *ryokan* option in Northern Higashiyama occupies a prime location, right beside Yasaka-jinja and a short walk from downtown (page 267).

★ **Yoshida Sansō:** This discreet luxury *ryokan,* close to nature in a quiet part of Northern Higashiyama near Ginkaku-ji, remains slightly off the radar (page 268).

★ **The Millennials Kyoto:** This sleek capsule hotel, with a shared lounge and workspace, is a great choice for young travelers on the go (page 268).

★ **Iori Machiya Stay Residence:** Rent a classic old *machiya* townhouse, with historic charm and modern creature comforts, in the heart of downtown (page 269).

★ **Ritz-Carlton Kyoto:** The Ritz offers a fantastic mix of luxury and convenience in the city center, with stellar amenities and a renowned *kaiseki* restaurant (page 270).

scattered around the city's oldest districts. Kyoto is also home to Japan's heaviest concentration of traditional artisans. This is the best place to shop for calligraphy scrolls, goods made from *washi* (traditional handmade Japanese paper), bamboo tea whisks, lacquerware, tea and sweets, textiles from kimono to *yukata* (lightweight summer kimono), and a variety of other accoutrements, from folding fans to the sorts of elegant hairpins worn by geisha.

ORIENTATION

Kyoto is laid out in a refreshingly simple grid pattern, and the main boulevards and some small side streets are often mercifully named, especially in the city center. This makes navigating the city easy. A series of main thoroughfares run east-west through the city, numbered from north to south in ascending order (e.g., Ichijō for "First Avenue," Sanjō for "Third Avenue," etc.). The streets running north-south through the city and intersecting these broad east-west avenues are likewise often named (e.g., Kawaramachi-dōri,

Senbon-dōri, etc.). The **Kamo River** also runs north-south through the city and serves as another geographic marker, with the culturally and historically rich neighborhoods of **Gion** and **Higashiyama** east of the river and **downtown** and the rest of Kyoto to the west. Looming to the east of the whole city, abutting the Higashiyama district, is the Higashiyama mountain range.

Kyoto Station Area

Virtually all visitors to Kyoto will first arrive at **Kyoto Station,** located a 10-minute walk west of the **Kamo River.** This mammoth complex of glass and steel can be a jolt and a visceral reminder that Kyoto is a thoroughly modern city with a population of 1.5 million. The cityscape surrounding the station, located in the city's south-central side, is dotted by drab concrete structures, from shopping malls to electronics emporiums. Perhaps the purest embodiment of this is the visually jarring **Kyoto Tower,** located a brief walk north of the station. There are also a few more attractive sights in the area,

A Word on Addresses in Kyoto

Though Kyoto is relatively easy to navigate compared to other large cities in Japan, the address system is a little quirky. In addition to the usual elements in Japanese addresses—the **building name**, the **number of a business, apartment, or house** ("-gō" or 号), the **area** ("-chō" or 町), the **city** ("-shi" or 市), the **ward** ("-ku" or 区), and **postal code** (〒)—Kyoto addresses also often include the **name of the nearest access road** (often, but not always "-dōri" or 通り) and the **cardinal direction** ("iri" or 入) from the access road where you'll find the address you're seeking.

HOW TO NAVIGATE

This twist, rooted in an ancient system, is unfortunately out of sync with Google Maps. The easiest way around this is to simply **input only the essentials**—city (e.g., Kyoto-shi), ward (e.g., Higashiyama-ku), and area (e.g., Shimokawara-chō), and leave out the rest. For example, to find the famed *kaiseki ryōri* restaurant Kikunoi Honten, simply input "459 Shimokawara-chō Higashiyama-ku" into Google Maps.

Most of the addresses in this chapter are written in this simplified way, although some do include extra directional information that could prove helpful to taxi drivers or locals well acquainted with the city's ticks. When in doubt, simply **type the name of a temple, restaurant or hotel,** and Google Maps will likely already have it in the system.

including the **Higashi Hongan-ji** temple complex. In terms of major roads in the area, **Shiokoji-dōri** runs east-west along the north side of the station, **Hachijo-dōri** runs east-west just to the south, and the northwest artery of **Karasuma-dōri** runs north of the station all the way up into downtown and the central part of the city.

Southeast Kyoto

Moving beyond the Kyoto Station area, the city's history remains preserved in bronze, bamboo, and wood, tucked down atmospheric, dense lanes around the edges of town. Beginning in Southeast Kyoto, located roughly 30 minutes' walk southeast of Kyoto Station, the major draw of this district is the spellbinding shrine complex of **Fushimi Inari-Taisha,** famed for its tunnel of vermillion *torii* gates that winds over a mountain trail. The splendid **Tōfuku-ji** temple complex is also located in the area, about 10 minutes' walk north of Fushimi Inari-Taisha.

To access this rich district, take the **JR Nara line** from Kyoto Station to **Tōfukuji Station** (for Tōfuku-ji) or **Inari Station** (for Fushimi Inari-Taisha). It's also possible to walk from Kyoto Station to Tōfuku-ji (25 minutes) or from Fushimi Inari-Taisha (40 minutes), or make either journey quicker by traveling on a bicycle.

Southern Higashiyama

Heading north from there, about 15 minutes on foot brings you to the southern edge of the large district of Higashiyama, which occupies most of the eastern half of the city. Southern Higashiyama's best-known sight is the crowd-pleasing temple complex of **Kiyomizu-dera.** Other notable spots in the area include the temple of **Sanjūsangen-dō,** which houses roughly 1,000 effigies of Kannon, Buddhism's goddess of mercy, and the huge complex of **Chion-in,** the head temple of the Jōdo school of Pure Land Buddhism.

The busy thoroughfare of **Shichijo-dōri** runs east-west along the southern edge of the area, with east-west **Sanjō-dōri** hemming in the northern edge. The **Higashiyama mountains** lie to the east. The crowded pedestrian thoroughfare of **Sannen-zaka,** which runs uphill to Kiyomizu-dera, is also found in this district. The easiest way to reach

Kyoto Area

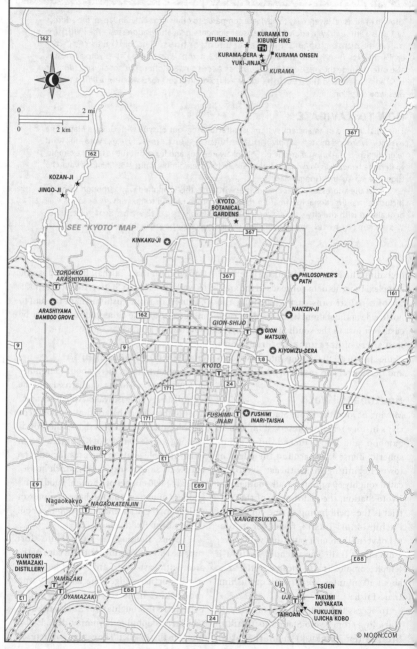

162

KIFUNE-JIINJA ★   KURAMA TO
                   KIBUNE HIKE
KURAMA-DERA ★   TH   ★ KURAMA ONSEN
YUKI-JINJA ☖   KURAMA

367

0   2 mi
0   2 km

162

KOZAN-JI ★
JINGO-JI ★

KYOTO
BOTANICAL
GARDENS
★

SEE "KYOTO" MAP

KINKAKU-JI ✪   367

TOROKKO
ARASHIYAMA   367   ● PHILOSOPHER'S
☖   PATH

ARASHIYAMA   NANZEN-JI
BAMBOO GROVE   ✪
●
162
                     GION-SHIJO
                     ☖ ● GION
                          MATSURI
9   9   KIYOMIZU-DERA ✪

                KYOTO ●
                ☖
                    24
             171
        171   E1
                FUSHIMI- ☖ FUSHIMI
                INARI   INARI-TAISHA

161

Muko ◇

E1

E9
                E89
Nagaokakyo ◇
         ☖ NAGAOKATENJIN

                ☖ KANGETSUKYO

1

SUNTORY
YAMAZAKI
DISTILLERY
☖ YAMAZAKI   E88
E1   ☖ OYAMAZAKI   E88
                                  Uji ◇
                                      ● TSUEN
24   UJI ☖ ● TAKUMI
                                           NO YAKATA
                                  TAIHOAN ● FUKUJUEN
                                           UJICHA KOBO

© MOON.COM

the area is via the **Karasuma subway line** from Kyoto Station, exiting at **Karasuma-Oike Station** and transferring to the **Tōzai line** to **Higashiyama Station.** From here, the district spreads out to the south.

Gion

About 5 minutes' walk southwest of Chion-in, **Yasaka-jinja** is the important shrine presiding over the district of Gion, the city's main entertainment district, along the eastern bank of the Kamo River just west of the northern edge of Southern Higashiyama. This area originally developed into an entertainment hub to cater to the earthly needs of the pilgrims who came to visit the grand Yasaka-jinja, and today, it remains the best part of the city to observe the sensuous "floating world" of nighttime pleasures that has developed over the centuries. Think **kabuki performances,** geisha flitting over cobblestone streets, well-heeled guests eating multicourse feasts, and bars where hostesses carouse with loose-lipped businessmen.

At the western edge of Gion is the avenue of **Kawabata-dōri,** running north-south beside the Kamo River. Running eastward from Kawabata-dōri, through the heart of Gion, is the main drag of **Shijo-dōri,** whose sidewalks are typically clogged by foot traffic. The Higashiyama mountains lie farther to the east, where the district ends. To get to Gion, take the **Keihan line** to **Gion-Shijō Station.**

Northern Higashiyama

Northern Higashiyama lies north of Gion and Southern Higashiyama. Major sights in this popular sightseeing district include the grand shrine of **Heian-jingū,** the wonderful temple complex of **Nanzen-ji,** and the vaunted **Philosopher's Path,** and at the northern edge of the district lie the beautiful temple grounds of **Ginkaku-ji.**

The Kamo River and Kawabata-dōri define this district's western edge, the east-west artery of **Sanjō-dōri** forms its southern boundary, the Higashiyama mountains stand to the east, and the **Katsura Rikyū** sits at its northern periphery. Starting at Kyoto Station, reach the area via the **Karasuma subway line,** transferring at **Karasuma-Oike Station** to the **Tōzai line** and exiting at either **Higashiyama Station** in the area's west, or **Keage Station** in the east, and walking north from either one.

Downtown and Central Kyoto

The vast swath of town north of Kyoto Station and along the western bank of the Kamo River, sitting opposite Gion and Northern Higashiyama, includes Downtown and Central Kyoto. Like the Kyoto Station Area, this part of town is more modern and less aesthetically pleasing. This large area's main sights include the dreamy cobblestone alleyway of **Ponto-chō** and the castle of **Nijō-jō.** Otherwise, this part of town makes up for its more generically modern face with an abundance of excellent options to wine, dine, and shop.

While Central Kyoto is a sizable chunk of the city, downtown is essentially a square zone. The Kamo River runs along its eastern boundary on a north-south axis; north-south **Karasuma-dōri,** which runs to Kyoto Station in the south, forms its western border; east-west Shijo-dōri hems in the area's south; and **Oike-dōri** runs east-west along its northern edge. This area is highly walkable and can be reached from Kyoto Station by riding the **Karasuma subway** line to **Shijo Station** near the southwest corner of the downtown area, or to **Karasuma-Oike Station** in the neighborhood's northwest corner.

Northwest Kyoto

Moving west of Downtown and Central Kyoto, the district of Northwest Kyoto is another major sightseeing area, despite its slightly farther-flung position. A few standout sights in the area include the famously gilt temple of **Kinkaku-ji** and the iconic Zen temple of **Ryōan-ji,** known for its classic rock garden. Nearby, the less thronged temple complex of **Myōshin-ji** also begs to be explored.

This vast area lies north of east-west

Kyoto

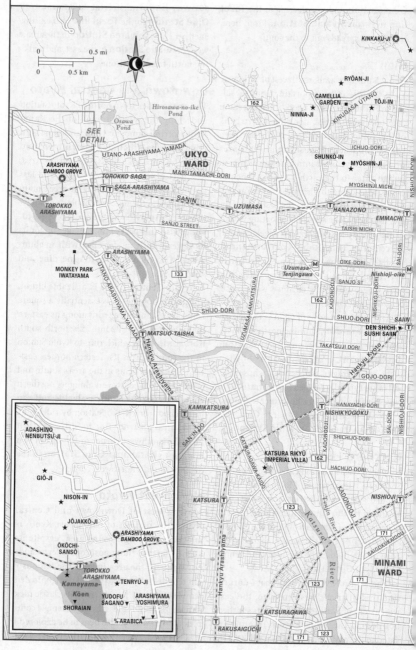

0   0.5 mi

0   0.5 km

KINKAKU-JI

RYŌAN-JI

CAMELLIA GARDEN

NINNA-JI

TŌJI-IN

KINUGASA UTANO

Hirosawa-no-ike Pond

Osawa Pond

SEE DETAIL

ICHIJO-DORI

SHUNKŌ-IN

MYŌSHIN-JI

UTANO-ARASHIYAMA-YAMADA

UKYO WARD

MARUTAMACHI-DORI

MYOSHINJI MICHI

ARASHIYAMA BAMBOO GROVE

TOROKKO SAGA

SAGA-ARASHIYAMA

SANIN

UZUMASA

HANAZONO

EMMACHI

TOROKKO ARASHIYAMA

SANJO STREET

TAISHI MICHI

MONKEY PARK IWATAYAMA

ARASHIYAMA

133

Uzumasa-Tenjingawa

ŌIKE-DORI

Nishioji-oike

SANJO ST

162

SHIJO-DORI

SHIJO-DORI

SAIIN

DEN SHICHI SUSHI SAIIN

MATSUO-TAISHA

TAKATSUJI DORI

Hankyu Kyoto

GOJO-DORI

KAMIKATSURA

HANAYACHI-DORI

NISHIKYOGOKU

SHICHIJO-DORI

KATSURA RIKYŪ (IMPERIAL VILLA)

162

HACHIJO-DORI

KATSURA

123

NISHIOJI

171

Tenjin River

MINAMI WARD

KATSURAGAWA

RAKUSAIGUCHI

171

123

Detail inset

ADASHINO NENBUTSU-JI

GIŌ-JI

NISON-IN

JŌJAKKŌ-JI

ŌKŌCHI-SANSŌ

ARASHIYAMA BAMBOO GROVE

TOROKKO ARASHIYAMA

Kameyama-Kōen

SHORAIAN

YUDOFU SAGANO

TENRYŪ-JI

ARASHIYAMA YOSHIMURA

% ARABICA

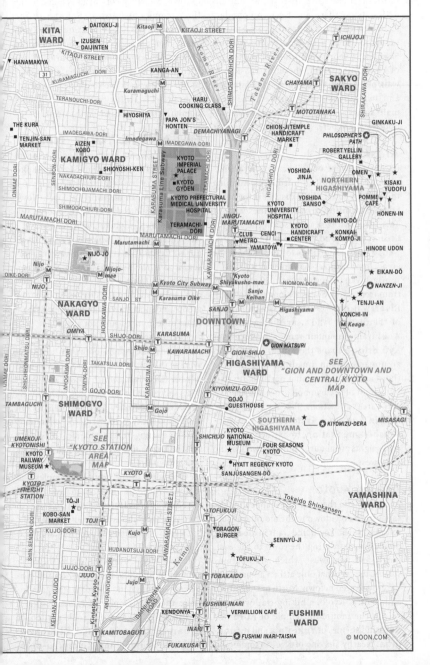

avenue **Imadegawa-dōri** and west of north-south oriented **Senbon-dōri.** Mountains define its northern and western boundaries. To reach the area from Kyoto Station, take the **JR San-in line** to **Hanazono Station,** a short walk south of the temple of Myōshin-ji, from where it's possible to walk or cycle north to Ryōan-ji (25 minutes) and then Kinkaku-ji (20 minutes). The area's main sights are spread out in the neighborhood north of here.

Arashiyama

In the far west of town, Arashiyama is among Kyoto's most crowded areas. Running through the heart of the district is the area's ethereal **bamboo grove,** with the temple of **Tenryū-ji** sitting near the south end and the dreamy house and gardens of the **Ōkōchi-Sansō villa** occupying a lofty spot above the area, affording great views of the city.

Arashiyama is located about 30 minutes by train from Kyoto Station, along the **Katsura River,** which flows along the southern edge of the district, and near the base of the Arashiyama mountain range. The **Tōgetsu-kyō bridge** spans the Katsura River, and an unnamed main drag lined with touristy shops and cafés runs on a north-south axis to the east of the bamboo grove and the rest of the area's attractions. Take the **JR Sagano/ San-in line** from Kyoto Station to **Saga-Arashiyama Station,** from where most of the area's sights are about 10 minutes' walk to the southwest.

Around Kyoto

Around Kyoto there are a few appealing escapes from downtown in the mountains surrounding town. You'll find trails in the nearby mountains bordering the town to the east, north, and northwest, which run to atmospheric temples that only attract a fraction of the crowds seen in town. North of Downtown and Central Kyoto, a hiking trail will take you to the mountain temple of **Kurama-dera** and shrines of **Yuki-jinja** and **Kifune-jinja.** Nearby sits one of Kyoto's top *onsen,*

Kurama Onsen. In the mountains northwest of town, the village of Takao is home to the three temples of **Jingo-ji, Saimyō-ji,** and **Kozan-ji,** a UNESCO site. South of Kyoto some great places to try two quintessential Japanese beverages: in the southeast, **Uji** is surrounded by tea fields and a great place to try the brew; in the southwest, **Suntory Yamazaki Distillery** is home to whiskies regularly named the best in the world.

PLANNING YOUR TIME

Like most of Japan, Kyoto is a highly seasonal destination. In **spring** (Mar.-May), an explosion of cherry blossoms bathes the city in a soft pink glow. In **autumn** (late Oct.-Nov.), foliage bursts into shades of red, orange, yellow, and brown—a photographer's dream. The city is besieged by the camera-wielding masses during *hanami* (cherry blossom viewing) season, and at the peak of *kōyō* in November, when autumn leaves reach their peak. If you don't mind sharing the city with large tour groups and other international travelers, these times of year are popular for a reason.

The off-seasons are the stuffy days of **summer** (June-Aug.)—note that June is on average the rainiest month of the year—and **winter** (Dec.-Feb.), which is cold and sometimes snowy but not overly harsh, with temperatures ranging from 1-11°C (34-52°F). If you don't mind sticky weather, summer offers long, glorious evenings that provide ideal conditions for strolling along the burbling Kamo River.

Even with only one day, you'll be able to see a handful of the city's key temples and shrines, which are clustered mainly around the Southern Higashiyama area and west of the city in the famous district of Arashiyama. But ideally, you'll have two to five days to explore the city.

It's easy to be overwhelmed by the sheer number of Buddhist temples—Zen and otherwise—throughout Kyoto. Highlights include the Zen temples of **Nanzen-ji** and **Gingaku-ji,** the famed rock garden of **Ryōan-ji,** the gold-plated **Kinkaku-ji** (Golden Pavilion), and **Kiyomizu-dera,**

Avoiding Kyoto's Crowds

Kyoto's treasures are well-known—and extremely crowded. Its most popular temples host almost Disneyland-level throngs. Its most crowded spots include the spellbinding shrine of **Fushimi Inari-Taisha** in the southeast; the hilltop temple of **Kiyomizu-dera** and **Ginkaku-ji** in Southern and Northern Higashiyama, respectively; **Nijō-jō** in the city center; the famed rock garden of **Ryōan-ji** and gold-plated **Kinkaku-ji** in the northwest; and **Arashiyama's bamboo grove** in the far west. These famous sights are still amazing, crowds aside, but given how popular Kyoto has become, having genuinely good offbeat alternatives to escape the crowds is very important. Throughout this chapter, strategies for escaping crowds will be covered, but here are a few general suggestions.

- **Avoid coming to Kyoto during its peak seasons:** late Mar.-early Apr. and Nov., and the Obon holidays of mid-Aug.

- **Visit attractions at off-peak times:** before 8am or after 4pm on weekdays.

- Keep in mind that some sights, including standouts like Fushimi Inari-Taisha and the Arashiyama Bamboo Grove, are **open 24/7,** meaning you can enjoy them almost alone if you're willing to visit at certain hours.

- Balance your itinerary with a mix of greatest hits and **lesser-known gems.** Most of Kyoto's busiest sites have stunning, less crowded options just a short walk away.

- Finally, no matter where you are, dare to discover your own version of the city by simply **veering off the beaten path** to discover charming shops, antique wooden townhouses, and local shrines well off the radar.

perched high above the city with stunning views. As for Shinto shrines, the one must-see is **Fushimi Inari-Taisha** with its hiking trail lined with more than 10,000 vivid *torii,* as the red gates seen at Shinto shrines are called. An equally striking sight is Arashiyama's magical **bamboo grove** on the outskirts of the city. When planning your time, one thing to keep in mind is the reality that you simply can't see everything that catches your fancy. To address this challenge, prioritize carefully. Avoid temple fatigue by exploring the city's **performance arts,** going on a **day trip, shopping** downtown, and having a *kaiseki ryōri* feast.

Itinerary Ideas

KYOTO ON DAY 1

On this first day, you'll explore the buzzing east side of town, from **Southern Higashiyama** to **Southeast Kyoto.** Some of Kyoto's most famous sights are found along this route, which can pleasantly be followed mostly **on foot.** There are also a few off-the-radar stops for balance.

1 Plan to start at **Chion-in,** arriving by 9am. Ascend its imposing stone steps that lead up to this vast temple complex, the "Vatican of Pure Land Buddhism," with numerous buildings, two gardens, and a stunning effigy of Amida Buddha (Buddha of Infinite Light) in the main hall.

Itinerary Ideas

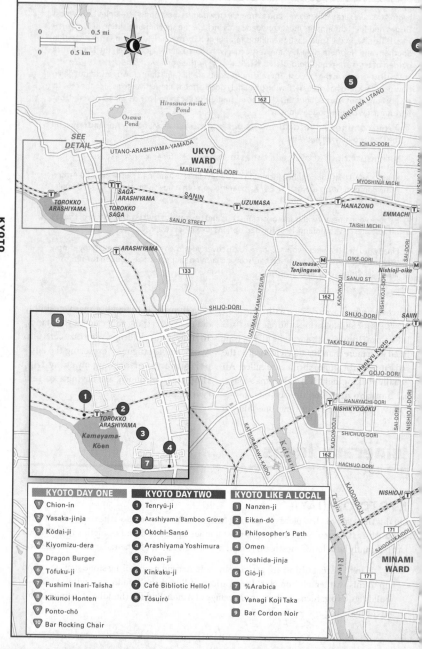

KYOTO DAY ONE	KYOTO DAY TWO	KYOTO LIKE A LOCAL
1 Chion-in	1 Tenryū-ji	1 Nanzen-ji
2 Yasaka-jinja	2 Arashiyama Bamboo Grove	2 Eikan-dō
3 Kōdai-ji	3 Ōkōchi-Sansō	3 Philosopher's Path
4 Kiyomizu-dera	4 Arashiyama Yoshimura	4 Omen
5 Dragon Burger	5 Ryōan-ji	5 Yoshida-jinja
6 Tōfuku-ji	6 Kinkaku-ji	6 Giō-ji
7 Fushimi Inari-Taisha	7 Café Bibliotic Hello!	7 %Arabica
8 Kikunoi Honten	8 Tōsuirō	8 Yanagi Koji Taka
9 Ponto-chō		9 Bar Cordon Noir
10 Bar Rocking Chair		

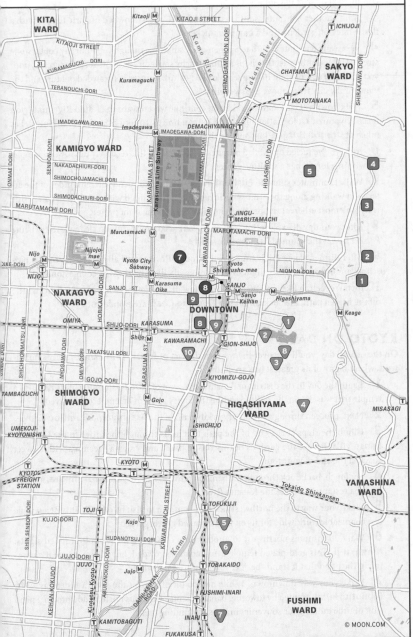

2 Continue on foot another 5 minutes through the leafy park of Maruyama-kōen, stopping at **Yasaka-jinja.** This handsome shrine sits perched atop an incline overlooking the commercial district of Gion.

3 Walk another 8 minutes southeast to **Kōdai-ji,** a less-crowded historic temple with a flashy interior, gardens, and a bamboo thicket.

4 Next, walk 6 minutes south to Sannen-zaka, an iconic though very touristy cobblestone street. Amble uphill, past the shops selling kitschy souvenirs and soft-serve ice cream, until you reach the magnificent hilltop temple of **Kiyomizu-dera.** It's crowded but fun, and the views of the city from above are sweeping.

5 Walk downhill via Chawan-zaka and continue west toward the Kamo River until you reach Kiyomizu-Gojō Station. Take the Keihan line to Tōfuku-ji Station (4 minutes). Eat lunch at **Dragon Burger,** just outside the station.

6 After you've fueled up, walk 5 minutes to **Tōfuku-ji.** This relatively uncrowded temple, set within a forest, has a sublime garden.

7 Walk 12 minutes south to **Fushimi Inari-Taisha** and spend the remainder of the afternoon walking along the atmospheric mountain path, lined with vermillion gates. This is Kyoto's most ethereal shrine, if not its most bewitching sight period.

8 After your day of exploration, return to your accommodation to clean up to try haute *kaiseki* fare at the vaunted **Kikunoi Honten.**

9 After dinner, take a nighttime stroll through **Ponto-chō** alley, soaking up the old-school ambience cast by the light of lanterns gently illuminating the cobblestone path.

10 If you're feeling like a nightcap, go for a few drinks downtown. For something a little off the beaten path, the cocktails at **Bar Rocking Chair** are wonderful.

KYOTO ON DAY 2

On the second day, you'll discover the western district of **Arashiyama** and the city's northwest, where many of its greatest hits are found.

1 Begin the day in the district of Arashiyama, west of the city, stopping by **Tenryū-ji,** a temple that was originally built to soothe the angry spirit of an emperor betrayed.

2 Next, proceed through the otherworldly path of the **Arashiyama Bamboo Grove.**

3 Climb the steps at the end of the path that leads through the grove to the **Ōkōchi-Sansō** villa. Peruse the gardens of this classic home and enjoy a green tea with a sweet snack at the end of your tour.

4 For lunch, backtrack through the bamboo grove to **Arashiyama Yoshimura,** a popular soba restaurant beside the Katsura River.

5 Make your way to the northwest side of downtown to visit **Ryōan-ji.** This Zen temple is recognizable worldwide for its enigmatic raked gravel garden.

6 Walk 20 minutes northwest to another one of Kyoto's most photographed sights: **Kinkaku-ji.** This gold-plated temple is undeniably crowded, but when you see it gleaming in the pond that it stands beside, you'll understand why.

7 Make your way downtown. While away a bit of time at the stylish hideaway **Café Bibliotic Hello!,** fronted by towering banana plants, which sits north of downtown. Spend a bit of time hunting for souvenirs in the surrounding area.

8 Eat dinner at **Tōsuirō**, a riverside restaurant with a terrace specializing in tofu and *yuba* (tofu skin). Follow dinner with an evening stroll along the Kamo River.

KYOTO LIKE A LOCAL

Now that you've taken in the bulk of the city's greatest hits, it's time to dig a bit deeper. The day begins in the (still) relatively popular area of Northern Higashiyama. It then veers into pockets of town that most tourists never see.

1 Start at the rambling Zen temple complex of **Nanzen-ji**. Behold its impressive main gate, then walk uphill and find the waterfall and sacred grotto on its backside.

2 Proceed on foot 5 minutes north to **Eikan-dō**, a serene temple with grounds crisscrossed by streams and containing a two-story pagoda, located at the southern edge of the Philosopher's Path.

3 Take your time ambling north along the **Philosopher's Path.** You'll pass mossy Hōnen-in temple, followed by the beautiful grounds of Ginkaku-ji ("Silver Pavilion").

4 Have *udon* (flour noodles) for lunch at **Omen.**

5 Walk about 10 minutes southwest of Omen to a quiet pocket of Northern Higashiyama. On the hill known as Yoshidayama, you'll discover off-the-beaten-path gems like the shrine of **Yoshida-jinja.**

6 From there, walk 20 minutes southwest to Higashiyama Station on the Tōzai subway line. Take the train to Nijō Station, then transfer to the JR Sagano line and ride to Saga-Arashiyama Station for a total trip of about 25 minutes (¥460). Walk 15 minutes northwest from Saga-Arashiyama Station to a cluster of hidden temples beyond the area's clogged bamboo grove. These quieter gems include thatch-roofed **Giō-ji.** You'll likely have the place to yourself.

7 Backtrack toward Arashiyama proper and regroup at **%Arabica,** sipping your coffee beside the Katsura River.

8 Have dinner downtown at **Yanagi Koji Taka,** a friendly standing *izakaya* set in an atmospheric alley.

9 Put a cap on the evening sipping whisky at **Bar Cordon Noir.**

Sights

KYOTO STATION AREA

Aside from a few temples hiding inside this slice of decidedly modern Japan, Kyoto's treasures lie in the districts beyond. View the station area as a means to an end: the city's entry and exit point, and a place to handle logistics and shopping.

Kyoto Tower
京都タワー
Karasuma-dōri, Shichijō-sagaru, Shimogyō-ku; tel. 075/361-3215; www.kyoto-tower.co.jp; 9am-9pm daily; adults ¥800, high school students ¥650, elementary and junior high school students ¥550, children over three ¥150; take JR lines to Kyoto Station, Karasuma central exit

Five minutes' walk north of Kyoto Station, you'll encounter an eyesore of a monument that Japanologist and author Alex Kerr once called "a stake through the heart of the city." Behold, 131-meter (430-foot) Kyoto Tower, built in 1963. You'll want to move outward toward the more historic districts, but if you must stop by, it is true

that there are great vistas from the viewing deck up top.

Higashi Hongan-ji
東本願寺

Karasuma-dōri, Shichijō-agaru, Shimogyō-ku; tel. 075/371-9181; www.higashihonganji.or.jp; 5:50am-5:30pm daily Mar.-Oct., 6:20am-4:30pm daily Nov.-Feb.; free; from Kyoto Station, take the Karasuma central exit

A short walk north from Kyoto Tower, up the main north-south artery of Karasuma-dōri, you'll find a stunning sight that is thankfully much more in line with what you'd expect to see in Kyoto: Higashi Hongan-ji. The main hall of this temple is one of the largest wooden structures on the planet.

Unfortunately, you can't glimpse much beyond the facade of this complex, which is closed to the public, so the altars and artwork remain shrouded from view. But the buildings themselves still induce a sense of awe, with both their scale and their elaborate gold-plated flourishes. This vast temple complex is by far the most splendid glimpse of Kyoto's illustrious past in the area surrounding the station.

Kyoto Railway Museum
京都鉄道博物館

Kankiji-chō, Shimogyō-ku; tel. 0570/080-462; www. kyotorailwaymuseum.jp; 10am-5:30pm Thurs.-Tues.; adults ¥1,200, university and high school students ¥1,000, junior high and elementary students ¥500, children over three ¥200; walk 20 minutes west of JR Kyoto Station, or take bus no. 205 or 208 from JR Kyoto Station to Umekōji-kōen-mae stop, or bus no. 104 or 110 to Umekōji-kōen/Kyoto Railway Museum-mae stop

If you're looking for a great rainy-day option, or you simply want a break from temple-hopping, head to the Kyoto Railway Museum. A hit with kids and train lovers, this museum traces train history from the steam engine all the way through to the bullet train. Old bullet-train models, commuter trains from days past,

and even steam locomotives are on display. It's also possible to hop aboard a steam loco-motive and go for a short ride (¥300 adults, ¥100 children).

Tō-ji
東寺

1 Kujō-chō, Minami-ku; tel. 075/691-3325; www. toji.or.jp; 8:30am-5pm daily Mar. 20-Sept. 19, 8:30am-4pm Sept. 20-Mar. 19; grounds free, kondo and kodo ¥500, treasure hall ¥500, pagoda (only 9am-4pm) ¥800; take the Kintetsu line to Tō-ji Station

Thanks to its towering pagoda, Tō-ji is one of the more visually prominent temples in the Kyoto Station area. Located southwest of the station, this wooden spire rises from a small sea of gloomy apartment blocks as a reminder that the heart of tradition still beats here, too. The best time to visit—perhaps the main reason—is its **Kōbō-san market,** held on the 21st of every month, an excellent stop if you're keen to visit a flea market.

SOUTHEAST KYOTO

Southeast Kyoto is dense in noteworthy sights, and slightly less crowded than Southern Higashiyama, to its north.

★ Fushimi Inari-Taisha
伏見稲荷大社

68 Yabunouchi-chō, Fukakusa, Fushimi-ku; tel. 075/561-1551; http://inari.jp; dawn to dusk daily; free; take JR Nara Line to Inari Station, or Keihan Railway line to Fushimi-Inari Station

If you only have time to visit one Shinto shrine during your stay in Kyoto, make it Fushimi Inari-Taisha. It is the head shrine for 40,000 shrines throughout Japan that are dedicated to Inari, the *kami* (god) of fertility, rice, *sake,* and prosperity.

Easily one of the most arresting sights in Kyoto, the bewitching complex spreads across a mountain, where more than 10,000 vermillion *torii* gates envelop a 4-km (2.5-mi) path through heavily wooded terrain. Hundreds of stone foxes with granary keys in their mouths stand watch over the complex, which consists of five shrines, numerous mausoleums, and

1: Higashi Hongan-ji 2: Tō-ji pagoda 3: Fushimi Inari-Taisha

Gion and Downtown and Central Kyoto

EBISUGAWA-DORI
EBISUGAWA-DORI

SHOYEIDO KYOTO
MAIN STORE

IPPODO

SAKE BAR
YORAMU

ZOHIKO

RITZ-CARLTON
KYOTO

CAFÉ BIBLIOTIC
HELLO!

NIJO-DORI

HONKE
OWARIYA

MIZUKI

KAMANZA-DORI
SHINMACHI-DORI
KOROMODANA-DORI
MUROMACHI-DORI
RYOGAECHO-DORI
KARASUMA STREET
KURUMAYACHO-DORI
HIGASHINOTOIN-DORI
AINOMACHI-DORI
TAKAKURA-DORI

NIJO DORI

OSHIKOJI-DORI

SAKAIMACHI-DORI
YANAGIBANBA-DORI
FUYACHO-DORI
TOMINOKOJI-DORI
GOKOMACHI-DORI
TERAMACHI-DORI
KAWARAMACHI-DORI

KAPPO
YAMASHITA

MUGHAL

Karasuma
Oike

OIKE-DORI
Kyoto City Subway

Kyoto
Shiyakusho-mae

KYOTO INTERNATIONAL
MANGA MUSEUM ★

Karasuma
Oike

HIIRAGIYA

SOLARIA NISHITETSU HOTEL
KYOTO PREMIER SANJO

TOSUIRO

ANEKOJI-DORI

KYUKYODO

BUTOH KAN

SAMA
SAMA

NAKAGYO
WARD

SANJO STREET

SANJO STREET

SANJO

URBANGUILD

BAR CORDON
NOIR

CROSS
HOTEL

ROKKAKU-DORI

SHOOTING
BAR M4

Karasuma Subway Line

SHINMACHI-DORI
MUROMACHI-DORI

TAKOYAKUSHI-DORI

MIYAWAKI
BAISEN-AN

MUMOKUTEKI
CAFÉ

THE MILLENNIALS
KYOTO

TAKAKURA-DORI
SAKAIMACHI-DORI
YANAGIBANBA-DORI
FUYACHO-DORI
GOKOMACHI-DORI
TERAMACHI-DORI

ROCKING
BAR ING

DOWNTOWN

NISHIKIKOJI-DORI

ARITSUGU

BAR KAZU

AIN SOPH.
JOURNEY
KYOTO

BEE'S
KNEES

KIYAMACHI-DORI

PONTO-CHO ★

NISHIKI
MARKET

KINMATA

SOUR

BARCODE

River

KEIHAN LINE

YANAGI
KOJI TAKA
KAWARAMACHI

SHIJO-DORI

KARASUMA

DAIMARU

HANKYU KYOTO LINE

SHIJO-DORI

Shijo

AYANO-KOJI

HOTEL GRAND BACH
KYOTO SELECT

TAKASHIMAYA

MINAMI-ZA

GION-SHIJO

TORA

SHIMOGYO
WARD

L'ESCAMOTEUR
BAR

SHINMACHI-DORI
MUROMACHI-DORI
HIGASHINOTOIN-DORI
TAKAKURA-DORI
SAKAIMACHI-DORI

MORITA
WASHI

BUKKOUJI-DORI

INOICHI

AOI HOTEL
KYOTO

CHIDORITEI

Kamo

TAKATSUJI-DORI

BAR ROCKING
CHAIR

TAKATSUJI-DORI

YANAGIBANBA-DORI
TOMINOKOJI-DORI
FUYACHO-DORI
GOKOMACHI-DORI
TERAMACHI-DORI

HOSTEL LEN KYOTO
KAWARAMACHI

KIYOMIZU-GOJO

MATSUBARA DORI

MATSUBARA-DORI

KIYAMACHI-DORI
KEIHAN LINE
YAMATO-OJI

MANJUJI-DORI

SUWACHO-DORI
KARASUMA ST

GUILO GUILO
HITOSHINA

KIYOMIZU-GOJO

GOJO-DORI

GOJO-DORI

YAMATO-OJI

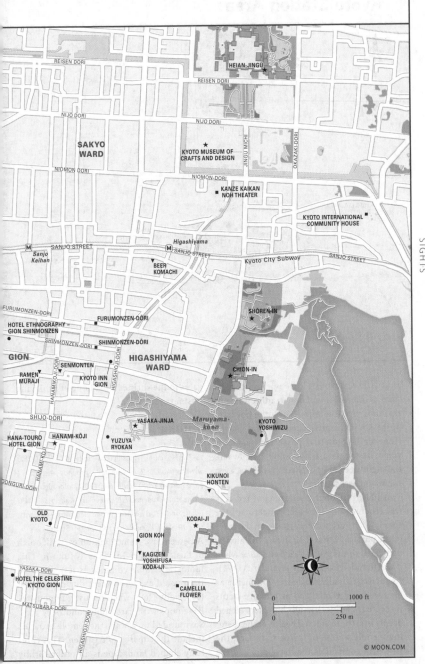

REISEN DORI

HEIAN-JINGU ★

REISEN DORI

NIJO DORI

NIJO DORI

SAKYO
WARD

KYOTO MUSEUM OF
CRAFTS AND DESIGN ★

NIOMON DORI

NIOMON-DORI

KANZE KAIKAN
NOH THEATER ■

JINGU MICHI

OKAZAKI-DORI

KYOTO INTERNATIONAL ■
COMMUNITY HOUSE

M Sanjo
Keihan

SANJO STREET

Higashiyama

M SANJO STREET

Kyoto City Subway

SANJO STREET

BEER
KOMACHI ▼

SHOREN-IN
★

FURUMONZEN-DORI

HOTEL ETHNOGRAPHY ■
GION SHINMONZEN

FURUMONZEN-DORI ■

SHINMONZEN-DORI

SHINMONZEN-DÕRI

GION

HIGASHIYAMA
WARD

CHION-IN
★

SENMONTEN ■

HANAMIKÕJI-DORI

HIGASHIÕJI-DORI

RAMEN ▼
MURAJI

KYOTO INN
GION

SHIJO-DORI

YASAKA-JINJA ★

Maruyama-
kōen

KYOTO
YOSHIMIZU ●

HANA-TOURO
HOTEL GION

HANAMI-KÕJI ★

HANAMI-KÕJI

YUZUYA ▼
RYOKAN

DONGURI-DORI

KIKUNOI
HONTEN ■

OLD
KYOTO ●

KODAI-JI
★

GION KOH ■

YASAKA-DORI

KAGIZEN ▼
YOSHIFUSA
KÕDA-IJI

HOTEL THE CELESTINE ●
KYOTO GION

CAMELLIA ■
FLOWER

MATSUBARA-DORI

HIGASHIÕJI-DORI

0   1000 ft

0   250 m

© MOON.COM

Kyoto Station Area

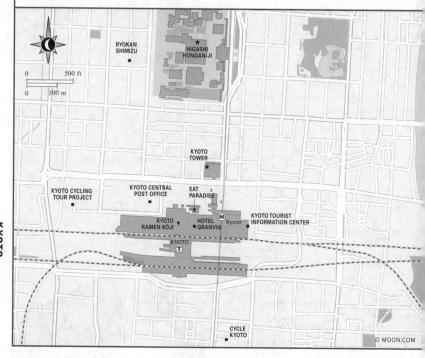

RYOKAN SHIMIZU

★ HIGASHI HONGAN-JI

0   500 ft
0 100 m

KYOTO TOWER ★

KYOTO CYCLING TOUR PROJECT ■

KYOTO CENTRAL POST OFFICE ■

EAT PARADISE ▼

KYOTO RAMEN KŌJI ▼

HOTEL GRANVIA ■

M *Kyoto*

KYOTO TOURIST INFORMATION CENTER ■

KYOTO T

CYCLE KYOTO ■

© MOON.COM

altars where devotees leave open cartons of *sake* as offerings. Japanese tradition deems the fox a mystical animal with the power to possess human beings by entering via the fingernails. Spiritual possession aside, if you're on the path as the sun begins to fall, the slightly eerie atmosphere may spook even the staunchest skeptic.

Ambling through the tunnel of red may feel ethereal, but the chief concerns of the shrine's deity are strongly rooted in the cares of the physical world. The site was originally dedicated to the gods of rice and *sake* when it was founded by the Hata family in AD 711. Its focus gradually shifted to commerce as farmers' clout waned and merchants' status increased. The black kanji characters etched deeply into the bright red beams of the seemingly endless rows of *torii* are, in fact, the names of companies that have donated the gates to the shrine in the hope of achieving business success.

Tōfuku-ji
東福寺

15-778 Honmahi, Higashiyama-ku; tel. 075/561-0087; www.tofukuji.jp; 9am-4pm daily; grounds free, Hōjō garden ¥400 adults and ¥300 junior high and elementary students, Tsūten-kyō and Kaizan-dō ¥400 adults and ¥300 junior high and elementary students; take JR Nara, Keihan lines to Tōfuku-ji Station

A Zen enclave about 20 minutes' walk north of Fushimi Inari-Taisha is Tōfuku-ji. This fantastic temple complex is less crowded than you'd expect—except during autumn (especially Nov.) when its justly famous foliage pops with earth tones and fiery reds. Surrounded by a wall, the temple grounds include the superb *Hōjō* garden. This carefully shaped landscape is an otherworldly expression of Zen, with mossy islands amid oceans of raked gravel, adroitly pruned shrubs, checkerboard patterns formed with natural elements, and misshapen stones suggesting imaginary mountains. This is a worthy stop and markedly less crowded than the great temples to the north in Higashiyama.

Sennyū-ji
泉涌寺

27 Yamanouchi-chō, Sennyū-ji, Higashiyama-ku; tel. 075/561-1551; www.mitera.org; 9am-5pm (last admission 4:30pm) daily Mar.-Nov., 9am-4:30pm (last admission 4pm) Dec.-Feb., treasure hall closed 4th Mon. of month; adults ¥500, junior high and elementary school students ¥300; take JR Nara, Keihan lines to Tōfuku-ji Station

After jostling through the camera-wielding masses at nearby Fushimi Inari-Taisha, this temple is a breath of fresh air. Uphill and well away from other tourists, about 5 minutes' walk northeast of Tōfuku-ji, it has a beautiful garden that is absolutely striking during autumn when the foliage turns.

Sennyū-ji gets its name (literally: "bubbling spring temple") from the freshwater spring flowing from its grounds. Situated at the foot of Mount Tsukinowa, this temple's illustrious history includes close ties to Japan's imperial family—hence its alternative name Mitera ("Imperial Temple"). A number of emperors' tombs sit within the walled-off mausoleum on the far side of the garden set deep into the grounds.

Inside the main Buddha hall (Butsu-den), reconstructed in 1668 and bearing architectural accents from China's Song Dynasty (960-1279), you'll find three golden Buddha effigies. Look up and marvel at the dramatic painting of a dragon, soaring overhead, by the master Kanō Tanyū of the illustrious Kano School of painting. There's also a **museum** (entrance fee included in temple admission) on the grounds, where you'll find sacred texts, art, and more on display.

To justify the uphill trek to this temple, visit its sub-temple, **Unryū-in** (雲龍院; 36 Yamanouchicho, Sennyū-ji, Higashiyama-ku; tel. 075/541-3916; www.unryuin.jp; 10am-5pm

(last entry 4:30pm) daily; ¥400), right next door. The epitome of Zen, this hushed and very well-hidden gem sees few tourists. Its sublime garden is known for its gorgeous autumn leaves. Inside, you're greeted by a large screen emblazoned with a twisting dragon (Unryū-in means "Cloud Dragon Temple"). For an additional ¥500, you can enjoy a tea with a sweet as you plop down on cushions on the tatami floor and bask in the serenity of the garden view.

SOUTHERN HIGASHIYAMA

The southern half of this district is the most jam-packed sightseeing area in all of Kyoto.

Sanjūsangen-dō
三十三間堂

657 Sanjusangendoma wari-cho, Higashiyama-ku; tel. 075/561-0467; http://sanjusangendo.jp; 8am-5pm daily Apr.-Nov. 15, 9am-4pm daily Nov. 16-Mar.; adults ¥600, high school and junior high school students ¥400, children ¥300; from Kyoto Station, take Kyoto City Bus 100 or 206 to Sanjūsangen-dō-mae bus stop, or Keihan line to Shichijō Station, exit 2

Inside Sanjūsangen-dō you'll find a surreal sight: around 1,000 statues of Kannon, the Buddhist goddess of mercy, standing like ethereal sentinels. (Strictly speaking, Kannon is not a goddess, but a bodhisattva, or an enlightened one who has voluntarily delayed entering nirvana to save others trapped in the wheel of suffering, or life, death, and rebirth.) At the center of these gold-plated beings is the thousand-armed Kannon, known as Senjū Kannon. Highly recommended at any time of year, and the fact that the treasures here are all under a roof make it a great choice for a rainy day.

Kyoto National Museum
京都国立博物館

527 Chaya-machi, Higashiyama-ku; tel. 075/525-2473; www.kyohaku.go.jp; 9:30am-6pm Tues.-Thurs. and Sun., 9:30am-8pm Fri.-Sat., closed following Tues. when Mon. is holiday; fee varies by exhibition; from Kyoto Station, take Kyoto City Bus

100 or 206 to Sanjūsangen-dō-mae bus stop, or Keihan line to Shichijō Station

Just across the street from Sanjūsangen-dō, you'll find Kyoto National Museum. Although the permanent collection is a little half-hearted, the museum often hosts stellar temporary exhibitions featuring some of the Japanese greats, such as the Edo-period woodblock print master Hiroshige. All information is clearly presented in bilingual displays. Like its neighbor Sanjūsangen-dō, the museum is also an excellent rainy-day option.

★ Kiyomizu-dera
清水寺

1-294 Kiyomizu, Higashiyama-ku; tel. 075/551-1234; www.kiyomizudera.or.jp; 6am-6pm daily (closing time varies by season); adults ¥400, junior high and elementary students ¥200; from Kyoto Station, take Kyoto City Bus 100 or 206 to Gojō-zaka or Kiyomizu-michi bus stop

Perched above the sight-dense district of Southern Higashiyama, Kiyomizu-dera is one of Kyoto's most iconic temples. Look beyond the crowds and you'll see a fantastic temple that offers sweeping views of the city below. If you happen to be at Kiyomizu-dera when the cherry blossoms are in bloom—ill-advised if you can't stand crowds—the nighttime illumination of the trees surrounding the temple is spectacular.

Coming from Higashi Ōji-dōri, proceed up either Matsubara-dōri or the Chawan-zaka ("Teapot Lane"), via **Gojō-zaka,** to the temple's main gate. Before entering the temple's main hall, keep your eyes open for **Zuigu-dō,** a separate hall on the temple's grounds with a hidden cave beneath it called the **Tainai-meguri.** The building itself is located to the left of the staircase leading up to the main temple. After paying ¥100 and removing your shoes, make your way down the stairs and through the pitch-black grotto, navigating with only the help of a rope. This sacred subterranean space symbolizes the womb of Daizuigu Bosatsu, a female bodhisattva

believed to have the power to grant wishes. Inside, there's a stone that is said to have the power to grant any wish.

After making your wish, continue to **Jishu-jinja,** a matchmaking shrine on the backside of the temple's grounds where you may see young students trying their luck at walking 18 meters (59 feet) between two stone pillars in the shrine's grounds with their eyes closed. If successful, the feat is believed to bring about luck in romance. From here, wander the complex, exploring its various temples, subtemples, rituals, and faithful masses.

Kōdai-ji
高台寺

526 Shimokawara-chō, Higashiyama-ku; tel. 075/561-9966; https://www.kodaiji.com/e_index.html; 9am-5:30pm daily; adults ¥600, high school and junior high school students ¥250, children free; take Kyoto City Bus 206 to Higashiyama Yasui bus stop

This Rinzai sect temple features exemplary gardens (raked-gravel and landscape). The main hall was once lacquered and graced with gilt designs, although the current incarnation is a simpler affair built in 1912. The grounds are illuminated in spring and autumn, conjuring a dreamy landscape (for details, visit https://www.kodaiji.com/e_illumi.html).

Originally built in 1606 in honor of Toyotoi Hideyoshi, one of Japan's three "great unifiers," it also enshrines his wife Nene. Both are honored in a mausoleum that sits atop a hill behind the main temple complex. The temple's interior contains plenty of flamboyance thanks to the financial backing of Tokugawa Ieyasu, who followed Hideyoshi as the founder of the Tokugawa shogunate. There are also two teahouses on the grounds, reached via a path that runs through a bamboo grove. The construction of one of these teahouses was overseen by none other than Sen no Rikyū, creator of the tea ceremony.

It's located between Kiyomizu-dera, which lies about 20 minutes' walk south, and Yasaka-jinja, 8 minutes' walk to the northwest. This temple is passed over by most tourists, making it a great place to go to escape the crowds of the area.

1: stone fox with granary key at Fushimi Inari-Taisha **2:** Tōfuku-ji's *Hōjō* garden **3:** Kiyomizu-dera

Chion-in
知恩院

400 Rinka-chō, Higashiyama-ku; tel. 075/531-2111;
www.chion-in.or.jp; 9am-4:30pm daily; outer grounds
free, adults ¥500, junior high and elementary school
students ¥250 for all inner buildings and gardens;
take Tōzai line to Higashiyama Station, or Kyoto City
Bus 206 to Chion-in-mae bus stop

Located just north of Yasaka-jinja and Maruyama-kōen, and about 8 minutes' walk north of Kōdai-ji, this massive temple is known as the "Vatican of Pure Land Buddhism." Besides being the head temple of the Jōdo sect of Pure Land Buddhism, the sheer scale of the complex is reminiscent of its Roman Catholic counterpart.

The sweeping front staircase was used in the film *The Last Samurai*. It also makes an appearance in *Lost in Translation*. There's very impressive joinery on display in the large Sanmon gate. With a height of 24 meters (78.7 feet) and a width of 50 meters (164 feet), it's the biggest wooden gate in the country. After passing through the gate, ascend the stairs to the temple's main grounds, centered on an expansive courtyard laced with stone paths.

It's free to enter the Miei-dō (main hall), which houses an effigy of Hōnen, the priest who founded the Jōdo sect, and the neighboring Amida-dō (Amida hall), in which you'll see a magnificent visage of the principle Buddha of the Amida Buddha ("Amida" is the Japanese version of the Sanskrit word for "Infinite Light"). Amida Buddha is the principle Buddha of the Pure Land sect, and is believed to have fashioned an afterlife paradise where anyone is welcome who faithfully chants Amida's name. You'll need to pay admission to venture farther inside.

Deeper within the temple precincts, alongside more buildings, you'll discover two gardens, **Yūzen-en** (9am-4pm daily; adults ¥300, children ¥150), a rock garden with a pond that sits southeast of the Sanmon gate, and **Hōjō-en** (9am-3:50pm; adults ¥400, children ¥200), a classic landscape garden dating to the mid-17th century that lies east of the temple's main hall. You can also pay to enter both gardens at a discounted rate (adults ¥500, children ¥250).

Shōren-in
青蓮院

69-1 Sanjōbōchō, Awataguchi, Higashiyama-ku; tel.
075/561-2345; www.shorenin.com; 9am-5pm daily;
adults ¥500, junior high and high school students
¥400, elementary school students ¥200; take Tōzai
line to Higashiyama Station, or Kyoto City Bus 5, 46,
or 100 to Jingū-michi bus stop

This is a hidden gem in the truest sense: Now a temple, it was originally built as villa for an abbot of the Tendai School of Buddhism. The temple also had longstanding ties to the imperial family: an empress temporarily called it home in the 18th century after a fire.

The first building you'll enter brings you to the tatami-floored Kachoden (drawing room). Here, you'll find sliding doors with paintings of natural scenes and court life, opening onto an exquisite garden centered on a pond filled with colorful koi. Wooden boardwalks link this building to other structures in the complex, including the Shijokodō, or compact main hall. Note that the two sacred paintings within the Shijokodō—a mandala (visual representation of the universe, according to Buddhist cosmology) and an image of Fudo Myō, a sword-wielding deity of wisdom enshrouded in flames—are usually veiled from public view.

After viewing the garden from within the drawing room, meander along the snaking path that laces it. It passes by a lovely **teahouse** (¥1,000, includes green tea and sweet; only open select days throughout year; for details, go to www.shorenin.com/english/tea), a shrine, and through an atmospheric bamboo grove. The grounds are lit up at night during spring and autumn (for details, go to www.shorenin.com/english/night). This is a recommended, largely crowd-free stop near Chion-in, from where it's about 5 minutes' walk north.

GION
祇園

To soak up the ambience of Kyoto's entertainment district, take a stroll down the cobblestone lane of **Hanami-kōji,** starting from the south side of Shijō-dōri, as dusk falls and the lanterns that hang in front of the wooden shopfronts flicker. Without an appointment to see a geisha performance or dine at a *kaiseki* restaurant, there's little in the way of casual entertainment here. You can enjoy the area by simply meandering through its lanes and breathing in the air of sophistication.

Yasaka-jinja
八坂神社

625 Gion-machi Kitagawa, Higashiyama-ku; tel. 075/561-6155; www.yasaka-jinja.or.jp; 24 hours daily; free; take Keihan line to Gion-Shijō, exit 6, or Kyoto City Bus 206 to Gion bus stop

In the heart of Gion, Yasaka-jinja is a grand shrine that is best known for hosting Kyoto's epic summerly **Gion Matsuri.** Despite its location in the heart of Kyoto's entertainment district, Yasaka-jinja is a dignified spiritual center. It's hard to miss, given its location in the heart of the southern half of Higashiyama, the city's most dense sightseeing district, and the steady flow of faithful who come for weddings, or to pray or make a New Year's Day request to the gods for a good year ahead. Religious proceedings aside, the shrine is a great place to stroll in serenity. It backs onto the excellent Maruyama-kōen, and at night it is lit by the soft glow of hanging lanterns.

NORTHERN HIGASHIYAMA

Northern Higashiyama has an abundance of spiritual sights, atmospheric paths, and gardens. It's also a bit less crowded than the neighboring districts.

Kyoto Museum of Crafts and Design

B1F Miyako Messe Bldg., 9-1 Okazaki Seishoji-chō, Sakyō-ku; tel. 075/762-2670; https://kmtc.jp;

9am-5pm, last admission 4:30pm daily; free; take Tōzai subway line to Higashiyama Station

A solid rainy-day option is this museum near Heian-jingū that shows off Kyoto's wide range of traditional crafts under one roof. It's commonly referred to as the Fureaikan. You'll find sterling examples of woodworking, basket weaving, textiles, metalwork, lacquerware, gold-leaf work, and more. To find this nicely curated—and importantly, free—museum, enter the gray Miyako Messe building, then ride the escalator to the first basement floor. English signage throughout.

Heian-jingū
平安神宮

97 Nishitennō-chō, Okazaki, Sakyō-ku; tel. 075/761-0221; www.heianjingu.or.jp; 6:30am-5:30pm daily Feb. 15-Mar. 14 and Oct., 6am-6pm daily Mar. 15-Sept. 30, 6am-5pm daily Nov. 1-Feb. 14; shrine grounds free, garden ¥600 adults, ¥300 children; from Kyoto Station, take Kyoto City Bus 5 to Okazaki-kōen/Bijutsukan bus stop, or Tōzai subway line to Higashiyama Station

Located in the heart of the Northern Higashiyama area, you'll find an imposing shrine known as Heian-jungū. Constructed in 1895 in honor of Kyoto's 1,100th birthday, it's a replica—5/8 in scale—of the city's ancient Heian Palace, where the earliest emperors resided. The shrine is a good place to begin a journey through this culturally rich neighborhood.

The approach to the shrine is unique in that the vermillion *torii* gate that marks its first entrance straddles and stands nearly 25 meters above the road that leads to the shrine, which sits in a park called Okazaki-kōen. After passing through the park, you'll find the shrine at the northern end of Jingū-michi, where it meets Nijō-dōri, running east to west.

Inside the shrine's main three-doored gate is an expansive gravel-covered space that fronts the main hall of the shrine. Near the entrance, amulets and talismans are sold by shrine maidens from windows, and myriad hanging wooden plaques are scrawled with visitors' wishes. Toward the back of the

Geisha

If you find yourself in Kyoto's Gion district in the mid-evening, a geisha in training, known as a *maiko,* may float past. This district, dating to the 16th century, remains one of the best places to spot one. These nostalgic entertainment quarters, called *hanamachi* (flower towns), are the traditional stomping grounds of the increasingly rare geisha (person of the arts), or *geiko* (child of the arts), as they're known in Kyoto.

Carried along by high-set *geta,* as her elevated wooden sandals are known, a *maiko* is easily recognized by her thick white makeup, charcoal-painted eyebrows, and deep-red lower lip. She is draped in an exquisite, flowery kimono tied with an elongated *obi* (belt) left to dangle from her waist as she walks.

TRAINING AND WORK

A common misconception is that geisha are prostitutes. Historically, some geisha would enter contractual relationships with wealthy patrons who would pay for their companionship, which would include a romantic dimension. The woman would often use the money earned to pay off her debt to her *okiya,* the matriarchal school where she spent five to six years acquiring her substantial talents: traditional dance, playing instruments such as the three-stringed *shamisen,* as well as singing and engaging in wide-ranging conversation.

Before World War II, some 80,000 geisha worked in *hanamachi* across Japan; today, a mere 1,000 work in this trade. In their heyday, geisha in training would enter an *okiya* as early as six years old. Today, the situation is more fluid, with geisha living where they want, dating whom they want, and entering—at the earliest—at 15 (the age when compulsory education is completed in Japan).

MEETING GEISHA

To be entertained by geisha, you more or less need to know somebody. They mostly flit to and

complex, locals approach the main altar to offer prayers.

Beyond the shrine's main building there's a garden that can be entered for a fee. Pay a visit to the shrine, but skip the garden, as better ones await nearby.

★ Nanzen-ji

南禅寺

86 Fukuchi-chō, Nanzen-ji, Sakyō-ku; tel. 075/771-0365; www.nanzen.net; 8:40am-5pm daily Mar.-Nov., 8:40am-4:30pm Dec.-Feb.; grounds free, Hōjō garden ¥500 adults, ¥400 high school students, ¥300 junior high and elementary school students, San-mon gate viewing platform ¥500 adults, ¥400 high school students, junior high and elementary school students ¥300; take Tōzai subway line to Keage Station

A personal favorite, Nanzen-ji is a magical temple complex that sprawls over a large area in Northern Higashiyama. Its grounds invite roaming and its paths lead up into the hills surrounding this lush site, transporting those who walk them to a hidden grotto and a smattering of subtemples with pristine gardens that most visitors to the site pass by. This 13th-century temple is the head temple of a strain of the Rinzai sect of Zen Buddhism

As you approach the temple grounds, take note of a couple of atmospheric, often missed subtemples: **Konchi-in** (86-12 Fukuchi-chō, Nanzen-ji, Sakyō-ku; tel. 075/771-3511; 8:30am-5pm daily Mar.-Nov., 8:30am-4:30pm daily Dec.-Feb.; adults ¥400, high school students ¥300, junior high and elementary school students ¥200) and **Tenju-an** (86-8 Fukuchi-chō, Nanzen-ji, Sakyō-ku; tel. 075/771-0744; 9am-5pm daily Mar.-mid-Nov., 9am-4:30pm mid-Nov.-Feb.; adults ¥500, children ¥300). Both boast sublime gardens that are only visited by a fraction of the crowd streaming into Nanzen-ji. The entrance to Konchi-in is located on the right side of the road leading up from exclusive parties at secretive inns, high-end restaurants, and in members-only teahouses. The other option is attending a public performance, often staged to coincide with cherry blossom season and autumn foliage in Kyoto. The most popular dances include **Miyako Odori** (held throughout Apr.), **Kyō Odori** (first three Suns. in Apr.), **Kitano Odori** (daily Apr. 15-25), **Kamogawa Odori** (daily May 1-24), and **Gion Odori** (daily Nov. 1-10). Ask your hotel concierge if your visit coincides with one of these occasions, and to help land tickets if it does.

If you're determined to experience an evening with geisha, some pricey options do exist. Check out the varied geisha experiences provided by **Maikoya** (https://mai-ko.com/geisha); the offerings of **Chris Rowthorn Tours** (www.chrisrowthorn.com/kyoto-geisha-tours), an outfit with deep ties to hard-to-access geisha houses; or **Gion Hatanaka** (www.gionhatanaka.jp/maiko/english/about.html), a Gion *ryokan* that hosts regular geisha dinners.

maiko in Kyoto

Finally, if you spot one in the street, don't interrupt her. She's a highly trained professional who is likely on her way to an appointment. The best places to catch a glimpse of a geisha or *maiko* in this candid way are **Ponto-chō** and **Gion** in Kyoto and **Ginza** in Tokyo.

to Nanzen-ji, about 40 meters (130 feet) before you come to the main gate to the Nanzen-ji complex. Proceed past the public restrooms on the right, and just beyond them, roughly parallel with the southern edge of Nanzen-ji's lofty San-mon Gate, you'll see the entrance to Tenju-an.

After soaking up the calm ambience at these two subtemples, explore Nanzen-ji's grounds at a contemplative pace. Note the aqueduct running through the grounds—a Meiji period (1868-1912) construction once used to transport goods and water between Kyoto and Lake Biwa northeast of the city. Facing the aqueduct from the temple's main grounds, up a stone staircase, is the subtemple **Nanzen-in** and its *Hōjō* garden. Follow the path leading uphill to the right, walking beside the canal as you go, for a great view of the city below.

If you cross under the canal from the main temple grounds and, instead, take a hard left,

following the road beside the stream, you'll reach a stone stairway that leads into the hills. Walk to the top—about 200 meters (656 feet) behind the temple grounds—where you'll discover **Okuno-in,** a sacred space containing a waterfall and a hidden grotto.

TOP EXPERIENCE

★ Philosopher's Path
哲学の道

After taking a stroll along the Philosopher's Path in northeastern Kyoto, the inspiration for its name—Tetsugaku-no-michi in Japanese—will be evident. This walking path begins in the south from about 100 meters (300 feet) north of the temple of **Eikan-dō** and ends at the foot of the approach to **Ginkaku-ji** in the north, for a total distance of about 1.8 km (1.1 mi). Walking at a leisurely pace, this stroll will take about 30 minutes, not accounting for stops at sights along the way.

This pathway runs beside a canal that directs a gentle stream of water through one of the city's most tranquil neighborhoods, and is surrounded by a wide range of foliage, including cherry trees that burst with color during *hanami* season. (Note that the path is thronged during springtime. Avoid visiting during daylight hours during the *hanami* rush. Instead, go after dusk when the trees are lit up for a few hours.)

The combination of the water and greenery make this path the ideal place for a contemplative stroll. This is exactly what Kyoto University philosophy professor Nishida Kitaro—who inspired the name of this path—did whenever he grew weary of trying to untangle some question and craved reconnection with his senses and the outside world.

The path winds through an area dotted with a host of atmospheric temples and shrines, some of them with stellar gardens. Rather than having a set agenda, I recommend ambling at your own pace and stopping at any that may catch your eye. In the spirit of its namesake, stroll the path with an open mind and see where your intuition leads.

Ginkaku-ji
銀閣寺

2 Ginkaku-ji-chō, Sakyō-ku; tel. 075/771-5725; www. shokoku-ji.jp/en/ginkakuji/; 8:30am-5pm daily Mar.-Nov., 9am-4:30pm Dec.-Feb.; adults ¥500, junior high and elementary school students ¥300; take Kyoto City Bus 5 or 17 to Ginkaku-ji-michi bus stop

Ginkaku-ji, or the "Silver Pavilion" is a stunning temple complex that boasts superb gardens and rambling halls. The temple, built in 1482, was originally the retirement villa of shogun Ashikaga Yoshimasa. Yoshimasa was the grandson of Ashikaga Yoshimitsu, who a few decades prior had built Kinkaku-ji (the Golden Pavilion) on the other side of town. It was repurposed into a Zen temple following Yoshimasa's death in 1490.

Located near the northern end of the Philosopher's Path, the grounds of Ginkaku-ji are classically Zen. On one hand, there's an intensely green, moss-covered garden. Contrasting this is a separate dry-gravel garden complete with a miniature representation of Mount Fuji and raked into geometric swirls. A still pond surrounded by gnarled pine trees frames the beautiful main hall, which is decidedly more rustic than the temple's gold-plated counterpart, Kinkaku-ji, across town.

Simply exploring and taking in the grounds via a circular loop and meandering through the buildings' dark wooden corridors makes a visit to Ginkaku-ji worthwhile. But be sure to also walk the path that leads up a hill behind the complex, affording a sweeping vista of the grounds and the surrounding area below. For better or worse, Ginkaku-ji is one of Kyoto's most popular spots. Aim to visit either just as it opens, or within an hour of closing to avoid the picture-snapping masses.

Eikan-dō
永観堂

48 Eikandō-chō, Sakyō-ku; tel. 075/761-0007; www. eikando.or.jp; 9am-5pm (last entry 4pm) daily, special hours during evening in autumn; adults ¥600, children ¥400; take Tōzai line to Keage Station, or Kyoto City Bus 5 to Nanzenji-Eikandō-michi bus stop

This tranquil Jōdo (Pure Lane) sect temple is 7 minutes' walk north from Nanzen-ji. It serves as the southern end of the Philosopher's Path and is famed for its autumn foliage, particularly its fiery maples. Originally the villa of a court noble during the Heian period (794-1185), it was converted into a temple originally known as Zenrin-ji. Its popularly used name of Eikan-dō is derived from an 11th-century priest named Eikan.

Its buildings, containing attractively painted sliding doors and linked by wooden walkways, sit beside a serene garden, criss-crossed by tiny streams that run into a pond with an island in the middle where a petite shrine stands. Standing above the grounds on a hill is the two-story Tahoto Pagoda,

1: Heian-jingū 2: Nanzen-ji 3: Philosopher's Path in autumn 4: Ginkaku-ji

Northern Higashiyama's Less Crowded Side

The quieter side of Northern Higashiyama is best seen on a hill known as **Yoshidayama,** about 25 minutes' walk northwest of Nanzen-ji, or 20 minutes west of the northern edge of the Philosopher's Path. Simply strolling through the grounds through these three sights (for free) will work its magic.

KONKAI-KŌMYŌ-JI

金戒光明寺

121 Kurodani-chō, Sakyō-ku; tel. 075/771-2204; www.kurodani.jp/en; 9am-4pm daily; grounds free, garden ¥600 (Nov.-early Dec. only)

Known for its atmospheric **Kurodani Garden,** this gem of a temple is ensconced on the southern side of Yoshidayama. To find it, walk west on Marutamachi-dōri. Walk about 200 meters (650 feet), then curl into the alley located just past on your right. Follow the alley, then at the end walk up the stairs, which lead to the temple. It's free to enter the main hall and walk through its grounds, where you'll find a pagoda and a graveyard. To enter the garden tucked away behind the temple that you must pay ¥600 throughout November and into the first week of December when autumn leaves have peaked.

SHINNYO-DŌ

真如堂

82 Shinnyo-chō, Jōdoji, Sakyō-ku; tel. 075/771-0915; https://shin-nyo-do.jp; 9am-4pm daily; grounds free, ¥500 main hall and inner garden, ¥1,000 during special periods of Mar. and Nov.-early Dec.

A brilliant place to see autumn foliage with a fraction of the crowds, this temple of the Tendai sect is about 5 minutes' walk uphill from Konkai-Kōmyō-ji (aka Kurodani). Established in 984, razed in the Onin War (1467-1477), and finally rebuilt and relocated to its current location in 1693, its grounds includes a main hall with a gilt canopy, sacred statues, paintings that alternate every half-year (one depicting the scene of Buddha's death, the other a mandala representing the Buddhist Pure Land), a three-storied pagoda, and an inner garden.

YOSHIDA-JINJA

吉田神社

30 Kaguraoka-chō, Yoshida, Sakyō-ku; tel. 075/771-3788; www.yoshidajinja.com; 9am-5pm daily; free

Standing above both temples is the secluded hilltop shrine of Yoshida-jinja, which was originally built by nobleman Fujiwara no Yamakage in 859 to ward off evil spirits from what was then the ancient capital of Heian-kyō. The shrine grounds contain one main hall (Hongū) and 10 other sub-shrines, dedicated to an array of *kami* (gods): one guarding from evil, one bringing good fortune, another boosting scholarship, and so on. The shrine is known for its annual **Setsubun Festival** (Feb. 2-4), the end of winter on the traditional calendar. Attendees throw soybeans at someone suited up in an *oni* (demon) costume while chanting *"Fuku wa uchi! Oni wa soto!"* ("Happiness come in! Demons go out!"). Sticklers will also eat the same number of soybeans as their age to protect from illness in the coming year.

which has a square base and a rounded second level. Climb the stairs to this structure and enjoy views over the temple grounds and city beyond.

Note that the cost of entry is raised during autumn, when the grounds are illuminated at night (second half of Nov.; ¥1,000 daytime, ¥600 nighttime). Be forewarned: The crowds are intense when the leaves turn, particularly in November. During other times of year, however, the temple is an appealing escape from selfie-stick-toting masses who congregate at many of the other more famous temples around town.

Hōnen-in
法然院

30 Goshonodan-chō, Shishigatani, Sakyō-ku; tel. 075/771-2420; www.honen-in.jp; 6am-4pm daily; free; take Kyoto City Bus 5 or 17 to Ginkaku-ji-michi bus stop

A hushed temple founded in 1680 just off the Philosopher's Path, tucked away in a lush grove dotted by pools of water, Hōnen-in is about 10 minutes' walk south of jam-packed Ginkaku-ji. The thatched-roof entrance gate, blanketed in moss, is approached via a leafy path, creating a magical atmosphere. Upon entering, walk between two sculpted rectangular mounds of sand, over a pond, and past raked-gravel gardens to a hidden grotto. The main temple, which houses a black statue of Amida Buddha, can only be entered from April 1-7 and November 1-7. There's also a gallery on-site that hosts local art exhibitions. This is a worthwhile stop off the Philosopher's Path that is mercifully free of crowds.

DOWNTOWN AND CENTRAL KYOTO

Roughly in the geographical heart of the city, downtown is a convenient place to shop, eat, go out in the evening, and sleep. Central Kyoto includes the areas beyond the southern and northern edges of downtown. **Kyoto Imperial Palace,** its large, leafy surrounding park of **Kyoto Gyōen,** and the city's

imposing castle, **Nijō-jō,** are found in this broad swath of town.

Ponto-chō
先斗町

If you've ever seen a photograph of a cobblestone alley in Kyoto—festooned with softly glowing red lanterns and flanked by dark wooden shopfronts with doors obscured by curtains—chances are the street in the image was Ponto-chō.

This pedestrian-only street is a sight in itself and evokes the quiet refinement of old Kyoto, perhaps better than any other lane in the city. Running along the west bank of the Kamo River, Ponto-chō extends from just south of Sanjō Station (Tōzai subway line, Keihan line) at its northern edge to bustling Shijō-dōri, near both Gion-Shijō Station (Keihan line) and Kawaramachi Station (Hankyū line) at its southern end.

For maximum impact, visit Ponto-chō after the sun sets, when the paper lanterns flicker and well-heeled patrons make their way into one of the alley's countless exclusive eateries and bars. By and large, it's not the kind of area you can casually pop in, but there are some restaurants and bars that are accustomed to serving foreign customers where you'll be relieved to meet staff who speak English and find menus in English.

Kyoto Imperial Palace
京都御所

3 Kyoto Gyōen, Kamigyō-ku; tel. 075/211-1215; https://sankan.kunaicho.go.jp/guide/kyoto.html; 9am-4:30pm Tues.-Sun. Mar.-Sept., 9am-4pm Oct.-Feb., last entry 40 minutes before closing; free; take Karasuma subway line to Imadegawa Station

Ensconced in the center of a large park, the Gosho, as it's known in Japanese, is the Imperial family's home away from their current home in Tokyo. It's the site various ceremonies infused with much pomp, including the ascension of each new emperor to the throne. Originally constructed in 794, the current complex was built in 1855, following numerous incarnations made necessary by fires. Surrounded by a wall and laced with gravel pathways, the palace does retain Japanese accents—low, sweeping rooflines, a mostly wooden shell—but it's otherwise quite modern. If you're a history buff and would like to see the emperor's old primary residence, it's worth a stop. You can either follow a simple route with English language signage or join a free group **tour** in English (1 hour; 10am and 2pm) by showing up at the Kunaicho (Imperial Household Office). Be sure to bring your passport, which is necessary to join one of the tours.

Nijō-jō
二条城

541 Nijōjō-chō, Nijō-dōri, Horikawa Nishi-iru, Nakagyō-ku; tel. 075/841-0096; http://nijo-jocastle.city.kyoto.lg.jp/?lang=en; 8:45am-5pm (last entry 4pm), Ninomaru Palace closed Tues. Dec.-Jan. and Jul.-Aug., closed Dec. 26-Jan. 4; adults ¥620, junior high school students and younger free for Nijō-jō only, adults ¥1,030, high and junior high school students ¥350, elementary school students ¥200 for Nijō-jō and Ninomaru Palace; take Tōzai line to Nijō-jō-mae Station

One of Kyoto's more eye-popping sights is its famed castle, Nijō-jō. This imposing compound—surrounded by stunning gardens and hemmed in by towering stone walls—is the city's most visible demonstration of the power that the military elite held over the emperor during the feudal Edo period (1603-1867).

Construction of the majestic complex began in 1603. It was intended to serve as the Kyoto home of the first shogun, Tokugawa Ieyasu, and was completed 23 years later by Ieyasu's grandson Iemitsu, who also built a five-story keep. When the Edo period came to a close in 1867 and power was restored to the emperor, the castle was then used as an imperial palace for a time, until it was donated to the city. Today it stands at the center of the ancient capital, a stellar example of Japanese castle architecture and one of the city's most popular sites. Avoid going during the middle of the day when the site is flooded with visitors. Try to arrive just as it opens to beat the rush.

The castle can roughly be split into four sections: the outer walls and moats, two inner layers of defenses that encircle the complex—the Honmaru, or main ring of defense, and the secondary layer, or Ninomaru—and a smattering of attractive classical gardens. The Honmaru is not usually open to the public, but the Ninomaru area is.

Be sure to visit the **Ninomaru Palace.**

entry of Nijō-jō

Inside you'll discover some of the defensive tricks employed by the shoguns to subvert would-be assassins, such as the legendary "nightingale floors" that squeaked in a way that vaguely resembles a bird call to warn of any attempted sneak attack. The palace is also covered in artistic flourishes, from floridly adorned ceilings to handsomely painted sliding doors, reflecting the opulent tastes of the shoguns. Outside the palace, be sure to meander through **Seiryū-en,** a beautiful landscape garden.

Kyoto International Manga Museum

京都国際マンガミュージアム

Karasuma-dōri, Oike-agaru, Nakagyō-ku; tel. 075/254-7414; www.kyotomm.jp/en; 10am-6pm Thurs.-Tues., closed Thurs. when Wed. is holiday; adults ¥800, junior high and high school students ¥300, elementary school students ¥100; take Karasuma, Tōzai lines to Karasuma Oike Station

For hardcore manga fans, this place is pretty special. It's essentially a massive library of manga. It's housed in a former school building and boasts an impressive 300,000 individual volumes, which can be freely read for the price of admission. There are also (mostly bilingual) exhibitions on the history of manga and how it's drawn. Storytellers known as *kamishibai*, who essentially read a story from a scroll of images, sporadically perform onsite; the *kamishibai* tradition began long ago with monks who used drawings on scrolls to teach the basics of Buddhism to peasants who couldn't read. An essential stop for manga fans and a good rainy-day option for anyone.

NORTHWEST KYOTO

More out of the way than other areas of the city, Northwest Kyoto is nonetheless home to a handful of significant temples. Besides heavy hitters like **Kinkaku-ji** in all its gilt glory, and **Ryōan-ji,** famed for its rock garden, there are a number of quieter gems like the serene temple compounds of **Myōshin-ji** and **Daitoku-ji.** East of the temples are the significant shrines of the grand **Shimogamo-jinja** (59 Izumigawa-chō, Shimogamo, Sakyō-ku; tel. 075/781-0010; www.shimogamo-jinja.or.jp/english/; 6:30am-5pm daily; free), surrounded by forest, and the untouristy **Kamigamo-jinja** (339 Kamigamo Motoyama, Kita-ku; tel. 075/781-0011; www.kamigamojinja.jp; grounds 24 hours daily, inside Romon gate 8:30am-4pm; free), set beside the east bank of the Kamo River. Between these two shrines is **Kyoto Botanical Gardens** (Shimogamohangichō, Sakyō-ku; tel. 075/701-0141; www.pref.kyoto.jp/plant/; gardens 9am-5pm (last entry 4pm) daily, conservatory 10am-4pm (last entry 3:30pm); adults ¥200, high school students ¥150, elementary and junior high school students ¥80, additional ¥200 for conservatory; take Karasuma subway line to Kitayama Station, exit 3), a pristine natural space brimming with bamboo, cherry trees, hydrangeas, peonies, plum trees, lotus flowers bobbing in ponds, and more.

Ryōan-ji

龍安寺

13 Goryōnoshitamachi, Ryōan-ji, Ukyō-ku; tel. 075/463-2216; www.ryoanji.jp; 8am-5pm daily Mar.-Nov., 8:30am-4:30pm daily Dec.-Feb.; adults ¥500, junior high and elementary school students ¥300; from Sanjō Keihan Station (Tōzai line), take Kyoto City Bus 59 to Ryōan-ji-mae bus stop, or Keifuku Kitano line from Arashiyama to Ryōan-ji-michi Station

The raked-gravel garden in the grounds of Ryōan-ji, with 15 rocks placed just so, is in many ways the embodiment of what most people think of when they hear the words "Zen garden." As with Ginkaku-ji, Ryōan-ji was once a villa, lived in by an aristocrat during the Heian period (794-1185). It became a temple of Zen Buddhism's Rinzai sect in 1450.

The origins of the temple's iconic rock garden are less clear. Though the precise meaning of the garden is an enigma, various stabs have been taken at theories on its meaning, from islands in the ocean to a mama tiger carrying her cubs across a pond to infinity.

One interesting point: When viewed from any angle, one rock will always be concealed from view.

Aside from this spiritual statement made in gravel, the head priest's former quarters (*Hōjō*) and the old kitchen (*kuri*) still stand. Take a peek at the compact gardens behind the *Hōjō*, as well as the beautifully painted sliding doors inside the *Hōjō's* tatami rooms.

To have a fighting chance of pondering the famed rock garden when it's not being mobbed by visitors, aim to arrive either just after the temple opens, or within an hour of closing.

★ Kinkaku-ji
金閣寺

1 Kinkaku-ji-chō, Kita-ku; tel. 075/461-0013; www. shokoku-ji.jp/en/kinkakuji; 9am-5pm daily; adults ¥400, junior high and elementary school students ¥300; from Kyoto Station, take Kyoto City Bus 205 to Kinkaku-ji-mae bus stop, or Kyoto City Bus 12 from Sanjō-Keihan Station (Tōzai line) to Kinkakuji-michi bus stop

Easily Kyoto's most recognizable temple, Kinkaku-ji cuts a striking profile, particularly on a sunny day. Its upper two stories are famously covered in gold, giving the site an ethereal glint and causing a mirage-like reflection to form in the pond surrounding its base. This Zen temple was originally built to serve as the villa of shogun Ashikaga Yoshimitsu, whose grandson built Ginkaku-ji in the northeast of town. The site was converted into a temple in 1408 upon Yoshimitsu's death.

Surrounded by greenery and fronted by a pond, Kinkaku-ji's design reflects the opulent Kitayama aristocratic culture at its height. The first floor was built in the style of a Heian-period palace—pillars made of timber, plaster walls painted white. The second floor is in the style of a samurai residence with statues of Kannon, the Buddhist goddess of compassion, and Four Heavenly Kings, mythological guardians of the four cardinal directions. The third floor is designed like a Zen Hall in the Chinese style. The roof is topped by a phoenix made of, yes, gold.

The grounds also include the former head priest's residence, or *Hōjō*, which can only be seen from outside, and a series of gardens that remain as they were when Yoshimitsu once strolled through them. If you see other visitors tossing ¥1 coins onto a statue—with a small fortune on the ground surrounding it—this is your chance to try to toss a few of your own. If you can throw a coin directly into the statue's lap, you'll be blessed with good luck.

As you exit the grounds, you'll pass a teahouse, some shops selling trinkets, and a small subtemple that contains a statue of one of the Five Wisdom Kings that is believed to have maybe been carved by Kobo Daishi (774-835), a monk and scholar of legendary proportions, and founder of the Shingon school of Buddhism.

As with many of Kyoto's top sights, it's worth trying to avoid going at the most popular times: midday any day of the week, and all day on weekends. Opening time on Monday or Tuesday mornings is a good time to visit.

Myōshin-ji
妙心寺

64 Myōshin-ji-chō, Hanazono, Ukyō-ku; tel. 075/461-5226; www.myoshinji.or.jp/english; 9:10am-11:40am (entry permitted every 20 minutes), 12:30pm (entry permitted once), 1pm-4:40pm (entry permitted every 20 minutes) daily, closed sporadically; adults ¥700, junior high and elementary school students ¥400; take JR Sagano San-in line to Hanazono Station, or Kyoto City Bus 62, 63, 65 or 66 from Sanjō Keihan Station (Tōzai line) to Myōshin-ji-mae bus stop

This sprawling Zen Buddhist complex of the Rinzai sect is just south of Myōshin-ji Station on the Kitano line. Besides the main temple of Myōshin-ji, the grounds are peppered with subtemples as well as a wonderful garden (at **Taizo-in**). Myōshin-ji is also notable for its *zazen* (seated meditation) classes (for prices and times, go to www.myoshinji.or.jp/english/zen/info.html).

1: Tourists meditate at the Zen garden in Ryōan-ji.
2: Kinkaku-ji

Northwest Kyoto's Less Crowded Side

Check out these two temples if you want to get away from the crowds:

NINNA-JI
仁和寺

33 Omurōuchi, Ukyō-ku; tel. 075/461-1155; www.ninnaji.jp/en; 9am-5pm daily Mar.-Nov., 9am-4:30pm daily Dec.-Feb.; grounds free, admission to Goten ¥500 adults, ¥300 junior high and elementary school students; take Kyoto City Bus 59 from Sanjō Keihan Station (Tōzai line), or Keifuku Kitano line from Arashiyama to Omuro-Ninna-ji Station

A 15-minute walk northwest of Myōshin-ji, this ancient temple (founded in 888) at the base of the mountains north of town is off the radar. It's a good place to escape the crowds of Ryōan-ji and Kinkaku-ji. A UNESCO World Heritage Site with a handsome five-story pagoda, its gardens are perfectly suited to a meditative ramble.

Be sure to visit the **Goten,** where the head priest once resided. Surrounding this building on the southeastern corner of the compound are idyllic gardens centered on ponds, bridges, a variety of trees and shrubs, and raked gravel. A good place to go in the northwest of town if you want to have somewhere to yourself or very close to it.

Note that around mid-April the late-blooming Omuro cherry tree blossoms and fills the temple's grounds with pink. This is the one time when the temple fills with visitors. Admission during this time increases to ¥600.

TŌJI-IN
等持院

63 Tōji-in Kita-machi, Kita-ku; tel. 075/461-5786; 9am-5pm daily; ¥500; take Keifuku Kitano line to Tōji-in Station

About 20 minutes' walk east of Ninna-ji, this temple is another good off-the-radar option. Founded by Shogun Ashikaga Takauji in 1341, with the present structures dating to 1818, the real star at this temple is its garden. The serene space contains two notable ponds: one shaped like the character for the word *shin* or *kokoro* (心), which means "heart" or "mind," and one that resembles a lotus blossom. There's also a superb teahouse on-site that was built in 1457, brilliantly exhibiting the *wabi-sabi* (shabby-chic plus Zen) aesthetic of the tea ceremony.

The temple complex was founded in 1337, originally as a villa for an abdicated emperor, and was later converted into a temple. Throughout the compound as it stands today, there are nearly 50 subtemples, most of which are closed to the public with four open year-round. The bulk of the major structures are grouped around the southern gate. Whether you enter from the north or south, wandering through the lanes that thread through the compound will leave you feeling enchanted.

Within the temple of Myōshin-ji itself, stop by **Hattō Hall,** where a huge painting of a dragon is emblazoned across its ceiling. Note that this building can only be entered on a guided tour (30 minutes, Japanese language only). Other buildings that can be entered in the compound include **Taizo-in** (9am-5pm daily; ¥500), a subtemple renowned for its stunning garden centered on a pond. The landscape garden at this subtemple was actually created in the mid-1960s, despite its classic appearance. Its rock garden, however, dates to the 15th century.

Two other subtemples within the complex that can be entered by the public are **Keishunin** (9am-5pm daily; ¥400), which has some alluring stroll gardens, and **Daishinin** (9am-5pm daily; ¥300) where you'll find a meditative rock garden.

Daitoku-ji
大徳寺

53 Daitoku-ji-chō, Murasakino, Kita-ku; tel.
*075/491-0019; http://zen.rinnou.net/head_*
temples/07daitoku.html; main temple and grounds
24 hours, subtemples various hours; free to enter
complex, subtemples charge separate admission fees;
take Karasuma line to Kitaōji Station

In some ways similar to Myōshin-ji, this sprawling, walled temple compound is one of Kyoto's prime Zen centers. This oasis of calm has some of the best rock gardens in Kyoto, minus the throngs of Ryōan-ji. Daitoku-ji is also home to **Izusen Daijinten,** a restaurant on the temple's grounds that is the best place to dine like a monk in Kyoto.

Enter through the main gate, located at the east side of the complex, then proceed to explore four magical subtemples with gardens: **Ryōgen-in** (9am-4:30pm daily; ¥300), **Zuihō-in** (9am-5pm daily; ¥500), **Kōtō-in** (9am-4:30pm daily; ¥400) and **Daisen-in** (https://daisen-in.net; 9am-5pm daily; ¥400). Daitoku-ji itself, after which the entire compound is named, is not open to the public.

Check out Ryōgen-in's raked-gravel garden (thought to be Japan's smallest) and moss garden, and don't miss Zuihō-in's stunning rock garden, designed in the 1960s by Shigemori Mirei. This is a fantastic alternative to the popular Ryōan-ji. Kōtō-in's inner temple grounds are home a garden and a humble tea room designed by Sen no Rikyū, founder of the tea ceremony. Daisen-in boasts two spectacular dry landscape gardens considered to be among Japan's most iconic examples of this this quintessential element of Zen culture, but be forewarned that there's a very strict no-photography policy.

ARASHIYAMA
嵐山

West of Kyoto proper, Arashiyama is dense with sights, centered around the atmospheric **Arashiyama Bamboo Grove.** The main unnamed thoroughfare running through the area that connects to the **Tōgetsu-kyō bridge,** which spans the Katsura River, is a tourist trap, to be passed over for the treasures beyond.

Tenryū-ji
天龍寺

68 Susukinobaba-chō, Saga Tenryū-ji, Ukyo-ku; tel.
075/881-1235; www.tenryuji.com; 8:30am-5:30pm
daily Mar. 21-Oct.20, 8:30am-5pm daily Oct.
21-Mar. 20; Hōjō garden ¥500 adults and high
school students, ¥300 junior high and elementary
school students, garden and buildings ¥800 adults
and high school students, ¥600 junior high and
elementary school students; take JR Sagano line
to Saga-Arashiyama Station, or Hankyū line to
Arashiyama Station

The best place to begin your exploration of Arashiyama is at the main act: Tenryū-ji. This important temple—the base of the Rinzai school of Zen Buddhism—has a wonderful garden beside the area's famed bamboo grove, which serves as a stunning example of the old Chinese gardening principle of drawing on "borrowed scenery."

This temple was built 1339-1345 by shogun Ashikaga Takauji (1305-1358), constructed in a ploy to appease the angry spirit of Emperor Go-Daigo. Takauji had once been Go-Daigo's ally, but later turned on him in his attempt to gain control of Japan. The original complex contained as many as 150 buildings, which have been ravaged by fire many times through the centuries. The structures that stand today were built during the Meiji period.

The garden, however, remains largely as it was when it was first designed by famed garden master Muso Soseki (1275-1331), the first head priest of the temple. Centered on an expansive pond surrounded by manicured pines and misshapen rocks, a bamboo-covered slope rises into the distance. The story goes that the garden was meant to reflect a Chinese myth about a koi (carp) that made its way up a waterfall and transformed into a dragon. Stones rising from the pond, which teems with koi, stretch up a hill strewn with large stones, said to resemble the legendary waterfall.

Arashiyama's Less Crowded Side

Although it may be hard to believe after a trip to the bamboo grove, a few pockets of Arashiyama remain surprisingly uncrowded. Unlike other districts, where there may be 2-3 less-crowded temples near the heavy hitters, Arashiyama is peppered with several smaller atmospheric temples, as well as a lovely park.

The simplest way to explore the area's lesser-known temples is to turn right at the T-junction at the western end of the path that leads through the area's thronged bamboo grove, near the entrance to Ōkōchi-Sansō. From there, walk straight ahead and pass the pond on your left. From here, it's possible to take a lovely 25-minute walk (one-way) passing through a rural area of rice paddies and residences, where you'll find some enchanting smaller temples well away from the crowds, including (in north-south order):

JŌJAKKŌ-JI

3 Saga Ogurayama, Ukyō-ku; tel. 075/861-0435; www.jojakko-ji.or.jp; 9am-5pm daily; ¥500
This discreet temple is a good place to come for some peace and quiet. Its mossy grounds contain a pagoda and lots of trees.

NISON-IN

27 Monzenchōjin-chō, Saga Nison-in, Ukyō-ku; tel. 075/861-0687; http://nisonin.jp; 9am-4:30pm daily; adults ¥300, ages 12 and under free
About 3 minutes' walk north of Jōjakkō-ji, Nison-in offers a similar experience. Leisurely strolling its grounds has a calming effect.

GIŌ-JI

32 Kozaka-chō, Saga Toriimoto, Ukyō-ku; tel. 075/861-3574; www.giouji.or.jp; 9am-5pm daily; adults ¥300, students ¥100
A 4-minute walk north from Nison-in, Giō-ji has a petite main hall topped by a thatched roof and a moss garden on its grounds. If you're going to pay admission to one of these temples, make it this one.

ADASHINO NENBUTSU-JI

17 Adashino-chō, Sagatoriimoto, Ukyō-ku; tel. 075/861-2221; www.nenbutsuji.jp; 9am-4:30pm daily Mar.-Nov., 9am-3:30pm Dec.-Feb.; adults ¥500, high school and junior high school students ¥400, elementary school students and younger free
This temple has some 8,000 stone effigies commemorating those who have died without any surviving kin. From here, it's a 40-minute walk southeast back to Arashiyama Station on the Keifuku line.

Arashiyama's quieter options are not limited to temples. There's also **Kameyama-kōen** (Kamenō-chō, Saga, Ukyō-ku; tel. 075/414-5326; www.pref.kyoto.jp/koen-annai/ara.html; 24 hours daily; free), a quiet park set on a hilltop on the northern bank of the Hozugawa River, which runs through Arashiyama. To reach it, just turn left—rather than right—at the T-junction at the western end of the path that leads through the famed bamboo grove, then walk uphill. Besides being a calm setting that offers beautiful views of the river below, the park is often host to troupes of monkeys.

Begin your tour of the temple by slipping off your shoes and exploring the interior of the main hall, or *Hōjō* (9am-5pm daily Mar. 21-Oct. 20, 9am-4:30pm daily Oct. 21-Mar. 20; ¥500), then meander through the garden. Drift toward the north gate of the temple complex, which deposits you right in the thick of the area's iconic bamboo grove.

TOP EXPERIENCE

★ Arashiyama Bamboo Grove
嵯峨野の竹林

Arashiyama, Ukyō-ku; 24 hours; free; take JR Sagano (San-in) line to Saga-Arashiyama Station, or Hankyū line to Arashiyama Station

Strolling through the Arashiyama Bamboo Grove feels like passing into another realm. The shoots reach skyward and extend deeply in all directions with no other competing forms of vegetation in view.

The real magic of this grove must be experienced first-hand. It doesn't always fully translate to photographs. You can almost imagine two martial artists lithely leaping between the supple sprouts—the largest being up to 40 meters (131 feet) in height and 35 cm (18 in) in diameter—evoking the famous scene from *Crouching Tiger, Hidden Dragon*. There

is an almost eerie glow to the light in this singular forest, which takes on an increasingly ethereal glow as dusk begins to fall.

I recommend entering this enchanted realm after first exploring Tenryū-ji. You'll find yourself in the midst of the bamboo as soon as you pass through the north gate of the temple. Once you pass through the gate, turn left and simply walk straight up the mountain path. The grove works its magic most intensely as you reach its final section, which terminates at the entrance to the alluring **Ōkōchi-Sansō** villa.

Ōkōchi-Sansō
大河内山荘

8 Tabuchiyama-chō, Saga Ogurayama, Ukyō-ku; tel. 075/872-2233; 9am-5pm daily; adults and high school students ¥1,000, junior high and elementary school students ¥500; take Hankyū line to Arashiyama Station, or JR Sagano line to Saga-Arashiyama Station

On the far side of the bamboo forest, you'll discover the highlight of Arashiyama: a dreamy mountaintop villa known as Ōkōchi-Sansō. Like many of Kyoto's beautiful places, Ōkōchi-Sansō was once the home of a figure of ample means, namely the movie star Ōkōchi Denjirō (1898-1962), famous for his

Arashiyama Bamboo Grove

roles in dramas set during the Edo period. This site is a bit of a walk from the nearest station through the area's iconic bamboo forest, but that's part of the fun.

When you reach the top of the famed bamboo grove, forge ahead to the ticket window at the start of a footpath leading up a slope before making your way toward the magnificent garden above. Simply follow the arrows indicating the order in which to explore the grounds, winding through dense tunnels of foliage and past a swath of earth overtaken by a verdant blanket of moss, revealing glimpses of downtown Kyoto spreading out in the distance below, as well as a mystical mountain vista seen from the other side of the peak. Try to spot the distant temple.

As you move through the grounds, also take time to savor the beautiful villa itself—built in a traditional Japanese residential style—as well as a serene teahouse oozing rustic charm. You can't enter either of these structures, but you can take a break at a modern teahouse that you come to at the end of the walking route. Here, hand over your entrance ticket to the kindly staff in exchange for a sweet and a warm cup of *matcha*.

Katsura Rikyū (Imperial Villa)
桂離宮

Katsura-Misono, Nishikyō-ku; tel. 075/211-1215; http://sankan.kunaicho.go.jp/english/guide/katsura.
html; by appointment (tours offered hourly 9am-4pm Tues.-Sun., not offered Tues. if Mon. is holiday); adults ¥1,000, ages 12-17 free; take Hankyū line to Katsura Station

Roughly 6 km (3.7 mi) southeast of Arashiyama's main drag and 5 km (3.1 mi) west of Kyoto Station in the rather drab suburban neighborhood of Katsura, this villa was built on a plot of land gifted by Shogun Toyotomi Hideyoshi, one of Japan's "three great unifiers," to a prince named Hachijō Toshihito. It's a stellar example of a traditional villa, boasting four teahouses and an exquisite garden. Visiting requires joining a 40-minute **tour** (English audio guides available; English tours offered at 10am, 11am, 2pm, and 3pm), held several times daily (except Mon.) through the grounds, looping around the pond at the center of the stroll garden. Buildings can't be entered and photos can only be shot from certain places.

To reserve a spot on one of the tours, you must apply in person—be sure to take your passport—at the **Imperial Household Office** (tel. 075/211-1215; 8:40am-5pm Tues.-Sun., closed Tues. if Mon. is holiday), located inside **Kyoto Gyōen.** There are also limited places up for grabs on the Imperial Household Agency's website (http://sankan.kunaicho.go.jp/order/index_EN.html), but they tend to get taken fast.

Entertainment and Events

THEATER

While it may not match the scope of Tokyo's performing arts scene, Kyoto is a good place to catch traditional theater performances, from flamboyant kabuki to enigmatic *Noh*. On the avant-garde side of things, the city is home to Japan's only theater dedicated solely to the grotesque, mesmerizing style of modern dance known as *butoh*. And of course, Kyoto is the best place in the country to see geisha perform seasonal dances or entertain over a meal or tea (page 228).

MINAMI-ZA

198 Nakano-chō, Shijō-dōri, Yamato-oji nishiiru, Higashiyama-ku; tel. 075/561-1155; www.kabukiweb. net/theatres/minamiza; performances from ¥5,000; take Keihan line to Gion-Shijō Station, exit 6

The premier theater for kabuki in Kyoto is Minami-za, an imposing building at the corner of Kawabata-dōri and Shijō-dōri. If kabuki intrigues you, it's possible to sit in for a few acts rather than watch an entire play, which can last upward of four hours. English audio guides available. Tickets can either be bought at the box office or online at www. kabukiweb.net. Ask your hotel concierge for help if you're unsure whether a performance is scheduled during your stay.

KANZE KAIKAN NOH THEATER

44 Enshoji-chō, Okazaki, Sakyō-ku; tel. 075/771-6114; www.kyoto-kanze.jp; performances from ¥2,000; take Tōzai subway line to Higashiyama Station, exit 1

The other form of traditional theater with a presence in Kyoto is the more refined—and enigmatic—*Noh*. The best place to watch this slow-paced, restrained artform is at the Kanze Kaikan Noh Theater. Performances on the stunning cedar-wood marvel of a stage are mainly held on holidays and weekends. Your best bet is to ask your hotel concierge whether a performance will take place during your stay, then for help with securing tickets.

BUTOH KAN

123 Tsukinuke-chō, Nakagyō-ku; tel. 075/257-2125; www.butohkan.jp; ¥4,200; take Karasuma or Tōzai line to Karasuma Oike Station, exit 6

For truly avant-garde dance experience, this theater run by legendary dancer Ima Tenko is the only space dedicated solely to the starkly emotive dance style known as *butoh*, which has made waves in the dance world since its birth in the late 1950s. It somehow feels fitting that this provocative performance art— raw, primal, erotic, grotesque—should find a home in an Edo period storehouse in the heart of ancient Kyoto, bastion of Japan's most traditional of arts, which *butoh* haughtily subverts. And with just enough seating for eight, the line between dancer and audience is thin indeed. At the time of writing, the theater had indefinitely stopped performances due to the coronavirus pandemic, but is intent to resume. Visit the website and contact the theater in advance to check on the status of any potential upcoming performances.

FESTIVALS
★ GION MATSURI

Gion; www.gionmatsuri.jp/manu/manual.html; throughout July; free

One of Japan's most iconic festivals, centering on the shrine of Yasaka-jinja, Kyoto's Gion Matsuri takes place each year during the sweltering month of July. The highlight is a parade of truly astounding floats pushed through Gion by revelers in traditional garb. Known

Gion Matsuri float

as *omikoshi,* the floats are up to 25 meters (82 feet) tall and weigh up to 10 tonnes (12 tons). Up to 30 of them slowly proceed along Shijō-dōri, representing individual neighborhoods scattered around the city.

The festival dates back to the 9th century, when it was born as a purification ritual to appease what were believed to be the angry gods responsible for fires, earthquakes, floods, pestilence, and plague. In 869, Emperor Seiwa ordered a mass prayer and ritual at Yasaka-jinja to appease the god of the shrine. It was officially made an annual event in 970. By the Edo period, extravagant touches added by the merchant class had made it an occasion devoted to the peacocking of wealth.

Today, the festival culminates July 14-17, when Kyoto's city center is blocked off to traffic and residents mill about in *yukata,* drinking beer and nibbling on grub from food stalls. The city is decorated with flowers and flags, and lit by hanging lanterns. The *yamaboko junkō* (grand procession of floats) occurs July 17 and 24. The city's accommodations are booked well in advance of the festival, so book as far ahead as possible.

DAIMON-JI GOZAN OKURIBI

Five mountains surrounding city (viewable from downtown); Aug. 16; free

Another iconic Kyoto summer festival, the Daimon-ji Gozan Okuribi, begins at 8pm on August 16 every year, an occasion to bid farewell to deceased spirits believed to visit the living during the holiday of Obon, celebrated in mid-August in Kyoto. Blazing fires in the shape of Chinese characters are lit and left to burn for about 40 minutes on the slopes of five mountains surrounding the city. The most famous one burns atop Daimon-ji-yama, a mountain looming over the northeastern side of the city. The best spot to view the blaze is from the Kamo River, between Sanjō-dōri in the south and Imadegawa-dōri in the north (best accessed via Sanjō Station, Tōzai subway line).

Sports and Recreation

PARKS

Kyoto is home to some serenely beautiful parks. Whether you're in the city during *hanami* season, want to spot wildlife, or simply want to have a picnic, there are plenty of good options.

MARUYAMA-KŌEN

Maruyama-chō, Higashiyama-ku; tel. 075/222-3586; 24 hours; free; from Kyoto Station, take Kyoto City Bus 100 or 206 to Gion bus stop, or Keihan line to Gion-Shijō Station, exit 1

Perhaps the city's most popular park, smack in the middle of Higashiyama, behind Yasaka-jinja. It features a pond, burbling brooks, and an array of cherry trees. Thronged during *hanami* season, the rest of the year, it's ideal for a picnic or stroll.

KYOTO GYŌEN

Kyoto Gyōen, Kamigyō-ku; tel. 075/211-6348; 24 hours daily; free; take Karasuma subway line to Imadegawa Station or Marutamachi Station

Kyoto Gyōen is another downtown oasis. Set in the center of town, the grounds of the former **Kyoto Imperial Palace** are the geographic heart of the city. It's another famed *hanami* spot, renowned for its beautiful collection of weeping cherry trees. It's a great place to meander on foot or sit down for a picnic with the former imperial palace looming beyond.

MONKEY PARK IWATAYAMA

8 Genrokuzan-chō, Arashiyama, Ukyō-ku; tel. 075/872-0950; www.monkeypark.jp; 9am-4:30pm daily, last entry 30 minutes before closing; adults ¥550, ages 15 and under ¥250; take JR Sagano line to Saga-Arashiyama Station, or Hankyū line to Arashiyama (transfer at Katsura Station)

For something wilder, there's Monkey Park Iwatayama in the west of the city. While it's certainly not a completely natural jungle out there, the Japanese macaques on this site in Arashiyama are essentially just going about their business. This is a good place to observe them close up. They're free to play and jump about, while the humans are enclosed.

KAMEYAMA-KŌEN

Saga Kamenō-chō, Ukyō-ku; tel. 075/701-0101; 24 hours daily; free; take JR Sagano line to Saga Arashiyama Station, or Hankyū line to Arashiyama Station

Across the Katsura River from the Iwatayama Monkey Park, this oasis of calm offers a refreshing escape from the crowds of the area. While there aren't as many as you'll see at Iwatayama, monkeys do hang around here, too. There are also sweeping views of the river gorge and much of Arashiyama below. To reach the park, simply turn left and walk uphill when you reach the T junction at the western end of Arashiyama's famed bamboo grove.

CYCLING

Kyoto is a fantastic city for cycling. In a basin ringed by mountains, downtown is mostly flat. Its clean grid pattern, wide boulevards, and relatively tame traffic also make navigation easy. For a wide range of detailed cycling itineraries, visit www.cyclekyoto.com/popular-cycling-routes.

KAMO RIVER CYCLING PATH

Cycling Distance: *16 km (9.9 mi) round-trip*
Cycling Time: *about 2 hours round-trip*
Information and Maps: *www.insidekyoto. com/cycling-kyoto*
Trailhead: *Kyoto Station*

A popular and easy cycling route is biking northward on the path for pedestrians and cyclists that runs along the Kamo River. There are numerous staircases, typically beside bridges, that lead down to a path that runs along both sides of the river. You'll need to

actually carry your bicycle down these stairs in most places, although you may spot ramps in some locations.

While simply riding along the river is pleasant in itself, there are many potential trips you can also make from the riverside path. For example, when you reach Sanjō-dōri, ascend to the street and cycle northeast into Northern Higashiyama. Head for Nanzen-ji, then from there, pedal north to Ginkaku-ji, via the Philosopher's Path. This trip takes about two hours from Kyoto Station, depending on your speed.

CYCLE KYOTO

7 Higashikujō, Nishi Sannōchō, Minami-ku; tel. 090/9165-7168; www.cyclekyoto.net; tours ¥7,000-12,000 per person; Kyoto Station Hachijō, east exit

While you may prefer to explore on your own, there are also some great cycling tours available. The most reputable agency is Cycle Kyoto. Alongside group tours of the city's north and south, it's also possible to arrange family tours (¥40,000), private tours (¥45,000-85,000), and custom tours (price varies; inquire for details).

KYOTO CYCLING TOUR PROJECT

552-13 Higashi-Aburanokoji-chō, Aburanokoji-dōri, Shiokoji-sagaru; tel. 075/354-3636; www.kctp.net; 9am-6pm daily; from ¥1,000 for standard bicycles; Kyoto Station, central exit

The most reliable rental shop in town is Kyoto Cycling Tour Project, which rents a variety of bicycles, including mountain bikes, city bikes, children's bikes, and more. Call the head office, where the staff speak English, to ask about availability. After riding around for the day, you can drop off your bike at one of the outfit's five terminals spread around the city.

HIKING

KURAMA TO KIBUNE HIKE

Hiking Distance: *5.2 km (3.2 mi) one-way*
Time: *1.5 hours one-way*
Information and maps: *www.insidekyoto.*

com/kurama-to-kibune-hike; https://patrickcolgan.
net/2017/01/15/hike-kibune-kurama

Trailhead: *Kurama Station*

This route is easy to access and is set in the mountains north of town. The combination of spirituality and a stunning natural setting imbue this hike up and over Mount Kurama, between two mountain hamlets, with a visceral power. Reached by train (about 30 minutes from downtown), the villages of Kurama and Kibune are well away from the masses; it's possible to walk between them in about 1.5 hours. To reach the starting point of the hike, Kurama Station, hop on the Eizan line at Demachiyanagi Station, which is the northern terminus of the Keihan line, then ride to Kurama Station (30 minutes; ¥420).

To get started, exit Kurama Station and walk by the large statue of the bright-red noggin of the mythical, improbably long-nosed Tengu (a prominent creature in Japanese folklore). Turn left onto Kurama's main thoroughfare, which leads to a set of stairs. Climb them and follow the path up Mount Kurama for about 10 minutes. You'll recognize the first sight of note, **Yuki-jinja** (1073 Kuramahonmachi, Sakyō-ku; tel. 075/741-1670; www.yukijinjya.jp; 24 hours daily; free) by the giant cedar tree at its entrance (instead of a vermillion *torii* gate). This is the guardian shrine of Kurama village.

Push on from Yuki-jinja and after about 5 more minutes of walking you'll come to the temple of **Kurama-dera** (1074 Kurama Honmachi, Sakyō-ku; tel. 075/741-2003; www.kuramadera.or.jp; 9am-4:30pm daily; free), which stands near the top of Mount Kurama. From here, the trail to Kibune is pretty clearly marked. Once you make it to Kibune, the one must-visit sight is **Kifune-jinja** (180 Kuramakibune-chō, Sakyō-ku; tel. 075/741-2016; http://kifunejinja.jp; 9am-5pm daily; free), a shrine approached via an ethereal stone staircase flanked by red lanterns.

From Kibune, you can either return to Kurama Station or board the train at Kibuneguchi Station, also on the Eizan line, to Demachiyanagi Station on the northern

edge of the city, where you can transfer to the Keihan line and head downtown.

There's also a fantastic mountain *onsen* with both indoor and outdoor pools at **Kurama Onsen** (520 Kuramahonmachi, Sakyō-ku; tel. 075/741-2131; www.kurama-onsen.co.jp; 11am-8pm (last admission 7pm) daily; ¥2,500 adults, ¥1,600 ages 4-12 for full use of facilities; ¥1,000 adults, ¥700 ages 4-12 for open-air baths only). Note that it's also possible to walk this route in reverse if you'd like to take a dip in the hot spring baths of Kurama Onsen after a hike. Kurama Onsen is about 12 minutes' walk north of Kurama Station, set beside the burbling Anba River. There's also Japanese fare served on-site at the *onsen's* restaurant (www.kurama-onsen.co.jp/plan01_e/index.html).

TAKAO TO HOZUKYŌ STATION HIKE

Hiking Distance: *11 km (6.8 mi) one-way*
Time: *6 hours one-way*
Information and maps: *www.insidekyoto.com/takao-hozukyo-hike-via-kiyotaki-kuya-no-taki-waterfall; https://tales-of-trails.com/2018/10/24/hiking-from-takao-to-hozukyo*
Trailhead: *Village of Takao*

Reached from downtown by bus (about 50 minutes), this village in the mountains has three fantastic temples, namely, **Jingo-ji** (5 Takao-chō, Umegahata, Ukyō-ku; tel. 075/861-1769; www.jingoji.or.jp; 9am-4pm daily; junior high school students through adults ¥600, elementary school students ¥300), a sprawling temple complex that's dotted by pagodas and that serves as a place to carry out the ritual of Kawarake-nage, in which you can throw clay shards known as *kawarake* to dispel unwanted karma. You'll also come across **Saimyō-ji** (1 Makinō-chō, Umegahata, Ukyō-ku; tel. 075/861-1770; 9am-5pm daily; adults ¥500, high school and junior high school students ¥400, elementary school students and younger free), a hidden temple with an enchanted little grotto behind it; and the most famous but actually least essential **Kozan-ji** (8 Toganō-chō, Umegahata,

Ukyō-ku; tel. 075/861-4204; https://kosanji. com; 8:30am-5pm daily; ¥800 grounds, additional ¥500 during autumn), a temple and UNESCO site, which can be skipped.

To reach Takao, you have three options. From Kyoto Station, find the JR3 bus stopping point and take the bus bound for either Toganoo or Shūzan. You'll need to get off at Yamashirotakao bus stop (50 minutes; ¥500). Alternatively, take bus Kyoto City Bus 8 from Nijō Station to Takao bus stop (40 minutes; ¥500).

From the village, begin the hike by descending to the Kiyotaki River. There's a sign near the bus stop that points the way to the hike and Jingo-ji. First, visit Saimyō-ji, before walking about 10 minutes west along the Kiyotaki River until you reach the grueling stairs that lead up to Jingo-ji. Once you've finally reached the temple, be sure to throw some of the clay discs known as *kawarake* (¥100 for 2) into the valley below to release any bad karma you're carrying around.

Leaving Jingo-ji, walk about 50 minutes southward along the Kiyotaki River until you reach Kiyotaki village. Continue following the Kiyotaki River until it joins the larger Hozu River. The last stretch of the hike involves following the Hozu River until you reach Hozukyō Station, where you can return directly to Kyoto Station on the JR Sagano line (¥240).

COOKING CLASSES
HARU COOKING CLASS
166-32 Shimogamo Miyazaki-chō, Sakyō-ku; www. kyoto-cooking-class.com; classes start from 2pm; from ¥6,900; take Eizan, Keihan Main lines to Demachiyanagi Station

At Haru Cooking Class, you can join bilingual cooking instructor and Kyoto food insider Taro at his home in the north of the city. Taro is well versed in both vegetarian and non-vegetarian cuisine, and he offers guided tours of the rambling realm of local food that is Nishiki Market. Lessons typically last up to four hours.

Shopping

KYOTO STATION AREA
Flea Markets
KŌBŌ-SAN MARKET
1 Kujō-chō, Minami-ku; tel. 075/691-3325; www.toji. or.jp; 8:30am-5pm (last entry 4:30pm) Mar.-Aug., 8:30am-4pm (last entry 3:30pm) Sept.-Feb.; free; take Kintetsu line to Tō-ji Station

On the 21st of every month, a great flea market known as the Kōbō-san Market is held at the temple of Tō-ji, southwest of JR Kyoto Station. Go in the morning before the good stuff is picked over.

GION

In the heart of Gion, the two parallel streets of **Furumonzen-dōri** and **Shinmonzen-dōri** are chock-full of businesses selling traditional Japanese art. You'll find landscape paintings, Buddhist sculptures, teapots and implements, and scrolls. Note that it's a fairly pricey area to shop, but if you mean business and could potentially buy something, the sellers welcome foreign customers. To get to these two streets, take the Tōzai subway line or Keihan line to Sanjō Keihan Station, exit 2.

NORTHERN HIGASHIYAMA
Flea Markets
CHION-JI TEMPLE HANDICRAFT MARKET
103 Tanaka Monzen-chō, Sakyō-ku; www. tedukuri-ichi.com/hyakumanben; 8am-4pm 15th of every month; free; take the Keihan line to Demachiyanagi Station

On the 15th of every month, a great place to shop for souvenirs is the Chion-ji Temple

Top Souvenirs: *Omamori*

If you discreetly glance around at the cell phones, purses or bags of the people around you in Japan, chances are you'll notice colorful handmade pouches dangling by white woven cords. These pouches are amulets, or talismans, known as *omamori*: small ornaments sold at shrines and temples generally believed to bring protection or good luck to the owner. Rectangular ones contain words penned on thin strips of wood or paper inside. Others come in a variety of shapes, from foxes to bells and gourds.

HISTORY AND SIGNIFICANCE

The belief in *omamori* stems from the idea that Shinto charms contain a sprinkling of the power of a *kami* (god) that is housed in the shrine, combined with Buddhism's amulet culture, readily visible throughout other parts of Asia (for example, in the ubiquitous tiny Buddha statues seen swinging from the rear-view mirrors of Bangkok taxis). Although Shinto shrine maidens known as *miko* were once responsible for crafting *omamori,* today they are largely produced in factories and blessed by priests upon arrival at shrines and temples where they're sold.

BUYING AN *OMAMORI*

You don't need to be a devotee to respectfully buy and keep an *omamori*. If you choose to pick one up, just be sure you handle it with the same amount of respect you would any religious object. While there's big business in souvenir shops hawking cutesy *omamori* featuring manga characters like Hello Kitty, some religious groups don't regard them as being authentic. A final note: Whatever kind of *omamori* you choose, resist the urge to loosen the straps and see what's inside! Opening the pouch is believed to drain the talisman of its power.

Handicraft Market. The market is fun, lively, and well-stocked with locally made goods. Show up early before the masses pour in.

Traditional Goods and Souvenirs
KYOTO HANDICRAFT CENTER

21 Shōgoin Entomi-chō, Sakyō-ku; tel. 075/761-8001; www.kyotohandicraftcenter.com; 10am-7pm daily; take Kyoto City Bus 206 to Kumano-jinja-mae bus stop, or take Keihan line to Jingu Marutamachi Station

Kyoto Handicraft Center is the best one-stop souvenir shop in the city. *Yukata,* ceramics, accessories, jewelry, woodblock prints, and more are available.

Ceramics
ROBERT YELLIN GALLERY

Ginkakuji-mae-chō 39, Sakyō-ku; tel. 075/708-5581; http://japanesepottery.com; take Kyoto City Bus 5 or 17 to Ginkaku-ji-michi bus stop

A stone's throw from Ginkaku-ji, you'll find one of Kyoto's best ceramics shops: the

Robert Yellin Gallery. The gallery is set in a beautiful traditional home, complete with a landscape garden. Yellin is an American expat based in Kyoto who has a masterful grasp on the Japanese *yakimono* (ceramics; literally "fired thing") tradition, and has amassed an eye-popping collection to prove it. To avoid sticker shock, have a look at the online gallery on the official website to get a sense of how much a quality piece can potentially cost. Note that there are no official hours, but Robert is a friendly host who welcomes visitors. Your best bet is to call or email ahead and confirm he's not out with clients or visiting kilns when you plan to visit. Otherwise, knock on the door if the gate is open and he'll be happy to greet you if he's there. Have a look at the access map, available on the website, before making the trip.

DOWNTOWN AND CENTRAL KYOTO

You'll find two grand department stores downtown: **Daimaru** (79 Tachiuri Nishi-machi, Shijō-dōri, Takakura Nishi-iru, Shimogyō-ku; tel. 075/211-8111; www. daimaru.co.jp; 10am-8pm daily) and **Takashimaya** (52 Shinchō, Shijō-dōri, Kawaramachi Nishi-iru, Shimogyō-ku; tel. 075/221-8811; www.takashimaya.co.jp; 10am-8pm daily). Both have a staggering selection of international brands and offer world-class service, along with stellar food floors in their basements. Stop by either one to browse and discover the phenomenon that is the Japanese department store. Take the Hankyū line to Karasuma Station, or the Karasuma subway line to Shijō Station. Both stores are within walking distance from there.

Shopping Districts
NISHIKI MARKET

www.kyoto-nishiki.or.jp; 9am-5pm daily; take Hankyū line to Kawaramachi Station or Karasuma Station, or Karasuma line to Shijō Station

One block to the north of Shijō-dōri, running parallel to the busy thoroughfare, Nishiki Market is an extensive smorgasbord of local edibles. Whether you aim to buy something or not, the covered pedestrian thoroughfare is a sight to behold.

EBISUGAWA-DŌRI

take Karasuma subway line to Muratamachi Station

This street two blocks south of Marutamachi-dōri that runs westward from Teramachi-dōri is the best place in the city to pick up a piece of antique furniture, such as a *tansu* (antique chest).

TERAMACHI-DŌRI

about 10 minutes' walk east of Muratamachi Station

Another great shopping street for old Japanese items, Teramachi-dōri is the street you'll come to when you reach the eastern end of Ebisugawa-dōri, or. It's heaving with shops selling Japanese antiques, tea ceremony implements, painted scrolls, and more. Consider coming to Teramachi-dōri after a stroll to Ebisugawa-dōri.

Traditional Goods and Souvenirs
KYŪKYODŌ

520 Shimohonnōjimae-chō, Teramachi-dōri, Aneyakōji-agaru, Nakagyō-ku; tel. 075/231-0510; www.kyukyodo.co.jp; 10am-6pm Mon.-Sat.; take Tōzai subway line to Kyoto-Shiyakusho-mae Station

For the best place to buy an assortment of traditional items related to the arts, from artsy stationery and calligraphy brushes to incense, an item with great history in the city's myriad Buddhist temples, head to Kyūkyodō. A great pick if your time is limited and you want to find anything you'd realistically desire under one roof.

MORITA WASHI

1F Kajinoha Building, 298 Ogisakaya-chō, Higashinotoin-dōri, Bukkoji-agaru, Shimogyō-ku; tel. 075/341-1419; www.wagami.jp; 10am-6pm Mon.-Fri., 10am-5pm Sat.; take Karasuma subway line to Shijō Station, or Hankyū line to Karasuma Station

The best place in the city to see art made of traditionally handmade paper—a craft with deep roots in Kyoto.

MIYAWAKI BAISEN-AN

80-3 Daikoku-chō, Rokkaku-dōri, Tominokōji, Higashi-iru, Nakagyō-ku; tel. 075/221-0181; www.baisenan.co.jp; 9am-6pm daily; take Karasuma or Tōzai subway line to Karasuma-Oike Station

Another traditional item that says "Kyoto" is the folding fan. For a superb selection, go to Miyawaki Baisen-an. This fan specialist has been in business since 1823.

SHOYEIDO KYOTO MAIN STORE

Karasuma Nijō, Nakagyō-ku; tel. 075/212-5590; www.shoyeido.co.jp; 9am-6pm daily; take Karasuma, Tōzai lines to Karasuma Oike Station, exit 1

It's a bit on the formal side, but if you're intent on getting a hold of high-grade incense—conjure the aroma that hits your nostrils when you step foot in a temple—this is one of the best stores in Kyoto.

AIZEN KŌBŌ

215 Yoko Ōmiya-chō, Nakasuji-dōri, Ōmiya Nishi-iru, Kamigyō-ku; tel. 075/441-0355; www.aizenkobo.jp; 10am-5:30pm Mon.-Fri., 10am-4pm Sat.-Sun.; take Karasuma subway line to Imadegawa Station

Aizen Kōbō is a family-owned shop selling only textiles dyed with indigo. Located near the old textiles district of Nishijin, the shop sells a wide range of elegant garments made of silk and cotton.

HIYOSHIYA

546 Dodo-chō, Horikawa Teranouchi-higashi-iru, Kamigyō-ku; tel. 075/441-6644; http://wagasa.com; 9:30am-5pm Tues.-Sun.; take Karasuma subway line to Imadegawa Station

Hiyoshiya is a family-owned shop that makes traditional wooden parasols with exquisite designs. They're more art pieces than functional umbrellas. They also create custom lampshades using the same technique.

Kitchenware and Food
ARITSUGU

tel. 075/221-1091; www.kyoto-nishiki.or.jp/stores/aritsugu; 10am-5pm daily

The best place to buy traditional Japanese kitchen knives, Aritsugu, is housed in Nishiki Market.

ZŌHIKO

719-1 Yohojimae-chō, Teramachi-dōri, Nijō-agaru, Nishigawa, Nakagyō-ku; tel. 075/229-6625; www.zohiko.co.jp; 10am-6pm daily; take Tōzai subway line to Kyoto Shiyakusho-mae Station

If you dine at a *kaiseki* restaurant, something that will leap out at you as much as the flavor is the visual power of the feast. Lacquerware is a major reason for this. To see an excellent selection of this classic Japanese craft, go to Zōhiko. This restaurant sometimes closes on random days, so be sure to call ahead.

IPPŌDŌ

Teramachi-dōri, Nijō-agaru, Nakagyō-ku; tel. 075/211-4018; www.ippodo-tea.co.jp; 9am-6pm daily; take Tōzai subway line to Kyoto Shiyakusho-mae Station

After sampling some of the different brews available at any number of the city's teahouses, you might be tempted to take home some high-grade tea. Ippōdō has the best selection of teas in the city.

SHIOYOSHI-KEN

180 Hidadono-chō, Kuromon-dōri, Nakadachiuri-agaru, Kamigyō-ku; tel. 075/441-0803; www.kyogashi.com; 9am-5:30pm Mon.-Sat., closed public holidays, irregular closings on Wed.; take Karasuma subway line to Imadegawa Station

Shioyoshi-ken is a historic shop that has a great selection of traditional Kyoto sweets, great with tea.

NORTHWEST KYOTO
Flea Markets
TENJIN-SAN MARKET

Bakuro-chō, Kamigyō-ku; tel. 075/461-0005; http://kitanotenmangu.or.jp; 5am-6pm 25th of every month Apr.-Oct., 5:30am-5:30pm 25th of every month Nov.-Mar.; take Kyoto City Bus 50 or 101 to Kitano-Tenmangū-mae bus stop

On the 25th of every month, Kitano-Tenmangū shrine in the north of the city holds the Tenjin-san Market. While there are plenty of merchants hawking touristy tripe, there are also some genuinely good finds. Wandering the beautiful shrine grounds in search of them is part of the fun.

Antiques
THE KURA

817-2 Kannon-ji Monzen-chō, Kamigyō-ku; tel. 075/201-3497; www.the-kura.com; open by appointment only; take Kyoto City Bus 50 or 101 to Kitano-Tenmangū-mae bus stop

If you have the money to spend and are keen to see a stunning collection of Japanese antiquities and traditional art, visit The Kura, with everything from artifacts of the Jomon period (14,000-300 BC) to samurai armor.

Food

Kyoto is most known for its painstakingly prepared, beautifully presented style of haute cuisine known as *kaiseki ryōri,* which evolved to complement the tea ceremony. But this only scratches the surface. Other dishes and cooking styles with a strong presence in the ancient capital include **shōjin-ryōri,** a vegetarian form of cooking used to nourish Buddhist monks; stellar soba and *udon* noodles; **traditional desserts** made with ingredients like azuki red bean paste, rice cake, and arrowroot noodles, perhaps paired with the city's endless supply of high-grade *matcha* (green tea).

KYOTO STATION AREA
Ramen
KYOTO RAMEN KŌJI

10F Kyoto Station Building, Higashi Shiokoji-chō, Shiokoji-sagaru, Shimogyō-ku; tel. 075/361-4401; www.kyoto-ramen-koji.com; 11am-10pm daily; ¥1,000
If you're in or near Kyoto Station and need a quick, cheap meal on the go, Kyoto Ramen Kōji is a good bet, with eight styles from all corners of Japan. To reach here, turn so that you're facing north toward Kyoto Tower while you're under Kyoto Station's main soaring atrium. Look to your left and you'll see a number of escalators. Follow them to the 10th floor. From this lofty perch, turn left and you'll see the hall of ramen before you.

Cafés and Light Bites
EAT PARADISE

11F Kyoto Station Building, Higashi Shiokoji-chō, Shiokoji-sagaru, Shimogyō-ku; tel. 075/352-1111; 11am-10pm daily; ¥1,500
If you're not a noodle aficionado, don't fret. There's also a food court with more variety on the 11th floor of Kyoto Station: Eat Paradise. The restaurants here, ranging from Japanese (tempura, *tonkatsu*) to Italian, are appropriate when you're in the mood for a proper meal

before hopping on the *shinkansen* or striking out for a day of sightseeing. To reach this food court, simply take the escalators one floor higher than where Kyoto Ramen Kōji is located and walk to the left until you reach the restaurants. Many restaurants here have English-language menus. Just pick the one that strikes your fancy.

SOUTHEAST KYOTO
Udon
KENDONYA

41 Fukakusa, Ichinotsubochō, Fushimi-ku; tel. 075/641-1330; https://kendonya.com; 11am-6pm Thurs.-Tues., random closing one day per month; ¥1,000; take JR Nara line to Inari Station
A worthwhile *udon* (flour noodle) restaurant about 5 minutes' walk from Fushimi Inari-Taisha. The shop serves a form of chewy al dente *udon* known as *koshi* in a flavorsome soup. The staff are bubbly, creating a welcoming atmosphere.

Cafés and Light Bites
VERMILLION CAFÉ

5-31 Kaidoguchi-cho Fukakusa, Fushimi-ku; tel. 075/644-7989; www.vermillioncafe.com; 9am-5pm daily; ¥1,000; take JR Nara line to Inari Station
A stone's throw from the army of fox statues and tunnel of vermillion *torii* gates snaking through the mountain where Fushimi Inari-Taisha stands, you'll find the aptly named Vermillion Café. This cozy café is located in the shrine area's backstreets and has a terrace overlooking a pond on the shrine's sprawling grounds. Excellent coffee and tasty baked goods are prepared on-site. This café is recommended for a great pit stop or a sit-down lunch.

International
DRAGON BURGER

13-243 Hommachi, Higashiyama-ku; tel. 075/525-5611; https://dragon-burger.com; 10am-11pm

daily; from ¥1,020; take Keihan, JR Nara lines to
Tōfuku-ji Station

Sometimes you just need a burger. Toppings range from wasabi and blue cheese to *tsukemono* (pickled vegetables), for which Kyoto is famed. Sets come with a side salad, fries, and a drink, and buns are made with domestically sourced ingredients. Good spot for a lunch or casual dinner near Tōfuku-ji or Fushima Inari-Taisha.

GION
Kaiseki
★ KIKUNOI HONTEN

459 Shimokawara-chō, Shimokawara-dōri, Yasakatoriimae-sagaru, Higashiyama-ku; tel. 075/561-0015; http://kikunoi.jp; noon-1pm (last order 12:30pm) and 5pm-8pm (last order 7:30pm) Wed.-Mon.; lunch ¥25,000 and up, dinner ¥30,500 and up; take Keihan line to Gion-Shijō Station

For a stunning example of a *kaiseki* feast, you won't be disappointed at Kikunoi Honten. Serving refined fare since it opened in 1912, Kikunoi is now run by Yoshihiro Murata, a third-generation in chefs. Located near Maruyama-kōen in the heart of Gion, Kyoto's historic entertainment quarter, this restaurant changes its menu and the décor with the seasons. To get a spot at the table, speak with the staff or concierge of your accommodations at least one month prior.

Japanese
SENMONTEN

380-3 Kiyomoto-chō, Higashi-gawa, Hanamikoji Shimbashi kudaru, Higashiyama-ku; tel. 075/531-2733; 6pm-2am Mon.-Sat.; from ¥530; take the Keihan line to Gion-Shijō Station, then walk 7 minutes

Fried dumplings (*gyoza*) and beer: If this sounds good and you're not overly concerned about caloric intake or a balanced diet, you can't go wrong with Senmonten. There's nothing else on the menu, and that's fine. The *gyoza*, served in batches of 20, are crispy outside and stuffed with juicy pork and scallions.

Ramen
RAMEN MURAJI

373-3 Kiyomotocho, Higashiyama-ku; tel. 075/744-1144; http://ramen-muraji.jp/en; 11:30am-3pm and 5pm-10pm dinner Mon.-Sat., 11:30am-8pm Sun. and public holidays; ¥850; take the Keihan line to Gion-Shijō Station, then walk 5 minutes

Ramen Muraji serves a mean bowl of ramen in a creamy broth made from chicken bones left to boil for hours then tossed with bamboo strips and chicken. Add an egg to make it more filling. Housed in a classic *machiya*-style building that's been tastefully spruced up and decorated; it's tucked down a cobblestone alley in Gion next to a canal; there's unfortunately no English sign. Keep an eye out for white curtains in front of the entrance. English-language menu available.

Sushi
CHIDORITEI

203 Rokken-chō, Donguri-dori Yamato-oji Nishi-iru, Higashiyama-ku; tel. 075/561-1907; www7b.biglobe. ne.jp/~chidoritei/index.html; 11am-8pm Fri.-Wed.; ¥2,000; take Keihan line to Gion-Shijō Station

Being landlocked, Kyoto isn't known for sushi, but the city is does serve a variety based on seasoned, marinated mackerel. The best place to try this is Chidoritei, a cozy family-run joint also serves good *chirashi* bowls (sashimi over rice) and eel.

Cafés and Light Bites
★ KAGIZEN YOSHIFUSA KŌDAI-JI

Kōdai-ji Omote-mon-mae Agaru, Higashi-yama-ku; tel. 075/525-0011; www.kagizen.co.jp; 9am-6pm Thurs.-Tues., last order 5:45pm; ¥1,000; take Keihan line to Gion-Shijō Station, or Hankyū line to Kawaramachi Station

Any traveler with a sweet tooth take note: Kagizen Yoshifusa Kōdai-ji is one of the city's most venerated traditional dessert cafés. The shop's most popular branch is right on Shijō-dōri in the heart of Gion. I prefer the Kōdai-ji branch in Southern Higashiyama; it's a calm place to sample traditional sweets, such as azuki red bean paste-stuffed pastries and arrowroot noodles dipped in black sugar, washed down with bitter *matcha* tea. This location is close enough to the bustling shopping streets leading uphill toward Kiyomizu-dera without being in the thick of it.

TORAYA

415 Hirohashidono-chō, Ichijo-kado, Karasuma-dōri, Kamigyō-ku; tel. 075/561-5878; https://global. toraya-group.co.jp; 10am-7pm, closed on irregular days; from ¥1,000; take the Keihan line to Gion-shijō Station, exit 6

Located on the first floor of the Minami-za kabuki theater in Gion, Toraya is an elegant place to sample a traditional sweet (think: rice cake stuffed with red bean paste) and a cup of *matcha* green tea—in summer, try it iced.

NORTHERN HIGASHIYAMA
Udon
HINODE UDON

36 Kitanobo-chō, Nanzen-ji, Sakyō-ku; tel. 075/751-9251; 11am-3pm Tues.-Sat.; from ¥750; take Tōzai subway line to Keage Station, exit 2

Another fantastic *udon* restaurant near the Philosopher's Path, this cozy family-owned shop is famous for its noodles served in flavorsome curry. The menu also includes more traditional *udon*, as well as soba noodle dishes. A great pick if you're feeling famished around the southern end of the Philosopher's Path, near Nanzen-ji and Eikan-dō. Queues do sometimes form but tend to move relatively fast. English menu available.

★ OMEN

74 Jōdo-ji, Ishibashi-chō, Sakyō-ku; tel. 075/771-8994; www.omen.co.jp; 11am-9pm (last order 8pm) daily; ¥1,200; take Kyoto City Bus no. 5 to Ginkakuji-michi

The formula is simple at Omen. A generous portion of seven varieties of vegetables are served along with white wheat-flour noodles (*udon*)—either hot or cold—with soup and a liberal hit of sesame (to be used as seasoning) on the side. Mix the vegetables into the soup and dunk the noodles. Delicious. This is a great choice for a meal when you're in the vicinity of Ginkaku-ji. You'll have a choice of sitting at the counter, at a separate table, or on a tatami floor.

Vegetarian
KISAKI YUDOFU

19-173 Jyodoji Minamida-chō, Sakyō-ku; tel. 075/751-7406; http://kyotokisaki.web.fc2.com; 11am-9pm Thurs.-Tues., open Wed. when it falls on holiday, last order 7:30pm; from ¥2,100; take Kyoto City Bus no. 32 to Minamida-chō bus stop

Kisaki Yudofu is a great place for a healthy vegetarian lunch near the Philosopher's Path. Set meals come with various iterations of tofu and *yuba*, dipped in batter or fried as tempura, served with pickled vegetables, or seasoned with sesame.

International
CENCI

44-7 Entomi-chō, Shōgoin, Sakyō-ku; tel. 075/708-5307; https://cenci-kyoto.com; lunch noon-3pm, last order 12:30pm, dinner 6pm-10:30pm, last order 7:30pm Tues.-Sun.; irregular closings on Sun.; lunch from ¥6,000, dinner from ¥12,000; take Keihan line to Jingu-Marutamachi Station, exit 4

This first-rate Italian eatery is one of the city's new "it" restaurants. As you pass through the tunnel, built with bricks made from the soil dug up from the site on which it stands, you emerge into a singular space that is faintly European, yet also Japanese. This reflects the menu. With Kyoto-born chef Ken Sakamoto at the helm, the kitchen rustles up fantastic Italian fare with a distinctly local twist, from *ayu* (sweetfish) instead of anchovies in the *bagna càuda* to liberal use of Japanese ingredients like buckwheat and *yuzu*. Produce is locally sourced—mushrooms and root vegetables foraged in the mountains nearby—and dishes are beautifully presented on smart tableware crafted by Japanese artisans. Word has gotten out, and the restaurant takes reservations up to two months in advance. Reserve as far ahead as you can. Inform the restaurant in advance if you're traveling with children under the age of 10.

Cafés and Light Bites
YAMATOYA

25 Sanno-chō, Shōgoin, Sakyō-ku; tel. 075/761-7685; www.jazz-yamatoya.com; noon-11pm Thurs.-Tues., closed second Tues. of month; from ¥650; take Keihan line to Jingu-Marutamachi Station, exit 4

This jazz café is the stuff of legend. It's been going strong for five decades, and the elegant interior of this cozy joint has a corner of floor-to-ceiling shelves overflowing with vinyl, dark wood furniture, stone walls, and antique lamps. But what really grabs you are the perfect tunes wafting through the stellar audio system. The coffee is top-notch, too. Recommended. Cash only.

POMME CAFÉ

144 Jodoji Shimominamida-chō, Sakyō-ku; tel. 075/771-9692; 11am-6pm Mon. and Thurs.-Sun., closed second and third Tues. every month; ¥1,000

A great option for a lunch near the Philosopher's Path is Pomme Café. This is a welcoming, friendly spot with baked goods, coffee, and other drinks. It's a terrific pit stop as you explore the area.

DOWNTOWN AND CENTRAL KYOTO
Kaiseki
GUILO GUILO HITOSHINA

420-7 Namba-chō, Nishikiyamachi-dōri-Matsubara-sagaru, Shimogyō-ku; tel. 075/343-7070; 5:30pm-11pm daily, closed last Mon. of month; dinner from ¥4,000; take Keihan line to Kiyomizu-Gojō Station, exit 3

At this chic, fun riverside restaurant in a two-story revamped warehouse, trendy young chefs in a tiny open kitchen whip up shockingly affordable *kaiseki* courses with a modern twist. The menu leans heavily toward simple, affordable, seasonal seafood and vegetables, with some curveballs like *gyoza* (dumplings) stuffed with broad beans, pea mousse, and caramel imbued with roasted green tea. Don't come here for a traditional feast; do come if you'd like to see the young, modern face of *kaiseki* without breaking the bank. The place gets packed, so reserve a month or more in advance. Cash only.

KAPPO YAMASHITA

491-3 Kami Korikicho, Nakagyō-ku; tel. 075/256-4506; 11:30am-1:30pm and 5pm-10pm Tues.-Sun.; lunch ¥5,000, dinner ¥15,000; take Tōzai line to Kyoto Shiyakusho-mae Station

In a culinary tradition as focused on refinement as *kaiseki,* Kappo Yamashita stands out for its down-to-earth atmosphere. The friendly chefs here are known to engage in banter with customers who sit at the counter—*kappo* means "counter style"—to watch them at work. The staff are also happy to field questions about the menu.

Tempura
MIZUKI

Kamogawa Nijo-Ohashi Hotori, Nakagyō-ku; tel. 075/746-5555; www.ritzcarlton.com/en/hotels/japan/kyoto/dining/kaiseki-mizuki; 11:30am-2pm (last order) and 5:30pm-8pm (last order) daily; lunch from ¥9,000, dinner from ¥12,000; take Hankyū line to Kawaramachi Station

The best tempura in Kyoto is arguably served at a large granite counter in the decidedly modern, luxurious setting of the Ritz-Carlton Kyoto; the atmosphere is sleek, in an elegant dining room with tableware made by artists. Diners at a large granite counter are treated by tempura maestro Chef Fujimoto, who has earned a Michelin star for his delicate seasonal and local creations, made with safflower oil instead of the heavier sesame oil used in most Tokyo kitchens. Alternatively, the hotel's innovative chefs also serve a *kaiseki* menu in the restaurant's main dining area. They aim to hit the principles of *go-mi* (five flavors), *go-shyoku* (five colors), and *go-ho* (five cooking methods).

Izakaya
YANAGI KOJI TAKA

577 Nakano-chō, Nakagyō-ku; tel. 075/708-5791; https://taka-kyoto-japan.net; 1pm-11pm (last order 10:30pm) Wed.-Mon.; dishes from ¥200, drinks from

Kaiseki Ryōri

summertime *kaiseki* cuisine

Kaiseki ryōri is one of the world's most aesthetically sophisticated and beautiful cuisines. This rarefied style of cooking embodies everything Japan does right in the kitchen, from selecting the very best, exquisitely fresh seasonal ingredients to artful presentation in elegant tableware.

BACKGROUND

Kyoto is at the center of the *kaiseki* tradition, the place of its origin. *Kaiseki* cuisine initially emerged as a complement to the tea ceremony, and was meant to be served as the meal before sipping the bitter green brew. A typical *kaiseki* meal consists of five or more dishes, beginning with sashimi and both grilled and steamed fish or vegetables. Next comes a soup and rice dish, with a light dessert to round out the meal. The preparation methods used in *kaiseki* cooking differ significantly from, say, gourmet French fare. Rather than adding new layers of taste with seasoning or sauce, *kaiseki* chefs are masters of letting the natural flavors of the ingredients speak for themselves.

WHAT TO EXPECT

Beyond the food itself, a staunch emphasis on hospitality (*omotenashi*) and the aesthetic dimension of the meal—involving gorgeous ceramic tableware and careful placement of individual courses—elevate a *kaiseki* meal to a multisensory experience. Unsurprisingly, this doesn't come cheap. Depending on the restaurant, expect to pay more than ¥20,000 for a full *kaiseki* meal. If you're serious about food and want to experience the higher end of Japan's menu, plan on budgeting for this splurge once on your journey, whether you dine in an old townhouse in Kyoto, a sleek modern restaurant in Tokyo, or a rural inn overlooking a stream or a garden. Note that reservations must be made at least a few weeks or a month ahead for any *kaiseki* meal.

WHERE TO TRY IT

- **Kikunoi Honten,** a stalwart in the heart of the Southern Higashiyama near Kōdai-ji and Maruyama-kōen (page 252).

- **Kappo Yamashita,** a laid-back restaurant with casual countertop seating in front of a kitchen run by gregarious chefs (page 254).

- **Shoraian,** in Arashiyama, an atmospheric restaurant that has a tofu-focused menu and is housed in a formerly private residence overlooking a river (page 259).

¥500; take Hankyū line to Kawaramachi Station, exit 6

After being trained in the art of *kaiseki*, followed by stints in Italy, Australia, and Denmark, the eponymous Chef Taka chose to launch this stylish *tachinomi* (standing bar) on the lantern-lit, cobblestone alley of Yanagi Koji in 2016. Besides an extensive yakitori menu, the popular eatery serves a number of fusion dishes—from seared beef to grilled fish and salads—that combine expertise in Japanese cuisine with tricks gleaned in Milan. There's a good Japanese craft beer and *sake* selection, with some Italian wines, too. English menu available.

Sushi
DEN SHICHI SUSHI SAIIN

Saiin, 4-1 Tatsumi-cho, Saiin, Ukyō-ku; tel. 075/323-0700; www.kushihachi.co.jp/denshichi-saiin. html; 11:30am-2pm and 5pm-10pm Tues.-Sun.; ¥2,000; take Hankyū line to Saiin Station

Get a sushi fix a bit west of downtown at Den Shichi Sushi Saiin. Enter to a hearty "welcome" from the chefs, who are busy carving behind the counter, where patrons sit. The quality is high and prices are reasonable, frequently attracting a queue. Try to show up early to avoid the rush. Showing up late means options may have already been picked over.

Ramen
INOICHI

1F, 528 Ebisuno-chō, Ebisuterasu, 528, Ebisunocho, Shimogyō-ku; tel. 075/353-7413; 11:30am-2pm and 5:30pm-10pm Tues.-Sun.; ¥1,200; take Hankyū line to Kawaramachi Station

Inoichi serves ramen with white (lighter) or black (fuller) soy sauce for your broth. Bamboo shoots and a delicious "red egg" marinated in soy sauce fill out the bowl, with the light yet robustly flavored broth being made with a mix of dried fish and kelp. If you don't mind waiting in the line that often forms outside, there's an English menu.

Soba
HONKE OWARIYA

322 Niomontsukinuke-chō, Nakagyō-ku; tel. 075/231-3446; https://honke-owariya.co.jp; 11am-4pm (last order 2:30pm) daily; from ¥880; take Karasuma or Tōzai subway line to Karasuma Oike Station, exit 1

This soba shop is an institution. Set in a historic building that embodies the classic Kyoto aesthetic, just south of the Kyoto Imperial Palace Park, this shop makes arguably the city's best soba noodles. It is the soba pick of choice for the imperial family when they come to town. It started as a confectionary shop in modern-day Aichi Prefecture, and the shop relocated to Kyoto to improve its business prospects and switched to making noodles, which ultimately proved more popular than their sweets. They haven't opened a Tokyo branch because the capital doesn't afford access to the particular well water they religiously use to make the restaurant's *dashi* (stock). The menu ranges from spare bowls of the buckwheat strands to filling sets with a slew of toppings: grated daikon, *nori*, leeks, wasabi, shrimp tempura, shiitake mushrooms, sesame seeds, and more. Friendly warning: Prepare to wait 15-30 minutes or more at peak lunchtime hours.

Vegetarian
MUMOKUTEKI CAFÉ

2F Human Forum Building, 351 Iseya-chō, Gokomochi-dori-Rokkaku-sagaru, Nakagyō-ku; tel. 075/213-7733; http://mumokuteki.com; 11:30am-10pm daily; from ¥1,000; take Hankyū line to Kawaramachi Station

If you're in search of a vegetarian or vegan restaurant downtown, head to the airy, elegant Mumokuteki Café. There's a clearly labeled menu (English available) that breaks down the ingredients in each dish. Options include set meals, a salad bar, and a good selection of items that can be ordered à la carte. Avoid the lunch rush by coming early or mid-afternoon.

AIN SOPH. JOURNEY KYOTO

538-6 Nakano-chō, Shinkyogoku-dōri Shijō-agaru, Nakagyō-ku; tel. 075/251-1876; www.ain-soph.jp/ journeykyoto; noon-8pm (last order 7pm) Mon.-Fri. and Sun., noon-9pm (last order 8pm) Sat.; from ¥1,000; take Hankyū line to Kawaramachi Station, exit 9

This elegant restaurant on a pedestrian lane downtown serves good vegan fare: vegan burgers topped with coconut cheese, tofu omelets, spinach curry, and surprisingly convincing desserts (vegan pancakes, soy ice cream, chocolate gateau, faux New York cheesecake).

★ TŌSUIRŌ

517-3 Kamiosaka-chō, Sanjō-agaru, Kiyamachi-dōri, Nakagyō-ku; tel. 075/251-1600; http://tousuiro. com; 11:30am-3pm (last order 2pm) and 5pm-10pm (9pm last order) Mon.-Sat., 11:45am-3pm (2pm last order) and 5pm-9:30pm (8:30pm last order) Sun. and holidays; lunch from ¥4,000, dinner from ¥5,000; take Hankyū line to Kawaramachi Station

Tōsuirō is a great place to explore the wonders of tofu and *yuba*—and surprising wonders they are. Multicourse meals consist of small variations in cooking method. Assorted sashimi brings a different element to the table. When the weather is warm, book ahead to get a seat on the veranda overlooking the Kamo River—a quintessential Kyoto experience.

KANGA-AN

278 Shingoryoguchi-chō, Karasuma-dōri, Kuramaguchi-Higahiiru, Kita-ku; tel. 075/256-2480; www.kangaan.jp; noon-3pm (last entry 1pm) and 5pm-9pm (last entry 7pm) daily; courses from ¥5,000; take Karasuma subway line to Kuramaguchi Station

To sample bona fide *shōjin-ryōri,* you have to go to a temple. Brought from China to Japan by the founder of Zen Buddhism, Dogen, *shōjin-ryōri* forgoes all meat, dairy, and even flavorful ingredients like garlic, onions, and spices. Arguably the best place to dine like a monk is the temple of Kanga-an in the city's north-central area. Diners are seated in private dining rooms divided by sliding paper doors and presented with a spread that is as aesthetically pleasing as it is healthy. Don't expect to be knocked out by flavor. Admire the delicacy instead. After your meal, move over to the bar next door.

International
SAMA SAMA

532-16 Kamiosaka-chō, Kiyamachi, Sanjō-agaru, Nakagyō-ku; tel. 075/241-4100; www.facebook.com/

soba and tempura

SamaSama0214; 6pm-2am Tues.-Sun.; ¥200 cover charge, dishes from ¥850; take Keihan line to Sanjō Station

A non-Japanese choice for spicing things up is Sama Sama. The kitchen at this cozy Indonesian restaurant and bar whips up a diverse menu of omelets, and rice dishes with lots of chicken and fish. The Balinese owner is friendly and makes guests comfortable with a bit of conversation. Guests sit on floor cushions, creating a very laid-back atmosphere.

MUGHAL

2F Airu Takeshima Bldg., Kiyamachi-dōri Oike agaru, Nakagyō-ku; tel. 075/241-3777; www.kyoto-mughal. com; noon-3pm (last order 2:30pm) and 5pm-11pm (last order 10pm) Wed.-Mon.; lunch from ¥1,000, dinner from ¥2,850; take Tōzai subway line to Kyoto Shiyakusho-mae, exit 3

As you eat your way through numerous rice, noodle, tofu, and fish-based meals, you might start to crave something different. Mughal, a spacious Indian restaurant beside the Kamo River near the northeast corner of downtown, offers a nice alternative. The excellent menu is mostly north Indian: curries, tandoori dishes, *biryanis,* and more.

Cafés and Light Bites
PAPA JON'S HONTEN

642-4 Shokokuji-chō, Karasuma-dōri, Kamidachiuri higashi-iru, Kamigyō-ku; tel. 075/415-2655; www. papajons.net; 10:30am-8pm daily; lunch from ¥850, dessert from ¥350; take Kurasuma subway line to Imadegawa Station

If you're near Imadegawa Station north of Kyoto Imperial Palace Park, Papa Jon's Honten is a good place for lunch—curry, quiche, sandwiches—or a coffee break with a slice of their famed cheesecake.

★ CAFÉ BIBLIOTIC HELLO!

650 Seimei-chō, Nijō-dōri, Yanaginobanba higashi-iru, Nakagyō-ku; tel. 075/231-8625; http:// cafe-hello.jp; 11:30am-midnight daily; ¥1,000; take Tōzai line to Kyoto-Shiyakusho-mae Station

With serious points for atmosphere—excellent lighting, exposed-brick walls lined with books, a globe lit from within—is the awesomely named Café Bibliotic Hello!. It's an appealing place to while away a few hours over a coffee, smoothie, or light meal with a book or laptop in hip surroundings. Just look for the red-brick exterior fronted by large banana plants.

NORTHWEST KYOTO
Soba
HANAMAKIYA

17-2 Kinugasa Gochonouchi-chō, Kita-ku; tel. 075/464-4499; https://hanamakiya.gorp.jp; 11:30am-7pm Fri.-Wed., irregular holidays; from ¥1,300; a few minutes' walk east of Kinkaku-ji's grounds

There is a surprising dearth of restaurants around Kinkaku-ji, but thankfully there's Hanamakiya. Come here for a quick, filling lunch at a good value. The restaurant serves handmade soba noodles, tempura, *unagi-don* (grilled eel over rice), and more. Seating is on tatami floors around low tables. It's busy at peak times, but queues move fast. English menu available.

Vegetarian
★ IZUSEN DAIJINTEN

4 Daitoku-chō, Murasakino, Kita-ku; tel. 075/491-6665; http://kyoto-izusen.com; 11am-4pm daily; from ¥3,500; from Kyoto Station, take Kyoto City Bus no. 204, 205, or 206 to Daitoku-ji bus stop

On the grounds of the atmospheric Daitoku-ji temple complex, Izusen Daijinten offers one of Kyoto's best *shōjin-ryōri* experiences. Great Buddhist vegan fare is served in a series of dishes that keep coming, one after the other. Surprisingly diverse in flavor—pleasing even non-vegans—the dishes are beautiful to look at, too. You can sit in a garden attached to the restaurant in good weather. Be sure to wander the vast temple grounds after you eat—highly recommended.

ARASHIYAMA
Kaiseki
★ SHORAIAN

*Sagameno-chō, Ukyō-ku; tel. 075/861-0123; www.
shoraian.com; 11am-5pm Mon.-Thurs., 11am-8pm
Fri.-Sun. and holidays; lunch from ¥3,800, dinner
from ¥6,300; take Hankyū line to Arashiyama, or JR
Sagano line to Saga-Arashiyama Station*

For a unique *kaiseki* experience in a more natural setting, try Shoraian. Set in the hills of Arashiyama, overlooking the Katsura River, the restaurant is housed in an old private residence. Climb a stone stairway through the forest, go inside and sit down on a tatami floor. The service is outstanding, making guests feel like they're dining at someone's home. The menu consists of set courses that are heavily tofu-based and surprisingly affordable by *kaiseki* standards. Reservations for dinner Fri.-Sun. and on holidays are required and must be made before 5pm on the day prior. That said, booking ahead a few weeks or even a month is wise to ensure a spot. Reservations aren't required for lunch, although booking a week or more in advance is recommended. Its location outside the city and its affordability make this a superb introduction to *kaiseki*.

Soba
ARASHIYAMA YOSHIMURA

*3 Saga-Tenryū-ji Susukinobaba-chō, Ukyō-ku; tel.
075/863-5700; http://yoshimura-gr.com; 11am-5pm
daily; from ¥1,300; take Hankyū line to Arashiyama
station*

Arashiyama Yoshimura is a local soba shop that sells soba (hot or cold) lunch sets with various side dishes. Located a few minutes' walk from the temple of Tenryū-ji, this popular restaurant has a nice view of the Hozu River rushing by outside. This is a good pick for a lunch before setting off on foot to explore the sights of the area. Note that it often attracts a queue, so try to avoid peak hours if you don't like to wait.

Vegetarian
YUDOFU SAGANO

*45 Sagatenryūji, Susukinobaba-chō; tel.
075/871-6946; www.kyoto-sagano.jp; tel.
075/871-6946; 11am-7pm daily; courses from ¥3,800;
take JR Sagano line to Saga-Arashiyama Station*

For a more casual tofu-based meal, another option in Arashiyama is Yudofu Sagano. The specialty here is simmered pieces of hot tofu known as *yudo*, served with side dishes of mountain vegetables, tempura, and more.

Cafés and Light Bites
%ARABICA

*3-47, Saga-Tenryū-ji Susukinobaba-chō, Ukyō-ku;
tel. 075/748-0057; https://arabica.coffee, 8am-6pm
daily; from ¥500; take Hankyū line to Arashiyama
station*

Just down the road from Arashiyama Yoshimura, you'll find %Arabica. This hip café, overlooking the Hozu River, serves artisanal coffee and makes for an ideal pit stop before or after exploring the area's sights. There's not much in the way of seating, but the area makes takeaway an appealing alternative.

Uji and Japanese Tea: A Primer

Tea has been imbibed in Japan since the 8th century, when it arrived from China. The small town of Uji, just south of Kyoto and home to the famed **Byōdō-in** temple (116 Uji-Renge, Uji-shi; tel. 0774/21-2861; www.byodoin.or.jp; grounds 8:30am-5:30pm (last entry 5:15pm) daily, Phoenix Hall 9:30am-4:10pm, temple museum 9am-5pm (last entry 4:45pm); adults ¥600, high school and junior high school students ¥400, elementary school students ¥300) seen on the back of the 10-yen coin, has deep ties to Japan's rich tea culture, particularly celebrated for green tea, which has been grown in the surrounding mountains since the 12th century.

BACKGROUND

In the Nara period (710-794), Buddhist priests and aristocrats began to quaff tea, which had then only recently been brought to Japan from China. By the Muromachi period (1333-1573), tea had trickled down to the masses. Tea drinking was infused with Zen sensibilities, and a detailed set of movements and social protocols began to grow around the simple act. These behaviors gradually became what we know today as the *sadō* or *cha-no-yu* (the way of tea), which is fully expressed in the act of the tea ceremony, or *chaji*.

Fast-forward to the present. Today, tea is ubiquitous in Japan, with some popular types including *ryokucha* (green tea), which can also be roasted (*hōjicha*) and combined with roasted brown rice (genmaicha); *matcha* (powdered green tea); and jasmine-cha.

TASTING TEA IN UJI

There are some wonderful opportunities to taste and learn about tea in Uji, which is just 20-30 minutes from Kyoto on the JR Nara line to JR Uji Station (¥240). Trains on the Keihan main line also run from downtown Kyoto (including Gion-shijō, Sanjō, and Demachiyanagi stations) to Keihan Uji Station (¥310-400). Note that some Keihan express trains traveling south from Kyoto to Uji may require a transfer to a Keihan local train at Chushojima.

Takumi no Yakata

17-1 Mataburi, Uji-shi; tel. 0774/23-0888; www.ujicha.or.jp; 11am-5pm (last order 4:30pm) Thurs.-Tues.; tasting sets from ¥800; Keihan Uji Station or JR Uji Station

Learn to brew your own tea with certified expert instruction at this teahouse beside the Uji River.

Fukujuen Ujicha Kobo

10 Yamada Uji-shi; tel. 0774/20-1100; www.ujikoubou.com; 10am-5pm (last order 4:30pm at teahouse) Tues.-Sun.; workshops from ¥2,000; Keihan Uji Station JR Uji Station

Come here for a range of hands-on tea workshops. You'll learn to grind tea leaves, whisk the powder you've created, and then quaff the resulting brew. Walk-ins are welcome. There's also a café on site that serves a variety of teas.

Taihoan

2 Togawa, Uji-shi; tel. 0774/23-3334; 10am-4pm daily, closed Dec. 21-Jan.9; ¥500; JR Uji Station or Keihan Uji Station

Come to this city-run traditional teahouse, a stone's throw from Byōdō-in, for a remarkably affordable tea ceremony. A member of staff will kindly guide you in proper etiquette.

Tsūen

1 Higashi-uchi Uji-shi; tel. 0774/21-2243; www.tsuentea.com; 9:30am-5:30pm daily; ¥1,000

a tea ceremony

Sitting at the corner of Uji-bashi bridge, in front of Keihan Uji Station, this riverside tea shop is the oldest purveyor of the brew in Japan. Stop here for teatime, with the option of adding a sweet *matcha*-flavored ice cream or even having a light meal.

TASTING TEA IN KYOTO

While a full-scale tea ceremony lasts up to four hours—from the preceding *kaiseki* feast to the ceremony itself—it's possible to experience a shortened version that simply consists of drinking one kind of *matcha* accompanied by a small sweet. To experience this Zen ritual in Kyoto in a relaxed yet refined setting, try **Camellia**, which has two locations. Book a spot on their website.

Camellia Flower

349-12 Masuya-chō, Higashiyama-ku; tel. 075/525-3238; www.tea-kyoto.com/experience/flower; 10am-6pm daily; shared tea ceremony ¥3,000 adults, ¥1,500 children ages 7-12, children under 6 free, private tea ceremony ¥6,000 ages 12 and up for group of 2 or more, children under 6 free
The bilingual woman who performs the 45-minute ceremonies here is informative and has a knack for putting guests at ease.

Camellia Garden

18 Ryōan-ji Ikenoshita-chō, Ukyō-ku; tel. 070/5656-7808; www.tea-kyoto.com/experience/garden; 11am-6pm Mon.-Sat.; ¥8,000 per person for group of 2 or more, free for children under 6 years old
Set in an old house with a lovely garden, this branch is also run by a charming bilingual woman with a masterful grasp on the art of tea. The dreamy setting and slightly longer time given for each session (1 hour) justifies the slightly higher price tag.

Bars and Nightlife

If you'd like to get acquainted with the city's breweries, check out **Kampai Sake Tours** (tel. 080/7045-8365; https://kampaisake-tours.com/tour/kyoto-sake; 3 hours; 2pm-5pm Wed.-Sun.; ¥8,500).

SOUTHERN HIGASHIYAMA
BEER KOMACHI

444 Hachiken-chō, Higashiyama-ku; tel. 075/746-6152; www.beerkomachi.com; 5pm-11pm Mon. and Wed.-Fri., 3pm-11pm Sat.-Sun.; take Tōzai subway line to Higashiyama Station

Beer Komachi is a friendly, laid-back spot to sample a range of Japan's craft beer offerings, with usually around seven types on tap. This spot also serves good nibbles, from beer-battered chicken to deep-fried blowfish.

NORTHERN HIGASHIYAMA
CLUB METRO

B1F Ebisu Building, 82 Shimotsutsumichō, Kawabata-dōrii, Marutamachi-sagaru, Sakyō-ku; tel. 075/752-4765; www.metro.ne.jp; 8pm-3am daily; fees vary by event; take Keihan line to Jingū-Marutamachi Station

Club Metro is a longstanding venue with a penchant for catering to a wide range of musical tastes, from big-name DJs to indie rockers and even art exhibitions. With room for about 250 people, the space has an intimate feel. Events change nightly, so check the calendar online before making the trip.

DOWNTOWN AND CENTRAL KYOTO
SOUR

607-19 Uradera-chō, Nakagyō-ku; tel. 075/231-0778; https://sour.jp; 3pm-midnight daily; take Hankyū line to Kyoto-Kawaramachi Station, exit 2

This chic, cramped standing bar offers a range of "sours," made with *shochū*, tonic, and infused with a range of fresh fruits. Staff are a bit

unengaged, but the mixed crowd is friendly. A good spot to start an evening if you're feeling social.

BEE'S KNEES

1F Matsuya Bldg., 364 Kamiya-chō, Agaru, Kiyamachi, Nakagyō-ku; tel. 075/585-5595; https://bees-knees-kyoto.jp; 6pm-1am (last order 12:30am) Mon.-Thurs., 6pm-2am (last order 1:30am) Fri.-Sat.; take Hankyū line to Kyoto-Kawaramachi Station, exit 1A, or Keihan line to Gion-Shijō Station, exit 4

Push open the door to "The Book Store," pull aside the black curtain, and enter this dimly lit space, which evokes a serious cocktail den. Friendly young bartenders in bowler hats mix drinks with ingredients like honey and citrus to mask the scent of the gin that delivers the punch. Prohibition-era black-and-white photos hang in golden frames on the walls and 1990s hip-hop permeates the air. The cocktails are all beautifully garnished, and some come with dry ice for dramatic effect.

ROCKING BAR ING

2F Royal Bldg., 288 Minamikurayama-chō, Nishikiyama-dōri, Takoyakushi-agaru, Nakagyō-ku; tel. 075/255-5087; www.kyotoingbar.com; 7pm-2am Sun.-Thurs., 7pm-5am Fri.-Sat.; take Hankyū line to Kyoto-Kawaramachi Station, exit 1A, or Keihan line to Sanjō Station, exit 6

If you like rock 'n' roll, this popular bar ticks the right boxes: guitars and Rolling Stones posters on the walls and tunes drift through the air, as a friendly international crowd swills cheap drinks and eats pub fare.

BAR KAZU

3F, 309 Bizenjima-chō, Nakagyō-ku; 9pm-5am daily; take Hankyū line to Kyoto-Kawaramachi Station, exit 3A

No sign, no phone number, this bar is the stuff of local legend. The minimal space is solely illumined by candlelight. The music selection and sound system are impeccable.

Suntory Yamazaki Distillery and Japan's Award-Winning Whisky

Museum in the Suntory Yamazaki Distillery

Japan's renowned spirit of craftsmanship, knack for detail, and fresh, flavorsome groundwater have all contributed to the country's success in the world of whisky. Aficionados credit the nation's four seasons with adding extra layers of texture to barrel casks that sit aging for years.

Japan's first domestically distilled malt whisky was bottled in 1924 at Suntory Yamazaki Distillery (5-2-1 Yamazaki, Shimamoto, Mishima District, Osaka Prefecture; tel. 075/962-1423; www.suntory.com/factory/yamazaki; 9:30am-5pm daily, sporadic closings) in Osaka Prefecture, between Osaka and Kyoto. Their **Yamazaki 12 Years single malt** was the first Japanese whisky to win a gold medal at the International Spirits Challenge in 2003. The success has snowballed from there, with Suntory's **Hibiki** taking the Best Blended Whisky in the World prize for the fourth time at the World Whiskies Awards in 2016. At the 2017 awards, Japan made the strongest showing of any country, snagging three prizes: World's Best Single Cask Single Malt (Chichibu Whisky Matsuri 2017); World's Best Blended (Hibiki 21 Year Old); and World's Best Grain (Fuji-Gotemba Distillery Single Grain 25 Year Old Small Batch).

If you visit Suntory Yamazaki Distillery, you can walk through on your own, with bilingual exhibits at an on-site **museum** about the history of the label, and sample the goods at a paid **tasting counter** (10am-4:30pm). Or, pay for a guided, behind-the-scenes **distillery tour** (80-100 minutes; ¥1,000-2,000) in English; **reserve ahead** at www.suntory.com/factory/yamazaki/info. To get here, take the JR Kyoto line to Yamazaki Station (30 minutes from Osaka Stationl ¥460; 15 minutes from Kyoto Station, ¥220), then walk 10 minutes west.

The eponymous owner—gregarious, generous, sometimes boisterously drunk—offers a hearty welcome to all who enter. Regulars include in-the-know locals and expats. Seats line the bar, with a roomier array of sofas around a large central table in the back.

Drinks are reasonably priced, too. It's one floor above **Elephant Factory Coffee** (309 Bizenjima-chō, Nakagyō-ku; tel. 075/212-1808; 1pm-1am Fri.-Wed.), a good spot for a caffeine hit during daylight hours in its own right.

L'ESCAMOTEUR BAR

138-9 Saito-chō, Saiseki-dōri, Shijō-sagaru,
Shimogyō-ku; tel. 075/708-8511; 8pm-2am Tues.-Sun.;
take Keihan line to Gion-Shijō Station, or Hankyū line
to Kawaramachi Station

For a cocktail, L'Escamoteur Bar is a known quantity. Bartenders wearing bowler hats and bow ties mix great cocktails, some of which look like magic potions. This fun and friendly bar is strewn with curios and has an air of enchantment.

BAR CORDON NOIR

3F Matsushimaya Building, 121 Ishiya-chō,
Nakagyō-ku; tel. 075/212-3288; 7pm-3am daily; cover
charge ¥500; take Tōzai subway line to Sanjō Station

Whisky aficionados, take note of this compact bar. It's not cheap, but the range of bottles is truly impressive, most of them either limited-edition or aged at least 17 years. The bartenders are friendly and highly knowledgeable, and cigars are sold.

BARCODE

3F Reiho Kaikan, 366 Kamiya-chō, Nishi-kiyamachi-
dōri, Shijō-agaru, Nakagyō-ku; tel. 075/221-7333;
8pm-5am daily; take Keihan line to Gion-Shijō
Station, or Hankyū line to Kawaramachi Station

Feel like crooning? Barcode is a fun place for a night of karaoke, which can be done for free with a machine and mics brought straight to your table. Sometimes this bar hosts international parties, which draw a diverse crowd.

URBANGUILD

3F New Kyoto Building, 181-2 Kiyamachi, Sanjō-shita,
Nakagyō-ku; tel. 075/212-1125; www.urbanguild.net;
6:30pm-1am daily; fee varies by event; take Tōzai
subway line to Sanjō Station

Urbanguild is the best place to catch a glimpse of Kyoto's underground scene. A bit of decay and a DIY spirit are on display, with an antique chandelier and furniture made from recovered wood. Think punk, avant-garde theater, noise, and experimental electronic music. Check the website's events page to see what's on and for the cover charge.

BAR ROCKING CHAIR

434-2 Tachibana-chō, Gokomachi-dōri,
Bukkoji-sagaru, Shimogyō-ku; tel. 075/496-8679;
www.bar-rockingchair.jp; 5pm-2am (last order 1am)
Wed.-Mon.; take Hankyū line to Kawaramachi Station

Bar Rocking Chair is a serious cocktail den. Bartender and owner Kenji Tsubokura is a renowned mixologist who uses homegrown ingredients in his flavorsome creations. A great pick for laid-back drinks in a classy, unstuffy atmosphere.

SHOOTING BAR M4

3F TN Building, 452 Matsugae-chō, Nakagyō-ku;
tel. 080/5350-0556; https://m4-kyoto.jimdo.com;
5pm-midnight daily; take Tōzai subway line to Sanjō
Station

At Shooting Bar M4 are friendly staff, affordable drinks, and a BB gun shooting range. What more can you ask for?

SAKE BAR YORAMU

35-1 Matsuya-chō, Nijō-dōri, Higashinotoin,
Higashi-iru, Nakagyō-ku; tel. 075/213-1512; www.
sakebar-yoramu.com; 6pm-midnight Wed.-Sat.;
from ¥1,600; take Tōzai or Karasuma subway line to
Karasuma-Oike Station

Make your way to Sake Bar Yoramu for a great introduction and *sake*-tasting course. Owned by an Israeli *sake* enthusiast, the bar is a cramped but friendly spot to glean a bit more insight into the joys of Japan's most iconic drink. Friendly forewarning: Yoram—his real name—takes the brew very seriously and has developed a reputation as an agitator due to the way he dispenses his opinions on the brew. If you go with an open mind and don't mind getting schooled in his own heretical tradition, you'll likely leave with a much more nuanced appreciation for *sake*—particularly of the aged variety.

Accommodations

KYOTO STATION AREA
¥10,000-20,000
RYOKAN SHIMIZU

644 Kagiya-cho, Shichijō-dōri, Wakamiya agaru, Shimogyō-ku; tel. 075/371-5538; www.kyoto-shimizu. net; ¥13,000 d with private bath; walk about 5 minutes from JR Kyoto Station's Karasuma central gate

Ryokan Shimizu is a great budget *ryokan*. There are no luxurious meals or landscape garden views, but the rooms are clean, and both English-speaking staff and friendly fellow travelers are happy to swap information. If you're content sleeping in a futon on a tatami floor, and proximity to Kyoto Station is important to you, this hotel is a good bet. Bicycle rentals available (¥700 per day). Note that there is a midnight curfew.

¥30,000-40,000
★ HOTEL GRANVIA

JR Kyoto Station, Central Exit, Karasuma-dōri, Shiokōji-sagaru, Shimogyō-ku; tel. 075/344-8888; www.granviakyoto.com; ¥35,000 d

Hotel Granvia has well-appointed rooms with chic décor. The hotel is literally in the JR Kyoto Station building, offering direct access to transport links. The views over the city (or train tracks) are notable, too.

SOUTHERN HIGASHIYAMA
Under ¥10,000
GOJŌ GUESTHOUSE

3-396-2 Gojōbashi Higashi, Higashiyama-ku; tel. 075/525-2299; http://gojo-guest-house.com; ¥2,000 dorm, ¥5,500 twin, ¥9,000 triple room; take Keihan line to Kiyomizu-Gojō

With its English-speaking staff, Gojō Guesthouse is a good budget option and is popular among backpackers. It is situated near the ever-popular Kiyomizu-dera and set in a century-old *ryokan* building. The rooms

are a mix of dorms and petite private rooms for up to three. All rooms share a bathroom and toilet.

¥10,000-20,000
KYOTO YOSHIMIZU

Maruyama-kōen, Bentendoue, Higashiyama-ku; tel. 075/551-3995; http://yoshimizu.com; ¥15,000 d; 10-minute walk from Gion bus stop

Set in the back of Maruyama-kōen, Kyoto Yoshimizu scores points for its natural setting within easy reach of the city. The inn is set in a traditional-style *ryokan* building but has both western-style and Japanese-style rooms. Breakfast is included.

Over ¥40,000
HYATT REGENCY KYOTO

664-2 Sanjūsangen-dō-mawari, Higashiyama-ku; tel. 075/541-1234; www.hyatt.com; ¥55,700 d; take Keihan line to Shichijō Station

The Hyatt Regency Kyoto is a fantastic hotel with luxury trimmings at a relatively reasonable price. In the southern edge of Higashiyama, the hotel has helpful staff and chic, spacious rooms, each with room service a touch screen away.

FOUR SEASONS KYOTO

445-3 Maekawa-chō, Myohoin, Higashiyama-ku; tel. 075/541-8288; www.fourseasons.com; ¥127,800 d; 10-minutes taxi ride from JR Kyoto Station

For a phenomenal luxury experience in the heart of Kyoto's most important sightseeing district, it's hard to outdo Four Seasons Kyoto. Elegant rooms with Japanese accents (paper lamps, painted screens) boast marble bathrooms with large tubs and views overlooking a gorgeous garden centered around a serene pond. There's excellent on-site dining, too. The hotel's staff are warm and helpful, and it's all located a short walk from key sights such as Sanjūsangen-dō.

Staying in a *Ryokan*

A stay in a traditional Japanese inn (*ryokan*) offers the chance to experience many elements of Japanese hospitality and comfort—spare traditional interiors, sleeping on a futon on a tatami floor, and haute dining in your room. Before the modern era, *ryokan* served as stopover points for anyone traversing the Tokaido Highway that once ran between the feudal capital of Edo (modern-day Tokyo) and the ancient capital of Kyoto. Many associate *ryokan* with the countryside, but fantastic *ryokan* are also found in virtually every city and town in the country.

WHAT TO EXPECT

Today, *ryokan* vary significantly, from modest family-run countryside pensions to luxe getaways. Some core elements shared by *ryokan* across the spectrum include simple **tatami-mat floors,** both private and shared **onsen baths,** and **excellent meals** delivered twice daily to your room, from breakfast (Japanese or Western, depending on the inn) to *kaiseki* spreads for dinner. (Some more modest digs serve meals in common areas.) Furniture will be simple: a low wooden table with floor-cushions to sit on, a futon for sleeping (usually laid out as you eat dinner). You'll notice that some *ryokan* rooms have nature-inspired names—flowers are common—rather than being numbered.

Perhaps what stands out most is the **relaxed pace** and impeccable *omotenashi* (hospitality) at the heart of a *ryokan* stay. Upon entering, slip off your shoes and ease into the slippers provided. In your room, be sure to take off your slippers before entering any tatami-mat area, where only socks or barefoot are acceptable etiquette. Ditch your day clothes in favor of a much more comfortable *yukata*.

Although it's by no means necessary or expected, upon leaving, nudge an envelope with a **cash tip** to the staff if their service impresses you. Tipping isn't customary in Japan, but *ryokan* are an exception due to the exceptional hospitality they often provide.

HOW TO CHOOSE A *RYOKAN*

Some factors to consider when choosing a *ryokan* to stay in will include whether the rooms have en-suite bathrooms or not, whether the inn has an *onsen,* whether you'd be sleeping on a futon or a bed, and what kind of food options will be included in your stay. Both **Japanese Guest Houses** (www.japaneseguesthouses.com) and **JAPANiCAN** (www.japanican.com) are excellent English-language *ryokan* portals that make browsing and reserving *ryokan* smooth and enjoyable.

GION
Under ¥10,000
GION KOH

475 Shimokawara-chō, Higashiyama-ku; tel. 075/561-0125; http://gion-koh.com; doubles from ¥7,300; take Keihan line to Gion-Shijō Station, exit 1

This charming guesthouse tucked down a quiet sidestreet near Kōdai-ji is a great choice if you're on a budget and want to stay in a place with some ambiance. There's a mix of Western (wooden floors, beds) and Japanese-style (tatami, futon) rooms—some sharing a bathroom, others with their own—an interior courtyard, and a shared kitchen. It's a little bit far from the nearest station, so either be ready for a bit of a walk with your luggage or to simply catch a taxi from the station.

KYOTO INN GION

435 Rinka-chō, Higashiyama-ku; tel. 075/330-6666; https://kyotoinngion.com; doubles from ¥9,500 with breakfast; take the Keihan line to Gion-Shijō Station, exit 8

This reasonably priced hotel is located smack in the center of Gion, right in front of the imposing entrance of Chion-in and a few minutes' walk from Yasaka-jinja and Maruyama-kōen. Staff are happy to help, rooms are spacious, and the atmospheric temples of Northern Higashiyama are a stone's throw away. A great budget pick.

¥10,000-20,000
HOTEL ETHNOGRAPHY - GION SHINMONZEN

219-2 Nishinochō, Shinmonzen, Yamato Ōji Hirashi-iru, Higashiyama-ku; tel. 075/708-7858; www.hotel-ethnography.com; rooms from ¥17,000; take Keihan line to Gion-Shijō Station, exit 7

Hotel Ethnography - Gion Shinmonzen is a boutique hotel a short walk from the east bank of the Kamo River. The interior is minimalist with tasteful Japanese accents, including local arts and crafts. Some rooms even look out onto private gardens. Friendly English-speaking staff are on call to help you navigate the city. Fantastic value.

¥30,000-40,000
OLD KYOTO

536-12 Komatsu-chō, Higashiyama-ku; tel. 075/533-7775; www.oldkyoto.com; from ¥32,000 per night, minimum 5-night stay; take Keihan line to Gion-Shijō Station, exit one

There are three charming *machiya* in the southeastern corner of Gion run by an aesthetically minded restoration organization called Old Kyoto. Up to four people can occupy the Gion House, Indigo House, or Amber House at any one time, with a requirement of at least five nights' stay. Spruced up retro Japanese-style interiors are complemented by fully modernized creature comforts, including decked-out kitchens and laundry facilities. Considering the space and amenities, as well as the charm and location, these homes are excellent affordable alternatives to the city's hotels.

★ HOTEL THE CELESTINE KYOTO GION

572 Komatsu-chō, Yasaka-dōri, Higashiōji-nishi-iru, Higashiyama-ku; tel. 075/532-3111; www. celestinehotels.jp; doubles from ¥33,580; take Keihan line to Gion-Shijō Station, exit 1

Hotel The Celestine Kyoto Gion is brand-new and sits in a sweet spot right in the heart of Gion. If you're seeking an excellent option at the higher end of the midrange, and convenience is a priority, this hotel is highly recommended. En-suite bathrooms are complemented by gender-separated public baths, and an on-site restaurant whips up Japanese and western offerings. The rooms are sleek and amply sized, and the hotel's location is excellent.

HANA-TOURO HOTEL GION

555 Komatsuchō, Higashiyama-ku; tel. 075/525-8100; doubles from ¥38,000; take Keihan line to Gion-Shijō Station, exit 6

Hana-Touro Hotel Gion is a sleek new boutique hotel smack in the middle of Kyoto's old geisha quarter. The rooms are modern, stylish, and clean, with balconies and wooden bathtubs. There's a rooftop terrace and a restaurant serving Japanese fare, and the front desk can assist with anything from attending geisha performances to renting bikes and kimonos.

Over ¥40,000
★ YUZUYA RYOKAN

Yasaka-jinja Minami-tonari, Gion-machi, Higashiyama-ku; tel. 075/533-6369; http://yuzuyaryokan.com; doubles from ¥60,000; take Keihan line to Gion-Shijō, exit 6

Yuzuya Ryokan is a sophisticated *ryokan* located right on Higashiōji-dōri, a stone's throw from Yasaka-jinja. The inn, discretely tucked away up a stairway right off the main drag, oozes refinement once you step inside. There's a charming garden for a relaxing stroll, excellent meals, wooden tubs in the rooms, and highly attuned staff. It's also very convenient, with downtown a mere 10-minute walk away and the sights of Southern Higashiyama arrayed all around it.

NORTHERN HIGASHIYAMA
¥30,000-40,000
★ YOSHIDA SANSŌ

59-1 Yoshida Shimōji-chō, Sakyō-ku; tel. 075/771-6125; www.yoshida-sanso.com; from ¥32,125 pp with breakfast; take a taxi from Kyoto Station (20 minutes), or Kyoto City Bus no. 5 to Ginkaku-ji Michi bus stop and walk 15 minutes

Yoshida Sansō has a whiff of secrecy and history about it. In a quiet corner of the city near Ginkaku-ji, on the summit of Mount Yoshida, this classic old *ryokan* was originally built during the Shōwa Period (1926-1989)—seen in the architectural blend revealing inspiration from both East and West—to serve as the home of a prince, Higashi-Fushimi, who was the uncle of Japanese Emperor Akihito. There's an atmosphere of elegant wear on the surfaces of this hideaway. A short walk from Northern Higashiyama's temple circuit, as well as a network of hiking trails, Yoshida Sansō is a *ryokan* set apart.

DOWNTOWN AND CENTRAL KYOTO
Under ¥10,000
HOSTEL LEN KYOTO KAWARAMACHI

709-3 Uematsu-chō, Shimogyo-ku; tel. 075/361-1177; https://backpackersjapan.co.jp/kyotohostel; dorms from ¥2,600, private rooms from ¥3,500 pp; take Keihan line to Kiyomizu-Gojō Station, or Hankyū line to Kawaramachi Station, exit 4

With a café, bar, and restaurant on-site, this trendy hostel is a popular choice for young, stylish travelers looking to mingle. It's near the west bank of the Kamo River a stone's throw from downtown, making it a good base. Room types range from dorms (mixed, female only) to private rooms—all with shared bath. There's also a shared kitchen and a library.

★ THE MILLENNIALS KYOTO

235 Yamazaki-chō, Nakagyō-ku; tel. 075/212-6887; www.themillennials.jp; single capsules from ¥2,800, adjoining capsules from ¥5,300; take Tōzai subway line to Sanjō Station, exit 6

The Millennials Kyoto is a hip "smart pod" (capsule hotel) aimed, as the name suggests, for young professionals on the go. Each "pod," just big enough to crawl in and comfortably crash, has a plug and USB socket, and its own iPod touch. There's a shared lounge, a shared workspace, and amenities including free Wi-Fi, free breakfast and coffee, and even free beer. Restrooms, showers, laundry facilities, and lavatories are all shared. If you're looking to mingle and don't mind sleeping in a capsule, this is a stylish option in a central location.

HOTEL GRAND BACH KYOTO SELECT

363 Naramono-chō, Shijō-dōri, Teramachi-nishiiru, Shimogyō-ku; tel. 075/221-2211; www.grandbach. co.jp/kyoto; doubles from ¥9,000; take Hankyū line to Kyoto-Kawaramachi Station, exit 11

This business hotel right in the center of things has a little more style than other digs in the same price range. Alongside spacious en-suite baths in all rooms, there's a gender-separated *sento* (public bath) on site. Japanese-style breakfast included. A great pick if proximity to sights and budget are high on your list. The hotel entrance is on Fuyachō-dōri.

¥10,000-20,000
CROSS HOTEL

71-1 Daikoku-chō, Kawaramachi-dōri Sanjō sagaru, Nakagyō-ku; tel. 075/231-8831; www.crosshotel.com/ kyoto; doubles from ¥12,000 with breakfast; take Keihan line to Sanjō Station or Tōzai subway line to Sanjō Keihan Station, exit 6

This chic, modern hotel smack in the heart of downtown is a great mid-range pick. The rooms are bright, clean, and while not massive, are larger than many similarly priced options. The bathrooms are well-appointed and roomy, with separated bath and toilet. The cheery staff are happy to help, and there's an appealing lounge with free coffee, as well as a bar. Breakfast is very decent, but you can safely pass on dinner.

★ IORI MACHIYA STAY RESIDENCE

various locations downtown; tel. 075/352-0211; www.
kyoto-machiya.com; from ¥13,000 pp

Iori Machiya Stay Residence offers the greatest range of *machiya* accommodations in Kyoto. An impressive 11 homes scattered around the downtown area, near the Kamo River's west bank, have been renovated to have all creature comforts, while retaining their original aesthetic character, with tatami floors, paper lanterns, alcoves housing scrolls and flower arrangements, and calligraphy. Some of the properties even boast private terraces overlooking the river. Alongside beautifully restored digs in the heart of downtown, a concierge service is also on call and is happy to answer any questions as well as arrange any number of experiences, from fine dining to the arts.

¥20,000-30,000
SOLARIA NISHITETSU HOTEL KYOTO PREMIER SANJŌ

509 Kamiosaka-chō, Kiyamachi-dōri Sanjō-agaru,
Nakagyō-ku; tel. 075/708-5757; http://solaria-kyoto.
nishitetsu-hotels.com; ¥24,000 d; take Tōzai subway
line to Kyoto Shiyakusho-Mae Station

Solaria Nishitetsu Hotel Kyoto Premier Sanjō opened in 2016 and is one of the city's best values. With a boutique feel, the property is smack in the middle of downtown, right next to the Kamo River. It commands stellar views of the river as well as the Higashiyama Mountains looming to the east. Rooms are well appointed, surprisingly chic for the price and quiet. The staff are friendly and speak English. A solid balance at a reasonable price.

¥30,000-40,0000
AOI HOTEL KYOTO

Reception at 145-1 Tenno-chō, Shimogyō-ku; tel.
075/354-7770; www.kyoto-stay.jp; doubles from
¥36,000; take Hankyū line to Kawaramachi stationto
reach reception

Aoi Hotel Kyoto is a great value. It has an excellent concierge service, and spacious rooms that are more akin to small studio apartments than to hotel rooms, with Japanese flourishes, including painted screens and flower arrangements. The hotel is right next to the Kamo River in the heart of downtown, within walking distance of heaps of good food options, nightlife, and a number of sights. Each room has ample amenities, including its own washer and dryer.

stay at Kyoto's Iori Machiya

Over ¥40,0000
KINMATA

Gokomachi, Shijō-agaru, Nakagyō-ku; tel. 075/221-1039; www.kinmata.com; ¥50,000 with 2 meals; take Hankyū line to Kawaramachi Station

Founded in 1801, this institution is both a high-end *ryokan* with seven Japanese-style rooms and a bastion of *kaiseki* dining (lunch ¥6,000-16,000, dinner ¥13,000-35,000). The *ryokan* rooms look the part: wooden interiors, opening onto an inner garden, tatami floors, and screens made of reed and paper. The restaurant is overseen by Chef Haraju Ukai, a seventh-generation culinary wizard. Classic, old-school, and exquisite.

AOI KYOTO STAY

Reception at 145-1 Tenno-chō, Shimogyō-ku; tel. 075/354-7770; www.kyoto-stay.jp; about ¥60,000 per night in each house; take Hankyū line to Kawaramachi station to reach reception (some properties offer pick-up service from Kyoto Station)

Run by the same folks who operate Aoi Hotel Kyoto, Aoi Kyoto Stay follows a similar concept, but extends it to the level of a house. Six phenomenal homes—most of them built in Kyoto's ubiquitous *machiya* townhouse style—dot the eastern side of the downtown area near Ponto-chō and the western bank of the Kamo River. Plush beds, heated floors, luxurious bathrooms, and tasteful Japanese décor give each residence an air of sophistication with an equal measure of comfort. If you want to stay downtown and price is no object, renting one of these homes will not disappoint.

HIIRAGIYA

Nakahakusan-chō, Fuyachō, Aneyakōji-agaru, Nakagyō-ku; tel. 075/221-1136; www.hiiragiya.co.jp; ¥34,000-90,000 pp with two meals; take Tōzai subway line to Kyoto Shiyakusho-mae Station, exit 8

While the vaunted Tawaraya *ryokan* across the road may be steeped in more mystique, the Hiiragiya is on par with its renowned neighbor and is, relatively speaking, easier to book.

From the outside, the inn looks exactly like you'd expect: earthen walls separate it from the street, with foliage poking over the top and black tiles on the roof. Inside, hushed tatami-mat rooms with sliding paper doors look onto private landscape gardens. Exquisite *kaisek ryori* meals are de rigueur, as is impeccable service. In a surprise twist, there is not only an old classic wing, but also a shiny modern one, offering a range of room types. Unlike at many of Kyoto's elite *ryokan,* is the staff here is accustomed to hosting visitors from abroad. To book a room, you'll need to submit a request online (in English) through the official website.

★ RITZ-CARLTON KYOTO

543 Hokoden-chō, Nijō-Ōhashi-hotori, Nakagyō-ku; tel. 075/746-5555; www.ritzcarlton.com; from ¥95,000; take Tōzai subway line to Kyoto Shiyakusho-mae Station

For an ideal balance of extravagance and convenience, the Ritz-Carlton Kyoto reigns supreme. It's right next to the western bank of the Kamo River in the center of the city, a bit north of the major artery of Nijō-dōri. It comes with all the sumptuous amenities you'd expect from this global luxury juggernaut. It also houses a fantastic *kaiseki ryōri* restaurant. Perhaps its biggest trait worthy of mention is that it blends in seamlessly with Kyoto's low-rise skyline.

NORTHWEST KYOTO
Under ¥10,000
SHUNKŌ-IN

42 Myōshinji-chō, Hanazono, Ukyō-ku; tel. 075/462-5488; www.shunkoin.com; ¥8,800 single, ¥7,500 double, ¥6,000 triple (all rates pp); take JR Sagano line to Hanazono Station

A chance to sleep in one of Kyoto's magnificent temples—well, at least in lodgings on its grounds. Bicycles and Wi-Fi are free, and the head priest speaks English, so guests can chance ask whatever they want to know about Zen.

Information and Services

TOURIST INFORMATION
Online Resources
Kyoto Travel Guide (www.kyoto.travel) is a great English-language resource online. The site introduces Kyoto's cuisine, culture, sights, neighborhoods, travel agents, and more. The **Deep Kyoto** (www.deepkyoto.com) blog unearths some of the city's hidden gems, from cafés to art exhibits. For inspiration both visual and written, head to the lush website of **Kyoto Journal** (https://kyotojournal.org), an award-winning nonprofit quarterly that's been going strong from the city since 1987. The staunchly independent magazine covers all of Asia but remains deeply rooted in its home, Kyoto. **Inside Kyoto** (www.inside-kyoto.com) is another great resource.

Information Centers
KYOTO TOURIST INFORMATION CENTER
2F Kyoto Station Building; tel. 075/343-0548; 8:30am-7pm daily

Your first port of call in Kyoto is the Kyoto Tourist Information Center on the second floor of Kyoto Station next to the entrance to Isetan department store. It's the best place in the city to pick up English-language materials pamphlets on the city's main attractions and maps of the extensive bus routes and guided walks. Be sure to pick up a copy of the **Kyoto Visitor's Guide** (www.kyotoguide.com), which gives a good rundown of sights, events, restaurants, and lodgings. Its English-language website is another great resource.

KYOTO INTERNATIONAL COMMUNITY HOUSE
2-1 Torii-chō, Awataguchi, Sakyō-ku; tel. 075/752-3010; www.kcif.or.jp; 9am-9pm Tues.-Sun.

Kyoto International Community House is located about 5 minutes' walk from Keage Station (exit 2) on the Tōzai subway line in Northern Higashiyama, a stone's throw from the sprawling temple realm of Nanzen-ji. This one-stop shop offers a library stocked with international periodicals, Internet access (¥200 for 30 minutes), a comfortable lounge, and a message board where people post accommodations information, calls for language exchange partners, flyers offering goods for sale, and more. Various classes on traditional arts, such as tea ceremony and calligraphy, are often hosted at the complex, too.

POSTAL SERVICES
KYOTO CENTRAL POST OFFICE
843-12 Higashishiokoji-chō, Shimogyō-ku; tel. 075/365-2471; 9am-9pm Mon.-Fri., 9am-7pm Sat.-Sun.

Kyoto Central Post Office is located just outside Kyoto Station's main exit on the north side. As soon as you leave the station, it will be the sixth-floor building fronted by rows of windows to the left.

PHARMACIES AND MEDICAL SERVICES
Pharmacies (*yakyoku*) are plentiful; simply look for the internationally recognizable red cross symbol out front. Call **AMDA International Medical Information Center**'s Osaka branch (tel. 050/3598-7574; http://eng.amda-imic.com; 9am-5pm Mon.-Fri.) for medical advice in the Kansai region, including Kyoto. The English-speaking operators are happy to help you navigate the Japanese medical system, referring you to doctors, hospitals, and so on.

If you need to visit a hospital, your best bet is **Kyoto University Hospital** (54 Shōgoin Kawahara-chō, Sakyō-ku; tel. 075/751-3111; www.kuhp.kyoto-u.ac.jp; 8:15am-11am Mon.-Fri. reception), located just east of the Kamo River in Northern Higashiyama. English-speaking assistance and quality of care are ensured here.

Also reliable, **Kyoto Prefectural Medical University Hospital** (Kawaramachi-Hirokoji, Kajii-chō, Kamigyō-ku; tel. 075/251-5111; www.kpu-m.ac.jp; 9am-3pm reception Mon.-Fri.), is located just west of the Kamo River next to Kyoto Imperial Palace. They offer English interpretation services from 9am-3pm on weekdays.

Transportation

GETTING THERE

If you're traveling to Kyoto from within Japan, the *shinkansen* (bullet train) is your best bet, particularly if you have a JR Pass. If you're coming from overseas and Kyoto is your first or only stop, there are also three airports within relatively easy reach, although none of them are actually in the city.

Air

The nearest flight hub to Kyoto is **Osaka International Airport** (tel. 06/6856-6781; www.osaka-airport.co.jp; information center 6:30am-9:30pm), also known as Itami Airport. Located roughly 50 minutes from the city by limousine bus, this hub is primarily a stop on domestic routes. But if you see a good flight deal that connects to the airport from another international airport in the country, don't hesitate. Some airlines offer connecting flights via Tokyo's Narita Airport. Flights from either Narita or Haneda Airport to Kansai International Airport (KIX) or Osaka International Airport (Itami) take about 1.5 hours and start from around ¥10,000 on budget airlines. Just be aware that you'll have to also pay for ground transport to Kyoto (bus, taxi, train) from the airport, and further, that travel times grow longer than taking the train with airport check-ins and ground transport.

Osaka Airport Transport (tel. 06/6844-1124; www.okkbus.co.jp; 55 minutes; ¥1,340) offers limousine bus services from the airport to Kyoto and vice versa. Tickets can be purchased from machines outside the arrivals area. **MK Taxi Sky Gate Shuttle** (tel. 075/778-5489; www.mk-group.co.jp; ¥3,000) will bring you directly to your lodgings. You'll have to share the journey with others staying elsewhere, so you may have a long ride if your stop is later in the route.

You can also fly directly to Osaka's **Kansai International Airport** (tel. 072/455-2500; www.kansai-airport.or.jp). Access to Kyoto is via express train via the **JR Haruka Airport Express** (80 minutes, ¥3,430). Note that this route is covered by the JR Pass. As with Osaka International Airport, Kansai International Airport is also serviced by Osaka Airport Transport (90 minutes; ¥2,600) and MK Taxi Sky Gate Shuttle (¥4,300). Finally, if you have a JR Pass and don't mind traveling by bullet train upon arrival, you can even consider flying into **Central Japan International Airport** (tel. 0569/38-1195; www.centrair.jp; 6:40am-10pm telephone center) in Nagoya. Although the distance between the two cities is 129 km (80 mi), the journey by bullet train from Nagoya to Kyoto—covered by the JR pass—is a mere 35 minutes (¥5,700).

Train

By far, the easiest way to reach Kyoto from Japan's other major transport hubs is the *shinkansen* (bullet train); from **Tokyo,** Nozomi trains (140 minutes; ¥14,170 reserved seat) and Hikari trains (160 minutes; ¥13,850 reserved seat) make the journey. Note that the JR Pass does not cover Nozomi trains.

From **Hiroshima,** take the Sakura *shinkansen* to Shin-Kobe Station, where you'll transfer to the Hikari *shinkansen* and travel the rest of the way to Kyoto Station (total trip: 1 hour 50 minutes; ¥11,100). Alternatively, if you're not using a JR Pass and don't mind paying out of pocket, you can also hop on the

Nozomi *shinkansen* and travel directly from Hiroshima Station to Kyoto Station (1 hour 40 minutes; ¥11,420).

From **Kobe,** take the Hikari *shinkansen* (30 minutes; ¥3,190), which departs from Shin-Kobe Station, which is covered by the JR Pass. A second option is the **Hankyu Kyoto/Kobe line,** which links Kobe-Sannomiya Station and Karasuma Station in downtown Kyoto with a transfer at Juso Station (70 minutes; ¥630).

Bus

Operators run buses during the daytime and overnight between **Tokyo** and Kyoto. The trip takes 7-8 hours one-way. One of the best-known operators is **Willer Express** (http://willerexpress.com), with fares from ¥4,000. Compare fares and book tickets via their website, **Japan Bus Online** (https://japanbusonline.com), or **Kosoku Bus** (www.kosokubus.com).

Car

It rarely makes sense to drive to Kyoto unless you happen to be traveling through Japan by car already and it's your only means of transport. The toll fees are not particularly cheap, reaching about ¥10,000 one-way. If you do happen to arrive in Kyoto in a rental car, visit www.parkme.com/kyoto-jp-parking to search for available **parking** spaces, rates, and more. Do not attempt to park along any random stretch of road, or in the lot of a business where you are not a paying customer, no matter how free a given space may look. Doing so could result in a fine.

GETTING AROUND

Some elements of Kyoto's public transport network leave a bit to be desired, at least compared to hyperconnected Tokyo: Only two subway lines run beneath the city. But aboveground trains also connect disparate parts of town, and Kyoto's easily navigable streets are ideally suited for getting around by bus, taxi, or better yet, on a bicycle or your own two feet.

As with anywhere in Japan, **prepaid IC cards** bought from ticket machines in both JR and non-JR railways stations (Suica cards, Pasmo cards, etc.) can be used across various transport networks in the city, from buses to the subway system. The local IC card variant purchased through JR stations in Kyoto is the Icoca. For an English-language **map** of the city's train and subway system, visit www.jr-pass.com/maps/map_kyoto_metro.pdf.

The city's streets can become crowded; jams are frequent during *hanami* season in late March and early April, as well as during the height of the *kōyō* (autumn leaves) season in November. Stick to subways and trains, or get around on a bicycle or on foot during these times to avoid getting stuck in a jam.

Bus

Originating from Kyoto Station, the green-striped **Kyoto City Bus** and red-striped **Kyoto Bus** companies serve different sections of the city. The bus system can be difficult to navigate, but it does have an extended reach, so buses can be useful when you need to reach sights that are not easily accessed by subway or train, are too far to reach by bicycle, or are too expensive to go by taxi.

Northwest Kyoto—home to sights like Ryōan-ji and Kinkaku-ji—is one part of the city that may call for a journey by bus. Likewise, sights dotting the area around Gingaku-ji in **Northern Higashiyama** are also best served by bus. That said, even these parts of town can be reached by train if you're willing to walk up to 10-30 minutes from the nearest station.

If you don't mind spending a bit of time puzzling out timetables and routes and you plan to use the bus system a lot, it's worth investing in a special bus pass (adults ¥600, children ¥300), sold at the **Kyoto City Bus & Subway Information Center** (tel. 075/371-4474; 7:30am-7:30pm), found just outside the central exit of Kyoto Station. Activate your pass by inserting it into the slot in the payment machine next to the driver's seat of all buses as you exit. The one-day bus pass covers unlimited rides on both Kyoto City Bus and Kyoto Bus routes for a day. If you plan to get around by bus, remember to pick up an English-language bus map (Bus Navi: Kyoto City Bus Sightseeing Map) at the Kyoto Bus Information Center or at any tourist information center around town.

To take a single journey, enter through the back door and pay upon exiting via the front of the bus. Fares within the city are generally a flat ¥230 (children ages 6-12 ¥120, children under 6 free), but go up for longer distances. Fares can be paid either with coins or any one of the types of IC cards available in Japan.

As its name suggests, the **K'Loop** (tel. 075/661-1234; http://kloop.jp; ¥500 adults one-day, ¥200 children one-day, 9am-6pm Mon.-Fri. call center) sightseeing bus makes a loop around the city, hitting a number of highlights (Kiyomizu-dera, Ginkaku-ji, Kinkaku-ji, Nijō-jō, etc.). Note that it only operates on Sat., Sun., and holidays.

Subway

Kyoto has an efficient if limited subway system, with the **Karasuma line** running north-south and the **Tōzai line** running east-west. The Karasuma line is named after the city's main north-south artery, Karasuma-dōri, under which the subway runs. This line passes through key stations downtown like Shijō and Karasuma-Oike. Sights near the Karasuma line include Daitoku-ji and Kyoto Imperial Palace. At Karasuma-Oike, you'll find the Karasuma line's junction with the Tōzai line, which brings you within easy reach of Nijō-jō in the west, and Gion and southern Higashiyama in the east.

Single journeys on the subway start from ¥210 (children ¥110). One-day unlimited subway passes (adults ¥600, children ¥300) are sold at subway station ticket windows and through ticket machines. The Kyoto Subway & Bus Pass allows you to hop on both subway lines and buses an unlimited number of times for one day (adults ¥900, children ¥450) or two days (adults ¥1,700, children ¥850). You can pick up one of these passes at the Kyoto City Bus & Subway Information Center, at

any commuter pass sales counter, or at the ticket window of any subway station. This pass doesn't cover rides on any of the aboveground train lines.

Train

Trains run by JR and a number of private operators serve Kyoto. The subway and bus systems provide more direct access to various sights and corners of the city, but a few areas—particularly the southeast around Tōfoku-ji and Fushimi Inari-Taisha (**JR Nara line**), and the sight-rich area of Arashiyama in the west (Sagano line)—are conveniently reached by train. The **Keifuku line** (aka **Randen line**) is essentially a sightseeing train that links Arashiyama in the west to the area in the city's northwest near Kinkaku-ji and Ryōan-ji.

Bicycle

Kyoto feels tailor-made for cycling. Its mostly flat, grid-pattern streets and the path-lined Kamo River burbling through the eastern half of town beg to be explored by bicycle. Many major sights have designated bicycle parking lots. Orderly traffic and a glut of bicycle rental shops make this an even more appealing proposition.

Before hiring a bicycle from a specialized rental shop, check to see if your accommodation happens to provide bike rentals for guests. Daily rentals typically cost ¥1,000-1,500 for standard city bikes, while paying around ¥2,000 will often get you an electrically assisted one, which can come in handy if you plan to go into any of the hillier districts dotting the eastern edges of town. **Cycle Kyoto** and **Kyoto Cycling Tour Project** are reliable rental options.

A few more thoughts to consider before pedaling through Kyoto's streets: It's illegal to park your bike in a spot that is not specifically a bicycle parking area. Illegally parked bicycles are routinely picked up in city-run sweeps. If your bicycle is gone after you've left it on a stretch of sidewalk outside a café or leaning against some random building, it's quite likely been impounded. If you experience this unfortunate fate, look for a paper affixed somewhere near where you parked your bicycle and use the map on it to make your way to where it's being kept. You'll typically pay ¥2,000 to get your bike back.

To avoid this fate, stick to parking your bike only in specifically designated bicycle lots outside major sights, train or bus stations. Or, leave it at one of the large parking lots found around town. A good example is the **Kyoto Wings** lot, found north of Daimaru department store in the heart of downtown, near the intersection of Takoyakushi-dōri and Higashinotoin-dōri. You can leave your bike here for ¥150 per day. For an extensive list of bicycle parking lots, which will keep you on the right side of the law, view the **map** at the bottom of this page: www.cyclekyoto.com/bicycle-parking.

Be aware that there are certain stretches of downtown Kyoto where it's illegal to ride a bicycle. For a detailed breakdown of exactly where you should not ride a bicycle, go to www.cyclekyoto.com/areas-to-avoid.

Taxi

Taking taxis is normally not advisable for those on a budget in Japan. Kyoto bucks this trend. The city is blessed with an over-abundance of taxis, and relatively short distances between sights ensures that most fares won't climb much above a few thousand yen. Thanks to Kyoto's thriving tourism industry, most drivers speak a smattering of English. There are now foreigner-friendly taxis plying the avenues of Kyoto with English-speaking drivers. There's a stand in front of the **Kyoto Century Hotel,** just outside Kyoto Station's central exit, to the right, specifically reserved for these English-friendly cabs.

Kansai 関西

Japan, in a sense, is bipolar. Its modern heart is, without a doubt, in Tokyo. Go deeper into the past, however, and Kansai is the cultural birthplace of the nation, from which the very notion of Japanese-ness emerged. This dichotomy is felt in daily life, with reality TV shows and books expounding on subtle differences in customs between the politically, economically, and pop-culturally mightier pole of Kantō (Greater Tokyo) and the historically rich region of Kansai a few hours by *shinkansen* (bullet train) to the west. There's very much a Kansai versus Kantō rivalry in Japan (think New York versus Los Angeles), with Kansai denizens—of whom there are about 22 million—known for their fierce local pride.

Kansai takes up a coast-to-coast chunk of the bottom third of

Highlights

Look for ★ to find recommended sights, activities, dining, and lodging.

★ **Dōtombori:** Eat yourself into a state of ruin on this famed food street, where fried, fatty, carbohydrate-laden goodies are sold by the plate, bowl, and skewer (page 303).

★ **Tōdai-ji:** The Buddhist temple known as Tōdai-ji, one of the largest wooden structures in the world, contains an awe inspiring 15-meter (49-foot) bronze statue of Buddha (page 310).

★ **Jazz in Kobe:** Experience this city's sophisticated and historic nightlife scene at one of its renowned jazz haunts (page 321).

★ **Himeji-jō:** This soaring white fortress is an architectural reminder of a time when Japan was under the rule of ruthless feudal lords (page 325).

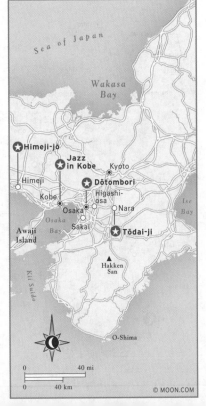

© MOON.COM

Kansai

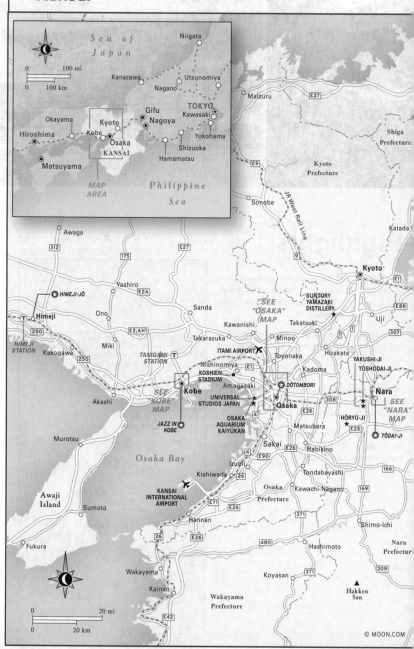

Sea of Japan

Niigata

Kanazawa
Utsunomiya

Nagano

Okayama
Gifu
Nagoya
TOKYO
Kawasaki

Hiroshima
Kyoto
Kobe
Osaka
KANSAI
Yokohama

Matsuyama
Shizuoka
Hamamatsu

MAP AREA

Philippine Sea

Maizuru E27

Shiga Prefecture

Kyoto Prefecture

Sonobe

JR West Rail Line

Katada

Awaga

312   175   E27

Yashiro
E2A

HIMEJI-JŌ

Himeji

Ono

Sanda
Kawanishi

Takarazuka

SEE "OSAKA" MAP

SUNTORY YAMAZAKI DISTILLERY

Takatsuki

Kyoto   E1

E88

Uji

307

HIMEJI STATION

Kakogawa
250

Miki

TANIGAMI STATION

250

Akashi

E2; AH1

Minoo

ITAMI AIRPORT

Toyonaka

Nishinomiya
E1

KOSHIEN STADIUM

Kobe

SEE "KOBE" MAP

Amagasaki

UNIVERSAL STUDIOS JAPAN

DŌTOMBORI

Osaka

E26

Hirakata

Kadoma

YAKUSHI-JI
TŌSHŌDAI-JI

Nara

SEE "NARA" MAP

308

HŌRYŪ-JI
E25

TŌDAI-JI

JAZZ IN KOBE

OSAKA AQUARIUM KAIYŪKAN

4

Matsubara

Murotsu

Sakai

4

E90

Habikino

Osaka Bay

Izumi

E26

Kishiwada

26

Tondabayashi

166

Osaka Prefecture

Kawachi-Nagano

169

KANSAI INTERNATIONAL AIRPORT

E71

E26

371

Awaji Island

Sumoto

Hannan

26

E26

480

Shimo-Ichi

Nara Prefecture

Fukura

Hashimoto

309

Wakayama

Koyasan

371

Hakken San

Kainan

E42

Wakayama Prefecture

© MOON.COM

Honshu, Japan's largest island. While Kyoto is technically in Kansai, the nearby cities of Osaka, Kobe, and Nara to the south make up the region's core, and are all within a short train ride of the ancient capital. A few short jaunts around the area add a dash of zest to the rarefied offerings of Kyoto.

The urban nucleus of the region, Osaka is a garish, boisterous, smaller-scale alternative to Tokyo. The city is famous for its decadent dishes, such as *takoyaki* (fried octopus dumplings) and *okonomiyaki,* a savory pancake stuffed with cabbage, meat, or seafood, and topped with all manner of sauces, fish flakes, mayonnaise, and more. To the west of Osaka, about 30 minutes by train, Kobe is a sophisticated city set between green hills and the Inland Sea. Notably more pleasing to the eye than Osaka, Kobe invites visitors to become urban explorers. Farther west still from Kobe, the city of Himeji is home to what is perhaps Japan's most recognizable castle, the soaring white fortress of Himeji-jō.

For a further look into to the region's past, turn to Nara, Japan's first permanent capital. A half-hour express train ride south of Kyoto and about an hour east of Osaka by train, Nara's main draw is Nara-kōen, a large park home to some 1,200 deer, and Tōdai-ji, a wooden temple with an awe-inspiring statue of Buddha.

ORIENTATION

Kansai accounts for a large part of Western Honshu. The cities covered in this chapter are mostly within quick reach of Kyoto, south of the ancient capital, from east to west: Nara, Osaka, Kobe, and Himeji. More specifically, **Nara** is about 40 km (25 mi) south of Kyoto; **Osaka** is about 50 km (31 mi) southwest of Kyoto and 35 km (22 mi) west of Nara; **Kobe** is around 30 km (19 mi) west of Osaka and 70 km (43 mi) southwest of Kyoto; and **Himeji** is roughly another 60 km (37 mi) west of Kobe. Geographically, Nara is bounded by mountains roughly 40 km (25 mi) inland from Osaka Bay to the west, while Osaka sprawls across a vast alluvial plain that fans out from Osaka Bay. Farther west, Kobe is wedged between Osaka Bay, where it operates a bustling port, and verdant mountains just behind downtown, while downtown Himeji sits about 5 km (3 mi) north of the Inland Sea.

PLANNING YOUR TIME

Most destinations in Kansai are best viewed as add-ons to Kyoto, given their proximity to the ancient capital. Otherwise, consider spending a few nights in a particular city or historical or cultural spot if it interests you and you have time to spare.

Plan to spend anywhere from a half day to two days in each of Kansai's hubs. **Osaka** and **Nara** are best as day trips, or you could visit Osaka just for dinner and drinks. Osaka, in the middle of the other main destinations, makes a good base for exploring the region, conveniently near **Nara,** as well as **Kobe** and **Himeji,** only about 30-40 minutes apart by train—you could even see both in one long day. If you have more time, Kobe is a pleasing place to stay the night, heading to Himeji the next day.

The most pleasant times of year to visit Kansai are in **spring** (Mar.-May) and **fall** (Oct.-Nov.). That said, **summer** (June-mid-Sept.) and **winter** (Dec.-Feb.) are not so extreme that it makes travel unwise. In the summer, be prepared to endure temperatures upward of 30°C (86°F) and patches of rainfall from mid-June through July; and in winter, lows of about 3-5°C (37-41°F) with the occasional dump of snow.

KANSAI

Where to Go from Kyoto

Destination	Why Go?	Getting There from Kyoto	Getting There from Hiroshima	How Long to Stay
Osaka	garish lights, greasy food, and fun; savory *okonomiyaki* pancakes; dough balls stuffed with octopus (*takoyaki*)	Train: 15-45 minutes, ¥570-¥2,660	Train: 1 hour 40 minutes, ¥10,220	One day
Nara	Tōdai-ji, the world's largest wooden structure, with the Great Buddha; Nara-kōen, a sprawling park with legions of deer; escaping the crowds	Train: 35 minutes-1 hour, ¥720-1,160	Train: 2 hours 40 minutes, ¥11,160	One day
Kobe	19th-century European-style architecture; urban walks; slower pace; Kobe beef; a buzzing jazz scene	Train: 30 minutes-1 hour, ¥1,100-3,190	Train: 1.5 hours, ¥10,000	Half day
Himeji	the best surviving example of a feudal castle in Japan	Train: 55 minutes-1 hour 40 minutes, ¥2,310-5,170	Train: 1 hour 10 minutes, ¥8,240	Half day

Itinerary Ideas

A WEEKEND IN OSAKA AND NARA

Day 1: Osaka

1 Before tromping through Osaka's array of colorful neighborhoods at street level, first behold the city's vastness from above with a trip to **Umeda Sky Building** in the city's Kita (north) side, which opens at 10am.

2 Walk to nearby ramen shop **Mitsuka Bose Kamoshi,** one of the best bowls of noodles in Osaka, for an early lunch before the office worker lunch rush.

3 Hop on the Midō-suji line at Umeda Station and ride south to Shinsaibashi, the northern gateway to the city's Minami (south) side. Grab a coffee at **Lilo Coffee Roasters.**

4 Walk south toward **Triangle Park** in the heart of youth culture mecca Amerika-mura. Spend your afternoon here and in the stylish nearby Horie district a couple of blocks southwest, people-watching and popping into shops.

5 Continue south to the Dōtombori-gawa canal. Walk along the river's northern bank until you reach **Ebisu-bashi,** the famous bridge at the heart of Dōtombori. Join the throngs taking selfies in front of the famous Glico "running man" billboard.

6 Cross the bridge and enter the famed Dōtombori arcade proper. As dusk sets, this strip becomes a surreal neon-soaked realm. Also stop by **Hōzen-ji,** an enigmatic temple in the heart of a consumerist frenzy.

7 Eat dinner in Dōtombori. Your choices are endless. *Okonomiyaki* is a very safe bet and an Osaka classic—try **Chibō.**

8 If you still have energy, explore Minami's nightlife. In Amerika-mura, try **Bar Nayuta** for a good cocktail.

Day 2: Nara

1 Aim to arrive at either JR Nara Station or Kintetsu-Nara Station around 10am. Take in views of Kōfuku-ji, a temple beside a pond known for its soaring pagoda, on your way to the beautiful garden **Isui-en.**

2 Walk northeast about 10 minutes to **Tōdai-ji,** one of Japan's most awesome sights.

3 Walk about 15 minutes south to **Le Case** for lunch. They serve great quiche.

4 Continue south from the restaurant to **Kasuga Taisha,** Nara's most important shrine. Set in a forest teeming with deer, this shrine's grounds beg to be slowly explored. After entering the shrine's main hall, spend some time wandering on the surrounding paths, flanked by myriad stone lanterns.

5 Gradually make your way west, crossing through the center of **Nara-kōen.** After walking about 20 minutes, you'll exit the west side of the park and find yourself back at Kōfuku-ji; look for its looming pagoda.

6 For dinner, try the excellent *izakaya* fare at **Kura** before returning to where you're staying via JR Nara Station or Kintetsu-Nara Station.

HIMEJI AND KOBE IN ONE DAY

1 Start your day in Himeji, aiming to arrive at stunning **Himeji-jō** by 10am—the earlier the better to dodge the crowds.

2 After exploring what is perhaps Japan's most beautiful castle and its grounds, hop on the train for Sannomiya, Kobe's bustling core, where you'll be spoiled for choice of lunch spots. **Grill Jūjiya** serves nostalgic Western food with a Japanese twist.

3 Make your way down to **Port of Kobe Earthquake Memorial Park,** passing through Chinatown on the way. This park gives a sense of the destruction caused by the 1995 earthquake, and the seaside promenade is peppered with benches if you're in need of a rest.

4 Hop back on the train a few stops to Shin-Kobe Station and walk north. You'll find

Osaka and Nara Itinerary Ideas

To
Umeda Sky Building
and Mitsuka Bose Kamoshi

YOTSUBASHISUJI

Shinsaibashi

Yotsubashi

Shinsaibashi

AMERIKA-MURA

YAOYAMACHISUJI

DOTOMBORI

Namba

NIPPOMBASHI

NAMBA

KITA   MIYAKOJIMA

JOTO

FUKUSHIMA   OSAKA
MAP AREA

NISHI   CHUO

HIGASHINARI

NANIWA

TAISHO   TENNOJI

IKUNO
WARD

NISHINARI

DAY ONE: OSAKA

1 Umeda Sky Building
2 Mitsuka Bose Kamoshi
3 Lilo Coffee Roasters
4 Triangle Park
5 Ebisu-bashi
6 Hōzen-ji
7 Chibō
8 Bar Nayuta

DAY TWO: NARA

1 Isui-en
2 Tōdai-ji
3 Le Case
4 Kasuga Taisha
5 Nara-kōen
6 Kura

0   500 ft.
0   100 m

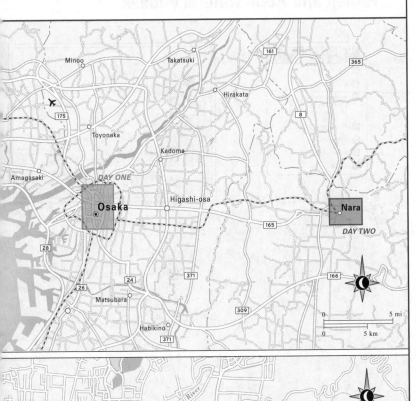

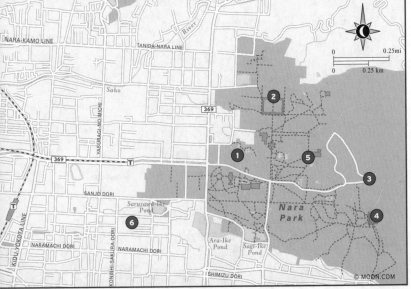

© MOON.COM

Himeji and Kobe Itinerary Ideas

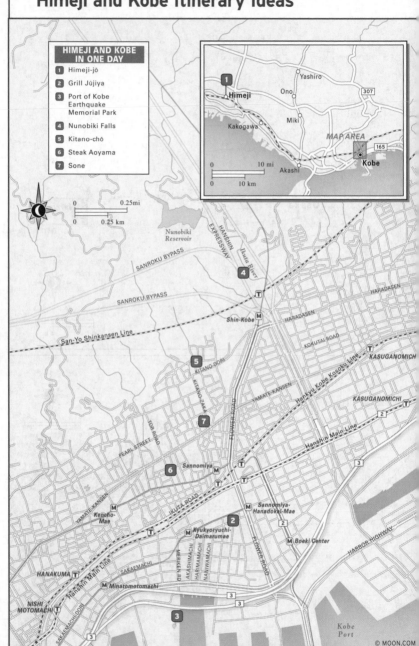

yourself at the foot of a forested slope. Walk along the steep path for about 400 meters (1,312 feet) until you reach the sublime **Nunobiki Falls,** which have inspired poets and artists for centuries.

5 Backtrack toward Shin-Kobe Station, walking southwest to the historic hilltop neighborhood of **Kitano-chō.** Amble through this upscale hillside neighborhood, dotted by elegant Western-style *ijinkan* ("foreigner's houses") that were once lived in by Kobe's well-heeled early foreign transplants.

6 Treat yourself to Kobe's famed beef for dinner at **Steak Aoyama.**

7 Finish off the evening by catching a show at legendary live jazz joint **Sone.**

Osaka   大阪

A concrete jungle in the truest sense, Osaka can't claim to be beautiful. But it exerts a strange kind of magnetism, emanating from Osaka-jō in the center of town, vast shopping arcades and entertainment centers in the south, and the bay on the west side of town where you'll find Universal Studios Japan and a massive aquarium. The beating heart of the city is in the area surrounding the large canal, Dōtombori-gawa, running through the south side of town, the domain of an army of street-food vendors, rowdy bars, and loudly dressed, disarmingly friendly locals who know how to have a good time.

Japan's third-largest city, Osaka is fundamentally a place of commerce that has been the region's economic core since the Edo period (1603-1868). Shunning pleasantries, the greeting shared by dyed-in-the-wool Osakans is "*mōkari makka?*" ("making any money?"). The cash does indeed flow into this bustling city, with Panasonic and Sharp among the commercial giants based here. Among its many monikers, Osaka has been called the City of Water and the City of 1,000 Bridges, alluding to the network of rivers crisscrossing the city that has long served as the circulatory system shipping goods in and out of this vast commercial organism.

Despite its reputation as a place for earning, Osaka remains notably cheaper than Tokyo or Kyoto. Instead of breaking the bank at a high-end sushi counter in Ginza or slowly savoring a rarefied *kaiseki* feast in a Kyoto townhouse,

in Osaka you'll more likely be standing in a street eating fried balls of battered octopus on a stick while kicking back a beer.

Similarly, Osaka's entertainment is of the earthy variety. Since *rakugo* (humorous storytelling) was born in the city in the Edo period, the city has been the center of Japan's comedy scene, from slapstick to saucy. All told, the city's food, drinking dens, and earthy locals add up to a fun, colorful escape from Kyoto when the temples all start to look the same. Beyond this, Osaka is an exciting city in its own right and begs to be experienced by insatiable urban explorers and gourmands with a taste for the deep-fried side of life.

ORIENTATION

The easiest way to get the lay of the land in Osaka is to think of it on a north-south axis. Buttoned-down **Kita** (north) Osaka encompasses the vast business district of Umeda, as well as Osaka and Shin-Osaka stations. The fun, chaotic image most associated with Osaka comes from the flashy **Minami** (south) side of town. Here, the vast shopping and entertainment districts of **Shinsaibashi, Dōtombori, Namba,** and **Amerika-mura** exude a hedonistic air. Shops and cafés rule the daylight hours, while food, drink, and entertainment in all its forms take center stage at night.

Osaka is split by many rivers. Its most prominent is the **Yodo River,** which hems in the northern edge of the city, flowing to the

Best Restaurants

★ **Ganso Kushikatsu Daruma Honten:** Discover the joys of nibbling just about any food item you can fathom skewered on a stick, breaded, and deep-fried at this greasy-spoon Osaka-favorite *kushikatsu* restaurant (page 298).

★ **Takotako King Honten:** Munch on fried balls of dough stuffed with bits of octopus meat at this boisterous bar-cum-*takoyaki* shop in Osaka (page 300).

★ **Ajinoya:** Come to this restaurant, just off the tourist trail, to sample Osaka's savory pancake dish known as *okonomiyaki* (page 300).

★ **Steak Aoyama:** Find out what all the fuss is about surrounding Kobe beef at this intimate, friendly family-owned steak restaurant, serving melt-in-your-mouth *wagyu* since 1963 (page 321).

REGIONAL SPECIALTIES

In Osaka, you'll find *okonomiyaki,* a savory pancake stuffed with cabbage, meat, and seafood and sprinkled with green onion; *takoyaki,* essentially a savory fried spherical donut containing hunks of octopus; and *kushikatsu,* or skewers of meat and vegetables that have been battered and deep-fried. Nearby, the port city of Kobe is known worldwide for the quality of its highly marbled beef, popularly known as *wagyu,* a term that refers to all forms of Japanese beef.

north of Umeda. Another river of note is the **Ō River,** which diverts southwest from the Yodo River and runs just past the northwestern corner of the grounds of **Osaka-jō.** Boats congregate along this stretch of water during the city's great summertime bash, the Tenjin Matsuri. Meanwhile, the concrete-canalled **Dōtombori River** runs through the heart of the pedestrian district of the same name in the south side of town.

SIGHTS
Kita
UMEDA SKY BUILDING
梅田スカイビル

1-1-88 Ōyodonaka, Kita-ku; tel. 06/6440-3855 (for Kuchu Teien); www.kuchu-teien.com; 9:30am-10:30pm (last entry 10pm) daily; adults ¥1,500, children ages 4-12 ¥700; 10 minutes' walk northwest from JR Osaka Station's north central gate, or 10 minutes' walk west from Umeda Station

One of Osaka's most impressive buildings, the Umeda Sky Building was once declared to be the "triumphal arch of the future." Whether triumphal or not, the structure certainly has

a futuristic layout, with a "floating garden" called the **Kuchu Teien** ("Garden in the Sky") on the 39th-41st floors. This is the place for striking views of the mammoth cityscape, with both outdoor and indoor observatories. Come during the evening when the city becomes a vast sea of lights. Buy tickets to the Kuchu Teien on the ticket counter on the 39th floor. You can reach the building either aboveground or via a well-marked underground walkway.

OSAKA-JŌ
大坂城

1-1 Osaka-jō, Chūō-ku; tel. 06/6941-3044; www.osakacastle.net; 9am-5pm (last entry 4:30pm) daily; grounds free, adults ¥600 or ¥1,000 combined with Osaka Museum of History, children under 15 free inside keep; take Tanimachi or Chūō subway line to Tanimachi 4-Chōme Station, or JR Loop line to Osaka-jō-kōen Station

The warlord Toyotomi Hideyoshi, Japan's great unifier of the 16th century, directed 100,000 laborers to construct his imposing castle, Osaka-jō. Even today, it looms over

Best Accommodations

★ **Intercontinental Osaka:** Perhaps Osaka's best hotel, the Intercontinental is top-notch in all respects, from the views and dining to its prime location (page 303).

★ **Edosan:** This family-owned *ryokan* in the heart of Nara-kōen has long been favored by artists as a soul-nourishing escape (page 313).

★ **Nara Hotel:** Luminaries like Albert Einstein and the Dalai Lama have slept at this historic property and wandered through its enchanting grounds (page 314).

★ **Oriental Hotel:** One of Japan's first hotels, this rebuilt waterfront tower offers a first-rate experience and stunning views of Kobe's appealing cityscape (page 323).

the eastern side of the city, dramatically illuminated at night.

Originally completed in 1583, the castle was soon after sacked by the forces of Tokugawa Ieyasu, the first shogun of the Tokugawa Shogunate, in 1614. Ieyasu simply rebuilt it block by block, ensuring its fortitude with even larger stones, each weighing up to 100 tonnes (110 tons), studding its wall. In 1931, citizens raised money to reconstruct the main tower. After being razed by bombing during World War II, the main structure was later refurbished in 1995. Thirteen structures from the 17th-century version built by Ieyasu remain in place. Even the concrete reproductions have enough visual oomph to make the castle one of Osaka's biggest draws.

The complex towers over a 106-hectare (262-acre) park that comes vividly alive in spring with the cherry blossoms. It's an excellent place to stroll or have a picnic. Inside the castle, there are displays with information about Osaka's history, the castle, and original builder Hideyoshi on the lower floors, and on the top floor, there's an observation deck looking over the eastern side of the city.

Minami

Less a place to take in sights than a neighborhood to people-watch and gawk at seemingly endless shopping arcades bathed in neon lights, Minami rewards aimless strolling.

EBISU-BASHI

1-6 Dōtonbori, Chūō-ku; 24 hours daily; free

This bridge straddling the Dōtombori-gawa is ground zero for Osaka's Minami (south) side. Tourists jostle for a spot in front of candy maker Glico's **Running Man** neon billboard hovering in the backdrop, and the area's famed deep-fried food zone starts from the south side of the bridge. Come here to feel the city's thrum and gawp at the neon light dancing in the intensely urbanized waterway below.

HŌZEN-JI
法善寺

1-2-16 Namba, Chūō-ku; tel. 06/6211-4152; http://houzenji.jp; 24 hours daily; free; take Midō-suji subway line to Namba Station, exit B-16

Walk two blocks south of the main culinary thoroughfare to a small atmospheric lane known as **Hōzen-ji Yokochō,** where you'll find Hōzen-ji, a temple frequented by those working in the *mizu shōbai* ("water trade"), as the sensual realm of nightlife is known. Peek inside the temple to see the moss-encrusted statue of the esoteric Buddhist deity Fudō Myō-ō.

TSŪTEN-KAKU
通天閣

1-18-6 Ebisu-higashi, Naniwa-ku; tel. 06/6641-9555; www.tsutenkaku.co.jp; 8:30am-9:30pm (last entry 9pm) daily; adults ¥800, junior high school and

Osaka

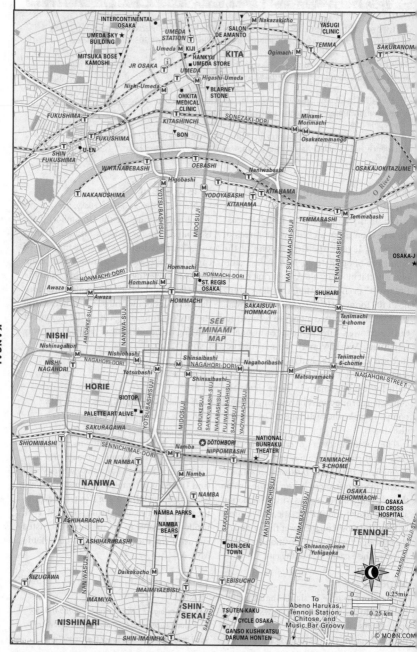

Minami

YOTSUBASHISUJI

Shinsaibashi
Ⓜ

Nagahoribashi
Ⓜ

NAGAHORI-DORI

Yotsubashi
Ⓜ

Shinsaibashi
Ⓜ

▼LILO COFFEE
ROASTERS

CAFE
ABSINTHE
▼

HOTEL
NIKKO
OSAKA
●

CLUB
CIRCUS

DOBUIKESUJI

SANKYŪBASHI-SUJI

NAKABASHISUJI

FUJINAKABASHISUJI

SAKAISUJI

YAOYAMACHISUJI

MIDŌ-SUJI

SHINSAIBASHI-SUJI

HOTEL
FELICE SHINSAIBASHI
BY RELIEF
●

TRIANGLE
PARK
■

BAR
NAYUTA
▼

MOMEN
▼

AMERIKA-MURA

CINQUENCENTO
▼

TAKOTAKO KING
HONTEN
▼

FARPLANE
▼

CROSS
HOTEL
OSAKA
●

EBISU-
BASHI

GANSO KUSHIKATSU
DARUMA HONTEN

✪DŌTOMBORI
★

Dotonbori   River

DOTONBORI
HOTEL
●

CHIBŌ
▼

EBISU-BASHI-SUJI

DŌTOMBORI

AJINOYA
▼

HŌZEN-JI
★

Namba
Ⓜ
Ⓣ

OSAKA NAMBA STATION
(KINTETSU/HANSHIN LINES)

NIPPOMBASHI
Ⓣ

NAMBA

Ⓜ Namba

MISONO
BUILDING
▼

KUROMON
ICHIBA
▼

ℹ

USHITORA
▼

DOGUYA-SUJI

NANKAI NAMBA
STATION
Ⓣ

FRASER RESIDENCE
NANKAI OSAKA
●

0   500 ft

0   100 m

© MOON.COM

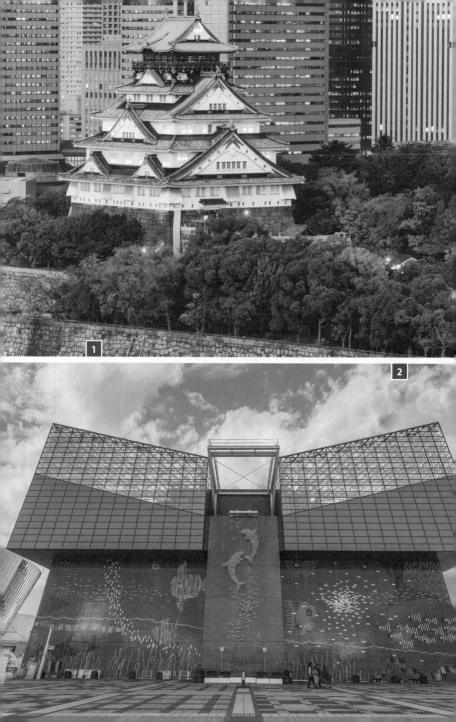

elementary school students ¥400, children under 5 free; take Sakai-suji subway line to Ebisu-chō Station, exit 3, or take Midō-suji subway line to Dōbutsuen-mae Station, exit 5

At 103 meters (338 feet) tall, this nostalgia-inducing tower stands in the heart of the tumbledown zone of Shin-Sekai, inspired in its layout by a mix of Paris and Coney Island. Originally built in 1912, it was once the second tallest tower in all of Asia at a mere 63 meters (207 feet). After being damaged by fire during World War II, it was rebuilt in 1956. Today, it has a fifth-floor viewing deck at 91 meters (299 feet) and an open-air one above that. An admitted eyesore, it is nonetheless a symbol of Osaka, similar in spirit to Tokyo Tower. This is not where the similarities between these two steel behemoths ends: Both were dreamed up by architect Tachū Naitō, who modeled them after the Eiffel Tower. Be forewarned: A show employing a captive monkey is sometimes held in the entrance area. If you feel squeamish about such spectacles, consider viewing the tower from the outside, and skip the observation deck.

ABENO HARUKAS
あべのハルカス

1-1-43 Abenosuji, Abeno-ku; tel. 06/6621-0300; www.abenoharukas-300.jp; 9am-10pm daily; adults ¥1,500, ages 12-17 ¥1,200, ages 6-11 ¥700, ages 4-5 ¥500; take Midō-suji, Tanimachi subway lines or JR Loop line to Tennoji Station, or take Kintetsu Minami Osaka line to Osaka-Abenobashi Station

A southern answer to the Umeda Sky Building in the city's north, the towering Abeno Harukas complex is Japan's tallest skyscraper at 300 meters (984 feet) and houses Osaka's highest observation deck, Harukas 300. Designed by Argentine-American architect Cesar Pelli of Petronas Towers fame, this hulking monolith in the southern hub of Tennoji is at the center of an urban renaissance sweeping through what was previously considered a dingy, dated side of town, giving the name Harukas ("clear up" or "brighten")

added meaning. Another good choice for jaw-dropping views of the urban sprawl.

The lower portion of the vast complex houses the **Kintetsu department store** (B2-14th floor; https://abenoharukas.d-kintetsu.co.jp; 10am-8pm daily), Japan's largest, including three stories of restaurants (12th-14th floors; 10am-11pm daily).

Osaka Bay Area
OSAKA AQUARIUM KAIYŪKAN
海遊館

1-1-10 Kaigan-dōri, Minato-ku; tel. 06/6576-5501; www.kaiyukan.com; 10am-8pm (last entry 7pm) daily; adults ¥2,300, ages 7-15 ¥1,200, ages 4-6 ¥600, ages 3 and under free; take Chūō subway line to Osakako Station

This excellent aquarium shows off the wildly diverse sea life of the Pacific Ring of Fire, from Antarctica and the Arctic to the Aleutian Islands, Monterey Bay in California, the Gulf of Panama, the Ecuadorian jungle, the Great Barrier Reef, and more. It is one of the world's largest aquariums, and its centerpiece is a massive tank that is large enough to accommodate a whale shark. Other residents of this impressive complex include bizarre jellyfish, penguins, manta rays, sea lions, coralfish, and many more.

Though the impact of coronavirus has thinned crowds, the aquarium has historically been notoriously packed on weekends. At the time of writing, the aquarium was only admitting visitors on a timed admission basis. All tickets must be bought online up to five days in advance and can only be used to enter at the set date and time. Should its entrance policy return to normal, visit on a weekday morning or evening to avoid the rush.

ENTERTAINMENT AND EVENTS
Bunraku

If you're going to watch one traditional performance in Osaka, make it *bunraku*. This singular form of puppet theater involves fully visible puppeteers dressed all in black, controlling the nearly life-size puppets onstage.

1: Osaka-jō **2:** Osaka Aquarium Kaiyūkan

Minami's Nightlife Zones

Minami, the southern part of Osaka that contains its garish, neon-lit nightlife districts, is vast. For the purposes of this book, it encompasses the large swath of the city between **Shinsaibashi Station** in the north down to **Tennoji Station,** roughly 4 km (2.5 mi) southwest of there. Hemming all of this in at the northern border is the major east-west thoroughfare of **Nagahori-dōri,** which is bisected by the north-south artery of **Midō-suji.**

SHINSAIBASHI
心斎橋

Calm by day, this large neighborhood along the north bank of the Dōtombori-gawa, sprawling south of Nagahori-dōri, shows its real face when the sun sets and its warren of bars, hostess clubs and restaurants comes to life. On any given evening, touts in flamboyant attire stand on the corners, while hostesses in cocktail dresses banter with businessmen using corporate expense accounts to cover lavishly priced drinks. Also roaming these streets are groups of 20-somethings on pub crawls and clubbers heading to the city's best music venues.

To reach Shinsaibashi, take the Midō-suji subway line to **Shinsaibashi Station.** Otherwise, if you're already in neighboring Dōtombori, simply cross any one of the bridges over the Dōtombori-gawa to Shinsaibashi just to the north.

AMERIKA-MURA
アメリカ村

Directly west of Shinsaibashi, Amerika-mura is an enclave of tattoo parlors, love hotels, and shops hawking everything from curios to street fashion. It occupies a number of blocks just west of the major above-ground traffic artery of **Midō-suji,** a few blocks north of Dōtombori and its namesake canal to the south. It's named for the brisk business selling U.S.-made goods in this area in the postwar years. It's an interesting place to wander and see what flavor of the month the pierced, hair-dyed youth of Osaka are into, with lots of bars and restaurants dotting the area. Particularly at night, the central **Triangle Park** (2-11 Nishishinsaibashi, Chūō-ku; 24 hours daily; free) is a popular hangout. Behold the faux Statue of Liberty perched atop a drab apartment block.

To reach Amerika-mura, take the Midō-suji subway line to **Shinsaibashi Station** and leave via one of the west exits. It's also a quick walk on east on Midō-suji from Shinsaibashi, or southeast from Dōtombori. If you cross north-south Yotsubashi-suji, which defines the western edge of Amerika-mura, you'll enter **Horie,** a fashionable district with slightly more refined offerings.

DŌTOMBORI
道頓堀

This mostly pedestrian area, named after the Dōtombori-gawa canal running through it, is the heart of Osaka's south side, where the bulk of the eating and partying takes place. Of the numerous bridges and walkways on the canal, the most famous is **Ebisu-bashi,** which offers the best vantage point of all the neon shimmering off the river, as well as the iconic Glico Running Man billboard. On the main thoroughfare running parallel to the canal on its south side, try to spot

The art form, listed as UNESCO World Intangible Cultural Heritage, was not born in Osaka but has thrived more in the city than anywhere else. The outsized puppets depict tales set in the pleasure quarters of old, where dramas played out among merchants and members of the sensually loaded *mizu shōbai* ("water trade").

NATIONAL BUNRAKU THEATER

1-12-10 Nipponbashi, Chūō-ku; tel. 06/6212-2531; www.ntj.jac.go.jp; from ¥2,400 for full performances, from ¥500 for single acts; take Sakai-suji subway line to Nipponbashi, exit 7

To learn more about this unique form of theater, or to see a performance, go to the National Bunraku Theater. Similar to kabuki,

Kuidaore Taro, the statue of a drumming clown in a red and white striped suit. While this area is touristy, you owe it to yourself to indulge in some *takoyaki* or some other fried treat while perusing Osaka at its most brash.

To reach Dōtombori, take the Midō-suji subway line to Namba Station, exit 14. For maximum sensory impact, take the Midō-suji subway line to Shinsaibashi Station instead, then walk south along the **Shinsaibashi-suji shopping arcade,** which leads directly to Ebisu-bashi.

NAMBA
難波

This sprawling district, brimming with restaurants, shops, and nightlife options, fans southward from Dōtombori. Similar to reaching Dōtombori, just go to Namba Station, exit 14, to reach the north side of this area, or Namba Station, exits E5 or E9. Better yet, walk south on any of the streets that run south from Dōtombori's pedestrian promenade, such as the frenetic covered shopping street of **Ebisu-bashi-suji.**

You'll find the temple of **Hōzen-ji** here, as well as **Doguya-suji** ("Kitchenware Street") and a clutch of restaurants and bars where locals flock in the evening. Just south of Namba Station is **Namba Parks** (2-10-70 Nanbanaka, Naniwa-ku; tel. 06/6644-7100; www.nambaparks.com; 11am-10pm daily), a cavernous shopping mall on the southern edge of the district; **Den-Den Town,** Osaka's main electronics zone, is about 5 minutes' walk southeast of Namba Station. About 10 minutes' walk north of Den Den Town, or 5 minutes' walk east of Namba Station, you'll come to **Kuromon Ichiba,** a bustling open-air culinary emporium.

SHIN-SEKAI
新世界

Farther south, get a sense of what the city imagined as the big, bright future around the turn of the 20th century. Shin-Sekai ("New World") is a rundown entertainment area dotted by gritty restaurants, garish pachinko parlors, dive bars, and old-timers playing mah-jongg. The centerpiece of the grizzled area is the 103-meter-tall (338-foot-tall) **Tsūten-kaku,** a retro steel tower bearing a heavy dose of neon. Get dinner at one of the area's famed *kushikatsu* restaurants, though keep to the main area: To the west and south are a homeless encampment and a red-light district.

Via JR, take the Loop Line to Shin-Imamiya Station; via subway, hop on the Sakai-suji line bound for Tengachaya and get off at Ebisucho; or, if you're taking the Midō-suji line, go to Dōbutsuen-mae.

TENNOJI
天王寺

About 15 minutes' walk southeast of Shin-Sekai, Tennoji Station has become a fashionable hub thanks to the March 2014 opening of the mammoth **Abeno Harukas** tower, looming over the area around Tennoji Station. It's the tallest building in Japan, and the observation deck atop this tower is a chance to get as high off the ground as possible.

the length of *bunraku* performances can test your endurance, with some clocking in at more than four hours. If that sounds like too much, non-reserved tickets for single acts are also available. If you want to sit through an entire play, reserve as far in advance as possible. Check the website for the performance schedule.

Festivals
TENJIN MATSURI
天神祭

Tenmangū shrine and Ō River; www.tenjinmatsuri. com; July 24-25; free

Along with Tokyo's Kanda Matsuri and Kyoto's Gion Matsuri, Osaka's Tenjin Matsuri is one of Japan's three blowout festivals.

Japanese Comedy: Lost in Translation?

Osaka is considered the epicenter for Japanese comedy. With a deep vein of sheer zaniness, Japanese comedy is often misunderstood by the outside world. One reason for this is the heavy use of puns and wordplay, completely lost to those who don't speak Japanese or understand the cultural context of a given joke. A little browsing on YouTube will quickly yield some fine examples of whacky Japanese talk shows, skits, and outlandish pranks, often played on unwitting participants in vulnerable moments. For example, unleashing an emu in a public restroom to walk up behind an unsuspecting salaryman at a urinal and filming it for TV. Or, launching a man clad in nothing but a towel and seated in a massage chair through the wall of a sauna and down a snowy mountainside in the dead of winter.

To be sure, there are some more universal examples of Japanese humor. There is a long history of comedy in Japanese art, from visual to performance and storytelling, from Buddhist priest Toba Sōjō's (1053-1140) satirical scrolls depicting sumo-wrestling animals to cheeky prints by great Edo period artists and masters of caricature such as Hokusai (1760-1849) and Kyosai (1831-1889). Satirical literary works were penned by esteemed authors such as Natsume Soseki (*I Am a Cat*, 1906) and Ryunosuke Akutagawa (*Kappa*, 1927). Perhaps the most widely known character in Japanese comedic history is Tora-san, a loveable underdog played by the late Kiyoshi Atsumi in the cinematic franchise *Otoko wa Tsurai yo (It's Tough Being a Man)*. More recently, the late Shimura Ken brought satire to television through his much-beloved variety show *Shimura Ken no Bakatono-sama*.

The main styles of comedic performance in Japan, which can be seen today, include the following:

- *Kyogen:* Stretching back to the 14th century, this slapstick style of comedic performance was used to break up the austere acts of Noh plays and is still performed using archaic Japanese even today. A common *kyogen* theme is the bumbling, cowardly samurai.

- *Rakugo:* The "fallen words" of these storytelling performances are delivered by a solo raconteur seated on a floor cushion, dressed in a kimono, facing the audience. These skilled performers weave lengthy, often complex tales that include dialogs between various characters.

- *Owarai:* This catchall term for modern-day comedy, literally meaning "laugh," includes anyone who climbs the ranks of the stand-up circuit. The types of performers seen on televised game shows, variety shows, and more would fall under this banner.

- *Manzai:* Think Abbott and Costello. One character plays the dimwitted *boke* character, while the counterpart *tsukkomi* character continuously jumps to correct the *boke's* confusion on a wide range of topics they quickly move between on a stage before an audience. Osaka is renowned as the epicenter of Japan's modern comedy machine, with its *manzai* acts leading the pack.

While seeing a traditional comedy performance in Japanese will just result in confusion, there are some English-speaking standup venues and troupes performing in Osaka and Tokyo. If you're interested in catching an English comedy show in Osaka, check out the website of the popular English-language comedy club ROR Comedy (www.rorcomedy.com). If you're in Tokyo, have a look at the website of The Pirates of Tokyo Bay (www.piratesoftokyobay.com), who host an occasional bilingual *Whose Line Is It Anyway?*-style show, or Standup Tokyo (www.standuptokyo.com), which hosts a range of English-language open-mic and standup events in the capital. At the time of writing, comedy shows had unfortunately ground to a halt due to coronavirus. Be sure to check a given troupe's website for updates before making plans to see any shows.

Taking place every July 24-25, practically all of the city participates in this massive festival—dedicated to Sugawara Michizane, the God of learning—which has a history that stretches back to the 10th century. The proceedings begin on the morning of the 24th at the shrine of **Tenmangū** (2-1-8 Tenjinbashi, Kita-ku; tel. 06/6353-0025; https://osakatemmangu.or.jp; take JR Gakkentoshi line to Osakatemmangu Station), located on the north side of town about 25 minutes' walk southeast of JR Osaka Station.

Following a ritual and prayers for the city's peace and prosperity at Tenmangū on the first day, the festival reaches a crescendo on the second day when (starting from around 3:30pm) locals wearing traditional garb pull opulent portable shrines the size of cars, known as *mikoshi*, from Tenmangū through the surrounding streets, then proceed to glide through the Ō River in swarms of boats. The evening ends with a huge fireworks show along the Ō River.

KISHIWADA DANJIRI MATSURI
岸和田だんじり祭

1-10 Miyamoto-chō, Kishidawashi; tel. 072/423-2121; https://osaka-info.jp/en/page/kishiwada-danjiri-festival; 6am-10pm Sat.-Sun. of third weekend in Sept.; free

In the Kishiwada Danjiri Matsuri, held on September's third weekend each year, scores of locals tug around 35 massive wooden floats called *danjiri*, weighing up to 3,000 kg (6,613 lbs), through the streets west of Kishiwada Station in far southern Osaka (reached via Nankai line from Namba Station in 25 minutes; ¥490). The floats, which resemble religious architecture, are ridden by revelers wearing white headbands and colorfully woven traditional threads. The timing of the festival always falls on the weekend (Sat.-Sun.) preceding a national holiday known as Respect for the Aged Day (third Mon. of Sept.). Visit www.city.kishiwada.osaka.jp/site/danjiri/danjiri-map.html for a map of the route that the floats typically take through the town's streets.

SPORTS AND RECREATION
Theme Parks
UNIVERSAL STUDIOS JAPAN

2-1-33 Sakurajima, Konohana-ku; tel. 0570/200-606; www.usj.co.jp/web/ja/jp; adults ¥7,800, children under 11 years old ¥5,400 for one-day pass, adults ¥15,400, children ¥10,500 for two-day pass; take JR Yumesaki line to Universal City

This sprawling counterpart to the popular U.S.-based parks draws daunting crowds, as the queues attest. But for some, especially those with kids, it's worth the wait. Located just southwest of downtown Osaka, the park's most popular attractions include "The Wizarding World of Harry Potter," a meticulous replica of Hogsmeade Village accessible by timed ticket, and the accompanying ride "Harry Potter and the Forbidden Journey," set in Hogwarts School. Other hit rides include a *Jaws* ride, a *Jurassic Park*-themed water ride, and an upside-down roller coaster called the "Flying Dinosaur."

Waiting for a few hours to reach some of the most popular rides isn't unheard of. To cut down the time, look into the various express passes offered at a considerable extra cost (www.usj.co.jp/e/ticket/express_pass.html). It's best to reserve tickets as far in advance as possible, using **Klook** (www.klook.com) or **Voyagin** (www.govoyagin.com).

Spas and Relaxation
SPA WORLD

3-4-24 Ebisu-higashi, Naniwa-ku; tel. 06/6631-0001; www.spaworld.co.jp; 10am-8:45am daily, closing hours vary for some bathing areas; ¥1,200 adults, ¥1,000 age 12 and under Mon.-Fri., ¥1,500 adults, ¥1,200 age 12 and under Sat.-Sun. for onsen and swimming areas; take Midō-suji, Sakai-suji subway lines to Dobutsuen-mae Station, or Nankai, JR Loop lines to Shin-Imamiya Station

At the southern end of Shin-Sekai you'll find this rambling smorgasbord of bathing options. Supplied with water drawn from deep within the earth, there are floors for European- (4th floor, with towel) and Asian- (6th floor, nude) style bathing, which alternate monthly by gender. Beyond *onsen* (hot-spring) pools, there are areas for swimming (8th floor; ¥600 bathing suit rental), and for an additional fee you can access eight types of *ganban-yoku* (stone sauna) options in a range of styles from around the world, from the Turkish *hamam* to the Russian *banya* (3rd floor; ¥800 adults Mon.-Fri./¥1,000 Sat.-Sun. and holidays). There's also a kid's play area (additional ¥500) and a smattering of restaurants on site. If you arrive between midnight and 5am or extend your stay during this window of time, you'll be charged an additional ¥1,300.

SHOPPING
Kita

On the north (Kita) side of town, the shopping options are mostly concentrated in **Umeda,** where department stores and chains of every stripe abound. The hip, artsy enclave of **Nakazakichō** on the east side of the JR Kyoto line tracks is filled with indie boutiques, stylish cafés, and bars set in retro Shōwa period (1926-1989) buildings draped in vines that somehow managed to evade bombing during World War II. The area rewards wandering. It's 5 minutes' walk east of Hankyū-Umeda Station, or 5 minutes' walk west of Nakazakichō Station (Tanimachi subway line).

GREEN PEPE

3-1-12 Nakazaki, Kita-ku; tel. 06/6359-5133; www. greenpepe3104.com; noon-7pm Wed.-Mon.

In Nakazakichō, check out Green Pepe, a quirky purveyor of vintage clothing and antique miscellany that is very in keeping with the ethos of the neighborhood.

HANKYŪ UMEDA STORE

8-7 Kakudachō, Kita-ku; tel. 06/6361-1381; www. hankyu-dept.co.jp/fl/english/honten; 10am-8pm Sun.-Thurs., 10am-9pm Fri.-Sat., 11am-10pm restaurant floors

This is the best department store in town. As the flagship of the Hankyū department store chain, this monument to high-end commerce

is suitably chic both in its atmosphere and offerings. Alongside pricey, stylish attire and a seemingly endless range of goods for home and life, there's a cavernous basement food hall and two restaurant floors on the 12th-13th floors. It occupies the building above Umeda Hankyū Station.

Minami

In the south side of Osaka, **Amerika-mura** (http://americamura.jp/en) is a rough approximation to Tokyo's Harajuku. This maze of lanes brims with shops selling streetwear, vintage threads, and hip-hop attire marketed to the city's fashion-conscious youth. Literally meaning America Village, the neighborhood has been a mecca for the city's 20-somethings for decades. To get here, take Midō-suji subway line to Shinsaibashi Station, exit 7.

A few blocks west of Amerika-mura, you'll enter a more mature, yet equally stylish neighborhood: **Horie.** Most of the boutiques in this area stock elegant attire and lifestyle goods produced in Japan.

SHINSAIBASHI-SUJI

East of Midō-suji, from Shinsaibashi Station in north to Dōtombori in the south; hours vary by shop; take Midō-suji subway line to Shinsaibashi Station, exit 5

This seemingly never-ending covered walkway, situated east of and running parallel to the major north-south artery of Midō-suji, is lined with shops of every kind: groceries, cosmetics, bookstores, cheap threads, cafés. In truth, it's mostly notable for its bustle rather than its shops. Walk down it on your way from Shinsaibashi Station to Dōtombori to people-watch and check the city's pulse.

DOGUYA-SUJI

14-5 Nanbasennichimae, Chūō-ku; tel. 06/6633-1423; https://doguyasuji.or.jp; hours vary by shop; take Midō-suji subway line to Namba Station, exit E-3, or Nakai line to Namba Station, south exit

This pedestrian emporium's name literally translates to "Kitchenware Street," which sums it up. Pick up things for the kitchen here, from cookery and sushi-shaped magnets for the fridge to high-grade knives. The shops are generally open daily from around 10am-6pm. The street runs north-south, parallel to Namba Station, which is a few minutes' walk west.

DEN-DEN TOWN

4-12 Nipponbashi, Naniwa-ku; tel. 06/6655-1717; www.denden-town.or.jp; hours vary by shop; take Sakai-suji, Sen-Nichimae subway lines to Nippombashi Station, exit 5, or Sakai-suji line to Ebisuchō Station, exit 2 or 5, or Nakai line to Namba Station, south exit,

Roughly 10 minutes' walk south of both Doguya-suji and Kuromon-Ichiba lies a shopping district where you'll find gadgets and various accoutrements of geekdom. If you're visiting Tokyo, then a trip to Akihabara will more than have these things covered. But if you're only going to be in Osaka and want to peruse cameras, electronics, computer parts, and pop-cultural artifacts (manga zines, anime figurines, cosplay outfits, retro video games, and more), then this is your place.

BIOTOP

1-16-1 Minamihorie, Nishi-ku; tel. 06/6531-8223; www.biotop.jp/osaka; 11am-11pm daily

A good starting point in upscale Horie is Biotop, a multistory shop with a café and greenhouse on the first floor, a garden on the roof, and a few floors of chic offerings from Japanese denim and bonsai trees to domestically fired ceramics.

PALETTE ART ALIVE

1-19-1 Minamihorie, Nishi-ku; tel. 06/6586-9560; http://palette-art-alive.com; noon-8pm daily

One-minute walk west of Biotop, the gallery-cum-fashion shop Palette Art Alive serves as a showcase for the next generation of Japan's bleeding-edge fashion designers.

FOOD
Kita

The greatest concentration of dining options in Kita can be found around Osaka and Umeda stations. One zone worth knowing about is **Shin-Umeda Shokudogai,** an atmospherically faded, rowdy network of eateries under the train tracks of JR Osaka Station. Other neighborhoods with a glut of dining options include the area around Umeda Sky Building, about 15 minutes' walk west of Osaka and Umeda stations; the hip youth zone of Nakazaki-chō, about 15 minutes' walk east of the Osaka and Umeda station area; the tightknit streets of Kitashinchi, about 10 minutes' walk south of Osaka and Umeda stations; and the Tanimachi area next to Osaka-jō.

The **Osaka Ramen Route** (www.osakaramenroute.com) is a fun brainchild of the Friends in Ramen (www.friendsinramen.com) blog. A stamp-collecting rally brings you to the city's best bowls of noodles and ends with a prize when you complete the circuit.

MITSUKA BOSE KAMOSHI

1-2-16 Ōyodominami, Kita-ku; tel. 06/6442-1005; https://mitsukabose.com; 11:30am-2:30pm and 6:30pm-11:30pm Tues.-Sat., 11:30am-2:30pm and 5:30pm-10pm Sun. and holidays; ¥1,000; take JR line to JR Osaka Station, central north gate

In a city with a wealth of ramen options, Mitsuka Bose Kamoshi is the best spot to try the miso-based variety. Soup stock options include everything from squid ink to burnt miso. Its location right next to the Umeda Sky Building makes it an appealing option either before or after heading skyward. This restaurant is on the **Osaka Ramen Route.**

SALON DE AMANTO

1-7-26 Nakazakinishi, Kita-ku; tel. 06/6371-5840; http://amanto.jp; noon-10pm daily; ¥1,000; take Hankyū-Kobe, Hankyū-Kyoto, Hankyū-Takarazuka lines to Umeda-Hankyū Station, or Tanimachi subway line to Nakazakichō Station

If you've got a soft spot for bohemian haunts, try this retro DIY space in the hip, somewhat hidden district of Nakazakichō about 10 minutes' walk east of Umeda. Set in a building that dates to the 1880s, by day it provides caffeine hits and simple, decent dishes like curry rice and chicken and egg on rice. By night, it turns into a bar that sometimes hosts music and art events.

SHUHARI

1-3-20 Tokiwamachi, Chūō-ku; tel. 06/6944-8808; http://shuhari.main.jp; 11:30am-3pm and 5:30pm-11pm daily; from ¥1,000; take Tanimachi subway line to Temmabashi Station, exit 2

If you've worked up an appetite after exploring Osaka-jō, Shuhari is a good spot for lunch. Located in Tanimachi 4-chōme near the park around Osaka-jō, this restaurant has a nice menu of soba sets served with tempura and fresh wasabi.

KIJI

9-20 Kakudachō, Kita-ku; tel. 06/6361-5804; 11:30am-9:30pm Mon.-Sat.; ¥1,500

For *okonomiyaki* on the north side of town, head to Kiji, a great *okonomiyaki* joint on the second floor of a building in the tightly packed Shin-Umeda Shokudogai restaurant district located between JR Osaka Station and Hankyū Umeda Station.

BON

1-3-15 Dojima; tel. 06/6344-0400; www. kitchen-dan.jp; 6pm-12:30am daily; from ¥15,000; take Yotsuhashi-suji subway line or JR Tōzai line to Kitashinchi Station, exit 11-5

Deep-fried goodies on skewers (*kushikatsu*) await at Bon, an expert shop in Kita-Shinchi, just south of JR Osaka and Umeda stations. This is the place to go for this local favorite in a refined setting.

Minami
KUROMON ICHIBA

2-4-1 Nipponbashi, Chūō-ku; tel. 06/6631-0007; https://kuromon.com/jp; hours vary by shop; take Sakai-suji, Sen-Nichimae subway lines to Nippombashi Station, exit 10

About 6 minutes' walk east of Doguya-suji, you'll find Osaka's largest food market. This covered walkway contains some 170 shops hawking culinary items of every type, from skewers of grilled meat and noodles to fresh fruits, vegetables, and fish sourced by restaurants around town. The market is inundated with tourists from around 10am, so aim to visit by around 9am.

If you'd like to sample something at the market, quaff a paper cup of rich, flavorsome (though unsweetened) soy milk from neighborhood tofu institution **Takahashi Shokuhin** (1-21-31 Nipponbashi, Chūō-ku; tel. 06/6641-4548; https://kuromon.com/en/takahashi-shokuhin; 8am-5pm Mon.-Sat.; ¥70). To reach this vendor, established in 1925, walk straight out of Nippombashi Station, exit 10, and take the first left. Takahashi Shokuhin will be on the right side of the first block of shops. From here, wander through the market, following your inspiration, and take in the atmosphere.

★ GANSO KUSHIKATSU DARUMA HONTEN

2-3-9 Ebisu-Higashi, Naniwa-ku; tel. 06/6645-7056; www.kushikatsu-daruma.com; 11am-10:30pm daily; single skewers from ¥110; take Midō-suji subway line to Dōbutsuen-mae, exit 5

If you prefer to eat *kushikatsu* right on Dōtombori, the Daruma shop there does a fine job. But to experience this dish in the gritty surroundings of its glorious origins, head farther south to Ganso Kushikatsu Daruma Honten. Set in the aged commercial development of Shin-Sekai, this shop claims to be where the dish originated.

LILO COFFEE ROASTERS

1-1-10-28 Nishi-Shinsaibashi, Chūō-ku; tel. 06/6227-8666; https://coffee.liloinveve.com; 11am-11pm daily; ¥280-750; take Midō-suji subway line to Shinsaibashi Station, exit 8

With its cozy patio and streetside seating, and baristas who know their stuff, this narrow, minimalist café is the place to go for a proper cup of coffee to fuel your stroll through Amerika-mura. A variety of beans are on offer, from single-origin to blends, in a range of roasts. They also sell light nibbles like croissants and hot dogs and have a few beers on tap.

"Eat Yourself to Ruin"

takoyaki

A stereotype exists across Japan that Osakans have a devil-may-care attitude toward indulging in earthly pleasures. Of all the seven deadly sins, gluttony, or at least something approaching it, tops the city's list. A jaunty attitude toward culinary excess has a long tradition in Osaka, which was historically referred to as "Japan's Kitchen." There's even a word for draining one's financial resources in the pursuit of scarfing down all the deep-fried goodies the city has to offer: *kuidaore* ("ku-ee-dao-rei"). After a night spent tipsily stumbling between rickety ramen stands and smoky yakitori (grilled, skewered chicken) joints, the risk of succumbing to *kuidaore* (literally: "eating oneself to ruin") becomes a distinct possibility. Here's a small sample of what you'll find:

- *Takoyaki:* Fried balls of dough stuffed with chunks of octopus tentacle.

- *Okonomiyaki:* Savory pancakes sizzling on an open griddle are stuffed with cabbage, meat, and seafood, and often topped with sweet sauce, bonito flakes, and mayonnaise.

- *Kushikatsu:* All manner of things on sticks—lotus root, sausage, eggplant, pork belly, mushroom—is dipped in panko, egg, and flour, then deep-fried in a vat of boiling oil until it's crispy on the outside.

- *Kaiten-zushi:* This is sushi delivered by conveyor belt.

- *Horumon:* This dish consists of discarded animal bits, including stomach, intestine, tripe, even uterus, grilled, thrown into stews or even deftly served raw.

- *Yaki-niku:* Thanks to its sizable Korean population concentrated in the neighborhood of Tsuruhashi, Osaka is also known for its Korean barbecue.

- *Kappō-ryōri:* In essence, this means *kaiseki* minus the fuss, with diners sitting directly at the counter to banter with the chef who serves up beautifully presented courses made from the finest seasonal ingredients.

For a guide into Osaka's culinary madness, try food-focused tour outfit **Ninja Food Tours** (www.ninjafoodtours.com; from ¥9,500 including dinner and two drinks) or **Backstreet Osaka Tours** (https://backstreetosakatours.com; tours from ¥6,500), which offers greasy spoon "soul food" tours and treks through the city's deep back alleys.

★ TAKOTAKO KING HONTEN

2-4-25 Higashishinsaibashi, Chūō-ku; tel.
06/6213-0098; https://takotakoking.com/honten.
html; 6pm-4am daily; ¥300-900; take Midō-suji
subway line to Shinsaibashi, exit 6

This is a great spot to indulge on one of Osaka's signature greasy-spoon dishes, *takoyaki* (fried balls of dough stuffed with octopus), away from the throngs of Dōtombori. This friendly local institution draws a crowd, especially on weekends, with its mix of affordable, delicious food made on the spot (*takoyaki, okonomiyaki,* and more), drinks, and lively ambience. There's both seating inside and on the sidewalk, and a takeout window. If this location is too crowded, there's an equally good branch 2 minutes' walk west on the same side of the same street (2-8-28 Higashishinsaibashi, Chūō-ku; tel. 06/6212-0079; https://takotakoking.com/honnishiten. html; 6pm-3am daily).

CHITOSE

1-11-10 Taishi, Nishinari-ku; tel. 066/631-6002;
www.bunjin.com/chitose; 11:30am-3:30pm
and 5pm-8:30pm Thurs.-Tues.; from ¥750;
Dōbutsuen-mae Station

If authenticity is what you're after, it's hard to beat this *okonomiyaki* spot set on a side street in a colorful corner of town that's seen better days. This legendary greasy spoon is run by cheerful staff who are happy to chat with customers in English. The interior looks like it hasn't been updated since the 1950s, with just a few solid tables and a couple of countertop seats. The chef works his magic just a few feet away.

CAFE ABSINTHE

1-2-27 Kitahorie, Nishi-ku; tel. 066/534-6635; www.
absinthe-jp.com/cafe-absinthe; noon-1am daily;
dishes from ¥900; Yotsubashi Station

Tired of deep-fried batter? This chic café, restaurant, and bar offers a nice balance of Middle Eastern and Mediterranean fare: salads, tapas, falafel, hummus, pizzas, couscous, mussaka, kebabs, and more. By day, fresh juices, teas, coffee, and smoothies are on offer, with cocktails served at night when a nice buzz settles in. Shisha is available, too, if you're so inclined. It's located just west of Amerika-mura, beside a bustling street that runs beneath an expressway.

★ AJINOYA

Gendai Koisan Bldg. 2F, 1-7-16 Namba, Chūō-ku;
tel. 06/6211-0713; http://ajinoya-okonomiyaki.com;
noon-10:45pm Tues.-Fri., 11:30am-10:45pm Sat.-Sun.;
lunch from ¥1,000, dinner from ¥2,000; take
Midō-suji subway line to Namba Station, exit 14

Just a few blocks south of Dōtombori, Ajinoya serves fantastic *okonomiyaki*. If the line for the nearby more touristy Chibō is discouragingly long, take heart. Queues form here, too, but they move quickly. The service is speedy and the quality of the food is excellent.

USHITORA

15-19 Namba Sennichimae, Chūō-ku; tel.
066/632-7830; 4pm-11pm daily; ¥3,000; Namba
Station, exit E9

This dimly lit standing bar, or *tachinomi,* occupies an inviting spot near the entry point into the backstreets of Namba. The menu consists of eclectic *izakaya* fare, from sashimi spreads to fried fusions, changing sporadically. If you feel like an evening of urban adventure, begin at Ushitora, then follow your inspiration.

MOMEN

2-1-3 Shinsaibashi, Chūō-ku; tel. 06/6211-2793;
5pm-10pm Mon.-Sat.; from ¥15,000; take Midō-suji
subway line to Shinsaibashi Station, exit 6

If all the deep-fried fare begins to feel fatiguing, remember that Osaka does have a refined side. Momen is an excellent *kappō-ryōri*—essentially *kaiseki* served more casually at a countertop—restaurant in Shinsaibashi, where patrons sit bantering with the chefs as they whip up seasonally inspired artistic creations with top-notch ingredients. The

---

1: Takotako King Honten **2:** fugu restaurant on Dōtombori **3:** Music Bar Groovy and owner Wataru Matsunaga

restaurant seats only nine, so reserve at least a few weeks in advance, if not earlier, to ensure a spot. Also note that the restaurant only accepts cash. It's not cheap, but it's an experience you will remember.

BARS AND NIGHTLIFE

Osaka is a fun city at night, with most of the action taking place in the southern half of the city. Cocktail bars, dance clubs, and live music are abundant in the bustling streets of Shinsaibashi and Namba.

Kita
BLARNEY STONE

6F Sonezaki Center Bldg., 2-10-15 Sonezaki, Kita-ku; 5pm-1am Mon.-Thurs., 5pm-5am Fri.-Sat., 3:30pm-1am Sun.; take Midō-suji or Tanimachi subway line to Higshi Umeda Station, exit 7

Blarney Stone is a good spot in the northern half of the city to mix with expats and locals over a pint or two. This faux Irish pub is especially lively during the after-work hours.

Minami
CINQUENCENTO

10-1-2 Higashi-Shinsaibashi, Chūō-ku; tel. 06/6213-6788; 8pm-5am daily; take Sakai-suji subway line to Nipponbashi, exit 2

Cinquencento is a lively martini bar with a reasonably priced menu (all drinks ¥500--*cinquencento* means 500 in Italian). It's a fun place to mingle with locals and expats before or after hitting the local clubs. Alongside domestic craft stalwart Minoh's offerings, a handful of other Japanese microbrews flow from 10 taps.

BAR NAYUTA

Mario Bldg. 5F, 1-6-17 Nishi-Shinsaibashi, Chūō-ku; tel. 06/6210-3615; http://bar-nayuta.com; 5pm-3am daily; take Midō-suji subway line to Shinsaibashi Station, exit 7

For great cocktails in a classic speakeasy atmosphere, head to Bar Nayuta. The man behind the bar, Hiro, is a master mixologist who puts a unique spin on his drinks. This is an excellent choice if you're seeking a place with a whiff of refinement. The bar is a little tricky to find. The elevator to the fifth floor is at the end of a corridor leading in from the street that runs along the left side of the building that houses the Cook Jeans shop on the first floor.

MISONO BUILDING

2-3-9 Sennichimae, Chūō-ku; hours vary; take Sakai-suji subway line to Nipponbashi Station, exit 5

For adventurous nightlife connoisseurs with a penchant for drinking in slightly grittier surroundings, head to Ura Namba's iconic Misono Building. Protected from the tourist onslaught on the backside (*ura* in Japanese) of Namba, the second floor of this dilapidated building is crammed with old bars that stay open into the wee hours. Choose the quirky facade that most strikes your fancy, then bar-hop from there.

CIRCUS

2F 1-8-16 Nishi-Shinsaibashi; tel. 06/6241-3822; http://circus-osaka.com; 11pm-late Fri.-Sat. nights and special events; take Midō-suji subway line to Shinsaibashi Station, exit 7

If you're seeking a club that takes its electronic music seriously, Circus is the best place in Osaka. The crowd goes more for the music than to see or be seen. An added bonus: The dance floor is non-smoking.

FARPLANE

East Village Bldg. 3F, 2-8-19 Nishishinsaibashi, Chūō-ku; tel. 06/6211-6012; http://farplane.jp/bar; 8pm-late daily; cover charges vary for special events; take Midō-suji subway line to Shinsaibashi Station, exit 8

For something outré, the appropriately named Farplane cannot be beat. This fetish bar with velvet-draped ceilings, chandeliers, and edgy posters on the walls grew out of what was once a shop selling sexy attire. Today, the city's weirdos flock to the space, run by bartenders in kinky outfits. It hosts occasional events like the monthly Creamy Banana Burlesque show and its annual Farplane Night (http://farplane.jp/farplane-night). For a full event schedule

☆ Eating Along Dōtombori

Eating along Osaka's Dōtombori canal is a quintessential part of a visit to the city. Although there are other purveyors of Osaka's signature dishes elsewhere in the city, there's something special about savoring them in this bright, bustling strip. Out of all the tacky signs demanding your attention (and yen), some of the shops really deliver on their promises.

- For great *okonomiyaki* right next to the canal, try **Chibō** (1-5-5 Dōtombori, Chūō-ku; tel. 06/6212-2211; www.chibo.com; 11am-1am Mon.-Sat., 11am-midnight Sun.; from ¥900). There's often a queue, but it moves fast.

- For excellent *kushikatsu* right on the main strip just a few doors down from Chibō, head to **Ganso Kushikatsu Daruma, Dōtombori** (1-6-4 Dōtombori, Chūō-ku; tel. 06/6213-8101; www.kushikatu-daruma.com; 11:30am-10:30pm daily; single skewers from ¥110).

- For very decent *takoyaki* along the lively thoroughfare, try **Takoyaki Jyuhachiban** (1-7-21 Dōtombori, Chūō-ku; tel. 06/6211-3118; 11am-9pm daily; ¥350 for six).

Eating along this neon-splashed canal is fundamental to any introduction to Osaka, but for some, the crowds and kitsch may be too much. If you prefer somewhere a little more subdued and authentic, there are loads of other great restaurants just off this main strip.

(Japanese only), go to http://farplane.jp/category/event.

NAMBA BEARS

3-14-5 Namba-naka, Naniwa-ku; tel. 06/6649-5564; http://namba-bears.main.jp; hours vary by event; take Midō-suji subway line to Namba Station, exit 4

If your musical taste is more of the rock variety, Osaka's go-to live venue is Namba Bears. DIY in spirit, the compact, bare-bones space hosts indie bands and punk rockers, providing sustenance to the city's underground scene. Bring your own booze.

MUSIC BAR GROOVY

1-6-12 Taishi, Nishinari-ku; tel. 080/4701-0022; www.musicbar-groovy.com; 7pm-1am daily; Dōbutsuen-mae Station, exit 8

This hip spot in a decidedly non-touristy part of town has a fantastic sound system, a massive record collection, and plenty of retro cultural memorabilia: Mick Jagger, *Harold and Maude*, Andy Warhol. The owner, a culture hound named Wataru with deep tastes in film and music, had a long stint working as a reggae producer in New York City.

Works well when combined with dinner at Chitose, just a few minutes' walk away.

ACCOMMODATIONS
Kita
U-EN

2-9-23 Fukushima, Fukushima-ku; tel. 06/7503-4394; www.hostelosaka.com; ¥2,800 dorm bed, ¥6,600 d; take Hanshin main line to Shin-Fukushima Station, exit 2

U-en is a stylish hostel set in an old renovated townhouse in the north of town. There are both Japanese-style private rooms and dorm beds. Flashes of traditional design—tatami floors, paper-screen doors—give it just the right amount of style. This is a great choice if you're on a tight budget.

★ INTERCONTINENTAL OSAKA

3-60 Ofuka-chō, Kita-ku; tel. 06/6374-5700; www.ihg.com; ¥48,000 d; take JR lines to Osaka Station, or Hankyū line to Umeda Station

A stone's throw from both JR Osaka Station and Umeda Station, the Intercontinental Osaka has all the amenities of a five-star hotel and is easily one of the city's best. This property is in an excellent location, with fantastic views and great restaurants on-site. Highly recommended.

Minami

HOTEL FELICE SHINSAIBASHI BY RELIEF

1-17-11 Higashishinsaibashi, Chūō-ku; tel. 066/281-8000; http://hotel-felice.com/shinsaibashi; ¥5,000 d; Shinsaibashi Station, exit 5

If you don't mind a petite room, this budget hotel in a convenient part of Shinsaibashi is easy on the eyes and the wallet. Despite the limited floor space, the well-stocked bathrooms feel relatively roomy. There's an optional breakfast buffet and a rooftop bar. The rooms may feel a bit tight for those traveling with kids, but for solo travelers or couples, it's a bargain.

DOTONBORI HOTEL

2-3-25 Dōtombori, Chūō-ku; tel. 06/6213-9040; http://dotonbori-h.co.jp; ¥12,000 d; take Sennichimae or Midō-suji subway line to Namba Station, exit 25

Beyond its quirky exterior fronted by pillars shaped like large human faces perched atop pairs of legs, Dotonbori Hotel is a solid, no-frills option in the center of Dōtombori. It's clean, modern, and convenient, and friendly staff are ready to help. This is a good pick for value, and a Japanese and Western-style breakfast buffet is available for an additional fee.

CROSS HOTEL OSAKA

2-5-15 Shinsaibashisuji, Chūō-ku; tel. 06/6213-8281; www.crosshotel.com; ¥17,000 d; take Midō-suji or Sennichimae subway line to Namba Station, exit 14

Cross Hotel Osaka is only a few minutes' walk from Dōtombori, Shinsaibashi, and Amerika-mura, putting street food, nightlife, and funky boutiques within easy reach. Rooms here are smart and clean, and the bathrooms are spacious compared to hotels in the same price range. It also has a bar and a few restaurants.

HOTEL NIKKO OSAKA

1-3-3 Nishishinsaibashi, Chūō-ku; tel. 06/6244-1111; www.hno.co.jp; ¥24,000 d; take Midō-suji subway line to Shinsaibashi Station, exit 8

The Hotel Nikko Osaka is a great pick if you want to stay near the heart of the action in Minami with a whiff of luxury. The hotel's quality breakfast spread, on-site dining options, and clean, stylish rooms put it a cut above the more budget-conscious options in the area. Its location directly above Shinsaibashi Station offers fantastic access to the attractions in the south part of the city.

ST. REGIS OSAKA

3-6-12 Honmachi, Chūō-ku; tel. 06/6258-3333; www.stregisosaka.co.jp; ¥27,000 d; take Chūō subway line to Honmachi Station, exit 3

Starting from its 12th-floor lobby, St. Regis Osaka exudes chic design sense throughout its 160-room property. Located on the prestigious Midō-suji shopping artery, this classy hotel has an outdoor Japanese garden and haute restaurants on-site (French, Italian). This is an excellent pick if you want to travel in style.

FRASER RESIDENCE NANKAI OSAKA

1-17-11 Nambanaka, Naniwa-ku; tel. 06/6635-7111; https://osaka.frasershospitality.com; from ¥27,000; take Namba Nankai line to Namba Nakai Station

If you prefer to feel "at home" in a hotel, check out Fraser Residence Nankai Osaka. Aside from being in the thick of the action in Namba, what sets Fraser Residence apart is that its rooms resemble apartments. This makes the hotel an especially appealing option for those who are traveling with kids or staying longer-term.

INFORMATION AND SERVICES

For information on how to connect to one of some 5,000 free Wi-Fi points around the city, see http://ofw-oer.com/en.

Tourist Information

These city-run centers have a good selection of English-language maps, brochures, and friendly bilingual staff who are happy to help you handle trip logistics, including booking accommodations.

For tourist information in the Kita (north) side of the city, head to **Tourist Information Osaka** (tel. 06/6131-4550; www.osaka-info.jp; 7am-11pm daily for tourist office, 9am-5:30pm daily for phone inquiries), located directly in front of the central ticket gates of JR Osaka Station.

In the Minami (south) side of the city, **Tourist Information Namba** (tel. 06/6131-4550; www.osaka-info.jp; 9am-8pm daily for tourist office, 9am-5:30pm daily for phone inquiries) is outside Nakai Namba Station and Namba Station on the first floor near the ticket gates for the Midō-suji and Sennichimae subway lines.

Medical Services

In the case of an emergency, the **Osaka Red Cross Hospital** has some English-speaking doctors on staff. (5-30 Fudegasaki-chō, Tennōji-ku; tel. 06/6774-5111; www.osaka-med.jrc.or.jp; 24 hours daily; take Kintetsu line to Osaka-Uehonmachi Station).

For less urgent situations, English-speaking doctors can be consulted at **Ohkita Medical Clinic** (1-12-17 Umeda, Kita-ku; tel. 06/6344-0380; 10am-7pm Mon.-Fri, 10am-1pm Sat.; take JR lines to Osaka Station, south-central exit) and **Yasugi Clinic** (1-75 Ikedachō, Osaka-fu; tel. 06/6353-0505; http://yasugi-clinic.com; 9am-11:45am Mon. and Wed.-Sat., 4:30pm-6:45pm Mon. and Wed.-Fri.; take Osaka loop line to Tenma Station). Both are on the north side of town.

Otherwise, the **Osaka Call Center** (http://ofw-oer.com/call/en; 24 hours daily) offers free English-language medical support, reachable directly through the website. To call, you must be connected to the internet.

Diplomatic Services

The **U.S. Consulate General Osaka** (2-11-5 Nishitenma, Kita-ku; tel. 06/6315-5900; https://jp.usembassy.gov; take Midō-suji subway line to Yodoyabashi Station, exit 1) is open weekdays 9am-5pm.

GETTING THERE
Air

Osaka is served by two airports. The larger of the two is **Kansai International Airport** (www.kansai-airport.or.jp), or KIX, located about 50 km (31 mi) southwest of town. **Itami Airport** (http://osaka-airport.co.jp) is located about 12 km (7 mi) northwest of the city. Though Itami is sometimes referred to as "Osaka International Airport," it only hosts domestic flights.

To shuttle back and forth between KIX and downtown, you can choose between a few trains and an airport limousine service. The most convenient is the twice-hourly **Nankai Rapid Limited Express** train (7am-10pm daily; ¥1,430), or "Rapi:t," which takes you from the airport to Namba Nakai Station (40 minutes) in the heart the Namba district in the Minami (south) side of the city. Another train running twice an hour is the **JR Kansai Airport Express Haruka** (6:30am-10pm), which runs to both Tenno-ji (30 minutes; ¥1,710) on the south side of downtown, and Shin-Osaka (45 minutes; ¥2,330) in the north. While one of these trains is generally the best way to go, if you happen to arrive after the train services stop, there's a limousine service called **KATE** (www.kate.co.jp) that runs between KIX and Osaka Station (1 hour, depending on traffic; ¥1,550) that runs once hourly after midnight. Worst case, you can hail a taxi, although this isn't recommended as fares to Namba in the city's south start from ¥14,000 and climb as you go north.

Traveling between Itami and downtown is done either by **Osaka Airport Limousine** (www.okkbus.co.jp) or **Osaka Monorail.** The former runs to Osaka Station (25 minutes; ¥640) in the city's north and Osaka City Air Terminal (35 minutes; ¥640) in the southern hub of Namba. The latter runs to Senri-Chūo Station, where you can transfer to the Hankyū

Senri line, which runs to Osaka Station, with connections to the rest of the city's train and subway lines.

Train

Coming from **Tokyo** (3 hours; ¥14,140) or **Kyoto** (15 minutes; ¥1,420) the **Tōkaidō-San'yō** *shinkansen* stops at **Shin-Osaka Station.** If you have a JR Pass, simply hop on.

Otherwise, take the **JR Kyoto line** from Osaka Station to Kyoto Station (30 minutes; ¥560), the **Hankyū Kyoto line** from Hankyū Umeda Station in Osaka's northern Umeda district to Kawaramachi Station (45 minutes; ¥400) in downtown Kyoto, or the **Keihan Main line** from Yodoyabashi Station in the center of Osaka (linked to the Midō-suji subway line) to Gion-Shijō (50 minutes; ¥410) and Sanjō (55 minutes; ¥410) stations in the heart of Kyoto.

Bus

If you don't mind taking the bus, it will save you a few thousand yen. **Willer Express** (www.willerexpress.com) has a center on the first floor of the east tower of the Umeda Sky Building (Tower East 1F, 1-1-88 Ōyodonaka, Kita-ku; https://willerexpress.com/en/wbt-umeda; 7:30am-11pm daily, 7:30am-2pm on third Thurs. of month). Willer runs buses to and from **Tokyo, Hiroshima, Hakata** (Fukuoka), and beyond. Operating out of the JR Osaka Station Highway Bus Terminal, just outside JR Osaka Station's north-central concourse, **JR West Highway Bus** (www.nishinihonjrbus.co.jp) operates along similar routes.

GETTING AROUND

Although Osaka does have an above-ground train network, its subway system is much more useful. Once you're on the ground in Kita

(Umeda), the Osaka-jō area, or in the core of the rambling Minami area (Shinsaibashi, Amerika-mura, Dōtobori, Namba), you'll find Osaka an enjoyable city to explore on foot. However, when shuttling between Kita and Minami, or to Minami's southernmost districts, you'll want to make use of the city's subway system.

Subway

Out of eight subway lines, you'll most likely only need the red-coded **Midō-suji line.** This line starts from Shin-Osaka in the north and runs southward through the business and entertainment zone of Umeda near Osaka Station, the entertainment districts of Shinsaibashi and Namba, and the relaxed southern hub of Tenno-ji. Trains depart every 3-5 minutes and run from early morning until around midnight, with single journeys costing from ¥180-370.

Bicycle

Osaka is an enjoyable place to ride a bike, thanks to its largely flat topography. That said, its main thoroughfares—Midō-suji, Sakai-suji, etc.—are crowded with traffic. Streets suited for cycling can be found in the calmer neighborhoods: Shinsaibashi, Amerika-mura, Horie, and around Osaka-jō.

Cycle Osaka (1-3-13 Ebisuhigashi, Naniwa-ku; www.cycleosaka.com; tel. 090/9165-7168; 10am-6:30pm daily) offers full-size cross bikes (¥1,500 per day) and more compact folding bikes (¥1,500 per day). It's possible to rent a bike and explore on your own or join one of the company's tours. It is necessary to book online. Do so at least two days ahead to ensure you get a bike. The bilingual staff also lead illuminating tours through the city's varied neighborhoods, bazaars, and culinary zones.

Nara

奈良

Nara has a lot to be proud of. This small city of about 360,000 can rightly claim to be the birthplace of Japanese culture as we know it. Founded in 710 and initially named Heijōkyō, or "citadel of peace," it was the first capital of Japan until 794, when the new nation's political center migrated to Kyoto. During its brief period as the nation's capital, religious, artistic, and architectural influences from China found fertile ground, and Japanese Buddhism emerged from the city.

Remnants of this eventful history are everywhere. Look no further than the myriad temples and gardens scattered throughout the city, particularly concentrated in the sprawling green space that is Nara-kōen, where you'll find a throng of docile deer in search of a handout and the towering temple of Tōdai-ji, housing one of Japan's most iconic sights, the Great Buddha, a statue standing 16 meters (53 feet) tall.

Beyond the grounds of Nara-kōen, a cluster of temples in the west side of town are also a draw, including Horyū-ji, which contains the world's oldest wooden buildings. You can also head to **Naramachi,** a brief stroll from the city's main railway hubs and fanning out from the southwestern edge of Nara-kōen, where Edo-period ambience oozes from the narrow roads lined by old whitewashed wooden buildings that now house a variety of restaurants, cafés, shops, and galleries. Overlooking it all is gently sloping **Mount Wakakusayama,** topped by a large grassy vantage point, standing at the north side of Nara-kōen. Also known as Mount Mikasa, it's more hill than mountain, at 342 meters (1,122 feet) high.

SIGHTS
Nara-kōen
奈良公園

http://nara-park.com; tel. 0742/22-0375; 24 hours daily; free; take Kintetsu line to Kintetsu Nara Station, or JR Nara, Yamatoji, Sakurai lines to JR Nara Station

Stretching from the eastern side of Naramachi and downtown Nara in the west to the hills at the eastern edge of town, Nara-kōen is an expansive leafy space dotted with important religious sites and crisscrossed by paths ideal for ambling and ponds full of colorful *koi* (carp). It's a wonderful place to stroll and is home to a number of impressive cultural properties harkening back to the beginnings of Japan.

The prized citizens of this green expanse are around 1,500 semi-wild deer, believed to be couriers of the gods in Shinto. Today they are doted on by visitors who feed them with deer crackers (*shika senbei;* ¥150), sold in the park. Forget Bambi—the deer here can become surprisingly aggressive in their quest for crackers. Don't be surprised if you're besieged as soon as you open a pack. It's best not to allow small children to feed them.

KŌFUKU-JI
興福寺

48 Noborioji-chō; tel. 0742/22-7755; www.kohfukuji. com; grounds 24 hours, Golden Hall 9am-5pm (last entry 4:45pm) daily; grounds free, ¥300 Tōkondō, ¥600 treasure hall; take Kintetsu line to Kintetsu Nara Station

Begin your exploration of Nara-kōen's Buddhist treasures at Kōfuku-ji, an illustrious temple complex with a lofty five-level pagoda and a more modest three-story one in the west side of the park.

Built in 669, it was relocated to Nara-kōen when the fledgling nation's capital moved to Nara in 710. In its heyday, some 175 structures dotted the grounds. Over the centuries, many of the buildings succumbed to fires and fighting between rivaling factions of the Fujiwara clan's temple-raised warrior monks, or between the Fujiwara clan and the invading Taira clan. Although Shogun Minamoto Yoritomo (1147-1199) had the complex rebuilt,

Nara

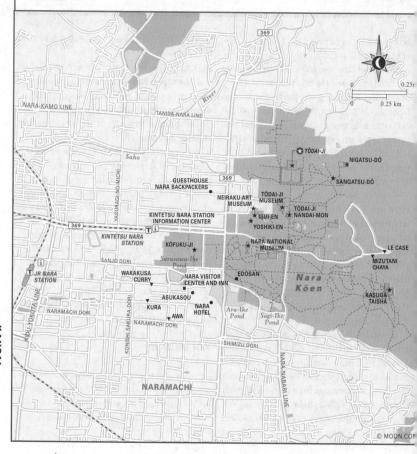

many of its structures succumbed to fire again in 1717.

Though the treasure hall does house some compelling Buddhist images, and the octagonal Tōkondō (East Golden Hall) is populated by impressive Buddha statues, I recommend just strolling through the grounds and taking in the atmosphere for free.

NARA NATIONAL MUSEUM
奈良国立博物館

50 Noborioji-chō; tel. 050/5542-8600; www. narahaku.go.jp; 9:30am-5pm (last entry 4:30pm)

Tues.-Sun.; adults ¥700, university students ¥350, high school students and younger free for permanent collection; take Kintetsu line to Kintetsu Nara Station
Just east of Kōfuku-ji, you'll find the excellent Nara National Museum. Its collection includes a wide array of Buddhist statuary, paintings, calligraphy, and other art, stretching from the 7th century to the Edo period, with quality English signage throughout. Pay ¥500 for the informative illustrated guide "Viewing Buddhist Sculptures," which

---

1: a woman selling snacks for the deer at Nara-kōen **2:** Tōdai-ji

will help you understand the symbolism in Buddhist art.

KASUGA TAISHA
春日大社

160 Kasugano-chō; tel. 0742/22-7788; www. kasugataisha.or.jp; 6am-6pm daily Apr.-Sept.; 6:30am-5pm Oct.-Mar.; free; take Kintetsu line to Kintetsu Nara Station

In the southeast corner of Nara-kōen, Kasuga Taisha is the most important Shinto shrine in the city. There's a *honden* (main hall) and a *haiden* (prayer hall), but the real magic is found by meandering along the paths on the shrine's grounds and exploring its subshrines. This is one of the most worthwhile stops in the park.

Since the Great Tohoku Earthquake struck the northeastern coast of Honshu in March 2011, a group of priests has been leading the faithful in morning prayers each day for the protection and peace of Japan. To witness this ceremony, which is open to the public, head to the *Naoraiden* (Ceremonial Hall) at 8:50am.

TOP EXPERIENCE

★ TŌDAI-JI
東大寺

406-1 Zōshi-chō; tel. 0742/22-5511; www.todaiji.or.jp; 7:30am-5:30pm daily Apr.-Oct., 8am-5pm Nov.-Mar. for Daibutsu-den, 9:30am-5:30pm Apr.-Oct., 9:30am-5pm Nov.-Mar. for Tōdai-ji Museum; adults ¥600, elementary school students ¥300 for Daibutsu-den, adults ¥600, elementary school students ¥300 for Tōdai-ji Museum, adults ¥1,000, elementary school students ¥400 for Daibutsu-den and Tōdai-ji Museum joint pass; take Kintetsu line to Kintetsu Nara Station

Northwest of Kasuga Taisha, Tōdai-ji is the centerpiece of Nara-kōen. This magnificent wooden temple houses the giant bronze Daibutsu statue. If you're only going to see one sight in Nara, make it Tōdai-ji's Great Buddha.

Emperor Shomu (701-758) directed the building of the temple for the sole purpose of hosting the towering bronze Vairocana, the cosmic Buddha from whom all worlds and beings are believed to emanate. Shomu held a ceremony for the unveiling of the statue; gifts from visiting monks from China and India are on display in the Nara National Museum today. The original structure was set ablaze during the wars that ultimately brought the Heian period to a close in 1185.

Approach the temple via the **Tōdai-ji Nandai-mon,** or Great South Gate, flanked by two fierce, muscular statues of Niō, a divine Buddhist guardian. These dramatic wooden sentinels stand 8 meters (26 feet) tall.

About 200 meters (656 feet) to the north is the **Daibutsu-den** (Great Buddha Hall), the world's largest wooden building and the home of the Daibutsu statue. Despite measuring 57 meters (187 feet) in width, 50 meters (164 feet) in depth, and 48 meters (157 feet) in height, the current structure, built in 1709, is only two-thirds the size of the original. The octagonal bronze lantern in front of the main hall dates to the 8th century. The spectacular Daibutsu statue weighs 500 tonnes (550 tons)—103 kg (290 lbs) of it gold—stands 16 meters (53 feet) tall, and exudes an uncanny sense of calm.

After basking in the presence of the Great Buddha, ascend a staircase to **Nigatsu-dō,** a subtemple atop a hill about 300 meters (984 feet) east of Tōdai-ji. The interior of this small structure is only glimpsed by elite priests, but you will be able to take in the stunning views over Nara from the veranda. Two minutes south, the oldest structure in the Tōdai-ji complex, **Sangatsu-dō,** houses a towering Kannon statue and more than a dozen other figures from the Nara Period.

ISUI-EN AND YOSHIKI-EN
依水園, 吉城園

74 Suimon-chō; tel. 0742/25-0781; https://isuien. or.jp; 9:30am-4:30pm (last entry 4pm) Wed.-Mon. Jun.-Mar., open until 5pm (last entry 4:30pm) Apr.-May, closed Wed. if Tues. falls on holiday; adults ¥1,200, university and high school students ¥500, junior high and elementary school students ¥300; take Kintetsu line to Kintetsu Nara Station

Isui-en has all the makings of an ideal landscape garden: abundant flowering plants and trees, a pond, and winding pathways. Access to the neighboring **Neiraku Art Museum,** which houses a collection of bronzes and ceramics from China and Korea, is included in the garden's admission fee. If you're taken enough by the scene to appreciate it while sitting on a tatami floor, there's a teahouse (cup of green tea and a sweet ¥850). Foreigners get in free to the garden next door, Yoshiki-en.

Western Nara

As if the impressive structures around Nara-kōen weren't enough, a cluster of temples of great historical import sits just southwest of town. With roots stretching back to the 7th and 8th centuries, when Buddhism was just being transplanted to Japanese soil, three particular temples are treasure troves of exquisite Buddhist art. Explore these gems if you have extra time in Nara and want to dodge crowds. You can visit all three temples in a half-day trip.

HŌRYŪ-JI
法隆寺

1-1 Hōryūji Sannai, Ikaruga-chō; tel. 0745/75-2555; www.horyuji.or.jp; 8am-5pm daily late Feb.-early Nov., 8am-4:30pm early Nov.-late Feb.; adults ¥1,500, ages 12 and under ¥750

Historically important and visually arresting, this sprawling complex was founded in 607 by Prince Shotoku (574-622), who is credited with drafting Japan's first constitution. The temple's Chūmon (Central Gate) is flanked by Japan's oldest effigies of Kongo Rikishi, the fearsome pair of deities with rippling muscles seen at temples throughout Japan. In fact, some of the original structures on the complex are among the world's oldest surviving wooden constructions. The recently built Gallery of Temple Treasures houses a vast wealth of paintings, relics, statues, and more, and the Yumendono (Hall of Dreams) houses a gilt-wooden life-sized effigy of Prince Shotoku, amid other treasures. This only scratches the surface of the wealth found at Hōryū-ji. For a comprehensive summary, pick up an English guide to the complex when you arrive.

From JR Nara Station, take the Yamatoji line to Hōryū-ji Station (12 minutes; ¥220), then hop on bus 72 (8 minutes; ¥190) to Hōryū-ji Sandō, or simply walk north from Hōryū-ji Station for 20 minutes. To return to Nara, take bus 97 from Hōryū-ji-mae bus stop.

YAKUSHI-JI
薬師寺

457 Nishinokyocho; tel. 0742/33-6001; www.yakushiji.or.jp/en; 8:30am-5pm (last entry 4:30pm) daily; adults ¥1,100, high school and junior high students ¥700, elementary school students ¥300

The temple of Yakushi-ji is likewise one of the oldest temples in Japan, having been built by Emperor Tenmu in 680 in hopes for the healing of his sick wife. The temple's sole surviving original structure is the East Pagoda, which underwent extensive renovation that was completed in mid-2020. The rest of the buildings date to the 13th century or are modern reconstructions, but the real treasures are found within them.

To reach Yakushi-ji from Hōryū-ji, take bus 97 from Hōryū-ji-mae (bus stand 2) to Yakushi-ji Higashiguchi (40 minutes). If you're coming directly from Kintetsu Nara Station, take the Kintetsu Nara line to Yamato-Saidaiji Station, then transfer to the Kintetsu Kashihara line and ride until Nishinokyō Station (25 minutes; ¥260). The temple is about a 1-minute walk southeast from there.

TŌSHŌDAI-JI
唐招提寺

13-46 Gojōchō, Nara; tel. 0742/33-7900; www.toshodaiji.jp; 8:30am-5pm (last entry 4:30pm) daily; adults ¥1,000, high school and junior high school students ¥400, elementary school students ¥200

Walk north from Yakushi-ji for about 10 minutes to reach Tōshōdai-ji, the youngest of the three temples, constructed in 759 by a visiting Chinese priest named Ganjin (Jian Zhen). Today, a wooden statue of the roving priest is brought before the public in the temple's Miedō (Founder's Hall) for a few days in early June, to commemorate the date of Ganjin's death on June 6. At any time of year, however, you can glimpse the 5-meter-tall (16-foot-tall) effigy of Kannon (Goddess of Mercy), complete with what are said to be 1,000 arms, towering within the main hall, or Kondō. The grounds are also laced with leafy footpaths.

To directly reach Tōshōdai-ji from Kintetsu Nara Station, take the Kintetsu Nara line to Nishinokyō Station (15 minutes; ¥260), then walk 500 meters (1,640 ft) north. Alternatively, take bus 78 from JR Nara Station (bus stand 6; 20 minutes; ¥260) or Kintetsu Nara Station (bus stand 8; 20 minutes; ¥260) to the Tōshōdai-ji bus stop. When returning to Nara, you must depart from the Tōshōdai-ji Higashiguchi bus stop on bus 77 or 97.

FESTIVALS
WAKAKUSAYAMA YAMAYAKI
若草山山焼き

At the base of Mount Wakakusayama, next to Nara-kōen; http://nara-park.com/yamayaki-en; around 5pm-evening fourth Sat. of Jan.; walk about 15 minutes east of Tōdai-ji and Kasuga Taisha

On the fourth Saturday of each January, fireworks are launched in town, and then the slope of Mount Wakakusayama is lit ablaze in this fiery festival. The action heats up from about 5pm when a procession of locals light their torches at a shrine in town, then proceed to the foot of Mount Wakakusayama to set the grass blanketing the slope on fire (in a safe, contained manner, of course!). The festival has been going for centuries, though its origins remain a mystery.

SHUNI-E
修二会

Nigatsu-dō; from sunset Mar. 1-14; walk 10 minutes west uphill from Tōdai-ji's main temple complex

This festival sees monks stand along the veranda of Nigatsu-dō, a subtemple of Tōdai-ji, from where they fling embers from around 10 huge flaming bundles of kindling onto a crowd of onlookers below. This is a 1,250-year-old ritual intended to spiritually cleanse the repentant recipients of the raining cinders. The ritual begins on each day of the period at around 6:30pm. Aim to arrive a few hours early if you want a good spot from which to receive the purifying sparks. On the 12th and 13th nights, around 1:30am-2:30am, priests ceremonially draw curative water (*omizutori*, or drawing water), said to only fill a nearby well at that time every year. Following the water drawing, a ritual known as Dattan is performed until about 3:30am inside Nigatsu-dō, involving the waving of torches, ringing of bells, and playing of horns.

FOOD
Nara-kōen
MIZUTANI CHAYA

30 Kasugano-chō; tel. 0742/22-0627; www. mizuyachaya.com; 10am-4pm Thurs.-Tues.; from ¥580; take Kintetsu line to Kintetsu Nara Station

Charming Mizutani Chaya is housed in a thatched-roof building and set in a grove of trees between Kasuga Taisha and Nigatsu-dō, the hillside sub-temple of Tōdai-ji. Alongside teahouse staples, the restaurant also serves rice dishes and bowls of *udon* with various toppings. It's nice, simple food with a classic ambience.

LE CASE

158 Kasugano-chō; tel. 0742/26-8707; http:// quicheteria-lecase.com; 11:30am-5pm (last order 4pm) Wed.-Mon., closed last Mon. every month; from ¥1,250; take Kintetsu line to Kintetsu Nara Station

A great choice for a meal while you're tramping between Nara-kōen's sights is Le Case. This eatery between Tōdai-ji and Kasuga Taisha serves French fare, including quiche (its specialty), as well as cheesecake. Given the dearth of restaurants in this part of town, this is highly recommended if you're hungry in the park.

Naramachi

WAKAKUSA CURRY

38-1 Mochiidonochō; tel. 0742/24-8022; www. wakakusacurry.jp; 11am-3:45pm (last order 3:15pm), 5pm-9pm (last order 8pm) Thurs.-Tues.; ¥700-1,280

This curry joint in the midst of Naramachi serves tasty curry and rice, from chicken and lamb curry to vegetarian and more. There are plenty of toppings, from cheese to breaded and fried pork cutlets. You can choose your spice level (0-25), too. A great place for lunch before or after traipsing through Nara-kōen.

AWA

1 Shonami-chō; tel. 0742/24-5699; www.kiyosumi. jp/naramachiten; 11:30am-3pm (last entry 1:30pm) and 5:30pm-10pm (last entry 8pm) Wed.-Mon.; lunch from ¥2,900, dinner from ¥3,900; Kintetsu Nara Station

This atmospheric restaurant is set in a restored townhouse in the heart of Naramachi. One seating area looks onto a garden, another has the aesthetic of a timeworn *kura*, or traditional storehouse once ubiquitous in Japan for storing grain, and another room has tatami floors. The menu is based on locally grown organic produce, grains including millet, local beef, and *sake* brewed nearby. Meals are beautiful collections of small dishes presented in *kaiseki* fashion. Reservations required. Aim to book a week or more in advance.

KURA

16 Komyoin-chō; tel. 0742/22-8771; 5pm-9:30pm daily; dinner from ¥4,000; take Kintetsu line to Kintetsu Nara Station

In the old-school section of downtown known as Naramachi, Kura is an *izakaya* that serves good food, from yakitori to fried pork cutlets and *oden* (vegetables and fishcake left simmered in broth and served with spicy mustard). Given that booze is a vital component here, this place may be best suited to dinner rather than lunch. Set in a white-walled building, the interior is composed of aged wood with a wraparound countertop. At first glance, it may look slightly intimidating, but step inside and the friendly staff will offer an English-language menu.

ACCOMMODATIONS

Nara-kōen

GUESTHOUSE NARA BACKPACKERS

31 Yurugichō; tel. 0742/22-4557; www. nara-backpackers.com; ¥2,400 dorm rooms, private rooms ¥3,800 pp; take Kintetsu line to Kintetsu Nara Station, exit 1

Guesthouse Nara Backpackers is perhaps Nara's best budget accommodation option. Set in the 90-year-old former home of a tea master, this hostel has many original design flourishes intact, such as its original glass windows, and some of the rooms look out onto a garden. Rooms range from mixed dorms and female-only dorms to a range of private rooms. There's also a shared lounge and kitchen (7am-11pm). The hostel does not accept guests younger than 10 years old. All guests share a common bath where towels can be rented and toiletries can be bought. Rental bikes are also on offer. Room rates drop with longer stays.

★ EDOSAN

1167 Takabatake-chō; tel. 0742/26-2662; www. edosan.jp; from ¥25,300 pp with dinner, from ¥29,700 pp with upgraded dinner plan

This dreamy *ryokan* set in the heart of Nara-kōen has deer ambling through its grounds. Still run by the family who founded a restaurant on the same spot in 1907, the inn prides itself on its exquisitely presented *kaiseki* cuisine. Each room is named after a musical instrument, a specimen of which can be found within (*dora* for the "gong" room, *taiko* for the "drum" room, etc.). It's no surprise that a number of creative luminaries have stayed at the inn, from writers and kabuki actors to painters and fashion designers. A highly atmospheric place to stay, dine, and disconnect from the modern world for a night.

Naramachi

ASUKASOU

*1113-3 Takabatake-chō; tel. 0742/26-2538; www.
asukasou.com; ¥35,000; take Kintetsu line to
Kintetsu Nara Station, exit 2*

For ease of access to the main sights of Nara-kōen, Asukasou is a great pick. It's located in Naramachi just a few minutes' walk from the southwest corner of Nara-kōen, and there's a Japanese restaurant on-site and a rooftop open-air *onsen* bath that can be reserved. Some rooms have futons on tatami floors while others have beds.

★ NARA HOTEL

*1096 Takabatake-chō; tel. 0742/26-3300; www.
narahotel.co.jp; ¥35,000 d; take Kintetsu line to
Kintetsu Nara Station, exit 2*

If you like the idea of staying in a truly historic hotel and don't mind parting ways with hard-earned cash, try the Nara Hotel. In business since 1909, this hotel's distinctive architecture is a fusion of Japanese and Western design. The rooms are expansive, the service top-notch, the grounds immaculate, and on-site dining is first-rate. Even the Dalai Lama and Albert Einstein bedded down at Nara Hotel when they passed through.

INFORMATION AND SERVICES

There are a few good tourist information centers with abundant English-language materials near both the main JR and Kintetsu stations. The **JR Nara Station Information Center** (tel. 0742/27-2223; www.nara-shikanko.or.jp; 9am-9pm daily) is just outside the east exit of JR Nara Station, while **Kintetsu Nara Station Information Center** (tel. 0742/24-4858; 9am-6pm daily) is near exit 3 of Kintetsu Nara Station. Closer to Nara-kōen, there's also the **Nara Visitor Center and Inn** (3 Iken-chō; tel. 0742/81-7461; www.sarusawa.nara.jp; 8am-9pm daily), which stocks ample information and even hosts cultural events sometimes. Friendly staff will be happy to answer questions at this center, which is attached to the Sarusawa Inn.

Online, a good downloadable guide with loads of suggestions, from food to historical sights, can be found at www.visitnara.jp.

GETTING THERE

To reach **JR Nara Station** from **Osaka,** take the JR Kansai line from Namba Station (45 minutes; ¥540) in the south side of Osaka. Also from Namba Station, you can take the Kintetsu Nara line to **Kintetsu Nara Station** (40 minutes; ¥560). From JR Osaka Station, you can take the JR Yamatoji line to JR Nara Station as well (55 minutes; ¥810). Several rapid trains run along this route hourly and stop at Tennoji Station in Osaka's Minami (south) en route (Tennoji to Nara: 30 minutes; ¥470). Another option is to take the JR Nara line from Shin-Osaka Station to JR Nara Station (1 hour; ¥940).

Coming from **Kyoto Station,** take the Kintetsu line to Kintetsu Nara Station (35-45 minutes; ¥1,160) or take the JR Nara line to JR Nara Station (45 miutes-1 hour 15 minutes; ¥720). From **Hiroshima,** first ride the *shinkansen* to Shin-Osaka Station (Sakura trains, 1 hour 40 minutes; ¥10,220), then transfer to the JR Nara line and ride the rest of the way to JR Nara Station (1 hour; ¥940).

It's also possible to arrive in Nara directly from both of Kansai's main regional airports. From **Kansai International Airport** (KIX), there's an hourly limousine run by **Nara Kōtsū** (www.narakotsu.co.jp). The ride takes 90 minutes and costs ¥2,050. Hourly Nara Kōtsū buses also make the 1-hour journey from Osaka Itami Airport (¥1,480).

GETTING AROUND

The easiest way to get around much of Nara is **on foot,** but there are two **buses** that run in a loop around the main sights in and surrounding Nara-kōen, with bus 1 running counterclockwise and bus 2 running clockwise (www.narakotsu.co.jp/language/en/sightseeing_bus/; runs every 10 minutes; ¥210 flat fee for single journey).

When venturing farther afield to the temples west of town, make use of the Yamatoji line, Kintetsu Nara line, or the city's bus network.

There's a **bus information center** (www.narakotsu.co.jp/language/en/pass.html; 8am-8pm Mon.-Fri., 8am-6:30pm Sat.-Sun. and holidays) on the second floor of JR Nara Station, right beside the ticket gate, and another (8:30am-8pm Mon.-Fri., 8:30am-7pm Sat.-Sun. and holidays) on the first floor of the Nara Line House building across from Kintetsu Nara Station. Inquire about **day passes** at either one (1-day passes for central Nara ¥500 adults, ¥250 children, for wider area, including Hōryū-ji, ¥1,000 adults, ¥500 children).

Kobe

神戸

Kobe ("God's Door") is situated on a slope that leads from the peak of Mount Rokko, looming to the north of the city, down toward the bay on the Inland Sea, where small islands are dotted by forests and fishing hamlets. Kobe has long been an important maritime center, having opened up to foreign trade during the Meiji Restoration (1868-1912). Beyond trade, the city became a conduit to the world beyond and was the first place in Japan to have a cinema or host jazz musicians. In a word, Kobe is cosmopolitan.

Mirroring its larger sibling near Tokyo, Yokohama, the city's mercantile past also led to the creation of a bustling Chinatown centered in the area of Nankinmachi (named after the city of Nanjing). Victorian architecture is still on display in the affluent neighborhood of Kitano-chō, once home to many members of the city's foreign traders and diplomats. The modern hub of Sannomiya, a short walk downhill toward the bay, is the city's modern heart. Excellent restaurants, ample shopping, and nightlife with a nice buzz are the draws of this neighborhood.

Though all indicators suggest that Kobe is thriving, in January 1995 the city was hit by a 6.9-magnitude quake that left 6,400 dead, 40,000 injured, and 100,000 homes along with much of the infrastructure in ruins. Thankfully, the city bounced back and its streets hum with life. The city still retains its global orientation with an expat population of around 50,000 and a host of multinational firms based in the city, particularly concentrated on manmade Rokko Island.

With many of Kobe's desirable neighborhoods within walking distance of each other, the city is an ideal place to stroll in search of a good café, a well-made meal, or perhaps a drink, while taking in views of the seaside in the distance.

ORIENTATION

Shin-Kobe Station, and next to it, the entrance to the path that leads uphill to **Nunobiki Falls and Herb Garden,** are at the northern edge of the areas covered here. Trundling about 10 minutes downhill to the southwest, you'll reach the neighborhood of **Kitano-chō,** perched on a hillside at the north end of downtown. Continuing downhill from Kitano-chō for another 15 minutes brings you to **Ikuta Jinja** and the bustle of **Sannomiya.** Fifteen minutes west, you'll pass through one of the most happening parts of town and end up in Chinatown. From there, **Kobe City Museum** is about 7 minutes' walk east, while **Meriken Park** and **Port of Kobe Earthquake Memorial Park** are 15-20 minutes' stroll to the south.

SIGHTS

Light on sights, Kobe is more of a place for a stroll. Be sure to spend some time in **Kitano-chō,** filled with the charming 19th-century Western-style brick residences of diplomats and merchants. Its atmospheric streets wind past cafés and bistros, and shops selling

Kobe

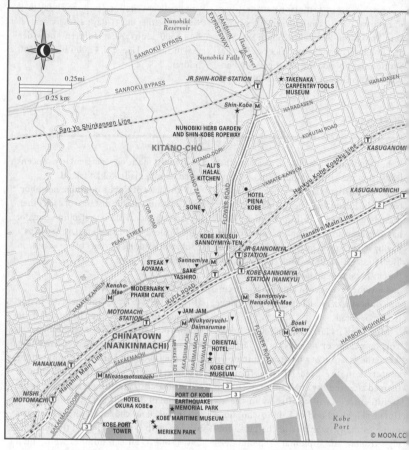

art, crafts, and fashion. The kitschy shops and food offerings of Kobe's **Chinatown** (Nankinmachi), illuminated by red lanterns at night, can seem a bit tired and overpriced, but it's a fun place to wander.

Nunobiki Falls and Herb Garden
神戸布引ハーブ園／ロープウェイ

1-4-3 Kitanochō, Chūō-ku; tel. 078/271-1160; www. kobeherb.com; herb garden only ¥200, Kobe Nunobiki Ropeway ¥950 one-way/¥1,500 round-trip, both including herb garden admission; take Seishin-Yamate line to Shin-Kobe Station

Not far from Shin-Kobe Station, a stone path leads 400 meters (1,312 feet) up a mountain where you'll find the strikingly pristine Nunobiki Falls, the serene Nunobiki Herb Garden, and zipping over it all, the Shin-Kobe Ropeway. You can either walk or ride the ropeway to the top and return down either way, too. The first leg of a walk up the mountain leads to Nunobiki Falls (24 hours; free; about 20 minutes from the bottom). Long the object of reverence and artistic inspiration, the falls vividly illustrate just how close to nature Kobe is.

Another 20 minutes' walk uphill from the

The Genius of Japanese Carpentry

Japan's relationship with carpentry is nothing short of extraordinary. When considering Japan's strong ties to the wooden arts, first dispense with the Western notions that nails, screws, and power tools are needed. Japan has been refining the painstaking art of **joinery** for more than a millennium. If you look under the surface of a traditional Japanese building, you'll discover a complex tapestry of interlocking joints that add up to a building without the use of a single nail.

A second key element of Japan's brilliant carpentry tradition is the importance of **selecting the right wood,** then ageing and treating it to make it last. For large-scale projects, like towering *torii* **gates** fronting ancient shrines and sprawling **temple complexes,** *hinoki* (cypress) is the go-to timber, thanks to its wonderfully smooth grain, ability to fend off rot, and tendency to strengthen with age.

EXAMPLES OF CARPENTRY IN KANSAI

Look no further than Nara Prefecture's **Hōryū-ji** (page 311) for a testament to the durability of Japanese carpentry. This temple complex dating to the 6th and 7th centuries contains the oldest wooden buildings in the world. Japan can also claim the world's largest wooden structure, the Nara-based treasure **Tōdai-ji** (page 310), a temple that houses the famed 16-meter-tall (53-foot-tall) Great Buddha bronze statue and is, shockingly, only two-thirds the size of the original.

THE TAKENAKA CARPENTRY TOOLS MUSEUM

7-5-1 Kumochi-chō, Chūō-ku; tel. 078/242-0216; www.dougukan.jp; 9:30am-4:30pm (last entry 4pm) Tues.-Sun., closed on following day when Mon. is a holiday; adults ¥500, age 65 and over ¥200, high school and university students ¥300, elementary and junior high school students free

For a captivating glimpse into the world of Japanese carpentry, head to Kobe's stunning Takenaka Carpentry Tools Museum, which does a phenomenal job of elucidating what could potentially be construed as a dry topic. It's located a stone's throw from Shin-Kobe Station. Pick up a free English-language audio guide that sheds light on the deep history, techniques, and masterful craftsmanship inherent in Japan's carpentry tradition, from intricate latticework to large-scale temple architecture.

KANSAI
KOBE

falls is the Nunobiki Herb Garden (10am-5pm Mon.-Fri., 10am-8:30pm Sat.-Sun. and holidays, only viewing platform is open after 5pm). This sculpted green space has lavender fields, glasshouses full of tropical blossoms, a café, and viewing platform.

The top station of the **Shin-Kobe Ropeway** (9:30am-5:15pm Mon.-Fri. and 9:30am-8:30pm Sat.-Sun. and holidays Mar. 20-Jul. 19 and Sept. 1-Nov. 30, 9:30am-8:30pm daily Jul. 20-Aug. 31, 9:30am-5pm daily Dec. 1-Mar. 19) lies just beyond the upper entrance to the herb garden, which is roughly 30 minutes' walk uphill from the lower entrance to the garden. You can access the trail that leads to Nunobiki Falls and beyond by exiting from the ground floor of Shin-Kobe Station, turning left, and walking beneath the station to

the beginning of the path. To access the lower station of the Shin-Kobe Ropeway, walk about 10 minutes' southwest of Shin-Kobe Station.

Ikuta Jinja
生田神社

1-2-1 Shimo-Yamate-dōri; tel. 078/321-3851; 7am-dusk daily; free; take JR line to Sannomiya Station

Ikuta Jinja is a surprisingly old shrine in the heart of Kobe's sleek Sannomiya area. It's remained standing through generations of war from the earliest days of the nation, World War II bombing raids, and even more recently, the 1995 earthquake that reduced much of the city to rubble. Some dating puts the shrine's age at up to 18 centuries. This pocket of calm in the midst of the bustle is a nice place for a breather as you walk through downtown.

Kobe City Museum
神戸市立博物館

24 Kyōmachi; tel. 078/391-0035; http:// kobecitymuseum.jp; 10am-6pm Tues.-Thurs. and Sun., 10am-8pm Fri., 10am-9pm Sat. (last entry 30 minutes before closing); first floor free, adults ¥300, high school students and younger ¥150 for second floor, up to ¥1,000 special exhibits; take JR line to Sannomiya Station

Housed in a Greek revival-style building dating from the pre-World War II years, the Kobe City Museum does a good job of documenting the history of the city's interactions with the west. The displays incorporate art and relics from the 19th century on, revealing the ways that Western culture gradually became part of the fabric of the city, from fashion to technology. An interesting example of this cross-cultural exchange is seen in the "Southern Barbarian" school of art, which emerged after Jesuit missionaries began to train Japanese artists in painting techniques from the West. There's sufficient English-language signage throughout.

Meriken Park
メリケンパーク

2-2 Hatoba-chō, Chūō-ku; tel. 078/321-0085; www. feel-kobe.jp; 24 hours daily; free; take Kaigan subway line to Minato Motomachi, or JR or Hanshin line to Motomachi Station

This harborside park is home to a few of the city's most popular sights, one being the Kobe Maritime Museum (2-2 Hatoba-chō, Chōu-ku; tel. 078/327-8983; www. kobe-maritime-museum.com; 10am-6pm Tues.-Sun.; adults ¥900, elementary school, junior high school, and high school students ¥400), easily recognizable with its white sailboat-shaped roofline. This museum contains displays on shipbuilding, cruise ships, the inner workings of ports, and well-made faux ships, including the types that plied Japan's waters during feudal days, but English information is limited.

Looming over the park and serving as an emblem of the city is the iconic hourglass-shaped Kobe Port Tower (5-5 Hatoba-chō, Chōu-ku; tel. 078/291-6751; www.kobe-port-tower.com/language/english.html; 9am-9pm (last entry 8:30pm) daily Mar.-Nov., 9am-7pm (last entry 6:30pm) daily Dec.-Feb.; adults ¥700, children ¥300). There's a 360-degree viewing deck atop the 108-meter-high (354-foot-high) high spire, offering good views of the city and surrounding harbor, with the lush mountains hemming in the city beyond.

Note that it's possible to buy a combination ticket that gives access to both the museum and the tower's observation deck (¥1,300 adults, ¥550 children).

About 10 minutes' walk west of Meriken Park, Harborland (1-3 Higashikawasaki-chō, Chūō-ku; tel. 078/360-3639; www.harborland. co.jp; 10am-9pm daily) is an entertainment and commercial complex on the waterfront with a number of shops and restaurants.

PORT OF KOBE EARTHQUAKE MEMORIAL PARK
神戸港震災メモリアルパーク

24 hours daily; free; take Kaigan subway line to Minato Motomachi, or JR or Hanshin line to Motomachi Station

If you make the trek to the harbor area, stop by the Port of Kobe Earthquake Memorial Park. Here you'll see a cluster of displays, with a video in English retelling the fateful events of the morning of January 17, 1995, when the 6.9-magnitude Great Hanshin Earthquake rocked the city, killing 6,000 and knocking down some 300,000 buildings. The most telling display is a section of the harbor left as it was immediately following the quake: The concrete tilted and partly submerged in water, with lampposts pointing in unnatural angles.

1: Nunobiki Herb Garden and Shin-Kobe Ropeway
2: Port of Kobe Earthquake Memorial Park

The Hanshin Tigers

Although the Hanshin Tigers are deeply associated with the city of Osaka in the popular imagination, the team's home stadium is in fact in Hyōgo Prefecture, just east of Kobe in the mid-sized city of Nishinomiya. The stadium is easily reached from either Osaka or Kobe, and the fans flock from each. The Tigers are not only Kansai's favorite baseball franchise, but in many ways Japan's highest profile team, mostly due to their zealous fan base. If you like sports, or fancy yourself an armchair cultural anthropologist, consider making time to catch a game if you're in Kobe or Osaka at the right time.

KOSHIEN STADIUM

1-82 Koshien-chō, Nishinomiya-shi; tel. 079/847-1041; www.hanshin.co.jp/koshien; tickets from ¥1,600 adults, ¥600 children; take Hanshin line to Kōshien Station

Built in 1924, this is the oldest baseball stadium in Japan and also likely the most famous. The home of the Hanshin Tigers is arguably the best place in Japan to catch a professional baseball game. Seating 47,000, the famously spirited home team side yells custom chants for each batter who steps up to the plate, then allows the opposing team to have their chance to do the same when the Tigers take to the field. Located between Osaka and Kobe in the city of Nishinomiya, the fans come from across the Kansai region.

HOW TO CATCH A GAME

Tickets begin from around ¥1,600, but go for as high as ¥4,800 for more coveted positions in the stands. The season runs from late March through October. Detailed information in English, including access to tickets, is available on the stadium's website. For an English-language guide to reserving tickets in advance visit www.hanshin.co.jp/koshien/global/en/ticket. To reach the stadium from Osaka, take the Hanshin line from Osaka-Umeda Station to Kōshien Station (about 15 minutes; ¥270). From Kobe, take the Hanshin line from Kobe-Sannomiya Station to Kōshien Station (about 20 minutes; ¥270).

FESTIVALS
KOBE JAZZ STREET FESTIVAL

Various locations around town, starting from north side of Hankyū-Kobe Sannomiya Station; www.kobejazzstreet.gr.jp; noon-5pm Sat.-Sun. during first half of Oct.; ¥4,600 1-day pass, ¥8,700 2-day pass

True to its cosmopolitan roots, Kobe is said to be the birthplace of Japan's first jazz group, the Laughing Stars, which formed in the city in 1923. After World War II, jazz giants like Louis Armstrong and Duke Ellington also jammed in the emergent jazz hub. Given its importance as a commercial port, Kobe's already international district of Kitano was fertile ground for a postwar jazz explosion. Today, the heart of the city's jazz scene still beats strong. Check the website for dates and times.

FOOD
GRILL JŪJIYA

96 Strong Bldg. 1F, Edo-chō, Chūō-ku; tel. 078/331-5455; www.grill-jujiya.com; 11am-8pm (last order 7:30pm) Mon.-Sat.; from ¥850; JR Sannomiya Station

Harkening back to Kobe's deep historic ties with the West, the interior of this eatery, founded in 1933, evokes a mid-20th-century diner. The menu consists of Japanese spins on Western fare, a style of cooking known as *yōshoku: omuraisu* (omelet stuffed with rice), beef stew, ham and egg sandwich, hayashi rice (demi-glace sauce slathered over beef hash and onions served over rice). A thoroughly modern complement: There's also a nice selection of craft beer from Osaka.

MODERNARK PHARM CAFE

3-11-15 Kitanagasadōri; tel. 078/391-3060; http:// modernark-cafe.chronicle.co.jp; 11:30am-10pm daily; food from ¥950, drinks from ¥500; take JR Tōkaidō line or Hanshin main line to Motomachi Station

Kobe also has a good range of healthier food options. For quality vegetarian fare in a laid-back café, Modernark Pharm Cafe is a good bet. The menu includes a vegetarian platter, bean burrito, various baked goods, organic beers, teas, juices, coffee, and more. Located north of Motomachi Station in the heart of downtown.

ALI'S HALAL KITCHEN

1-20-14 Nakayamatedōri, Chūō-ku; tel. 078/891-3322; www.aliskitchen.jp; lunch 11am-3pm, dinner 5pm-8pm daily; lunch ¥750-1,500, dinner ¥2,500-5,000; take JR Kobe, Hankyū-Kobe, Hanshin Main, Port Island lines to Sannomiya Station

The owner and chef at this cozy halal spot whips up excellent Pakistani and north Indian food, from tandoori prawn to mutton masala to biryani. There's also a nice range of middle eastern fare, such as *fattoush*, a type of Lebanese salad containing cucumbers and tomatoes, and *kabsa* (basmati rice with a mix of meat and veg). A great pick if you're feeling like something different. It's also an interesting place to get a glimpse of the city's thriving South Asian community.

★ STEAK AOYAMA

2-14-5 Nakayamate-dōri, Chūō-ku; tel. 078/391-4858; www.steakaoyama.com; noon-2:30pm and 5pm-9pm Thurs.-Tues.; lunch from ¥1,600, dinner from ¥2,700; take Hankyu Kobe, JR Tokaido, Seishin Yamate subway line to Sannomiya Station, east exit 3

For an affordable Kobe beef experience, you can't go wrong with Steak Aoyama. This family-owned restaurant, serving succulent slabs of meat since 1963, is the stuff of local culinary legend. Its masterful chef makes pleasant conversation with guests without resorting to cheesy teppanyaki grill sideshows. Set meals come with soup, locally prepped vegetables, tofu, and dessert, all complemented by a great wine selection. To snag one of the eight seats offered in four rounds of meals per day, book at least a month, if not two, in advance via phone or the restaurant's Facebook page.

KOBE KIKUSUI SANNOMIYA-TEN

1-20-13 Kitanagasa-dōri, Chūō-ku; tel. 078/392-1770; https://kobe-kikusui.com; 10am-9pm Mon.-Sat., 10am-8:30pm Sun. and holidays, closed third Tues. of month; average lunch ¥3,150, average dinner ¥6,600; take Seishin-Yamate subway line to Sannomiya Station, East exit 8

Housed on the second floor above a butcher shop, this is a low-key spot to sample Kobe's legendary beef, less expensive than many of the more prominent purveyors of the city's famously well-marbled meat and something of a local favorite. The beef, cooked on the countertop griddle in front of you, comes with grilled vegetables, miso soup, pickles, rice or pilaf, and dessert. Great food, no fuss. Reserve online (https://kobe-kikusui.com/reserve) up to three days in advance.

BARS AND NIGHTLIFE

When it comes to nightlife, Kobe is best known for its jazz haunts. The city is also home to a thriving *sake* brewing district, **Nada,** with some 40 breweries. If you'd like to get acquainted with the city's breweries and do a fair bit of tasting during daylight hours, before a night of jazz perhaps, check out **Kampai Sake Tours** (tel. 080/7045-8365; https://kampaisaketours.com/tour/sake-kobe; 3.5 hours; 1:30pm-5pm Tues.-Sun.; ¥7,700).

★ Jazz
SONE

1-24-10 Nakayamate-dōri, Chūō-ku; tel. 078/221-2055; http://kobe-sone.com; 5pm-midnight daily; ¥1,140 cover, meals from ¥2,500; take Hankyu Kobe, JR Tokaido, Seishin Yamate subway line to Sannomiya Station, east exit 8

Kobe has a long association with jazz, and Sone is the best place to experience the rhythm of the city. This live house—pronounced "so-nay"—has been hosting gigs for the musically discerning since it held its first

Kobe Beef

Rare indeed does a slab of meat have such a household name that simply uttering it, anywhere from New York to Paris, will invoke an air of reverence. Even rarer is a cut of beef so famous that it's more recognizable to many than the city after which it is named. Such is the power of Kobe beef. A taste will convince the hardest skeptic: Beyond well-marbled, it has fat so soft that it actually melts in your mouth.

BACKGROUND

The legendary quality of Japanese beef can be traced back to the 1880s when several European cattle breeds were brought to Japan and mixed with breeds native to the islands. Four strains emerged that remain the backbone of Japan's beef industry even today. While Kobe beef is indeed delicious, there are equally great strains of beef in Matsusaka, Mie Prefecture, northwest of Ise; Sendai and Hokkaido up north; and Miyazaki, down south in Kyushu. A mere 3,000 head of a breed of Tajima

Kobe beef

cattle, as the famed breed raised in Hyōgo Prefecture is known, are officially recognized as the source of bona fide Kobe beef. These legendary cows are fattened up on a choice diet of grass, dried pasture forage, and supplements, and even occasionally massaged, although their troughs are not filled with beer, nor are the bovines serenaded with classical music.

WHERE TO TRY IT

To taste what all the fuss is about, there's no better way than eating it in the place of its origin. Try **Steak Aoyama** (page 321). A small cut at the cheap end of the scale will set you back around ¥7,000, while choicer steaks cost upward of ¥20,000; you may find more reasonable prices during lunchtime—typically from around ¥2,000 at the cheaper end.

spontaneous jam session in 1969. Even today, the venue gets hopping during its four nightly performances and is regarded as Kobe's preeminent jazz den. Recommended for serious jazz aficionados. Performances start at 6:50pm.

JAM JAM

B1, 1-7-2 Motomachi; tel. 078/331-0876; www. facebook.com/jamjam.jazz.kobe; noon-11pm daily, closed first and third Mon. of month; take JR Kobe, Hanshin lines to Motomachi Station

This subterranean jazz bar has a phenomenal sound system and two separate seating areas: one for those who want to listen in peace, and another for those who want to talk quietly. The drinks are good and the

soundtrack sets a perfectly laid-back mood. Enjoy the tunes and note that no song requests are taken.

Sake Bar
SAKE YASHIRO

Fujiya Bldg. 1F, 1-1-5 Shimoyamate-dōri, Chūō-ku; tel. 078/334-7339; 4pm-11:30pm daily; take Hankyu Kobe, JR Tokaido, Seishin Yamate subway line to Sannomiya Station

Kobe's Nada district in the east part of the city is one of Japan's biggest producers of *sake* (rice wine), supplying about one-third of the country's stock. A great place to sip some of the *sakes* made in Kobe is at the laid-back bar of Sake Yashiro, a stone's throw from Ikuta-Jinja. The bar's extensive seasonal menu includes nibbles as well as 90-plus varieties of *sake* from around Japan, with about half of them coming from Kobe. This is a great place for an introduction to the world of *sake*.

ACCOMMODATIONS

HOTEL PIENA KOBE

4-20-5 Ninomiyachō, Chūō-ku; tel. 078/241-1010; www.piena.co.jp; ¥13,000 d; take Hankyu Kobe, JR Tokaido, Seishin Yamate subway line to Sannomiya Station

If you're looking for a clean, centrally located hotel in the midrange budget range, Hotel Piena Kobe is a cut above. Although they look slightly tired, the Western-style rooms are a good size compared to many mid-level hotels in the city and have touches of chic design. There's a good breakfast buffet, too.

HOTEL OKURA KOBE

2-1 Hatoba-chō, Chūō-ku; tel. 078/333-0111; www.kobe.hotelokura.co.jp; ¥25,000 d

For something a bit more luxurious, the Hotel Okura Kobe is a one of Kobe's best. Situated beside Meriken Park, the rooms in this 35-story tower are well-equipped and comfortable, with many boasting great views of the city and harbor. Staff are helpful and the dining room serves a good breakfast, too. The hotel shuttles guests from Kobe Sannomiya Station by bus for free.

★ ORIENTAL HOTEL

25 Kyōmachi, Chūō-ku; tel. 078/326-1500; www.orientalhotel.jp; ¥39,000 d; take Hankyu Kobe, JR Tokaido, Seishin Yamate subway line to Sannomiya Station

The Oriental Hotel is a graceful property closely linked to Kobe's cosmopolitan past. Although it was rebuilt following the Great Hanshin Earthquake of 1995, the hotel still retains a sense of history as one of Japan's first hotels, having originally opened in 1870. Friendly, bilingual staff, well-appointed rooms with plush furnishings and great views, and elegant on-site dining make it one of the best places to stay in the city. Room

rates appear steep on the hotel's website, but look at various booking sites and you may find a good deal.

INFORMATION AND SERVICES

For a range of English-language maps and other information on the city, as well as the "Kobe Welcome Coupon" booklet—which offers discounts for museums, transport, and various activities around the city—the best place to stop is the **Kobe Information Center** (8 Kumoi-dōri, Chūō-ku; tel. 078/322-0220; http://hello-kobe.com; 9am-7pm daily). English-speaking staff are on hand to help with recommendations and bookings. The office is just outside the east exit of JR Sannomiya Station. If you enter Kobe via *shinkansen,* there's also a smaller counter with English-speaking staff and a modest selection of resources in front of the main *shinkansen* ticket gate of JR Shin-Kobe Station.

GETTING THERE

Air

Arriving via **Kansai International Airport,** the **limousine bus** to Kobe is more comfortable than the longer train journey via Osaka. The bus journey (75 minutes; ¥2,000) ends right at **Sannomiya Station** in the heart of downtown Kobe. Buy bus tickets on the spot at the airport; just follow the signs for the bus limousine in the arrivals hall.

If you're flying into **Osaka Itami Airport,** the **limousine bus** is also the way to go. This ride, which goes to Sannomiya Station, takes 40 minutes and costs ¥1,050 per person. From the smaller **Kobe Airport,** which only handles domestic flights, take the **Portliner** (18 minutes; ¥330), which goes straight to Sannomiya Station. Buy tickets on-site in the arrivals hall in both airports.

Train

If you're traveling to Kobe via *shinkansen*—whether on the Sanyō or Tōkaidō line—you'll arrive at **Shin-Kobe Station,** slightly north of downtown. Transfer to the Seishin-Yamate line to travel south from Shin-Kobe Station to the more central **Sannomiya Station** (8 minutes; ¥210).

Coming from Osaka Station, you can easily arrive at Sannomiya Station in less than 30 minutes. If you're using a JR Pass, take the JR Kobe Line (22 minutes; ¥410 without JR Pass). Another option is the private Hankyū Kobe line, which runs from Hankyū Umeda Station in Osaka to **Hankyū Kobe-Sannomiya Station** (28 minutes; ¥320).

From Kyoto, you'll need first to travel to Osaka and change trains to either the JR Kobe line at Osaka Station, or the Hankyū Kobe line at Umeda Station.

From Hiroshima Station, ride the *shinkansen* to Shin-Kobe Station (1 hour 15 minutes; ¥10,200), then transfer to the city's subway or other local train lines to reach Sannomiya or elsewhere from there.

Bus

Like Osaka, Kobe can be reached from a number of stations in **Tokyo** or Yokohama on a highway bus. The trip takes about 8.5 hours and fares start from ¥5,400. Check **Willer Express** (http://willerexpress.com) for details. Willer Express also offers bus journeys from **Hiroshima** to Kobe (6 hours; ¥3,300).

GETTING AROUND
Train

Kobe's relatively small scale means short walk-times between most places and the nearest train station, making its **train network** the easiest way to get around. It's only about a 25-minute walk between Kitanochō in the

north and Chinatown in the south. There are also three above-ground lines and two subway lines running through the city.

Starting from Sannomiya Station in the east, the **JR, Hanshin,** and **Hankyū lines** run westward across the city. The Seishin-Yamate subway line runs north from **Sannomiya Station** to **Shin-Kobe Station,** and from there all the way up to **Tanigami Station.** The Kaigan subway line runs from **Sannomiya-Hanadokeimae Station** southward through downtown toward the bay, where a handful of other stations are located.

For a **map** of the city's train lines, visit www.westjr.co.jp/global/en/timetable/pdf/map_kobe.pdf. Subway fares start from ¥210; all aboveground lines start from ¥130. Purchase tickets from machines near the ticket gates at any station.

Bus

Beyond the rail network, there's also the **City Loop bus** (https://kobecityloop.jp; adults ¥260, children under 12 ¥130 for single ride; adults ¥660, children under 12 ¥330 for one-day pass). The green buses with a retro flair do a lap around the city's most touristed areas, including Sannomiya, Meriken Park, Harborland, and Kitanochō. The easiest place to hop onto one of these buses is at the stop on the north side of Sannomiya Station. Pay for a single journey at the machine next to the driver's seat as you exit the bus. If you plan to use a one-day pass, buy one at the **Kobe Information Center** outside JR Sannomiya Station's east exit.

Himeji

姫路

In the sleepy city of Himeji, home to some 500,000 people, you'll find the most stellar surviving example of a castle in all of Japan. If you're going to see one castle during your time here, make it Himeji-jō. Looming over the downtown area, this stunning example of feudal architecture is downright imposing, even today.

Today, Himeji's downtown is centered on **Otemae-dōri**, a broad avenue 1 km (0.6 mi) long, running straight from Himeji Station to the castle, with side streets spreading out to the east and west from there. The city's history is closely entwined with its famed fortress, which it grew around. After much of Himeji was razed by Allied bombers during World War II, amazingly leaving the castle intact, the city was rapidly rebuilt in the postwar years to become one of Hyōgo Prefecture's key manufacturing centers.

But drawing visitors to the castle is what the town does best. The towering white citadel is not only the best preserved and most handsome of all Japan's medieval fortresses, it is also the largest. Gawping at it, it's hard

to deny that its official status as both a national treasure and UNESCO World Heritage Site are well deserved. After visiting the castle, the town of Himeji is a pleasant place to have lunch.

SIGHTS
★ Himeji-jō
姫路城
68 Honmachi; tel. 079/285-1146; www.city.himeji. lg.jp/castle/index.html; 9am-5pm daily Sept.-Apr., 9am-6pm May-Aug. (last entry one hour before closing); adults ¥1,000, high school students and younger ¥300

"White Heron Castle," as it is also known, describes Himeji-jō well. Refined and nearly unconquerable, this luminous white fortress atop a hill is hands-down the most stunning citadel in Japan. Aside from being a brilliant example of Japanese castle architecture, it is one of the few original structures left intact—a miracle in itself, considering that Himeji was nearly razed by Allied bombers during World War II.

Built by warlord Toyotomi Hideyoshi in 1581, the trusty stronghold was expanded

KANSAI
HIMEJI

Himeji-jō

Japanese Castles 101

Ensconced on mammoth stone foundations, built many stories high with enormous timber planks, painted white or black on the outside and dimly lit on the inside, and topped by gently sweeping roofs, Japanese castles cut a striking profile.

HISTORY AND CASTLE TYPES

During the turbulent Sengoku (Warring States) Period, roughly from the mid-15th-early 17th century, the country was divided between a number of small independent fiefdoms that were locked in a seemingly endless squabble for power. The nearly constant state of war necessitated the building of hilltop fortifications known as *yamajiro* ("mountain castles"), solely for defense.

As Japan became more unified, castles known as *hirayamajiro* ("flatland mountain castles") were built on hilltops and used for administrative affairs more than defense. By the time Tokugawa Ieyasu (1543-1616) brought all of Japan under one central power with the dawn of the Edo period (1603-1868), castles known as *hirajiro* ("flatland castles") were simply built on flat land, as their overtly martial roots faded.

With the Meiji Restoration of 1868 and the dawn of the modern age, many of these magnificent complexes were razed following a government decree that sought to do away with the reminders of the country's feudal past. Others still were bombed to smithereens during World War II. Today, only 12 castles retain their original keeps, while a slew of others are concrete reconstructions.

THE CASTLE LAYOUT

A classic Japanese castle layout revolved around concentric rings, with the *homaru* ("main circle") at the heart and containing the *tenshukaku*, or main keep or castle tower, usually between two and five stories high; surrounded by the *ninomaru* ("second circle"), where the nobles often lived; in turn surrounded by the *sannomaru* ("third circle"). The outer reaches of a castle consist of a series of moats and walls, punctuated by strategically placed guard towers known as *yagura* and heavily fortified entrance gates.

in the 16th century by Ikeda Terumasa, shogun Tokugawa Ieyasu's son-in-law. It served as the home and fortress of almost 50 lords until 1868 when the Meiji Restoration brought Japan's feudal era to an end and ushered in the modern age. Renovated in 2015, it looks as good as new.

The castle's main five-story keep and a few smaller keeps are all surrounded by moats and stone walls featuring defensive openings for arrows, bullets, boiling oil, or water to be sent the enemy's way. The castle's ceramic roof tiles are believed to impart supernatural protection upon the fortress. Some of them are *onigawara* ("ogre tiles"), which bear the visages of ogres believed to fend off evil spirits and misfortune. Between the castle's various buildings, well-landscaped grounds full of flowering plants

and well-sculpted trees also make for an appealing stroll.

If you have time and want to extend your time in Himeji by an hour or two, cross the castle's western moat and enter Kōkō-en (9am-6pm daily May-Aug., 9am-5pm Sept.-Apr. (last entry 30 minutes before closing); adults ¥310, children ¥150, adults ¥1,050, children ¥360 with Himeji-jō combination ticket). These reconstructed samurai homes and gardens are thick with feudal-period ambience—a recommended addition to your exploration of the castle.

FOOD

MENME

68 Hon-machi; tel. 079/225-0118; noon-5pm Thurs.-Tues.; from ¥550; walk 10 minutes north of Himeji Station

This cheap, popular *udon* (flour noodles) shop is a good choice for a quick lunch on the main drag leading to the castle from Himeji Station. Coming from the station, you'll find it on the left side of Ōtemae-dōri. Out front, there's a row of stools for the occasional queue, and a white *noren* curtain hangs in front of the door.

LE CHAT BOTTÉ

71 Shirogane-machi; tel. 079/280-3107; https:// lechatbotte.owst.jp; 11:30am-2pm and 5:30pm-9pm (last order 8:30pm) Tues.-Sat., holidays, and days before holidays, 11:30am-2pm Sun.; lunch from ¥1,200, dinner courses from ¥4,200; walk 6 minutes north of Himeji Station

This authentic French bistro serves great lunch sets and larger meals for dinner. Lunch options include a mix of soup, appetizers, quiche or a main dish, bread, and coffee or tea. Dinner items include soup, appetizers, a main course (*wagyu*, or Japanese beef, steak, roasted duck, lamb stew, etc.), and dessert. Reserving a day ahead is recommended.

GETTING THERE

Visiting Himeji-jō is best approached as a jaunt from nearby Kobe, Osaka, Nara, or Kyoto, or as a stop on a longer westward journey to Okayama or Hiroshima aboard the San'yō *shinkansen*.

Train

Himeji Station is a straight shot on the JR Tōkaidō line from **Kobe** (40 minutes; ¥970). It's also possible to take the same train from **Kyoto Station** as a special rapid express train bound for Banshuako Station (90 minutes; ¥2,270), or as a special rapid express train from **Osaka Station** (1 hour; ¥1,490). From **Hiroshima,** *shinkansen* trains run directly to Himeji Station (1 hour; ¥8,440).

Getting Around

To reach the castle, exit the north side of JR Himeji Station and **walk** 25 minutes north along Ōtemae-dōri. Alternatively, you can take advantage of the city's local bus network, run by **Shinki Bus** (www.shinkibus.co.jp). Buses depart directly in front of JR Himeji Station's north exit. Bus fares, including for the trip from Himeji Station to Himeji-jō, start from ¥100. For detailed routes and fares, visit www.himeji-kanko.jp/files_foreign/pdf/ transportation_guide.pdf.

Between Kansai and Hiroshima

The stretch of Western Honshu's southern

(San'yō) coast borders one of the world's loveliest seascapes, the Seto Naikai (Inland Sea). This thoroughly modern shoreline, from Kansai's western edge in the east to Hiroshima in the west, is conveniently served by bullet train. Yet, a nostalgic air hangs over the antique streets and ageing harbors of its historic towns.

Starting in the east, Okayama Prefecture is known for its sublime landscape garden Kōraku-en, overseen by a castle, and the nearby town of Kurashiki, famed for its canal district that oozes Edo-period charm. West of Kurashiki, in Hiroshima Prefecture, the classic port town of Onomichi effortlessly enchants. Beyond the fishing boats docked in the harbor and mom-and-pop sushi shops, a mountainside strewn with

Highlights

Look for ★ to find recommended sights, activities, dining, and lodging.

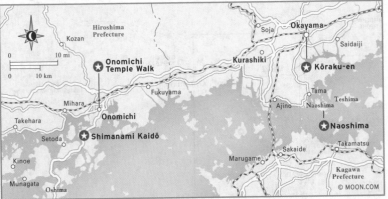

© MOON.COM

★ **Kōraku-en:** Wander this sprawling landscape garden and see why it safely claims a spot among Japan's top three gardens (page 339).

★ **Naoshima:** Take a ferry to this idyllic island for its rustic charm and bohemian ethos as much as for its collection of world-class art museums (page 346).

★ **Onomichi Temple Walk:** This hilly route meanders above the idyllic port town of its namesake, taking in 25 historic temples and offering gorgeous views of the Inland Sea below (page 356).

★ **Shimanami Kaidō:** Cross the sparkling Inland Sea by bicycle, following a series of bridges over a string of isles between Honshu and Shikoku (page 364).

Between Kansai and Hiroshima

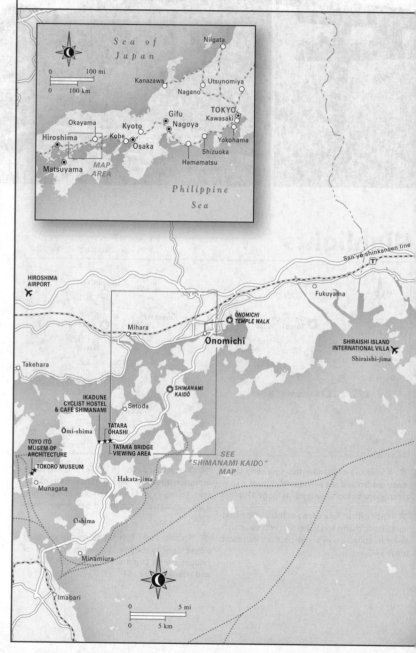

Sea of Japan

Niigata

Kanazawa

Utsunomiya

Nagano

Gifu

TOKYO

Okayama

Kyoto Nagoya

Kawasaki

Hiroshima Kobe

Osaka

Yokohama

Shizuoka

Hamamatsu

Matsuyama

MAP AREA

Philippine Sea

0 100 mi
0 100 km

San'yō shinkansen line

HIROSHIMA AIRPORT

Fukuyama

Mihara

ONOMICHI TEMPLE WALK

Onomichi

SHIRAISHI ISLAND INTERNATIONAL VILLA

Shiraishi-jima

Takehara

IKADUNE CYCLIST HOSTEL & CAFE SHIMANAMI

Setoda

SHIMANAMI KAIDŌ

TATARA ŌHASHI

Ōmi-shima

TATARA BRIDGE VIEWING AREA

TOYO ITŌ MUSEM OF ARCHITECTURE

SEE "SHIMANAMI KAIDŌ" MAP

TOKORO MUSEUM

Munagata

Hakata-jima

Oshima

Minamiura

0 5 mi
0 5 km

Imabari

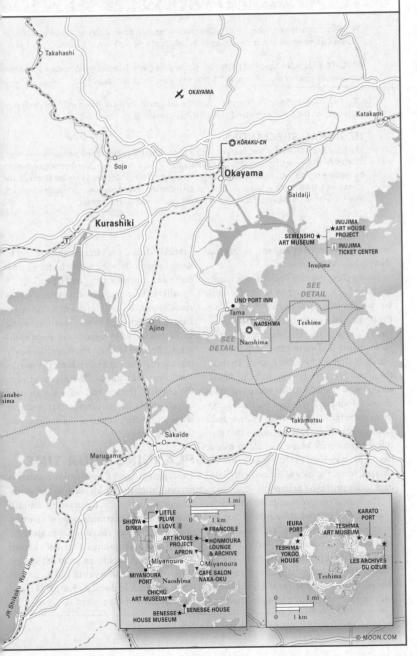

Takahashi

✈ OKAYAMA

★ KŌRAKU-EN

Okayama

Soja

Saidaiji

Katakami

Kurashiki

INUJIMA
★ ART HOUSE
PROJECT

SEIRENSHO ★
ART MUSEUM

ℹ INUJIMA
TICKET CENTER

Inujima

SEE
DETAIL

UNO PORT INN

Tama

Ajino

NAOSHIMA

Teshima

SEE
DETAIL

Naoshima

anabe-
ima

Takamatsu

Sakaide

Marugame

JR Shikoku Rail Line

0   1 mi

0   1 km

SHIOYA ●
DINER

▼ LITTLE
PLUM
■ I LOVE 湯

ART HOUSE ★
PROJECT
APRON ▼

● FRANCOILE

■ HONMOURA
LOUNGE
& ARCHIVE

▼ Miyanoura

MIYANOURA
PORT

▼ Miyanoura

Naoshima

○ CAFÉ SALON
NAKA-OKU

CHICHŪ
ART MUSEUM ★

BENESSE ★
HOUSE MUSEUM

■ BENESSE HOUSE

KARATO
PORT

IEURA
PORT

TESHIMA
★ ART MUSEUM

TESHIMA
YOKOO
HOUSE

LES ARCHIVES
DU CŒUR

Teshima

0   1 mi

0   1 km

© MOON.COM

Best Restaurants

★ **Takadaya:** Dine on skewers of grilled chicken, washed down with your booze of choice, at this old-fashioned yakitori shop in the delightfully nostalgic old town of Kurashiki (page 344).

★ **Café Salon Naka-oku:** Escape to this cozy spot, which serves great home-cooked fare and stays open after the throngs of day-trippers leave Naoshima (page 350).

★ **Hassakuya:** Savor an orange-stuffed rice cake made by hand at this wildly popular confectionary on the citrus-rich island of Inno-shima (page 361).

REGIONAL SPECIALTIES

The islands of the Inland Sea, blessed with a sunny and mild climate, are renowned for their **citrus fruits**—particularly lemons and oranges—as well as **olives.** Unsurprisingly, the sea blesses the region with an abundance of freshly caught **fish** of all types. There are also regional spins on **ramen,** such as the style popular in Onomichi, served in soup made with soy sauce, *dashi* (dried fish stock), and chicken, with the occasional addition of pork fat.

temples and guarded by an army of cats rises sharply behind downtown.

Facing these towns is the wistfully beautiful Inland Sea. The narrow body of water is bounded by Honshu to the north, Shikoku to the south, and Kyushu to the west, and is entered via four straits. The beauty of this calm, blue expanse is often mentioned in the same breath as Greece's majestic Aegean. In truth, these two great waterways differ in fundamental ways. Donald Richie remarked in his classic travelogue *The Inland Sea* that "a castaway, given the choice between a Greek and a Japanese island, would swim toward the latter. It looks like a place where it would be nice to live." This is evident in the region's timeless villages, where the pace of life and salty, laidback locals invite you to unplug.

The most accessible islands are Naoshima, Teshima, and Inujima, Naoshima being the most popular. These three "art islands" have added creative dimensions—world-class museums, local art projects, and more—to revitalize the quaint villages hugging their shores. Nearby, off-the-radar Shodo-shima and, farther west, tiny Shiraishi-jima and

Manabe-shima, are ideal escapes. A trip to any of them offers the ideal chance to slow down and experience the "real Japan."

Still farther west, a 70-km (43-mi) scenic route known as the Shimanami Kaidō starts from Onomichi and moves south, crossing six islands linked by some of the world's longest suspension bridges. The route ultimately leads across the sea and ends on the northwest corner of Shikoku. To fully experience the magic of this course, make the journey on two wheels. Riding through this maritime scene must surely be one of the world's prettiest bicycle trips.

PLANNING YOUR TIME

The region between Kansai and Hiroshima is part of **Chūgoku,** which takes up the southernmost tip of Honshu, Japan's main island. It makes for a great intermediary leg of a journey that starts in either Tokyo or Kyoto and ultimately ends in Hiroshima. On what's known as the **San'yō,** or southern, coast of Honshu, it's possible to see **Okayama** and its famous landscape garden, nostalgic **Kurashiki,** and the port town of **Onomichi** in 2-3 days. To

Best Accommodations

★ **Ryokan Kurashiki:** With top-end meals and plush rooms, this old-school *ryokan* is the best place to stay in Kurashiki's atmospheric old town (page 345).

★ **Benesse House:** Sleep amid the works of world-famous artists at Naoshima's luxury museum-cum-hotel, which offers sweeping views of the Inland Sea (page 351).

★ **Ōmi-shima Ikoi-no-Ie:** This singular lodging, stylishly designed by architect Toyo Itō and set in a former schoolhouse with many retro fixings intact, beckons from a remote corner of Ōmi-shima (page 370).

visit any of the **Inland Sea's** idyllic islands, plan to add 1-2 days extra per island, depending on your itinerary. The same goes for cycling the **Shimanami Kaidō:** Add 1-2 days, depending on whether you plan to do a one-day return trip, stay overnight on one of the islands, or travel all the way across to Shikoku.

Sany'yō is one of the sunniest parts of Japan. Long, pleasant springs (Mar.-May) roll into hot, muggy summers, with rainy *tsuyu* (rainy season) hitting in June and July. Like spring, autumns are agreeable, while winter (Dec.-Feb.) temperatures can drop to as low as 2°C (36°F), but seldom fall below freezing. Overall, **April-May** and **October-November** are the most desirable times to visit, with cherry blossoms popping in late March and early April, and the leaves taking on an elemental palette as autumn wears on. While the crowds won't overwhelm in most of the region—Naoshima being an exception—try to **book accommodations a few months in advance** if you plan to travel at these more popular times of year.

Itinerary Ideas

ONE DAY IN OKAYAMA AND KURASHIKI

1 Start your day with a midmorning trip to **Kōraku-en,** Okayama's justifiably praised landscape garden, in the shadow of Okayama-jō.

2 For lunch, head to nearby **Okabe** and enjoy a healthy tofu-based set meal prepared at this cozy local spot.

3 After lunch, head to JR Okayama Station to make the brief trip to the nearby town of Kurashiki. Make your way to the Bikan Historical Quarter. Begin your exploration of the area at **Ōhara Museum of Art.** Spend the rest of the afternoon strolling through the streets surrounding the historic district's dreamy canal.

4 For a late-afternoon coffee break, swing by the atmospheric **Kurashiki Coffee-kan.**

5 For dinner, feast on excellent yakitori at **Takadaya.** Either return to Okayama for the night or sleep in Kurashiki to enjoy the romantic canal-side ambience once the day-trippers leave.

Itinerary Ideas

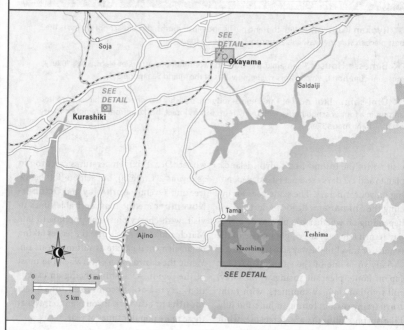

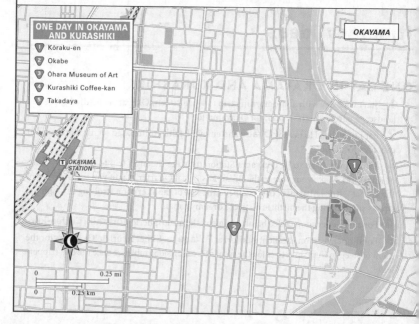

ONE DAY IN OKAYAMA AND KURASHIKI

1 Kōraku-en
2 Okabe
3 Ōhara Museum of Art
4 Kurashiki Coffee-kan
5 Takadaya

OKAYAMA

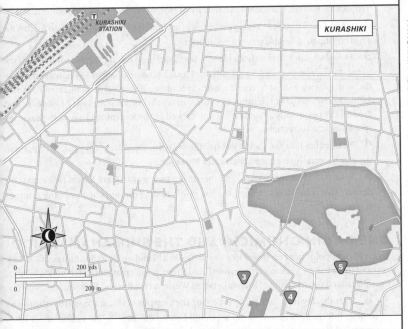

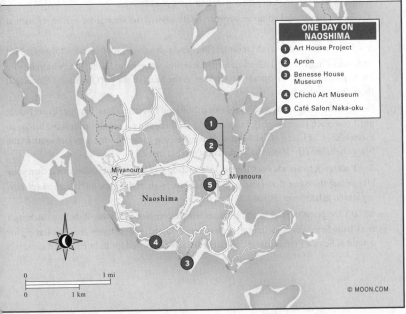

ONE DAY ON
NAOSHIMA
1 Art House Project
2 Apron
3 Benesse House
   Museum
4 Chichū Art Museum
5 Café Salon Naka-oku

© MOON.COM

ONE DAY ON NAOSHIMA

1   Begin your exploration of Naoshima's art scene at the various sites of the **Art House Project** around the traditional community of Honmura, on the east side of the island.

2   Once you've finished visiting the pieces of art built into the village, head to **Apron** for a healthy lunch in bright, artsy surroundings.

3   Fueled up, catch the bus from Honmura to Tsutsuji-sō bus stop on the south side of the island. Walk from the bus stop to **Benesse House Museum,** about 15 minutes on foot to the west, passing a stone *torii* gate scenically standing before the sea and Yayoi Kusama's iconic *Yellow Pumpkin* sculpture en route. Survey the impressive range of works in and around the beautifully situated museum, as well as the sweeping views of the seascape spreading in all directions.

4   Next, either take the shuttle bus from Benesse House Museum or walk 15 minutes to the architecturally stunning **Chichū Art Museum.**

5   Return to Honmura by bus, and then make your way to **Café Salon Naka-oku** for dinner. This cozy nook is among the few places to dine on the island once the sun goes down.

ONE DAY IN ONOMICHI AND THE SHIMANAMI KAIDŌ

To avoid disappointment on this active day in Onomichi and cycling the Shimanami Kaidō, **reserve your bike** a week in advance from Setoda Tourist Information Center on Ikuchi-jima, the third island on the string of islands between Western Honshu and Shikoku.

1   Start the day in Onomichi by following the **Temple Walk,** starting from the town's tourist information center, on the steep hill behind downtown. The entire circuit takes about 2-3 hours on foot, depending on how long you linger.

2   You've likely worked up an appetite. Walk toward the waterfront and have lunch at **Yamaneko Cafe.**

3   Sated, make your way to Onomichi Port and ride a ferry for 40 minutes to Setoda Port on Ikuchi-jima, the third island along the beautiful Shimanami Kaidō. Rent a bicycle from the **Setoda Tourist Information Center** in the heart of the port town's old Shiomachi shopping street area.

4   Cycle 8.5 km (5.3 mi) southward along the island's western shore, passing Sunset Beach, until you reach the imposing **Tatara Bridge,** where you can cross the hulking bridge to the neighboring island of Ōmi-shima. Make your way to the viewing area just south of the bridge to behold the sheer size of the construction marvel.

5   Backtrack to Setoda Port Tourist Information Center by 5pm so you can return your bike before the office closes and grab a quick bite to-go in the area, followed by a refreshing lemon gelato from **Dolce.**

6   If time permits, stop by the singular temple complex of **Kōsan-ji,** before catching a ferry from Setoda back to Onomichi (last ferry 6:30pm). Alternatively, consider staying for a night at Setoda Private Hostel, on Sunset Beach, renowned for its burning red sunsets.

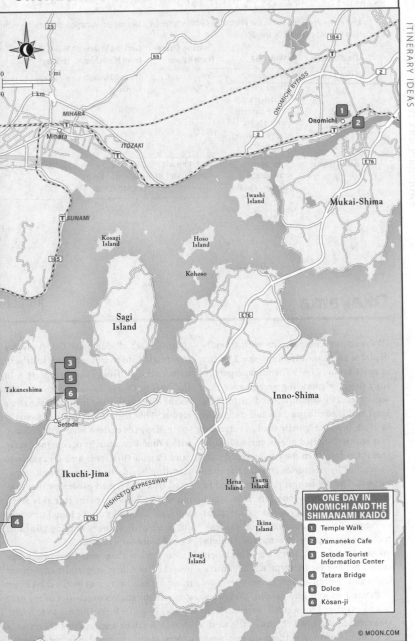

Onomichi and the Shimanami Kaidō

Where to Go from Kyoto and Hiroshima

Like in much of the region, the **Nozomi** *shinkansen* will be the fastest option, but keep in mind that it is not covered by the JR Pass.

Destination	Why Go?	Getting There from Kyoto	Getting There from Hiroshima	How Long to Stay
Okayama	Kōraku-en, considered one of Japan's top three gardens, with a black castle looming nearby	Train: 1 hour, ¥7,790	Train: 40 minutes, ¥6,550	Half day
Kurashiki	Edo-period townscape, a dreamy canal	Train: 1 hour 15 minutes, ¥8,120	Train: 35 minutes-1 hour, ¥5,940-6,150	Half day

Okayama 岡山

Okayama is a compact city with friendly denizens and a mostly sunny sky. The city is most famous for its landscape garden Kōraku-en, a sprawling green space that was originally commissioned in 1687 by local lord Ikeda Tsunamasa and completed in 1700. It was originally used to entertain and host well-heeled guests during Japan's feudal heyday, when the garden could only be reached by aristocrats crossing the river by boat. The public was only permitted to enter on special occasions until 1884, when its doors were flung open. Alongside typical elements of a classic *shūyū* (stroll garden), such as walking paths, streams, and a hilltop meant for surveying the scene, Kōraku-en is also notable for its atypically expansive lawns and even an archery range.

Beyond its sublime garden, Okayama is a pleasant city for a stroll. Surrounding Okayama Station, which sits in the western side of downtown, the main east-west thoroughfare of Momotarō Ōdōri divides the town into northern and southern halves straight from Okayama Station in the west to Okayama-jō in the east. The Asahi River is another feature of the city's layout. This wide waterway runs north-south along the eastern edge of downtown, with Kōraku-en actually occupying a large sand bar on this river and Okayama-jō standing beside its western bank, separated from the famed garden by the flowing water. Walking paths line this river, and wide sidewalks can be found throughout much of downtown, making Okayama a good place for a flaneur.

More often than not, Okayama is approached as a brief stop and a convenient transport hub, serving as both a *shinkansen* stop and the station to transfer to the only railway line that links Honshu to Shikoku. Though it can be seen in a day, Okayama is a pleasant place to spend the night. There's a

Destination	Why Go?	Getting There from Kyoto	Getting There from Hiroshima	How Long to Stay
The Art Islands	unconventional spaces designed by cutting-edge architects, natural beauty, world-class artwork	Train and Ferry: 2 hours, ¥8,650	Train and Ferry: 1.5-2 hours, ¥6,800-7,010	Overnight-a long weekend
Onomichi	a classic Japanese port, temples that beg to be explored on foot	Train: 1.5 hours, ¥9,220	Train: 45 minutes, ¥4,840-5,470	Half day
Shimanami Kaidō	a scenic, six-island bicycle journey leading over roads and bridges	Ferry and Bicycle: From Onomichi Port, 10-40 minutes; ¥70-1,200	Ferry and Bicycle: From Onomichi Port, 10-40 minutes; ¥70-1,200	One day-overnight

nice buzz in the air in the area near the city's main train station in the evening.

SIGHTS
★ Kōraku-en
後楽園

1-5 Kōraku-en, Kita-ku; tel. 086/272-1148; https:// okayama-korakuen.jp; 7:30am-6pm (last admission 5:45pm) daily Mar. 20-Sept. 30, 8am-5pm (last admission 4:45pm) Oct. 1-Mar.19; ages 15 and over ¥400, combined admission to castle ¥560, under age 15 free

Long considered one of Japan's top three gardens, alongside Mito's Kairaku-en and Kanazawa's Kenroku-en, Kōraku-en straddles the Asahi River. It was originally built in 1700 by local lord Ikeda Tsunamasa, whose former home, **Okayama-jō** (2-3-1 Marunouchi; tel. 086/225-2096; https:// okayama-kanko.net/ujo; 9am-5:30pm daily; adults ¥300; children 6-14 ¥120), sits beside the lush landscape garden. This black fortress, nicknamed "crow castle," has accents of white and golden fish ornaments curling upward on the corners of its eaves. If you're most interested in seeing it from the outside, the view from the garden suffices.

The garden was opened to the public in 1884, following the dawn of the Meiji era. Although floods in 1934 and World War II bombing marred the grounds, they have been returned to their former state. The main structure on the grounds is the reconstructed **Enyo-tei House,** once a living quarters for the local lord. There are also a series of open-air pavilions, a large central pond, streams and smaller pools of water inhabited by colorful *koi,* and a few secluded teahouses. Groves of plum, cherry, apricot, and maple trees, flowers from azaleas to rhododendrons, and a tea field draw the eye, while shrines and a *Noh* stage add a dose of culture. There's a crane aviary, too. Cherry blossom season in spring and the coming of autumn foliage are popular times to visit the grounds, but they're expansive enough never to feel thronged.

The gardens occupy 14 hectares (2.5 acres), which should take you a few hours to explore, depending on how much you stop to soak in the views and snap photos. Meander along the paths, admiring the wide range of viewpoints, from bridges, rest houses, and atop the prominent hill. Kōraku-en's layout is wonderfully open: you can see most of the garden from almost anywhere you look.

The garden is about 25-30 minutes' walk northeast of Okayama Station. You can also take the Higashiyama tram line to Shiroshita stop (10 minutes; ¥100), from where the castle is about 10 minutes' walk east and the garden's main gate is 10 minutes' walk northeast (via the large bridge). Alternatively, catch the bus that runs several times hourly from Okayama Station bus stop 1 to Kōrakuen-mae bus stop (15 minutes; ¥100), which puts you directly in front of the garden's main gate. Enter via the main entrance, located near the **Okayama Prefectural Museum** (1-5 Kōraku-en, Kita-ku; tel. 086/272-1149; www. pref.okayama.jp/site/kenhaku; 9am-6pm Tues.-Sun.; ¥250), or via the south entrance, near Okayama-jō.

FOOD
TORIYOSHI

5-8 Honmachi, Kita-ku; tel. 086/233-1969; 4pm-midnight daily; ¥250-850 per plate; walk 3 minutes east of Okayama Station

This boisterous *izakaya* is a great place to drink and eat with locals. The menu includes staples like yakitori (grilled chicken on skewers), side salads, grilled fish, sashimi, and more. Come here if you want to supplement your dinner with a steady flow of booze (beer, *sake*, whisky soda, etc.) and mingle with friendly locals. English menu available.

OKABE

1-10-1 Omote-chō; tel. 086/222-1404; http:// tofudokoro-okabe.com/shokujidokoro; 11:30am-2pm Mon.-Wed. and Fri.-Sat.; ¥880-970; take the Higashiyama tram line to Kencho-dōri tram stop

This homey tofu-focused lunch spot is a good option before or after visiting Kōraku-en. There are just three set meals on offer: deep-fried tofu, tofu skin over rice, and the assorted Okabe original set. The food is reasonably priced and tasty. Note that the food is not vegan, as some fish stock is used in the preparation. English-language menu with pictures is available.

ICHIRIN SHUZO

2-16 Honmachi, Kita-ku; tel. 086/231-0690; www. ichirinshuzo.com; 5pm-midnight Mon.-Sat., open Sun. and closed Mon. if Mon. falls on holiday; ¥285-1,142 per dish, courses ¥3,000-4,000; walk 3 minutes east of Okayama Station

Across the street from Toriyoshi, this seafood *izakaya* is a popular spot serving creative seafood concoctions and more, from fermented soybeans atop squid sashimi to salted mackerel and black pepper-infused pork spare ribs. It gets busy, especially on the weekends, so reserve ahead to be safe.

J'S EN

2-10-11 Hokan-cho, Kita-ku; tel. 086/251-0088; http://js-kitchen.jp; 4pm-midnight (last order 11:30pm) daily, 11:30am-2pm (last order 1:30pm) Sat.-Sun. and holidays; lunch sets ¥1,000-2,200, dinner ¥4,000-5,000; walk 10 minutes northwest of Okayama Station

This friendly Korean barbecue (*yakiniku*) joint is an excellent place to sample Okayama beef. The meat is balanced by a healthy range of salads, cabbage, soups, and more. The welcoming staff go out of their way to help you, too. Reserve a day in advance if you can.

ACCOMMODATIONS
TORII-KUGURU GUESTHOUSE AND LOUNGE

4-7-15 Hōkan-chō, Kita-ku; tel. 086/250-2629; http:// toriikuguru.com; dorms (mixed and female-only) ¥3,240, private singles ¥4,860, private doubles ¥7,020; walk 13 minutes northwest of Okayama Station

This laid-back, welcoming guesthouse, in an old-school shopping district on the quieter side of town, is a great option for those traveling on a tight budget. The interior is clean and bright with wood floors, tasteful lighting, and

---

1: Kōraku-en 2: Okayama-jō

shared bathrooms. Uniquely, the guesthouse is situated in Nawate, a petite complex that also includes a lounge and bar. You'll know you've found it when you reach the *torii* gate left over from a shrine that once stood on the plot next to the reception desk.

KŌRAKU HOTEL

5-1 Heiwachō, Kita-ku; tel. 086/221-7111; https:// hotel.kooraku.co.jp; ¥15,000 room only, ¥17,000 with breakfast; walk 5 minutes east of Okayama Station

This clean, bright midrange hotel has airy, modern rooms with well-appointed bathrooms. The common areas are stylish with a boutique vibe, and there's a restaurant serving Japanese fare on the second floor. Breakfast plan optional. This is a good mid-priced option in the heart of the entertainment district.

ANA CROWNE PLAZA OKAYAMA

15-1 Ekimoto-machi, Kita-ku; tel. 086/898-1111; www. anacpokayama.com; ¥15,750 room only

This upper-range business hotel just outside the west side of Okayama Station is a great value. The plush rooms are spacious and tastefully decorated. There are three restaurants and a bar with striking views over the city. If you've got the means, book one of the south-facing premium rooms for the best views and the added space.

INFORMATION AND SERVICES

Keeping with the theme of the region's favorite folk hero, the **Momotarō Tourist Information Center** (tel. 086/222-2912; www.okayama-kanko.net; 9am-8pm daily) is situated near the east exit of bustling Okayama Station, in the underground shopping complex. Staff speak some English. This is the best place to pick up information on the city and surroundings. Online, the official **Explore Okayama** website (www.okayama-japan.jp/en) is a useful resource, too.

GETTING THERE

Its position on the *shinkansen* line and local JR San'yō line makes Okayama easily accessible by **rail**. Coming from the east, a number of major hubs are accessible via *shinkansen*: **Osaka** (50 minutes; ¥6,020), **Kyoto** (1 hour; ¥7,850), and **Tokyo** (3 hours 30 minutes; ¥17,340). Lying to the west is **Hiroshima** (40 minutes; ¥6,230). Okayama Station sits on the western side of downtown, roughly 25 minutes' walk from Kōraku-en, which sits on the eastern side of downtown, alongside the Asahi River and Okayama-jō.

GETTING AROUND

Okayama is a very **walkable** city. Kōraku-en is about 20 minutes on foot from the main station. To cut your walking time to a manageable level, hop on the city's efficient **tram network** (all rides within downtown ¥100). The Higashiyama line runs all the way up the main thoroughfare of **Momotarō Ōdōri** to the gently flowing **Asahi-gawa** near both the garden and castle.

Another good way to get around is on two wheels. There are many **bicycle** rental shops scattered around the east side of the station. Try **Eki Rinkun** (1-1 Ekimotomachi; tel. 086/223-7081; 7am-9:45pm daily; ¥350 per day).

Kurashiki   倉敷

Less than 20 minutes west of Okayama by train, the Bikan historical district in the town of Kurashiki looks like it was designed for a leisurely stroll. The "Kura" ("storehouse") in Kurashiki relates to the fact that the town was replete with storehouses full of rice during the Edo period (1603-1868). The charming canal that runs through the center of downtown Kurashiki was one of the arteries used to transport rice to port.

Peach Boy Momotarō

Okayama Prefecture, along with Kagawa Prefecture on Shikoku, are said to be where Momotarō, one of Japan's most beloved folk heroes, sprang from a peach, and then grew up to save his homeland from marauding ogres. Momotarō—literally "Peach Tarō"—holds special status in Japan's rich mythology, along with other heroes and monsters from Astro Boy to Godzilla. You won't have to look far in this region to see his cherubic face plastered on buses, billboards, and manhole covers.

Momotarō characters on a manhole

THE LEGEND

Our hero was said to have been discovered by chance when the peach in which he descended to earth was plucked from a river by a childless elderly woman, who was washing clothes as the fruit bobbed by. When she and her husband went to eat the fruit, out popped Momotarō. After the kindly older couple raised the boy, he embarked on his hero's journey by venturing to a faraway island to fight a band of three-eyed ogres that plundered the locals' wealth and even ate villagers. Along the way, Momotarō teamed up with a dog who could talk, a pheasant, and a monkey. Together, the motley crew routed the ogres in their lair on a distant isle. They reclaimed the loot previously stolen by the demons and took the chief ogre hostage. Everyone lived happily ever after.

WHERE TO SEE MOMOTARŌ

You'll see Momotarō and peach motifs all throughout Okayama, from the hero's visage emblazoned on peach-flavored confectionary packaging to peach-shaped trinkets. A prominent **statue** of the beloved peach-boy is right outside the east exit of Okayama Station, gazing into the distance with his dog, pheasant, and monkey companions. As you walk around town, keep your eyes open and you'll soon grow familiar with his boyish countenance.

If you have time, interest, and want to dig deeper into the nuts and bolts of the legend itself, check out the English-language website **Momotarō Ura** (https://momotaro-ura.jp/en/), which provides Momotarō-related itineraries (https://momotaro-ura.jp/en/course/list/) and information on a number of spots around the region with ties to the story (https://momotaro-ura.jp/en/point/map/).

The quaint townscape left over from the town's affluent heyday has attracted a bustling tourist trade. The most scenic part of the canal district is the **Bikan Historical Quarter,** spanned by stone bridges and fringed by hanging willow branches. Starting at the canal's northern end at the Ōhara Museum of Art, slowly amble beside the canal and take in the old-world ambience conjured by the white-plaster storefronts and black-tile roofs. A number of small museums with

collections of folk crafts and old-fashioned toys are housed in some of the district's old storehouses, along with cafés, restaurants, and boutiques. Also atmospheric, Kurashiki's **Ivy Square** is a former spinning mill whose ivy-covered brick buildings now house restaurants, small museums, and a hotel.

The Bikan neighborhood is located about 10 minutes' walk southeast of JR Kurashiki Station. Though the town can easily be seen in a day, it can get packed in the afternoon.

To experience its subtler magic, try to stay for one night at one of the town's many charming *ryokan*. After the tourists depart, take a long stroll along the canal and you'll be mesmerized by the soft light from the street lamps dancing in the water. A caveat: If you choose to visit Kurashiki, avoid arriving on a Monday, when many of the town's shops close.

SIGHTS

Ōhara Museum of Art
大原美術館

1-1-15 Chūō; tel. 086/422-0005; www.ohara.or.jp; 9am-5pm (last admission 4:30pm) Tues.-Sun.; adults ¥1,500, students ¥500; walk 12 minutes southeast of Kurashiki Station

If you've traveled in Paris or visited some of New York's fantastic museums of Western art, this charming complex in Kurashiki may slightly underwhelm. But this was the first museum in Japan dedicated to Western art, founded in 1930. Local textile tycoon Ōhara Magosaburō (1880-1943) and local artist Kojima Torajirō (1881-1929) teamed up to assemble a collection of works by artists including Picasso, Gauguin, Modigliani, Matisse, Rodin, El Greco, Pollock, Warhol, and more. Even a canvas containing some of Monet's immortal water lilies resides here, apparently purchased directly from the French Impressionist himself. The Western art is concentrated in the **Main Gallery.** The museum is spread across three buildings that sit side-by-side along the canal.

For a change of pace, two buildings adjacent to the Main Gallery house the museum's **Craft Art Gallery,** which displays Japanese works from woodblock prints to pottery, while the **Asiatic Art Gallery** exhibits antiquities from China and from countries as far away as Egypt. The museum has instituted a list of coronavirus-related precautions and rules, outlined on its website.

FOOD

KURASHIKI COFFEE-KAN

4-1 Hon-machi; tel. 086/424-5516; www.kurashiki-coffeekan.com; 10am-5pm daily; ¥570-980; walk 13 minutes southeast of Kurashiki Station

In this 19th-century building with a warm interior—exposed brick, dark-wood countertop, exposed wooden beams—the brew is high-grade, with prices to match. The menu only includes coffee, both hot and iced, so this is just a spot to take a quiet break from the crowds. When the weather's nice, there's an atmospheric inner courtyard with outdoor seating. Look for the arched doorway, fronted by a red iron gate facing the canal.

★ TAKADAYA

11-36 Hon-machi; tel. 086/425-9262; www3.kct. ne.jp/~takataya_ikunoya/index.htm; 5pm-10pm (last order 9:30pm) Tues.-Sun.; skewers ¥120-420, courses ¥1,000-2,000; walk 15 minutes southeast of Kurashiki Station

This cozy restaurant oozes retro charm. The outside is appropriately storehouse-chic, while its interior is mostly dark wood, with slightly dim lighting and plenty of crumbling beer posters. The menu includes all forms of meat on skewers, alongside varied side dishes of vegetables, tofu, rice, and more. There's a good list of cocktails on offer as well. There's seating at tables, in tatami rooms, and at the counter. English menu available. Look for the blue *noren* (curtain). It's about 4 minutes' walk from Ōhara Museum of Art. Recommended.

MIYAKE SHOTEN

3-11 Hon-machi; tel. 086/426-4600; www. miyakeshouten.com; 11:30am-5pm (last order 4:30pm) Mon.-Fri. and Sun., 11am-8pm (last order 7:30pm) Sat.; set meals ¥900-1,450, desserts ¥500-950; walk 13 minutes southeast of Kurashiki Station

This shop serves one main dish and does it well: Japanese-style vegetable curry over brown rice. The set meals include side dishes of pickled vegetables. The menu also includes coffee and desserts. The ambience is cozy and classic: wood beams and furniture, *fusama* (sliding doors), and a mixture of seating at tables and on the floor. It's tucked behind a classic storefront with a white *noren* bearing the restaurant's name. This is a good spot for a healthy lunch, situated on a street running parallel to the canal.

ACCOMMODATIONS

NAGI KURASHIKI HOTEL & LOUNGE

1-14-3 Achi; tel. 050/5210-8506; https://nagi-kurashiki.com; singles from ¥10,000 with breakfast, doubles from ¥20,000 with breakfast

This chic brand-new boutique hotel right in front of JR Kurashiki Station is a comfortable and exceedingly convenient choice if access to the train station is important for you. It's about 12 minutes' walk from the Bikan historic district, but that's just fine since the hotel provides free bicycles for guests. The hotel's eight artfully designed rooms are spacious, easy on the eye, and have well-stocked private bathrooms. A continental breakfast is included, and the friendly English-speaking staff provide concierge services.

★ RYOKAN KURASHIKI

4-1 Honmachi; tel. 086/422-0730; www.ryokan-kurashiki.jp; ¥36,000 pp with 2 meals

Right next to Kurashiki Coffee-kan, this luxurious timepiece is the finest accommodation in town. The buildings were once storehouses for sugar and rice. Each room has a Western-style bedroom, private bathroom, and tatami-floor lounge, plus tastefully chosen artwork, calligraphy, flower arrangements, and antique furniture. The kimono-clad staff are supremely attentive and speak some English. Meals served are of the haute *kaiseki* (multicourse) variety, featuring locally caught seafood and seasonal ingredients. If you want to splurge, this is the best place to do so in Kurashiki.

INFORMATION AND SERVICES

There's a tourist information center is just outside Kurashiki Station inside **Kurashiki City Plaza** (1-7-2 Achi; tel. 086/424-1220; 9am-6pm daily). Alternatively, head to the information center housed in a Meiji-period building beside the canal in the heart of the historic district (1-4-8 Chūō; tel. 086/422-0542; 9am-6pm daily). You can also visit the town's **Kurashiki Sightseeing Web** (www.kurashiki-tabi.jp), which provides information on what to see and where to shop, eat, and sleep.

GETTING THERE AND AROUND

Kurashiki Station is on the JR San'yō line, southwest of **Okayama Station** (15 minutes; ¥320) and east of **Onomichi** (1 hour; ¥1,140). About 10 km (6.2 mi) southwest of Kurashiki Station is **Shin-Kurashiki,** a stop on the *shinkansen* line that is directly accessible from **Hiroshima** to the west, but only by Kodama trains (1 hour 15 minutes; ¥5,370).

Given that Shin-Kurashiki Station is only accessible by Kodama *shinkansen* trains, it's easiest to reach Kurashiki via Okayama Station instead. Okayama Station can be accessed directly by *shinkansen* from **Hiroshima Station** (40 minutes; ¥6,350), **Shin-Osaka Station** (45-80 minutes; ¥6,140-6,350, depending on *shinkansen* type), and from **Kyoto Station** (1-1.5 hours; ¥7,670-7,990 depending on *shinkansen* type; some itineraries may call for transfer to different *shinkansen* train type at Shin-Osaka or Fukuyama). From Okayama Station, just take the JR San'yō line to Kurashiki Station (15 minutes; ¥330).

Once you're in Kurashiki, exploring the town **on foot** is the only way to go. The narrow back lanes and lazy canal call for sauntering.

The Art Islands

Gliding through the blue-green expanse of the Inland sea south of the San'yō coast, the view from a ferry approaching any one of the thousands of alluring islands in this waterway is archetypally maritime. Boats tethered to weather-beaten docks bob on gentle waves. Fishermen empty barnacle-encrusted fishing nets of their daily catch. Squid hang to dry on wires in the open air like garments on clotheslines. In town, octogenarian aunties run corner stores and greasy-spoon restaurants, while stray cats prowl nearby for scraps.

The island of Naoshima in particular has become a jewel of the Inland Sea, combining beautiful natural surroundings, a fabulous design sense, and a forward-looking spirit of artistic experimentation. Easily accessed from Uno Station on Honshu, a sleepy stop on the JR Uno line about 22 km (13.7 mi) southeast of Kurashiki and 21 km (13 mi) south of Okayama, Naoshima is a must-visit for any trip to the area. Beyond offering a deep-dive into contemporary art, the island's communities are charming, authentic, slow-paced, and mellow, and the seaside views are stunning.

The artistic development of Naoshima has set something larger in motion in the region. Nearby, the tiny islands of Teshima and Inujima are two more "art islands" that are brilliantly following Naoshima's lead. These art-studded isles are the most famous in this glittering seascape. But venture a bit farther out to sea and you'll discover a constellation of quieter isles that radiate a distinct charm at once magnetic and subtle. Experiencing this slower, unsung side of Japan firsthand is the Inland Sea's greatest draw. You'll be amply rewarded with solitude and feel as if you've taken a trip back in time if you hop on a ferry bound for some of the sea's lesser-known gems, like Shodoshima, Shiraishi-jima and Manabe-shima.

★ NAOSHIMA
直島

Roughly 7.8 square km (3 square mi), with a population of around 3,300, this sublime isle is awash with art, mostly funded by the big pockets of the language-study and test-prep company Benesse Corporation as Benesse Art Site Naoshima (http://benesse-artsite.jp). Soichiro Fukutake, the chairman of Benesse, is a native of nearby Okayama and a keen patron of the arts. Since 1992, when the Benesse House Museum opened as a boutique hotel-cum-museum where guests are permitted to roam unfettered at night, Naoshima has been transformed from a dwindling fishing community into an immersive, world-class art hub. As the island's profile rose, other creatives came to launch cafés, bed-and-breakfasts, and restaurants.

The minimalist structures in this area that were created by Pritzker Prize-winning architect Tadao Ando are works of art themselves, not to mention the outdoor sculptures dotting the landscape, and works by Jackson Pollock, Claude Monet, Jasper Johns, and David Hockney scattered around the island's museums.

If you time your visit carefully, you can visit Naoshima on a day trip. But if you have the funds, consider staying on the island for a night. After the legion of day-trippers depart, quiet falls across the island and Naoshima returns to its slower native rhythm. A caveat: Avoid visiting on Monday, when most museums are closed. If Monday happens to be a holiday, things close on Tuesday instead.

Orientation

Naoshima can be reached via two ferry ports: the more popularly used **Miyanoura Port** on the west side of the island, and **Honmura Port** in the east. Ferries run between Miyanoura and Takamatsu in

Shikoku's northeast, Uno on Honshu, and Ieura Port on the tiny isle of Inujima, another art-studded island roughly 25 km (15.5 mi) northeast of Naoshima. Meanwhile, only sporadic ferries travel between Uno and Honmura Port.

Miyanoura is the more popularly used port of these two ports and has a well-stocked information center, a number of food and accommodation options, and several bicycle rental shops. That said, Honmura also has a range of restaurants, inns, and, significantly, is the location of the **Art House Project,** a premier art installation strewn throughout the village of Honmura, which abuts the eponymous port. The rest of the island's major museums are clustered along the southern side of the island, southeast of Miyanoura and southwest of Honmura. These include **Benesse House Museum** and **Chichū Art Museum.**

Buses shuttle once or twice hourly (all rides ¥100) from Miyanoura Ferry Terminal to Honmura (10 minutes), on to Tsutsujiso bus stop (15 minutes), with Benesse House about 10 minutes' walk west from there. On the walk from Tsutsujiso bus stop to Benesse House, you'll also pass Yayoi Kusama's famed *Yellow Pumpkin* seaside sculpture. If you'd like to avoid too much walking, you can also take a free shuttle bus from Tsutsujiso bus stop to Benesse House (3 minutes) and Chichū Art Museum (7 minutes).

The most appealing way to see the island when the weather cooperates is by bike. Bicycles can be rented in Miyanoura and to a lesser extent in Honmura (single-speed from ¥300, multi-speed from ¥500, electrically assisted from ¥1,300). The island is hilly in parts, so an electrically assisted bicycle is a good option if you can manage to snag one: It's a very popular option, so you'll need to either arrive at one of the rental shops by 8:30am or reserve a bike in advance. It's also possible to explore the island on foot, but the hills are a bit daunting.

Sights
ART HOUSE PROJECT
家プロジェクト

Various locations in Honmura; http://benesse-artsite. jp/en/art/arthouse.html; 10am-4:30pm Tues.-Sun., closed Tues. when Mon. is holiday; ¥1,050 multi-site admission, ¥420 admission to single site; take a bus from Miyanoura Port to Honmura (¥100), or walk 3 minutes' west from Honmura pier

The Art House Project in the traditional community of Honmura, on the island's east side, presents a series of conceptual artworks incorporated into unassuming old structures dotting the village. Art lovers find these works by following a walking route like a treasure hunt, with map in hand. The traditional buildings in which they appear range from homes and workshops to a shrine and a temple. The works are eclectic: LED lights illuminating a pool of water inside a home, underground chambers in hillsides looking onto glass staircases emerging up through the surface of the earth, a two-story Statue of Liberty replica jutting up through a former dentist's home, and more.

Honmura is a good place to visit during the morning or early afternoon. That way, you can combine your art walk here with a stop at one of the area's homey cafés or restaurants, serving fresh, healthy nosh. For more information on the individual artists and their creations spread around the village, and to purchase a ticket to enter the various sites of the Art House Project, stop by the **Honmura Lounge** (850-2 Naoshima; tel. 087/840-8273; http:// benesse-artsite.jp/en/art/arthouse.html; 10am-4:30pm Tues.-Sun., closed Tues. when Mon. is public holiday), located near the town's main bus stop.

BENESSE HOUSE MUSEUM
ベネッセハウス ミュージアム

tel. 087/892-3223; https://benesse-artsite.jp/en/art/ benessehouse-museum.html; 8am-9pm (last entry 8pm) daily; ¥1,050, age 15 and under free; take a bus from Miyanoura Port, via Honmura, to the Tsutsujiso bus stop

This well-known complex doubles as museum and high-end accommodation. It's the jewel in Benesse Corporation's crown on Naoshima, designed by architectural giant Tadao Ando. The sprawling property on the south side of the island includes a museum, a building called the Oval, a park, and a beach.

Beyond art featured in the rooms and museum—David Hockney, Gerhard Richter, Hiroshi Sugimoto—the grounds are dotted by outdoor pieces that suit the surroundings, such as Yayoi Kusama's avant-garde take on a giant pumpkin that looks as if it's been plopped onto a pier. Guests can peruse the museum's collection 24/7. The views over the Inland Sea from the hill outside the museum are phenomenal at any time of day, but the sunsets are especially stunning.

At the time of writing, the museum had reduced its hours to 10am-6pm daily in an effort to curb the spread of coronavirus.

CHICHŪ ART MUSEUM
地中美術館

*http://benesse-artsite.jp/en/art/chichu.html;
10am-6pm (last entry 5pm) Tues.-Sun. Mar.-Sept.,
10am-5pm (last entry 4pm) Tues.-Sun. Oct.-Feb.;
¥2,100, age 15 and under free; take the bus from
Miyanoura Port, via Honmura, to the Tsutsujiso bus
stop, then walk (30 minutes) or take the free shuttle
bus (10 minutes), or walk east from Miyanoura Port
(35 minutes) or cycle over (10 minutes)*

This museum is a mind-bending, almost completely subterranean complex lit mostly by natural light filtered through skylights of various shapes and sizes. This is one of Naoshima's highlights, one of many structures designed by all-star architect Tadao Ando. Natural light changes throughout the day in a seamless dance with the artworks on display. The collection is not huge, but it includes heavy hitters like Claude Monet and Walter De Maria. On Friday and Saturday evenings, the "Open Sky Night Program" is held, in which the sunset can be viewed from within the subterranean space.

Tickets must be reserved in advance to enter the museum. Visit the museum's official webpage to find a link to the English-language online reservation system. You can reserve even a day before visiting, but reserve a week or more ahead to be safe. You must leave any luggage or cameras in one of the lockers provided at the ticket center.

Spas and Relaxation
I LOVE 湯 ("I LOVE YU")

*2252-2 Higashicho, Naoshima-chō; http://
benesse-artsite.jp/en/art/naoshimasento.html;
1pm-9pm Tues.-Sun., closed Tues. if Mon. is holiday;
adults ¥660, children 2-15 ¥310, ages 2 and under
free; walk 4 minutes east of Miyanoura Port on the
island's west side*

For an experience beyond ogling art, why not bathe in it? I Love Yu (*Yu* meaning "hot water") is a funky *sento* (bath house) designed by artist Shinro Ohtake, whose quirky spin on the neighborhood bath is a natural fit on the island. In place of the de rigueur mural of Mount Fuji, you'll find a life-sized elephant walking overhead, white tiles emblazoned with blue undersea visions of divers, jellyfish and octopuses on the walls, and a ceiling made of vividly stained glass.

Events
SETOUCHI TRIENNALE

*https://setouchi-artfest.jp; 3-season passport to most
art sites adults ¥4,800, 16-18 ¥3,000, under 15 free,
single-season passport adults ¥4,000, 16-18 ¥2,500,
under 15 free*

This massive happening features performances (dance, music, drama) and visual spectacles. Taking place every three years on Naoshima and an array of other islands in the Inland Sea, the proceedings are generally broken into seasonal programs in spring, summer, and autumn. The website has thorough English-language information on everything from the event, the islands involved, ferry links, and more. If you intend to catch this world-famous arts and culture event, book your accommodation as far in advance as

1: *torii* gate on Naoshima **2:** Benesse House Museum

you can—six months ahead or more. If you have trouble landing a room, check out potential options around Takamatsu on Shikoku or Uno in Okayama Prefecture.

Food

Naoshima's restaurants and cafés tend to close on the early side. Plan your mealtimes carefully and be sure a given restaurant is open before making the trip.

★ CAFÉ SALON NAKA-OKU

1167 Honmura; tel. 087/892-3887; https://cafesalon-naka-oku.jimdofree.com; 11:30am-3pm (last order 2:40pm) and 5:30pm-9pm (last order 8:30pm) Wed.-Mon., some irregular closings; set lunches ¥650-800, ¥480-980 per dish

Much of Naoshima shuts down on Monday, giving this inviting café added cache. Its nicely aged wooden interior and home-cooked menu of classics like *karage* (fried chicken), *omuraisu* (omelet stuffed with fried rice), Japanese-style curry rice, and cakes, are a winning combination. There's also a good selection of booze if you want a drink in the evening. It's at the top of a hill on the backside of the village of Honmura, away from the bustle.

SHIOYA DINER

2227 Naoshima; tel. 087/892-3290; www.facebook.com/Shioya-Diner-437280336290995; 5pm-8:45pm (last order 8pm) Tues.-Sun.; ¥400-1,000; walk 4 minutes inland from the port, around the corner from I Love Yu bathhouse

As advertised, this is a diner in the classic sense, and the retro décor and soundtrack straddling rockabilly and oldies reinforces this. Run by a friendly Japanese couple smitten by Americana, it's homey and funky, with just the right amount of kitsch. The menu includes comfort foods like chicken breast and mashed potatoes, tacos, hot dogs, burgers, and fries, plus there's beer on tap and Corona in the bottle. This is a great place to dine on the Miyanoura Port (west side) of the island, particularly if you're feeling like a break from Japanese fare.

APRON

777 Naoshima-chō Ichien; tel. 090/7540-0010; www.facebook.com/aproncafe.naoshima; 11am-4pm Tues.-Sun.; ¥1,100-1,580; near the Ando Museum down one of the footpaths that snake through inner Honmura

This bright, friendly café in the heart of Honmura is a great place for a healthy lunch. Stylish furniture, potted plants, art on the walls, and a chilled-out soundtrack create a relaxed vibe. The inventive lunch plates contain many small dishes: organic salads with fresh herbs, quiche packed with local produce, multigrain and black rice, cheese gratin, quinoa, vegetable curry, and scones made with cranberry and coconut.

Accommodations

If you can manage to snag a room on the island, be prepared for a surprisingly quiet night. The whole island closes down by around 7pm, save for a convenience store each in Honmura and Miyanoura, and a smattering of vending machines. That said, experiencing the island minus the tourist hordes is a revelation. You'll feel as if you could be on any one of the myriad sleepy isles dotting the Inland Sea.

Naoshima's lodgings are often fully booked, so be sure to conduct an exhaustive search (www.naoshima.net/stay). If the island's lodgings are full, aim to stay either on Honshu or Shikoku near either ferry port. It's simple to shuttle between Naoshima and Uno (Honshu) or Takamatsu (Shikoku) for a day trip or two.

UNO PORT INN

1-4-4 Chikko, Tamano; tel. 0863/21-2729; http://unoportinn.com; ¥11,800 d; take the JR Uno line to Uno Station

With a cozy café on site serving nibbles and coffee, English-speaking staff, and petite, clean rooms (both Western and Japanese-style), this welcoming inn near the port on the Honshu side is a good place to stay for a night either before or after a trip to Naoshima. All rooms—each with a unique Japanese cinema-inspired theme—have a private bathroom, with most of them accessed through separate doors at the end of the hallway on each floor. Free Wi-Fi and laundry facilities are available.

FRANCOILE

953-2 Sonota, Naoshima-chō; tel. 090/4375-1979; www.francoile.com; ¥17,000 d

On the Honmura side, this bed-and-breakfast is a great place to stay for a night. There are just two rooms in this modern, well-decorated lodging on the backside of the village. Both rooms have good lighting, spacious private bathrooms, and two twin beds. There's also a café (2pm-5pm Tues.-Thurs. and Sat.-Sun.) on the first floor serving good pour-over coffee and muffins. The place is run by a young Japanese couple with an amazing sense of hospitality, one of whom speaks great English. With only two rooms, peace and quiet are a given. But it also means you'll need to reserve well in advance. Recommended.

★ BENESSE HOUSE

tel. 087/892-3223; http://benesse-artsite.jp/en/stay/ benessehouse; ¥32,000 d

In the island's museum-studded south, this luxury property has rooms spanning four sites, all of which sit near the museum at the center of the Benesse art empire. All four complexes are paragons of the art gallery-cum-hotel concept. These include the beachside Benesse House Park and Beach, with its spa and library; the museum itself, which can be wandered by guests after hours; and the most-expensive Oval, which is perched on a hill above the museum and reached by monorail. The rooms are stylish yet minimal—televisions are notably absent—and feature artwork that belongs in the museum's private collection. If you have the means, this is the most luxurious, visually stunning accommodation on the island. Book as far in advance as you can.

Information and Services

Pick up one of the clearly marked English maps at the **Naoshima Tourism Association** (tel. 087/892-2299; 8:30am-6pm daily), an information desk in the lively Miyanoura ferry terminal on the west side of the island. If you arrive via Honmura port on the east side of the island, stop by the **Honmura Lounge & Archive** (850-2 Naoshima; tel. 087/840-8273; 10am-4:30pm Tues.-Sun.).

Getting There

You can reach Naoshima by **ferry** from both Honshu and Shikoku. If you're coming from **Okayama Station** (Honshu), you'll need to take the Marine Liner (13 minutes; ¥770) or the JR Seto-Ohashi line (22 minutes; ¥240) to **Chayamachi Station.** Both lines are covered by the JR Pass. At Chayamachi Station, transfer to the JR Uno Port line (50 minutes; ¥1,100) to **Uno Station,** then walk 3 minutes south to **Uno Port** where you'll catch a ferry (20 minutes; ¥290). Note that ferries bound for **Miyanoura Port** on the south side of Naoshima depart from Uno Port once or twice hourly, while those running to **Honmura Port** on the north side of Naoshima leave five times per day. For a full ferry timetable to and from Naoshima, and additional information on how to reach these ports, visit http://benesse-artsite.jp/en/access.

Getting Around

Your best options for getting around Naoshima are either by **bus** or **bicycle.** There's a convenient bus that runs from Miyanoura in the island's west, through Honmura on the east side, around to Benesse House and the Chichū Art Museum (all rides ¥100).

There are loads of bicycle **rental shops** (single-speed from ¥300, multi-speed from ¥500, electrically assisted from ¥1,300) around the port in Miyanoura, as well as a few shops in Honmura, but be forewarned: The bicycles often run out very early in the day. If you want to rent a bicycle, plan on showing up at either port around 8:30am, or making a reservation. For a list of rental shops on the island, including information on which ones allow advanced reservations, visit www.naoshima.net/en/access/rental.

TESHIMA
豊島

Of Naoshima's two sister islands, Teshima and Inojima, Teshima is the larger and more popular, sitting between Shōdo-shima to the east and Naoshima to the west. The thinly populated green isle, which is the second largest in the Inland Sea after Shōdo-shima, is dotted by three fishing villages and swathed in citrus trees.

Since it has emerged as one of the leading lights of the Inland Sea's art scene in recent years, Teshima serves as one of the main venues of the Setouchi Triennale. This is a dazzling success story when considering the fact that the island was at the center of a scandal involving the dumping of hundreds of thousands of tons of toxic waste near its western coast in the 1980s, for which cleanup was finished in 2017.

Compared to Naoshima, which runs on tourism, Teshima still has the feeling of a living, breathing fishing community. Besides striking, conceptual artworks set amid a lovely natural environment, you'll also find terraced rice fields, weather-beaten coastline, and a forested interior. The relatively smaller number of tourists, at least compared to Naoshima, gives you the chance to relax and feel time slow down. The artworks found on Teshima have an enigmatic quality. The standout sight is **Teshima Art Museum,** in the island's northeast, which enchants visitors with its seamless blend of simple geometry framing the island's natural beauty. Other prominent artworks include the abstract creation that is the **Teshima Yokoo House** near Ieura Port, and the archive of sound recordings of visitors' heartbeats at **Les Archives du Cœur** in the island's far east.

Plan on spending a half day or full day exploring Teshima, depending on how slowly you want to go. To enjoy the island to its fullest, rent an electrically assisted bicycle at Ieura Port in the island's northwest, then pedal through the rural landscape. If you can't manage to get an electric bike, a standard bicycle will suffice. But be forewarned the island is quite hilly in parts. If you've got a full day, it's also possible to walk.

Sights
TESHIMA YOKOO HOUSE
豊島横尾館

2359 Teshimaieura; tel. 0879/68-3555; http://benesse-artsite.jp/en/art/teshima-yokoohouse.html; 10am-5pm (last entry 4:30pm) Wed.-Mon. Mar.-Oct., 10am-4pm (last entry 3:30pm) Wed.-Mon. Nov., 10am-4pm (last entry 3:30pm) Fri.-Mon. Dec.-Feb.; ¥520

Built inside a traditional house near Ieura Port, the Teshima Yokoo House complex was designed by architect Nagayama Yuko. The house showcases works on life and death by the artist Yokoo Tadanori, after whom it is named. Outside, a classical Japanese rock garden strewn with multicolored rocks and mosaic tiles was built by locals. Inside, carp swim through a pond under a plexiglass floor. Inside an attached tower with mirrored floor and ceiling, the 14-meter-tall (46-foot-tall) walls are plastered with nearly 1,000 waterfall postcards. Look up or down for a simulated glimpse of infinity. Even the bathrooms' chrome interiors create a disorienting effect.

TESHIMA ART MUSEUM
豊島美術館

607 Karato; tel. 0879/68-3555; http://benesse-artsite.jp/en/art/teshima-artmuseum.html; 10am-5pm (last entry 4:30pm) Wed.-Mon. Mar.-Oct., 10am-4pm (last entry 3:30pm) Wed.-Mon. Nov., 10am-4pm (last entry 3:30pm) Fri.-Mon. Dec.-Feb.; ¥1,570

This mesmerizing water droplet-shaped structure sits beside a rice terrace on a hill. A joint-collaboration by artist Naito Rei and architect Nishizawa Ryūe, this shell is punctuated by openings in the ceiling that reveal the sky and lush backdrop of the island's verdant topography. To enter, you must take off your shoes. Inside, look down and observe the captivating rivulets of water that periodically spring from the floor and dance around the space. This is a place to slow down and observe the beauty of the island itself, which is the true star of this exhibit. Attached, there's a glass-roofed café that maintains the same hours as the museum.

At the time of writing, the museum was requiring advance reservations to combat the spread of coronavirus. Check the website for the current admission policy and to book a ticket if needed.

LES ARCHIVES DU CŒUR

2801-1 Karato, Teshima, Tonosho-chō; tel.
0879/68-3555; http://benesse-artsite.jp/en/art/
boltanski.html; 10am-5pm (last entry 4:30pm)
Wed.-Mon. Mar.-Oct., 10am-4pm (last entry 3:30pm)
Wed.-Mon. Nov., 10am-4pm (last entry 3:30pm)
Fri.-Mon. Dec.-Feb.; ¥520

Come here to hear a singular archive of heartbeats recorded around the globe. Step into the special darkened room where thousands of heartbeats are piped through a mesmerizing sound system. You can also record, register, and get a CD of your own heartbeat for ¥1,570.

Food

Eateries on Teshima close early, so plan ahead. For a list of the island's scant eateries, visit https://teshima-navi.jp/en/restaurants/.

TESHIMA NO MADO

2458-2 Ieura, Teshima, Tonosho-chō;
teshimanomado@gmail.com, www.teshimanomado.
com; 11am-4pm Sun.-Wed.; from ¥900

Five minutes' walk inland from Ieura Port and next to Teshima Yokoo House, this cafe occupies a renovated building made with tin sheets that was once a seaweed processing workshop. The menu includes good coffee and bread, respectively roasted and baked in house, light meals (curry and rice dishes, salads, and more), and desserts.

SHIMA KITCHEN

1061 Karato, Teshima, Tonosho-chō; tel.
0879/68-3771; www.shimakitchen.com; 11am-3:30pm
Sat.-Mon. and holidays, lunch time until 2pm, café
time until 3:30pm; from ¥1,200

About 12 minutes' walk south of Teshima Art Museum, this restaurant is set in a formerly abandoned house redesigned and refurbished into a restaurant and art space by architect Abe Ryo in 2010 as part of the Setouchi Triennale. Today, it's run by locals who have trained under chefs from a four-star hotel in Tokyo to whip up a healthy menu of dishes such as curry and rice, fish, vegetable medleys, and desserts. Ingredients are gathered from around the island, from rice and produce to fruits, olives, and fish caught offshore. There are tables with floor cushions arrayed around a wooden veranda, and occasional events are hosted on the large open terrace, which is a great place to socialize with other diners.

UMI NO RESTAURANT

525-1 Ieura, Teshima, Tonosho-chō; tel.
0879/68-3677; https://il-grano.jp/umi/; 11am-5pm
(last order 4:30pm) daily Mar.-Nov., 11am-4pm (last
order 3pm) daily Dec.-Feb.; dinner courses (from 6pm
daily Mar.-Nov., 5pm daily Dec.-Feb.) also available
with at least 2 days' advance reservation, irregular
holidays; lunch ¥3,000, dinner course ¥8,800

About 15 minutes' walk east from Ieura Port, this stylish beachside eatery set in a minimalist, white structure serves Italian cuisine made with local ingredients, from produce to fish. The pies are made in a wood-fired Neopolitan pizza oven, and seating is available both inside and on an open-air terrace that overlooks the sea.

Accommodations

Teshima has limited accommodation options, but if you inquire in advance, you may be able to secure a room at one of the island's inns, which range from family-owned *minshuku* to chic private residences. For a full list of options, visit https://teshima-navi.jp/en/accommodation.

Information and Services

On Teshima, you'll find English-language maps and other materials at the **information** desk (9am-5pm Wed.-Mon.; tel. 087/968-3135) in the Ieura Port ferry terminal. Online, check out the island's tourism portal, **Teshima Tourism Navi** (https://teshima-navi.jp/en).

Getting There

On Teshima, the main ports are **Ieura** on the northwest shore and **Karato** in the northeast. Ferries run between Ieura and **Miyanoura** on Naoshima (22 minutes; ¥620) and **Uno** on Honshu (40 minutes; ¥770), and some continue on to **Karato** (1 hour; ¥480). If you're coming directly from Uno, take either the Marine Liner (13 minutes; ¥770) or the JR Seto-Ohashi line (22 minutes; ¥240) to **Chayamachi Station,** then transfer to the JR Uno Port line to Uno Station (50 minutes; ¥1,100), then walk 3 minutes to Uno Port. Ferries run from Uno to Ieura on Teshima every 1-2 hours. Separately, ferries sailing from **Tonosho** on Shōdo-shima sail to both Karato (20 minutes; ¥770) and Ieura (35 minutes; ¥770). Note that some of these ferries do not run every day. For a full ferry timetable to and from Teshima, and additional information on how to reach these ports, visit http://benesse-artsite.jp/en/access.

Getting Around

Once you've reached Teshima, sporadic **buses** (¥200) run between Ieura and Karato, stopping at some sights, including the Teshima Art Museum, along the way. See the bus schedule online at https://benesse-artsite.jp/en/uploads/access/map_201903.pdf. Alternatively, and recommended, rent a **bicycle** at the port in Ieura (standard ¥500 per day, electric ¥1,000 four hours, ¥100 each additional hour). Given the hilliness of the island's terrain, it's worth paying a bit extra for an electrically powered bicycle.

INUJIMA
犬島

This diminutive island (literally "Dog Island") lies to the north of Naoshima and Teshima, closer to Okayama than the northern shore of Shikoku. Here you'll also find galleries with stunning seaside vistas, the Seirensho Art Museum, and the Inujima Art House Project, akin to the one on Naoshima.

Inujima's backstory is rather industrial. The small isle was the source of large granite blocks used in castle construction during Japan's feudal heyday. It turned its industriousness to refining copper in the early 20th century, but the copper boom was short-lived due to a steep drop in prices for the metal. The ruins of the island's once bustling refinery now serve as the basis for its largest attraction, the **Seirensho Art Museum.**

Of the three art islands, Inujima is the smallest and has the fewest inhabitants. Unlike Teshima and Naoshima, Inujima lacks public transport and is best explored on foot. Its manageable scale and rustic setting make it an appealing, offbeat option if you've already seen Naoshima and Teshima or would like to explore on foot in a relatively uncrowded environment. You can smoothly see the island in a half day.

From December 1, 2020, Inujima's art sites are only open Friday-Monday from March through November (open Tues. when Mon. is national holiday; otherwise, open on national holidays and closed the following day). From December through February, the island's art sites are completely shuttered. Check for updates on the official website of Benesse Art Site Naoshima (https://benesse-artsite.jp/en/) which also includes information for Inujima, before planning a trip.

Sights
SEIRENSHO ART MUSEUM
精錬所美術館

327-4 Inujima; tel. 086/947-1112; http://benesse-artsite.jp/en/art/seirensho.html; 9am-4:30pm (last entry 4pm) Fri.-Mon. Mar.-Nov., open Tues. when Mon. falls on holiday, closed Dec.-Feb.; ¥2,100, including admission to Inujima Art House Project and Seaside Inujima Gallery

The top sight on Inujima, much less visited even than Teshima, is the dreamlike, highly interactive Seirensho Art Museum. Built around the shell of a former copper refinery, this museum explores environmental crises and the contradictory nature of modernization in Japan through the artwork of Yanagi Yukinori. Among the materials Yanagi used to create the works housed in the museum are the remnants of the house once lived in by Mishima Yukio, a controversial, conflicted literary figure who is widely considered one of the most important Japanese novelists of the 20th century. It's worth noting that the architect Sambuichi Hiroshi had the museum built according to strict eco-friendly standards, using locally sourced granite and waste left over from the process of smelting copper. Plan your lunchtime around your visit to the museum. The attached café serves great lunches made with ingredients sourced from the island.

INUJIMA ART HOUSE PROJECT

Various locations around island; tel. 086/947-1112; http://benesse-artsite.jp/en/art/inujima-arthouse. html; 9am-4:30pm (last entry 4pm) Fri.-Mon. Mar.-Nov., open Tues. when Mon. falls on holiday, closed Dec.-Feb.; ¥2,100 including admission to Seirensho Art Museum and Seaside Inujima Gallery

The island's 50 or so inhabitants have fully embraced the "art island" concept, which has overtaken the main village in the form of five "art houses" and a few installations. As with the Seirensho Art Museum, the island's past and locally available materials figure heavily in the works on display. A good example is Asai Yusuke's installation *Listen to the Voices of Yesterday Like the Voices of Ancient Times*, which is built on the spot where a stonecutter's home once stood, using stone and other materials collected around the island, juxtaposed with images of plants and animals reminiscent of ancient cave paintings scrawled across the ground where the house once stood.

Food

Restaurants and cafés on Inujima close early on days they are open for business, and close on days when ferries do not run to the island, or when the main art sites are closed.

TREES INUJIMA

324 Inujima; tel. 086/947-1988; www.trees-rest.com/ shop/inujima; 11:45am-3pm Wed.-Mon., otherwise closed on days when ferry does not run and other irregular holidays; ¥1,000

This restaurant set in a wooden building by the water has indoor seating and an open-air deck that is ideal for warm, sunny days. The simple menu consists of chicken curry and rice, salad made with local vegetables, and pudding made in house. Try the craft beer brewed on the island (¥600).

UKI CAFE

293-2 Inujima; tel. 086/947-0877; www.facebook. com/Ukicafe; 10am-5pm Wed.-Mon. Mar.-Nov.; ¥1,000

This cozy restaurant set in a traditional wooden home has tatami-floor seating at low tables. The menu consists of good salads and pasta dishes made with local ingredients, from vegetables to octopus caught nearby. It's a good pick for lunch or an early dinner.

Information and Services

On Inujima, pick up English-language information at the **Inujima Ticket Center** (10am-4pm Wed.-Mon. Mar.-Nov., 10am-4pm Fri.-Mon. Dec.-Feb.).

Getting There and Around

Inujima's one main port is on the northeast corner of the island. Ferries connect the island to **Miyanoura** on Naoshima (55 minutes; ¥1,880), via **Ieura** on Teshima (25 minutes; ¥1,250), and Okayama's **Hoden port** (10 minutes; ¥300). To reach Hoden port by train, take the JR Ako line from Okayama Station to Saidaiji Station (20 minutes; ¥240; 2 trains per hour), then transfer to a bus and ride to Nishi-Hoden (東宝伝) bus stop (1 hour; ¥540; 3-4 buses daily). Hoden port is about 2 minutes on foot south of there. Three buses also run between Okayama Station and near Hoden port (50 minutes; ¥760; daily during Setouchi Triennale, otherwise Sat. and Sun. only). Be aware that not all of these ferries run every day, with limited capacity in winter, among other times. For a full ferry timetable to and from Inujima, and additional information on how to reach these ports, visit http://benesse artsite.jp/en/access.

Once on Inujima, it's possible to see all of its main sights in about three hours **on foot**

Onomichi

尾道

This seaside town is full of retro storefronts, traditional homes, and aging fishing boats floating in the harbor. A vintage shopping arcade houses a mélange of old and new: classic *kissaten* (old-fashioned coffee shops), bakeries, trendy fashion boutiques, and art galleries. In temple-studded neighborhoods spread across the slopes behind the town, an army of cats makes itself at home. Many films, including Yasujiro Ozu's timeless masterpiece *Tokyo Story,* and TV dramas have been shot in Onomichi, which has also produced its fair share of auteurs. This artistic cred makes sense as you stroll around town and up through the hills behind it. Rather than ticking off boxes of sights, Onomichi feels ready-made to wander and follow where inspiration leads.

To take in the spiritual side of the town, there's the temple walk. If you're of a more literary bent, there's also a path marked by poetry-inscribed stones that intersects the temple walk and pays homage to literary figures who were inspired by the town, haiku master Matsuo Bashō among them. Onomichi also serves as the starting point of the Shimanami Kaidō, a 70-km (43-mi) series of bridges across the Inland Sea that links Honshu and Shikoku. This scenic journey can be made by car or bicycle and traverses a string of rural islands en route.

HIKING
★ TEMPLE WALK
Distance: 2.5 km (1.6 mi) one-way
Time: 1-3 hours (depending on time spent at temples)

Information and maps: *Tourist Information center (1-1 Higashigosho-chō)*
Trailhead: *North of first bridge that goes over train tracks east of Onomichi Station*
This famed walking route leads to 25 temples which were built using donations from well-heeled merchants during the town's heyday as a major port city. Aside from including some spectacular architecture, the walk offers stunning views of the Inland Sea and rustic townscapes. You'll walk up and down steps and slopes, and through residential areas. The temples range from petite and deserted to vast complexes.

Senkō-ji (千光寺; 15-1 Higashitsuchido-chō; tel. 0848/23-2310; www.senkouji.jp; 9am-5pm daily), said to have been built by Kōbō Daishi (aka Kūkai) in 806, is the most iconic temple. This complex sits below a park that is reachable by ropeway and offers fantastic views of the city and sea below. Another notable temple is **Jodo-ji** (浄土寺; 20-28 Higashikubo-chō; tel. 0848/37-2361; https://ermjp.com/j/temple; 9am-4pm daily), the last one on the walk; it is said to have been built in the early 7th century, making it the oldest on the route. The temple has a two-story pagoda and lovely garden, both of which are officially designated National Treasures by the Agency for Cultural Affairs. If you prefer to go straight to the town's highest viewing platform without breaking a sweat, hop on the **Senkō-ji Mountain Ropeway** (tel. 084/822-4900; http://onomichibus.jp/ropeway; 9am-5:15pm daily; ¥320 one-way, ¥500 round-trip) to **Senkō-ji-kōen,** the park located above the temple of the same name. The bottom station of the ropeway is about 15 minutes' walk

The Inland Sea's Quieter Side

Naoshima and the other creative hubs nearby on Inujima and Teshima are undeniably the most accessible—and consequently, crowded—places to experience this gorgeous swath of sea. Other islands beckon from just beyond the tourist trail for those who yearn to experience the Inland Sea's charm at a much more intimate level, less impacted by the encroachment of mass tourism. Here are a few of the best slivers of land to get a taste of this simpler way of life.

SHŌDO-SHIMA
小豆島

To sink deeply into the Inland Sea's island time and immerse yourself in the local rhythms, the climatically mild Shōdo-shima, east of Teshima, is a good starting point. Here you'll find olive groves, citrus trees, walking trails, soaring cliffs, and lovely seascapes. Visit www.town.shodoshima.lg.jp for information about activities on the island and detailed access information.

While a day trip to Shōdo-shima is possible, an overnight stay will allow you to fully soak up the laid-back pace. A great spot to do this is the **Sen Guesthouse** (687-15 Tanoura Otsu; tel. 0879/61-9980; www.senguesthouse.com; ¥12,000 d with shared bathrooms, dorms ¥3,400). Run by a friendly English-speaking couple, this property has a private beach, barbecue area, balcony with seaside views, a shared kitchen, and more. Another good pick option on the island is the **Shōdo-shima Olive Youth Hostel** (1072 Nishi-mura, Uchinomi-chō; tel. 0879/82-6161; www.jyh.gr.jp/shoudo; dorms ¥3,400).

KASAOKA ISLANDS
笠岡諸島

Farther west, the Kasaoka Islands also make for a great escape. Accessed from Kasaoka Port, located about 45 minutes by local train on the JR San'yō line from Okayama (¥760) and 30 minutes from Kurashiki (¥500), two of the most charming islands are **Shiraishi-jima** (www.kasaoka-kankou.jp/en/island/shiraishijima) and **Manabe-shima** (www.kasaoka-kankou.jp/en/island/manabeshima/), one of Japan's famed "cat islands," where felines rule the roost.

Both islands make for a pleasant day trip, while the **Shiraishi Island International Villa** (tel. 086/256-2535; www.international-villa.or.jp; ¥3,500 pp) is a great place for a serene overnight stay. The International Villa's generous staff are happy to recommend points of interest on either island, such as the mini-version of Shikoku's 88-temple pilgrimage spread across Shiraishi-jima, or to introduce the island's limited food options. (Stocking up on some snacks on the mainland before making the trip is recommended.) If you're on Shiraishi-jima during the warmer months, swing by the beachside **Moooo! Bar** (www.moooobar.com; daily July-Aug., Sun. June and Sept.). It's a great place to sip a cocktail in the summer heat or watch as the sun dips below the horizon. As for Manabe-shima, the best way to visit is by staying on Shiraishi-jima for two nights and making a day trip to Manabe-shima on one of the days. For detailed access information on both islands, visit www.kasaoka-kankou.jp/en/access.

northeast of Onomichi Station. The easiest way to approach the trek is with an English-language **map** from the tourist information center in hand.

As you make your way along the Temple Walk, you'll notice a number of sizable stones gracefully inscribed with poems and songs (Japanese only). These markers line the **Path of Literature,** which celebrates a handful of literary luminaries, some of whom are also seen along the way in statue form, who have either lived in or been inspired by Onomichi over the centuries. Most prominent among them is the wandering haiku master Matsuo Bashō (1644-1694) who drew inspiration from the town and its surrounding seascape. As you walk along the path, near the fourth temple of **Hōdo-ji** (宝土寺; 10-3 Higashi, Tsuchidō-chō; tel. 0848/22-4085), you'll come to the **Onomichi Literature Museum** (13-28

Higashi, Tsuchidō-chō; 10am-4pm, last entry 3:30pm, Wed.-Mon., closed Wed. if Tues. falls on holiday; ¥310).

SHOPPING
ONOMICHI HONDŌRI

3-17 Higashigosho-chō; tel. 0848/23-5001; www. okaimonomichi.com; street open 24 hours daily, shop hours vary

Many Japanese towns have covered pedestrian shopping streets known as *shōtengai* running through their downtowns. Today, most *shōtengai* are lined by chain stores where mom-and-pop stores once did brisk business. Onomichi Hondōri, however, retains its roots as a thriving piece of the local economy and has its mid-20th-century ambiance fully intact. The street's western edge begins about 4 minutes' walk east of Onomichi Station and continues eastward, through the center of downtown for 1.2 km (0.7 mi), making it a particularly rambling example of this classic style of shopping arcade. Be sure to wander along this retro time capsule to admire the nostalgic shop fronts and weave in and out of the lanes that branch off from it. Rather than set out for a particular shop, just wander down this street, stop anywhere that catches your eye, and enjoy getting a little bit lost.

FOOD
Sushi
YASUHIRO

1-10-12 Tsuchidō; tel. 0848/22-5639; https://yasuhiro. co4.jp; 11:30am-2pm and 5pm-9pm (last order 8:30pm) Tues.-Sun., closed Tues. if Mon. is holiday; lunch sets from ¥1,650, dinner courses from ¥5,400; walk 6 minutes east of Onomichi Station

This mom-and-pop sushi shop near the waterfront has been in business for upward of five decades. The menu includes a good range of rice bowls, sushi platters, tempura, set meals, and more. The quality of the fish used has garnered a loyal following. Lunchtime prices are more affordable. There's a good English-language menu on the website.

Cafés and Light Bites
KITSUNEAME

2-11-17 Kubo; www.facebook.com/kituneame; 9am-11am (last order 10am) and noon-6pm (last order 5pm) Fri.-Mon.; from ¥600; walk 18 minutes northeast of Onomichi Station

Tucked down a side street that branches off of the town's nostalgic Hondōri *shōtengai* (covered shopping street), this hushed old-school café is a classic example of a *kissaten*: dark wood tables, chandeliers, lights behind stained-glass windows. The menu includes items like parfait, French toast, pizza toast (a Japanese spin on pizza) tea, coffee, simple pasta dishes, pancakes, and basic Japanese set meals. Look for the white sign with two foxes under an umbrella and the cafe's name (キツネ雨) under a sign simply saying "Coffee" on the outside.

YAMANEKO CAFE

2-9-33 Tsuchidō; tel. 0848/21-5355; https:// ittoku-go.com; 11am-10pm Tues.-Sun.; dishes from ¥700, set meals from ¥1,300; walk 12 minutes northeast of Onomichi Station

This hip café with an old-school interior is a great spot for a coffee and small dessert or a light, healthy lunch near the waterfront. Western and fusion dishes, from curry-rice to pasta are served, alongside Japanese-style set meals and some vegan items.

Ramen
ONOMICHI RAMEN ICHIBANKAN

2-9-26 Tsuchidō; tel. 0848/21-1119; www.f-ichibankan. com; 11am-7pm Sat.-Thurs.; from ¥580; walk 13 minutes northeast of Onomichi Station

In a town famed for its ramen, this shop is among the most accessible places to eat the town's signature spin on the dish. Springy medium-sized noodles are served in a hearty broth made from soy sauce, *dashi* (fish stock), and chicken, enriched by fatty cuts of pork. Side items like *gyoza* (fried dumplings), fried rice, and *karage* (fried chicken) are also served.

1: view of Onomichi from Senkō-ji 2: Senkō-ji

ACCOMMODATIONS

Onomichi is a peaceful place for an overnight stay, either while traveling between Kyoto or elsewhere in Kansai and Hiroshima, or before or after a jaunt on the Shimanami Kaidō. For a full list of accommodations, visit www.ono-navi.com/accommodations.

MIHARASHI TEI

15-7 Higashitsuchido-chō; tel. 0848/23-3864; http://miharashi.onomichisaisei.com; dorms from ¥3,000, private rooms from ¥10,000

Ensconced on a cliff near Senkō-ji temple, this inn occupies a once abandoned hilltop villa originally built a century ago during the town's *saen* ("tea culture") boom, when well-heeled residents built vast residences geared toward drinking tea with guests in beautiful surroundings. It served as an inn for a time after World War II, then fell into disrepair for almost three decades, until an extensive project to breathe new life into the property was launched in 2015. There are both dorms (mixed and women-only) and private rooms, all with tatami-mat floors, futon bedding, and shared bathroom, a café with sweeping views, and friendly English-speaking staff. A caveat: It's located about 20 minutes' walk from Onomichi Station and involves a climb up some 370 stone steps, so taking a taxi from the station is recommended if you're arriving with heavy luggage. Direct the taxi driver to Senkō-ji, as you can't drive directly to the inn, then walk 10 minutes downhill from there. Children under 6 are not permitted.

HOTEL CYCLE ONOMICHI

Onomichi U2 complex, 6-15 Nishigosho-chō; tel. 0848/21-0550; www.onomichi-u2.com; twins from ¥18,200

About 9 minutes' walk west of Onomichi Station on the waterfront, this modish hotel is set within a large complex called Onomichi U2 that is housed in a former row of warehouses. The rooms are all twins (deluxe size available) and have a minimalist design sense and well-stocked, spacious bathrooms. More importantly, guests can keep their bicycles in their rooms or tune them up with various tools provided in the hotel's lounge area. Beyond the hotel itself, the U2 complex also houses restaurants, cafés, shops, and a **Giant** store offering bicycle rentals.

INFORMATION AND SERVICES

You can stock up on English-language information at Onomichi Station's **tourist information counter** (1-1 Higashigosho-chō; tel. 0848/20-0005; www.ononavi.com 9am-6pm daily). Visit the town's official tourism portal, **Ononavi** (www.ononavi.com).

GETTING THERE

Onomichi's core centers around **Onomichi Station,** which is served by local trains on the **JR Sany'ō line.** Coming from Hiroshima, you can take the *shinkansen* to Fukuyama, then transfer to the local JR San'yō line bound for Mihara (1 hour; ¥5,280). Coming from the east, you can take the JR San'yō line directly from both Kurashiki (1 hour; ¥1,140) and Okayama (1 hour 20 minutes; ¥1,320). From Kyoto, take the *shinkansen* to Fukuyama (1 hour 15 minutes to 2 hours; ¥8,570-8,890 depending on train type), then transfer to the JR San'yō line and ride until Onomichi (20 minutes; ¥420).

GETTING AROUND

Once you've arrived in Onomichi, the easiest way to get around is either **on foot** or **bicycle.** There are bike rental shops surrounding the ferry terminal. And if you happen to be in town on the weekend, the **Skip Line** is a bus route that runs clockwise through the heart of town, starting from Onomichi Station. Buses leave every 30 minutes (9:30am-4:30pm Sat.-Sun.; single ride ¥140, 1-day pass ¥500).

Shimanami Kaidō しまなみ海道

Extending southward from Onomichi, a route known as the Shimanami Kaidō (Shimanami Sea Route) links six picturesque islands via nine massive bridges, terminating in the town of Imabari in northwest Shikoku's Ehime Prefecture. The roadway takes in sublime stretches of the Inland Sea and reveals snapshots of bucolic island life, as well as more industrialized areas. Though this route makes for a spectacular scenic drive (roughly 60 km/37 mi; 1 hour), one-way tolls add up to about ¥5,000. An even more breathtaking way to enjoy it, when the weather cooperates, is by bicycle.

INNO-SHIMA
因島

Awash in flowers, this island is the second one you'll reach as you travel southward from Onomichi along the Shimanami Kaidō. It is linked by the **Inno-shima Bridge** to Mukai-shima to the east, beyond which lies Onomichi, and by the **Ikuchi Bridge** to Ikuchi-jima to the west. As with many of these isles, the soil of Inno-shima yields a glut of citrus fruit, most notably oranges. Due to the fact that English-speaking staff or printed materials are scarce on Inno-shima, your best bet is simply to stock up in Onomichi, where English-language material is available for all of the islands along the Shimanami Kaidō cycling route.

Sights
MOUNT SHIRATAKI
白滝山

Shigei-chō; tel. 0845/26-6212; www.ononavi.jp/sightseeing/showplace/detail.html?detail_id=313; 24 hours daily; free

Dotted by 700 stone Buddhist statues, including those depicting Buddha's 500 disciples, this modest peak offers stunning views of the surrounding sea. To reach the top, pedal about 2 km (1.2 mi) from Shigei-Higashi Port,

then walk another 10 minutes to the top. After visiting the mountain, swing by the nearby **Inno-shima Flower Center** (1181-1 Inno-shima Shigei-chō; tel. 0845/26-6212; 9am-5pm Wed.-Mon., closed Wed. if Tues. is holiday; free) for a breather. There's a greenhouse and flowers in bloom everywhere you turn here, as well as an observatory with beautiful views of the sea. It's located just west of the mountain.

INNO-SHIMA SUIGUN CASTLE
因島水軍城

3228-2 Nakanosho-chō; tel. 0845/24-0936; www.ononavi.jp/sightseeing/showplace/detail.html?detail_id=247; 9:30am-5pm Fri.-Wed.; high school students and older ¥330, junior high and elementary school students ¥160

Continuing another 3.7 km (2.3 mi) to the southeast, this former pirate's castle is worth a quick stop. The Inland Sea once teemed with "pirate" ships, and the vessels of the Murakami Kaizoku (clan) were atop the pecking order from the Muromachi (1336-1573) through the Sengoku (aka "Warring States") (1467-1615) periods. While pirates are normally infamous for plundering wealth from other ships, the Murakami clan were, relatively speaking, a force for good, primarily maintaining order and providing safe lanes for the sea's traffic. The remains of their maritime prowess are scattered throughout the region, with this castle being a prime example. The structure itself is only mildly interesting, but make a quick stop if you're curious to see its stash of old weapons. If you want to kit up in samurai armor, you can do that, too.

Food
★ HASSAKUYA

246-1 Ohama-chō; tel. 0845/24-0715; http://0845.boo.jp/hassaku; from 8:30am until sold out Wed.-Sun., closed mid-Aug.-early Oct.; from ¥150

Soon after reaching the island from Mukai-jima, be sure to stop at this citrus-focused

Shimanami Kaidō

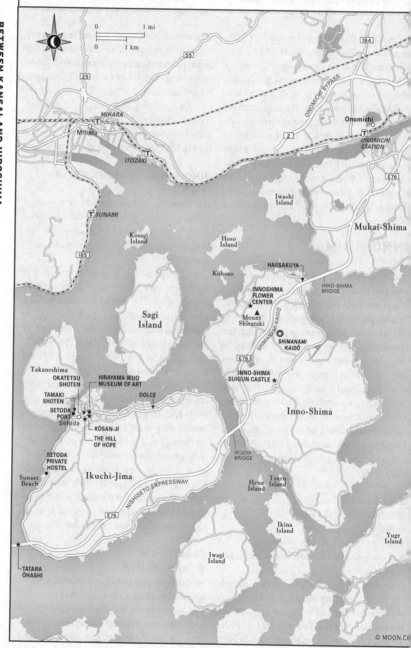

confectionary. This shop sells rice cakes stuffed with the island's famously juicy, mildly bitter *hassaku* oranges. The sweetness of the cake and mildly bitter zest of the orange mingle beautifully. After eating a cake or two at the shop, you'll likely want to buy extras for the road. Directions for reaching Hassakuya can be confusing; the shop's website has a detailed map (http://0845.boo.jp/hassaku/access/index.html). Note that the shop closes once the treats are sold out for the day, and shuts down from mid-August until early October.

Getting There

Inno-shima is best reached on two wheels, as part of the Shimanami Kaidō route. It's about 22 km (13.7 mi), or a 2-hour ride, from Onomichi. To begin, first take a short **ferry** ride from Onomichi to Mukai-shima, where the route officially begins (5 minutes; ¥100, ¥10 extra with bicycle; departs every 5-10 minutes).

IKUCHI-JIMA

生口島

Yet another island sprinkled with citrus trees, with a preponderance of lemons, Ikuchi-jima is the most visited isle of the Shimanami Kaidō. Linked to Inno-shima by the **Ikuchi Bridge** in the north, and to Ōmi-shima via the imposing **Tatara Bridge** in its south, the bulk of the action is clustered around the Setoda area on the island's west side. Shops and hotels are particularly dense around the **Shiomachi** shopping street, and along **Setoda Sunset Beach**—which, as its name suggests, is known for its fiery dusk. Among the area's charms are a curious marble walk-through artwork named *The Hill of Hope,* and the **Ikuo Hirayama Art Museum**—all within 1 km (0.6 mi) of **Setoda Port.**

Sights
KŌSAN-JI
耕三寺

553-2 Setoda-chō; tel. 0845/27-0800; www.kousanji. or.jp; 9am-5pm daily; adults ¥1,400, university students ¥1,000, high school students ¥800, junior high school students and younger free; walk 10 minutes east of Setoda Port along Shiomachi shopping street

This curious temple complex was envisioned by a local businessman who directed the building of each structure in the 1930s in honor of his mother's memory. Each building on the grounds is modeled after an iconic temple found elsewhere in Japan—historic and spiritual hot spots like Kyoto and Nikko make appearances, to name a few. After admiring the skillful reproductions, bravely descend into the subterranean passageway filled with vivid imagery of Buddhist hell.

To lighten things after your virtual journey into the underworld, ascend the hilltop behind the temple and walk through the unique—and glaring in the daytime—artwork known as the *Heights of Eternal Hope for the Future* (*Miraishin no Oka*; 未来心の丘; entrance included in temple admission). This walk-through was wrought by Kazuto Kuetani, a sculptor who imported giant slabs of marble from Italy to actualize his vision. While it may sound lofty, this is a secular artwork on the temple grounds rather than a direct extension of the temple itself.

There's also a bright, airy, on-site café, appropriately white marble throughout, called **Cafe Cuore** (tel. 0845/27-0755; 10am-4:30pm daily; from ¥500). It's a good spot for a light lunch or coffee break with sea views.

HIRAYAMA IKUO MUSEUM OF ART
平山郁夫美術館

200-2 Sawa, Setoda-chō; tel. 0845/27-3800; http:// hirayama-museum.or.jp; 9am-5pm (last entry 4:30pm) daily; adults ¥920, university and high school students ¥410, junior high and elementary school students ¥210; walk 10 minutes east of Setoda Port along Shiomachi shopping street

This museum showcases the paintings of favorite local son, after whom it is named. Hirayama, who passed away in 2009, was the foremost modern practitioner of the *Nihon-ga* style of traditional watercolor painting, which came into vogue

TOP EXPERIENCE

☆ Cycling the Inland Sea

There's no "right" way to travel the classic Shimanami Kaidō Inland Sea bicycle route, but whether you cycle part or all of it, it's sure to be memorable.

ISLANDS AND BRIDGES

The islands crossed on the Shimanami Kaidō, from north to south, are **Mukai-shima, Inno-shima, Ikuchi-jima, Ōmi-shima, Hakata-jima,** and **Oshima.** The bridges that link them are engineering marvels. The **Tatara Bridge,** which spans Ikuchi-jima and Ōmi-shima, has the fourth longest main span of any cable-stayed bridge in the world, with a center span of 890 meters (2,920 feet) and a total length of 1,480 meters (4,855 feet). Bridging Ōshima and Imabari, the **Kurushima Kaikyōu Bridge** is one of the world's longest suspension bridges at a staggering 4 km (2.5 mi). Tolls for cyclists have been waived on the bridges for some time, although there's a chance they could be in effect in the future (up to ¥200 per bridge).

THE ROUTE

The recommended Shimanami Kaidō cycling course is well marked. If you want to cycle all the way from Onomichi to **Imabari** on Shikoku, the 70 km (43 mi) trip takes about 8 hours without pit stops. Many cyclists prefer to spend a night on one of the islands, **Ikuchi-jima** being a prime spot. Others go partway, and then take the ferry back to Onomichi.

Starting in Onomichi, you'll first need to hop on a **ferry** to nearby **Mukai-shima** (¥70-110 pp with bicycle). The bridge linking Onomichi to Mukai-shima doesn't allow pedestrians or cyclists. From Mukai-shima, you're free to pedal all the way to Imabari. Note that **Setoda Port** on Ikuchi-jima is the island farthest from Onomichi that can be reached by ferry (40 minutes; ¥1,200; boats depart every hour or two); this is an important consideration if you plan to return to Onomichi by ferry on the same day (last ferry 6:30pm). You'll need to pay up to an additional ¥300, depending on the route, to bring a bicycle aboard a ferry.

RENTING A BIKE

You can rent a bicycle and pick up a map of the route at a variety of **bicycle terminals** in Onomichi, a short walk toward the waterfront from the main train station, and on some of the islands (¥1,100 per day, plus ¥1,100 deposit, refundable if bicycle is returned to same terminal). Electrically assisted bicycles are on offer at some of these terminals (up to 6 hours; ¥1,600, ¥1,100 deposit; must be returned to same terminal). **Reserving a bicycle online** is recommended during high season and must be done at least a week in advance. For a full list of terminals or to reserve a bicycle in advance, visit http://shimanami-cycle.or.jp/rental/english. If you prefer a fancier steed and don't mind paying a premium, **Giant** (https://bicyclerental.jp/en; from ¥4,000 per day) has rental outlets in both Onomichi and Imabari. Advance reservation and an extra ¥3,000 is required if you want to drop off one of Giant's road bikes at a non-Giant terminal.

during the Meiji period (1868-1912). Much of Hirayama's work reflects visions of his travels in remote desert corners of the former Silk Road. Closer to home, he also documented with his brush the construction of the Shimanami Kaidō, which he watched being built in the late 1990s. Delving deeper into Hirayama's life story, the museum also explores the impact that witnessing the bombing of Hiroshima had on him, as well as his subsequent illness. These harrowing experiences inspired him to adopt Buddhism,

Shimanami Kaidō bike path

CYCLING TIPS

A few brief tips before setting out. First, be sure to always **stay on the left side of the road** and avoid hogging the lane. Second, set out with enough **cash** for your needs, as the small mom-and-pop businesses, from *izakaya* to *ryokan,* likely won't take other forms of payment. Finally, if you plan to stay overnight in a *ryokan* on any of the islands, **arrive by 5pm** so you are in time for dinner. Besides being disappointing, missing a meal in your inn could leave you without many options once the sun goes down, as shops close early on the islands.

You can also leave your luggage in a locker at most bicycle terminals if you plan to do a return trip. If you plan to forge onward, a popular luggage forwarding service is **Kuro Neko** (www.kuronekoyamato.co.jp; from ¥1,000), which sends packages overnight to and from select convenience stores. Catering specifically to the Shimanami Kaidō, **Sagawa Express** (www.sagawa-exp.co.jp/stc/english/) allows you to send luggage between participating hotels in both Onomichi and Imabari.

MORE INFORMATION

For general information on the route, including a downloadable English **map,** visit www.go-shimanami.jp. Another helpful free resource, which includes information on bicycle rentals, accommodation across the islands, maps, and summaries of things to do is this downloadable **guide:** https://shimanami-cycle.or.jp/cycling/assets/pdf/shimap-en.pdf. And of course, the friendly **tourist information office** in Onomichi can also provide any information you need, as well as help with booking accommodations on the islands.

an influence that is evident in his work. Recommended.

Beaches
SETODA SUNSET BEACH
瀬戸田サンセットビーチ

1506-15 Tarumi, Setoda-chō; tel. 0845/27-1100; www.onomichi-sunset-beach.jp; 24 hours daily; free

Commonly referred to simply as Sunset Beach, this admittedly touristy stretch of sand along Ikuchi-jima's west side is renowned for its brilliant skies at dusk. And that says a lot for a region where just about every island can justly brag about its sunsets. At 0.8 km (0.5 mi) long, the beach has ample amenities—showers, lockers, stand-up paddleboard rentals, tent rentals, paid barbecue spaces, a café, and more—outlined on the website in Japanese. Swimming is permitted, but that comes with a caveat. While it's a sandy beach, there are plenty of shells and small stones throughout the area, so venture out with footwear if you want to avoid stepping on something sharp.

Food

Cafés and restaurants are clustered along the **Shiomachi** shopping arcade east of Setoda Port. You'll notice plenty of lemon ice cream, orange juice served directly in hollowed-out orange peels, juicy roast chicken, and various forms of octopus on offer. Given that this is among the more touristed islands of the region, you can trust the queues—the longer they are, the more likely a restaurant is to deliver.

OKATETSU SHOTEN
517 Setoda-chō; tel. 0845/27-0568; 8:30am-6:30pm daily, irregular closings

A stone's throw from Tamaki, you'll come to another great takeout spot. The specialty at this former butcher is beef croquette. The outer shell is crispy and freshly fried. The mouthwatering inside is stuffed with sweetened ground beef and potato. This winning combo has landed the little shop on Japanese television more than 70 times and counting. It closes when the goods sell out.

DOLCE
20-8 Setoda-chō; tel. 0845/26-4046; www. setoda-dolce.com; 10am-5pm daily; from ¥350

If you're approaching by bicycle from Innoshima, after pedaling through the first few industrialized kilometers of the island, you'll come to this well-loved gelato shop. The gelato made with locally sourced lemons is fantastic and very refreshing after working up a sweat on your bike. Be sure to avail yourself of the shop's free supply of lemon water

before hitting the road again, too. There's also a branch (546 Setoda-chō; tel. 0845/26-4036; 10am-5pm daily) in Setoda proper, located on the main drag between Kōsan-ji and the Hirayama Ikuo Museum of Art.

TAMAKI SHOTEN
511 Setoda-chō; tel. 0845/27-0239; 9am-6pm daily; from ¥380

Also on the main Shiomachi shopping street, this popular shop serves delicious roast chicken to-go. It's crunchy on the outside, soft on the inside, and slathered in sweet and spicy sauce. Search for "Tamaki Deli" in Google Maps.

Accommodations

SETODA PRIVATE HOSTEL
58-1 Tarumi, Setoda-chō; tel. 0845/27-3137; http:// setodashimanami.web.fc2.com/eshimanami.html; ¥3,000 pp stay only, ¥4,800 with 2 meals

Private tatami rooms, an *onsen* built by the friendly owner that faces the beach, and tasty home-cooked meals sourced mostly from the sea. For the price, what more can you ask for? The no-frills rooms are basic, but clean. If you're not craving luxury, the place can't be beat for location or local charm. Reserve ahead by telephone (basic English spoken) or via this online booking service: www.travelarrangejapan.com/Accommodations/setoda-tarumi-onsen/. Cash only.

Information and Services

The **Setoda Tourist Information Center** (200-5 Setoda-chō; tel. 0845/27-0051; 9am-5pm daily) is about 10 minutes' walk from Setoda Port, along a classic shopping street, near the Ikuo Hirayama Museum of Art. Pick up English-language maps, rent bicycles (¥1,100 per day with ¥1,100 deposit), or store your belongings in a locker. Free Wi-Fi available.

Getting There

If you're approaching the Shimanami Kaidō entirely by bicycle, you'll reach Ikuchi-jima from Inno-shima, lying to the east, via the

ŌMI-SHIMA
大三島

Lying west of Ikuchi-jima, this quiet, hilly island is reached via the dazzling Tatara Bridge. In the same spirit of the "art islands" speckled throughout the eastern side of the Inland Sea, Ōmi-shima also has its share of well-designed architectural gems. Located in the island's southwest and envisioned by "starchitect" Toyo Itō, two notable stops include an eponymous architecture museum, which celebrates the island's community and beauty, and a rejuvenated former schoolhouse that has morphed into a stylish modern *ryokan*. Beyond these modern wonders, the island is also home to **Ōyamazumi-jinja,** one of the oldest Shinto shrines in all of Western Japan. Given its distance from Onomichi, the island is a great place to stop and rest for a night, either before returning to the mainland the following day, or perhaps forging on to Imabari on the other side of the Inland Sea.

Sights
TATARA BRIDGE VIEWING AREA
多々羅展望台

*Tatara-shimanami Park (多々羅しまなみ公園); tel.
0897/87-3000; www.imabari-shimanami.jp/tatara/;
24 hours daily; free*

Located within Tatara Shimanami Park, this is just like what it sounds: a vantage point at which to stop and gaze upon the massive feat of construction that is the Tatara Bridge, which you will have crossed over from neighboring Ikuchi-jima by now. Views of the surrounding seascape are stunning.

ŌYAMAZUMI-JINJA
大山祇神社

*3327 Miyaura, Ōmi-shima-chō; tel. 0897/82-0032;
8:30am-5pm daily; ¥1,000 Treasure Hall and Kaiji
Museum*

In the island's heart stands this significant and very ancient shrine. Housed within is Ōyamazumi no Okami, god of mountains, oceans, and war, and brother of the sun goddess Amaterasu, from whom Japan's imperial line is believed to have sprung. Underscoring

---

kuchi Bridge. From Onomichi, the trip is 31 km (19.3 mi) and takes about 3-4 hours, depending on how leisurely you pedal and how many stops you make.

Like Inno-shima, it's also possible to take a **ferry** from Onomichi, arriving at Setoda Port (722-2411 Setoda-chō Ikuchi-jima; 8am-6pm daily) in Ikuchi-jima's northwest (20 minutes; adults ¥650, children ¥330 one-way; running roughly 6:30am-6:30pm). The ferries, also run by **Setouchu Cruising** (tel. 0865/62-2856; www.s-cruise.jp) follow the same route as those traveling to Shigei-Higashi Port on Inno-shima, leaving seven times daily, roughly hourly, from just in front of Onomichi Station at **Onomichi Ekimae Port** (9-1 Higashigosho-chō), a short walk from JR Onomichi Station. View https://s-cruise.jp/timetable-eng to see an English-language timetable.

Getting Around

Once you're on the island, explore by bicycle. Either rent your bicycle in Onomichi before setting out, or in Setoda if you arrive by ferry. There are cycle rental shops, including for electric bicycles, scattered around the port town, as well as on Setoda Sunset Beach.

In town, the easiest place to rent (and return) a bicycle is the **Tourist Information Center** (200-5 Sawa, Setoda-chō; tel. 0845/27-0051; www.ononavi.jp/sightseeing/infooffice/detail.html?detail_id=399; 9am-5pm daily; daily rates ¥1,100 standard bicycles, ¥1,600 electrically assisted bicycles, ¥1,300 tandem bicycles). On Sunset Beach, there's also a **terminal and rental shop** (1506-15 Tarumi, Setoda-chō; tel. 0848/22-3911; www.onomichi-sunset-beach.jp/activity.html; 9am-5pm daily; daily rates ¥1,100 standard bicycles, ¥1,600 electrically assisted bicycles, ¥1,300 tandem bicycles).

You can reserve a bicycle to be picked up either in town at the Tourist Information Center or at the terminal on Sunset Beach online at https://shimanami-cycle.or.jp/rental/english-reservation. You must book at least four days in advance of your planned trip.

A Taste of Shikoku

Kurushima Kaikyō Bridge

The smallest and least populated of Japan's four main islands, Shikoku has always felt remote from the Japanese mainland. It's much easier to access now, thanks to a series of bridges linking Honshu with Shikoku's northern coast, but a sense of otherness pervades the island nonetheless. Its deep mountainous interior has limited public transportation, and its dramatic coastline rolls on seemingly without end. As remote as the island's interior and southern half may be, its northern coastline is within relatively easy reach from many points in the Inland Sea region. If you complete the full **Shimanami Kaidō route,** passing over the final **Kurushima Kaikyō Bridge,** among the world's longest suspension bridges at 4 km (2.5 mi), you'll land in the city of Imabari, located in Ehime Prefecture in the island's northwest. Here are a few ways to rejuvenate yourself before returning back to Honshu:

· Drop off your bicycle and stay for a night at **Sunrise Itoyama** (2-8-1 Sunaba-chō, Imabari; tel. 0898/41-3196; www.sunrise-itoyama.jp; single ¥4,400, twin with shared bathroom ¥6,600), a hotel right by the bridge that is a designated drop-off point for bicycles.

· Ride your bike the last 30 minutes or so from the bridge to **JR Imabari Station** and drop it off there, then walk 6 minutes southwest of the station to soak your weary muscles at hot-spring complex **Shimanami Onsen Kisuke no Yu** (1-2-30 Nakahiyoshi-chō, Imabari; tel. 0898/22-0026; www.kisuke.com/yu-imabari; 6am-9pm daily; weekdays ¥600, weekends and holidays ¥650, towel rental ¥300).

the shrine's age, the shrine was founded in 594, although its current structure was constructed in 1378. For added temporal impact, note that the mammoth camphor tree in its courtyard has been there for 26 centuries.

Given that the shrine's resident deity is the god of war, it's no surprise to learn that it was frequented by warriors seeking victory in battle since time immemorial. Samurai

who emerged triumphant developed a tradition of leaving their armor and weapons as offerings to the sun goddess's brother. As a result, today around 80 percent of Japan's entire cache of samurai relics of war, distinguished as National Treasures and Important Cultural Properties, are stashed away in this shrine's Treasure Hall. Among this martial bounty are some legendarily massive *ōdachi* (great swords), clocking in at 180 cm (71 in) in length and weighing almost 5 kg (11 lbs).

TOKORO MUSEUM
ところミュージアム大三島

2362-3 Urado, Omishima-chō; tel. 0897/83-0380; www.city.imabari.ehime.jp/museum/tokoro; 9am-5pm Tues.-Sun.; adults ¥310, students ¥160

Located atop a steep incline, roughly 9 km (5.6 mi) southwest of Ōyamazumi-jinja in the island's southwest, this peculiar modern museum is remarkably simple in its design. Two concrete walls, standing parallel and linked by a curved wooden lattice frame at the top, are sheltered by a translucent roof. The structure is oriented in a downhill fashion so that you descend as you proceed through the museum, one level at a time. Within this unique space, you'll find an assortment of sculptures, some cheeky, crafted by artists such as Ikeda Munehiro, Giacomo Manzù, Noe Katz, and Marisol. When you reach the lowest level of the museum, you'll emerge onto an open-air terrace with sweeping views out to sea—arguably the most stunning piece of all.

TOYO ITŌ MUSEUM OF ARCHITECTURE
今治市伊東豊雄建築ミュージアム

2418 Urado Omishima-chō; tel. 0897/74-7220; www. tima-imabari.jp; 9am-5pm Tues.-Sun.; ¥800

Just down the road, within eyesight of Tokoro Museum, this conceptually brilliant building celebrates the local culture and landscape of this picturesque island. Designed by Pritzker Prize-winning architect Toyo Itō, the highly original complex is divided into two main buildings. The polyhedral-shaped **Steel Hut** showcases a collection of photographs of the island and its people, as well as images illustrating Itō's creative process at work. The **Silver Hut** is a reconstruction of Itō's celebrated Tokyo home that he built in 1985. And of course, throughout the museum guests are met with yet more awe-inspiring views of the surrounding sea.

Food

There are a number of restaurants serving locally caught seafood dotting the area around Ōyamazumi-jinja. Otherwise, your best bet is to fuel up soon after you arrive on the island at one of the eateries near the Tatara Bridge.

seafood meal at a roadside restaurant along the Shimanami Kaidō

IKIDANE CYCLIST HOSTEL & CAFE SHIMANAMI

7345-1 Kamiura-chō Inokuchi, Imabari; tel.
0897/72-8308; https://shimanami.bike/
caferestaurant/; 11:30am-9pm (last order 8:30pm)
daily; set meals from ¥1,080

This bright, chic café attached to a stylish hostel serves good Japanese set meals, ranging from fish to *tonkatsu*, with salad, rice, and miso soup. On an island where dining options are slim, this is a good option for a meal soon after crossing the nearby Tatara Bridge.

Accommodations

IKIDANE CYCLIST HOSTEL & CAFE SHIMANAMI

7345-1 Kamiura-chō Inokuchi, Imabari; tel.
0897/72-8308; https://shimanami.bike; single
¥12,000, twin ¥14,000, dorm ¥9,000

Alongside housing a good café, this complex is also a comfortable place to bed down for a night. There are a mix of single and twin rooms with bunk beds, as well as mixed dorms, all with shared bathrooms and toiletries provided. Note that even the "private" rooms are only separated by curtains. Lockers are provided.

★ ŌMI-SHIMA IKOI-NO-IE

5208-1 Omishima-chō Munakata, Imabari; tel.
0897/83-1111; www.ikoinoie.co.jp; dorms with 2 meals
from ¥5,000, doubles with two meals from ¥15,000

Housed in an old wooden elementary school, this modern guesthouse is a peaceful hideaway on the more remote southern side of the island. Developed by architect Toyo Itō, who also designed the Toyo Itō Museum of Architecture, just a 10-minute bicycle ride to the north, this unique property is the brainchild of a local family who saw an opportunity to revitalize the island amid an exodus of young residents. Many of the school building's original fixings, such as wooden classroom signs, remain in place, evoking a whiff of nostalgia. The room styles include both modern (with beds) and Japanese (with futons and tatami floors). This is a great pick if you plan to make your way to the remote far side of the island, coming from Onomichi, and want to rest before either returning to Onomichi the next day or proceeding all the way across to the city of Imabari on Shikoku. Excellent meals, heavy on locally caught seafood, are included.

Getting There and Around

Ōmi-shima does not have any direct ferry links. If you want to cut the time it takes to reach the island from Onomichi, take the ferry to **Setoda Port** on the neighboring island of Ikuchi-jima. Otherwise, the island takes 3-4 hours to reach from Onomichi by bicycle.

The most sensible and appealing way to see Ōmi-shima, as with the other islands of the Shimanami Kaidō, is from the seat of a **bicycle.** You can either rent a bike in Onomichi, or travel to Setoda by ferry to shave a few hours off the journey, and then rent one there.

Hiroshima and Miyajima

Though the cities on Western Honshu's south-ern San'yō ("sunny side of the mountain") coast present a modern face, you'll find they're balanced by a nice degree of old-time charm. Conveniently served by bullet train, the manageable cities and fishing towns along this coastline unveil a slower side of Japan—a breath of fresh air after jetting through Tokyo or Osaka.

The top destination of the San'yō coast is Hiroshima, a city whose destruction by atomic bomb during World War II left a scar that will never fully heal. But its energetic modern incarnation is an inspiring testament to the power of the human spirit. Hemming in the city to the south is the wistfully beautiful Seto Naikai (Inland Sea), a narrow body

Look for ★ to find recommended sights, activities, dining, and lodging.

Highlights

★ **Peace Memorial Park:** Pay your respects to Hiroshima's harrowing past with a visit to its sobering collection of atomic bomb monuments (page 379).

★ **Food in Hiroshima:** Most associate the savory pancake known as *okonomiyaki* with Osaka, but Hiroshima has its own fried-noodle-infused spin on the dish (page 386).

★ **Itsukushima-jinja:** Take in one of Japan's quintessential views, the "floating" vermillion *torii* gate of Miyajima (page 394).

© MOON.COM

Hiroshima and Miyajima

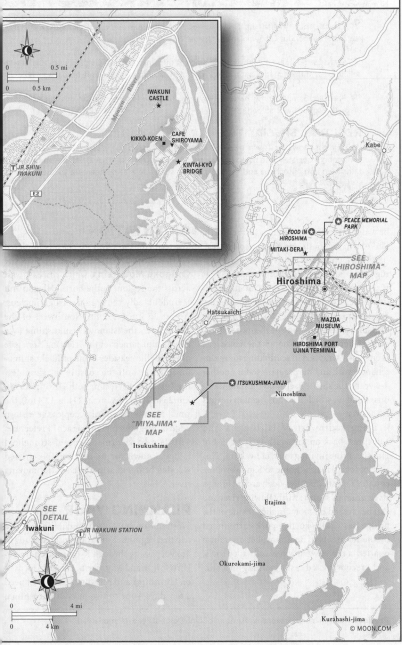

IWAKUNI CASTLE

KIKKŌ-KOEN

CAFE SHIROYAMA

KINTAI-KYŌ BRIDGE

JR SHIN-IWAKUNI

E2

0   0.5 mi
0   0.5 km

Matsuyama River

Kabe

FOOD IN HIROSHIMA

PEACE MEMORIAL PARK

MITAKI-DERA

SEE "HIROSHIMA" MAP

Hiroshima

Hatsukaichi

MAZDA MUSEUM

HIROSHIMA PORT UJINA TERMINAL

ITSUKUSHIMA-JINJA

Ninoshima

SEE "MIYAJIMA" MAP

Itsukushima

Etajima

SEE DETAIL

Iwakuni

JR IWAKUNI STATION

Okurokami-jima

Kurahashi-jima

0   4 mi
0   4 km

© MOON.COM

Best Restaurants

★ **Okonomiyaki Lopez:** This hallowed Hiroshima joint serves *okonomiyaki* made by a masterful, gregarious Guatemalan chef (page 387).

★ **Cafe Lente:** Eat a healthy, simple lunch at this smart café as you gaze through floor-to-ceiling glass at the famed "floating" *torii* gate of Itsukushima-jinja just offshore (page 397).

★ **Kakiya:** Sample freshly harvested oysters, from raw to deep-fried, in this chic restaurant on picturesque Miyajima (page 397).

REGIONAL SPECIALITIES

Hiroshima is known for its own take on *okonomiyaki,* in which the savory pancake dish more commonly associated with Osaka is topped with *yaki-soba* (fried soba) noodles and also contains fried egg. Hiroshima and the surrounding seascape is also known for the quality of its **oysters.**

of water bounded by Honshu to the north, Shikoku to the south, and Kyushu to the west.

Nearby, one of the jewels in this shimmering seascape is the island of Miyajima. This virgin-forested isle is famed for its semi-domesticated deer—you can feed them by hand—and most of all, the "floating" *torii* gate of Itsukushima-jinja, one of the most photogenic shrines in Japan. Though the fabled gate is currently wrapped in scaffolding for maintenance work and may remain so for another 4-5 years, the shrine itself, and the mountainous island on which it stands, remain beautiful as ever.

Lying southwest of Hiroshima and Miyajima, back on the south-facing coast of Honshu, is the inviting town of Iwakuni. This slice of local Japan is home to Kintaikyō, the country's most famous wooden arched bridge. Its five humps span a swiftly flowing river and can be crossed on foot. On the far side of the bridge lies Kikko-kōen, a park surrounded by the remnants of an atmospheric samurai quarter, complete with white walls, tiled roofs, and a reconstructed castle looming on a hill.

ORIENTATION

Western Honshu's **San'yō** coast is Bordered by the **Inland Sea** to the south and the **Chūgoku Mountains,** which run east-west across the region, to the north. **Hiroshima** is undoubtedly the region's urban nucleus. About 25 km (15.5 mi) southwest of the city proper, the island of Itsukushima (aka **Miyajima**), famed for the "floating" *torii* gate of the idyllic seaside shrine of Itsukushima-jinja, lies just off the coast in the shimmering Inland Sea. West of both Hiroshima (40 km/25 mi) and Miyajima (20 km/12.4 mi), the small town of **Iwakuni** occupies the eastern edge of neighboring Yamaguchi Prefecture. This laid-back former samurai stronghold is best known for its massive five-arched wooden bridge that spans a swiftly moving river.

PLANNING YOUR TIME

Western Honshu is often the culmination of a trip that begins in Kanto or Kansai, starting in Tokyo, passing through Kyoto, and ending in **Hiroshima** and **Miyajima.** For a trip focused on Hiroshima and Miyajima, you'll just need a few days—one to two days in Hiroshima,

---

Previous: Itsukushima-jinja; *okonomiyaki*; Atomic Bomb Dome at Peace Memorial Park.

Best Accommodations

★ **Rihga Royal Hotel Hiroshima:** A pleasant stroll from Peace Memorial Park, this well-priced, stylish hotel with cheerful staff and plenty of amenities is a great base in the heart of Hiroshima (page 390).

★ **World Friendship Center:** This welcoming B&B, run by friendly American hosts, is an ideal place to make sense of your time in Hiroshima, from its tragic past to its dynamic present (page 390).

★ **Iwasō Ryokan:** This historic *ryokan* in Miyajima is surrounded by maple trees that become a kaleidoscope of color in fall (page 398).

and one day on Miyajima. If you'd like to go deeper, consider an additional side trip to **Iwakuni,** which is easily explored in half a day. The highlights of Hiroshima are undoubtedly the **Peace Memorial Park** (commonly referred to as Peace Park) and **Peace Memorial Museum.** However, the city has its lesser-known gems, with the temple of **Mitaki-dera** hidden in a mountain forest outside town atop the list. Miyajima is justly famous for its watery shrine of **Itsukushima-jinja,** known for its "floating" shrine gate, and a trip to the top of **Mount Misen,** offering stunning vistas from the summit of the island's core, is also high on most itineraries.

The easiest way to reach the region is via *shinkansen*, which runs to Hiroshima from Tokyo, Kyoto, Osaka, and all stops in between and beyond on the JR Tōkaidō-San'yō line.

Once you're in the region, you'll be using local train lines and trams within Hiroshima and regional train lines to reach Miyajima-guchi and Iwakuni.

Your best choice for a base is Hiroshima, which has the widest range of accommodations. If you have the leisure of time, you can consider staying one night on atmospheric Miyajima, too. It's possible to visit both Miyajima and Iwakuni in one long day trip from Hiroshima, or perhaps to visit Iwakuni after staying in Miyajima overnight.

San'yō is one of the sunniest parts of Japan. **Summers** (June-Sept.) are hot and humid (27-32°C/81-90°F), with the rainy season rolling in throughout June and July. Temperatures drop in **winter** (Dec.-Feb.) to as low as 2°C (36°F), but rarely dip below freezing.

Itinerary Ideas

DAY ONE: HIROSHIMA

1 Start your day at **Peace Memorial Park.** Pay your respects at the memorials strewn throughout this serene place, from viewing the sobering Atomic Bomb Dome to prayerfully ringing the Peace Bell. Take your time and let the gravity of the city's past sink in.

2 Proceed to the **Peace Memorial Museum.** Give the emotive displays your full attention. Allow the added context to inform your views of history and the horrors of war, as well as deepen your appreciation for the thriving city that Hiroshima is today.

3 Shift gears back to the present and make your way to nearby greasy spoon **Okkundo**

Hiroshima Itinerary Ideas

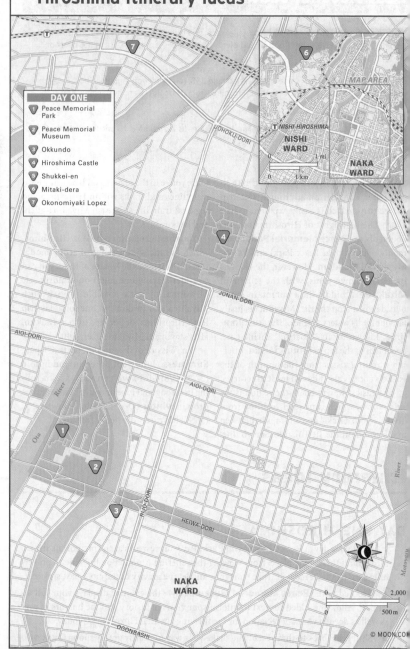

DAY ONE

1. Peace Memorial Park
2. Peace Memorial Museum
3. Okkundo
4. Hiroshima Castle
5. Shukkei-en
6. Mitaki-dera
7. Okonomiyaki Lopez

NISHI-HIROSHIMA

NISHI WARD

NAKA WARD

MAP AREA

JOHOKU-DORI

JONAN-DORI

AIOI-DORI

AIOI-DORI

Ota River

RIJO-DORI

HEIWA-DORI

NAKA WARD

OGONBASHI

Motoyasu River

River

0   2,000
0   500m

0   1 mi
0   1 km

© MOON.COM

for lunch, roughly 7 minutes' walk away. This shop serves tasty noodles in a light sauce with various trimmings.

4 Fueled up, walk to nearby Chūden-mae tram stop. Ride the tram line (numbers 3 or 7) to Kamiyachō-nishi tram stop, then walk 10 minutes north to **Hiroshima Castle.** Amble through the castle grounds and get close to the reconstructed keep for a photo.

5 From the castle grounds, walk 10 minutes east to **Shukkei-en.** Wander the winding paths and enjoy discovering the numerous views of this nicely shaped landscape garden—nature in miniature—which incredibly sprang back to life soon after it was razed by the A-bomb.

6 Continue on foot to Hiroshima Station, 6 minutes to the east. Take the JR Kabe line to Mitaki Station (8 minutes). Trundle uphill to **Mitaki-dera,** an enchanting, delightfully uncrowded temple complex just outside the city. This mystical realm is soothed by the whoosh of water from three waterfalls that spill down the verdant mountainside it clings to. You'll likely want to explore for an hour or two here. This is one of the city's best-kept secrets.

7 You've likely worked up an appetite. Walk back down to Mitaki Station, then ride the JR Kabe line to Yokogawa Station (3 minutes). Walk 7 minutes east to **Okonomiyaki Lopez.** This unlikely institution, run by a kind Guatemalan chef and his Japanese wife, serves fantastic *okonomiyaki*, Hiroshima-style, complemented by a nice range of Latin American appetizers.

DAY TWO: MIYAJIMA

1 Strike out for the sacred isle of Miyajima in the morning. Alighting on the hallowed island, make your way on foot down the shore, passing deer and large stone lanterns as you go, for about 10 minutes to **Itsukushima-jinja.** Although the iconic "floating" shrine gate is currently wrapped in scaffolding for maintenance work, the seaside shrine is still a bewitching place. Stroll its wooden passageways, festooned by lanterns, with open views onto the Inland Sea.

2 Miyajima contains other holy sites beyond Itsukushima-jinja. To discover one that many visitors miss, walk inland (south) and uphill for about 10 minutes until you reach **Daishō-in.** Climb the stone staircase that leads to the temple, spinning prayer wheels as you go. Founded by the great saint Kūkai in 806, this temple is packed with iconography, statues, and colorful nooks and crannies to explore.

3 It's lunchtime. Walk about 15 minutes northeast, back into the sleepy town near the port, and make your way to oyster specialist **Kakiya.**

4 Sated, walk inland (southeast) for about 15 minutes, passing through leafy Momijidani-kōen until you reach the bottom station of the **Miyajima Ropeway.** Ride the ropeway to the top (15 minutes), then walk to the summit, where you'll come to a temple where Kūkai meditated for 100 days, with stunning views of the seascape spreading out below.

5 Descend to sea level. If you're feeling like a coffee break and maybe a light bite before returning to Hiroshima, head to **Cafe Lente,** a stone's throw from Itsukushima-jinja. Enjoy the beautiful views from the café's wall of windows.

6 Return to Hiroshima by ferry and train. When dinnertimes comes, make your way to **Nikuchan,** an energetic *izakaya* serving great meat and side dishes made at a teppanyaki counter in the heart of Hiroshima's nightlife zone.

7 Depending on your staying power, the city's nightlife is within walking distance. The friendly drinking den of **Koba** is a good starting point.

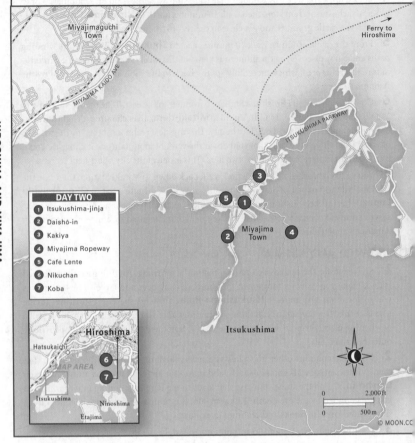

Miyajima Itinerary Ideas

DAY TWO
1. Itsukushima-jinja
2. Daishō-in
3. Kakiya
4. Miyajima Ropeway
5. Cafe Lente
6. Nikuchan
7. Koba

Hiroshima 広島

To fully experience Hiroshima, you must take in its past and present in equal measure. When you make the somber trip to Peace Memorial Park, fully give your attention to its call for a world without atomic weaponry. Feel the weight of the unimaginable destruction that occurred here on August 6, 1945.

As you leave the park, however, prepare to switch gears. While history must be honored

and the Peace Park should be at the top of any Hiroshima itinerary, its modern downtown is a revelation. Friendly locals, broad leafy avenues, a buzzing restaurant scene, and lively nightlife beckon you to enjoy the city as it lives and breathes today. Some of Hiroshima's sights have also been rebuilt, including the castle and Shukkei-en landscape garden.

To properly take all this in, avoid treating

Hiroshima like a whistle-stop. Instead, plan to stay for a night. Few cities in the world offer such a poignant message on the human ability to overcome tragedy and bring about rebirth.

ORIENTATION

Hiroshima is relatively compact, with almost everything you'll be seeking just west of **Hiroshima Station.** The city, which *Hiroshima* author John Hershey described as being "fan-shaped," sprawls across six main islands in the **Ōta-gawa** river delta. Upon exiting the main train station, you'll most likely be heading west into the city's inner core, about 5 minutes away by tram.

Downtown, also known as **Naka-ku** ("middle ward"), contains the central business district and most major sights. Among them, the garden of **Shukkei-en** lies about 7 minutes' walk west of Hiroshima Station, with **Hiroshima Castle** situated another 10 minutes farther west. **Peace Memorial Park** is about 20 minutes' walk southwest of the castle, with the **Peace Memorial Museum** at the far southern edge of the park. The bulk of the city's best restaurants, accommodations, and nightlife also lie within this area. North and west of downtown lies **Nishi-ku** ("west ward"), where you'll find the remote temple of **Mitaki-dera,** while **Minami-ku** ("south ward") encompasses the area south and southeast of Hiroshima Station, including the **Mazda Museum** and **Mazda Zoom Zoom Stadium.**

The city's main thoroughfare is **Hon-dōri,** a covered pedestrian arcade that runs 0.6 km (0.4 mi) eastward from Peace Memorial Park through the heart of downtown. Running parallel to the north of Hon-dōri is **Aioi-dōri,** the main artery for cars and trams running between Hiroshima Station and the western edge of downtown.

The city's major train lines include the **JR Kabe line,** which runs west and then north of Hiroshima Station, and the **JR San'yō line,** which runs southwest along the coast, linking Hiroshima Station with Miyajima-guchi, the gateway to the island of Miyajima, and Iwakuni. Most of downtown is woven together by the city's vast **tram network,** Japan's most extensive with 8 lines.

SIGHTS
Naka-ku

★ PEACE MEMORIAL PARK
広島平和記念公園

1-1 Nakajimachō, Naka-ku; www.city.hiroshima.lg.jp/www/contents/1483699383190/index.html; 24 hours daily; free; from Hiroshima Station, take tram line 2 or 6 to Genbaku-Domu Mae

The park that contains all of the memorials of the atomic bombing of Hiroshima occupies a sprawling 12-hectare (30-acre) green space that was once the city's commercial and political hub—precisely the reason that the area was targeted in the bombing. The city waited four years before declaring that the area would become a place of remembering and learning rather than be redeveloped.

Begin your exploration of Peace Memorial Park at the **Atomic Bomb Dome,** Hiroshima's most famous sight. The blackened architectural shell stands beside the Motoyasu River, as one of only a few buildings to miraculously remain standing despite being within 2 km (1.2 mi) of the center of the blast. The iconic skeleton was once a much larger handsome red-brick building that housed the Prefectural Industrial Promotion Hall. In order to preserve its architectural integrity, the UNESCO World Heritage Site cannot be entered.

From the Atomic Bomb Dome, walk north to the T-shaped Aioi Bridge, which crosses the point where the Ōta and Motoyasu rivers merge. From here, enter on the north side of the park and approach the **Peace Bell** (24 hours; free), cast by national treasure, bronze artist Masahiko Katori. Note the world map without borders emblazoned on the outer surface of the bell. In a spirit of quiet

Hiroshima

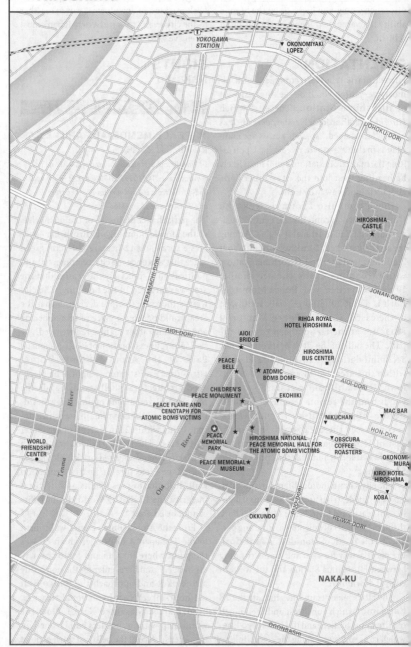

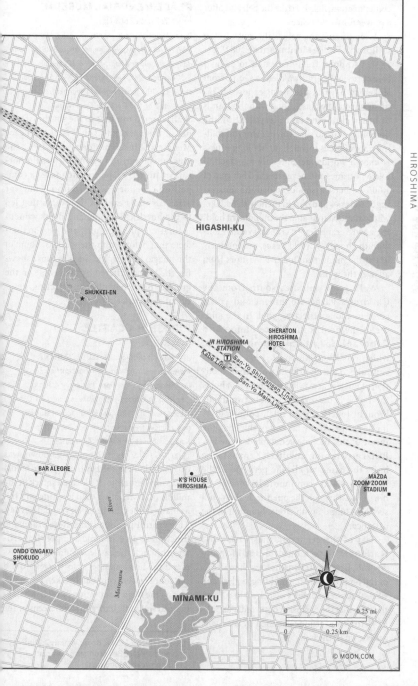

© MOON.COM

contemplation, lightly strike the bell and offer a prayer for world peace.

After ringing the bell, walk south to the **Children's Peace Monument** (tel. 082/242-7831; 24 hours; free) dedicated to Sadako Sasaki, a young girl who died at age 12 from leukemia, 10 years after being exposed to radiation from the blast, along with thousands of other children tragically killed by the bombing. Sadako's harrowing story of folding paper cranes throughout her long illness is known worldwide. She only managed to fold 644 cranes and never reached her goal of 1,000, so her classmates folded the remaining 356 cranes and buried them with Sadako, whose statue stands atop the monument holding a wire crane. Paper cranes, synonymous with the hope for world peace, are routinely left at the monument today by visitors from all over the world.

Walk a few minutes south from the Children's Peace Monument and you'll come to a long reflecting pool. In the middle of the pool is the **Peace Flame and Cenotaph for Atomic Bomb Victims,** which was lit on August 1, 1964, and will continue to burn until the worldwide abolition of nuclear arms. The platform that holds the flame is meant to resemble two hands brought together with open palms pointing skyward. At the far end of the pool, the inside of this moving cenotaph designed by Pritzker-winning architect Kenzo Tange bears the names of all who perished in the bombing. Names continue to be added even now. Gaze through the open arch and you'll see the Atomic Bomb Dome looming in the distance.

East of the cenotaph, the **Hiroshima National Peace Memorial Hall for the Atomic Bomb Victims** honors the victims of the bomb. Inside the building, a glass and steel structure resembles a clock set to 8:15am, the time that the explosion occurred. Portraits of victims and tributes penned by survivors are shown in the hall.

PEACE MEMORIAL MUSEUM
広島平和記念資料館

Peace Memorial Park, 1-2 Nakajimachō, Naka-ku; 082/241-4004; http://hpmmuseum.jp; 8:30am-6pm daily Mar.-July and Sept.-Nov., 8:30am-7pm Aug., 8:30am-5pm Dec.-Feb.; adults ¥200, high school students ¥100, junior high and younger free; take tram line 2 or 6 to Genbaku-Domu Mae

Walk about 3 minutes to the southeast corner of the park, and you'll find the Peace Memorial Museum. Opened in 1955, the museum powerfully communicates the horrors of atomic weaponry and makes a compelling case for a world without nuclear arms. Exhibits explain the events that led to the horrific bombing and display documentation, photographs, and personal effects that belonged to the victims. Some of the images are graphic, such as those showing the burns suffered by the people on the ground. Be prepared for an affecting, emotional experience.

HIROSHIMA CASTLE
広島城

21-1 Motomachi, Naka-ku; tel. 082/221-7512; www.rijo-castle.jp; 9am-6pm (last entry 5:30pm) daily Mar.-Nov., 9am-5pm (last entry 4:30pm) Dec.-Feb.; grounds free, main keep adults ¥370, high school students ¥180, junior high school students and younger free; take tram lines 1, 2, or 6 to Kamiyachō-nishi or Kamiyachō-higashi

"Carp Castle," as it's popularly known, was originally built in 1589 by the powerful feudal lord Mori Terumoto. It's located smack in the middle of town, rather than looming on a hill as many castles did in Japan's feudal heyday. This central position hints at its pragmatic function as an economic and political center. Although the castle was only partly dismantled when a number of fortresses around the country were completely taken down following the Meiji Restoration of 1868, what remained was sadly blown to smithereens by the

1: Cenotaph for Atomic Bomb Victims **2:** students ringing the Peace Bell **3:** origami cranes at Children's Peace Monument

atomic bomb. A concrete reproduction was built in 1958, with an exterior partly made of wood, along with a few structures of the *ninomaru* (second circle of defense).

Entering from either the south or east, on the grounds you'll find a smattering of ruins and a shrine where romantic hopefuls pray for luck in love. Inside the five-story keep, there are displays (with limited English) outlining the history of the castle and the city, and elucidating the finer points of Japanese castles more broadly. At a minimum, it's worth meandering through the leafy grounds and taking a quick look at the castle's handsome wooden exterior for free if you're already in the area, say, walking from the Peace Park to the garden of Shukkei-en. You can pass on paying to see its sterile, modern interior, unless you're keen to glimpse the vistas from the top. Thanks to its downtown location, the views of the castle's impressive moat, bridges, and the cityscape below are worth the charge of admission.

In case you're wondering, the castle's nickname was inspired by the old name for the surrounding region, which was once called Koi-no-ura ("Carp Sea Shore"). Naturally, a multitude of colorful *koi* now swims in the moat that wraps around the castle. And the hometown baseball club is known as the Hiroshima Carp, too.

SHUKKEI-EN
縮景園

2-11 Kaminoborichō, Naka-ku; tel. 082/221-3620; http://shukkeien.jp; 9am-6pm (last entry 5:30pm) daily Apr.-Sept., 9am-5pm (last entry 4:30pm) Oct.-Mar.; adults ¥260, high school students ¥150, junior high and elementary school students ¥100; from Hiroshima Station, take tram line 9 to Shukkeien-mae stop, or walk 8 minutes northwest to the garden from JR Hiroshima Station or 10 minutes east to the garden from Hiroshima Castle

Shukkei-en, which roughly translates to "contracted view garden," lives up to its name, emulating peaks, woodlands, islands, and valleys in miniature form. Paths wind through these natural scenes with ease, just as Lord Asano Nagaakira had in mind when he appointed tea master Ueda Soko to create a green escape for him in 1620. The garden was all but flattened in 1945, but some vegetation miraculously flourished the year after the bombing, and the natural space was eventually revived. Today, its striking layout, with a variety of alluring footpaths, plum and cherry blossoms, teahouses, and island-studded pond, make it one of the city's loveliest spots.

Nishi-ku
MITAKI-DERA
三瀧寺

411 Mitaki-yama, Nishi-ku; tel. 082/237-0811; 8am-5:30pm daily; free; from Hiroshima Station, take JR Kabe line to Mitaki Station

Well off the tourist track, Mitaki-dera is one of Hiroshima's most prized hidden gems. Aside from autumn—the turning leaves reach their fiery peak in November—the temple is often delightfully uncrowded. This is surprising, given its bewitching atmosphere and impressive backstory. The temple was founded in 809 by Kūkai, founder of the Shingon sect of Buddhism, who recognized the holiness of the place and perceived the spirit of Kannon in Mount Mitaki's three waterfalls (Mitaki literally means "three waterfalls"). Today, the hallowed site is one of 33 pilgrimage stops in the Chūgoku (Western Honshu) region where Kannon devotees travel to worship the goddess.

Entering the grounds of Mitaki-dera feels like passing into an enchanted forest: moss-caked bodhisattvas carved from rock, rows of stone *jizō* guardians wearing red caps and bibs, an ancient two-tiered pagoda, stone staircases leading past rock walls etched with Buddhist deities, a large bronze bell, lifelike effigies of Buddhist saints, a clifftop shrine, lush embankments awash with ferns, and the constant burble of water.

Above all else, this is a watery realm; visiting the temple on a rainy day makes it even more atmospheric. The water offered in the annual Hiroshima Peace Memorial

August 6, 1945

At 8:15am, on August 6, 1945, just as Hiroshima hummed to life on what would have seemed like an ordinary day, a rotund capsule named *Little Boy* was dropped over the city by a U.S. bomber plane called the *Enola Gay*, triggering an event of horrific magnitude never seen before or since. In an instant, a blinding, incinerating flash consumed the sky and half the city was flattened. The other half soon went up in flames.

Thousands upon thousands died in an instant, while thousands of brutally charred victims sought relief by throwing themselves into the Motoyasu River, swelling the waterway with hundreds of corpses. Those who survived the first wave of horrors would soon contend with lethal drops of "black rain," pregnant with radioactive fallout. All told, some 140,000 died in the world's first nuclear bomb attack.

Hiroshima had the unfortunate distinction of being an ideal target for the bomb. For starters, the U.S. military sought a city with a downtown core that measured more than 4.5 km (3 mi) around. Hiroshima was on a short list that also included Niigata, Kokura, and Nagasaki. Hiroshima's grim fate was sealed partly due to the fact that U.S. forces did not think any American prisoners of war were being kept in the city.

On that fateful morning, the skies were clear. The bombers used the T-shaped Aioi Bridge, which crosses the Ōta and Motoyasu rivers, as their target. This bridge stands—rebuilt and now bustling with traffic, like the rest of the city—just north of the Atomic Bomb Dome in Peace Memorial Park, near the hypocenter of the blast.

On each anniversary of the city's decimation, around 50,000 people fill Peace Memorial Park to commemorate those who died that day. Alongside locals and travelers, foreign dignitaries and ambassadors amass to hear speeches by Japan's top officials, offering pleas for world peace.

The day's proceedings begin at 8:15am, when temple bells chime, sirens wail, and all citizens observe a somber moment of silence to honor those who perished in the blast and its aftermath. The solemnity is softened in the evening when 10,000 floating lanterns are released onto the Motoyasu River. Seeing myriad floating lights, gently flowing past the Atomic Bomb Dome, is an undeniably haunting, ethereal sight.

Ceremony to commemorate the bombing of the city is drawn from one of the three waterfalls.

Among the buildings strewn throughout the complex, note the vermillion, two-storied **Tahōtō pagoda.** Although dating to the Muromachi period (1392-1573), the structure was moved to the site from Wakayama Prefecture in 1951 to console the souls of the victims of the atomic bombing. The temple is also dotted by memorials to those who lost their lives to the atomic bomb, and its waters are believed to contain healing powers. There's also a rustic **teahouse** on the temple grounds serving tea, simple Japanese fare, and desserts. Altogether, aim to spending a few hours here. It's an extensive site with lots of nooks to explore.

To reach the temple's entrance, you'll need to walk about 20 minutes uphill from **Mitaki Station** on the JR Kabe line, two stops from Hiroshima Station. Exiting Mitaki Station, walk to the left with the station at your back until you reach the crossing, where you'll turn right and start walking uphill. When you reach a fork in the road in front of Saigan-ji temple, veer right and continue walking straight ahead, veering left when you reach the next fork. Walk past the small park on your right-hand side and continue walking uphill until you reach the dead end with the temple entrance right in front of you. Alternatively, catch **bus no. 22** from Hiroshima Station and ride until the Mitaki-kannon bus stop.

Minami-ku
MAZDA MUSEUM
マツダミュージアム

1-1 Nihookimachi, Minami-ku; tel. 082/252-5050; www.mazda.com/en/about/museum; English-language tours at 10am Mon.-Fri.; from Hiroshima Station, take JR San'yō line to Mukainada Station

Since its founding a century ago, Mazda has maintained its corporate headquarters in Hiroshima. Like Toyota for Nagoya, the automaker plays a vital role in the local economy. Also like Toyota, it welcomes visitors to take a peak under the hood of its operations. Near its HQ, along a stretch of coastline south of Hiroshima Station, the automobile giant runs factories, shipping facilities, and labs where its engineering and design wizards carry out R&D. The company welcomes visitors to a museum and to join English-language tours of a section of one factory where a daunting assembly line snakes 3.4 mi (7 km). To join one of the one-hour **tours** in English, you must reserve in advance, up to a year ahead of time, either via the website (www.mazda.com/en/about/museum/reservations/) or by calling ahead (8:30am-noon, 12:45pm-5pm Mon.-Fri.). At the time of writing, the museum was temporarily closed to prevent the spread of coronavirus. Check the website for updates before planning a trip.

FESTIVALS AND EVENTS
TŌKASAN YUKATA FESTIVAL
とうかさん大祭

Chūō-dōri and around; www.toukasan.jp; noon-11pm for three days starting first Fri. of June; free

The streets of downtown fill with denizens in *yukata* (lightweight cotton kimonos) during this lively annual festival. Expect to see *yatai* (street food stalls), games (think fish scooping and shooting at targets with airsoft guns), dancing, beating on *taiko* drums, and more.

PEACE MEMORIAL AND PEACE MESSAGE LANTERN FLOATING CEREMONIES

Peace Memorial Park; www.city.hiroshima.lg.jp/site/english/115509.html; 8am-9am and 6pm-9pm Aug. 6; free

On the morning of August 6, officials give speeches imploring for world peace, the Peace Bell and temple bells are rung, sirens are

sounded, and 1 minute of silence is observed out of respect for those who died at 8:15am that same morning in 1945. Seating begins at 6:30am. Arrive *early* if you want to get a spot. In the evening, a more casual, visually moving tribute is paid when people release lanterns into the Motoyasu River to console the souls of the victims of the bombing. Make your way to the river at dusk to witness this poignant sight.

BASEBALL
MAZDA ZOOM ZOOM STADIUM

2-3-1 Minami-Kaniya, Minami-ku; tel. 082/568-2777; www.mazdastadium.jp; from JR Hiroshima Station, walk 12 minutes southeast

They may not have the same clout nationally as the Tokyo's Yomiuri Giants or Kansai's Hanshin Tigers, but Hiroshima's hometown baseball team, the Carp, have a fierce following. Visit www.japanball.com to see the schedule in English, and inquire at one of the tourist information centers in JR Hiroshima Station about getting **tickets,** which start from around ¥2,000.

★ FOOD

The two most popular items on Hiroshima's menu are **oysters** hauled in from the bay and the local style of *okonomiyaki* (a savory cross between a pancake and an omelet), loaded with cabbage, seafood, meat, soba noodles, bean sprouts, and a slathering of mayonnaise, bonito flakes, sweet sauces, and other condiments. If you aim to try one local dish in Hiroshima, make it *okonomiyaki*.

Naka-ku
OBSCURA COFFEE ROASTERS

3-28 Fukuro-machi, Naka-ku; tel. 082/249-7543; https://obscura-coffee.com; 9am-8pm daily, closed third Wed. every month; ¥290-570; take Astram line or tram lines 1, 3, 7 to Hondori tram stop

Originally launched in Tokyo, this café chain was founded by three coffee lovers from Hiroshima. For a quick pick-me-up or pastry, to be enjoyed in the café or taken away, this artisanal café is a great bet. The minimalist interior is offset by rugs and wooden furniture. If you're seeking a calm break, it fits the bill nicely, but might not be the place to go with young kids. Note that there's a 45-minute limit if you stay at the café.

OKKUNDO

Sansan Bldg. 3-3-3 Otemachi, Naka-ku; tel. 082/246-1377; www.powerland.co.jp; 11am-11pm daily; ¥520-1,060; take tram lines 1, 3, 7 to Chūden-mae tram stop

Serving up generous helpings of *mazemen*—flavorful noodles mixed with a light sauce topped with soft-boiled egg, leek, roast pork, and more—this shop is a good option if you've had your fill of *okonomiyaki* and seafood. There's also a good side menu of items like *gyoza* (fried dumplings) and onion rings, too. It feels like a hole-in-the-wall, but the service is friendly.

OKONOMI-MURA

5-13 Shintenchi, Naka-ku; tel. 082/241-2210; www. okonomimura.jp; 11am-2am daily; from ¥800-1,300; take tram lines 1, 2, 6 to Ebisu-chō tram stop

It's firmly on the tourist track, but this is a great place to enter the world of *okonomiyaki*. Some 25 stalls serve up the city's signature dish in this cramped, boisterous "Okonomiyaki Village" spread across the second through fourth floors of the building. Situated within a bar district, this place hops late at night, but it's good any time of day. Among the glut of purveyors, Hasshō on the second floor stands out, but follow your inspiration and you'll likely be satisfied wherever you choose.

EKOHIIKI

1-7-20 Ōte-machi, Naka-ku; tel. 082/545-3655; http://ekohiiki.com; 11:30am-2pm and 5pm-11pm Tues.-Sun.; plates from ¥580-1,500, set meals ¥800-2,000; take Astram line or tram lines 1, 3, 7 to Hondori tram stop

This restaurant just east of Peace Memorial Park is a great place to sample the city's famed oysters. The consistently plump, juicy oysters are prepared any way you like: raw, grilled, deep-fried, and more. There's also a good range of side dishes, from chicken wings to sashimi, and a diverse alcohol selection, too. Service is friendly, and there's a good English-language menu.

NIKUCHAN

1-12 Shintenchi, Naka-ku; tel. 050/5596-8777; https:// hirokawaya.co.jp/nikuchan; 6pm-3am daily; à la carte ¥990-1,790, courses ¥4,000 courses; take tram lines 1, 2, 6 to Ebisu-chō tram stop

This smoky, boisterous corner *izakaya* in the heart of the nightlife district is hard to resist. It's overflowing with friendly locals during primetime, seated at the wraparound teppanyaki-style counter, where cooks throw various cuts of meat, offal, and more on the iron griddle as frosty mugs of beer are swilled in all corners. It's just the kind of friendly hole-in-the-wall you'd expect to find in the neighborhood, and the food is good. A sound pick if you've had your fill of *okonomiyaki* and oysters.

Nishi-ku

★ OKONOMIYAKI LOPEZ

1-7-13 Kusunoki-chō, Nishi-ku; tel. 082/232-5277; 11:30am-2pm Tues. and Fri., 4:30pm-11pm Mon.-Fri.; from ¥650; take JR San'yō line to Yokogawa

This *okonomiyaki* joint is a Hiroshima institution run by Guatemalan-born chef Fernando Lopez and his Japanese wife, Makiko. Lopez has lived in the city for more than two decades and learned from the *okonomiyaki* maestro Ogawa Hiroki. The friendly husband-wife team exude warmth, engaging in lighthearted conversation while adroitly flipping *okonomiyaki*; their food is among the best *okonomiyaki* in a city crazy about the dish. Portions are generous, too.

BARS AND NIGHTLIFE
Naka-ku
MAC BAR

Borabora Bldg. 3F, 3-4 Tatemachi, Naka-ku; tel. 082/243-0343; www.facebook.com/pages/Mac-Bar/845730498970349; 6pm-late daily; take tram lines 1, 2, 6, 9 to Tatemachi tram stop

If you like classic rock and want a mellow evening out with a 40s-and-up crowd, this is your place. Tucked away in a nondescript building, this is the third incarnation of this local institution, which has been in business for more than four decades. With its remarkable CD collection and solid sound system, it's a laid-back spot for a drink.

BAR ALEGRE

Cony Bldg. 3F, 1-32 Horikawa-chō, Naka-ku; tel. 082/545-5295; www.facebook.com/alegre.hiroshima; 7pm-2am Mon.-Sat.; ¥500 cover charge; take trams 1, 2, 6 to Ebisu-chō tram stop

The talented mixologists at this cozy bar make serious craft cocktails. The bar is well-stocked and the atmosphere evokes a speakeasy. It's a great place to go if you want something sophisticated but not fussy.

KOBA

Rego Bldg. 3F, 1-4 Naka-machi, Naka-ku; tel. 082/249-6556; www.facebook.com/Koba-211406912214710; 6pm-2am Thurs.-Tues.; take trams 1, 3, 7 to Fukuromachi tram stop

This heavy-metal bar's affable owner Bom-san makes instant friends with all his customers. The soundtrack leans heavy, with occasional live performances. Currency notes from around the world dangling above the bar attest to just how many friends he's made. The drinks are good and reasonably priced, and Bom-san is handy in the kitchen, too. The bar is a little tricky to find. Walk down the corridor next to the Stussy shop and then walk upstairs.

ONDO ONGAKU SHOKUDO

Ondo Onsen Bldg. B1, 6-3 Tanaka-machi, Naka-ku; tel. 082/245-9563; www.ongakushokudoondo.com; 6pm-3am daily; take trams 1, 2, 6 to Ebisu-chō tram stop

This cozy basement-level music bar and restaurant is tucked beneath a public bath, Ondo Onsen, on the south side of Hiroshima's sprawling Nagarekawa nightlife zone. Alongside a serious sound system—*Ongaku* means "music"—the owners whip up good home-cooked fare using healthy ingredients—*Shokudo* denoting "canteen." There's a respectable collection of vinyl behind the bar, extending to reggae, jazz, and soul, and the bar hosts occasional live shows on weekends. A relaxed spot to mingle with a crowd who is friendly yet in-the-know.

okonomiyaki, Hiroshima style

Sake Side Trip to Saijō

Less than an hour by train east of Hiroshima, the town of Saijō is a *sake*-brewing powerhouse, with seven local breweries opening their showroom doors to visitors.

THE BREWERIES

Saijō's history as a *sake* center can be traced to its abundance of spring water, which flows into town from Mount Ryuo-zan to the north. If you spot people filling bottles with water from fountains along the main street of Sakagura-dōri (Sake Brewery Street), they are taking some of that very mountain water from the wells of each brewery. The actual production facilities of these breweries are not open to the public, but each one has a showroom where they explain their methods and history, and provide *sake*-tasting.

A good starting point is the brewery of **Kamotsuru** (9-7 Saijō-honmachi; tel. 082/422-2122; www.kamotsuru.jp; 9am-6pm Mon.-Fri., 10am-6pm Sat.-Sun.), known for its spacious tasting room and diverse selection. In business since 1623, it had a moment in 2014 when Prime Minister Shinzō Abe and President Barack Obama said *kampai* ("cheers") over a variety brewed here. If you happen to be in town in autumn, look out for the seasonal *hiya-oroshi,* lauded for its perfectly balanced taste and mild aroma.

Another stalwart with roots stretching back to the Edo period (founded in 1675) is **Hakubotan** (15-5 Saijō-honmachi; tel. 082/422-2142; www.hakubotan.co.jp; 9:30am-4pm Mon.-Fri., 10:30am-4pm Sat.-Sun., closed 2nd and 4th Sat. and public holidays). In its tasting room, attached to a building dating from feudal times, an original woodblock print by famed artist Shiko Munakata clings to a wall. Famously, novelist Natsume Sōseki was said to love the *sake* made here.

SAKE MATSURI

On the second weekend of every October, a festival celebrating the tipple is held. Sake Matsuri (西条酒まつり; mid-Oct.; https://sakematsuri.com; from JR Hiroshima Station, take JR San'yō line to Saijō Station) is a great chance to drink, be merry, and discover what this major *nihonshū*-making town has to offer.

LEARN MORE

To find out more, visit www.saijosake.com. This excellent English-language introduction to the town's breweries has an interactive map with detailed breakdowns of what makes each brewery unique. Note that some of the breweries require advanced bookings, so be sure to inquire ahead using the contact details on the website to ensure a smooth trip.

GETTING THERE

The trip to Saijō from Hiroshima is easy. Just take the JR San'yō line directly from Hiroshima Station to Saijō Station (35 minutes; ¥590).

ACCOMMODATIONS

Naka-ku

KIRO HOTEL HIROSHIMA

3-21 Mikawa-chō, Naka-ku; tel. 082/545-9160; www. thesharehotels.com/kiro; ¥6,000; take tram lines 1, 2, 6, 9 to Hatchobori tram stop

This stylish new hotel in the heart of the action, yet tucked down a side street, is a great mid-range choice. It offers a bit more space than most hotels at a similar price point. There's an on-site restaurant, a shared kitchen and a shared lounge, and free Wi-Fi throughout. The design sense is simple and modern, and the staff are friendly, young, and hip. Compared to many petite "unit baths," the separated toilet-bath style bathrooms are well-stocked and large. Great bang for buck in a very convenient location.

★ **RIHGA ROYAL HOTEL HIROSHIMA**

6-78 Motomachi, Naka-ku; tel. 082/502-1121; www. rihga.co.jp/hiroshima; ¥15,000; take Astram line to Kencho-mae Station

The rooms at this classy hotel are spacious, and many boast fantastic views. It's conveniently located between the castle to the north and Peace Park to the south, and the friendly concierge is happy to assist guests with restaurant bookings and more. There's an on-site restaurant, a rooftop bar, an indoor pool, fitness center, laundry services on offer, and more. A recommended upper mid-range pick.

Nishi-ku
★ **WORLD FRIENDSHIP CENTER**

8-10 Higashi Kan-on, Nishi-ku; tel. 082/503-3191; http://wfchiroshima.com; ¥4,200 pp; take tram lines 2, 3 to Koami-chō tram stop

This no-frills guesthouse, owned by an American couple, is a good place for those interested in peace activism to engage directly with those affected by the A-bomb. Besides providing good, clean, and private tatami rooms, with a shared bathroom and breakfast, you'll have the opportunity to talk with survivors of the attack. The friendly hosts also impart generous local knowledge to all guests.

Minami-ku
K'S HOUSE HIROSHIMA

1-8-9 Matoba-chō, Minami-ku; tel. 082/568-7244; https://kshouse.jp; dorms from ¥2,000, double with en suite bath ¥2,680-6,450; take tram lines 1, 2, 5, 6 to Matobachō tram stop

Located an 8-minute walk southwest of Hiroshima Station, this hostel has mixed dorm rooms, private tatami rooms, and rooms for two. All rooms share a bathroom, lounge, kitchen, and laundry facilities. This is a good place to meet fellow travelers and exchange tips, and it's an affordable, convenient home base.

Higashi-ku
SHERATON HIROSHIMA HOTEL

12-1 Wakakusa-chō, Higashi-ku; tel. 082/262-7111; www.marriott.com/hotels/travel/hijsi-sheraton-grand-hiroshima-hotel; ¥30,380 d; take any JR line that runs to Hiroshima Station

If you're willing to spend a bit more, this luxurious hotel is conveniently located right outside the north exit of the main station. Rooms are notably larger than the norm in Japan and very well-appointed, and staff are cheerful and eager to please. There's a breakfast buffet (¥2,750 pp) and a Japanese restaurant on-site. Recommended.

INFORMATION AND SERVICES
Tourist Information

You can pick up English-language information and get recommendations from one of three **tourist information centers** in Hiroshima Station. The first one is next to the ticket gate for *shinkansen* (bullet train) arrivals and departures at the north side of the station (tel. 082/263-5120; 6am-midnight daily). The other information counters are next to the north exit (8:30am-6:30pm daily), and the south exit (9am-6pm daily). Also useful is the pleasant **Hiroshima Peace Memorial Park Rest House** (1-1 Nakajima-machi, Naka-ku; tel. 082/247-6738; www.hiroshima-resthouse.jp; 8:30am-7pm daily Aug., 8:30am-6pm Mar.-July and Sept.-Nov., 8:30am-5pm Dec.-Feb.), which sits at the northeast side of Peace Memorial Park beside the Motoyasu-bashi bridge.

For information online, from restaurant and nightlife listings to transportation breakdowns, check out the helpful websites **Visit Hiroshima** (http://visithiroshima.net) and **Hiroshima Navi** (www.hiroshima-navi. or.jp), or the webzine **Get Hiroshima** (www. gethiroshima.com), run by expats.

Postal Services

The biggest post office in town is the **Hiroshima Central Post Office** (1-4-1 okutaiji-machi, Naka-ku; tel. 057/000-356; 9am-7pm Mon.-Fri., 9am-5pm Sat., am-12:30pm Sun.), which sends parcels verseas.

Pharmacies and Medical Services

For a good rundown on hospitals and clinics where English-speaking doctors are on staff, visit http://gethiroshima.com/lifestyle/medical-reference/. To ensure you reach the right doctor at the right time and place, your best bet is to call the city's free English-language medical hotline, which can be reached by dialing 0120/169-912. Alternatively, visit the official nationwide English-language online medical portal of the Japan National Tourism Organization (JNTO) at www.jnto.go.jp/emergency/eng/mi_guide.html. This website helps foreign visitors find hospitals where English is spoken from anywhere in the country.

For a medical emergency, dial 119. English-speaking interpreters are available. However, be forewarned that you'll need to have someone who can speak Japanese first explain to the operator that you need an English interpreter.

Safety

A list of police stations in Hiroshima Prefecture, including the city of Hiroshima, can be found at www.kurunavi.jp/en/syako/syako_kankatsu_hiroshima.html. However, English-language service is often limited. If you need to report a crime, your best bet is to speak to a representative at a tourist information office. In the event of an emergency for which you need to reach the police, dial 110 and have a Japanese speaker request an English interpreter.

Internet Access

It's possible to use free Wi-Fi in 30-minute blocks of time for an unlimited period of time anywhere a "Hiroshima Free Wi-Fi" sticker is placed. You must first register with either your email address or a social media account.

These Wi-Fi points are typically found at major tourist spots.

GETTING THERE
Train

Sitting on the east side of downtown, **Hiroshima Station** is served by the *shinkansen,* running to and from **Tokyo** (4 hours; ¥19,080), **Shin-Osaka** (1 hour 30 minutes; ¥10,440), and **Kyoto** (1 hour 40 minutes; ¥11,410) in the east, and **Fukuoka** (Hakata Station; 1 hour; ¥9,150) in the west. Local trains on the JR San'yō line also stop at the station, with the train route beginning from **Himeji** in the east and heading westward to Honshu's far-western fringe.

Air

Both international and domestic flights serve **Hiroshima Airport** (tel. 082/231-5171; www.hij.airport.jp), about 45 km (28 mi) east of downtown. Overseas routes include Dalian and Shanghai in China, as well as Hong Kong, Taipei, and Seoul, though it doesn't make much sense to fly into Hiroshima from any of the domestic destinations described in this book, which are so well-connected by bullet train. **Shuttle buses** connect the airport to Hiroshima Station (45 minutes; 8:20am-9:40pm from the airport to downtown, 6am-7:20pm from Hiroshima Station to airport; ¥1,340).

Bus

Hiroshima is well-connected by highways, with buses making the journey to the city from all around Japan. Some buses use **Hiroshima Bus Center** (6-27 Motomachi; www.h-buscenter.com), accessed via the third floor of the Sogō Department Store in the heart of downtown. A number of bus companies offer overnight trips between Tokyo and Hiroshima, with one-way journeys ranging from ¥6,000-13,000 depending on timing and the type (read: comfort level) of a given bus. Buses also run between Kyoto and Hiroshima (7 hours; ¥3,200-4,200). **Willer Express** (https://willerexpress.com/en) is a good provider. You can conduct a blanket search on **Japan Bus Online** (https://japan-busonline.com/en).

GETTING AROUND

Hiroshima's scale makes it ideal to explore **on foot.** That said, some sights are just far enough that you may want to hop on the city's efficient tram network, avail yourself of a tour bus, or pedal around on a bike.

Operator **Setonaikai Kisen Ferry** (tel. 082/253-1212; www.setonaikaikisen.co.jp) travels in and out of **Hiroshima Port Ujina Terminal** (1-13-26 Ujinakaigan, Minami-ku; tel. 082/253-6907). Boats running to and from **Miyajima** (30 minutes; ¥1,850) also serve this port, which is located south of downtown and accessible by Ujina-bound tram lines 1, 3, and 5 (all ¥160).

Tram

Hiroshima is well-served by the handy **Hiroden tram network** (www.hiroden.co.jp; single ride ¥190, one-day pass ¥640, one-day pass with Matsudai ferry to Miyajima ¥840), which has a total of eight lines. Trams 2 and 6 are particularly useful, linking the area around Peace Memorial Park. To take a single ride, board from the back and deposit your fare in the machine beside the driver's seat when you exit from the front. Passes ca be bought at the tram terminal in Hiroshim Station.

Tour Bus

The city's *meipurū-pu* **Sightseeing Loo Bus** (www.chugoku-jrbus.co.jp; single rid ¥200, one-day pass ¥400) traces two color coded routes (orange and green) aroun town, both starting from the north side o the station near the *shinkansen* concourse The orange route passes by the Shukkei-e landscape garden, the castle, and some mu seums, while the green bus takes in temple dotting the north side of town. Both link t Peace Memorial Park. JR pass holders can rid both buses for free.

Bike

If you'd like to **cycle** around town, staying in an accommodation that offers cycle rent als is your best bet. The city does have a bi cycle rental system, with 20-plus cycle-ports around town, but it's a little complicated to operate. If you'd like to try **Peacecle** ("peace" + "cycle"), check out the English instructions at https://docomo-cycle.jp/hiroshima/en/ Here, you'll find step-by-step instructions and a map with cycle-ports throughout the city.

Miyajima

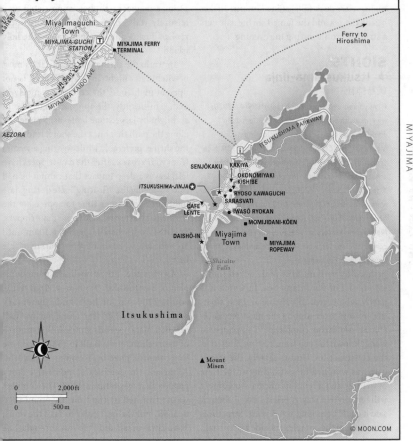

Miyajima　　　　　　　　　　宮島

The island of Miyajima (officially named Itsukushima) may not be a household name in the West, but the scene of the vermillion *torii* gate rising directly from the sea at the shrine of Itsukushima-jinja is widely hailed as one of Japan's three best views. Beyond this famously "floating" shrine gate, the island is defined by low-lying mountains dotted by temples and laced with good walking trails

up Mount Misen, where you'll find a cluster of temples and shrines.

Similar to Nara-kōen, Miyajima is also known for its population of alarmingly tame deer, whose heads are topped with tiny horns. Don't be surprised if they walk right up to you, and don't feed them unless you want to be mobbed.

Miyajima is easily visited on a day trip from Hiroshima, less than an hour away. But if you'd like to avoid the crowds and soak up its ethereal atmosphere, consider staying overnight. After dusk falls, stone lanterns flicker beside the sea and the famed shrine gate cuts a striking profile during the evening.

SIGHTS
★ Itsukushima-jinja
厳島神社

1-1 Miyajima-chō, Hatsukaichi; tel. 0829/44-2020; www.itsukushimajinja.jp; 6:30am-5:30pm daily Jan.-Feb. and mid-Oct.-Nov., 6:30am-6pm Mar.-mid-Oct., 6:30am-5pm Dec.; adults ¥300, high school students ¥200, junior high and elementary school students ¥100 for the shrine, adults ¥300, high school students ¥200, junior high and elementary school students ¥100 for the treasure hall, adults ¥500, high school students ¥300, junior high and elementary school students ¥150 for combination ticket; walk 10 minutes southwest from Itsukushima ferry terminal

Fringed by verdant hills and tucked into a small inlet of the Inland Sea, in which it is partly submerged, this shrine and its "floating" *torii* gate are among the most recognizable Shinto shrine complexes. Camphor-tree wood, known to keep from rotting, is used in the construction. Unfortunately, the iconic gate was wrapped in scaffolding at the time of writing, and it remains unclear how long it will remain that way. A priest I asked about it said it could be as long as 4-5 years. Structures elsewhere in the complex include a main hall, prayer hall, and *Noh* theater stage, linked by a series of boardwalks.

Although the shrine was originally founded as early as the 6th century, it was rebuilt in 1168 by then Heike clan leader Taira no Kiyomori, who selected the site to be the location of his family shrine. The *Noh* stage next to the shrine was constructed in 1680.

The shrine's peculiar construction can be attributed to the belief that the island is hallowed ground. Traditionally, only the priestly class were permitted on the island and were required to approach by boat.

To see the shrine and its famed gate "floating," arrive at high tide. Inquire at the ferry terminal for a tide forecast. If you stick around for sunset, the gate and shrine are lit up until 11pm: a magical sight best appreciated on leisurely walk, preferably from your local *ryokan* during an overnight stay on the holy island.

In truth, the shrine is arguably at its most bewitching at night anyway. While it is not open at nighttime, the complex is nicely lit and, significantly, the approach is bathed in soft light by large stone lanterns. Sauntering along the path that hugs the shore, leading to the shrine, preferably while wearing a *yukata* from your *ryokan*, after the day-trippers have left, leaves a deep impact that cannot be had by only seeing the "floating" gate during daylight hours. Another time to appreciate the shrine is by arriving *before* the day-trippers anytime from when it opens at 6:30am until around 8am, when tour groups start to trickle in.

As an aside, the sprawling shrine complex of **Senjōkaku** (8:30am-4:30pm daily adults ¥100, junior high and elementary school students ¥50) (the name means "hall of 1,000 mats") stands atop a hill just north of Itsukushima-jinja. Built in 1587, the shrine was commissioned by Toyotomi Hideyoshi. Alongside the complex stands a five-story pagoda that was built in 1407. The complex wasn't finished by the time Toyotomi died in 1598, and the next ruler to take the reins, Tokugawa Ieyasu, didn't follow through. The shrine remains incomplete, as reflected in the lack of an official front gate.

Daishō-in
大聖院

210 Miyajima-chō, Hatsukaichi; tel. 0829/44-0111; https://daisho-in.com; 8am-5pm daily; free; walk 20 minutes southwest from Itsukushima ferry terminal

About 10 minutes' walk south of Itsukushima-jinja, sitting at the foot of heavily wooded Mount Misen, this intriguing temple is worth seeing if you plan to hike up or down

1: Itsukushima-jinja **2:** Momijidani-kōen **3:** prayer wheels of Daishō-in

1

2

3

the mountain. It is one of the most important in the Shingon sect, founded by Kōbō Daishi (aka Kūkai), who called for the building of the temple in 806.

At the temple, you can see prayer wheels; a cave festooned with lanterns that feature images depicting the 88 pilgrimage stops of the famed Shikoku pilgrimage; 500 statues of a disciple of Amida Nyorai (Buddha of Infinite Light) named Rakan, each with an individual facial expression; an 11-headed effigy of Kannon (Goddess of Mercy); a mandala sand painting done by visiting Tibetan monks; and more.

To accelerate your own Buddhist scholarship, reach out and spin the prayer wheels bearing the inscriptions of sutras (scriptures) as you walk up the temple's main staircase. This action is said to equate to reading the content of the sutras emblazoned on each prayer wheel, and receiving the blessing contained therein.

Miyajima Ropeway

www.miyajima-ropeway.info; 9am-5pm daily; adults ¥1,000 one-way/¥1,800 round-trip, children ¥500 one-way/¥900 round-trip

If you'd rather not work up a sweat getting to the top of Mount Misen, simply hop on the (recommended) Miyajima Ropeway to the top. The lower ropeway station is about 10 minutes' walk from Momijidani-kōen, from where the ride to the upper station, with a transfer midway at **Kayatani Station,** takes about 15 minutes. From there, it's another 30-minute hike uphill to the summit. If you've got time, and are a glutton for punishment, you can trundle up the verdant peak on foot.

SPORTS AND RECREATION
Parks
MOMIJIDANI-KŌEN

Miyajima-chō, Hatsukaichi; www.miyajima.or.jp/ english/spot/spot_momiji.html; 24 hours daily; free

Momijidani-kōen sits at the foot of Mount Misen, the island's highest peak at 535 meters

(1,755 feet). It's justly known for its autumn foliage. Bisected by a stream, spanned by arched bridges, and lined by stone lanterns, with tame deer roaming freely, it's near the **ropeway** that takes you within a 30-minute walk of the summit of Mount Misen.

Hiking
MOUNT MISEN HIKE

Hiking Distance: 2.5 km (1.5 mi) one-way
Hiking Time: 1.5-2 hours one-way
Information and Maps: *www.miyajima.or.jp/ english/course/course_tozan3.html; www.miyajima. or.jp/english/map/map_misen.html*
Trailhead: *Momijidani-kōen*

Mount Misen offers phenomenal views of the Inland Sea, stretching to Hiroshima and even as far away as Shikoku on cloudless days. You can hike to the top, passing through thick forest, where a temple marks the spot where Kūkai meditated for 100 days. A flame housed at the **Reikadō** (Hall of the Spiritual Flame) was lit by Kūkai and has been continuously burning for 1,200 years. The Peace Flame at Hiroshima's Peace Park was lit with this fire.

To reach the summit of Mount Misen, one option is to start in Momijidani-kōen. This is the shortest yet steepest trail to the top of the peak. There are also two other trails, one that starts behind **Daishō-in** temple (2.6 km/1.6 mi; 1.5-2 hours), which is the least strenuous of the lot and arguably boasts the prettiest views; and the third starts at **Omoto-kōen,** a park behind **Omote-jinja** (10 Miyajima-chō, Hatsukaichi; 0829/44-2020; www.hiroshima-jinjacho.jp/month01; 24 hours daily; free), a shrine located about 7 minutes' walk west of Itsukushima-jinja (3.4 km/2.1 mi; 2-2.5 hours), the longest and least crowded climb of the three. The **Miyajima Tourist Association** has information on all the routes online in English.

You'll likely find yourself panting if you hike to the top. To avoid biting off more than you can chew, take the **Miyajima Ropeway** up, then trundle down one of the three trails on your return. Maintenance work is ongoing along the trail that starts from Momijidani-kōen, scheduled to finish at the end of March 2021.

FESTIVALS AND EVENTS

MIYAJIMA WATER FIREWORKS FESTIVAL
宮島水中花火大会

tel. 0829/44-2011; www.miyajima.or.jp/english/event/event02.html; 7:40pm-8:40pm second to last Sat. of Aug.; free

Some 300,000 spectators, many dressed in *yukata*, throng to Miyajima and the adjacent coastline of Honshu to watch this spectacular fireworks festival every summer. Some 5,000 fireworks burst over the water between the island and the mainland. Special ferries shuttle between the mainland and the island until around midnight to account for the crowds making their way back to Hiroshima. A good strategy is to take the train one stop toward Iwakuni, then transfer to the next Hiroshima-bound train to beat some of the crowds to the train so you can at least attempt to snag a seat. Note that the festival has been postponed by a week or canceled due to rain during some years.

FOOD

SARASVATI
407 Miyajimacho, Hatsukaichi; tel. 0829/44-2266; https://itsuki-miyajima.com/shop/sarasvati; 8:30am-7pm daily; drinks from ¥350, sandwich sets ¥950; walk 2 minutes east of Itsukushima-jinja

This stylish café a stone's throw from the shrine serves great coffee, tea, and desserts. It's located in the midst of the tourist buzz but is a good place to escape the crowds.

★ CAFE LENTE
1167-3 Kitaonishi-chō, Miyajimachō; tel. 0829/44-1204; www.lente-miyajima.com; 11am-4pm Fri.-Mon.; drinks from ¥500, dishes from ¥800; walk 7 minutes west of Itsukushima-jinja

This is a chic little oasis with nearly floor-to-ceiling windows that offer great views of the pine-studded shore and iconic floating *torii* gate beyond. They serve good coffee, tea, desserts, and a smattering of light, healthy meals.

OKONOMIYAKI KISHIBE
483-2 Miyajima-chō, Hatsukaichi-shi; tel. 0829/44-0002; 11am-2pm Sat.-Sun. and 5pm-9pm Wed.-Sun.; ¥650-1,250; walk 4 minutes northeast of Itsukushima-jinja

Like oysters, *okonomiyaki* is as good on the island as it is on the neighboring mainland. If you haven't had your fill in Hiroshima, this mom-and-pop shop serves Hiroshima-style *okonomiyaki* as well as ramen. This is a good place for a homey meal.

★ KAKIYA
539 Miyajima-chō, Hatsukaichi-shi; tel. 0829/44-2747; www.kaki-ya.jp; 10am until oysters are sold out daily; ¥1,200-3,000; walk 5 minutes northeast of Itsukushima-jinja

If you haven't already sampled oysters in Hiroshima, or if you want more, this is a great spot to try them in their various guises (deep-fried, raw, grilled) in the heart of the island's small town.

ACCOMMODATIONS

Staying overnight on Miyajima is a great way to experience the island's subtle charms that are often missed amid the crowds of day-trippers. If you have the time and budget, there are some wonderful traditional lodgings tucked away in the island's small village.

RYOSO KAWAGUCHI
469 Miyajimacho, Hatsukaichi; tel. 0829/44-0018; http://ryoso-kawaguchi.jp; doubles from ¥14,630 with breakfast and dinner; walk 3 minutes east of Itsukushima-jinja

This welcoming inn, tucked away in the heart of the village east of the shrine, is a great mid-range pick. The guesthouse itself is quite old but well-maintained, with private rooms sharing two private *onsen* (hot spring) tubs (one for couples, one for singles). The host is warm and helpful, and the meals (breakfast and dinner) are tasty and filling. Recommended.

★ **IWASŌ RYOKAN**

345-1 Minamimachi, Miyajimacho, Hatsukaichi; tel. 0829/44-2233; www.iwaso.com; ¥22,000-28,000 pp with breakfast and dinner; walk 4 minutes southeast of Itsukushima-jinja, heading toward Momijidani-kōen

This renowned high-end *ryokan* has history and a magical ambience. In business since 1854, the property is divided into three wings with a handful of cottages. Some rooms use a shared bathroom. All rooms have access to a shared *onsen*. Two lavish meals are served daily to the exquisite tatami rooms. It's located about 15 minutes' walk east of the Miyajima-sanbashi Pier. There's also an optional courtesy shuttle bus pickup from the pier. You'll have to reserve six months or more in advance to snag a room in autumn, when the leafy gorge behind the property explodes with red, orange, and yellow.

INFORMATION AND SERVICES

For English information on Miyajima, stop by the **tourist information booth** in the island's ferry terminal (tel. 0829/44-2011; http://visit-miyajima-japan.com; 9am-6pm daily).

GETTING THERE AND AROUND

Miyajima is accessible by ferry from **Miyajima-guchi Station,** a stop on the JR San'yō line, about 20 km (12 mi) southwest of Hiroshima (30 minutes; ¥410). From

Miyajima-guchi's **ferry terminal,** two companies operate ferries to and from Miyajima: **JR** (tel. 0829/56-2045; www.jr-miyajimaferry.co.jp; departures from Miyajima-guchi 6:25am-10:42pm daily) and **Matsudai** (tel. 0829/44-2171; www.miyajima-matsudai.co.jp; departures from Miyajima-guchi 7:15am-8:35pm daily). Note that while both operators charge the same fare (10 minutes; ¥180 one-way), you can ride the JR ferry for free if you have a JR pass.

If you'd like to zip straight to the island from Hiroshima's core in about 30 minutes, serving Hiroshima's **Ujina Port** is hydrofoil operator **Setonaikai Kisen** (tel. 082/253-1212; www.setonaikaikisen.co.jp; departures from Ujina Port 9:25am-4:25pm Mon.-Fri., 8:25am-4:25pm Sat.-Sun.; ¥1,850 one-way). Ujina Port can be reached from downtown via tram numbers 3 and 5 (20 minutes; ¥160).

Aqua Net Ferry (tel. 082/240-5955; www.aqua-net-h.co.jp; departures from Peace Memorial Park 8:30am-5:10pm daily) whisks away passengers directly from Peace Memorial Park (45 minutes; ¥2,000 one way, ¥3,600 return). You'll find the dock on the opposite side of the Ōta-gawa river from the Peace Memorial Park.

While **taxis** do trundle through the island's quiet lanes, plan to explore Miyajima **on foot.** All sights of interest are within a comfortable stroll from each other.

Iwakuni 岩国

This town of 135,000, just across the prefectural border in neighboring Yamaguchi, is best known for its iconic Kintai-kyō bridge. This five-arched marvel of pre-modern engineering spans the Nishiki River, and has been a symbol of the town since it was first built in the 17th century. Just beyond the bridge, you'll also find the remnants of a charming samurai quarter, centered on the appealing park, Kikkō-kōen, with a modern

reconstruction of Iwakuni Castle looming from a hilltop in the backdrop. The lanes running between white-walled homes surrounding Kikkō-kōen—some once occupied by samurai—are dotted by old shrines and temples, evoking Iwakuni's time as a feudal domain during the Edo period. Iwakuni makes for an appealing side trip from Hiroshima, whether by itself or combined with Miyajima on a longer day trip.

SIGHTS
Kintai-kyō Bridge
錦帯橋

1 Iwakuni; tel. 0827/41-1477; http://kintaikyo.
iwakuni-city.net; 8am-5pm daily; adults ¥310,
elementary school students ¥150 for round-trip on
bridge, adults ¥970, elementary school students
¥460 for combination ticket with cable car and
castle entry

This massive arched bridge, boasting five humps connected by large stone pillars, was originally built in 1673 by Kikkawa Hiroyoshi, the third lord of the Iwakuni domain. The local noble called for its construction after the Nishiki River had repeatedly wiped out less robust bridges over the occasionally raging waterway. Once constructed, only members of the elite were permitted to cross during feudal times. After standing for almost three centuries, it buckled after a fierce typhoon in 1950, but was rebuilt by 1953 and saw its most recent renovations in the early 2000s.

The bridge is an impressive sight any time of year, but it cuts an especially striking profile during *hanami* (cherry blossom viewing) season around late March and early April, when clusters of cherry trees along the river banks burst with pink. It's also a romantic scene around dusk when hanging lanterns along the riverside flicker on. As an added bonus, if you arrive after its official opening hours, it's worth noting that you can still cross the bridge, as many locals do, for free.

Just beyond the bridge lies the former samurai quarter surrounding the park of **Kikkō-kōen.** At the northeast corner of the park you'll find the lower ropeway station that leads up to the hilltop where **Iwakuni Castle** looms in its reconstructed glory.

Iwakuni Castle
岩国城

3 Yokoyama; tel. 0827/41-1477; http://kankou.
iwakuni-city.net/iwakunijyo.html; 9am-4:45pm
(last entry 4:30pm) daily, cable car 2pm-5pm daily,
irregular closings; adults ¥270, elementary school
students ¥120 castle only, ¥560 ropeway round-trip,
adults ¥970, elementary school students ¥460
bridge, ropeway, and castle

A combination ticket for both the bridge and the cable car also gives access to the reconstructed four-story citadel perched on the hill beyond the park. The fortress was first built in 1608, but forcibly razed by a decree of the shogun only seven years later. Rebuilt in 1962, its interior is underwhelming, with a collection of swords and armor. But good views of the town, roughly 200 meters (656

Kintai-kyō Bridge

feet) below, can be had from its grounds. You can also walk to the top via a path that starts from the park's western end in about 45 minutes. Note that the castle is another 5 minutes' walk northeast of the upper ropeway station.

SPORTS AND RECREATION

KIKKŌ-KŌEN
吉香公園

2-6-51 Yokoyama; 24 hours; free

On the other side of the bridge, you'll come to this pleasant park. Upon entering the green expanse, you'll be met with a statue of lord Kikkawa in samurai garb. The park itself is a leisurely place to stroll, with some temples and shrines dotting its outskirts. It also contains a number of modest museums with collections of feudal-era artifacts that are not must-sees. If you happen to be traveling with kids, it may be worth a brief stop at the **White Snake Museum** (2-6-52 Yokoyama; tel. 0827/35-5303; http://shirohebi.info; 9am-5pm daily; adults ¥210, children ¥100), which showcases the unique albino species that slithers through the area. Some of the homes in the area were once lived in by samurai and retainers of the Kikkawa family.

FESTIVALS

KINTAI-KYŌ FIREWORKS FESTIVAL
錦帯橋花火大会

tel. 0827/41-2037; http://iwakuni-kanko.jp; 8pm-9:30pm first Sat. in Aug.; free

Miyajima's blowout is not the only fireworks show in the region each summer. When the heat reaches a boiling point in August, locals in *yukata* flock to the riverside near Kintai-kyō for one of Japan's most glorious fireworks shows. The atmosphere is highly festive, with a glut of *yatai* food stalls set up along the banks of the river, which is filled with boats of revelers. To secure a spot worthy of the trip, aim to arrive very early in the day—1pm is a good target—and leisurely enjoy the merry-making leading up to the main event.

FOOD

For a town its size, Iwakuni boasts diverse dining options, mainly clustered around JR Iwakuni Station and the area around Kintai-kyō and Kikkō-kōen.

CAFE SHIROYAMA

2-4-23 Yokoyama; tel. 0827/43-2554; 11am-4:30pm Mon., Wed.-Fri., 11am-5pm Sat.-Sun.; ¥1,000

This classic cafe in the heart of Kikkō-kōen is a good option for lunch, or a caffeine hit with dessert, near the bridge. The menu is a mix of western-style set meals, coffee, and light desserts. The classic café ambiance evokes the mid-20th century, with its slightly dated (though inviting) interior—old wooden furniture—and its chipper staff dressed in crisp white shirts.

VITAL YAWD

2-2-2 Marifu-machi; tel. 0827/24-4100; www.facebook.com/pages/Vital-Yawd/334301609981332; 6pm-1am Mon., noon-1am Tues.-Fri., noon-3am Sat.-Sun.; ¥1,500; walk 2 minutes west from JR Iwakuni Station

For something unexpected near JR Iwakuni Station, this Jamaican restaurant run by a couple of veritable reggae heads doesn't disappoint. The Rasta décor and dubby soundtrack will make you wonder if you have been transported to Kingston. The dense menu includes many variations of jerk chicken, Thai curry, and rice-bean combos. There's also a well-stocked bar and a towering speaker stack pumping out a steady thump of bass.

INFORMATION AND SERVICES

If you're coming via the San'yō line, stop by the **tourist information booth** in JR Iwakuni Station (tel. 0827/24-9071; 10am-5pm Tues.-Sun.). If you're coming by *shinkansen*, there's also one at JR Shin-Iwakuni Station (10:30am-3:30pm Thurs.-Tues.).

Near Kintai-kyō you'll find a visitors center set in a mid-19th-century house called **Honke Matsugane** (1-7-3 Iwakuni; tel. 0827/28-660; www.honke-matsugane.jp; 9am-6pm daily

Apr.-Aug., 9am-5pm Sept.-Mar.; free). It's just as worth dropping in here to get an intimate view of the inside of a historic home as it is to glean information on Iwakuni from the friendly English-speaking staff who can give brief tours of the home and answer any questions you may have.

GETTING THERE AND AROUND

It's easy to reach Iwakuni from either **Hiroshima** or **Miyajima.** From either starting point, take the JR San'yō line to **JR Iwakuni Station** (55 minutes from Hiroshima, ¥760; 22 minutes from Miyajima, ¥330). If you're traveling from Hiroshima with a JR Pass and feel like saving a bit of time,

you can also take the *shinkansen* to **Shin-Iwakuni Station** (15 minutes; ¥1,620). Once you're in either JR Iwakuni Station or Shin-Iwakuni Station, you'll need to hop on a bus to reach Kintai-kyō. Buses depart in front of JR Iwakuni Station (20 minutes; ¥300) and from bus stop no. 1 outside Shin-Iwakuni Station (15 minutes; ¥350).

It's also possible to make the journey to Kintai-kyō from Hiroshima directly by **bus** (50 minutes; ¥930 one-way, ¥1,700 round-trip). A total of 12 buses make the trip daily, departing from bus stop no. 1 of the Hiroshima Bus Center.

Once you're in the area around the bridge, everything of interest is within walking distance.

Background

The Landscape

GEOGRAPHY

Despite the insistence of many Japanese people, their country is not a small place. At 377,915 square km (145,914 square mi), it's a bit larger than Germany and slightly smaller than California. From the northeastern tip of Hokkaido to far southwestern Okinawa, the bow of islands extends 3,008 km (1,869 mi), or roughly the same length, north to south, as the continental United States. This gives the country a wide range of climates and landscapes, and a vast coastline.

The island of Honshu is not only Japan's largest and most central,

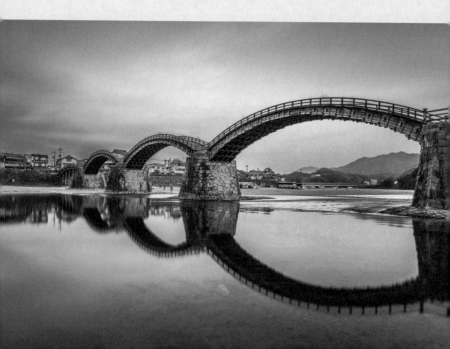

but also its cultural heartland. Just about any archetypally Japanese image you may conjure in your mind's eye is likely found here, from the neon rush of Tokyo and Mount Fuji's perfect cone to Kyoto's nimble-footed geisha and Hiroshima's Atomic Bomb Dome. Honshu is the world's seventh largest island (227,960 sq km/88,020 sq mi) and the second most populous (after Java in Indonesia). Some 100 million inhabitants are mostly crammed onto the fertile plains that hug its vast coastline, which rolls on for 10,084 km (6,266 mi). Greater Tokyo alone is home to 30 percent of the island's residents.

The large, mountainous island can be split into a number of distinct regions, with the vast wilds of Tōhoku in the north; Greater Tokyo (aka Kantō), including Tokyo, Yokohama, Kamakura, Hakone, and Mount Fuji, southwest of there; west of which lies the mountainous central core known as Chūbu, encompassing the Japan Alps, Nagoya, Kanazawa, and more; with Kansai (Kyoto, Nara, Osaka, Kobe) west of there; and Western Honshu (aka Chūgoku), home to Hiroshima, Miyajima, and the sparkling Inland Sea along its southern shore, in Honshu's far southwest.

Oceans and Coastline

Perhaps the most constant feature is the ocean. The Sea of Japan lies to the west, with the Korean peninsula and China on the other side. The Pacific stretches eastward, with the United States mainland lying more than 8,000 km (5,000 mi) to the east. The lack of land borders has allowed Japan to develop its unique cultural universe.

Thousands of islands comprise Japan, but four make up the bulk of the nation's landmass: the main island of Honshu; Hokkaido in the north; and bordering the Inland Sea with Western Honshu in the nation's southwest: rustic Shikoku and volcanic Kyushu.

All told, some 27,000 km (16,777 mi) of coastline encircle these islands.

Mountains

Inland, the landscape is roughly 70-80 percent mountainous, pushing people and agriculture to the coastal fringes, comprising 20-30 percent of the land. Honshu's geographic heart is in the Japan Alps (North, Central, and Southern), where you'll find most of the nation's tallest peaks, some of which top 3,000 meters (9,800 feet). Elsewhere on Honshu are the Hida and Kiso ranges, as well as Japan's tallest and one of the world's most recognizable peaks, the sublime Mount Fuji (3,776 meters/12,388 feet). As you move to the southwest or northeast of Honshu, the mountains dip to rolling foothills.

Geothermal Activity and Volcanoes

Geothermal activity is rife in the country. Part of the Ring of Fire, Japan is located directly on the Pacific Plate ridgeline. The country's share of volcanic eruptions and earthquakes attest to that fact. Even Fuji itself is a volcano, which last erupted in 1707. All told, about 70 volcanoes dot Japan. That said, though occasional eruptions send shivers down the public's collective spine, cataclysmic events are rare. The Japanese take advantage of the country's intense geothermal activity by periodically plunging into the waters of a hot *onsen* bath.

Rivers and Lakes

Notable rivers in the area covered in this book include the Tonegawa, which runs from Niigata to Chiba east of Tokyo and serves as a major source of freshwater for the capital region; Tokyo's Sumidagawa, running through the old part of downtown (Shitamachi); Osaka's concrete-embanked Yodogawa, a key historic lane of commerce; and Kyoto's pleasant Kamogawa, lined with paths well-suited for a summer evening stroll. To the chagrin

Previous: Kintai-kyō Bridge.

of many environmental activists, a major proportion of the country's waterways have been dammed for electricity, water storage, irrigation, or other industries.

Japan's largest lake is Lake Biwa (Biwa-ko), which lies northeast of Kyoto. Other prominent lakes in this book include the Fuji Five Lakes (Lake Kawaguchi and Lake Yamanaka being most famous), which frame the iconic peak.

CLIMATE

The vast majority of Japan has four neatly delineated seasons, but there are variations. The northern extremities of the country, particularly Hokkaido, fall into the Northern Temperate Zone, producing conditions similar to those of New England. Meanwhile, Okinawa and much of the far southwest enjoy subtropical warmth most of the year.

Several distinct climatic zones are delineated by mountain ranges and ocean straits. From northern Kyushu to Shikoku and up the eastern half of Honshu, the climate is defined by mild springs; hot, sticky summers; cool autumns; and chilly, crisp winters with the occasional dusting of snow or (even more rare) heavy snowfall.

Central Honshu

In the mountainous interior of Central Honshu, a highland climate prevails. Snow piles up in the Japan Alps and surrounding ranges during winter, producing excellent winter sports conditions. Summers are warm, but less intensely humid than the coastal population centers. As a general rule of thumb, the temperature dips about 5°C (9°F) for every 1,000-meter increase in altitude

Inland Sea

Moving south, the Inland Sea region, which includes northern Shikoku and the southern Sany'yō coast of Western Honshu, has a distinct climate of its own. This idyllic section of the country is largely sunny, but droughts can occur in the region. Moreover, the overwhelming floods that ravaged this

mostly sun-drenched region in 2018 are a reminder that it's not immune to inclement weather.

Tsuyu

From late May or early June, *tsuyu* (rainy season) descends on much of the country. Showers vary from heavy to nonexistent during this period. Then, from July through September, typhoons that begin farther south in the tropical Pacific begin to work their way across Japan, starting in Okinawa and moving north. These storms often batter the southern half of the country, before gradually tapering off as they reach Tohoku. Hokkaido, separated from Honshu by the Straits of Tsugaru, is generally spared. These midsummer squalls can be unpleasant and can occasionally turn dangerous. Take any forecasted typhoon into consideration when planning a trip, but not to the extent of avoiding the country altogether.

Extreme Weather Events

In recent years, in line with broader climate change sweeping the globe, Japan has had record-high temperatures in summer and winters that are either short and mild, or in some cases bitterly cold. Extreme rainfall, including floods and landslides, have also spiked in recent years. Most notably, in the summer of 2018 floods devastated large swaths of western Japan. The cataclysmic floods killed nearly 200 people, left thousands without water and electricity, and forced millions to evacuate.

ENVIRONMENTAL ISSUES

At a glance, Japan is stunning, with craggy spines blanketed in forest, pristine rivers coursing through steep ravines, and sweeping seaside cliffs plummeting into unspoiled bays. Look closer, however, and blemishes reveal a harsh truth: The postwar development rush has not been kind to the environment. The country's environmental issues are many, afflicting both land and sea.

Construction and consumer waste have

blighted the landscape, and sustainable forestry has been supplanted by boundless *sugi* (cedar) plantations. Offshore, the oceans have been severely depleted by overfishing, Japanese ships sustain a highly contentious whaling industry, and smaller boats execute a deplorable dolphin hunt. Meanwhile, the nuclear catastrophe flowing out from Fukushima has seeped into the surrounding earth and spread to all corners of the planet, carried by ocean currents.

Waste and Pollution

The proliferation of plastic and staggering levels of consumption of every kind make waste management a perennial challenge. All told, 45.4 tons of municipal solid waste are generated annually in Japan, the eighth highest worldwide, with 20.8 percent of that being recycled. Disposable wooden chopsticks (*waribashi*), which are dispensed freely by restaurants and convenience stores, further contribute to the excess of waste. About 130 million pairs of chopsticks are discarded daily; to avoid wasting wood and adding to the landfill, consider picking up a pair of "my hashi" (my chopsticks), which are stored in a case and reused. These chopsticks kits are sold in lifestyle shops like Tokyu Hands and Loft, and in some convenience stores. For perspective, some estimates place the toll for the production of these throwaway chopsticks at 400,000 cubic meters of forest annually.

Fukushima and Nuclear Power

The ongoing nuclear crisis in Fukushima is the most pressing environmental issue facing Japan today. When the mega-quake struck off the coast of Tohoku on March 11, 2011, six reactors melted down. Since then, radioactive fuel has been leaking from the complex, into which up to 150 tons of groundwater leaks daily. And this is an improvement. The figure once stood at 400 tons before TEPCO installed pumps and its $300 million ice wall.

Aside from the region immediately surrounding Fukushima's reactors, the country is officially deemed safe for visitors and citizens. Nonetheless, groups of concerned citizens, scientists, and activists have taken radiation monitoring into their own hands. To find current radiation levels (from non-government sources), visit Safecast (https://blog.safecast.org) or the Citizens' Nuclear Information Center (www.cnic.jp) online.

Meanwhile, there are signs of hope that a deeper environmental consciousness is slowly taking hold. Civil consciousness surrounding nuclear energy has taken off significantly in the years following Fukushima. Protestors routinely gather in Tokyo's public squares and in front of government offices to voice their opposition to the use of nuclear power. But under former Prime Minister Shinzo Abe, who resigned in September 2020, the government pushed to keep nuclear power. It's hard to say what will happen under the new PM, Yoshihide Suga.

Plants and Animals

When it comes to flora and fauna, it helps to think of Japan as being divided into three broad regions: temperate in the center (Honshu, Shikoku, and Kyushu), subarctic in the north (Hokkaido), and subtropical in the far southwest (Okinawa and the other southwestern island chains). Within these three zones, remarkable variations exist in plant and wildlife. To delve deep into the archipelago's natural world, **Japan Nature Guides** (www.japannatureguides.com) offers a range of services to help with birdwatching tours and other excursions, as well as in-depth guidebooks about wildlife of the islands.

TREES

Roughly two-thirds of Japan is forested, even after the post-World War II construction boom. While forests envelope much of Japan today, around half of this cover is comprised of *matsu* (pine) and *sugi* (cedar) plantations.

These cookie-cutter forests once served the lumber industry, falling into disuse in the 1970s when the nation began to import timber from its tropical neighbors at an eyebrow-raising rate. Historically, the Kiso Valley of Nagano Prefecture has been famous for its prized timber. The imperial seal of approval has meant that the wood from this region has long been used in the construction of key structures, with Tokyo's most venerable shrine, Meiji Jingū, among them.

Beyond the ubiquitous pines and cedars, other common species include hinoki (Japanese cypress), a smattering of bamboo varieties, and a host of deciduous trees, from oaks to maples that blaze with color every autumn, and, of course, the beloved cherry tree, famed for vivid pink petals that dazzle every corner of the nation every spring.

FLOWERS

Japan has a reverence for flowers. Plum blossoms, which bring winter to a close, are soon followed by waves of pink *sakura* (cherry blossoms): nature's way of announcing the arrival of spring. The unofficial national flower of Japan, *sakura* has an outsized presence in the nation's psyche.

Meanwhile, violet wisterias bloom around the end of April; hydrangeas and irises flourish in June; and lotus blossoms, sunflowers, and lavender cover fields like patches of a quilt in July and August. These waves of summer blooms draw enthusiasts to wildflower hot spots, while hikers marvel at similar displays in mountain meadows nationwide.

Heading into autumn, spider lilies unfold their spindly arms in September and October, while the chrysanthemum, Japan's official national flower, blooms from September to November.

MAMMALS

A vast range of mammals inhabit Japan. Kyushu, Shikoku, Honshu, and Hokkaido fall into the Palaearctic region, home to temperate and subarctic mammals, many of which have links to East Asia. Kyushu and the Okinawa Prefecture fall into the Oriental region, a balmier zone inhabited by subtropical and tropical animals linked to Southeast Asia.

The iconic Japanese macaque (also referred to as a "snow monkey"), which is endemic to Japan, is perhaps the most recognizable mammal of all. These ornery primates live in an area that stretches from the northern periphery of Honshu to the emerald island of Yakushima, off the southern coast of Kyushu. Atop Honshu's food chain is the Asiatic black bear, smaller than its cousins in Hokkaido. Some 15,000 of these bears are believed to roam the forests and mountains of Honshu.

Other land-dwelling mammals include the endemic Japanese serow, which looks like cross between a goat and an antelope, and lives in mountains and forests from northern Honshu to Shikoku and northern Kyushu; the wild boar (*inushishi*); Japanese sika deer; the tanuki, or raccoon dog; and red foxes, which feature heavily in Shinto myth. (Note that the "fox villages" found in some parts of Honshu are sad affairs with cooped-up foxes and are not worth visiting.)

It's also worth noting that Japan has a few native dog breeds, namely the medium-sized shiba and the larger akita, which are both Spitz types (pointed ears, thick fur). Cats are ubiquitous and beloved across Japan as well.

SEALIFE

All told, some 3,000 species of aquatic life inhabit Japan. This remarkable diversity of marine life is partly due to a few distinct ocean currents. Warm water flows from Taiwan to Okinawa and the southwest islands, branching off into two separate currents when it hits Kyushu. Meanwhile, coming from the north, the cold waters move toward northeastern Hokkaido, veering south toward northeastern Honshu. In the Pacific south of Shikoku and Honshu swim Loggerhead turtles, dugongs, and dolphins. And elsewhere, a range of marine life teems in the oceans surrounding

Japan, from dolphins and flying squid to sea bream, surgeonfish, tuna, seabass, sting rays, sharks, and snappers, to name but a few. Freshwater fish living in the nation's rivers, lakes, and streams include carp, *ayu* (sweet fish), eel, and more.

BIRDS AND REPTILES

Throughout the country, there are many types of ducks, geese, swans, herons, kingfishers, pheasants, black kites, and cormorants. Turtles and small lizards such as geckos are found throughout much of Japan, but make their strongest showing in the subtropical islands of Okinawa.

All told, some 50 species of snake live in Japan. As one of the Chinese zodiac's 12 animals, snakes are potent symbols in Japan, and elsewhere in East Asia, where they are traditionally thought to serve as divine messengers. While most of them are harmless, there are a few poisonous species in the islands extending southward from Kyushu.

INSECTS AND ARACHNIDS

To the chagrin of many residents in Japan's urban centers, *gokiburi* (cockroaches) are common any time of year in humid parts of the country, and most common during summer in drier climes. Another insect that sometimes finds its way into homes is the *gejigeji* (house centipede), which looks positively terrifying, though it's harmless and is only interested in eating other insects.

Outdoors, the hum of cicadas peaks at around 120 decibels during summer, making a walk through a forest or park as loud as a rock concert. Mosquitoes can be a nuisance in the warmer months and near any fresh water source.

Generally speaking, Japan's insects are relatively harmless and few are poisonous. Most of Japan's spiders are also harmless. The most dangerous spider found in Japan is the red-back spider, believed to have been introduced from Australia by cargo ships carrying wood chips. A bite from a redback can occasionally be deadly. Unfortunately, these spiders have been seen in more than 20 of Japan's prefectures, largely toward the west of the country.

AMPHIBIANS

Around 40 frog species live in Japan, including the Japanese rain frog, Japanese tree frog, and American bullfrog, which is common in ponds. A number of toad species are also found across the country. An amphibian of particular note is the Japanese giant salamander, the second-largest salamander in the world. Endemic to the rocky bottoms of swiftly flowing streams in southwestern Japan, the giant salamander reaches up to 1.5 meters (5 feet).

History

ANCIENT CIVILIZATION

For a period of time around 18,000 BC, there was a land bridge linking Japan to the Asian continent. Japan's first inhabitants traveled over this bridge from the mainland. This overland link to the rest of Asia vanished when sea levels rose around 10,000 BC. Architectural touches and some facial features of the Japanese population today suggest that Polynesian seafarers may also have made the long journey north to the islands in the ancient past. In truth, the origins of Japanese people are highly complex and debated, with genetic input believed to originate in groups all around Asia, from Tibetans and Koreans to Han Chinese.

Jōmon Period

The earliest civilization emerged in Japan during the Jōmon period (14,000-300 BC), a hunter-gatherer culture known for its "cord-marked" pottery made by pressing cords onto wet clay. This pottery tradition is thought to be among not only the oldest in East Asia, but the whole world.

Yayoi Period

During the following Yayoi period (300 BC-AD 300), rice cultivation techniques and metalworking arrived from mainland Asia. The period's name is derived from the place in present-day Tokyo where bronze artifacts dating to the period were first unearthed.

EARLY HISTORY
Yamato Period (250-710)
KOFUN PERIOD (250-538)

The first section of the Yamamoto period, the Kofun period was named after a type of burial mound used for the period's elite. These megalithic tombs ranged from relatively modest square-shaped mounds to massive mounds shaped like keyholes hundreds of meters long, surrounded by moats and laden with sometimes thousands of artifacts. All told, more than 160,000 Kofun have been discovered around Japan, with a heavy concentration around modern-day Kansai and Western Honshu.

During this period, the Shinto religion began to take shape, its principles and practices growing from older beliefs from the Yayoi period. During the Kofun period, a plethora of small kingdoms existed in Japan. The Yamato clan, which would eventually become the imperial family, rose to the top of that power structure. Contact with China and Korea also grew, with Japan taking on a more formal political identity of its own.

ASUKA PERIOD (538-710)

As the Kofun period drew to a close, the Yamato clan had fully established itself as the imperial family of Japan. The key features of the Asuka period were the introduction of Buddhism in the mid-6th century and the adoption and adaptation of Chinese characters to form Japan's own written script. Coinage, in the form of the *Wado kaiho*, was also introduced. Japan began to borrow heavily from China, perceived as a highly civilized role model. The period is named after Asuka, the capital during the period, today in the northern Nara Prefecture.

The first bona fide historical emperor rose to power during this period, Emperor Kimmei (509-571). Empress Suiko (554-628) and Prince Shōtoku (574-622) were by far the period's most prominent leaders. As Suiko's regent, Shōtoku initiated government reforms, stamped out corruption and entrenched nepotism, and established embassies with the Chinese Sui Dynasty around 607.

Shōtoku is believed to have drawn up Japan's first constitution, the Jushichijo-kenpo (Seventeen Article Constitution) in 604. This document centralized Japan's government and emphasized the Confucian principle of *wa* (harmony).

Shōtoku heavily promoted Buddhism, erecting 46 monasteries and temples, including Hōryū-ji in modern-day Nara, the only monastery still standing that was originally built in the Asuka period. This initial push to adopt Buddhism would significantly alter Japan's spiritual development over the longer term and signal to its more powerful neighbors that the country had "arrived." In addition to an increasingly sophisticated system of government and a deeper spiritual life, the Asuka period also saw a creative boom as music and literature flourished in and around the imperial court.

Within this milieu, the upstart Fujiwara clan rose to prominence through a coup in AD 645, wresting power from the Soga clan, which had controlled the government since 587. Inspired by China, Emperor Kōtoku reshaped the new government through the Taika Reform of 645, shortly after the death of Shōtoku. The sweeping changes of these reforms included introducing a codified system of law, nationalizing land, replacing forced labor with a tax system, reshuffling social classes, introducing an examination-based recruitment system for the civil service, and establishing the emperor's absolute authority. With the elevation of Emperor Tenjin

(626-672), along with his senior minister Nakatomi no Kamatari (614-669), who was granted the surname Fujiwara, the Fujiwara clan ascended to a position of great power, where they would remain for centuries to come.

Nara Period (710-794)

During the brief Nara period, the capital relocated to Nara during 710-784. Until this time, the capital moved every time an emperor or empress died. Tōdai-ji, the world's largest wooden building, which houses the towering Great Buddha, was built during this time. By the end of the Nara period, the capital's population swelled to around 200,000.

Two seminal texts were penned during the Nara period, placing the nation's mythical founding in the ancient past. According to the legends recorded in the 8th century, the Kojiki, Japan's oldest written chronicle, and the Nihon Shoki (aka Nihon-gi), the second oldest, say that the mythical first emperor, Jimmu Tenno, established the nation of Japan on February 11, 660 BC. This is why the National Foundation Day holiday is held on February 11 each year. Others put his actual existence, if he existed at all, closer to AD 100.

In many ways, the Nara period saw a continuation of trends that began in the Kofun and Asuka period. The city itself, then known as Heijokyō, was modeled after the Tang Dynasty's capital of Chang-an and was laid out on a Chinese grid pattern. Its architecture was similarly Chinese in appearance. A Confucian university was built and the government became increasingly bureaucratic, mimicking the mandarins of the Tang court.

Smallpox outbreaks (735-737) killed 25-35 percent of the population. Faced with widespread poverty, and occasionally struck with famine, the remaining citizens became resentful of the increased meddling of the Yamato court in Japan's outlying areas, and the largely agrarian provinces grew restless. The government in Nara responded by establishing military outposts in the provinces. Fujiwara no Hirotsugu raised an army in Dazaifu, Kyushu, then led a rebellion in 740 that was quashed by a 17,000-strong army sent by Emperor Shomu (724-749).

It's worth noting that three empresses ruled during the Nara period: Gemmei ruled 707-715; Gensho ruled 715-724; and Koken ruled 749-758 and again as Shōtoku 764-770. This would be the last empress for 800 years. Women were also able to own land during this time.

Heian Period (794-1185)

As the Nara period drew to a close, Emperor Kammu (736-806) moved the capital in 794 to Heiankyō (modern-day Kyoto), where the imperial court remained for more than a millennium, and marking the start of a pivotal stage in Japan's history. During this time, Japan began to wean itself off Chinese influence, taking on an isolationist stance that would greatly intensify in the ensuing centuries. Although the flow of cultural and commercial exchange did continue, Japan became less politically engaged with China. Exchanges between Japanese and Chinese scholars, monks, and creatives gradually wound down, however, and Japanese civilization began to take on its own distinct characteristics.

During this time, Shinto and Buddhism began to fuse, becoming both the state religion as well as the faith of commoners. Buddhism flourished, with Shingon Buddhism being founded by Kūkai (774-835), or Kobo Daishi. The Tendai sect was also founded during this era by Saicho (767-822).

It was during this period that Japan began to hone its own artistic style. Courtiers in elaborate silk costumes and poets engaged in trysts and intrigue, leading to a remarkable leap forward in the literary arts, with the penning of classic works of literature in the early 11th century such at *The Tale of Genji* by Lady Murasaki Shikibu and *The Pillow Book* by Sei Shōnagon. Beyond literature, court artists actively developed the arts of screen paintings, scrolls, calligraphy, and music, and enjoyed teasing their intellects with the complex strategy board game known as *go*.

Politically, the period was marked by significant influence exerted by the Fujiwara clan, who eventually fell into a feud with lesser nobles, including the Taira (aka Heike) and Minamoto (aka Genji) families. Under the helm of Taira no Kiyomori (1118-1181), the Taira clan challenged the Fujiwara and Minamoto, and emerged victorious in 1160, ruling for 20 years. Taira rulers succumbed to corruption and vice and were supplanted by the victorious Minamoto clan, led by Yoritomo Minamoto (1147-1199), in the Genpei War (1180-1185), waged for control of the imperial throne.

Following the war's final conflict, the Battle of Dannoura, Tomomori, who led the Taira forces, and Antoku, the would-be young Taira emperor, committed suicide. Yoritomo then granted himself the title of Shōgun (Generalissimo) upon the death of Emperor Go-Shirakawa in 1192, an honor normally only granted to a general. With this bold move, the illustrious Heian period came to an end, ushering in the beginning of Japan's military-dominated feudal age.

FEUDAL JAPAN
Kamakura Period (1185-1333)

Japan's long, tumultuous feudal era would last seven centuries, beginning with the Kamakura period. Major political change came with this new era, including control of the government falling under the newly declared shogunate and military ruler, Yoritomo Minamoto.

Although Yoritomo officially operated under the distant emperor, in truth, he was the new de facto head of government. While the emperor remained in Heiankyō (Kyoto), Yoritomo set up his new *bakufu* (tent government) in Kamakura. A lord-vassal system emerged, and the age of the samurai was born. Staunch loyalty was a hallmark of the new cultural ethos, which was markedly militaristic in tone.

When Yoritomo died under suspicious circumstances in 1199, his widow, Masako, began to lay the foundation for the Hōjō

Shogunate, under her own family. By the late Kamakura period, the state was tried by invasion attempts by Kublai Khan, who first led forces from Mongolia across the Sea of Japan in 1274. He tried again in 1281, bringing with him a 100,000-strong armada. This time Japan was spared by a kamikaze (divine wind) that sunk half of the mighty fleet, while spirited warriors in Kyushu finished the job.

Still, Japan began to unravel internally due to increased regional infighting. Emperor Go-Daigo and his court made efforts to bring full control of the government under the throne, hatching a plot to do away with the *bakufu*. When the conspiracy was discovered, Go-Daigo was exiled to far-flung Oki Island off the coast of modern-day Shimane Prefecture.

Meanwhile, local chieftains in the Kinai area, comprising Kyoto and Nara today, assembled an army and took the Kamakura *bakufu* by storm. Two vassals of the ruling Hōjō clan who had become disgruntled, Ashikaga Takauji and Nitta Yoshisada, helped clinch the victory for the imperial forces, wiping out the majority of Hōjō elites. This effectively brought the Kamakura period to a close.

Muromachi Period (1333-1568)

Following the overthrow of the Kamakura *bakufu*, Emperor Go-Daigo returned from exile to Kyoto and swiftly instituted reforms aimed at restoring imperial rule, sending family members to serve as administrators in the outlying provinces. Many warriors felt that Go-Daigo unfairly rewarded his own family, while neglecting the men who fought on his behalf. In response, Ashikaga turned on Go-Daigo and forced the emperor to the Yoshino Mountains outside Nara in 1336. Go-Daigo then established the Southern Court near Nara, while Ashikaga appointed a puppet emperor in Kyoto. These two rival courts were engaged in an ongoing feud for the next six decades, until Takauji's grandson Yoshimitsu finally settled the score in 1392, after which the imperial line descended through the Northern Court of Kyoto.

When Go-Daigo fled to Yoshino, Ashikaga Takauji established a *bakufu* of his own in Kyoto. From Kyoto, Takauji's grandson Yoshimitsu neutralized all rivals and was declared prime minister. He resuscitated trade and diplomatic relations with China, then in the Ming Dynasty.

Despite these advancements, the era was largely characterized by an ongoing state of civil war between regional lords (*daimyo*) and their loyal armies of *bushi* (samurai warriors). There was also widespread economic instability, famine, and disagreement over who would become the next shogun.

Combined, these developments created the perfect conditions for the breakout of the Onin War (1467-1477), which erupted around the midway point of the Muromachi period, marking the beginning of the Sengoku (Warring States) period (1467-1600). The eastern Hosokawa faction, backed by the shogun and emperor, clashed with the western Yamana faction, supported by the powerful Ōuchi family. Fires raged in the capital, decimating temples and grand homes. Fighting gradually bled into the provinces, where local samurai led defensive uprisings against *shugo* (military governors) who oversaw large swaths of land. Amid the chaos, some of these samurai ended up establishing themselves as local lords.

The warrior class set the cultural tone during this period. The ideals of Zen Buddhism, such as austerity, simplicity, and self-discipline, meshed well with the samurai class. This led to the rise of refined arts such as *ikebana* (flower arrangement), *Noh* theater, *renga* (linked verse) poetry, and the painstaking social ritual that is the tea ceremony. Many priests and aristocrats fled the volatile capital to surrounding towns, spreading Kyoto's rarefied culture to the outlying provinces.

In 1543, a Portuguese ship was blown ashore on the small island of Tanega-shima, off the southern coast of Kyushu. The exotic foreigners, the first Europeans to arrive in Japan's history, came bearing guns and Christianity. This disruptive foreign faith took off. Many *daimyo* adopted the new faith in hopes of facilitating commerce with European merchants and accessing the revolutionary weapons the Europeans brought with them.

True to the violent times, the arcane art of musket construction became prized knowledge among *daimyo,* who clamored to get their hands on the new military technology. A warlord with a particular affinity for firearms was the ruthless Oda Nobunaga (1534-1582). Although he never became shogun, he did manage to topple Kyoto and seize control of it in 1568, deposing Ashikaga Yoshiaki in 1573 and effectively bringing the Ashikaga shogunate to a close. This made Nobunaga Japan's de facto supreme leader.

Azuchi-Momoyama Period (1568-1600)

During this short period, Nobunaga and his brilliant successor, Toyotomi Hideyoshi (1537-1598), brought order to the chaos. Hideyoshi, one of Nobunaga's favorite, most brilliant generals, swiftly consolidated power and started the practice of requiring *daimyo* families to reside in Kyoto, effectively as hostages. Castles, built and refortified by regional *daimyo,* mushroomed around Honshu and Kyushu during this turbulent period.

Hideyoshi's main rival was Tokugawa Ieyasu (1543-1616), a local lord originally from a domain near modern-day Nagoya. Ieyasu decided to pledge his fealty to Hideyoshi, who allowed Ieyasu to remain in charge of his own domain. Meanwhile, Ieyasu diligently built up and strengthened his domain. In 1586, he moved his base farther east, away from Hideyoshi, where he laid in wait for his time to pounce.

Toward the end of his life, Hideyoshi became feverish with expansionist dreams. He launched two invasions of Korea, with the hopes of going on to topple China and control Asia. This had long been the dream of his predecessor Nobunaga. The attempted invasions failed miserably, however, and severely damaged ties between Japan and Korea.

Following Hideyoshi's death, his young son Hideyori was placed behind the protective walls of Osaka Castle until he was old enough to rule. This, however, was not to be. Ieyasu seized power in the Battle of Sekigahara (1600), widely considered one of the most epic battles in Japanese history.

Edo Period (1603-1868)

In 1603, Tokugawa Ieyasu became shogun and established his base in Edo, which would one day become Tokyo. Under the Tokugawa Shogunate, Japan enjoyed relative peace for more than 250 years. A policy called *sankin kotai* forced *daimyo* and their families to alternate between the new capital Edo and their home state, controlling the *daimyo* and keeping any hidden ambitions in check.

During this time, Japan strictly enforced the *sakoku* (closed country) policy, spurred by meddling by foreign missionaries. Christianity was flat-out banned following the Shimabara Rebellion (1637-1638). In 1638, all foreigners were kicked out of the country, save for a cadre of Dutch traders who swore allegiance to commerce above religion. As a result, all Western medical and scientific knowledge came via the Dutch during this age of intense isolation.

By the early 18th century, Edo had a population of more than 1 million, making it the world's largest city at the time, as it is today. Osaka became a mighty mercantile center, while Kyoto became a hub of leisure and luxury. Four social classes emerged: the samurai, farmers, artisans, and merchants. These social classes were based on the ancient Chinese ideal of the "four occupations," derived from Confucian thought. Existing above these classes were the emperor, imperial court, shogun, and *daimyo*.

The merchants, at the bottom of the hierarchy, were viewed as self-serving and less crucial than farmers and artisans, but this didn't stop them from carving out a vibrant place in society. Increasingly rich merchants indulged in the arts, entertainment, and culinary pursuits. Woodblock prints known as *ukiyo-e* depict many of the favored pastimes from this *ukiyo* (floating world), including sumo tournaments, kabuki, and sprawling pleasure quarters.

By the early 19th century, the shogunate's power had begun to wane, just as the merchant class saw its influence rise. Moreover, foreigners began trying to make contact. Commodore Perry's Black Ships sailed into Edo Bay on July 8, 1853, gunboat-diplomacy style. After firing blank shots from 73 cannons—which Perry claimed was in celebration of American Independence Day—Perry sent a letter to the shogunate threatening to destroy them if they didn't comply, promising to return again a year later.

Only six months later, Perry returned with a crew of 1,600 men aboard 10 ships. They sailed into Kanagawa and negotiated the Convention of Kanagawa on March 31, 1854. The treaty granted access to the ports of Shimoda, Shizuoka Prefecture and Hakodate on Hokkaido. Soon after, Townsend Harris was appointed the first American diplomat to Japan. Other countries and ports followed.

From the time of Perry's arrival until the Meiji Restoration, sentiment against foreign powers and the shogunate grew. The public increasingly yearned for the emperor to be put atop the government again. On the other hand, there was also a growing sense that adopting Western science and military technology was the only hope for Japan in the new age. The tension between these two contradictory impulses set the stage for the next major sea change in Japan's history.

MODERN HISTORY
Meiji Period (1868-1912) and the Lead-Up to World War II

By 1867, the Tokugawa shogunate was crumbling under internal politics and anti-shogunate sentiment. Emperor Mutsuhito (1852-1912), posthumously renamed Emperor Meiji, was reinstalled as the head of state in the Meiji Restoration of 1868. With this monumental gesture, the feudal age came to a close and the radically transformative Meiji period began.

In the early Meiji years, real power was wielded by oligarchs from Tokyo, renamed (Tokyo literally means Eastern Capital) and officially made the new capital. There was a sense that Japan desperately needed to play technological, economic, and political catch-up with the West to resist colonization. Japanese scholars were sent West, and Western scholars were invited to Japan.

The ensuing changes were swift and dramatic. The first railway was built, linking Yokohama to Tokyo. A new constitution was drafted, based on Prussian and English models, and nationalized industries were formed, then sold to chosen entrepreneurs. This led to the rise of conglomerates known as *zaibatsu,* many of which still exist today, such as Mitsubishi, Sumitomo, and Mitsui.

Amid these developments, State Shinto replaced the Shinto-Buddhist mix that had been in favor for centuries, a symbolic return to a "purer" Japanese state, with the emperor at the top. The ban on Christianity was lifted and the rigid four-tier class system was disbanded. This led to massive upheaval for a few years, but ultimately all, save for the imperial class, were equal under the law, though women were neglected.

Japan also became militarily expansionist, annexing Korea after the Sino-Japanese War (1894-1895). Next came the Russo-Japanese War (1904-1905), which Japan also won. This victory elevated Japan's reputation as a force to be reckoned with, and won Taiwan and Liaoning peninsula as colonies.

By historical standards, the Meiji period ended with the death of the emperor on July 30, 1912. The decades that followed, leading up to the outbreak of World War II (1939-1945), were defined by Japan's increasing military and economic confidence, solidifying Japan's newfound status as the preeminent power in East Asia.

When World War I (1914-1918) broke out, Japan sided with the Allies. In 1914, Japan gave Germany an ultimatum: Remove all ships from the waters of Japan and China and let go of the port city of Tsingtao in China's northeast. Germany agreed, and by extension Japan was able to gain control over China, laying the groundwork for Japan to exploit China's vast pool of labor and natural resources.

World War II (1939-1945)

In the years leading up to the outbreak of World War II, Japanese forces became embroiled in a growing number of skirmishes in Manchuria. By 1937, Japan was engaged in all-out war with China, with imperial troops sacking Shanghai and advancing on Nanjing. Over several months, a staggering number of people were raped and murdered in what would become known as the Rape of Nanking. The total number of victims in the atrocity perpetuated by Japanese troops in Nanking is still debated by scholars, with some estimates as high as 400,000.

As war officially broke out in Europe, and France was defeated in 1939, Japan swooped in and overtook French Indo-China. When Japan came to blows with the U.S. over demands that Japan stop its advance through China, the U.S. halted oil exports to Japan. This led to Japan's devastating attack on Pearl Harbor (December 7, 1941), which officially brought the U.S. into the war. In 1942, an emboldened Japan proceeded to occupy a number of other countries in the region, including the Philippines, Dutch East Indies, Burma, Malaya, Hong Kong, and Guam, among others.

The turning point came in June 1942 at the Battle of Midway, in which the Allied forces managed to wipe out most of Japan's carrier fleet. After Midway, U.S. forces proceeded to route Japan's lines of support, advancing toward the Japanese archipelago itself. By 1944, U.S. planes were bombing Japanese cities, including devastating firebombing over Tokyo.

The war came to a dramatic, decisive end when the U.S. dropped atomic bombs on Hiroshima (August 6, 1945), and then Nagasaki (August 9, 1945). Both bombs killed tens of thousands in an instant, and hundreds of thousands more through subsequent fires and radioactive fallout. Faced with utter ruin, Emperor Hirohito formally surrendered on August 15, 1945, via radio. This was the first time that the Japanese people had ever heard the voice of the emperor, who until then had been believed to be a god. Along with surrendering, the emperor renounced his divine status.

Emperor Hirohito was loathed across Asia until his passing in 1989. To this day, the barbaric Battle of Nanking is a source of intense friction between the governments of Japan and China. In Korea, Japan's wartime use of Korean "comfort women," who were forced to serve as sex slaves, is still a source of ire.

Post-War Japan

After the war, the U.S. military occupied Japan and the imperial military and navy were completely disbanded. Under General Douglas MacArthur, a new postwar constitution was written and came into effect in 1947. The constitution created a parliamentary system that gave adults age 20 and over the right to vote. The document included a pacifism clause, under which Japan was forced to pledge not to have a military with the intent or capability of waging war. The emperor's status was brought that of a ceremonial figurehead. In 1951, Japan inked a peace treaty with the U.S. and other former foes. Japan was finally given independence and the U.S. withdrew, although a handful of U.S. military bases remain.

From the late 1940s to the early 1950s, Japan was heavily engaged in rebuilding. From the nuclear bombing of Hiroshima and Nagasaki to firebombing raids across the nation, much of urban Japan was in shambles. Many citizens were on the verge of starving.

American influence began to creep into everything from pop culture to the nation's diet—most notably, bread and wheat products—which led to an explosion of cheap, homegrown dishes like ramen, and the take-off of Japan's own music and pop cultural

sensibility. The 1950s were also the dawn of what would become known as an "economic miracle," with Japan's industry and economy astonishingly ascending to become the world's second-largest after the U.S. by the 1960s. Economic growth roared through the 1970s and early 1980s. At the peak of Japan's growth, people were splashing around ¥10,000 bills in the way most would spend a ¥1,000 note today.

The 1950s also saw major realignment in international relations, with Japan joining the United Nations in 1956. It went on to hold the 1964 summer Olympics in a radically transformed Tokyo and unveiled the first *shinkansen* (bullet train) that same year. In 1972, the Japanese prime minister went to China, normalizing relations, and Japan closed its embassy in Taiwan. A decade later, in 1982, Honda opened its first factory in the U.S.

Emperor Hirohito was never tried for war crimes; he passed away on January 7, 1989, marking the end of the Shōwa Era, which was the longest of any in Japan's long history.

Contemporary History

Rule passed on to Hirohito's son Akihito, giving birth to the Heisei (Peace Everywhere) Era. To the shock of diehard traditionalists, the emperor married a commoner. To top it off, there was no male heir for a long stretch, spurring talks of a female to ascending to the throne for the first time in millennia.

From around 1986 the economy reached "bubble" proportions, fueled by inflated real estate and stock prices, until it popped in 1992. Stagnation stretched from 1991 until 2010, a period that is often called the "lost decades."

Underscoring the downturn were a series of calamities, starting with the 6.9-magnitude Great Hanshin Earthquake that struck Kobe on January 17, 1995. This natural disaster was followed two months later by the heinous sarin nerve gas attack on the Tokyo subway, carried out by members of the Aum Shinrikyo doomsday cult on March 20. Another major disaster rocked the nation 16 years later on March 11, 2011, when the 9.0-magnitude

Great Tohoku earthquake and tsunami not only killed an estimated 18,000, but also triggered the ongoing meltdown at Fukushima's nuclear plants.

Japan's relations with its neighbors, namely, Korea and China, began to improve in the early 2000s, beginning with Prime Minister Koizumi Junichiro's visits to Seoul in 2001 and Pyongyang in 2002. Then Chinese Prime Minister Wen Jiabao addressed Japan's parliament and touted the two nations' strengthening ties in April 2007, by which point Shinzo Abe had succeeded Koizumi as Prime Minister.

To the dismay of peaceniks, the government approved a reinterpretation of the pacifist Article 9 of the postwar constitution in July 2014. This reinterpretation calls for allowing Japan to come to the aid of allies if attacked. This controversial shift in tone has ignited furious debates. Prime Minister Abe has declared that 2020 would be a deadline to finalize the revision of the article. At the time of writing, the revision was not yet finalized. Prime Minister Abe's decision to step down from power in September 2020 left the agenda hanging, although his replacement, Prime Minister Yoshihide Suga, has expressed his intention to clarify the status and existence of Japan's Self-Defense Forces. However, some commentary suggests he is less enthusiastic in the matter than his predecessor. A national poll conducted in June 2020 revealed that 69 percent of the population opposed the move to revise the article.

Emperor Akihito shocked the nation in August 2016 with a televised address in which he expressed his desire to abdicate: the first time this has been done in about two centuries. The Heisei era finally ended on April 30, 2019, with the dawn of the Reiwa period on May 1, 2019. On that day, Crown Prince Naruhito officially ascended to the throne to become the 126th emperor of Japan.

Naruhito has broken with tradition in a number of ways, having studied overseas at Oxford, married a commoner, and been surprisingly candid about the struggles that he and his wife, Empress Masako (nee Owada), have had with their attempts to have a male heir. Soul searching about the legacy of the turbulent Heisei era is ongoing. Only time will tell what the tone of the new era will be.

Government and Economy

ORGANIZATION

Japan is a constitutional monarchy with a parliamentary system. According to the postwar constitution, the emperor is head of state, but is expressly restricted from participating in politics. Pacifism is a key element of the constitution. Japan is banned from having atomic weaponry or maintaining a standing army, although it does maintain self-defense forces, which in recent years have gone on missions abroad but never engaged in combat.

The government is led by a prime minister who is elected from a majority ruling party of the government, known as the National Diet (legislative), plus Cabinet members (executive). The Diet is split between two parts, the House of Representatives, which is more powerful in practice, and the House of Councillors. Together, both houses draft and ratify all bills. The judiciary is headed by the Supreme Court, with three levels of lesser courts under it. A majority vote is needed to elect an official or pass a bill.

POLITICAL PARTIES

In theory, a range of parties occupy Japan's political spectrum. In practice, the Liberal Democratic Party (LDP), which leans toward the conservative edge of the spectrum, has ruled the roost more or less from the time it formed in 1955, with only brief interludes. At the time of writing, the Prime Minister is

Yoshihide Suga. He took the place of Shinzo Abe in September 2020, when Abe brought to an end his stint in power, which began in 2012, making him the longest-serving prime minister in Japanese history. Another party that wields significant influence is the Komeito. This small fringe party is a stalwart coalition party of the LDP, as well as the political arm of the mainstream religious group Soka Gakkai, to which many ascribe cultish undertones.

The main opposition party was once the Democratic Party (DP), which was virtually wiped out in the 2017 general elections, and splintered into two factions: the Constitutional Democratic Party of Japan (CDP) and the Democratic Party for the People (DPP). Further toward the fringe are the Japanese Communist Party (JCP) and the Social Democratic Party of Japan (SDPJ).

Scandals have swirled around former Prime Minister Abe; among them was his alleged donation to a nationalist elementary school, which was able to buy government land for a fraction of its price. Abe's image took another hit when his friend and former Administrative Vice Finance Minister Junichi Fukuda was accused of committing sexual harassment in 2018. Abe has also been revealed to be a member of Nippon Kaigi (Japan Conference), a right-wing group of lobbyists intent on restoring Japan to the supposed glory of its pre-World War II imperial days; that would mean trashing the postwar constitution as well as human rights, doing away with sexual equality and booting out foreigners.

ELECTIONS

Japan holds three types of elections: a general election for the House of Representatives (supposed to occur every four years, but snap elections are common); an election for the House of Councillors, held every three years; and local government elections held every four years.

Recent voter turnout has been lackluster. In the 2017 election for the House of Representatives, election turnout was around 54 percent, just above the nearly 53 percent turnout of 2014, which was the lowest in postwar Japanese history. Since 2018, citizens aged 18 and over have a legal right to vote. Despite the drops in voting age, young people remain largely unengaged, except for short-lived examples like the Students Emergency Action for Liberal Democracy (SEALDs), which led anti-LDP protests in 2015 and 2016.

In September 2020, Yoshihide Suga, the former prime minister Shinzo Abe's cabinet secretary, became Japan's 99th prime minister. Abe announced in August 2020 he would stepping down due to health issues after occupying the role for more than eight years over the course of two terms, the longest-serving PM in the country's history. PM Suga faces a daunting host of issues across the social, political, and economic spectrum, all exacerbated by the coronavirus pandemic. Time will tell how his tenure shapes up.

AGRICULTURE

Japan conjures images of rice fields and rolling tea plantations. Yet, very little of Japan's land is actually suitable for cultivation, and it's shrinking—from 15.4 percent of the country in 1961 to 11.5 percent in 2015. Terrace farming allows for maximum use of limited space. Japan has one of the highest levels of crop yield per area of any country in the world.

Due to a decline in rice consumption and wheat production facing a setback due to typhoon damage, the nation's food self sufficiency dropped to 38 percent in 2016, the lowest in 23 years. The government has set an ambitious target of raising that figure to 4 percent by 2025.

Japan's agriculture sector is highly subsidized, even coddled, and sheltered from outside influences. Japanese farmers always take precedence, even if it means consumers paying top yen. This is particularly true for rice, by far Japan's most protected crop, with tariff of up to 778 percent. Quotas have at least expanded through recent trade deals under the Trans-Pacific Partnership (TPP) and with the European Union.

INDUSTRY

Toyota. Honda. Sony. Nintendo. Nikon. Canon. Fuji. Toshiba. Panasonic. Softbank. Nippon Steel. Shiseido. Uniqlo. Muji. The list goes on. Japan is known globally as a juggernaut of industry and commerce, producing vehicles, electronics, ships, (bio)chemicals, machine components, tools, and increasingly softer items like snacks, cosmetics, fashion, lifestyle goods, and so much more. By far, Japan's main exports are vehicles, followed by machinery. As of 2012, Toyota was the largest vehicle producer in the world.

From the Meiji period through WWII, a cluster of *zaibatsu* exerted an outsized influence on the Japanese economy. The four biggest zaibatsu were still-surviving Mitsubishi, Mitsui, Sumitomo, and the disbanded Yasuda group. Sumitomo is the oldest of the lot, having been founded during the Edo period in 1615.

Following World War II, the *keiretsu* ("system" or "grouping of enterprises"), a new form of business grouping that is arranged horizontally and vertically, emerged. The members of these newer business groupings all own shares in each other's stock and are served by the same bank at the center, the idea being to reduce the risk of stock market turbulence and any potential takeover attempts. Former *zaibatsu* Mitsubishi, Mitsui, and Sumitomo have lived on as members of the "Big Six" *keiretsu,* along with Fuyo, Sanwa, and the Mizuho Financial Group.

When Sony released its Walkman in 1979, the product represented a major turning point for personal gadgets, ultimately leading to the ubiquitous MP3 player. While Japan has been knocked off its pedestal somewhat by electronics brands in South Korea and China, it remains a giant in the field.

DISTRIBUTION OF WEALTH

Japan has a robust middle class, with GDP per capita at $34,428.10 in 2017, making it 23rd globally. On paper, it is among the most equal economies in the world, but poverty does exist. Generally speaking, there is a widespread attitude among Japanese that it is virtually immoral for company executives to receive the kinds of exorbitant salaries that are commonplace in the West.

Under current laws, part-time workers do not have the same access to nationalized healthcare or to the pension system, leaving those not adequately plugged into the system in a precarious position. For those who do pay into the pension system, the returns are miniscule. For this reason, some elderly people can't afford to stop working, and many of them reside in rural areas, where resources are dwindling due to depopulation.

TOURISM

Before the COVID-19 pandemic struck, tourism had been a bright spot in Japan's otherwise sluggish economy in recent years. When the 2011 Tohoku earthquake and tsunami battered the country's economy and morale, inbound tourist numbers dipped to 6.2 million. When Tokyo won the bid to host the 2020 Summer Olympics, the government set about to change that trend, aiming to attract 20 million annual visitors by 2020. By 2015, the number of overseas visitors positively exploded, shooting up to 19.7 million. The figure just kept climbing, hitting 31.2 million in 2018 and 31.9 million in 2019.

With the initial target already long surpassed, the government had set its sights on a target of 40 million inbound visitors by 2020. This, unsurprisingly, has been completely derailed by the COVID-19 pandemic, with tourism numbers plummeting to essentially zero from the spring of 2020. At the time of writing, the government has made efforts to incentivize domestic travel in 2020 to try and breathe some life into the ravaged industry. It is also considering ways to slowly lift its entry ban on foreign tourists leading up to the rescheduled 2021 Olympics, but nothing is final.

This year's devastating blow to tourism aside, there's been a corresponding flood of positive press about Japan as a travel destination in recent years, from glossy travel magazine features to travel documentaries. It's appropriate that Mount Fuji itself, primordial symbol of the nation, and *washoku* (Japanese cuisine) as a whole were both bestowed heritage status by UNESCO in 2013.

The downside to this massive boost in soft power is that some places are now routinely clogged with camera-toters. Kyoto, which is visited by 25.9 percent of international visitors to Japan, is a prime example. From 2013 to 2017, Kyoto saw international tourist numbers surge by 279 percent. Tokyo (visited by 46.2 percent of inbound travelers) and Osaka (38.7 percent) have also been flooded by international tourists. With this surge comes a shortage of accommodation, especially during high season, and a high likelihood that you'll be gazing upon the more famous sights with a multitude of others. Prominent restaurants and shops are often overrun, too.

People and Culture

DEMOGRAPHY AND DIVERSITY

Japanese society is exceptionally homogenous, with less than 2 percent being foreign-born. The refrain of *ware ware Nihonjin* (we Japanese) is commonly heard, though the tone might be humble or proud. At the far-right end of the spectrum, it's downright xenophobic, underlying a pervasive belief that being 100 percent ethnically Japanese is a thing to be desired.

Zainichi

Chinese and Koreans have a long history of living on the fringes of Japanese society. The *Zainichi* Korean community took shape after World War II, when Koreans living on Japanese soil were stripped of their nationality, becoming essentially stateless. Many of these unfortunates caught up in geopolitical chaos were thrown out with the bathwater when Korea was divided into North and South, forcing people to choose sides. Even today, members of the *Zainichi* community are often treated as outcasts and second-class citizens. Until the 1980s, they were forced to relinquish their Korean names and adopt Japanese names to become Japanese. Although the majority have naturalized, discrimination remains entrenched.

Burakumin

The community that's faced, perhaps, the most discrimination in Japan, however, is the *burakumin* (hamlet people). Akin to India's "untouchables," this class comprises people employed in professions deemed "unclean," from sanitation staff to slaughterhouse workers, undertakers, and even executioners (the death penalty is still enforced in Japan). Today those of *burakumin* descent still face discrimination in everything from marriage to employment prospects, often being pushed into unskilled labor and low-income jobs. The government passed a law in 2016 that was meant to discourage discrimination against *burakumin*. Many have criticized the bill, however, saying it lacks teeth, because violators cannot be fined or imprisoned.

Immigration

Demographics and economics are forcing things to change. Japan's complex relationship with *gaikokujin* ("foreigners"; sometimes called by the more colloquial, slightly derogatory *gaijin*) is gradually evolving. A recent influx of Asian immigrants, hesitantly encouraged by the government due to labor shortages, is coming from Nepal, Vietnam, the Philippines, and beyond. This new wave of immigrants, which is often forced to speak Japanese at a higher level than many Westerners who come to work in Japan, is visible in the service industry, and many attend Japanese universities.

One trend indicating a change in Japan's

makeup is the rise of mixed-race and mixed nationality marriages. The growing number of *haafu* ("half" or mixed) people has become a hot topic in the media. At best, mixed Japanese are put on a pedestal for their "exotic" looks. At worst, mixed-birth Japanese are treated like foreigners in their own country. To put a human face on this social problem, check out the documentary *Hafu—The Mixed-Race Experience of Japan,* directed by Megumi Nishikura, a filmmaker born to a Japanese mother and American father.

Population Decline

Recent immigration trends may be the tip of a much larger iceberg. For the first time in recorded history, Japan's population began to decline in 2016, when the census counted 127.1 million, down 0.7 percent from 2010. Estimates vary, but some numbers peg Japan's projected population in 2060 at around 87 million. At that point, 40 percent of the population will be 65 and up. This has myriad implications, from a smaller workforce to increased reliance on imports, which will in turn limit the growth of GDP.

The rise in retirees will also strain the government's pension system. Japan has the second-largest debt load—and growing—of any nation. One government response has been to raise the retirement age from 60 to 65 for employees in the private sector. While there's still time to find solutions, these trends paint an unsettling picture.

RELIGION

There's a saying that most Japanese are born Shinto, are (sometimes) married Christian (aesthetically, anyway), and die Buddhist. In many ways, this truism is a good summary of the nation's spiritual life, which is highly pragmatic and involves a lot of mixing. Today, ask someone in Japan if they're religious and chances are they'll say they're not. Many will go as far as saying that Japan as a whole is not a very religious country. Yet, you won't have to look far to see throngs at Buddhist temples where they wave holy incense smoke around

their heads and bodies, or at Shinto shrines where they toss coins into wooden boxes, ring bells to summon the resident *kami* (god), bow, clap their hands, and pray.

In the distant past, Shinto and Buddhism, Japan's two key faiths, mingled freely. Shrines and temples were often combined into single complexes until the late 19th century when they were crudely ripped apart. This government action set the stage for what would eventually become the creation of State Shinto. During the years leading up to World War II, the state labeled Buddhism and Christianity, among others, as religions, but conspicuously left Shinto off the list, classifying the Japanese system of nature worship as more of a proto-philosophy than a religion. This status was nullified after the end of the second world war, when the emperor publicly broadcasted that he relinquished claims to divinity. From that point on, Shinto was classified as a religion like any other. Nonetheless, the notion that Shinto is the spiritual fabric of the Japanese nation, beyond any kind of religious faith, persists.

Shinto

Of the two primary religions that color life for the vast majority of Japanese—Buddhism and Shinto—Shinto can claim to be the indigenous faith. Literally translated as "way of the *kami*," Shinto is predicated on the belief that *kami* (deity, gods, or divine beings) live in all things. *Kami* are believed to inhabit natural objects, from rocks to mountains to trees.

Today, shrines remain busy as ever, due to the widely held belief that *kami* can be called upon for help through prayer, or through specific rituals that often involve music and dance. Before beseeching a *kami*, purification is key. You'll notice water basins with bamboo scoops near the entrance to any shrine. All visitors to shrines are expected to carry out a simple purification ritual at these *temizuya* (water ablution pavilions). Known as *jinja, jingū,* or sometimes simply bearing the suffix *-gū,* shrines are usually open-air, save for an inner sanctum or main hall, which can only be entered directly by priests. Shrines at the more elaborate end are approached via expansive paths lined by imposing *torii* gates. Meanwhile, small roadside structures are often fronted by a single, humble *torii* gate.

Famous shrines include Ise Jingū, Shinto's holiest spot; Izumo Taisha, the grand shrine in Shimane Prefecture; Miyajima's Itsukushima-jinja, famed for its "floating" *torii* gate; Tokyo's Meiji Jingū; and Nikkō's opulent Tōshō-gū. Most ordinary Japanese visit shrines for births, to celebrate various rites of passage, sometimes for traditional weddings, for purification rites, or to receive blessings for things ranging from new homes to business ventures and new cars.

Buddhism

By far the foreign faith with the most lasting impact on Japan has been Buddhism, specifically the Mahayana ("Great Vehicle") strain. First brought to the country from Korea in the 6th century, it's been both demonized and patronized by different governments. Buddhism saw major leaps in sophistication from the 7th through 9th centuries, largely benefitting from its deepening in China. It was essentially combined with Shinto for centuries, until the two were split in the late 19th century. Even

today, many Japanese may scratch their head if you ask them to explain the difference between a temple and a shrine.

Contrasting with Shinto's here-and-now focus on life—births, blessings, rites of passage, *matsuri* (festivals)—Buddhist temples are associated with the hereafter. Most Japanese ultimately have Buddhist funeral rites. Graveyards are often situated next to temples. It's also common, especially in rural Japan, to see a small Buddhist altar, usually kept in an elaborate wooden cabinet, known as a *butsudan*, prominently displayed in a family's living space. These miniature altars, which often contain statues of the Buddha or various deities and scrolls inscribed with sacred text, are meant to honor deceased loved ones.

Known as *(o)tera* or simply having the suffix *–ji*, temples range from towering wooden edifices housing giant bronze bells to small structures akin to local chapels in the West. Famous temples include Nara's massive Tōdai-ji; Kinkaku-ji, Kyoto's postcard-perfect gilt icon; as well as Kyoto's hillside complex Kiyomizu-dera; the mesmerizing cluster of temples and adjacent cemetery atop the mountain sanctuary of Kōya-san; and Hase-dera, known for its towering wooden statue

the famous "floating" *torii* gate of Itsukushima-jinja

of Kannon (goddess or bodhisattva of mercy) in Kamakura, a town littered with majestic temples.

The main Buddhist sects include Tendai, the nation's oldest, founded at Hiei-zan in Kyoto; the more esoteric Shingon, founded at Kōya-san; Jodo, or Pure Land, which emphasizes faith in the Buddha over ritual; Nichiren, named for its founder, the monk Nichiren, centered on habitually reciting sections of the Lotus Sutra; and the austere school of Zen, heavily weighted toward strict meditation and asceticism, and once prized by the samurai class.

Christianity

Christianity received a tepid greeting upon reaching Japanese shores. Arriving with Portuguese merchants and missionaries in Kyushu in 1542, it was initially tolerated, but in 1587, Toyotomi Hideyoshi banned missionary activity and had 26 people executed in Nagasaki. The faith was outright banned by Tokugawa Ieyasu following the Shimabara Rebellion (1637-1638), after which thousands of Christians went into hiding for more than two centuries until the arrival of Commodore Perry's fleets in 1853-1854. With the Meiji Restoration of 1868, freedom of religion was declared.

Today, Christianity has only a minor presence in Japan, representing about one percent of the population. Faith aside, Christian wedding ceremonies are big business even among unbelieving Japanese. Held at mock wedding chapels, these ceremonies are often officiated by token foreigners playing the role of priest or pastor. Moreover, Christian holidays like Christmas and Valentine's Day have gained a purely secular, commercial foothold.

New Religious Movements

Alongside the mainstays of Shinto and Buddhism, a number of *shinshukyō* (new religions) have mushroomed in Japan since the mid-19th century. These new faiths are often centered around a charismatic leader, and range from bona fide religions to downright cults. Given this reputation, *shinshukyō* have an unsavory reputation among much of the public.

The most famous new religion is Soka Gakkai, a strain of Nichiren Buddhism with a major presence overseas. The influential group has claimed celebrity members such as rock star Courtney Love, actor Orlando Bloom, and jazz legend Herbie Hancock. Many who have left the group have brought attention to its cultish tendencies, as well as the right-leaning agenda being pushed by its political arm, the Komeito party.

The most infamous is Aum Shinrikyō ("supreme truth," often shortened as "Aum"), formed in 1984 by Shoko Asahara (birth name: Chizuo Matsumoto), who was born into a poor family of tatami mat makers. Asahara, who was blind since childhood, claimed divinity. The doomsday cult he founded combines teachings from Buddhism, Hinduism, and apocalyptic Christian prophecies. Aum made global headlines on March 20, 1995, when a group of its members carried out the worst terrorist attack in Japanese history, using sarin nerve gas during morning rush hour on the Tokyo subway. The chemical attack killed 12 commuters and forced some 6,000 others to seek medical help. Asahara and six followers were executed by hanging in July 2018. Six other members remain on death row at the time of writing. At its peak, Aum had tens of thousands of members around the globe. Today, under the new name of Aleph, it still operates at the fringes, underground, with some estimates claiming its membership numbers 1,500 and growing.

LANGUAGE

As far as linguists can tell, Japanese is related to the Altaic language family, but is not officially included in it. Together with the Ryūkyū languages, Japanese falls under the standalone Japonic language family. It is grammatically similar to Korean, but has no other clear links. The Japanese language has a reputation as being difficult to learn. In truth, it's not too hard to get the hang of the highly systematic Japanese pronunciation system.

Although the Tokyo dialect is the official version of Japanese, dialects known as *ben* maintain a strong hold on many parts of the country. Moving to the margins—rural Tohoku or southern Kyushu, for example—the chance that something may be lost in translation, even among two Japanese, is very real.

The written language is a convoluted affair, requiring much effort to master. In any selection of Japanese text, you'll likely see a combination of three scripts: kanji, hiragana, and katakana. The most complicated aspect of learning to read and write Japanese is coming to grips with thousands of kanji, derived from Chinese characters that were adapted to fit the Japanese pronunciation system. Although there are around 50,000 kanji in use, Japanese are supposed to learn about 2,100 by the time they graduate from secondary school.

Making matters more complex, there is also hiragana, originally called *onnade* (women's script), a cursive script derived from Chinese characters originally created so that women could have the ability to write. By the 10th century, it was ubiquitous throughout Japanese society. The other syllabary, katakana, is also derived from Chinese characters. These boxy, angular characters are now primarily used to write foreign loanwords, onomatopoeia, and scientific terms, or to emphasize a given word or phrase.

LITERATURE
Traditional

With roots stretching back more than a millennium, Japan is rightly proud of its literary tradition. In the 8th century, a collection of orally transmitted ancient myths known as the *Kojiki* was written down, as well as a chronological account of Japan's origins, the *Nihonshiki*.

Some of Japan's earliest literature was written in verse. In the Asuka period (538-710), much of the poetry was being penned that would later be compiled in the *Manyoshu*

(Collection of 10,000 Leaves). This poetry anthology, which actually contains about 4,500 (not 10,000) poems, was put together around 760 CE, the first anthology in Japanese literature.

By the Heian period, women of the imperial court were writing groundbreaking works that would form the foundation of the novel. Specifically, *Genji Monogatari (The Tale of Genji)*, considered the world's first novel, was penned by Lady Murasaki Shikibu, the pen name of an unidentified courtesan who lived in the late 10th and early 11th centuries. Another notable example, *The Pillow Book* was written by courtesan Sei Shōnagon (966-1017 or 1025). Essentially a diary, the book offers an intimate glimpse of the intricacies and indulgences of Heian court life. In the 13th century, the dramatic recounting of the battles between the Heike and Genji clans was put down in written form in *Heike Monogatari (The Tale of the Heike)*. The saga tells the story of the Heike losing to the Genji clan in 1185. This classic story forms the basis of many theatrical performances.

By the Edo period, starting from 1682, writer Iharu Saikaku began scrawling the comedic tome *The Life of an Amorous Man*, based loosely on *The Tale of Genji*. Equally renowned for his poetic prowess, Saikaku worked in what was known as *haikai renga* (or *hokku*), or linked-verse, which laid the groundwork for haiku. Although the name "haiku" didn't stick until the 19th century, the form emerged as a response to Japan's older, more rarified forms. They're composed of three unrhymed lines, split into five, seven, and five syllables, respectively. More than anyone else, the wandering poet Matsuo Bashō immortalized Japan through his masterful haiku in the later 17th century, exploring themes related to nature and the transient beauty of life. Later haiku masters include Buson (1716-1784), Kobayashi Issa (1763-1828), Masaoka Shiki (1867-1902), Kawahigashi Hekigotō (1873-1937), and Takahama Kyoshi (1874-1959).

Modern

In the late-19th and early-20th centuries, forward-thinking scribes began to write short, naturalistic stories with noticeable Western influence. Among the first authors of "I-novels," as first-person accounts were called in Japan, was Natsume Sōseki (1867-1916). His most famous works include *Wagahai wa Neko de Aru (I Am a Cat)*, *Botchan*, and *Kokoro*.

The end of the 19th century and start of the 20th also saw the first reports by Western scribes who were eager to mystify their compatriots back home with tales and musings from the newly opened country. Writer Lafcadio Hearn (1850-1904), who was born to a Greek mother and an Irish father, was the first great Western interpreter of things Japanese. Moving from the U.S. where he worked as a journalist to Japan in the final decade of the 19th century, he lived in Matsue for 15 months. After marrying a woman from a local samurai family, he went on to write classics like *Glimpses of Unfamiliar Japan*. For an introduction, check out *Lafcadio Hearn's Japan: An Anthology of his Writings on the Country and Its People*.

Moving into the early 20th century, other giants from the early modern period include Jun'ichirō Tanizaki (*The Makioka Sisters*) and Ryunosuke Akutagawa (*In a Grove*). Yasunari Kawabata (*The Izu Dancer, The Scarlet Gang of Asakusa, Snow Country*) became the first Japanese writer to win the Nobel Prize in Literature in 1968.

Writers who were working in the mid- to late 20th century include the controversial Yukio Mishima (*Confessions of a Mask, The Sound of Waves, The Sailor Who Fell from Grace*), a raging nationalist who visited the Tokyo headquarters of the Japan Self-Defense Forces calling for them to restore the emperor to power and overturn the pacifist constitution. He summarily committed *seppuku*—ritual suicide samurai-style—on a balcony as shocked troops watched from below. A singular writer who came to prominence in the 1960s was Abe Kobo (*Woman in the Dunes*), a surrealist master who often draws comparisons to Franz Kafka. Oe Kenzaburo, whose work is interwoven with a deep strain of humanism, won the Nobel Prize in Literature in 1994.

Contemporary

Contemporary literature in Japan is dominated by the post-modern juggernaut Haruki Murakami (*The Wind-Up Bird Chronicle, Norwegian Wood*, the *1Q84* trilogy, and *Kafka on the Shore*). His whimsical world of talking frogs, psychic prostitutes, dancing gnomes, and scenarios wherein the supernatural and strange intrude onto the workaday in bizarre, often comical and even erotic, ways has amassed a giant following worldwide. A contemporary giant with a much darker gaze is Ryū Murakami (*Almost Transparent Blue* and *Coin Locker Babies*).

There are also a number of influential female writers making their mark in Japanese literature today. Some of the biggest include Yoko Ogawa (*The Diving Pool*); Banana Yoshimoto (*Kitchen*); Risa Wataya, who became the youngest author ever to win the Akutagawa Prize in 2003 for her novel *Keritai senaka;* Hitomi Kanehara (*Snakes and Earrings*), who shared the Akutagawa Prize in 2003 with Wataya; Sayaka Murata (*Convenience Store Woman*); and the novelist Mieko Kawakami (*Breasts and Eggs, Ms. Ice Sanwich*), a writer's writer whom Haruki Murakami has praised for her work, which spans many genres and is often written in her native Osaka dialect.

To dig deeper into contemporary literature, seeking out recent winners of the semi-annual Akutagawa Prize for up-and-coming writers is a good starting point. *Monkey Business* is an excellent anthology of short stories published annually.

Manga

Manga ("whimsical pictures"), as graphic novels or comics are known, accounts for nearly a quarter of all book sales in Japan. The popularity of this form of storytelling can loosely be traced back to the country's long history of caricature, seen in the woodblock prints known as *kiboyoshi*. The transition to manga came with the introduction of American comic books during the postwar occupation. In the ensuing decades, the form took on a life of its own. Topics range from high school antics to the psychedelically grotesque creations of visionary artists like Shintaro Kago to infamously graphic porn.

Popular manga series, some running for many years, can be collected in massive volumes known as *tankobon*. The sprawling, violent, cyberpunk masterpiece *Akira*, which explores dystopian themes in a post-apocalyptic future, was serialized from 1982 to 1990. *Ghost in the Shell*, a brilliant post-cyberpunk sci-fi franchise that explored the nature of consciousness through a counter-cyberterrorist organization active in the mid-21st century, ran from 1989 to 1990.

VISUAL ARTS

Japan has a vibrant arts tradition, ranging from ancient Buddhist sculptures and landscape paintings of austere beauty to cheeky postmodern sculpture. Among Japan's most notable arts are painting, calligraphy, woodblock prints (*ukiyo-e*), ceramics, lacquerware, *ikebana* (flower arrangement), and a bleeding-edge contemporary scene.

Concepts
WABI-SABI

Of the many concepts to be aware of when viewing traditional Japanese art, a recurring aesthetic ideal is *wabi-sabi*. A remarkably deep principle, it is the appreciation of things that are blemished, rustic, earthy, asymmetrical, incomplete, transient, authentic, and, in a word, imperfect. This sensibility is deeply Buddhist, in its positing that there is no inherent eternal essence to things, and further, that life is impermanent. *Wabi-sabi* took root in Japan in the 15th century, when tea ceremony founder Sen no Rikyū and others sought to rebel against the extravagant tastes of the time.

MA

Another key element that runs throug[h] much Japanese art is the spatial concept o[f] *ma* (negative space). This idea highlight[s] the importance of the empty space or ga[p] between objects in a scene. You'll notic[e] a preponderance of blank space in man[y] landscape paintings and calligraphy scrolls evoking the scene at hand all the more dra[-]matically. This sensibility also accounts fo[r] the visual power that a simple flower ar[-]rangement or scroll exudes in an otherwis[e] spare tatami-mat room.

Traditional Art Forms
PAINTING

Painting in Japan began with ink or blac[k] paint landscapes on *washi* paper, with dee[p] influence from China. From the Heian perio[d] on, paintings that would later be known a[s] *yamato-e* tended to depict court life. Startin[g] in the Muromachi period, the ruling clas[s] began to patronize the arts, and the Tosa an[d] Kano schools took shape.

The Tosa school shared characteristics with the older *yamato-e* tradition, with fine brushwork depicting elegant historic scenes. The Kano school, meanwhile, set the scene fo[r] marvelous sliding doors, folding screens, temple ceilings, and more, splashed with paintings of nature, and mythological creatures such as dragons and phoenixes.

Following the Edo period, contact with the West shook up Japanese painting, which split into the schools of *yōga* (Western-style painting) and *nihonga* (Japanese-style painting). *Nihonga* is distinct from older styles with its Western techniques, such as shading.

CALLIGRAPHY

Originally imported from China, *shodo* (calligraphy) is deeply entrenched in the Japanese psyche. Throughout Japan's history it's been prized by the upper classes and is essentially the first art form taught to elementary school students today, along with learning kanji and kana characters. There are a variety of styles, from the blocky, clear-cut *kaisho* to *gyosho* (running hand, informal, semi-cursive) to *sosho* (fully cursive, formal, illegible to all but the initiated).

UKIYO-E (WOODBLOCK PRINTS)

Ukiyo-e (pictures of the floating world) evoke the fleeting pleasures and realm of the senses. These paintings became synonymous with the pleasure quarters of the Edo period. As such, they depict almost crude scenes in vivid colors. Kabuki, sumo, geisha, as well as landscape scenes are figure prominently in *ukiyo-e*. This style inspired the Japonisme movement in the West, which attracted such luminaries as Van Gogh and Manet.

CERAMICS

Jomon-era pottery is some of the oldest fired clay in human history. What began as functional over time took on added layers of complexity and beauty starting with the advent of the tea ceremony in the 16th century. Potters often worked deep in the mountains, where ideal clay was readily available, and Koreans with superior techniques were often employed in the early days.

LACQUERWARE

Shikki (lacquerware), also referred to sometimes as *nurimono*, is a delicate art form done by applying layer upon layer of sap from the lacquer tree to an object, from Buddhist statues and painted panels to tea pots and bento lunch boxes. Once an object is lacquered, pigments are added—often black and red—and the object is sometimes spruced up with inlays of silver, gold, or pearls. Aside from being beautiful, lacquerware is durable; lacquered wood is known to endure millennia.

IKEBANA

Likely introduced along with Buddhism, the art of *ikebana* (flower arrangement) involves the careful placement of flowers, usually in a vase, in a way that uses the flowers as well as the empty space around them to elicit a certain aesthetic response. An arrangement can also carry symbolic meaning. Several distinct schools have evolved, each with its own philosophy.

Contemporary Artists

Much of contemporary Japanese art has a pop touch. Perhaps the biggest name overseas from Japan's contemporary scene is Yayoi Kusama. Active since the 1950s, Kusama has created a singular body of colorful, polka-dotted tentacle-like sculptures, geometric, dot-infused abstract paintings, and immersive installations. Takashi Murakami, whose work is heavily influenced by manga and anime, is another heavyweight. He launched a postmodern artistic movement known as Superflat, which seeks to "flatten" a range of artistic forms, from graphic art and animation to pop culture and the fine arts. For something uplifting, check out the color-drenched photographs of Ninagawa Mika. Also worth noting is provocateur Aida Makoto, who works in a variety of mediums and tackles the bugbears of Japanese history, dark facets of the nation's psyche, and more.

Plenty of biennales and triennales (art festivals held every other year, or every third year, respectively) highlight Japan's buzzing contemporary art scene. Some of the most prominent ones are the Echigo-Tsumari Art Triennale (www.echigo-tsumari.jp), the Setouchi Triennale (https://setouchi-artfest.jp), and the Yokohama Triennale (www.yokohamatriennale.jp).

MUSIC
Traditional

Japan's musical heritage can be traced back to a troupe of Korean musicians who made the journey to Japan in the mid-5th century, and the arrival of Buddhism a century later. With the religion came a range of instruments, including the three-stringed *shamisen*, akin to a banjo; the *biwa*, a four-stringed lute shaped like a pear with a short neck often played by wandering monks; the *koto*, a 13-stringed zither; a variety of wind instruments, from the *shakuhachi* (five-holed bamboo flute) to panpipes to the oboe; and a range of percussion instruments from gongs to taiko drums of various sizes. (If you enjoy a good percussion show, check out the infectious beats of Kodō, a Sado Island-based taiko troupe of world renown.)

Contemporary

Japan is a country of audiophiles and deeply informed connoisseurs. Today, Tokyo is one of the best cities in the world to listen to music, with its deep network of dedicated DJ bars, jazz joints, classical music cafés, and thumping techno clubs. Likewise, record stores overflowing with rare vinyl of all genres dot the city. This isn't limited to the capital, however, with thriving music scenes found in Osaka, Kyoto, and Kobe (known for jazz).

ENKA

More than a century ago, trailblazing Japanese singers began to blend Western and Japanese music into a new genre that would become *enka* (roughly meaning "speech song" or "performance song"). Still immensely popular today, *enka,* particularly from the postwar years, is the go-to genre for drunk salarymen at hostess bars where mama-sans know and can skillfully croon all the classics. The nostalgic themes of *enka* songs cover the usual range of topics that were routinely touched upon in Western music in the early to mid-20th century, such as heartbreak, homesickness, and loneliness.

Some of *enka's* leading lights include early pioneer Koga Masao, who composed a staggering 5,000 songs in his lifetime, and Misora Hibari, a legendary songstress who began performing from age nine. The younger cadre of *enka* stars includes "prince" Hikawa Kiyoshi and Jerome Charles White, Jr. (aka Jero), a young singer from Pittsburgh of Japanese and African American ancestry, known for performing in a hip-hop getup.

J-POP

Meanwhile, youth culture hatched J-Pop (Japanese pop), a bubblegum juggernaut of a genre popularized by Hamasaki Ayumi, the queen, and boy-band SMAP, helmed by all-purpose celebrity Kimura Takuya. When SMAP disbanded in 2016 it was a national event. Kyary Pamyu Pamyu is a recent J-Pop singer whose saccharine hit songs and colorful fashion sense helped popularize Harajuku's kawaii aesthetic.

Another spin on the J-Pop shtick is the idol group genre, with acts like AKB48, comprising nearly 140 young female members; and Arashi (Storm), a five-member boy band, atop the heap. Meanwhile, the irresistibly catchy kawaii metal group Babymetal is composed of three young female members clad in goth-Lolita style outfits, singing bubbly tunes to a metal soundtrack, energetically dancing and beaming lots of smiles.

DJS

Digging a bit deeper, DJ Krush is a renowned spinner of jazz, soul, and hip-hop instrumentals; while DJs like Ken Ishii and Satoshi Tomiie, and deeper still, Nobu, Wata Igarashi, So, Hiyoshi, Haruka, Takaaki Itoh, and so many more, provide the soundtrack of Japan's burgeoning techno, house, and underground music scenes.

THEATER
Noh

With elaborate wooden masks and enigmatic music, *Noh* is a highly refined and regimented form of theater that is downright baffling to the uninitiated. Truth be told, the arcane language (even for Japanese), long periods of inaction, and rarefied atmosphere of *Noh* are not everyone's cup of tea. But with patience, the world of *Noh* proves fascinating.

Noh plays take place on a beautiful, yet austere stage, traditionally made of *hinoki* (cypress) and backed by the painted image of a single pine tree. Much of the story in a *Noh* play is told through an arcane system of gestures, movements, and subtle expressions.

There are two main characters in a play: a *shite* (pronounced "she-te"), which is often a restless ghost; and a *waki,* which steers the *shite* to the climax of the play. The roots of *Noh,* Japan's oldest form of theater, are found in ancient Shinto dances. It is traditionally a male-dominated art, although women are gradually making headway in the modern age. Traditionally, female and otherworldly roles are depicted with the masks that Noh is known for, while male roles are done without masks. There are prominent families of *Noh* actors in Japan, well ensconced in society's upper rung.

There's an accompanying form of theater known as *kyōgen,* performed during the intermission of a *Noh* play. *Kyōgen* actors perform short humorous skits meant to both add context or comment on the happenings of the ongoing *Noh* play, but also to serve up a bit of comedic relief.

Kabuki

What began with former shrine maidens dancing would eventually become the theatrical art form known as kabuki (song-dance-skill). The pivotal moment came in 1603 when former shrine maiden Izu no Okuni and a number of other female dancers arrived in Kyoto and invoked the ire of the authorities with their suggestive performances. After several crackdowns, the government decreed that only adult men could play roles in kabuki. Hence the creation of the *onnagata* (men who play women's roles), a mainstay in the kabuki world to the present day.

Typical kabuki stories revolve around betrayal, samurai clashes, and dramatic suicides. Kabuki reached its apex in popularity during the Edo period, when it was voraciously patronized by the moneyed merchant class. Today, the style of theater is by far Japan's most recognizable overseas, thanks to its elaborate attire; heavily made-up actors; intense music known as *nagauta* (long song), played on *shamisen,* taiko drums, and flutes; and dramatic style of acting.

Bunraku

Bunraku is a style of theater that emerged in Osaka in the early part of the 17th century,

employing puppets that are up to half the size of a grown adult. Rather than being manipulated by strings, a *bunraku* puppet is controlled by three puppeteers. *Bunraku* grew out of the older tradition known as *jōruri,* in which minstrels told legends accompanied by a *shamisen* or *biwa.* The story being told, typically involving heroic feats and legends, is chanted by a narrator with exceptional vocal range who is separate from the puppeteers. Many of these tales were penned by Chikamatsu Monzaemon (1653-1724), regarded as Japan's very own Shakespeare.

The puppeteers, meanwhile move the puppets to reflect the story as it unfolds with a *shamisen* being strummed in the background. The result is a surprisingly lifelike performance with theatrical precision and flair that most would never imagine possible with puppets.

Contemporary Theater

Starting in the 1960s, coinciding the countercultural explosion taking place globally, new currents reached the theater scene, spawning the *angura* (underground) scene and, soon after, the "fringe theater" movement. Playwrights and thespians with an eye on creative revolution staged performances in public places, basements—anywhere they could.

Alongside those who favored overturning convention, there were some artists who connected with Japan's well of tradition. Director and playwright Kara Jūrō, for one, noted how kabuki was initially performed in the open-air. *Noh* was also. Other playwrights who were central to the *angura* period included Shūji Terayama; Abe Kōbō, the novelist of *Woman in the Dunes* fame; Shimizu Kunio; and Minoru Betsuyaku, famous for advancing "theater of the absurd" in Japan.

CINEMA

Japan's film history is peppered with illustrious names. As early as the 1930s, Japan was pumping out around 500 feature films annually.

Notable Directors

One of the earliest masters to emerge was Mizoguchi Kenji, who had been active since the 1930s but is best known for his 1954 samurai drama *Ugetsu Monogatari*.

The golden age of Japanese cinema was the 1950s. Akira Kurosawa (*Rashōmon, The Seven Samurai, Yōjimbō, Ran*) would cement his universally revered reputation during this time, along with Ozu Yasujirō (*Tokyo Story, An Autumn Afternoon*). The 1950s also saw the release of the original *Gojira (Godzilla)*.

The 1960s saw the birth of a new genre of *yakuza* (mafia) flicks, many of which were directed by Suzuki Seijun, whose unflappable depiction of slick violence would later inform directors from Quentin Tarantino to compatriot Kitano Takeshi. The classic Tora-san series of films, among Japan's highest grossing of all time, debuted in 1969 with *Otoko wa Tsurai yo (It's Tough Being a Man)*. The series ran until 1996, when the actor who played Kuruma Torajirō (Tora-san) passed away.

Kitano Takeshi (aka Beat Takeshi), a man of many talents from standup comedy to acting, made his first big directorial splash with *Hana-bi (Fireworks)* in 1997. Also gaining stature around this time were Japanese horror directors like Nakata Hideo *(Ring)* and Takashi Shimizu, who directed the *Ju-on (The Grudge)* series.

Takashi Miike, a director with a cult following whose splatter quotient would put Quentin Tarantino's most violent work to shame, also came to prominence in the mid-1990s and early 2000s, with films like the horror romance *Audition*, adapted from Ryū Murakami's novel of the same name; *yakuza* tale *Dead or Alive*; and hyper-violent *Ichi the Killer*, for which vomit bags were distributed ahead of its screening at film festivals in Toronto and Stockholm.

New voices have since emerged such as Kiyoshi Kurosawa, whose film *Tokyo Sonata* garnered praise at the Cannes Film Festival in 2008. Takita Yōjirō's *Departures* won the Oscar for best foreign-language film in 2009. And in 2013, Hirokazu Kore-eda snagged the 2013 Jury Prize in Cannes for his excellent *Like Father Like Son*.

Anime

Like manga, anime is geared toward all age groups and social classes in Japan. It covers everything from history to love stories, to surreal fantasy, sci-fi, and entertainment for kids. In many ways, anime achieved liftoff in the 1960s with the legendary Tezuka Osamu's *Astro Boy* television series. Sharing the airwaves with *Astro Boy* were a host of other hit shows with names like *Space Battleship Yamato* and *Battle of the Planets* were beginning to cast a spell over Japan's youth.

Other developments in the early days of anime included some of Toei's big releases, beginning with *Hakujaden (Tale of the White Panda)* in 1958. The Toei animated flick *Little Norse Prince* was directed by the late Takahata Isao (1935-2018), who would form Studio Ghibli with the genius director Hayao Miyazaki in 1985.

The anime film adaptations of *Akira*, directed by Ōtomo Katsuhiro, and *Ghost in the Shell*, directed by Oshii Mamoru, are both mind-expanding explorations of metaphysical and post-apocalyptic themes, interlaced with plenty of bizarre characters, psychedelic imagery, and philosophical speculation. The late anime master Kon Satoshi (1963-2010) also produced a challenging and unique body of work in his short life.

Looming above all these names, however, is anime maestro Hayao Miyazaki, the oft-grinning, bespectacled genius and cofounder of Studio Ghibli. Although he'd been churning out brilliant films since the 1980s, Miyazaki finally broke onto the international stage by winning the Oscar for best animated feature in 2001 for his masterpiece *Spirited Away*. From his deep oeuvre, some of the other standouts include *Princess Mononoke, My Neighbor Totoro*, and more recently, *The Wind Rises*, which has stoked controversy over the implications of its antiwar tone.

A director who has achieved wild success in recent years and who has been touted as "the new Hayao Miyazaki" is Makoto Shinkai, whose smash-hit romantic fantasy *Your Name* remains the third-highest grossing anime film of all time.

DANCE
Traditional

Buyō is the umbrella term for all forms of traditional Japanese dance. It extends from the dances performed by geisha to the theatrical movements of kabuki and *Noh*. All forms of *buyō* ultimately stem from ancient folk and Shinto dances. The movements of traditional Japanese dance tend to be slow, graceful, and contained. This is largely due to the fact that they were traditionally performed while wearing a kimono, which restricts movement. All told, there are a few hundred different varieties of *buyō* today.

Contemporary

Japan's contemporary dance scene exists on a spectrum between the gleeful, all-female musical extravaganza known as the Takarazuka Revue and the evocative, grotesque form of dance known as *butō*, which emerged from the urge to discard the stringent rules found in most forms of traditional Japanese dance, while tapping into something more ancient and primal. Visionary dancer Hijikata Tatsumi performed the first *butō* dance in 1959. A *butō* dancer is in an intensely vulnerable state, usually naked or close to it. Unsurprisingly, *butō* has been considered scandalous by many. This has only inspired many dancers to push even harder against boundaries and discover more cracks in the edifice of society.

Essentials

Transportation

GETTING THERE
From North America

Tokyo's Narita International Airport (NRT) and Haneda Airport (HND) are linked by direct flights to a number of North American cities. Some carriers also fly direct to Osaka's Kansai International Airport (KIX). Delta also offers limited direct flights to Nagoya's Chubu Centrair International Airport (NGO).

Generally speaking, prices vary widely, with flights from the West Coast of North America being slightly cheaper than those from the

Getting to Japan from North America

Departure Airport	Arrival Airport	Carriers
New York City (JFK)	Tokyo (NRT)	Delta Air Lines
Detroit (DTW)	Tokyo (HND)	United Airlines
Chicago (ORD)		American Airlines
Los Angeles (LAX)		Air Canada
San Francisco (SFO)		All Nippon Airways
Honolulu (HNL)		Japan Airlines
Vancouver (YVR)		
Toronto (YYZ)		
Detroit (DTW)	Nagoya (NGO)	Delta Air Lines
Honolulu (HNL)		Japan Airlines

East. Although less convenient in terms of access to Tokyo proper, Narita is usually cheaper than Haneda. Deals can be found if you're willing to endure layovers. Moreover, avoiding peak season and buying as far in advance as possible (aim for three months or more) will naturally drive fares down. To fly economy from anywhere in North America, have a rough budget in mind of about $1,000 US, give or take. A stopover can bring prices down to as low as $500 US during off-season from some airports.

From Europe

Direct flights to and from the United Kingdom are getting cheaper. Carriers offering direct flights from London Heathrow (LHR) include British Airways (to NRT and HND), All Nippon Airways (to HND), and Japan Airlines (to HND). British Airways now flies direct to Osaka's KIX, too. It's generally cheaper to transfer in another European or Asian city en route.

Various carriers provide direct flights to Japan (mostly NRT and HND, but also sometimes KIX and NGO) from many European cities, including: Amsterdam (AMS), Brussels (BRU), Paris (CDG), Munich (MUC), Frankfurt (FRA), Zurich (ZRH), Vienna (VIE), Copenhagen (CPH), Helsinki (HEL), Madrid (MAD), Rome (FCO), Milan (MXP), Warsaw (WAW), and Moscow (SVO and DME).

Broadly speaking, if you're flying from Europe the budget is in the same ballpark as what it is from North America. Plan on spending roughly €850 (£750) for an economy class seat. A stopover will bring that figure down, and if you book several months in advance—three months or more is a good benchmark—you may land a bargain.

From Australia and New Zealand

It's possible to fly direct to Tokyo from Sydney, Melbourne, Perth, Brisbane, and Cairns in Australia, while most (but not all) flights from New Zealand first route through Australia, usually Sydney. Most of these flights land in NRT, although some do service HND. Carriers servicing these routes include Japan Airlines, All Nippon Airways, Qantas, and budget Japanese airline Jetstar, in addition to Air New Zealand from Auckland. There are limited direct flights to Osaka's KIX from Sydney, Cairns, and Auckland.

A stopover in another Asian city will likely make a flight significantly cheaper, but will

Coronavirus in Japan

At the time of writing in October 2020, Japan was moderately impacted by the effects of the coronavirus, but the situation was constantly evolving. The country had so far been relatively lucky, with a comparatively low death rate that has left experts scratching their heads. For perspective, as of early July 2020, coronavirus deaths had not yet even hit 1,000 in Japan, while the number soared over 100,000 in the United States.

Japan never implemented a true lockdown: A state of emergency was declared in Tokyo and six other more affected prefectures on April 7, expanded nationwide on April 15, with the government "requesting" citizens to minimize trips outside and for bars and restaurants to close. The government also encouraged avoiding the "three Cs": closed, poorly ventilated spaces; crowded public places; and close contact when people cough, sneeze, or speak. The state of emergency was lifted in late May, and life has returned to something resembling normal. Businesses that may have closed have largely reopened, with some voluntarily implementing a policy of socially distancing. Masks, already a regular feature in Japan during cold and flu season, remain ubiquitous, and products like hand sanitizer are often placed at shop entrances and have flown off the shelves.

At the time of writing, traveling within Japan was freely permitted. Overseas tourists were barred from entering the country starting from April. Starting September 1, 2020, legal foreign residents were allowed to re-enter the country after controversially being stuck for months if they happened to be outside Japan when the border closed. Starting October 1, 2020, the government lowered entry restrictions for business travelers and those with visas of more than three months. A slew of rules and conditions that varied by country were put in place, following a 4-tier rating system (4 being most dangerous). Travelers are required to take a coronavirus test upon landing, and then quarantine for 14 days in a designated location.

These conditions and rules will inevitably have changed as the situation evolves. When planning your own trip, check the JNTO's coronavirus page (www.japan.travel/en/coronavirus) for an up-to-date breakdown on travel restrictions and entry requirements by country. If anything feels unclear, inquire with your local embassy or consulate. Better safe than sorry.

Now more than ever, Moon encourages its readers to be courteous and ethical in their travel. We ask travelers to be respectful to residents, and mindful of the evolving situation in their chosen destination when planning their trip.

NOTE ON THE OLYMPICS

Perhaps the most dramatic example of the effect of the coronavirus on Japan has been the gut-wrenching decision to postpone the Olympics, which are tentatively now scheduled to take place in Tokyo in the summer of 2021. At the time of writing, it was unknown if the event would be open to foreign spectators.

BEFORE YOU GO

· Check websites and resources (listed below) for **local restrictions** and the **overall health status** of the destination and your point of origin. If you're traveling to or from a COVID-19 hotspot, you may want to reconsider your trip.

· If possible, take a **coronavirus test** with enough time to receive your results before your departure. Some destinations may require a negative test result before arrival, along with other tests and potentially a self-quarantine period, once you've arrived. Check local requirements and factor these into your plans.

- If you plan to fly, check with your airline and the Japanese Ministry of Health, Labour and Welfare (tel. 03/3595-2176; www.mhlw.go.jp/english) for updated **travel requirements.** Some airlines may be taking more safety precautions than others, such as limited occupancy; check their websites for more information before buying your ticket, and consider a very early or very late flight, to limit exposure. Flights may be more infrequent, with increased cancellations.

- Check the website of any museums and other venues you wish to patronize to confirm that they're open, if their hours have been adjusted, and to learn about any specific visitation requirements, such as **mandatory reservations** or **limited occupancy.**

- Pack **hand sanitizer,** a **thermometer,** and plenty of **face masks.**

- **Assess the risk** of entering crowded spaces, joining tours, and taking public transit.

- Expect **general disruptions.** Events may be postponed or cancelled, and some tours and venues may require reservations, enforce limits on the number of guests, be operating during different hours than the ones listed, or be closed entirely.

RESOURCES

- Japan's **Cabinet Secretariat** (https://corona.go.jp/en) supplies daily case numbers, breakdowns of policies and recommended safety measures, and coronavirus-related links.

- The **Japan National Tourism Organization** (JNTO; www.japan.travel/en/coronavirus) has provided an extensive breakdown of case numbers, travel and safety tips, information on getting 24/7 medical assistance in foreign languages, and an up-to-date breakdown of screening and quarantine procedures. The JNTO also runs a 24/7 coronavirus-related hotline in English (tel. 050/3816-2787).

- The **Japan Times** (www.japantimes.co.jp/liveblogs/news/coronavirus-outbreak-updates) provides a continuously updated roundup of coronavirus-related news stories.

- The **Tokyo Metropolitan Government** has created a chart (https://japan2.usembassy. gov/pdfs/covid19-what-to-do-e.pdf) that shows just what to do if you think you may have contracted coronavirus.

- **Time Out Tokyo** provides a useful online guide to staying safe in Tokyo (www.timeout.com/ tokyo/things-to-do/how-to-go-out-safely-in-tokyo-plus-social-distancing-rules-explained). They also maintain an archive of articles on COVID-related news (www.timeout.com/tokyo/ things-to-do/live-updates-the-covid-19-coronavirus-situation-in-tokyo-and-japan-right-now), as well as a continuously updated list of businesses that were temporarily closed, but have since reopened (www.timeout.com/tokyo/things-to-do/attractions-in-tokyo-and-japan-that-are-closed-due-to-covid-19-coronavirus).

- **Osaka Prefecture** (www.pref.osaka.lg.jp.e.agb.hp.transer.com/iryo/osakakansensho/ corona.html), **Kobe City** (www.city.kobe.lg.jp/a74716/kenko/coronavirus_en.html), and **Kyoto Prefecture** (www.pref.kyoto.jp/kokusai/coronavirus_update.html) all maintain a coronavirus page.

tack on quite a bit of travel time. Rock-bottom prices can occasionally be snagged through budget carriers like Jetstar or AirAsia, but don't expect a plush ride. Again, try to book tickets three or more months in advance to avoid paying top dollar.

Given that Japan is about the same distance from Australia and New Zealand as it is from North America or Europe, the budget is similar. Plan on paying about A$1,400 (NZ$1,500) for an economy class seat.

South Africa

There are no direct flights between South Africa and Japan, making for a very long journey. Major Middle Eastern carriers do fly to Tokyo from South Africa's major airports, Johannesburg (JNB) and, to a lesser extent, Cape Town (CPT). These carriers include Emirates, requiring an interchange in Dubai; Etihad, with a layover in Abu Dhabi; and Qatar Airways, with a transfer at Doha. It's also possible to fly from South Africa to Tokyo on Singapore Airlines via Singapore, Cathay Pacific via Hong Kong, or British Airways via London.

As with booking flights from other regions, try to buy tickets three or more months in advance to avoid price gouging. Expect to pay similar to the other regions described above: R150,000 for an economy seat. Tickets from Cape Town tend to be slightly more expensive than from Johannesburg.

GETTING AROUND

At the time of writing, in October 2020, public transportation across the country was mostly unaffected by coronavirus-related restrictions. Many long-distance bus routes and *shinkansen* services were temporarily shut down, but reopened from June 1.

Train

Japan's rail network is world-famous for its cleanliness, safety, and punctuality. It's extensive, linking northernmost Hokkaido to far-flung southern Kyushu. It can be daunting to get the hang of all the transfers and ticket deals, but thankfully, it's possible to catch on fast.

The main train operator nationwide is **Japan Railways** (JR), which has numerous regional branches. There is also a slew of private operators—**Odakyu, Tokyū, Hankyū, Kintetsu,** and more—each with their own fare and ticketing system. Regardless of the train network you're on, larger stations will have their own ticket office. Buying tickets at these offices is often the way to go if the machines feel too daunting (though most ticketing machines can be switched to English). The staff at ticket counters are generally experienced with helping overseas travelers. However you buy it, once you've got your ticket in hand, simply put it in the slot at the ticket gate, and then pick it back up after passing through. Hold on to your ticket for the duration of the trip, as you'll need to insert it again at the ticket gate of your destination. If you happen to lose a ticket, there's a chance you may have to pay for your journey again on arrival.

Another factor of train travel in Japan is speed: Some routes are local, and others are express or limited express train (slightly faster), while the *shinkansen* (bullet trains that reach up to 30kmph/199 mph) is the way to go for long-haul trips. To save on fare, the **Japan Rail Pass** is a good idea if you plan to travel extensively over long distances. A number of regional passes are also sold.

If all this sounds intimidating, don't fret. Staff at train stations are happy to help and comfortable with overseas travelers. Just be ready to bridge the communication gap with a smile and a sense of humor.

SHINKANSEN

Shinkansen run on an altogether different rail network than regular trains. There are two classes: **ordinary** (already a pleasant experience) and the pricier **Green Car,** akin to first class. Most of the cars of a *shinkansen* have reserved seats, which can be secured either at a ticket office or a ticket vending machine. Even if you have a Japan Rail Pass, you'll still need

The Almighty IC Card

Your first order of business on entering a Japanese train station for the first time should be to get a rechargeable smart card, known as an IC card in Japanese. These touch-cards are available from select vending machines at a station's ticketing counter. If you have an IC card, you can recharge it any time you are running low on funds at one of the IC card vending machines at any station.

Each region has its own, with **Suica** and **PASMO** being the variety sold in the JR East network, which includes Tokyo. The JR West network, including the Kansai region, issues the **ICOCA** card, but the cards are largely swappable, no matter where in Japan they are purchased. The **Suica** card, available at stations in the JR East network, is perhaps the most flexible.

IC cards will allow you to travel on local, rapid, and express trains, as well as subway networks in most cities. For *shinkansen* (bullet train) or limited express train journeys, you'll need to buy a ticket in advance or have the **JR Rail Pass.** The added bonus of having an IC card is that you can use it at vending machines inside stations and to make purchases at many convenience stores, whether inside a station or deep in a residential area.

to stop by the ticket office if you want to sit in a reserved seat. For an unreserved car, you can simply queue and board with the JR pass in hand. Reserved seats are recommended as unreserved cars often fill up completely.

Note that *shinkansen* often depart and arrive from entirely different areas within a station and sometimes from altogether separate stations. If *shinkansen* trains run through the same station also serviced by local trains, you'll likely have to go through another set of gates to enter the *shinkansen* area. Allow at least 10 minutes to get to get to the correct platform and find the correct car.

One more point to be aware of is that the ticketing system for *shinkansen*, as well as for limited express (see below), means that you will have two tickets instead of one. There's a *joshaken* (base fare ticket), which covers the journey itself, and the *tokkyūken* (special fare ticket), which allows you to travel aboard one of the more expensive, high-speed trains. Counterintuitively, you'll need to simultaneously put both tickets into the ticket machine as you enter the gate.

LOCAL, RAPID, EXPRESS, AND LIMITED EXPRESS TRAINS

There are several different categories of local trains. Local (普通, *futsū / kaku-eki-teisha*), trains are the most common. Local trains are the slowest and make the most stops. Rapid

(快速, *kaisoku*) trains skip some stations, while express (急行, *kyūkō*) trains generally skip even more, thus speeding up the journey. There's no extra expense to hop on either a rapid or express train.

To ride a limited express (特急, *tokkyū*) train, fares do jump. Moreover, these trains often have both unreserved and reserved seating, akin to the *shinkansen*, and carry a surcharge that can be bought on board or at the ticket office in advance. Like the *shinkansen*, limited express trains also require an additional ticket—one to cover the journey, the other to cover the added expense of riding in an extra-speedy train. Insert both into the machine at the ticket gate as you enter, and hold on to both tickets for the duration of your journey.

JAPAN RAIL PASS

The Japan Rail Pass (JR Pass; www.japan-railpass.net) can be purchased for either one, two, or three weeks, during which pass holders are able to travel freely on all JR lines, including *shinkansen*, as well as local buses in the JR network nationwide and the JR-West ferry that runs to Miyajima. Simply flash the pass to the staff each time you pass through the ticket gates at any JR station, bus station, or ferry terminal in the case of Miyajima, and hop aboard.

There are two grades available for the

pass: regular and Green Car (first class). For the ordinary seat level, one week costs ¥29,650 per pass, two weeks costs ¥47,250, and three weeks will set you back ¥60,450. Upgrading to the Green Car will cost ¥39,600 for one week, ¥64,120 for two weeks, and ¥83,390 for three weeks. For children ages 6-11, rates are lower, while children under six can ride for free as long as they are accompanied by an adult with a JR Pass and no other passenger needs their seat.

Note that the fastest categories of *shinkansen*, known as Nozomi and Mizuho, are not covered by the pass. Another thing to be aware of is that even with the JR Pass, you'll still need to go to the ticket office to get a ticket for the reserved seat.

For many travelers, the pass is a no-brainer. Even a Tokyo-Kyoto round-trip on the *shinkansen* will justify the seven-day pass for most travelers after taking into account the additional travel done on JR lines within either city. That said, the JR Pass isn't for everyone. Consider whether you will be doing enough travel to justify the cost of the pass. If you're traveling on a sumptuous budget, it's doubtful that the savings made with a JR Pass will feel worthwhile in exchange for the hassle of having to take on the limitations of the pass. If money is no object, you'll likely be happier booking transportation when and in what form you desire it.

If you'd like to book a JR Pass, you must be a **foreign traveler** entering Japan on a "temporary visitor" tourist visa. After you've bought a pass online and chosen a starting date for the pass, you'll receive a voucher at your home address, which can be exchanged for a proper pass at selected train station offices once you've arrived in Japan.

The JR Pass can only be purchased **outside Japan**—you cannot purchase it once you are in country. Also, you have to exchange the purchase voucher for the actual pass within three months of purchasing the voucher, so don't buy it too early.

INTERNET RESOURCES

There are some very useful sites to be aware of when it comes to train travel in Japan. **HyperDia** (www.hyperdia.com) provides step-by-step route information. All you do need to do is input the station you're leaving from and where you're going. You can also adjust the date and time, selected for either departure or arrival. **Jorudan** (https://world.jorudan.co.jp/mln/en) does the same thing. When all else fails, **Google Maps** (www.google.com/maps) is not only a trusty way to navigate a city street by street, but also allows you to compare how long it would take to make a journey by train, taxi, or on foot.

Bus

Traveling by bus is less comfortable and slower than train or plane, but it scores points for value, and sometimes it's the only option for reaching remote areas. Most towns and cities have their own local bus networks, which can come in handy in some places, but in others, it's quicker to simply walk or pay a bit more and take a taxi.

For longer journeys, highway buses operate during both daytime and nighttime, often arriving and departing near major train stations. Main bus terminals are sometimes set apart in slightly inconvenient spots, so be sure you know where your bus terminal is before a major journey.

There are eight regional variants of **JR Bus**. Some JR Bus routes can be booked at the website of **Japan Expressway Bus Net** (www.kousokubus.net/JpnBus/en). **Willer Express** (http://willerexpress.com/en) is another major highway bus operator, which offers some good deals. It's one of the few highway bus operators in Japan that allows for relatively easy online reservations in English. Willer also offers the **Japan Bus Pass** (http://willerexpress.com/st/3/en/pc/buspass), which covers all long-distance journeys for either three days (¥10,200 Mon.-Thurs., ¥12,800 all days), five days (¥12,800 Mon.-Thurs., ¥15,300 all days), or seven days (¥15,300 Mon.-Thurs.).

A number of other regional discount bus

Addresses in Japan

Addresses in Japan can be baffling to the uninitiated. Addresses in Japan can be baffling to the uninitiated. General elements include the **postal symbol (〒)** and **postal code, prefecture, municipality, subarea,** and three numbers separated by dashes, with the name of the business, name of the resident and so on underneath all of that. The piece that's notably missing is a street name. Though some major thoroughfares do have names, such as Tokyo's Meiji and Yasukuni-dōri, most streets are unnamed.

Instead, when written in Japanese, addresses are organized by **district, block,** and **building,** indicated by the three numbers following the prefecture and municipality. Compounding the confusion, districts and blocks tend to be numbered in a relatively logical geographic progression, while the buildings that make up the blocks aren't numbered according to their physical placement in the block but rather according to when they were built, with the oldest building on a given block being numbered 1, and so on.

As an example, take the Nezu Museum's address: 6-5-1 Minami-Aoyama, Minato-ku, Tokyo. Minato-ku is the ward that Minami-Aoyama is a part of, and Tokyo is the prefecture. The "6" refers to district number 6 of the area known as Minami-Aoyama, the "5" refers to the block number within that district, and the "1" is the building number.

If you're a bit confused, you're not alone. Even taxi drivers end up scratching their heads and doing a few extra laps around an area before finding some destinations—mercifully often stopping the taxi meter at the point where they lose their way so as not to hike up the fare. It helps immensely to have a **printed map** of where you're going, a clear set of directions based on **landmarks,** or best yet, a data-only SIM card so you can simply punch an address into **Google Maps,** which will get you where you're trying to go.

passes are available, including: the **Hokkaido Budget Bus Pass** (www.budget-buspass.com/purchase), the **Tohoku Highway Bus Ticket** (www.tohokukanko.jp/en/transport/detail_1001089.html), the **Shoryudo Highway Bus Ticket** (www.meitetsu.co.jp/eng/ticket-info/shoryudo.html), covering much of Central Honshu, and the Kyushu-centric **SunQ Pass** (www.sunqpass.jp).

It's recommended to reserve seats ahead for any long journey, particularly if it's on a popular route. Unfortunately, many bus reservation websites are only usable in Japanese. A few exceptions to this rule include the website of Willer (see above), and the websites of **Japan Bus Lines** (http://japanbuslines.com/en).

For more information on the various types of buses and how to make them work for you, visit the website of the **Nihon Bus Association** (www.bus.or.jp/en).

Car

Given Japan's fantastic rail network, renting a car can be downright inconvenient in urban areas, where you'll be contending with traffic, lots of narrow one-way streets, and extortionate rates for parking, which is often hard to find.

If you're traveling in a part of the country where having your own wheels makes sense, roads are well-paved and maintained, and most drivers are conscientious and follow traffic laws, speed limits aside. Driving is on the **left** side of the road like it is in the UK, which may be challenging for drivers from the United States and Canada. Traffic laws are essentially the same as what you'd expect anywhere else. If you're on a motorcycle, you'll need a helmet.

Drivers from most countries need an **International Driving Permit** (IDP). Apply for it in advance in your home country or the country of your driver's license.

SPEED LIMITS

The average speed limit hovers around 30 kilometers (19 miles) per hour on smaller streets, 40 kilometers (25 miles) per hour on medium-sized streets in cities, 80-100 kilometers (50-62 miles) per hour on expressways, and 50-60 kilometers (31-37 miles) per hour elsewhere. Signage is usually in Japanese and *romaji* (Roman alphabet). This comes in handy when navigating the country's extensive expressway network. Tolls are often hefty.

GAS

Gas stations, known as *gasorin sutando* ("gasoline stands"), are plentiful in most towns and at service areas (rest stops), dotting all expressways. They are often full-service, although self-service is increasingly common, and they may close at night. Gas prices have ebbed and flowed in recent years, but tend to hover around ¥140 per liter (0.26 gallon). Credit cards (*kurejitto kaado*) and cash (*genkin*) are both accepted. To keep matters simple, just request *mantan* ("full tank") when pulling into a full-service station. Note that rental car companies require all cars to be brought back with the tank full.

CAR RENTALS

Typically, car rentals start from ¥5,000 per day, plus daily insurance fees. Some car rental agencies give discounts for multiday rentals. Many rental cars from major agencies have navigation systems with English-language functionality. Having this set up before you hit the road will drastically simplify the task of navigating. Politely ask the car rental staff to switch the GPS system to English before you leave the agency—you'll be grateful you did later. If there's no English option for a given car's GPS, don't panic. The easiest solution is to punch in the phone number of your destination.

Japan's biggest car rental outlets include **Toyota Rent-A-Car** (https://rent.toyota. co.jp), **Nippon Rentacar** (www.nipponrentacar.co.jp), **Nissan Rent-A-Car** (https://nissan-rentacar.com), **Orix Rent-A-Car** (https://car.orix.co.jp), **Ekiren** (www.ekiren. co.jp), and **Times Car Rental** (https://rental. timescar.jp).

Although most of these agencies have some kind of English-language reservation system, **Japan Experience** (www.japan-experience. com/car-rental-japan) assists foreign travelers with making car rental reservations. **Rental Cars** (www.rentalcars.com) and **ToCoo! Travel** (www2.tocoo.jp/en) also offer English support with car rentals.

Ferry

Although Japan's main islands are linked by bridges and undersea tunnels, ferry is the only option for reaching many islands in the Inland Sea. You can usually buy tickets through individual ferry companies or through major travel agencies. Note that the water on some ferry routes can be notoriously choppy, so it pays to ask about this if you're prone to sea sickness.

Visas and Officialdom

PASSPORTS AND VISAS

Travelers from 68 countries, including the United States, Canada, UK, Australia, and New Zealand, as well as most European nations, receive short-term visas on arrival in Japan. The majority of these visas are for 90 days, with extensions of up to 90 days possible for a handful of countries, including the UK, Germany, and Switzerland, with a trip to the immigration office required. For a full list of visa-exempt nations, visit www.mofa go.jp/j_info/visit/visa/short/novisa.html Note that South African nationals must apply for a tourist visa at their nearest embassy or consulate.

Before traveling to Japan, check your passport's expiration date. It must be valid for at least six months from the date of your flight and entry into the country. Further, an onward ticket is required to enter the country.

Customs

Upon arriving in Japan, you'll be asked to fill out a customs declaration form. For this, have the address and phone number of where you plan to stay ready at hand. Simply writing the name of a city where you'll be staying won't be accepted.

A few official limitations to be aware of at customs: up to three 760-mililiter bottles of alcoholic beverages; 400 cigarettes, regardless of origin; all goods meant for personal use besides these two items may not exceed ¥200,000 in total value; a maximum amount of cash or travelers checks on hand no higher than ¥1 million; no more than 1 kilogram (2.2 pounds) of gold.

VACCINATIONS

Japan has an advanced medical system and is extremely safe from the perspective of communicable illnesses. No immunizations are required. At the time of writing in October 2020, the national government had announced its intention to provide coronavirus vaccinations for all members of the public in Japan for free by June 2021. There are currently no regulations yet in place related to coronavirus vaccinations for overseas visitors. Check the various official coronavirus-related resources available online (page 432) for any updates to this continuously evolving situation.

Festivals and Events

SPRING
KANDA MATSURI

Tokyo; weekend closest to May 15

One of Tokyo's three biggest festivals with hundreds of floats and *omikoshi* (portable shrines) carried by sweaty participants to the great shrine of Kanda Myōjin. It's a spectacle to behold.

SANJA MATSURI

Tokyo; third weekend of May

The largest festival in Tokyo celebrates the three founders of Tokyo's most famous Buddhist temple, Sensō-ji in Asakusa. The most visually stunning aspect is about 100 elaborate *mikoshi* (portable shrines), which symbolically house deities. The neighborhood around Sensō-ji overflows with *yatai* (foot stalls), games, and plenty of locals beating drums, playing bamboo flutes, and milling around in *yukata* (lightweight kimono).

SUMMER
GION MATSURI

Kyoto; throughout July

One of Japan's most iconic festivals, Kyoto's Gion Matsuri takes place during the sweltering month of July each year. It is rounded off with a parade of truly astounding floats pushed through the streets of Gion by revelers in traditional garb. The festival culminates July 14-17, when Kyoto's city center is blocked off to traffic and residents mill about in *yukata*, drinking beer, and nibbling on grub from food stalls.

TENJIN MATSURI

Osaka; July 24-25

Regarded as one of Japan's three blowout festivals, practically all of the city participates in this massive festival. Following a ritual and prayers on the first day, the festival reaches a crescendo on the second day when (starting from around 3:30pm) locals wearing traditional garb pull opulent portable shrines the size of cars, known as *mikoshi*, from Tenmangū through the surrounding streets, then proceed to glide through the Ō River in swarms of boats. The evening ends with a huge fireworks show along the Ō River.

DAIMON-JI GOZAN OKURIBI

Kyoto; Aug. 16

Another iconic Kyoto summer festival, this is

an occasion to bid farewell to deceased spirits believed to visit the living during the holiday of Obon, celebrated in mid-August in Kyoto. Blazing fires in the shape of Chinese characters are lit and left to burn for about 40 minutes on the slopes of five mountains surrounding the city.

KŌENJI AWA ODORI
Tokyo; last weekend of Aug.

Kōenji Awa Odori is a pulsating, fun, and rowdy festival, by far Tokyo's best *awa-odori* dance festival. Although not quite as large as the one in Tokushima, more than 1 million people flock to the suburb of Kōenji to watch as troupes of drummers, flutists, *shamisen* players, and dancers weave through the neighborhood's streets. This is one of my personal favorites.

FALL
TOKYO JAZZ FESTIVAL
Tokyo; Sept.

Tokyo Jazz Festival brings together a world-class lineup of jazz stars from Japan and abroad for Japan's biggest jazz event. It's definitely recommended for serious devotees of the art.

Recreation

BIKING

Japan's relatively tame streets make exploring by bicycle an attractive option. Rental outfits and tour operators are plentiful in many places, from Tokyo to Kyoto and Osaka. If you'd like to undertake a longer journey, consider the gorgeous **Shimanami Kaidō.** This 70-km (43-mi) succession of bridges and roads allows cyclists to pedal their way across the Inland Sea, via six scenic islands, starting from the port of Onomichi on Honshu and ending in the town of Imabari in northwestern Shikoku.

For a good introduction to some of Japan's more popular cycling routes, visit the websites of **Japan Cycling Navigator** (www.japancycling.org/v2/) and Kansai-centric **KANCycling** (www.kancycling.com). Note that bicycle frames in Japan are often on the petite side for taller foreign travelers. If you're over 180 centimeters (5'11") tall, you may need to seek out a rental or tour outfit with larger frames available.

HIKING

While heavy-duty expeditions fall outside the scope of this book's terrain—for that, look to the loftier peaks of the Japan Alps, the wilds of Hokkaido, or volcanic Kyushu, to name a few—there are still some great hikes in the regions surrounding Tokyo and Kyoto, often somewhat urban and involving a decent amount of temple-hopping. The most strenuous hike in the region surrounding Tokyo, Kyoto, and Hiroshima is undoubtedly also Japan's most iconic: **Mount Fuji.**

SPECTATOR SPORTS

Though soccer and sumo each exert their own pull among the Japanese, baseball is by far Japan's favorite sport.

Soccer

Soccer—*sakkaa* ("soccer") or *futtobōru* ("football")—has gained traction over the past few decades. Since 1993, there's been a professional **J-League** (www.jleague.jp/sp/en), or J1 League, with 18 teams and a season that runs March-October. Japan has also been sending its **Samurai Blue** to the World Cup since 1998. After a rough entry, the team has since battled their way into the quarterfinals three times (2002, 2010, 2018). Japan's stellar women's team, **Nadeshiko Japan,** were the 2011 Women's World Cup champions and came in second place in 2015. Soccer matches are televised on various sports channels, which are sometimes only available on

Baseball in Japan

Japan may be the most baseball-crazed country on the planet. Known in Japanese as *yakyū* ("field ball"), baseball was first introduced to the country in 1873 by Horace Wilson, an American English lecturer in Tokyo. The sport began to take feverish hold of the country during the first half of the 20th century, when a few exhibition games starred the likes of Babe Ruth, Lou Gehrig, and Joe DiMaggio. Throw in the vigorous indorsement of American GIs in the postwar years, which inspired Japanese corporations to begin funding teams, and you had all factors needed for the sport to enthrall the nation.

JAPANESE VERSUS AMERICAN BASEBALL

While the game in Japan stays mostly true to its American roots, there are a few differences. For one, the ball used is slightly smaller and more tightly wound. And in terms of play, there's less emphasis on thwacking home runs. In Japan, strategic strikes by the batter—just enough to keep teammates moving around the bases—are revered.

In terms of the viewing experience, watching fans can be as interesting as the game itself, joining in elaborate, choreographed cheers that vary by team and player. Rally towels are waved in synchrony, while balloons, umbrellas, and more dance rhythmically in the air, as cheerleaders prance around the perimeter of the field. For sustenance, "beer girls" patrol the stands bearing beer kegs weighing as much as 35 pounds, while food stands sell the classics (think: hot dogs, peanuts), alongside local options like *yaki-soba* and ramen.

SEASONS, LEAGUES, AND TEAMS

Nippon Professional Baseball (http://npb.jp) is split into the Central and Pacific leagues, with six teams on each. The season runs from late March-October, when the Nippon Series (Japan's World Series) has the nation glued to its television sets for the final showdown between the top team from each league. By far, the most popular teams are Tokyo's **Yomiuri Giants** and their main rivals, Kansai's **Hanshin Tigers,** whose home base is 55,000-seat Koshien Stadium, between Kobe and Osaka. Other teams with healthy followings include the **Hokkaido Nippon-Ham Fighters,** Tokyo's **Yakult Swallows,** and Fukuoka's **SoftBank Hawks.** Although the Giants have the strongest record in Japan's pro-baseball history, with 45 titles to date (combined Central and Japan Series wins), the Tigers undoubtedly have the most ferocious fans.

HOW TO CATCH A GAME

If you're keen to watch the pros play, your best bet is trying to catch a game either in Tokyo (Yomiuri Giants, Yakult Swallows) or outside Osaka (Hanshin Tigers) at Koshien Stadium. Tickets start from as low as around ¥1,000 for the standing section and up to ¥6,000 or more for prized seats near the field. And for a fascinating, in-depth look at the quirks of the game as it's played in Japan, with a generous helping of humor, check out Robert Whiting's classic book *You Gotta Have Wa.*

---

cable. There's also the **Emperor's Cup,** held between September and New Year's Day, in which literally any team, including ambitious high schoolers, can suit up.

Sumo

The most quintessentially Japanese of all sports, sumo is a singular spectacle. Huge men known as *rikishi* (professional sumo wrestlers), sporting impeccably styled hairdos and donning *mawashi* (padded loin cloths),

slam their bodies against each other with tremendous force in the center of a circular *dōyo* (ring) as an elaborately attired *gyōji* (referee) wielding a wooden war-fan known as a *gunbai* looks on.

The rules are relatively simple: Whoever gets pushed out of the ring or touches the ground with anything but their feet first loses. Grand tournaments known as *bashō* are held six times per year in different locations. In January, May, and September, Tokyo is where the clash occurs, while Osaka hosts in March, Nagoya in July, and Fukuoka does the honors in November. Attending one of these tournaments is a highlight and a rare glimpse into something deeply Japanese.

Martial Arts

Japan has a rich *budō* (martial way) tradition. Perhaps the most recognizable of all Japan's martial arts is **karate.** Literally meaning "empty hand," karate originated in Okinawa and reflects it with its fusion of Okinawan and Chinese techniques. Various styles have splintered off the original, and today many flock to Japan to study the iconic fighting art on its home turf. Appropriately, karate is on the bill for the 2021 Olympics to be hosted in Tokyo.

Among the other schools, **aikidō's** aim is to use the opponent's own force and strength against them. The name of this fighting school translates to "way of harmonious spirit." Founded relatively recently in the early 20th century by Morihei Ueshiba, it combines elements of karate, judō, and kendō. **Jujitsu,** which focuses on combat in close quarters and involves lots of on-the-mat tussles, is an ancient art that first emerged during the Warring States period (1467-1600). **Judō** is a gentler spinoff of jujitsu. Like karate's induction into the Olympics in 2021, judō was added to the roster of sports, where it remains, in Tokyo's first Olympic games in 1964. Derived from sword fighting, **kendō** sees participants kitted out in *bōgu* (armor) use bamboo swords known as *shinai* lunge, strike, and roar spirited shouts known as *kiai* as they land blows.

While these varied styles of fighting are more a participatory than spectator sport for many, **tournaments** occasionally draw large audiences. Large tournaments are occasionally held at **Nippon Budōkan** (2-3 Kitanomaru-kōen, Chiyoda-ku; tel. 03/3216-5100; www.nipponbudokan.or.jp), a huge indoor arena near Tokyo's Imperial Palace.

ONSEN

Of all quintessential experiences in Japan, submerging yourself to the shoulders in water heated by magma in the earth may be the most revelatory. Iceland may have given us the word "geyser," but the ritual of soaking in hot water has arguably seeped more deeply into Japan's collective psyche than anywhere else on earth. Hot springs, or *onsen* ("hot water spring"), are found in every region of this exceedingly volcanic country, with the sulfuric resort town of Hakone atop the list within the scope of this book.

Technically speaking, the water gurgling up into the pools of an *onsen* must be at least 25°C (77°F), although it usually hits around 39-42°C (102-107.5°F) or even more scalding levels. It must also contain at least one of the naturally occurring chemical elements on a list of 19—many of which are believed to possess healing powers to smooth skin, boost circulation, and more.

These pools, often made with marble, granite, or cypress wood, are found in a range of settings: indoors (often attached to *ryokan*), outdoors (aka *rotenburo*), next to rivers, on mountainsides, in steamy valleys, and next to the ocean. They are typically segregated by gender—though not always!—and must be entered in the buff. Unsurprisingly, as with many things in Japan, a complex code of etiquette governs bathing in an *onsen*; here are a few of the basics:

- Upon entering, **slip off your shoes** and deposit them at lockers or shelves near the door.

- **Enter the appropriate changing room** (men: 男; women: 女).

- **Bathe and rinse off before getting in the pool** in the separate area for washing.

- Most onsen will provide or rent **towels,** though simple ones will not (in which case you will need to bring your own). You may use a small modesty towel to cover up on your way to the bath, but this is not necessary, and should not be brought into the water.

- **Never put your head underwater;** if you have long hair, wrap it up in a towel or tie it up in a hairband.

- **Don't be rowdy;** alcohol is frowned upon, though pleasant in moderation if you have access to a private baths.

- When you exit the bath, **wipe off excess water** before returning to the changing room.

- Many onsen have a strict policy against **tattoos.** Cover up small ones with band-aids or medical tape, or visit https://blog.gaijinpot.com/how-to-onsen-if-you-have-tattoos for a list of tattoo-friendly hot springs.

If this all sounds intimidating, many *ryokan* and *onsen* resorts have private tubs available for rent. Whatever type of *onsen* pool you choose, you'll be greatly rewarded if you take the plunge. As an aside, public bathhouses called *sento* are also ubiquitous across Japan, typically in more urban settings. The difference is that the water in a *sento* tub is artificially heated.

Food and Drink

Widely regarded as one of the best national cuisines in the world, Japanese food is too wide-ranging and varied to describe in any level of detail here. Here are some of the mainstays you'll find in restaurants across the region covered in this book, and the country as a whole.

On the casual end of the spectrum, popular options when dining out include **donburi** (rice bowls topped with various types of meat or fish) and a glut of noodles, from **ramen** (typically thin noodles) to **udon** (thick noodles made of wheat flour) to **soba** (thin noodles made from buckwheat). It's worth noting that ramen alone is said to have 26 varieties, served in a range of soups (*tonkotsu*, or pork bone-based, miso-based, soy sauce-based, etc.). *Udon* and soba can also be served in broth, or separately and dipped in a side bowl of broth or sauce. Another heartier casual option is **tonkatsu**, or breaded and deep-fried pork cutlet often served with rice, shredded cabbage, and various condiments and sauces. Another great casual mainstay is the **yakitori** shop. Here you'll find most parts of a chicken (and many vegetables) slow-grilled on skewers over charcoal.

For a (slightly) longer list of regional specialties in the region stretching from Tokyo to Hiroshima, see page 34.

EATING OUT

The sheer range of restaurant offerings in Japan can be daunting. Many restaurants in Japan specialize in only one type of dish. Many meals that leave a lasting impression will likely be from a chef who embodies the traits of a *shokunin*, someone who brings a sense of pride to their work. Another thing to note is an emphasis on seasonality.

Some general restaurant types include:

- **"Family restaurants"** (think: Denny's and similar), where a range of set meals and items can be ordered à la carte.

- *Shokudo* **canteens,** which are essentially cafeterias that serve simple set meals of home-cooked Japanese fare.

- **Cafés,** in the modern sense, and their antecedents, *kissaten,* which are nostalgic coffeehouses preserved with their old brewing methods and atmosphere intact since the postwar years.

- *Izakaya,* or pub-cum-restaurants with sometimes quite extensive food offerings, featuring lots of small dishes that are

Izakaya and Kissaten

There are a few eating establishments central to social life in Japan that you may be encountering for the first time if it's your first visit to the country: *izakaya* and *kissaten*. Here's how to make the most of a visit at either one.

IZAKAYA

These gathering places are essentially akin to a pub, but different in subtle ways. Alcohol is central to the experience, from the volume quaffed to the fact that the food served tends to pair well with booze. Think lots of small plates bearing skewers of grilled meat (chicken, pork, etc.), french fries, small servings of stew, sashimi, salads, and more. The alcohol on offer usually includes draft beer, *sake* (aka *nihonshū*), and *shōchū*.

There are many spins on the *izakaya* concept, from an open space with many separate tables to private rooms where people sit on tatami floors. Another common format is the *tachinomi* (literally "stand-drink") where people hover around a bar or small separate tables, eating and drinking on their feet. There's often a seating charge (around ¥300-500), for which you'll generally receive a small dish known as *otōshi*, which usually includes a bit of fish or meat. Finally, many *izakaya* impose a time limit (normally around two hours), and the option of *tabehōdai* (all you can eat) and/or a *nomihōdai* (all you can drink) for a flat fee (around ¥4,000 is common). You'll be able to fill up as much as possible until your time is up, when your party will have to make way for the next group.

KISSATEN

Another unique enterprise found throughout Japan without an exact overseas counterpart is the *kissaten*. These are essentially nostalgic cafés dating to the Shōwa period (1926-1980), with the dated décor—dark, aged wood or tile dating to the 1950s—and old-school preparation methods to prove it. At a *kissaten*, you can expect to receive a proper cup of coffee that's been meticulously and slowly prepared by a master of the bean, often with the use of tools that are all but extinct. Try to visit one of these time capsules while you're in Japan. Given the rarefied nature of such a space, expect to pay a bit more than you normally would for a caffeine hit. A safe benchmark is something in the range of ¥700, or even more. Savor it—don't swill it down and run.

typically shared by the whole table (think grilled meat on sticks and various dishes that pair well with booze).

- The humble **yatai,** or street stall commonly seen at traditional festivals.

- The **yokochō,** or culinary alleyway, is another phenomenon abundant throughout Japan.

When entering a restaurant, you'll be greeted with *Irasshaimase* ("Welcome, come in"). A server will likely come to you and ask *Nan mei sama desu ka?* ("How many are in your party?"). While answering in Japanese may feel like an achievement, it's perfectly fine to just hold up the number of fingers to indicate how many you'll be dining with. Now is the time to either request a smoking seat (*kitsuen seki*) or non-smoking (*kin-en seki*).

Note that many restaurants permit smoking anywhere, so you may have to endure a bit of secondhand smoke.

A vast range of seating styles are found at restaurants in Japan. Besides tables (or counters) and chairs, some restaurants have tables that sit close to the ground with seating that ranges from thin cushions on a tatami floor, known as *zashiki* style, to sunken spaces in the floor beneath the table where diners put their legs. Always remove your shoes before stepping on the tatami mats.

A common feature of a restaurant meal is being presented with a wet towel known as an *oshibori*, which is often either chilled or heated (depending on season). Use this to clean your hands before eating; resist the urge to wipe your face or neck with it.

If dining with a group, once everyone has

placed their order, it's considered good manners to wait until everyone's food has arrived to begin eating. When it comes time to call for the check, call over a server again with a polite *sumimasen* ("excuse me"), then say *o-kaikei onegaishimasu* ("check please"). Japan is still very much a cash-based society. Unless you're at a high-end restaurant, plan on paying with cash. **Tips** are simply not accepted in Japan. Be aware, however, that some upscale restaurants may add a 10 percent service charge or a seating charge ranging from ¥200 to upward of ¥1,000 at swankier establishments.

Unless you're going to a 24-hour chain restaurant or convenience store, you're unlikely to find good food outside typical opening times. Breakfast is usually eaten at home, but cafés will often serve "morning sets" from around 8am until 10am or 11am. Lunch is typically served from 11:30am to 2pm or 3pm, while dinner hours are usually from 5pm or 6pm until 10pm or 11pm.

To make a reservation, language barrier can be a real challenge. Your best bet is to ask the staff at your accommodations to call on your behalf.

EATING IN

Eating a meal at someone's home in Japan is a great pleasure and a revelatory cultural experience. Most Japanese don't expect foreigners to have expert command of the multitude of nuanced table manners, but mastering a handful of small things will make a first-rate impression on your hosts. (Note that most of the following also holds true for eating at restaurants.)

First things first, if alcohol is being served, the meal will normally begin with a toast. In a Japanese home, more often than not, meals consist of many shared dishes, clustered in the center of the table. In this situation, turn your chopsticks around and use the opposite ends to take food from the individual shared dishes. Alternatively, some dishes may have chopsticks, or other utensils, solely used for serving. Use these instead of your own chopsticks if they are available.

A few pointers on chopsticks. Try to practice using them before making your trip. You'll feel more confident and will enjoy dining situations more. Western utensils will often simply not be available. Don't use your chopsticks to point or gesticulate. It's also considered rude to spear any form of food with chopsticks. While you'll want to use your chopsticks to lift the food to your mouth from each small dish, when eating from a small bowl of rice in particular, it's customary to lift the bowl close to your mouth and take the rice from there with your chopsticks. In the case of miso soup, sip it directly from the small bowl. But don't lift other bowls in this manner, especially larger ones. Another point: Put soy sauce or any other kind of dipping sauce into a small dish that will be provided with the rest of the dishes, rather than pouring sauce directly onto your food, especially white rice.

When drinking, it's considered good manners to refill the glass of anyone sitting next to you. They will likely offer to do the same. Try not to leave food uneaten—as much as you can manage. Counterintuitively, slurping noodles is encouraged, especially when served in soup. Finally, at the end of a meal try to put all your dishes back in their original places. Then, give your complements to the host with a hearty *gochisōsama deshita* ("It was a feast!").

A final word on coming prepared for a meal at someone's home: Bring a bottle of booze (wine, *nihonshū*, etc.), some nicely packaged tea, or a dessert that everyone can share. If you'd like to experience a meal at someone's home during your trip, **Nagomi Visit** (www.nagomivisit.com) matches travelers and English-speaking locals living across Japan for a home-cooked meal.

DRINKS AND ALCOHOLIC BEVERAGES

The legal drinking age in Japan is 20. It's worth saying a few words about Japan's most famous alcoholic beverage, *nihonshū* (rice wine; literally "drink of Japan"). Although *nihonshū* is widely referred to overseas as *sake*, this word literally just means "alcohol."

Umami: The Fifth Taste

"Deliciousness"—the word used to describe the sensation of savoriness. It's slowly seeped into the West's culinary vocabulary, so it's worth expounding up on it, commenting on other traditional flavors and principles that pop up in Japanese cooking.

While most of the above will be prepared by a chef and served to you at a table or counter, you'll also prepare some types of meals at your table. Common examples include **okonomiyaki,** a savory pancake stuffed with vegetables, seafood, meat, cheese, and more, cooked on a griddle built into your tabletop, then dabbed in a sweet, savory sauce; **sukiyaki,** a hotpot dish containing choice thin cuts of beef and vegetables, thoroughly boiled in a pot then dipped in a dish of raw egg (it's safe!); **shabu-shabu,** which is similar to *sukiyaki,* but the meat (and sometimes fish) is merely parboiled then dipped in sauce infused with sesame or citrusy *ponzu.* Another DIY classic is **yakiniku** (Korean barbecue), which consists of meat, vegetables, and more, brought to your table where you'll cook them at a grill that is either built into the table or on a brazier that will be brought to you by the staff.

At the haute end of the spectrum, **kaiseki ryōri,** which grew out of the traditional tea ceremony, is essentially a multicourse banquet, often served at a plush *ryokan* or exclusive restaurant. *Kaiseki* dishes are highly seasonal and include a range of often inventive concoctions made with all manner of ingredients that are only limited by the imagination of the chef. Tempura, a style of cooking in which vegetables, seafood, and more are battered and deep-fried, can also get pricey at the higher end of the spectrum. And of course, the price of an upmarket sushi or sashimi spread can be exorbitant.

Breweries across the islands make *nihonshū* every winter using a mix of water, a special type of polished rice, and a yeast extract known as *koji.*

While a sommelier approaches *nihonshū* with the same level of nuance you'd expect of wine in the West, at a the most basic level, *nihonshū* is usually described as being either *kara-kuchi* (dry) or *ama-kuchi* (sweet). Typical ways of drinking it include *jō-on* (room temperature), *reishu* (chilled), or *nuru-kan* (heated). It's often poured from a small ceramic flask known as a *tokkuri* into drinking cups known as *o-choko.* When it comes to choosing *nihonshū,* as well as how to drink it, your best bet will be to simply ask for a recommendation from the staff at a bar or restaurant. It's easy to get carried away when drinking *nihonshū,* which can be deceptively smooth, but be careful: It ranges in strength from 15 to 22 percent.

O-cha is the general term for tea, and the default is green tea. While **matcha** is the type of tea around which the tea ceremony is based, there are a number of other teas to sample in Japan. Roasted *matcha* is known as *hōjicha,* which is a darker brown color and less caffeinated. Warm *hōjicha* is often served for free at restaurants. A refreshing tea that tastes great chilled is *mugicha,* made with roasted barley. Sometimes you'll come across *kōcha* (black tea) too, although the aforementioned types of the beverage are more common.

DIETARY RESTRICTIONS

Eating out in Japan can admittedly be tricky if you've got dietary restrictions, from being vegetarians or vegan, to dealing with gluten intolerance or other allergies, to having religious commitments that forbid certain products (halal, kosher). To smooth things, consider carrying cards that explain in Japanese exactly what you can't eat. **Just Hungry** provides free printable cards that do just that (www.justhungry.com/japan-dining-out-cards). In a pinch, simply saying you have an allergy to a specific ingredient will ensure that the restaurant staff does due diligence to confirm whether it's present in a specific dish or not.

A good option for vegetarians is *shōjin-ryōri*, served at Buddhist temples. *Kaiten-zushi* (conveyor belt sushi) provides a surprising number of veggie sushi (cucumber roll, pickled vegetable sushi, etc.), as well as some side dishes and desserts. Convenience stores are another unlikely option, selling a range of salads, pickled vegetables, tofu dishes, egg sandwiches, and more.

A few other good resources for finding food options with dietary limitations include the website **Happy Cow** (www.happycow.net), a global database of vegan restaurants, and the online Japan-specific restaurant guide **Bento** (https://bento.com), which allows you to apply vegan or vegetarian filters to search results. **Halal Gourmet** (www.halalgourmet.jp) is a good source for Muslim-friendly dining options. If you must avoid gluten, be aware that some types of soy sauce may contain wheat. The **Legal Nomads** website has compiled a good guide to eating gluten-free in Japan (www.legalnomads.com/gluten-free/japan).

Accommodations

Japan has an eclectic range of accommodations, ranging from hyper-modern to traditional, with all types available for every budget. Even modest accommodations are usually well-maintained. Moreover, travelers are routinely wowed by Japan's justifiably famous hospitality (*omotenashi*).

That said, room rates in Japan can run quite high, and the rooms quite small. To avoid being charged sky-high rates, plan and book as far in advance as possible, especially during peak season (*hanami*, or cherry blossom season, in late March or early April; Golden Week holidays in late April and early May; or the Obon holidays in August).

The following websites tend to be particularly helpful for reserving accommodations in Japan, particularly *ryokan* and *minshuku*:

- **Travel Rakuten** (https://travel.rakuten.com)
- **Japanese Guest Houses** (www.japaneseguesthouses.com)
- **Ryokan Collection** (www.ryokancollection.com)
- **Japanese Inn Group** (www.japaneseinngroup.com)
- **Jalan** (www.jalan.net)
- **Japan Hotel Association** (www.j-hotel.or.jp)

- **JAPANiCAN**, run by travel agency giant JTB Group (www.japanican.com/en)
- **Japan Hotel & Ryokan Search**, run by Japan National Tourism Organization (www.jnto.go.jp/ja-search/eng/index.php)

HOTELS

There is a plethora of different types of Western-style hotels. At the cheaper end of the spectrum, **business hotels** are compact, no-frills options that are normally located near transport hubs. What they lack in soul, they make up for in reasonable rates. Singles tend to go from around ¥8,000, while doubles usually go for about ¥12,000 per night. There's often an optional breakfast buffet on offer.

Midrange options are readily available in Tokyo and Kyoto, where hotels with a truly boutique touch are only recently gaining more traction. At the higher end, the sky is the limit to how much you could spend on a luxury room.

RYOKAN

A *ryokan* is the most quintessentially Japanese accommodation: tatami-mat floors, futons instead of beds, and meals served to your room, all within the walls of a creaky, old wooden building. A deep sense of hospitality is something that respected *ryokan* are known for. A *ryokan* is much more than just a place to sleep. Most offer the option of an elaborate dinner and breakfast, often served to your room where you eat while lounging in a *yukata* (lightweight kimono).

Ryokan are often located in *onsen* towns. As such, many have a private, in-house *onsen* (hot spring), which can typically be rented hourly for ¥2,000-4,000, or a shared, gender-separated *onsen* that can be used by guests and sometimes visitors during specific hours only.

Both cheap and expensive *ryokan* exist. For the full experience, expect to spend in the range of ¥15,000-25,000 per person.

BED-AND-BREAKFASTS

A traditional Japanese bed and breakfast, or *minshuku,* is typically family-owned and often set in a private home that's been converted into a lodging. They're similar to *ryokan* but tend to charge more affordable rates, and are often clustered around ski resorts, mountain towns, and hot-spring areas. More often than not, guests share toilet and bathroom facilities. Expect to pay in the range of ¥5,000-12,000 per person.

HOSTELS

If you don't mind sharing bathroom facilities and potentially even the room itself, there are a growing number of hostels in Japan, particular in larger cities. Most hostels are either part of the **Japan Youth Hostel** (JYH) network (www.jyh.or.jp/e) or operate independently or as part of a small chain. Bedding will be included in the price. Room types include both dormitory and private, with a private room in an independent hostel costing around the same or more than a private room in a business hotel. This is worth considering if you're keen to have privacy, as a business hotel room has the added benefit of a private bathroom.

JYH membership gives you a discount on prices of member hostels (usually starting around ¥3,300 for members, from ¥4,000 for non-members). JYH-member hostels often offer food (breakfast and dinner) for a small fee, but the kitchen can't be used freely by guests. They may also have a curfew. Check the JYH website to see what properties are available. Make sure you've read the fine print so that you're not surprised by strict conditions around points like the timing for check-in and check-out or whether there's a curfew.

At independently run hostels, dorm beds tend to start from around ¥2,000 at the low end, although a more realistic starting figure is ¥3,000. Normally, private hostels will have a shared kitchen and lounge. Curfews will be less common, too. Chains include **J-Hoppers** (https://j-hoppers.com), **K's House** (https://kshouse.jp/index_e.html), and **Khaosan** (http://khaosan-tokyo.com/en).

CAPSULE HOTELS

A night spent in a capsule hotel could be either a matter of urban survival for a drunk salaryman or a one-off novelty for the experience-seeking traveler. A capsule hotel is literally what its name suggests: a capsule or pod in which you can bed down for a night, with lockers outside for your luggage. You'll likely have just enough room to crawl in and lay down.

Naturally, you'll be using a shared toilet and bath. Most capsules have air-conditioning, a power outlet, and a small television. Don't expect much in the way of privacy, and note that not all chains accept female guests. If a chain does accept female guests, the floors are usually segregated by gender.

Given their nature, a capsule hotel isn't a practical choice for more than an overnight stay. If you plan to stay in one of these cubes for more than a night, you'll have to actually check out each morning and then check back in. Prices hover around ¥3,500-6,000 or a bit higher for more stylish options.

TEMPLE STAY (*SHUKUBO*)

The *shukubo* (temple stay) phenomenon allows travelers to sleep in a temple. This highly recommended experience is a great way to see inside a Buddhist temple and offers guests a chance to potentially join in morning meditation or some form of ritual, such as prayers or fire ceremonies.

Love Hotels

Another "only-in-Japan" accommodation is the ubiquitous love hotel. As the euphemistic name suggests, these establishments are geared toward those engaged in the pursuit of "love." Let's face it—space and privacy are hard to come by in many Japanese homes, hence the explosion of this novel form of accommodation. Appropriately, they tend to be clustered around entertainment districts or near highway exits.

These hotels have increasingly snuck onto mainstream booking websites. The easiest way to tell if you've stumbled upon a love hotel listing will be if it happens to say "adults only" or something to that effect in the description. These rooms will usually contain an array of condoms and sex toys (handcuffs, blindfolds, whips), and are often decked out in lavish (if dated) bathing facilities. Don't worry—the cleaning crews are said to do a legendarily thorough job.

On the street, the easiest way to spot a love hotel is by its placard out front containing by-the-hour rates. More often than not, rather than dealing with a receptionist (the shame!) you'll be selecting your room from an electronic board that shows vacancies. Note that same-sex couples aren't always admitted, and multi-night stays usually aren't allowed. Prices can differ wildly depending on the area and rise dramatically on the weekends or for overnight stays. Generally speaking, renting a room to "rest in" for a few hours usually costs from around ¥3,000, while overnight stays start from about ¥6,000.

Despite the overtly risqué nature of love hotels, they can actually make for a fun experience. Rooms are often decked out in whacky themes and offer a firsthand glimpse into Japan's collective private life.

Two meals will be served of the Buddhist vegetarian variety known as *shōjin-ryōri*, and rooms tend to be traditional (tatami mat, futon, with *yukata* for guests to wear). Depending on the temple, both shared and private rooms can be chosen, of which some have private bath and toilet facilities, while others are shared. While there are temples around the country that offer *shukubo* lodgings, the best place to experience a temple stay is in one of the dozens of temples that offer lodgings in the sacred hermitage of Kōya-san.

AIRBNB

Despite making massive inroads to so many tourism hot spots around the globe, Airbnb's footprint in Japan is notably small. This is largely due to new accommodation laws that came into effect in 2018, which imposed more stringent laws for shared accommodations, from making it mandatory for all rented rooms to have clearly marked emergency exits to requiring those running Airbnb rooms to have a license number. This doesn't mean that Airbnb isn't an option. Have a look on the website and peruse rooms if you're a fan of the service. Just be aware that the company's reach isn't as deep in Japan as it is in most places around the world.

Conduct and Customs

Japanese people have a reputation for being a bit buttoned-up. There is some truth to this, as seen in the complex etiquette that governs social interactions. While foreigners are granted quite a bit of leeway, if you observe basic customs it will be reciprocated with friendliness and appreciation. Keeping things as simple as possible, here are some fundamentals.

GENERAL TRAVEL ETIQUETTE

One important area of etiquette in Japan revolves around footwear. **Remove your shoes** in the *genkan* (entryway) of anyone's home you visit, without fail. Some restaurants will also require patrons to remove their footwear at the entrance, and castles or old-school *ryokan* also require you to slip out of your shoes at the door.

On the subject of floors, be sure to carefully handle **luggage** indoors. Try not to roll, let alone drag, any luggage across wooden or tatami floors. In fact, try to avoid putting luggage on tatami floors altogether, whether at someone's home or in an old *ryokan*.

In public, use common sense when it comes to **noise** levels. Keep your voice down on public transit, especially if you get onto a train or bus and no one around you is talking.

It's also worth noting that eating and drinking when walking around in public or riding on public transportation is considered impolite. This doesn't apply to high-speed trains such as *shinkansen* or any others with reserved seating, due to the more private nature of each given seat.

If you'd like to have a guide to etiquette that accounts for any situation you'll likely encounter, the playfully illustrated book *Amy's Guide to Best Behavior in Japan: Do It Right and Be Polite!* is a great resource that doesn't overwhelm.

Greetings

When greeting someone in Japan, lightly bow and offer a friendly *yoroshiku onegaishimasu*. Or, simply use English if your new acquaintance seems comfortable with it. If you happen to be in a business situation, extend a business card with two hands as you bow, ensuring that the text is facing the recipient's direction so they can read it when they receive it. Don't be shocked if you are simply met with a handshake, which is commonly offered to foreign guests. The one thing you want to avoid doing is embracing or kissing on the cheek

Mediterranean-style. Doing so would only cause awkwardness and discomfort.

HOUSES OF WORSHIP

When visiting shrines (Shinto) and temples (Buddhist), the etiquette is quite similar. At a **shrine,** bow before walking through the *torii* gate that marks the entrance. After passing through the *torii*, walk along either side, but not the center, of the path that leads to the shrine. It's believed that the *kami* (gods) proceed down the center of the path. After walking farther into a shrine's ground, you'll come to a water basin, where it's customary to fill the ladle resting on the basin, pour a small amount of water on your left hand, followed by your right, and rinse your mouth with it. Finally, tilt the ladle upright so the small remaining bit of water runs down the handle, thus cleansing the ladle itself. If you want to say a prayer, toss in a coin (¥5 is standard), then ring the bell hanging over the offering box, deeply bow twice, clap your hands two times, pray silently, then bow once more and walk away.

When visiting a **temple,** you can essentially follow these same guidelines, minus clapping your hands. Note that not all temples have purification basins. Some have large incense burners where you can purchase incense as an offering for a small fee (usually around ¥100). If you choose to do so, light the incense from the other incense already protruding upright from within the ash that fills the burner, wave it around your head and body, then stick the bundle of incense sticks into the burner along with the others.

Photography can be limited at shrines and temples. Watch out for signs and heed them.

ATTIRE

On the subject of attire, aim to dress slightly more formally than you may be used to. On average, Japanese people are quite dapper and, cutting edge trendsters aside, modest. You'll notice that many men wear suits, especially while working, while women tend to dress in classic cuts.

SMOKING

Be aware the smoking is still considered very normal in Japan. That said, smoking on the street isn't permitted, except in designated areas. Frustratingly for many, smoking is often permitted indoors, including in restaurants and bars. Some restaurants will have a smoking (*kitsuen*) and non-smoking (*kinen*) sections.

PHOTOGRAPHY

Ask before taking photos of people. Not only out of courtesy, but also the law. Taking photos in which people in public spaces are visibly recognizable and publishing them without their permission is illegal.

Also, watch out for places, especially at religious structures and museums, where photography is forbidden.

Health and Safety

Japan sets a high benchmark for cleanliness and safety. Your chances of encountering any serious physical danger in the country are very low. Nonetheless, arm yourself with basic knowledge on a few things to be aware of during your trip.

MEDICAL EMERGENCIES

If you need emergency medical assistance, dial 119. Most operators only speak Japanese, but they will transfer your call to someone who speaks English. Japanese hospitals and clinics only accept Japanese medical insurance. Foreigners will generally be asked to pay upfront and claim it back after returning home. Just be sure to get medical/travel insurance before your trip. If you do find yourself in need of medical assistance, the standard of care is high, but little English is spoken. Large university-affiliated hospitals, typically in major cities, tend to have more English-speaking doctors on staff, as do pricey international clinics, which are also usually in urban centers.

CRIME

Alongside being a very clean, safe place in terms of health, Japan is also blessed with some of the lowest crime rates in the world. Still, resist the temptation to lull yourself into a false sense of security. To call the police about a crime or accident, dial 110. For English-language help with emergency services assistance, available 24/7, dial 0120/461-997 (www.jhelp.com/en/jhlp.html). Alternatively, contact your embassy if you're not in immediate danger. On the flipside, if stopped by police, be polite and cooperative. If they ask to see your ID, you are legally obligated to show them. Sometimes foreigners are stopped in this manner. The more cooperative you are, the quicker you'll likely be on your way.

Petty theft is thankfully a rarity. If you've lost something, or suspect if may have been stolen, go to the closest *kōban* (police box). Chances are someone has handed it in. Likewise, if you lose something on a train, go report the matter to the station staff when you get off the train. Tales of kindly train attendants recovering wallets and high-end cameras are commonplace.

One common crime is drink spiking, which occurs routinely in small, dodgy corners of select nightlife zones such as parts of Tokyo's Roppongi and Kabukicho districts. If you happen to go out in one of these two areas, keep an eye on your drink to be safe. Also, never follow a tout into any establishment in either neighborhood

ILLICIT DRUGS

When it comes to drugs, beware that Japan has a zero-tolerance policy, with even first-time offenders usually charged (and jailed) or deported. In the event of arrest, try to contact your local embassy. They won't provide legal aid but may be able to recommend a lawyer or translator. You may not be given this option, however, with Japanese detention laws being rather severe, with police having the right to detain anyone without charges for up to 23 days. Japan's controversial detention practices were dramatically revealed in the high-profile detention saga of Brazilian-born French ex-chairman and CEO of Nissan, Carlos Ghosn, in 2018.

NATURAL DISASTERS

Being caught up in a natural disaster is more likely than falling victim to a crime in Japan. Foremost, there are regular earthquakes, which are usually small, but the "big one" always looms. If you happen to be unlucky enough to be in the country when the next big one strikes, drop close to the ground, cover your head and neck—either under a table or under your backpack; whatever is at hand—and hold onto something to keep your footing steady.

While rare, devastating tsunamis do sometimes strike after significant tremors. Typhoons, which sweep through the country from July through early October, as well as occasional landslides, volcanic eruptions, extreme heat waves at the peak of summer, and occasional snowstorms in the depths of Tohoku and Hokkaido during winter are other potential natural dangers.

Information on weather, earthquakes, and more is available in English on the website of the Japan Meteorological Agency (www. jma.go.jp/jma/indexe.html). The same information is also disseminated by the national broadcaster, NHK, in up to 18 different languages on their NHK World website (www3. nhk.or.jp/nhkworld).

Practical Details

WHAT TO PACK

First things first, note that storage on public transport is often limited, so you should opt for a small bag if possible. Also, before packing anything else, be sure to take a small **gift**—something linked to where you're from is best—for anyone whose home you may be visiting. This little gesture goes a long way in Japan.

When it comes to attire, everyday dress tends to be a bit more **formal** than you may be used to. For perspective, many salarymen go to work in a suit every day. For dinner in an upscale restaurant, men should pack a dress shirt; for women, a smart-casual dress or blouse should do the trick. And, of course, be sure to pack for the season. Depending on where you're going and when, you may need proper winter attire or only loose, breathable clothing. Layers that you can add or remove are almost always a good bet.

Bring a **plug adapter** from home if you're traveling from a country with a different system. (Outlets in Japan are two-prong, like in the United States.) You can check if you'll need an adapter at https://world-power-plugs. com/japan. Most electronic stores will sell them, but may only have the Japan to international version if you're not in a tourist hot spot/large city.

To be on the safe side, bring all **medicines** with you that you may need during your trip, preferably in the original packaging. Pharmacies (*yakyoku*) are plentiful—simply look for the internationally recognizable red cross symbol out front—but there are fewer over-the-counter medicines in Japan than overseas. In a pinch, most pharmacists can usually speak limited English and will likely be able to read and write some, too. On that subject, certain antidepressants and pain-killers, which are mostly legal overseas, are illegal in Japan unless they're under a certain strength. To learn more, read the information on classes of drugs and how to bring those that are legal into the country, as explained by the

Japanese Convenience Stores

From a citydweller's perspective, Japanese convenience stores (*konbini*) are one of the wonders of the modern world. Ubiquitous (more than 50,000 individual stores dot the archipelago), operating at all hours, and remarkably diverse in their offerings, these smooth-operating institutions can be an unexpected revelation for many foreign travelers.

The biggest *konbini* chains, in order of market share, are **7-Eleven, Family Mart,** and **Lawson. Natural Lawson,** a Lawson spinoff that has been gaining steam in recent years, stocks products made with healthier ingredients. There's also a smattering of smaller players such as **MiniStop, New Days, Circle K Sunkus,** and **Daily Yamazaki.**

Food and drinks are the main thing on sale, from snacks and canned coffee to *bento* (boxed meals): sandwiches, salads, *onigiri* (rice balls), candy, dairy products, ice cream and frozen food, beverages of every kind (soft drinks that change with the season, energy drinks, vitamin drinks, alcohol, etc.), warm foods like fried chicken and *oden* (a variety of foods boiled in soy-flavored broth), snacks, instant noodles, bread, and more. Recently, many *konbini* have started selling surprisingly good (and cheap at around ¥100-200) coffee (café latte, Americano, etc.).

Convenience stores in Japan also tend to stock a surprising array of **products used in daily life:** batteries, household goods, toiletries, cosmetics, body care products, neckties, undershirts, pantyhose, and umbrellas. Some bigger convenience stores even have areas to sit down and eat, some even alfresco in warmer months. Alongside edibles and drinks, there are always well-stocked **magazine racks,** filled with serialized manga and women's magazines sitting next to pornography (sealed shut with tape).

Ministry of Health, Labour and Welfare (www.mhlw.go.jp/english/policy/health-medical/pharmaceuticals/01.html), which has also provided a helpful Q&A page on the matter (www.mhlw.go.jp/english/policy/health-medical/pharmaceuticals/dl/qa1.pdf).

Another item that you may want to consider bringing is a handkerchief or hand towel. Its uses will be myriad. Particularly in summer, you'll spot people of all ages occasionally wiping their brow. Beyond this, some restrooms in shops, restaurants, train stations will not have any means of drying your hands. This trend has increased during the coronavirus pandemic, as many air dryers have been sealed shut to prevent the spread of germs. If you forget to pack one, don't fret. Once you're in Japan, you'll see no shortage of colorfully designed *tenugui* (all-purpose traditional hand towels) at souvenir or lifestyle shops, or the plain cotton variety on convenience store shelves just about anywhere.

BUDGETING

Japan isn't the cheapest country, but it's less prohibitively expensive than what its reputation suggests. Your main costs will come from transportation and accommodation. **Book in advance** to increase your chances of landing a deal. Further, if you'll be traveling long distances in a short period of time, it will likely pay to get a **rail pass.** Otherwise, budget quite a bit more (at least ¥10,000 per leg) for transportation—*shinkansen* in particular are pricey, and it doesn't take long for a taxi meter to top ¥2,000. Food, drink, and entertainment costs can be as high or low as you like, as the proliferation of Michelin stars going to affordable ramen restaurants attests.

A good baseline daily budget would be around ¥8,000. This will typically get you a hostel bed (¥3,000), three cheap meals a day (¥500-1,000 each), basic transportation, and perhaps one splurge such as a café pit stop or a moderate entry fee. A good midrange daily budget would be around ¥10,000-25,000 (business hotel or private room in guesthouse from ¥8,000, dinner ¥3,000 per person at an *izakaya* or restaurant, and extra funds of roughly ¥6,000-9,000 for miscellaneous things like admission fees or local tours). For a bit more luxury, the prices jump quite a bit. A night in a good hotel will likely start from around ¥25,000, while an upmarket dinner will likely cost at least ¥10,000 per person.

To trim food costs, try to eat a big lunch. Many good restaurants offer ¥1,000-2,000 lunch sets that can be surprisingly satisfying. Alternatively, see what surprisingly substantial food items convenience stores sell, or go to a supermarket or department store food hall around 30 minutes to an hour before closing time to hunt for discounted *bento* (boxed meals).

- **Sandwich:** ¥300-500
- **Cup of coffee:** ¥300-500
- **Beer:** ¥500 for draft beer at local *izakaya*
- **Lunch:** ¥1,000 for a rice bowl topped with meat or fish
- **Dinner:** ¥1,500 for midrange meal without drinks; ¥3,000 for a meal at an *izakaya* with drinks
- **Train ticket (local):** from around ¥180 if traveling only a few stops
- **Train ticket (regional):** ¥3,000-8,000 for journeys on limited express trains; ¥8,000-25,000 for longer *shinkansen* trips
- **Hostel bed:** ¥3,000
- **Business hotel or private guesthouse:** ¥8,000
- **Small *ryokan* (often with 2 meals):** ¥12,000

MONEY

Japan's currency is known as the yen (pronounced "*en*"). Its symbol is ¥, and its abbreviation is JPY. Banknotes come in denominations of ¥1,000, ¥5,000, and ¥10,000. Coins include the small, lightweight silver ¥1, the copper ¥5 (with a hole in the center), the copper ¥10, the nickel ¥50 (with a hole in the center), the nickel ¥100, and the hefty copper-nickel blend worth ¥500. Vending and ticketing machines will often take ¥10, ¥50, ¥100, and ¥500 coins, but not ¥1 or ¥5. Generally, shops do not let you break bills

without purchasing something. But, whe paying, most shops will have change for ¥10,000 note, unless you're at a flea marke or street stall.

At the time of writing, the exchange rat was as follows for a range of currencie US$1 = ¥107, £1 = ¥132, €1 = ¥117, AU$1 ¥72. Check for latest rates at www.xe.com c www.oanda.com. Note that ATM exchang rates are often better than those offered b money changers, especially those at the ai port. Reputable, but smaller exchange office in big cities, close to train stations, will ofte have better rates. For U.S. travelers, thinkin of ¥100 as US$1 makes the conversion easier– just think of the last two digits of any pric as cents, and you have a U.S. dollar estimate ¥1,750 is roughly $17.50.

ATMs are on nearly every corner in th downtown of most big cities. Give a pre-tri travel notice to your card provider, and you' likely not have an issue using your card a select ATMs. Be aware that making a with drawal may incur a small fee (¥216). A goo rule of thumb is to look out for 7-Eleven ATM (Seven Bank), which tend to be the most ac cessible for those with overseas cards. Beyon the cities, ATMs are a bit harder to find. I you're heading into the countryside, withdraw enough cash to cover you until you plan to b back in a larger town.

Japan is quite slow to the credit card gam A surprising number of businesses still onl accept cash. To be safe, plan on paying for th bulk of your trip with cash.

COMMUNICATIONS
Cell Phones

To dial a number in Japan from overseas, firs dial your country's exit code (00, 011, 001 depending on country), then Japan's coun try code (81), followed by the number. If th number you're trying to dial begins with a 0 drop that digit, then dial it from the secon digit on. To dial direct to an overseas lin from Japan, follow the same procedures yo would if calling Japan from overseas. First dial the international dialing access cod

)10), followed by the country code where ou're calling (e.g., 1 for dialing to the US), len the number. To dial a domestic number om within Japan, just dial it as is.

Japan's largest players in the mobile mar- et are **NTT Docomo** (www.nttdocomo. o.jp/english), **Softbank** (formerly Vodafone; ww.softbank.jp/en/mobile), and **au** (owned y KDDI; www.au.com/english).

Assuming you have a cell phone that is oth unlocked and works on a Japanese net- york, you can also buy a **prepaid Japan IM card** for it. Note that SIM cards on offer or foreign travelers often only allow for data sage. This means you'd only be able to make oice calls on internet-based apps like Skype nd WhatsApp. If your phone has Wi-Fi con- ectivity, of course you'll be able to access the nternet anytime you have Wi-Fi access.

The best prepaid card on offer right now is vailable through **Mobal** (www.mobal.com). ou'll get unlimited cellular data, English- anguage support, and the ability to make and eceive voice calls—a rarity among the main repaid SIM card options—for any plan above he 30-day option (¥7,500). They send their IM cards worldwide, so you can place your rder and receive it before ever setting foot n a plane. Alternatively, you can reserve in dvance, then fetch it on arrival at the airport.

For something a bit less expensive, but vithout voice calls and with limits on data sage, vending machines stocked with **J-Mobile SIM cards** (for one or two weeks) re found scattered around Narita Airport. ou can also just walk into a major electronics hop (Bic Camera, Yodobashi Camera, Labi) nd pick up a store-branded prepaid SIM card vith limited data and no voice calls. These ards tend to run around ¥4,000 for a week r so of use.

nternet Access

)espite its high-tech reputation, finding Ni-Fi in Japan can be surprisingly challeng- ng. It's often available in cafés, at some res- aurants, and even in some public spaces (at rain stations, etc.), but it tends to be slow or require an inconvenient amount of hoop- jumping to get what is often only 30 minutes to 1 hour of very patchy access. As a saving grace, most accommodations do offer some form of internet, whether Wi-Fi in the rooms or (bare minimum) a shared computer for emails and basic web surfing in a shared lounge.

The best way around this is to rent a pocket Wi-Fi router for internet access when you're on the go. The best pocket Wi-Fi provider is **Ninja WiFi** (https://ninjawifi.com), which of- fers up to 10GB of daily data use from ¥900 per day. Conveniently, it's possible to rent a Ninja WiFi pocket router along with a JR Pass, allowing you to pick up both of them at once at the airport or have them delivered to your accommodation. You can read more about this option at www.jrpass.com/pocket-wifi.

Shipping and Postal Service

Post offices are widespread throughout Japan, as are red post boxes often seen sitting beside the road. Post offices and post boxes alike are marked with a 〒 symbol. **Japan Post** (www. post.japanpost.jp/index_en.html) runs a use- ful English-language website where you can search for the nearest post office. It's easy to send letters, postcards, and packages any- where on the globe for reasonable rates from any Japan Post branch. You'll have the option of attaching a tracking number to your ship- ment and more.

When you're on the ground, Japan's well- oiled luggage forwarding service, known as *takkyūbin*, is a major boon. This service eliminates the need for you to lug your bag- gage up steep staircases or through crowded train stations. Most service desks provid- ing this service can be found at airports and train stations. Be aware that you'll need to fill a day-pack with your necessities if using one of these services, as you'll likely be waiting for your bag the day after you've sent it. To learn more about this handy service, check out the helpful **Luggage-Free Travel** website (www. luggage-free-travel.com). Rates tend to be around ¥2,000, give or take, per item.

OPENING HOURS

All offices are closed on **public holidays,** but many businesses (shops, museums, restaurants, cafés) will often be open but closed on the day after the public holiday. Department stores and many shops often operate from around 10am-8pm daily. Museums and galleries likely stay open 9am-5pm, with last entry around 4:30pm or even 4pm. They are often closed on Monday, unless Monday is a public holiday, in which case they close on Tuesday.

Bars tend to open from 5pm at the earliest, but more often start serving from around 6pm or later, then stay open until midnight or in some cases, much later. **Restaurants** normally open for lunch from 11:30am-2pm or 3pm, then again open for dinner from 6pm-10pm or 11pm (last orders tend to be taken 30 minutes or even 1 hour before closing time). Later opening hours tend to be more common in cities or for chains.

Banks tend to be open from 9am-3pm (counter can be until 5pm as well) Monday-Friday and are closed on public holidays. Some banks may be closed on Sunday and only open until 5pm or earlier on other days. Meanwhile, **post offices** are usually open 9am-5pm Monday-Friday, with some large branches maintaining longer hours and offering services on Saturdays and sometimes even Sundays (limited hours). Truly large ones will have pickup points for mail that are open 24/7.

Public Holidays

Restaurants, shops, and most tourist attractions are still open on national holidays, with the exception of New Year, when almost everything closes down. Another point to be aware of: holidays are moved to the following Monday if they happen to fall on a Sunday. Further, if there are two national holidays within two days apart, the day between them also becomes a holiday. This sometimes happens during **Golden Week** in late April to early May, when a handful of holidays are clustered close to each other.

- Jan. 1: New Year
- Jan. (second Mon): Coming of Age Day
- Feb. 11: National Foundation Day
- Feb. 23: The Emperor's Birthday
- Mar. 20 or 21: Spring Equinox Day
- Apr. 29: Shōwa Day
- May 3: Constitution Day
- May 4: Greenery Day
- May 5: Children's Day
- Jul. (third Mon): Ocean Day
- Aug. 11: Mountain Day
- Sept. (third Mon): Respect for the Aged Da
- Sept. 22 or 23: Autumnal Equinox Day
- Oct. (second Mon): Health and Sports Da
- Nov. 3: Culture Day
- Nov. 23: Labor Thanksgiving Day

OBON

Ancestors who have passed on are believe to return to the land of the living durin this important Buddhist holiday. Lantern are festooned in front of homes and aroun towns intended to guide the spirits to the destination, dances are performed at loca festivals by everyone from children to the el derly, and people tend to the graves of thei ancestors and leave offerings of food at tem ples and home altars. The festival is brough to a close by releasing floating lanterns int rivers, lakes, and the ocean to light the wa back to the spirit world for the ancestors wh have visited.

This day was traditionally celebrated form the 13-15 on the seventh month of the yea on the lunar calendar (August). Today, how ever, many regions follow the solar calendar which makes it fall in July (July 13-15). Semi officially, August is the month that is treate like a holiday, with August 10-17 being one o the busiest tourist seasons in Japan, as com panies nationwide let their staff take off. It' best to either avoid traveling during this peal time, or to book accommodations, flights and more *well* in advance.

WEIGHTS AND MEASURES

Japan is on the **metric system.** All weights, measures, and distances on road signs will be in metric units.

When it comes to voltage, **100V** is the norm, unlike the 110-120V standard for the U.S. or Europe's 220-230V. That said, the plugs are the same type as those used in the US, with two flat prongs.

TOURIST INFORMATION

More often than not, you'll find a little tourist information center inside or near main train stations or close to popular tourist spots. Staff tend to be more proficient in English on average in bigger cities, but English-language help becomes hit or miss in the countryside. Thankfully, there are usually a healthy number of English-language leaflets.

While you can't expect every tourist office to handle all of your logistical needs, many helpful members of staff will be willing to assist with things like booking onward travel, booking tickets, reserving accommodations, and more.

Traveler Advice

ACCESS FOR TRAVELERS WITH DISABILITIES

The keyword for accessibility when traveling with a disability is *baria-furii* ("barrier free"). Accessibility in Japan is improving in cities, mostly due to an aging population and the Olympics, but the issues remain in rural areas.

On the street, traffic lights are synced up with different songs that indicate when it's safe to cross. And train platforms have raised dots and lines worked into the pavement as tangible guidance. A good rule of thumb for wheelchair users would be to contact any tourist sites or restaurants ahead of time to ask about access such as a separate entrance with a ramp. Many sites marked as "accessible" will unfortunately still have gravel pathways or sharply inclined slopes.

Most train lines will have a car or several cars for wheelchair users, while the priority seats at each end of the carriage, near the doors, are reserved for elderly, pregnant, and disabled people. Also note that most trains have a gap between train and platform. To board, the best thing to do is often inform a staff member. They will then bring a portable ramp to lay down and help you on. They will also call ahead to the station you're getting off at, where another member of staff will be there at your car with a ramp to help you get off. Buses usually have priority seats, too, which are sometimes stowaway seats that are often marked with a different color of upholstering.

The multilingual **Japan Accessible Tourism Center** website (www.japan-accessible.com) has extensive information about wheelchair accessibility. It also includes good information about hotels and more for a number of cities. For accommodations that do have barrier-free rooms, book as far in advance as you can to secure them.

WOMEN TRAVELERS

Japan is a very safe country, including for women travelers. There are incidences of groping or unwanted contact on crowded trains, but they are not common. In cities, trains and metros often have dedicated women-only cars to decrease the possibility of inappropriate behavior from men. Open harassment, such as catcalls and gestures, is practically nonexistent.

Although sexism is in many ways still rooted in Japanese society, it primarily affects women living in Japan. Some capsule hotels don't allow women guests, but otherwise, there are few ways in which women travelers are limited in their experience of the country.

TRAVELING WITH CHILDREN

There's plenty of kid-friendly stuff to do in Japan, from beaches and attraction parks to arcades, pop culture sites, outdoor activities, and more.

Be aware that you'll likely end up walking significant distances in big cities. Further, there are often elevators in train stations, but few ramps exist near many tourist sites. Children ages 6-11 receive half-price train fare (including for the *shinkansen*), while those under 6 are free. There is priority seating and trains and city buses for pregnant women and those with small children.

When dining out, note that picky eaters can be placated with Western-style foods like sandwiches at convenience stores, cafés, and more. There are plenty of bakeries and family restaurants with kids menus in Japanese towns, too. Note that highchairs aren't ubiquitous in Japan.

When choosing accommodation, be aware that hotels can usually provide cots, assuming there's space. Even double rooms can be quite small in Japanese hotels. Quad rooms or two double beds are rare, although triple rooms are occasionally available. For these reasons, staying in a traditional accommodation such as a *ryokan* or *minshuku* might be easier if you want everyone to be in one room. A room in one of these traditional digs will probably be one large tatami room with several futons.

If you're traveling with an infant or a toddler, when it comes time to change a diaper, changing stations are usually found in the women's bathrooms in (large) train stations, department stores, larger shops, and malls. You can pick up diapers and other basics at larger pharmacies and at some larger supermarkets. Breastfeeding in public isn't common

and is somewhat frowned upon. It will likely go unnoticed if you find a corner and cover up.

SENIOR TRAVELERS

With its aging population, Japan has relatively good infrastructure for senior travelers. Be aware, though, that there are still lots of steps and little ledges (often unmarked) that you'll have to navigate. There are priority seats for seniors on trains and buses. Some tourist attractions offer discounts (even some domestic travel tickets), but are often either unmarked or only explained in Japanese.

LGBTQ TRAVELERS

LGBTQ travelers are unlikely to encounter any discrimination, especially in urban areas like Tokyo and Osaka. If anything, Japan is relatively accepting, although prejudice does still exist. Homosexuality is legal, but gay marriage isn't. Foreign marriages aren't recognized in Japan, but partnership certificates are available in several cities or districts.

Same-sex couples should not have a problem getting reservations or staying in a hotel. Regardless of sexual orientation, overt displays of affection are not very welcome in public. For trans people, the main issue may be *onsen* and bathrooms, as you'll be expected to go to one that matches your physical sex. The best solution is to rent a private *onsen*.

By far, Tokyo is Japan's main LGBTQ hub. The city's LGBTQ community throws the large **Tokyo Rainbow Pride** (https://tokyorainbowpride.com) parade in May each year as part of a multiday celebration.

For up-to-date information on what's happening in Japan's LGBTQ community, particularly in Tokyo, check out the website of **Utopia Asia** (www.utopia-asia.com) LGBTQ groups on Meetup.com are active in Tokyo, too.

TRAVELERS OF COLOR

Only about 2 percent of Japan's population is foreign-born. There's not a whole lot in the way of diversity, especially of those

ho look significantly different. People are
ostly polite to foreigners, although the oc-
asional microaggression and even overtly
acist behavior do occasionally occur. Those
ith East Asian features will be assumed to
peak Japanese. Expect some confusion if
ou don't. In general, this can make visiting
apan more of an "invisible tourist" experi-
nce for those of East Asian descent. Sadly,
hose perceived to have Korean features re-
ort having been the victims of derogatory
omments from older Japanese.

Some travelers report that if you're black
r brown, some people may appear to avoid
itting next to you on trains—this may hap-
en to foreigners of other ethnicities, too,
nd in some cases, small children may stare.

Unfortunately, blackface makes an occa-
ional appearance on primetime television.
he situation is changing, though, and so-
ial discourse around diversity is on the rise.
ood references for black travelers are the
Black Eye column in *The Japan Times*, writ-
en by American expat Baye McNeil; **The
lack Experience Japan** (www.blackexjp.
om), where you'll find videos, interviews
nd more; as well as Facebook groups and
ages such as **Black in Japan** (www.face-
ook.com/groups/BlackinJapan).

OUR GUIDES AND OPERATORS

or a service that can connect you with vari-
us professional tour guides who can also
erve as interpreters on the go, there is the
apan Guide Association (tel. 03/3863-
895; www.jga21c.or.jp; fee varies by tour).
ts website allows you to search for licensed
uides nationwide. The Japan National
ourism Organization (JNTO) also offers a
ystem of goodwill guides who work on a

volunteer basis around the country. If you
employ their services, just be aware that
you will need to cover their transportation,
admission to any sites or events, and meals
eaten during the tour. For a nationwide list
of goodwill guide groups, visit www.japan.
travel/en/plan/list-of-volunteer-guides.

For a more tailored experience, there are a
number of stellar bespoke trip outfits:

Boutique Japan (https://boutiqueja-
pan.com) excels in this area. This small
Japan-focused tour operator specializes in
immersive private itineraries throughout
the country. They offer high-end trips, especially for travelers deeply interested in
off-the-beaten-path cultural and culinary
experiences. Each trip is completely unique.

Be Here (http://behere.asia) operates
with a similar philosophy, albeit with less
of a focus on high-end accommodation and
food (although these things can be part of
a tour, too!). These tours tend to put travelers in touch (literally) with local arts and
crafts, and put a premium on learning in a
hands-on way by taking a cultural deep dive
into out-of-the way corners of the country.

As its name suggests, **Walk Japan**
(https://walkjapan.com) offers a variety of
trips through the country, undertaken on
your own two feet. Self-guided and custom
tours are possible.

If you'd prefer to get around by bicycle,
there are a number of tour providers that
both lead tours and create self-guided tour
plans, as well as rent touring bicycles. **Cycle
Japan** (https://cyclingtoursjapan.com) and
Bike Tour Japan (https://biketourjapan.
com) both offer enticing rural journeys,
including both led and self-guided. If you
prefer to design your own tour, check out
Japan Cycling (www.japancycling.org).

Resources

Glossary

annaijo (案内所)**:** information desk

bijutsukan (美術館)**:** art museum

cha (茶)**:** tea; often *o-cha*

chūi (注意)**:** caution

dōzo: please, go ahead

eki (駅)**:** train station

futsū (普通)**:** regular; for trains, *futsū* means local, making all stops

-gai (街)**:** district

gaijin: shortening of *gaikokujin;* although often casually used, it is an impolite term for foreigner

gaikokujin: foreigner

genkin: cash

geta: traditional Japanese wooden sandals; shoe storage closets are called *getabako* (*geta* box)

gohan: rice

goran kudasai: please look around; often heard in shopping areas

goyukkuri: please take your time (often used with *dōzo*)

hakubutsukan (博物館)**:** museum

hashi (橋)**:** bridge, sometimes changes to *-bashi* when part of a name

hashi (箸)**:** chopsticks, often *o-hashi*

hiragana: Japanese phonetic alphabet used for Japanese words

irrashaimase: Welcome! Often heard when entering an establishment

izakaya: Japanese pub with bar bites but not full meals

jiyūseki (自由席)**:** open seating, as opposed to reserved (e.g., on trains)

kaikei: bill, check (at restaurant)

kaiseki ryōri: traditional Japanese multi-course meal

kaisoku (快速)**:** rapid (for trains)

kaku-eki-teisha: local train; literally, stopping at all stations

kami: god

kanji: Chinese character-based Japanese writing system

katakana: Japanese phonetic alphabet used to write foreign words

kawa (川)**:** river, sometimes changes to *-gawa* when part of a name

kawaii: cute

kin-en (禁煙)**:** no smoking

kissaten: café

kitsu-en (喫煙)**:** smoking

kōban (交番)**:** neighborhood police booth

kōen (公園)**:** park

koto: Japanese zither

kushikatsu: deep-fried pork skewers

kyūkō (急行)**:** express (for trains)

madoguchi (窓口)**:** ticket window

maiko: geisha in training

maki: form of sushi with items rolled into the center of a tube of rice and seaweed

manga: comic book

matsuri: festival

-meisama: party of [number], e.g., *nimeisama* is party of two; this is only used by restaurant employees when confirming the number of customers in a party, not the other way around—use *futariseki* to ask for a table of two

minasan: everyone (often heard when addressing, or trying to get attention from, group)

misoshiru: miso soup

mochi: sweet rice cake, often *o-mochi*

nigiri: form of sushi with an oblong ball of rice topped with a piece of fish

okonomiyaki: Japanese savory pancake

okyakusan/okyakusama: customer

otsumami: snacks

otsuri: change (when making a purchase)

rotenburo: open-air *onsen*

ryokan: traditional Japanese inn

ryokō/ryokōsha: travel/traveler

sakura: cherry blossom

shakuhachi: traditional Japanese flute-like instrument

shamisen: traditional Japanese guitar-like instrument

shima (島)**:** island; *shima* sometimes changes to *-jima* when paired with the name of the island

shinkansen: bullet train

shiteiseki (指定席)**:** reserved seating (e.g., on trains)

shosho omachikudasai: please wait a momment

shōjin-ryōri: Buddhist vegetarian food

shokuji: meal

shukubo: temple lodging

takoyaki: octopus dumpling

tera: temple; often *o-tera*; *tera* sometimes changes to *-dera* when paired with the name of the temple

tokkyū (特急)**:** limited express (for trains)

tomare (止まれ)**:** stop

tonkatsu: pork cutlet

torii: gate at Shinto shrines

uketsuke (受付)**:** reception desk

washiki: Japanese-style (e.g., toilet)

yakiniku: grilled meat

yakitori: grilled chicken on skewers

yama (山)**:** mountain; 山 is also read *san* and sometimes *zan* when paired with the name of the mountain

yakuza: Japanese mafia

yokochō: culinary alleys; side streets lined with food stands

yōshiki: Western-style (e.g., toilet)

yukata: lightweight kimono worn in the summer or as loungewear at *ryokan*

Japanese Phrasebook

ALPHABETS AND WRITING

The phonetic alphabets used in Japanese (hiragana and katakana) are made up of five vowels, same as English (*a, i, u, e, o*), 39 consonant-noun pairs (*ka, ki, ku, ke, ko, sa, shi, su, se, so,* etc.), plus one single consonant (*n*) and one single particle (*o*). The consonants *k, s, t, n, h, m,* and *r* are paired with each of the five vowels, with a few exceptions: there's *shi* instead of si; *chi* instead of ti; *tsu* instead of tu; *fu* instead of hu. *Y* is only paired with *a, u,* and *o* (*ya, yu, yo*); and *w* is only paired with a (*wa*).

This base 46-letter alphabet is extended with symbols that look like straight quotes (") on the k set to make the g sound (*ka* becomes *ga, ki* becomes *gi,* etc.); the s set to make the z sound (except for *shi,* which becomes *ji*), the t set to make the d sound (except for *chi,* which

becomes *ji,* and *tsu,* which becomes *zu*), and the h set to make the b sound. A symbol that looks like the degree symbol (°) also can appear with the h set to make the p sound.

Kanji is the writing system that uses Chinese characters and is not phonetic. Kanji is what makes reading even the most basic signs and notices, let alone newspapers, a bit intimidating. (For reference, 2,136 characters are listed as *jōyō kanji,* or commonly used kanji.) Latin characters are called *romaji* in Japanese, and many signs are also written in *romaji,* especially in cities.

PRONUNCIATION

Despite the difficult-looking characters, Japanese words are pronounced phonetically, so try saying them the way they look, and you won't be as far off as you might think. Following the

Hiragana and Katakana

English	wa	ra	ya	ma	ha	na	ta	sa	ka	a
hiragana	わ	ら	や	ま	は	な	た	さ	か	あ
katakana	ワ	ラ	ヤ	マ	ハ	ナ	タ	サ	カ	ア
English		ri		mi	hi	ni	chi	shi	ki	i
hiragana		り		み	ひ	に	ち	し	き	い
katakana		リ		ミ	ヒ	ニ	チ	シ	キ	イ
English		ru	yu	mu	fu	nu	tsu	su	ku	u
hiragana		る	ゆ	む	ふ	ぬ	つ	す	く	う
katakana		ル	ユ	ム	フ	ヌ	ツ	ス	ク	ウ
English	-n	re		me	he	ne	te	se	ke	e
hiragana	ん	れ		め	へ	ね	て	せ	け	え
katakana	ン	レ		メ	ヘ	ネ	テ	セ	ケ	エ
English	o	ro	yo	mo	ho	no	to	so	ko	o
hiragana	を	ろ	よ	も	ほ	の	と	そ	こ	お
katakana	ヲ	ロ	ヨ	モ	ホ	ノ	ト	ソ	コ	オ
English					ba/pa		da	za	ga	
hiragana					ば"/ぱ°		た"	さ"	か"	
katakana					バ"/パ°		タ"	サ"	カ"	
English					bi/pi		ji	ji	gi	
hiragana					び"/ぴ°		ち"	し"	き"	
katakana					ヒ"/ヒ°		チ"	シ"	キ"	
English					bu/pu		dzu	zu	gu	
hiragana					ふ"/ぷ°		つ"	す"	く"	
katakana					フ"/フ°		ツ"	ス"	グ"	
English					be/pe		de	ze	ge	
hiragana					へ"/へ°		て"	せ"	け"	
katakana					ヘ"/ヘ°		テ"	セ"	ゲ"	
English					bo/po		do	zo	go	
hiragana					ほ"/ぽ°		と"	そ"	ご"	
katakana					ホ"/ホ°		ト"	ソ"	コ"	

pronunciation tips below, especially for the vowels, will increase your success.

Vowels

Speakers of Spanish will have no problem pronouncing the vowels in Japanese, as they are pronounced the same way. Japanese puts vowels in a different order than in English, and we've used the Japanese order.

SHORT VOWELS

a   pronounced *ah*, like ta-da

i   pronounced *ee*, like saying the vowel "e" in English

u   pronounced *oo*, like food; sometimes reduced or silent when at the end of a word (e.g., *desu* often sounds like *des*)

e   pronounced *eh*, like *e*ducate

o   pronounced somewhat like *oh* but with a lighter touch; words like "go" and "no" in English end with a slight "u" sound—the same words/syllables with a short "o" in Japanese are pronounced without that "u" at the end

LONG VOWELS

Long vowels in Japanese are indicated by a macron over the vowel (ō) or by a repeated letter (aa, ii, uu, ee). When a macron hasn't been used, the long o is spelled either *oo* or *ou,* depending on its hiragana spelling. Long vowels are pronounced by simply holding the sound of the short vowel for longer. (There is a slight pronunciation difference between *oo* and *ou,* but not one beginners should worry about.)

VOWEL COMBINATIONS

Vowel combinations are essentially pronounced as each vowel would be individually, although a few are more distinct.

ai pronounced like a long *i* in English, e.g., *tai* is pronounced tie

ao pronounced somewhat like *ow,* like in renown

ei pronounced like a long *a* in English, like in ace

Consonants and Consonant-Vowel Combinations

Consonants in Japanese are generally pronounced as they are in English, keeping the following notes in mind. Note that the Japanese alphabet does not use the consonants c by itself (although ch is used), l, q, v, or x. Nor is the sound "th" used.

g at the beginning of a word, always hard, as in *game,* no matter what vowel follows it; in the middle of a word, often pronounced like the g in *song,* but pronouncing it as a hard g in all cases is fine

r somewhere between the English r and l, but just pronouncing it as an English r is fine

tsu this combination is rare in English, but there is a Japanese word commonly used in English that includes it: tsunami

When two consonants are together, there is usually a slight pause between them.

In some cases, when preceded by a certain sound, words that would normally be said/written with a *k* are pronounced/written with a *g,* an *s* with a *z,* a *t* with a *d,* and an *h* with a *b* or a

p. An example of this is *hyaku* (100) changing to -*byaku* in some cases (as in *sanbyaku* or 300) or -*pyaku* in others (as in *roppyaku* or 600).

Intonation

Japanese is not a tonal language, and stresses on syllables are subtle. Beginners should try to speak without putting too much emphasis on any particular syllable.

PHRASES

Although macrons are used in the rest of the book, long vowels in this phrasebook are depicted with repeated letters (or ou when relevant) to help with pronunciation. The particle *o* (を in hiragana) is spelled "wo" in romaji, but in this phrasebook "o" is used since that is how it is pronounced. Similarly, the particle は is spelled with the *ha* hiragana, but in this phrasebook, it's spelled "wa" to reflect the pronunciation.

Many Japanese nouns below start with "o," although if you were to look them up in an English-Japanese dictionary, the word without the "o" would appear. The "o" prefix makes the word more polite.

General

Excuse me Sumimasen
Do you speak English? Eigo o hanasemasu ka?
Hello (during the day) Konnichiwa
Hello (after dark) Konbanwa
Good morning Ohayougozaimasu (only said first thing in the morning)
Good night Oyasuminasai (literally, get rest; only said when turning in for the night)
Good-bye Sayounara
Thank you Arigatou (casual)/arigato gozaimasu (polite)
please onegaishimasu (literally, "I wish for this")
I'm sorry Gomennasai
yes hai
no iie
I don't understand Wakarimasen
I don't speak Japanese. Nihongo o hanasemasen.

Could you write that down? Sore o kaitekuremasen ka?

Where is/where are…? …wa doko desu ka?

Where are the restrooms? Otearai wa doko desu ka?

Do you have this in Latin characters/ English? Romaji/Eigo de kaitearu no arimasu ka?

I would like…/may I have… … kudasai (literally, "please give me") or ….onegaishimasu (e.g., *miso ramen kudasai* is "I would like/may I have the miso ramen")

I'm looking for… …o sagashite imasu (e.g., deguchi o sagashite imasu—I'm looking for the exit.)

How much is this? Ikura desu ka?

Can you take our picture? Shashin o totte kuremasenka?

Note: "How are you" is a useful phrase in English, but it is not as ubiquitous in Japanese conversation and does not have an easy Japanese equivalent. The closest is *genki desu ka?*, which translates to "are you healthy?" and would be odd to say to someone upon entering a shop, for example.

Terms of Address

In Japanese, the terms "I," "me," and "you" are generally omitted from sentences. "You," in particular, should be avoided. When you are being addressed by a salesperson or someone in the service industry, most likely you will be called *okyakusama* (customer) or, if your name is known, by your last name with -*san* or -*sama*.

Mr./Mrs./Ms. … …-san (regular), -sama (very polite, used for people in a higher station than the speaker); for example, Ms. Suzuki is Suzuki-san or Suzuki-sama

I/me watashi

My name is … …to moushimasu (Note: Japanese people go by their last names, and first names are generally only used with friends and family. Foreigners can use either to introduce themselves—use whichever name you would like to be called by.)

adult otona

child kodomo

Directions and Transportation

(travel) information desk (ryokou) annaijo（旅行）案内所

map chizu　地図

here koko

there soko

over there asoko

left hidari　左

right migi　右

up ue　上

down shita　下

straight massugu

north kita　北

south minami　南

east higashi　東

west nishi　西

entrance iriguchi　入口

exit deguchi　出口

in front of mae

behind ushiro, ura

next to tonari

road douro/-douri (as part of a name) 道路/通り

street michi　道

signal shingou

bridge hashi/-bashi　橋

address juusho　住所

bicycle jitensha　自転車

car kuruma　車

taxi takushii　タクシー

subway chikatetsu　地下鉄

train ddensha　電車

train station eki　駅

train platform hoomu　ホーム

[Number] track number [number]-ban sen　[number character]番線

[Number] train car [number]-gousha [number character]号車

What track number/train car? Nan ban sen/nan gousha desu ka?

plane hikouki　飛行機

airport kuukou　空港

bus basu　バス

bus stop/station basu tei

ticket window madoguchi　窓口

How do I get to…? Douyatte…ni ikimasuka?

How far is it to… …wa dono gurai desu ka?

Is it close/far? Chikai/toi desu ka?

I want to go to… …ni ikitai desu.

kilometer kiro (also used for kilogram)
キロ

**I would like [one, two, etc.]
(tickets)** (Kippu) [ichi, ni, etc.]-mai kudasai.
Note that including *kippu* is optional since
what you are requesting would be clear
from the context.

one-way katamichi 片道

roundtrip oufuku 往復

luggage nimotsu 荷物

Accommodations

hotel hoteru ホテル

traditional inn ryokan 旅館

key kagi 鍵

room heya 部屋

single room hitoribeya

double room futaribeya

**western-style rooms (i.e., beds
not futons)/Japanese-style
rooms** youshitsu/washitsu

I want to check in. Cheku in
onegaishimasu.

I want to check out. Cheku aoto shimasu.

Can I get another key? Kagi mou hitotsu
onegaishimasu. (If asking for more than one,
change "hitotsu" to the counter number you
want.)

**Can I get another towel/
blanket?** Taoru/Moufu mou ichimai
onegaishimasu. (If asking for more than one,
change "ichi" to the number you want.)

I can't get into my room. Heya ni
hairemasen.

**Is breakfast/are meals
included?** Asagohan/shokuji tsuki desu
ka?

**What time does breakfast start/
end?** Asagohan wa nanji kara/made desu
ka?

Food and Drink

breakfast asagohan 朝ご飯

lunch hirugohan 昼ご飯

dinner bangohan 晩ご飯

restaurant resutoran レストラン

A table for one/two, please. Hitori/futari
seki onegaishimasu. (if asking for more than
two people, change *hitori-/futari* seki to
[number]-nin seki)

chopsticks ohashi

fork fooku

spoon supuun

knife naifu

napkin napukin

menu mennyu

water omizu お水

coffee koohii コーヒー

tea ocha お茶

cream kuriimu

beer biiru ビール

sake osake 酒

wine wain

milk gyuunyuu/miruku

bread pan

egg tamago 卵

fish sakana 魚

shrimp ebi 海老

Meat niku 肉

pork buta 豚肉

beef gyuuniku/biifu 牛肉

chicken toriniku/chikin 鶏肉

ramen ramen ラーメン

sushi sushi 寿司

sugar sato

I would like to order. Chuumon
onegaishimasu.

I would like the check. Okaikei
onegaishimasu.

to eat taberu 食べる

to drink nomu 飲む

I cannot eat… …o taberaremasen.

I cannot drink… o nomemasen.

vegetarian/vegan bejitarian/biigan

Money and Shopping

money okane お金

bank ginkou 銀行

post office yuubinkyoku 郵便局 (Note:
Post offices in Japan perform banking
functions and are a reliable place to find an
ATM.)

shop mise 店

How much is this? Ikura desu ka?

Can I pay by credit card? Kaado de harattemo ii desu ka?

Can I try this on? Shichaku shitemo ii desu ka?

postcard hagaki

souvenir omiyage

Problems and Health

Help me! (emergency) Tasuketekudasai!

I lost… …o nakushimashita

My…was stolen. …ga nusumaremashita.

wallet saifu

phone/cell phone denwa/keitai denwa

passport pasupouto

I don't feel well. Guai warui desu.

I feel sick to my stomach. Onaka ga itai desu.

(I need to go to the) hospital/ doctor. Byouin/isha (ni ikanakereba narimasen). 病院/医者

It/that hurts. Itai desu.

fever Netsu 熱

drugstore yakkyoku 薬局

medicine kusuri 薬

earthquake jishin 地震

typhoon taifuu 台風

embassy taishikan 大使館

police keisatsu 警察

Numbers

1	ichi	一
2	ni	二
3	san	三
4	yon/shi	四
5	go	五
6	roku	六
7	nana/shichi	七
8	hachi	八
9	kyuu/ku	九
10	juu/too	十
14	juuyon (not juushi)	十四
17	juushichi/juunana (both okay)	十七
20	nijuu	二十
30	sanjuu	三十
40	yonjuu	四十
50	gojuu	五十
60	rokujuu	六十
70	nanajuu	七十

80	hachijuu	八十
90	kyuujuu	九十
100	hyaku	百
300	sanbyaku	三百
400	yonhyaku (not shihyaku)	四百
600	roppyaku	六百
700	nanahyaku (not shichihyaku)	七百
800	happyaku	八百
1,000	sen	千
10,000	man	万

For numbers greater than 10, just combine the words for each digit. For example, 14 is juuyon: juu for the 10s digit and yon for the 1s digit. Similarly, for three-digit numbers, combine the various units: 256 is nihyaku gojuu roku.

Counting

Counting is complicated in Japanese because how you count depends on what you are counting. For example, the counter for small items (e.g., small fruits) is -ko (ikko, niko, sanko, etc.), the counter for flat items is -mai (e.g., tickets, postcards, shirts, etc.), for long narrow items (e.g., bottles of beer) is -hon (which changes to -pon for three and six), and the list goes on. A good default is -tsu, which is also meant for small items but only goes up to nine items. Beyond nine items, just try using the number with no counter.

1	hitotsu
2	futatsu
3	mittsu
4	yottsu
5	itsutsu
6	mutsu
7	nanatsu
8	yattsu
9	kokonotsu

Time

day nichi 日

today kyou 今日

yesterday kinou 昨日

tomorrow ashita 明日

morning asa 朝

before noon/am gozen 午前

noon hiru 昼

Afternoon/pm gogo　午後

evening ban　晩

night yoru　夜

[number] o'clock [number] ji (e.g., goji) [number] 時

What time is it? Nanji desu ka?

What time are we leaving? Nanji ni shuppatsu shimasuka?

Days of the Week

Monday getsuyoubi　月曜日

Tuesday kayoubi　火曜日

Wednesday suiyoubi　水曜日

Thursday mokuyoubi　木曜日

Friday kinyoubi　金曜日

Saturday doyoubi　土曜日

Sunday nichiyoubi　日曜日

Months

January ichigatsu　一月

February nigatsu　二月

March sangatsu　三月

April shigatsu (not yongatsu)　四月

May gogatsu　五月

June rokugatsu　六月

July shichigatsu (not nanagatsu)　七月

August hachigatsu　八月

September kugatsu　九月

October juugatsu　十月

November juuichigatsu　十一月

December juunigatsu　十二月

Dates

To express dates, the first part of the month doesn't follow the same pattern as the rest of the month. After the 10th, the dates follow the pattern *number + nichi*. There are a few exceptions, which are listed below. Also, except for *tsuitachi*, the dates also double as the counter for the number of days.

1st tsuitachi　一日

2nd futsuka　二日

3rd mikka　三日

4th yokka　四日

5th itsuka　五日

6th muika　六日

7th nanoka　七日

8th youka　八日

9th kokonoka　九日

10th tooka　十日

14th juu-yokka　十四日

17th juu-shichinichi　十七日

20th hatsuka　二十日

21st nijuu-ichinichi　二十一日

24th nijuu-yokka　二十四日

27th nijuu-shichinichi　二十七日

Suggested Reading

HISTORY

Embracing Defeat: Japan in the Aftermath of World War II (John W. Dower, 1999). This engaging tome explores Japan's rough road to recovery through the prism of the years after World War II. The book draws on numerous first-person accounts, documentary photographs from the period, and piercing historical analysis. This book, which won both the Pulitzer and the National Book Award for Nonfiction, is a powerfully focused lens onto the ways that World War II altered Japan's psyche and destiny forever.

CULTURE

A Geek in Japan: Discovering the Land of Manga, Anime, Zen, and the Tea Ceremony (Hector Garcia, 2019). Just released in revised and expanded form, this hit explores Japanese pop culture from A to Z. It also unravels many arcane social constructs and rituals, and elucidates topics ranging from architecture to video games. It's beautifully illustrated with hundreds of photos, too, making it a great visual primer on contemporary Japan as a whole.

Yokai Attack! (Hiroko Yoda and Matt Alt, 2012). This fun, light series consists of three books: *Yokai Attack: The Japanese Monster Survival Guide, Ninja Attack: True Tales of Assassins, Samurai, and Outlaws,* and *Yurei Attack: The Japanese Ghost Survival Guide.* Each volume explores a different aspect of Japan's rich lore, ranging from the supernatural (*Yokai Attack* and *Yurei Attack*) to historical figures (*Ninja Attack*) with serious battlefield cred. Playful illustrations breathe life into the outlandish tales contained in the books.

Zen and Japanese Culture (D.T. Suzuki, 1938). Originally published in 1938, this scholarly masterwork is a deep dive into the evolution of Zen Buddhism and its profound influence on Japan's traditional culture and arts. Samurai swordsmanship, haiku poetry, tea ceremony, painting, calligraphy, architecture––it's all there. It's been refreshed numerous times over the decades and no version will disappoint. For an up-to-date version, the edition published in the Princeton Classics series (2019) is a good pick.

SOCIETY

Tokyo Vice: An American Reporter on the Police Beat in Japan (Jake Adelstein, 2010). In this colorful memoir, American investigative journalist Adelstein tells all about his 12 years of reporting on Tokyo's underworld, from murder and corruption to human trafficking and plenty of *yakuza* (mafia). As he goes deeper and deeper, he encounters more danger than he bargained for.

FOOD AND DRINK

Rice, Noodle, Fish: Deep Travels Through Japan's Food Culture (Matt Goulding, 2015). This lauded book is written in a literary voice and comes with a visual feast of images from across Japan's exceptional culinary world. Goulding explores the food culture of Japan's great cities—Tokyo, Osaka, and Kyoto—but also ventures farther afield to Hiroshima, Fukuoka, Hokkaido, and the remote Noto Peninsula.

Food, Sake, Tokyo (Yukari Sakamoto, 2010) This book follows chef, sommelier, an writer Yukari Sakamoto through Japan vast capital, exploring its department stor food halls, sake bars, *izakaya*, markets, an more. The book brilliantly decodes arcan dishes, explains a range of exotic ingredi ents, gives the lowdown on which fish ar in season at various times of year, gives *sake* primer, and introduces Tokyo's dee food culture.

TRAVEL WRITING

The Inland Sea (Donald Richie, 1971). Thi timeless book, written by Japan's foremos interpreter of the 20th century, is an ele giac hymn to the joys of traveling in "ol Japan"—specifically, the dazzling Inlan Sea. Part memoir, part travel narrative Richie muses on what was then—and onl more so now—a vanishing way of life. H describes the seascape, the tiny islan towns, and his encounters with a host o characters with great humanity, humor and warmth. The result is a dreamlike trav elogue on Japan that remains unsurpassed

The Roads to Sata: A 2,000-Mile Walk Throug Japan (Alan Booth, 1997). This insightful often hilarious travelogue recounts the au thor's walk from the northern tip of Hok kaido to Kyushu's far south, along back country lanes. His poignant descriptions o rural Japan, and the people he met along the way—from fishermen to bar owners—reveal a salty side of Japan that remains hidden to the vast majority of foreign visitors.

Another Kyoto (Alex Kerr with Kathy Arlyn Sokol, 2018). If you're keen to delve beneath Kyoto's surface, this "spoken book" contains decades of insight, spoken by Kerr and then transcribed by Kathy Arlyn Sokol, into the overlooked details of the ancient capital, from its gardens to its architecture and customs, gleaned from the city's priests, monks, art dealers, and intellectuals.

MEMOIR

ost Japan: Last Glimpse of Beautiful Japan (Alex Kerr, 1993). This beautifully written and award-winning book—impressively first written in Japanese, then translated into English—weaves together three decades of the author's rich life experience in Japan. Kerr takes readers deep into the kabuki theater scene, Tokyo's boardrooms during the heady 1980s (before the bubble had popped), Kyoto's rarefied traditional arts, and the remote Iya Valley of Shikoku where he would ultimately make a home. Juxtaposing all this beauty is a sense that Japan's ancient traditions and natural splendor have been blemished by the country's race to modernize.

The Lady and the Monk: Four Seasons in Kyoto (Pico Iyer, 1992). This book recounts the year that celebrated travel writer Pico Iyer first came to Japan to study Zen Buddhism at a monastery—a goal that didn't last long—and ultimately fell in love with a woman who would eventually become his wife. The book is very much a love letter penned by a besotted young Iyer. He followed up this work recently with *Autumn Light* (2019), a deeply mature, meditative book on the passage of time, ageing, and how decades living in Japan have informed his outlook on life.

Internet Resources and Apps

TRAVEL

www.japan.travel/en

The Japan National Tourism Organization (JNTO) promotes travel to Japan and provides a good deal of English-language information on its website. It's a good place to go for trip ideas and suggested itineraries, and to download maps (www.japan.travel/en/things-to-do).

www.outdoorjapan.com

Outdoor Japan's website and full-color seasonal print magazine cover Japan's wild side. It's a great resource for discovering outdoor adventure opportunities in off-the-radar areas.

NEWS AND MEDIA

www.japantimes.co.jp

The Japan Times is Japan's largest English-language newspaper. It's a good resource for keeping up on news, learning about local happenings, and checking out event listings.

https://gaijinpot.com

GaijinPot is a portal for the foreign community in Japan that runs great content on everything from culture and travel to what it takes to set up a life in Japan. Its Japan 101 section is packed with practical information on topics ranging from banking to doctors. Its sister site **Japan Today** (https://japantoday.com) is a good source for news.

www.kansaiscene.com

In addition to the website, Kansai Scene free print zines are found at more than 300 pickup points in Kyoto, Osaka, Nara, Hyogo, Shiga, and Wakayama prefectures. It's a great portal into the Kansai region, including features about culture and happenings in the region, food and nightlife options, and event listings.

FOOD

https://tabelog.com/en

Tabelog's national restaurant database is comprehensive, including information like business hours, average prices, etc. You can search restaurants by location and cuisine type, as well as make informed decisions on where to eat based on user rankings. Anything with a rating above 3.5 stars tends to be dependably good.

https://gurunavi.com

Gurunavi is a good supplement to Tabelog, which scores points for its user rating system (allowing for discernment), but is more limited in its English-language coverage. Gurunavi, however, lacks Tabelog's useful user rating system. If you use both websites creatively, you'll usually be able to find a good choice for a meal anywhere you go.

TICKET RESERVATION SERVICES

www.ticketsgalorejapan.com

Tickets Galore Japan, a ticket proxy service, is a godsend. Basically, you contact the service about ticket(s) for an event you'd like to attend. The service then buys the ticket(s) on your behalf, charging a reasonable service fee. This saves massive hassle and potentially losing out on great events, as buying tickets for events in Japan—let alone from overseas—can be quite convoluted at the best of times.

TRANSPORTATION

www.hyperdia.com/en

While in Japan, Hyperdia, a user-friendly train trip-planning website, will quickly become your new friend. The website allows you to input your starting point and destination, then gives you a full itinerary for a train journey, accurate to the minute. There are many other search options, such as boxes where you can select what categories of train (local, express, etc.) you'd like to include in the search results. Note that it is available as a smartphone app for both Android and iOS.

ONLINE LANGUAGE SERVICES

https://jisho.org

Denshi Jisho, and easy-to-use online dictionary, has a mercifully simple user interface. It'll come in handy when you're searching for the name of a dish or asking for medicine at a pharmacy.

https://translate.google.com

It may seem too obvious to mention, but Google Translate also does a great job with translating on the fly.

MONEY

www.xe.com

XE is a user-friendly, up-to-date currency conversion website that also has an app for both Android and iOS. Download it so you can convert prices in yen on the fly.

HEALTH

Japan Hospital Guide

In case you need to find a hospital on the road, this app draws on data from Google Maps to provide information on hospitals and clinics. All pertinent details—opening hours, phone numbers, and more—are given. Be aware that you'll have to allow your smartphone to know your location for the app to work.

CHAT APPS

https://line.me/en

If you plan to make any new friends in Japan, forget WhatsApp. The chat app of choice here, hands down, is Line. It's available on both iOS and Android, and has an English option, so downloading it and setting it up is pretty self-explanatory.

Index

List of Maps

Photo Credits